CITIES OF DESTINY

ARNOLD TOYNBEE
SIR MAURICE BOWRA
J. R. HALE
HAROLD ACTON
W. H. BRUFORD
CLAIRE PRÉAUX
JÉRÔME CARCOPINO
ARTHUR F. WRIGHT
SIR STEVEN RUNCIMAN
A. J. ARBERRY
DAVID DOUGLAS
IGNACIO BERNAL
LAURENCE LOCKHART
PERCIVAL SPEAR
TAMARA TALBOT RICE
ALAN PRYCE-JONES
ROGER FULFORD
ALLAN NEVINS
ANDREW SINCLAIR
CONSTANTINOS A. DOXIADIS

542 illustrations
157 in color
385 photographs, drawings
maps, plans and diagrams

CITIES
OF DESTINY

EDITED BY ARNOLD TOYNBEE

WEATHERVANE BOOKS
New York

Designed and produced by Thames and Hudson, London

MANAGING EDITOR: Stanley Baron MA

ART EDITOR: Ruth Rosenberg D PHIL

EDITORIAL ASSISTANTS: David Britt BA, Anthony Fagin BA,
Nathaniel Harris BA, Emily Lane BA

ASSISTANT ART EDITOR: Dian Crawford-Johnson

RESEARCH: Susan Bakker, Doreen Beck, R. Davidson-Houston BA, FRAI

SPECIAL PHOTOGRAPHY: Martin Hürlimann, Martin Weaver,
Martin Frishman, Josephine Powell, Richard Heimann

PROCESS WORK: Schwitter AG, Zurich

Printed in the Netherlands

This edition is published by Weathervane Books, a division of
Imprint Society, Inc., distributed by Crown Publishers, Inc.
by arrangement with Thames and Hudson, London

PREFACE

ARNOLD TOYNBEE

THIS BOOK is addressed to the world-wide public and its field is the whole world since the earliest cities made their appearance. The broadness of the field has made it impossible for the treatment of the subject to be comprehensive. It has necessarily been selective. The aim has been to give samples of the principal types of city that have arisen so far, and this only in some particular phase of each city's history that has been great in the sense that it has made a mark on the subsequent history of civilization.

Some of the cities that are dealt with in this book have been so important that they have had more great ages than one. Venice, for instance, had a great age in the thirteenth century, as well as in the fifteenth, and the Paris of Danton and Robespierre might put in a claim to have been as great as the Paris of Abelard and St Louis. Yet even Paris and Venice might have been replaced, in our selection, by other cities that would have served equally well to illustrate the kind of great age of a historical city that medieval Paris and Renaissance Venice represent respectively. The intellectual awakening of medieval western Christendom took place, not only in Abelard's Paris, but in contemporary Bologna, and crusaders as eminent as St Louis rode out from the capitals of other medieval western kingdoms besides France. Again, the combination of naval, military, commercial, artistic, and literary creativity, for which fifteenth-century Venice stands, could have been illustrated from some phase in the history of some other city-state: for instance, from the history of Renaissance Lübeck or of Ur in the third millennium BC.

The historic cities selected for treatment in this book are thus only samples – though eminent samples – of the types that they respectively represent. But they have been taken from all quarters of the civilized world, and they do represent some, at least, of the principal types of city that have emerged so far. For instance, the city-state, in which city and state are identical and sometimes actually conterminous, is represented by Athens, Venice, Florence and Weimar. The political capital of a large state is represented by Alexandria, Rome, Changan, Constantinople, Cordoba, Paris, Mexico, Isfahan, Delhi-Agra, St Petersburg and Vienna. The type of Megalopolis is illustrated by London, the American City, New York and (projecting into the future) Ecumenopolis.

Some historic cities have achieved greatness in a single field only. New York, for example, has become pre-eminent in the single field of commerce and finance. It will be noticed, however, that most of the great ages of historical cities that are surveyed in this book were great in several fields of activity simultaneously.

There are various other types – such as the holy city and the industrial city – that would have deserved to be represented in this volume if there had been space. Rome has had a great age as a holy city since she ceased to be the political capital of an empire; and, indeed, Peter and Paul have given Rome a spiritual empire that is far wider than the military empire that Antonine Rome had inherited from Augustus. The empire of Augustus and of the Antonines was confined to the perimeter of the Mediterranean Sea; the Pope today has ecclesiastical subjects in every continent. As for the industrial city, this is represented, to some extent, by Alexandria, Constantinople and Florence. But our survey does not include any city whose *raison d'être* is industry. This is a type of city of which Manchester, the two Birminghams, and Pittsburgh are examples.

If we look again at the set of cities with which the present book does deal, we shall notice another difference of type which cuts across the differences that we have already considered. There are cities that have become historic, and have achieved greatness in one or more fields, by a gradual process that has been the work of innumerable and mostly unidentifiable people; and there are cities that have been created – or, short of this, have been raised to greatness – by the deliberate act of some famous individual. Alexandria was called into existence by Alexander the Great, Isfahan by Shah Abbas, St Petersburg by Peter the Great, and it was the less than great Duke Karl August who established the glory of Weimar, which influenced, and advanced, the culture of Germany and the whole Western world, by persuading so great a man as Goethe to take service with him. On the other hand, Athens and Florence were already historic before Pericles and the Medici came on to the scene; and, if Pericles and the Medici had never been born, Athens and Florence would still have achieved greatness.

CONTENTS

INTRODUCTION
CITIES IN HISTORY

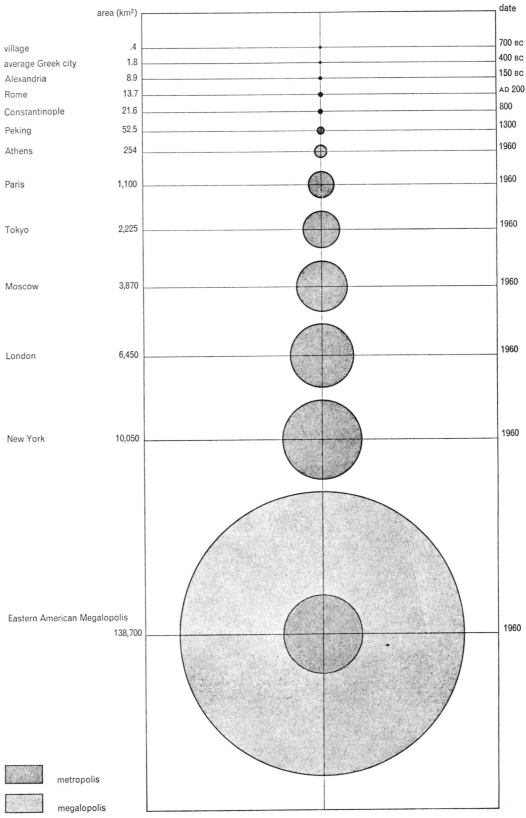

area (km²)

village .4

average Greek city 1.8

Alexandria 8.9

Rome 13.7

Constantinople 21.6

Peking 52.5

Athens 254

Paris 1,100

Tokyo 2,225

Moscow 3,870

London 6,450

New York 10,050

Eastern American Megalopolis
138,700

date

700 BC

400 BC

150 BC

AD 200

800

1300

1960

1960

1960

1960

1960

1960

1960

Evolution of the size of the city. (By per-mission of Doxiadis Associates, Athens.)

 metropolis

megalopolis

ARNOLD TOYNBEE

CITIES HAVE BEEN PLAYING an ever greater part in human life in the most recent age of human history – that is to say, during the last eight or nine thousand years, if the archaeologists are right in their dating of the lowest and oldest of the successive layers of the city of Jericho. But before we try to follow the rise of cities from that date up to the present day, we have to make clear to ourselves what we mean by the word.

What is a city?

The first ideas that the word 'city' evokes in our minds are concrete and visual. We picture a cluster of buildings that stand so close together, and that house a population that is massed so thick on the ground, that the inhabitants of the city cannot raise their food supply within the city's limits. They have to import it from the surrounding open country, and consequently they have to produce goods or services, or both, that the rural food-producers will accept in exchange for the quantity of food that the townspeople need to obtain from them. On the whole this physical picture holds good for cities in most parts of the world at most times within the last eight or nine thousand years. But a city is never just the habitat of a crowd that has to buy food by selling something else in exchange for it. Close settlement does not constitute a city unless the inhabitants of the built-up area are citizens in the non-material sense of having, and being conscious of having, a corporate social life. This need not necessarily take the institutional form of a mayor and corporation. A formal civic constitution may be lacking. What is essential is that the inhabitants of the city should be a genuine community in fact. The existence of this sense of community, where it does exist, is usually proclaimed by the presence of public buildings; a defensive city wall, with towers and gates; a meeting-place (agora, forum, piazza, plaza, maidan) for the transaction of common commercial and political business; at least one temple for the city's tutelary god; and perhaps a hall to provide office-room for the city's administrators, if the city's government has reached that degree of organization.

If this criterion of what constitutes a city is accepted, the civic centres of the pre-Columbian Maya society in northern Guatemala and in Yucatan would rank as cities, even if it were to be proved that only a handful of priests and rulers was permanently domiciled in each of them. On the other hand, the same criterion might require us to deny the title 'city' to a mere aggregation of thirty or forty thousand agricultural workers, such as one finds at, say, present-day Minervino and other similar agricultural workers' dormitories in south-eastern Italy; and a dormitory does not become a city when its denizens are industrial workers – as in the built-up environs of Gary, Indiana – or when they are rentiers, as in Los Angeles or in Miami. Los Angeles may swell physically to the size of a sub-continent, but the tropical luxuriance of its physical growth may never succeed in making a city of it. In order to become a city, it would have also to evolve at least the rudiments of a soul. This is the essence of cityhood. Many, perhaps most, of the world's historic cities have also practised a division of labour; and, in the diversification of their citizens' vocations, they have produced a small class with the leisure to think, plan, invent, and create – or alternatively to waste on luxuries, frivolities and wars the precious spare time that has been won for them by the surplus product of other people's daily work. The presence of a leisured class is perhaps evidence that a society has reached the stage of culture that we label 'civilization'. But there can be a city without a leisured class, so long as there is some kind of corporate life there. The inhabitants of the first city of Jericho may have had no spare time left over from the cultivation of their oasis, but the wall and the tower that they built survive to testify that they constituted a civic community nevertheless.

Cities, in the sense of civic communities, have had the destiny of the grain of mustard-seed in the parable. The earliest cities were thinly sown specks on the face of the earth. They were an exceptional form of human settlement, and their abnormality was signalized and symbolized by the wall that demarcated a primitive city's diminutive area from the vast surrounding countryside. Behind and within these physical defences, a new form of social life could, and did, take shape. The Greek word for city – *polis* – originally meant a citadel, and this citadel might consist of nothing but a ring-wall surrounding the crown of a hill, or a ridge between two converging ravines, or some other type of natural fortress. It was, in fact, not so much a city as 'a city of refuge' in which the surrounding rural population could find shelter for themselves, their families, flocks, herds and harvest if the open country was being overrun by an enemy with superior forces. The word for city in Greek indicates that the Greek city stood for security first and foremost; but security gives an opportunity for freedom. In medieval Germany there was a saying that 'city air makes one free'. This civic security and freedom were exceptional blessings at first. They were so exceptional that the rare cities were the greatest wonders of an incipient man-made world. But, because they were wonders, they had an innate tendency to radiate and grow and spread. The original polis at Athens became the 'acropolis', meaning 'the summit citadel', when a populous open city crystallized round the foot of the rock. The tiny Sumerian city Ur earned its living by extending its commercial operations right down the Persian Gulf into the Indus basin and right up the valleys of the Euphrates and Tigris into Anatolia and Kurdistan.

Irresistible urban expansion

These were precocious foretastes of the reversal in the physical relations between city and countryside that is coming to pass in our time. Today it is the countryside, not the city, that is becoming the exceptional feature in the human occupation of the earth's surface. It is not so long ago that the world's cities were still being protected by walls against the danger of being reabsorbed into the countryside. The name 'Wall Street' preserves a memory of this primeval stage in the physical structure of the city of New York. In Germany right into the nineteenth century, and in China right into the twentieth, the cities were still walled and the gates through their walls were closed at night-time. Paris was re-fortified in the eighteen-thirties, and these nineteenth-century ramparts were not demolished until after the First World War (they had not saved Paris from falling in 1871, and they would not have saved her in 1940 if they had been still in existence then). But, within the last hundred years, the open country has fallen into danger of being counter-attacked and overrun by cities that have burst their traditional bounds in a headlong career of territorial aggression. We no longer try to confine our cities within walls. The cities would not now submit to this. But we do try to fence off our parks and our green belts in the hope that we may be able to save them from being obliterated by encroaching houses and streets. It is the exceptional open space, nowadays, whose air makes one free from the oppressive atmosphere of the fast-coagulating world-city; and the most insecure places in the present-day world are no longer the surviving jungles and deserts; they are the urban slums. The slum-dwelling human gangster has become a more formidable predator on urbanized man than the lions and tigers that are preserved behind bars in a city's zoo. Within the brief span of eight or nine thousand years, the diminutive Jerichos and Urs have rankled into monstrosities on the scale of our gigantic Los Angeles and Tokyo.

In the history of this period, increasing urbanization of the earth's surface has been one of the main threads in the spinning of the web of human destiny. The progress of urbanization has been closely linked with the progress of technology, and its fortunes have been hardly less intimately affected by the more capricious play of politics and war. (Social relations have been man's most dismal failure, in contrast to technology, which has been his most brilliant success.) The history of cities is an integral part of the history of human affairs as a whole; and ideally it should be viewed within this context. But for practical purposes it is possible and convenient to distinguish this particular thread of human destiny from the other threads with which it is interwoven. We can now trace the history of the world's cities from Jericho to Megalopolis. The grain of mustard-seed has taken no more than eight or nine thousand years to grow into a tree that overshadows the earth. What is this world-encompassing city going to do to human life in the course of the two thousand million years during which it is said this planet will remain habitable for human beings if, in our time, we refrain from liquidating mankind by fighting an atomic world war? If we manage to exorcize the menace of the mushroom-shaped cloud of a genocidal thermonuclear explosion, the menace of the grain of mustard-seed that has grown to the dimensions of Megalopolis is going to hang over us for as far ahead as we can peer into the future. We need not despair of the possibility of surmounting this menace in its turn. Man has shown himself resourceful and indomitable, so far, in responding to the successive challenges with which he has been faced. The concluding chapter of this book offers some constructive proposals for making life possible and tolerable in the world-wide city of the future. We have no time to lose if we are to grapple with this formidable problem effectively. But the best – and, indeed, the necessary – introduction to the coming world-city's two thousand million years' expectation of life is to look back, in retrospect, over the eight or nine thousand years during which there have been such things as cities in our human world.

For the first nine hundred thousand years, or thereabouts, of human history, man has been a food-gatherer, such as some of the aboriginal inhabitants of Australia still are today. It is only within the last nine or ten thousand years that man has taken the initiative in his perpetual struggle with Nature to win his living from her. The cultivation of plants and the domestication of animals is no older than that, and the dawn of civilization is more recent still. Before the exploration of the mound accumulated by the building of successive cities at Jericho, it was believed that city-life was no older than civilization was. But the lowest stratum at Jericho has proved to date from the early Neolithic period, and some of the Black Pottery (*Lung Shan*) Culture Neolithic sites in northern China come near to being cities, in so far as their material remains allow us to guess at the kind of life that was lived in them. The Neolithic cultures of China are young compared to those of the 'Fertile Crescent' in south-west Asia; and we could also have guessed, with some assurance, that Neolithic Jericho was not unique, even if the excavation of its site had not produced evidence that there was at least one contemporary city whose citizens were a match for the original Jerichoans. There is archaeological evidence that the earliest community at Jericho was supplanted there by invaders who appropriated the site and introduced a distinctive culture of their own after having exterminated, evicted or assimilated the previous inhabitants.

Sumer: public works on the grand scale

This evidence for the existence of more than one city in the 'Fertile Crescent' in the Neolithic age is, so far, a matter of inference, though the inference is warranted by the change in material culture that we find when we pass from the lowest stratum at Jericho to the next. When we move on into the age of civilization and shift our attention from the semicircle of oases skirting the lower basin of the Euphrates and Tigris rivers to this basin itself, we meet with a whole cluster of cities that gained a living for themselves on an unprecedentedly affluent standard, in spite of their being so thick on the ground. They achieved this relative affluence by carrying out public works that must have required organization and direction of human labour on the grand scale. They transformed an inhospitable jungle-swamp into navigable canals and irrigated fields. The combined area of the territories of these Sumerian city-states is tiny by comparison with the total habitable area on the surface of the globe; but its magnitude, compared with the size of the Jericho oasis, is none the less significant as a portent of the world-wide urbanization that was to come and that is, in fact, bearing down upon mankind in our day. So far as we know, Sumer – the subsequent Babylonia and the present-day Iraq – was the first region in the world to produce a whole cluster of cities. This had already happened here by about the year 3000 BC, and it is significant that it did not remain an isolated phenomenon. Within the next century or two, a second cluster of cities came into existence in the lower valley of the River Nile, as a result of an achievement in water-control that rivalled what had been accomplished by the Sumerians.

By about half-way through the third millennium BC, there were cities in another, and much larger, tract of reclaimed jungle-swamp, namely the middle and lower basin of the River Indus. Simultaneously with the rise of Mohenjo-daro and Harappa here, cities arose on the islands of the Aegean Sea and round its continental coasts – such famous cities as Knossos and Phaestos in Crete; Mycenae, Pylos, Thebes and Orchomenos in continental European Greece; and Troy on the continental Asian side of the Dardanelles (the Hellespont). By the thirteenth century BC there was a city at Anyang in relatively remote northern China; and the case of Anyang is like the case of Jericho. Though, for its own place and date, it is a unique archaeological discovery so far, we can infer from the archaeological evidence – supported, here in China, by a posthumous literary tradition – that a number of contemporary Chinese cities are awaiting disinterment by the archaeologist's spade. Thus, within about eighteen hundred years of the emergence of the Sumerian cities in the Tigris-Euphrates basin, the urban form of human settlement had spread eastwards and westwards across the Old World almost to within hailing-distance of the Pacific and Atlantic oceans.

The same span of about eighteen hundred years had not only seen the expansion of the area sown with cities in the Old World; it had also seen a differentiation of these cities' political roles.

City-states at war

At the dawn of civilization in the Tigris-Euphrates basin, each of the Sumerian cities that had been planted in the land won from the primeval jungle-swamp was, in political terms, a city-state – that is to say, it was the physical nucleus and the administrative centre of a surrounding territory that was extensive enough to be able to provide food for this single city's population. Though the Sumerian city-states had a common culture which distinguished them, all alike, from the societies on the Sumerian world's fringes that were still in the pre-civilizational stage of cultural development, each of the Sumerian city-states was sovereign and independent in the sense of being free to go to war with any of the others. Presumably they had not come into serious collision with each other in the early days of the hard and slow process of reclamation. At that stage the territory which each city-state had reclaimed so far would have been insulated, by tracts of still virgin jungle-swamp, from the territories that were being reclaimed simultaneously by that particular state's nearest neighbours. The eventual completion of the reclamation of the lower Tigris-Euphrates basin was a triumph for the Sumerians' skill in organization and in technology; but it confronted their sovereign city-states with a political problem that they failed to solve. Their territories were now in immediate contact with each other. Disputes between them over the possession of territory and over water-rights inevitably arose; and, since they were sovereign, they dealt with these disputes, in the last resort, by going to war. Wars are the subject of some of the earliest of the Sumerian documents that archaeologists have disinterred; and the record – fragmentary though the relics of it are – suffices to inform us that these fratricidal wars became more frequent, more violent, and more destructive as time went on until they were eventually brought to an end, at least temporarily, by the imposition of a single victorious state's domination upon all the others. This replacement of a constellation of separate sovereign city-states by a single world-state, the empire of Sumer and Akkad, gave peace, at last, to the Sumerian world; but the price of obtaining peace through successive rounds of warfare, culminating in a 'knock-out blow', was disastrously high in terms of the destruction of life, wealth, happiness and standards of conduct.

Most of the other civilizations that have arisen and have run their course within these last five thousand years have started, like the Sumerian civilization, as constellations of local sovereign independent states and have ended by being incapsulated politically in a world-state as the culmination of a series of devastating wars. This was, for instance, the political history of the Graeco-Roman civilization, in which the original political units were city-states, as they were in the Sumerian society. The Graeco-Roman world ended by being united politically in the Roman Empire as a result of Rome's wars of conquest. The local states of China, at the eastern end of the Old World, and those of pre-Columbian Middle America and Peru in the New World, had a similar history. Pre-Columbian Peru had been united for several generations under the Inca Empire, and pre-Columbian Middle America was on the verge of being united under the Aztec Empire, when the Spaniards interrupted the process by breaking in. The contending local states of the Chinese world were forcibly united by one of their number – the state of Ch'in – within the eleven years 231–221 BC; and, though the Ch'in Empire quickly broke up, it was as quickly reconstituted again by the founder of the Han dynasty, and it has revived, sooner or later, after each subsequent collapse. Its latest breakdown was in AD 1911; its latest reconstitution was in AD 1929; and, since then, it has survived the Japanese attempt to conquer China and the civil war between the Communists and the Kuomintang. Under the present Communist régime, the continental Chinese world-state is a lineal successor of the one that was established by the Emperor Ch'in Shih Hwangti in 221 BC.

The Egyptian world-state

On this evidence, so far as it goes, the pattern of the Sumerian civilization's political history appears to have been the standard one. There is, however, one signal and significant exception; and that is the political history of the Egyptian civilization, which is second only to the Sumerian civilization itself in point of age. Egypt, like Sumer, started life politically as a constellation of separate local communities; but, in the Egyptian world, the local communities were united, by conquest, into a world-state at the dawn of civilization in the lower Nile valley. Instead of waiting to unite, as the Sumerian and most other civilizations have waited, until a series of wars between local states had reached an intolerable pitch of violence and destructiveness, the Egyptian civilization incorporated itself in an Egyptian world-state at the start. In Egypt, civilization and political unification were coeval.

As a consequence of this exceptional structure of the Egyptian civilization's political history, the cities of Egypt never developed, as self-conscious corporate communities, to the degree that was attained by the cities of the Sumerian, Graeco-Roman, Canaanite and medieval Western worlds. They became economic and administrative and religious centres, but they did not ever become sovereign city-states. This political development was precluded, for them, by the establishment of an Egyptian world-state at the very beginning of the post-Neolithic epoch. In Egypt, political unity did not persist continuously without any breaks. In Egyptian political history, as in Chinese, there were occasional 'intermediate periods' in which the world-state temporarily disintegrated. But in Egypt, as in China, political unity was invariably re-established. In Egypt, too, political unity was the rule, and political disunity was the exception, when once unity had been established. The Egyptian world-state lasted,

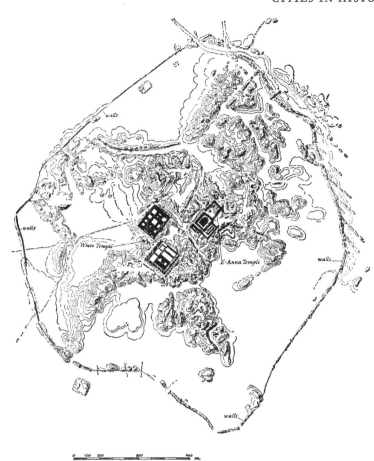

Plan of Uruk,
a Sumerian walled city of the fourth and third millennia BC.

off and on, for about 3,000 years, and in an expanded form – the Roman Empire – it survived the extinction of the Egyptian civilization itself. In China, likewise, the world-state has already lasted, off and on, for more than 2,000 years, and it is still a living reality today.

The exceptional precocity of the Egyptian civilization in achieving political unity makes Egyptian history the classic field for the study of a new political role for the city, which it played in the Egyptian world earlier than anywhere else. In the initial fractured political structure of the Sumerian world, each Sumerian city had been the nucleus of a local city-state of its own. In the initial unified political structure of the Egyptian world, there was no place for local city-states, but there was a need for a capital city to serve as a seat for a world-government to which the whole Egyptian world, including all the provincial Egyptian cities, would be subject.

The history of the series of capitals of the Egyptian world-state is the story of a tug-of-war between Upper and Lower Egypt. The original unification of the Egyptian world in the so-called 'Old Kingdom', and its subsequent re-unification, first in the 'Middle Kingdom' and then in the 'New Kingdom', was carried out, on each occasion, from a base of military operations in Upper Egypt. This was natural, considering that the Egyptian world was more open to invasion from her southern frontiers than it was either from Libya or from Asia. For this reason, the wardens of the Egyptian world's southern region tended to be better exercised in warfare, and more military-minded, than the inhabitants of the comparatively sheltered interior. Thus the forcible unification and re-unification of Egypt, first from Hieraconpolis and then, twice over, from Thebes, is what we should expect. It proved, however, more difficult to rule a united Egyptian world from this world's southern extremity than it had been to unify it by force of arms from there. Accordingly, the Old Kingdom had no sooner been established than the capital of the newly united Egyptian world was moved from the empire-builder's home town Hieraconpolis, in the far south, to Memphis, at the point where the Nile valley begins to splay out into the Delta – a location that was much more convenient geographically for serving as an administrative centre for a state that embraced Egypt as a whole. For the same reason, when Egypt was reunited in the Middle Kingdom, this time by an empire-builder from Thebes, the capital was quickly moved from Thebes to a new site at Ith-Taui, not far above the Delta's head. It was only after the second re-unification of Egypt in the New Kingdom, by another empire-builder from Thebes, that this city succeeded in remaining the capital for all Egypt, and even then it did not retain this position permanently. After Thebes had held its own for two hundred years, the revolutionary Emperor Akhenaton moved the capital to a new site in the interior, at Tell el-Amarna; and though Thebes temporarily became the capital again soon after Akhenaton's death, an increasing military and political pressure on Egypt from south-west Asia resulted in a second transfer of the capital of the New Kingdom – this time to Tanis, at the north-eastern corner of the Delta, at a point which lay in the path of any would-be invader of Egypt from Palestine.

This neighbourhood had already been the site of a capital of Egypt during the Second Intermediate period between the Middle and New Kingdoms. In that period, Egypt had been subjugated by Asian invaders, the Hyksos, and these alien rulers had planted their capital at Avaris, which covered their line of communications, across the eastern desert, with their home base in Palestine and Syria. Another and more famous capital of a foreign régime in Egypt was Alexandria, at the north-west corner of the Delta, which was the obvious site for conquerors whose reservoir of military man-power lay, not overland in Asia, but overseas in Greece. Egypt was ruled from Alexandria, first by the Ptolemaic successor-state of the Persian Empire, and then by the Roman world-state, for nearly a thousand years, running from the conquest of Egypt by Alexander the Great in the fourth century BC to its capture from the Roman Empire by the Muslim Arabs in the seventh century of the Christian era.

China's shifting capitals

Thus several different types of capital city are represented in the political history of the Egyptian civilization, and examples of these same types occur elsewhere. For instance, the tug-of-war between a site in the marches and a site in the interior is illustrated, at later dates, in the history of China. Anyang, the final capital of the Shang Empire – the oldest Chinese capital city that has been disinterred so far – lay in the interior of the Chinese world, in the middle basin of the Yellow River; but China was unified by the Chou dynasty, and was reunified by the Ch'in, from a base of operations in the Wei valley – that is to say, in China's north-western marches, over against the formidable barbarians who were perpetually pressing upon China from that direction. Unification, however, had the same sequel in China as it had had in Egypt. In China, too, it was regularly followed, sooner or later, by a transfer of the capital from a city in the Wei valley to a city in the middle basin of the Yellow River. This happened in the history of the Chou dynasty, and it happened again in the history of the Han, who were the Ch'in's more lasting successors. In the course of time, as the Chinese world expanded southwards into the Yangtze basin and beyond it to the south coast of the east Asian subcontinent, the main geographical axis of the Chinese world shifted from its original east–west alignment to a north–south one; but the tug-of-war between the marches and the interior remained a constant factor in the Chinese world's political history. The east–west pull between Changan and Loyang was succeeded by a north–south pull between Peking and Nanking. There are other examples of the pattern of Egyptian history being closely followed in China. Peking had previously been the capital of a foreign régime, established by China's Mongol conquerors, before it was adopted as their capital by the Mongols' indigenous Chinese successors, the Ming; and, in Shanghai, China has had a counterpart of Egypt's Alexandria. For a century, ending in the temporary Japanese occupation, Shanghai was the beach-head from which China was dominated, not only commercially but politically too, by Western foreign invaders from overseas.

Mongol Peking is an example of the same type of city as Hyksos Avaris. It was a 'cantonment' of barbarian foreign conquerors which was planted on the fringe of the conquered civilization's domain to cover the conquerors' line of communications with their home base of operations and reservoir of military man-power. In the history of the Sumero-Akkadian world, this 'cantonment' type of city is represented by Babylon. This 'Gate of the Gods' was planted, at about the end of the third millennium BC, by Amorite Semitic-speaking barbarian invaders of Akkad. Coming as they did from the steppes of northern Arabia, like their Akkadian predecessors, these Amorites sited Babylon on the western (i.e., the Arabian) side of the Euphrates,

where it covered their line of communications with their original homeland. The Amorite invaders of the Sumero-Akkadian world became assimilated to this world's previous inhabitants, and Amorite Babylon had the same destiny as Mongol Peking and Hyksos Avaris. After having started as a barbarian foreign cantonment, it eventually became the capital of an indigenous world-state. The Babylonian Amorite empire-builder Hammurabi was not the first political unifier of the Sumero-Akkadian world. In the course of the second half of the third millennium BC, he had been anticipated first by the Akkadian dynasty of Agade and then by the Sumerian Third Dynasty of Ur. Neither of these two previous unifying régimes had been long-lasting, and the régime of the Amorite First Dynasty of Babylon did not last long either. But the city of Babylon achieved the imperial destiny that Agade and Ur had failed to secure for themselves. For the greater part of a millennium and a half, running from the eighteenth or seventeenth century to the fourth century BC, Babylon continued to be the capital of a series of empires based economically on the surplus product of the irrigated lands in the reclaimed lower basin of the Tigris and Euphrates; and, after Babylon itself had passed its zenith, its role continued to be played by neighbouring cities that, officially, were new foundations, but in truth were merely avatars of Babylon itself. The Babylon of the Seleucid Greek successor-state of the Persian Empire was the city of Seleucia-on-Tigris. The Babylon of the Arsacid Iranian successor-state of the Seleucid Empire, and of the Sasanian Iranian successor-state of the Arsacid Empire, was Ctesiphon, the suburb of Seleucia on the Iranian side of the River Tigris. The Babylon of the 'Abbasid Arab successor-state of the Sasanian Empire was Baghdad, on the same side of the Tigris as Ctesiphon, a short distance higher up-stream. The 'Abbasid dynasty's reservoir of military manpower, like the Arsacid dynasty's, was Khorasan (previously known as Parthia), so they planted their avatar of Babylon on the Iranian fringe of their Babylonian economic power-house, on the eastern side of the two rivers.

'Abbasid Baghdad, Sasanian and Arsacid Ctesiphon, Amorite Babylon, and Hyksos Avaris are so many examples of the cantonment-city. But the classic examples of this type are the cantonment-cities planted in the seventh century of the Christian era by the Muslim Arabs to secure their hold on the vast empire, stretching away eastward to the upper Oxus, and westward into north-west Africa, which they had conquered within the amazingly short time-span of little more than a single generation. Like the Amorites at about 2000 BC, and like the Hebrews and Aramaeans in and after the thirteenth century BC, the Arabs in the seventh century of the Christian era had broken out of the Arabian Peninsula on two fronts simultaneously – invading Palestine and Syria to the north-west, as well as Iraq to the north-east. Unlike the previous waves of Semitic-speaking conquerors from Arabia, they had gone on to conquer Iran and central Asia beyond Iraq, and Egypt and north-west Africa beyond Palestine. On the fringe of each of the cultivated and civilized regions that they had conquered, the Arabs planted cantonment-cities along the borderline between the desert and the sown. They planted four of these along the desert borders of Syria and Palestine. They planted Fustat ('The Tents') at the head of the Nile Delta on the Arabian side of the river's easternmost arm, on a site a little way upstream from present-day Cairo. They planted Qayrawan on the south-eastern edge of the green belt in Tunisia. But the most important Muslim Arab cantonments of all were Basrah and Kufah on the Arabian fringe of Iraq. These two Arab cantonments were sited, like Amorite Babylon, on the west side of the Euphrates, where they were not cut off by any waterway from their reservoir of manpower in the Arabian peninsula. Under the Umayyad dynasty the Muslim Arab conquerors dominated not only Iraq but Iran and central Asia as well from Kufah and Basrah, while the Umayyad capital of the entire Arab Empire was located at Damascus, which was one of the four Arab cantonments on the Arabian fringes of Palestine and Syria. When the Umayyad dynasty, with its Arab soldiery, was supplanted by the 'Abbasid dynasty, with its Khorasani Iranian soldiery, the Khorasani cantonment at Baghdad, on the Iranian side of the Tigris, not only replaced Damascus as the capital of the empire but also supplanted Kufah and Basrah, on the Arabian side of the Euphrates, in the role of controlling the empire's north-eastern dominions. (Continued on p. 25)

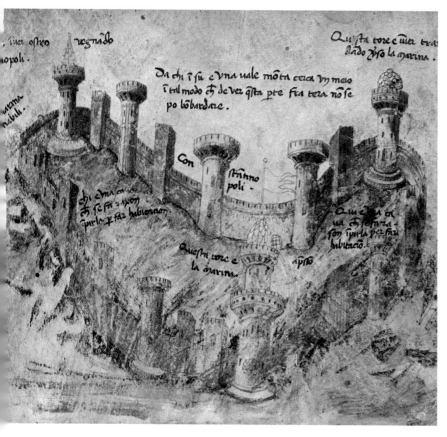

The medieval walled city

idealistically portrayed by contemporary artists. This depiction of the siege of Constantinople (above) was an illustration made shortly after the fall of the city in 1453. The Italian hill-town with its crenellated walls (above right) is a detail from *The Finding of the True Cross*, one of Piero della Francesca's fresco series in the Church of St Francis, Arezzo. The seaside city (below), a fragment by the fourteenth-century Sienese artist, Ambrogio Lorenzetti, shows the medieval city protected from all sides by its fortifications. (1, 2, 3)

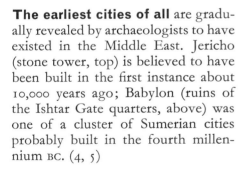

The earliest cities of all are gradually revealed by archaeologists to have existed in the Middle East. Jericho (stone tower, top) is believed to have been built in the first instance about 10,000 years ago; Babylon (ruins of the Ishtar Gate quarters, above) was one of a cluster of Sumerian cities probably built in the fourth millennium BC. (4, 5)

The designs of early planned cities are best appreciated from the air. Nördlingen in Bavaria (right top) is an almost perfect circle. The walls of Aigues-Mortes, in southern France (centre), enclose a rectangle. Palmanova (bottom), built by the Venetians in 1593, has ramparts which form a star and provide ideal defence. (6, 7, 8)

18

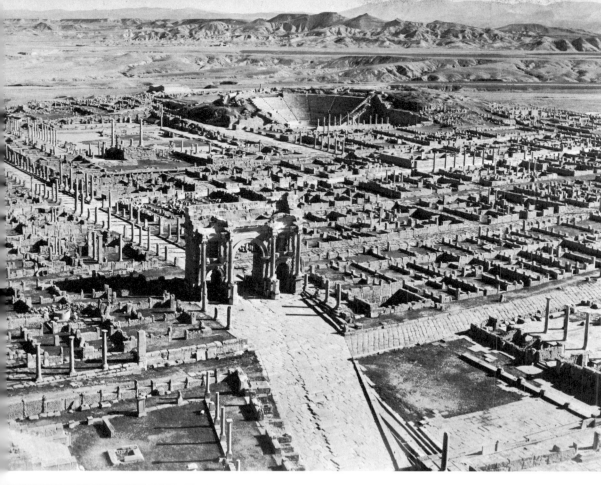

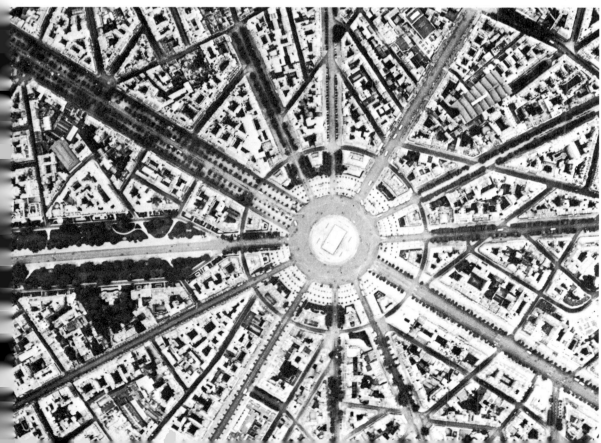

Beauty plus utility: the planned city without walls. Timgad, in modern Algeria (left), was founded by the Romans in AD 100; its remains show the typical imperial mixture of a rational street-grid, triumphal arches and arena for games. Bath (left centre) is the most impressive example of Regency England's taste for terraces, crescents and circles in a harmonious design. Baron Haussmann's nineteenth-century scheme for Paris (the Étoile, below left), with its radiating boulevards, offers multiple long vistas and wide thoroughfares for the parades and ceremonial occasions which give Paris the appearance of a great capital. (9, 10, 11)

The irrational city, which simply expanded without plan or restriction, is illustrated by Los Angeles (below), which has spread in all directions since it was first founded in 1781. (12)

In ancient Athens, the Acropolis, with its white marble temples, was a monument, a landmark and a beacon seen from afar. During the centuries that have passed since then, and especially in recent times, the city has grown so prodigiously that it has had to climb up the hill, thus robbing the Acropolis of its distant majesty and monumental character (left). (13)

One modern solution to the ever-increasing population density of most big cities is the housing estates or developments which have been built in all parts of the world. Alton East Estate at Roehampton (top right), a dormitory suburb south-west of London, was one of the earliest attempts of the London County Council to provide apartment housing in a rational and comprehensive plan, with individual units of varying heights set within open green areas (1954–6). The example for the units had been set in 1947–52 by Le Corbusier in his famous 'Unité d'Habitation' apartment block in Marseilles (top far right). Domino-shaped buildings in a variety of relationships have replaced the nineteenth-century rows of identical houses. In the new capital of Brazil, the city of Brasilia, designed by Oscar Niemeyer and Lucio Costa (right), great areas of such blocks form part of the city plan. (14, 15, 16)

The defacement of cities and their degeneration into slums is known throughout the world; efforts of revival and improvement are also universal. Depressed housing, such as existed in 1937 at Forsyth and East Houston Streets on the Lower East Side of New York (left top), is gradually but slowly disappearing and being replaced by 'high-rise' apartment buildings. In areas devoted to seasonal tourists, like Miami Beach (left below), the proliferation of competitive ugliness is more difficult to control, except by strict zoning laws – and it may already be too late for that. (17, 18)

Planned developments attempt to make the facts of daily urban or suburban life more agreeable, convenient and productive. The Eastland Shopping Center in Detroit (below) is intended to concentrate shops of all kinds within an easy walking radius. The same idea of organizing the problems of shopping was incorporated in the rebuilding of Rotterdam after the Second World War. The Lijnbaan (far right), in the centre of the city and designed by the architectural firm of Van den Broek and Bakema, is restricted to pedestrian traffic, and is also equipped with arcades against rain and snow. The housing estate in Hässelby Gard, a suburb of Stockholm (right above), follows the most popular pattern of contemporary housing, combining apartment houses with shopping centre; whereas Welwyn Garden City, within commuting distance of London, evolves from the principle of individual family dwellings within a green-belt area. (19–22)

Pointers to the future. The new capital of Punjab, Chandigarh, is being built at the foot of the Himalayas in several stages from the master plan developed in 1951 by a number of architects under the general supervision of Le Corbusier. If all goes as projected, the city will eventually be able to accommodate a population of half a million. The Palace of Justice (above) has been in use since March 1956.

The University City of Mexico City, just south of the capital, was begun in 1950 after the comprehensive plan had been established by Carlos Lazo. One of the most successful buildings in this complex is the Cosmic Ray Building (right above), designed by Felix Candela.

For the Olympic Games of 1964, Tokyo, the host city, built an elaborate and spectacular sports park, of which the Memorial Tower and the supports of Komazawa Stadium are shown at right (below). (23, 24, 25)

The city-state survives

The course taken by the evolution of cities has been determined by the progress of technology. At each successive stage in its advance, technology has been increasing the scale of its operations. This relation between urbanization and technological progress doomed the city-state to be superseded by the capital city of the would-be world-state which included dozens or hundreds of provincial cities within its frontiers. The accelerating advance of technology in our time is now threatening the political capitals in their turn. Even the capitals of the largest local states are now on the way to being merged in a Megalopolis that will be virtually coextensive with the whole of the habitable part of the earth's surface. The city-state, which was the earliest and the smallest of the successive social structures in which cities have played a part, has not proved to be 'the wave of the future'. Only a century or two after the earliest cluster of city-states had come into existence in Sumer, the emergence of a second cluster of them in Egypt was forestalled by the precocious political unification of the Egyptian world into a single empire ruled from a single imperial capital by which all the provincial cities were over-shadowed. The political unification of the Egyptian world portended the city-state's eventual disappearance, but this earliest form of polity in mankind's urban age has died hard.

Though the Sumerian cluster of city-states failed to reproduce itself in Egypt, there has been a series of subsequent constellations of city-states on scales that dwarf the Sumerian cluster's dimensions. The last millennium BC saw a new world of Greek, Etruscan, and Phoenician city-states spring into life round the shores of the Mediterranean and its backwaters. This new world of Mediterranean city-states not only spread westwards to the Atlantic coasts of north-west Africa and western Europe; it also spread eastwards as far in that direction as Alexander the Great and his successors succeeded in extending the bounds of the Hellenic world. The greater part of this vast area was subsequently united politically in the Muslim Arab Empire, and, throughout the Arab Empire's dominions, the galaxy of city-states enjoyed a second period of brilliance in the 'Abbasid age. Before the end of the first millennium of the Christian era, a new world of city-states had arisen along the inland waterways of Russia, between the Baltic and the Black Sea, in a region which had been cityless till then. The second millennium of the Christian era had hardly begun before a renaissance of city-life started in Italy and in north-western Europe, an outlying region which had relapsed into a rustic way of life after the decline and fall of the Roman Empire in these then semi-barbarian provinces. From the twelfth century to the fourteenth century of the Christian era it looked as if the Western world, like the former Graeco-Roman world, might become a galaxy of city-states, instead of becoming the mosaic of nation-states that it did become and continues to be today. In 1967 the only surviving sovereign independent city-states in the Western world are Liechtenstein, Andorra, San Marino, and the Vatican City, while the only surviving non-sovereign Western city-states, now that Hamburg, Bremen and Lübeck have been merged into larger *Länder* of the German Federal Republic, are some of the cantons of the Swiss Confederation – for instance Geneva, Basle, Zürich and Berne. Yet, even after the victory of the nation-state over the city-state in the Old World homeland of Western civilization, the Spaniards, whose municipal liberties were being extinguished in Spain itself by Charles V, planted hundreds of new self-governing cities in the vast new empire that they were winning for Spain in the Americas. They superimposed these on the pre-Columbian cities of Middle America and Peru. At Cuzco, the former capital of the Inca Empire, the super-imposition is literal and is visually dramatic. Here Spanish superstructures in the Renaissance or the Baroque style rest upon courses of magnificent Inca masonry.

The Greek, Etruscan, and Phoenician constellations of city-states were in competition with each other for the winning of the central and western basins of the Mediterranean. Their demographic bases and their economic objectives were diverse. The Greeks had numbers on their side. A population explosion in the Greek world, that had started at least as early as the eighth century BC, did not die down till part-way through the second century BC; and, during the intervening half-millennium, the Greek city-state world had expanded as far westwards as the Mediterranean coasts of Gaul and Spain and as far eastwards as the Oxus-Jaxartes basin and the Indus basin. The Greeks' original objective in expanding was to win agricultural land overseas for close settlement. In Greek economic life, trade and manufacture did not begin to take precedence over agriculture till the seventh and sixth centuries BC, and even then this only happened in a few of the many hundreds of Greek city-states. By contrast, the Phoenicians were weak in numbers, even allowing for the possibility that they may have augmented their supply of manpower by drawing on their Israelite kinsmen in their Palestinian hinterland. The Phoenicians sought, not new fields, but new trading-posts and new mines. Their cities were tiny, both at home and overseas. They were planted on small offshore islands such as Tyre and Aradus (the present-day Ru'ad) off the coast of Canaan; Utica off the north coast of Tunisia; and Motye off the west coast of Sicily. As a second choice, the Phoenicians planted their cities on promontories such as Sidon in Canaan and Carthage in north-west Africa. Jerusalem and Samaria, the capitals of the rural and relatively backward states of Israel and Judah in the Phoenician cities' hinterland, were large by comparison – though the Phoenician cities made the most of their confined space by building their houses six storeys high. As for the Etruscans, they must have been stronger in numbers than the Phoen-icians, since they penetrated deep into the interior of Italy, and this eventually in Campania, as well as in Etruria itself. In Campania and south-eastern Etruria they acquired agricultural land that was as good as any that the Greeks acquired – at Sybaris, Leontini and Selinus for instance. In north-west Etruria (the territory of Populonia and the island of Elba), the Etruscans acquired one of the three richest sources of minerals in the western basin of the Mediterranean. (The other two were south-western Sardinia and south-western Spain, both acquired by the Phoenicians.)

An instrument of colonization

The three rival peoples' objectives and ways of life thus differed from each other markedly, yet they had one policy and procedure in common which was perhaps a new departure. All three of them planted colonial city-states deliberately and purposefully. Indeed, this was the principal instrument that they all employed in their competition with each other. The Greek colonial city-states in the Mediterranean basin were planted by city-states situated in the homeland of the Hellenic civilization round the shores of the Aegean Sea, in the Archipelago and on the mainland of European Greece. These sep-arate, and in some cases rival, Greek colonizing activities were co-ordinated, to some extent, by the oracle at Delphi – a Pan-Hellenic religious centre which was always consulted on this matter. After the temporary subordination of the city-states of European Greece to the Greek Kingdom of Macedon by King Philip II, and after the subsequent overthrow of the Persian Empire by Philip's son Alex-ander, a new crop of Greek city-states was planted in Egypt and in Asia by Alexander and his successors. Alexander concentrated on the colonization of the north-eastern provinces of the Persian Empire, where the resistance to Greek conquest had been strongest. Some of Alexander's Greek colonists in this region drifted back home after his death. But the Bactrian Greek successor-state of the Seleucid Greek state which followed the Persian Empire in the territories that now constitute Soviet and Afghan Uzbekistan, together with Soviet Tajikistan, seems to have been one of the most effectively Hellenized regions in south-west Asia, notwithstanding its relative remoteness from the heart of the Hellenic world. Other patches of Asian territory in which colonial Greek city-states struck root and flourished were the Decapolis, a cluster of ten Greek colonial city-states in Palestine, most of them to the east of the River Jordan; the Seleucis in northern Syria, which was the metropolitan area of the Seleucid Empire; and the hinterland of the old-established Greek city-states along the west coast of Anatolia.

The world of Greek city-states eventually absorbed and assimilated the Etruscan and Phoenician worlds, partly by sheer weight of num-bers but also because of the superiority of the Greek way of life over the other two in intrinsic attractiveness. The Palestinian Jews and Samaritans alone were neither charmed by the attractiveness nor overwhelmed by the numbers. The whole of this vast Hellenic or Hellenized world was never united politically in a single world-state. However, the parts of it that lay to the west of the River Euphrates were eventually incorporated politically in the Roman Empire. The Romans had adopted the Hellenic city-state culture, partly at second hand from the Etruscans and partly direct from the Greeks themselves, and Rome came to play the same part in Greek history that Babylon had played in Sumerian history. Though Rome began life as a semi-barbarian city-state on the fringe of the Hellenic world, she became the capital of an empire that was the nearest approach to an Hellenic world-state that was ever achieved. When Rome declined, this eventual role was transferred to Constantinople – a new capital city planted, on the site of the Megarian Greek colony Byzantium, in a more commanding strategic position that was also nearer to the centre of the Hellenic world. Like Babylon in the Sumero-Akkadian world, Constantinople became *the* city of the Hellenic world. Its present-day Turkish name, Istanbul, is derived from a phrase in the Doric Greek dialect of Byzantium's Megarian founders. It means 'to the city' – a direction which a local Greek peasant or fisherman would give to a traveller by land or water who was asking his way to a city that had come to be thought of as the city *par excellence*.

Dark ages dispersed

The flowering of the Hellenic city-state culture from the ninth and eighth centuries BC onwards was surprising, because it had been preceded by a long drawn-out dark age that was the sequel to the catastrophic end of the pre-Hellenic Aegean civilization. This age was so dark that the Minoan systems of writing had fallen out of use, except for an adaptation of them that survived on the island of Cyprus; and, when the Greek-speaking world became literate once again, it did not revive either of the Minoan syllabaries, but adopted the Phoenician alphabet. The rise of the medieval Western city-state culture was surprising for the same reason. It, too, flowered unexpectedly in a region where the fall of the Roman Empire had left darkness behind it. Anyone who had set out to survey the cities of the Old World about the year AD 900 would have found urban life vigorous in China, in India, in the Islamic world from central Asia and Sind to Spain, and in the Eastern Roman Empire. Here Constantinople was not, after all, unique, in spite of its having come to be known as *the* city. Caesarea in eastern Anatolia and Thessalonica on the Aegean coast of Macedonia were also impressive cities at this date, and so were the Russian cities that were linked together politically under the hegemony of Kiev. These outposts of urban life in the northern wilderness lived by trade and had an economy based on currency like the contemporary Eastern Roman Empire and Arab Caliphate. Tenth-century Italy and north-western Europe would have looked like an exceptional patch of non-urban territory on the map of the Old World at this date. This derelict fragment of the Roman Empire had sunk back into a primitive economy of subsistence farming. Yet, within the next few centuries, northern Italy and Flanders each gave birth to a cluster of city-states that could challenge comparison with the Sumerian cluster at its zenith. Venice and Genoa planted colonies in the Levant and round the shores of the Black Sea that rivalled the former colonies of Greek Miletus, Megara and Chalcis in the intensity of their commercial activity. The host of Hansa towns on the rivers and coasts of the north German plain opened up the Baltic and imposed their domination on Scandinavia, while, in south Germany, chains of commercial city-states were conjured into existence by the overland trade between Italy and the Low Countries.

The failure of these dynamic medieval Western city-states to become the standard form of polity in the Western world is no less surprising than the suddenness of their original emergence out of the post-Roman dark age; and, here too, the history of the Western city-states resembles the history of their Hellenic counterparts. The rise of local nation-states in the Western world at the beginning of the modern age of its history had the same effect on the fortunes of cities as the political unification of the Egyptian and Sumerian and Hellenic worlds had. It depressed the city-states and brought capital cities to the fore. But, in the history of Western cities, this has not been the end of the story; for, in the West, the application of science to technology has precipitated the Industrial Revolution, and the Industrial Revolution is now on the way towards engulfing the political capitals of the West in a world-wide Megalopolis.

Science spreads the world-city

Megalopolis is a new phase in the history of urbanization, and it is confronting mankind with problems that have no precedents. The earliest cells of Megalopolis were spawned in Britain and in Belgium at the turn of the eighteenth and nineteenth centuries; and from these original north-west European nuclei the world-city of the future has been spreading, like a rank weed, over the face of the earth, not only in the Old World but in the Americas as well, and not only in Western civilization's domain but ubiquitously. The application of science to technology is swelling the population of Megalopolis at a prodigious rate through the combined effect of two different movements. The application of science to agriculture – especially since the close of the Second World War – is enabling us to produce more food and more vegetable fibres per acre with the employment of fewer hands; and the rural labour that is thus becoming redundant is drifting into the cities to find in urban factories and offices the employment that is no longer offering itself on the land. In the second place, the application of science to the technique of preventive medicine and to the organization of public health has been significantly reducing the death-rate. This is causing a population explosion all over the world, especially in the economically and socially backward countries. In these countries, too, the death-rate has been reduced, but the age-old habit of breeding up to the limit, as an offset to the former high mortality, has so far persisted almost unabated. In consequence, the world's population is going, by the end of the century, to become twice or three times as great as it is today, if we are to give credence (as we must) to the statisticians' forecasts; and this huge additional population is going to silt up in the most poverty-stricken and hungry and insanitary districts of Megalopolis, namely the shanty-towns that are now pullulating in southern and eastern Asia.

How are human beings to live in a 'conurbation' that is going to smother the land-surface of the planet? An uncouth new word like 'conurbation' is needed for conveying an appalling new fact. It is premature to call Megalopolis a 'city', if we have been right in defining a city as something more than a mass of buildings housing a crowd of human beings. We have defined it as being an association of human beings who have a feeling that they constitute a community, and who have succeeded in translating this feeling into the terms of a practical corporate life. To call Megalopolis a city in this sense would be to beg the fateful question that has been raised by its advent. The question is whether the physical Megalopolis can ever be made into a city in the social sense. During the last two centuries there has been a race between the proliferation of Megalopolis and the humanization of the conditions of life in it; and, so far, we do not know whether, in this grim race, it is brute matter or humanizing form that is going to come out the winner. This still undecided question is putting a premium on the art of town-planning.

Town-planning of some sort is as old as urban life itself. The primeval cities were planned, in a sense, when they were surrounded and confined by defensive walls, even if the alleyways inside the walls were allowed to twist and turn like rabbit-runs and there was no public sanitation and no public water-supply. The alignment of the town-walls will have been determined, in early days, by physical features – by the contours of a hill or by the shore-line of an islet of dry land in the midst of a marsh. Thousands of years passed before any cities were laid out, all of a piece, on some regular plan, such as the rectangular pattern of Nebuchadnezzar's Babylon, Hippodamus' Peiraeus and the colonial cities planted by the Etruscans and their Roman pupils. A city that is deliberately created for a purpose, to be a colony or a capital, can be planned, and will invite planning. The layout of a city that has grown gradually, without premeditation, cannot be rationalized without razing the original city to the ground and rebuilding it entire; and, even when the ground has been cleared providentially by fire, flood, earthquake or enemy action, site-values may be so high as to prevent would-be planners from making a new start. After the Great Fire of London, this financial consideration defeated Sir Christopher Wren. The City of London was rebuilt as the rabbit-warren that it had been before, and Wren's design for broad converging avenues, leading up from all directions to the new St Paul's, remained a dream. Only for a few years, after the surroundings of St Paul's had been levelled by bombing during the Second World War, was it possible to see Wren's work as its author had wished it to be seen. This is also the story of the rebuilding of Rome after she had been sacked by the Gauls. Rome was rebuilt as she had been built before; and, when eventually Augustus did bring some

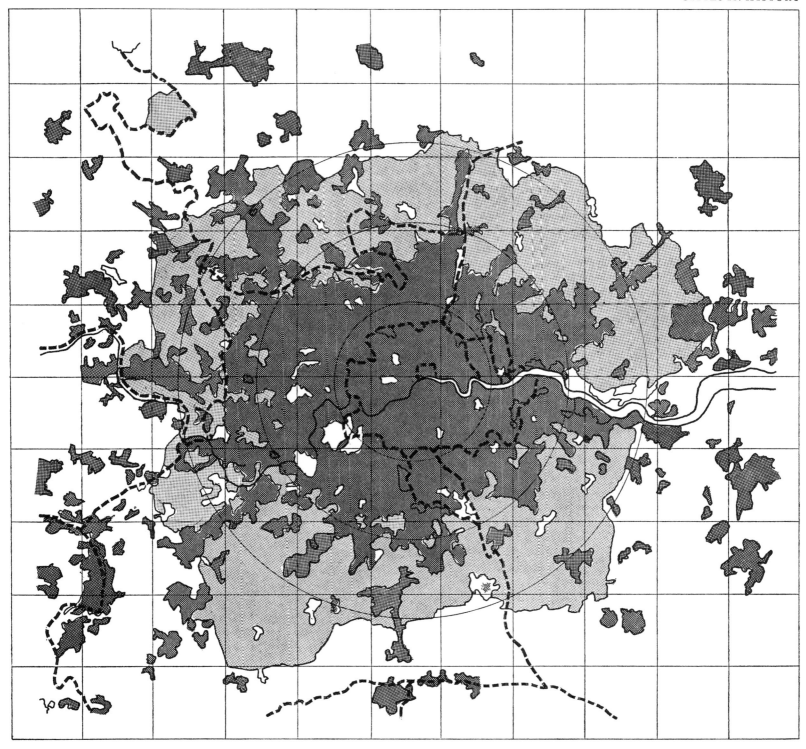

Proposition of 1954–8 for a green belt around London: an attempt at a static solution for a dynamic problem.
(By permission of Doxiadis Associates, Athens.)

order out of Rome's chaos, his task was as formidable as Haussmann's when he set out to rationalize nineteenth-century Paris.

City walls are works planned for defence; boulevards, avenues and piazze are planned to combine utility with beauty. In Megalopolis we shall have to plan for all these things – but in new ways, to cope with a situation that is unprecedented.

Man at the mercy of his creations

City walls were for defence against dangers that were external and tangible. The enemies that had to be kept out were wild beasts or, if human beings, they were barbarians or aliens. In Megalopolis, the need for defence is going to be more urgent than it ever was in Tiryns or in Troy, but the enemy now will be internal and the danger will be psychological. Man is paying for having overcome external dangers by becoming a still greater danger to himself. He is the victim of his triumphant science, technology and organization. Technology has inflated the material setting of human life to an inhuman scale. Man is being dwarfed by his apparatus and stifled by his numbers, and this heavy physical pressure on the individual is in-

flicting a severe psychic distress. The problem of defence in Megalopolis is the problem of how to rehumanize life when it has to be lived in a man-made infinity of people, buildings and streets. Megalopolis is going to encompass the earth. In material terms there is going to be no escape from it. Liberation from it will have to be sought by turning inwards from the physical world to the psyche and to the ultimate spiritual presence that is 'the dweller in the innermost' besides being the creator and sustainer of the universe. This way of salvation would have been less difficult for modern Western man's medieval forebears to take than it is for their present-day descendants; for, since the beginning of the modern age of Western history, Western man has been investing his efforts and his treasure in the mastery of his material environment. Now that his achievement of this mastery is forcing him back upon himself in self-defence against the dehumanized world that his technology has conjured up, he finds himself at a loss; and the non-Western majority of the human race is going to fall into the same straits as it becomes more and more deeply implicated in the 'extrovert' modern Western way of life. Megalopolis is going to swallow up human beings of all cultures, religions and races; for all of us, the problem of having to live in Megalopolis will have to be solved in spiritual terms. The town-planner cannot do our spiritual work for us; but perhaps he can help by mitigating the pressure of the physical environment. Perhaps he can articulate the endless chaos of buildings and crowds into human-sized quarters within which we can, once again, enter into personal relations with a limited circle of neighbours. Perhaps he can plan these quarters so that we can go about our daily business on foot, and our children can come and go between home and school without being made to risk death through being compelled to cross speed-ways infested with high-powered mechanized traffic. In fact, we need town-planners with the human imagination and the professional skill to re-create Weimars and Cranfords for us as cities of refuge in Megalopolis's shapeless wilderness. This was the solution which was suggested, half playfully, by Chesterton in *The Napoleon of Notting Hill* in the early years of the twentieth century, when the roar of the coming Megalopolis was already audible to a sensitive soul's inner ear.

Spiritual defences for life in Megalopolis can be found, and they can be as effective as the physical defences of Jericho were till Joshua's trumpets sounded, and as those of Troy were till its walls were wantonly breached to make an entry for the wooden horse. Change is of the essence of life. We have exposed ourselves to a revolutionary agency of change in learning, all too well, how to accelerate the progress of technology; and any response to a challenge that we may make today is hardly likely to hold good for the next two thousand million years. In any case, defences – even when successful – are never enough, and this is also true of defences against life in Megalopolis. Aristotle mantains that cities were brought into existence originally to make life possible, but that the ultimate purpose of them is to make life worth living. This dictum reads ironically today, when Megalopolis is the city in which we are going to have to live. Yet Aristotle is surely right. Mere existence on the defensive cannot satisfy human beings; so we have to make life worth living, even in Megalopolis, and this means making spiritual room, in Megalopolis, for the inner life of human feelings, ideas, ideals and purposes. Since this field of life is a spiritual one, each human soul has to find salvation in it for himself. But, here again, the town-planner, if he has the imagination and the skill, can help the citizens of Megalopolis to win their spiritual battle. He can help by providing them, in inspiring visible forms, with material symbols of these invisible spiritual treasures.

What will survive?

At the beginning of this chapter, it has been suggested that a city is the embodiment of a community, and that a community expresses its corporate consciousness in public monuments. These visible tokens of our common humanity which have graced the cities of the past will be needed, more than ever, in Megalopolis. But, in Megalopolis, will it be possible for even the most arresting public monuments to stand out? A classic example of an arresting public monument is the Acropolis of Athens. I visited Athens for the first time in 1911, and at that time the Acropolis still caught and held one's eye, and lifted up one's heart, as it had been doing for successive generations ever since it had been crowned with temples and surrounded by a city. The Acropolis was beautiful and inspiring intrinsically, but its beauty and nobility were arresting because the city at its feet was on a physical scale that was proportionate to the scale of the rock that gave it its character. Half a century later, the physical ratio between the city and the Acropolis had been changed radically, and this change had been to their mutual detriment. The human-sized city of Cecrops and Hadrian had been inflated to the size of Los Angeles. In its explosive expansion it had surged up the slopes of the nearest mountains and on, over their crests, into the next valleys, to assault the next mountains in turn. The sharply accentuated natural features that had been distinctive of the Greek landscape had been smothered and effaced by the works of man, as devastatingly as if Attica had been just another Surrey or just another Orange County, California; and the tide of encroaching streets and houses was still in full flow. In this new Megalopolitan panorama, the Acropolis was being stifled to the point of being effaced. It had dwindled from being the throne of the goddess Athene, the Keeper of the City, to becoming a pocket-sized exhibit in a museum. On my next visit, I shall perhaps find it enclosed in a glass case (present-day technology might be capable of doing that job); and a monument in a museum is one that has been desecrated and sterilized.

If Megalopolis has already proved itself to be more than a match for the Acropolis of Athens, is there any monument in the world that can hope still to hold up its head? Some of the famous monuments of Italy and India seem doomed to suffer the Acropolis's fate. How is the Taj Mahal going to fare when Agra has coalesced with New Delhi? And how is the Duomo of Florence going to fare when Florence itself has surged along the stupendous new speedway over the Apennines to melt into Bologna and Milan? Are not all the historic symbols of human endeavours and achievements going to founder in the world-slough into which Megalopolis is converting the earth's landscape, including the monuments of pre-Megalopolitan man? Will any of the historic peaks still stand out above this already man-made morass? If any do, we may guess that these survivors will be cities that have become holy cities after their material power and glory have come and gone. If any Rome succeeds in retaining its identity and its appeal, this will be the Rome of Peter and Paul, not the Rome of Augustus and Romulus. If any Jerusalem survives, this will be the Jerusalem of the Wailing Wall and the Holy Sepulchre and the Dome of the Rock, not the Jerusalem that has been David's and Godfrey's and Ben Gurion's secular capital city. Mecca and Medina, Benares and Bodh Gaya, the shrine of the Virgin of Guadalupe, and the monasteries on Koya San among their giant cryptomeria trees – these, too, have the same chance of surviving the coming deluge. These prospective survivors are few in number by comparison with the past wealth of monuments that were symbols of religion. They are few, but let us pray that they may be enough to keep life human, even in the inhuman environment of Megalopolis.

PART ONE
THE CITY-STATE

ATHENS

VENICE

FLORENCE

WEIMAR

FOREWORD

THE CITY-STATE is the oldest form of state and also the oldest political setting for a city. The city-state is, indeed, as old as civilization itself. One of the first places in which civilization was achieved was the lower valley of the Rivers Tigris and Euphrates, in the south-eastern part of what is now Iraq. At the beginning of the history of the Sumerian civilization here, we find the Sumerian world fractured politically into a number of separate city-states. Each of these was politically independent of the others, though the citizens of all of them spoke the same language, worshipped the same gods and, in general, followed the same way of life.

The distinctive feature of a city-state is that the government of the city and the government of the state are identical. The city dominates the state. The life of the state, including the life of its rural area, is focused on the city. Defence, administration, trade, manufacture, religion have their centre within the city walls.

Trade is, of course, a *sine qua non* for any city, because a city has to buy its food from the countryside and has to pay for this food in goods and services that the countryside will accept in exchange. Many city-states have been more or less self-sufficient economically. The local trade between the urban and the rural section of the state's territory has met both parties' economic needs. However, the Sumerian city-states were not in this position. Their territories had been reclaimed from a primeval swamp; the soil was alluvial; and, though it was marvellously good for agriculture, there was no stone, metal, or timber to be got from it. These raw materials were indispensable for the Sumerian civilization, so the Sumerian city-states had to import them from the highlands, and the highlands nearest to Sumer were far away. Accordingly, the Sumerian city-states' trading operations ranged far afield from the start.

Trade has sometimes led to empire, and there have been city-states that have built up colonial empires for themselves out of a network of trade-routes and trading-posts. Carthage's colonial empire was comparable to modern ones in its geographical scale. Medieval Genoa's colonial empire extended as far as the Crimea, and medieval Venice's as far as Crete. The colonial empire of the medieval Russian city-state Novgorod was carried by Novgorod's fur trade deep into Siberia.

Some city-states have built up empires over neighbouring city-states. City-state empires of this kind have mostly been short-lived. They have been based, not on trade, but on naval or military power, and the subjugated city-states have usually resented the loss of their political independence and have tried to regain it at every opportunity. The empires over fellow-city-states that were imposed by Athens and Sparta and by medieval Milan did not last long. Those imposed by Venice and by Florence proved more durable. Rome and Mexico-Tenochtitlan, originally city-states – and also the Sumerian city-state Ur, under its Third Dynasty – managed to enlarge their empires to the dimensions of a world-state.

Though the city-state seems to have been a Sumerian invention, it has been the standard form of state in other regions besides Sumer, and at later dates than the third millennium BC. The Sumerian city-states have had more recent, and mostly more familiar, counterparts in the city-states of Canaan, Greece, medieval Russia, and the Western world – medieval and later. The most famous of the Canaanite city-states are Tyre and Sidon and Byblos. Byblos was exporting timber to Egypt at an early date in the third millennium BC. Tyre founded Carthage. Judah, in the hinterland of these Phoenician maritime cities, became the city-state of Jerusalem after the secession of Israel and the centralization in Jerusalem of the worship of Judah's god Yahweh. The leading city-states of the Greek world – Athens, Sparta, Argos, Thebes, Miletus, Syracuse, Tarentum, Marseilles – are as familiar and as famous as those of the Canaanite world. It is perhaps less well known that Russia started life in the early Middle Ages as a string of city-states along the waterways and portages that link the Baltic with the Black Sea.

In the medieval Western world, the densest clusters of city-states were those in northern Italy and in Flanders. These two clusters were linked to each other by a belt of city-states in western Germany; and another belt of them, the Hansa towns, stretched eastwards across northern Germany and along the southern and south-eastern shores of the Baltic. In the twelfth and thirteenth centuries this network of medieval Western city-states pushed the larger but more backward Western nation-states into the background, as the nation-states of Greece had once been pushed into the background by the rise of city-states there. However, in the Western world, the city-state proved not to be 'the wave of the future' (it had not been 'the wave of the ultimate future' in the Greek world either). From the fourteenth century onwards, nation-states began to assert themselves in the Western world at the city-states' expense; but at the same time they took over from the city-states many of their ideas and institutions. The way of life that was developed in the medieval Western city-states has thus made a major contribution to modern Western civilizations. Still more important, perhaps, has been the contribution of city-states, such as Venice, Florence and Weimar, which survived the pressure of the nation-states to reach their great ages in the Renaissance or in the Age of Enlightenment.

ARNOLD TOYNBEE

ATHENS
IN THE AGE OF PERICLES

'An education to Greece'

is what Pericles proudly called his own city, Athens, in his famous oration at the funeral of dead warriors in 431 BC. More than two millennia later, the Athens of Pericles' time remains an education to the world: a unique moment in the history of Western civilization. For in this small city-state, with a relatively insignificant population by more recent standards (about 200,000), occurred an unprecedented outburst of artistic creativity, an appreciation of the dignity of man, and a democratic use of power, which have made Athens an ideal for subsequent civilizations.

Athens was for long one of several independent Greek cities and achieved its extraordinary ascendancy only during the fifth century BC. After freeing itself from the tyrant Hippias, it embarked on a century of democratic rule; but the full flowering of Athenian genius is associated with the years when Pericles was the city's leading citizen, its annually elected General, between 443-430. This was the period of Sophocles, Herodotus and Phidias; during these years were built those mutilated but indestructible monuments on the Acropolis.

The goddess Athene, born of Zeus, was the city's protective deity as well as the source of its name. Known as the goddess of war, she was the primary symbol of Athens' military and naval successes, and was accordingly glorified and worshipped by all citizens. In a cup-painting (detail opposite) by Douris (*c.* 487–470 BC) she is depicted with spear, Attic helmet and a scale-armour collar. The owl in her hand is a proverbial emblem of Athens, and the Gorgon's head on the collar (like an evil-eye to one's enemy, since the Gorgon turned men to stone) is a device used frequently in classical Greek painting. (1)

The Parthenon,

dedicated to Pallas Athene, the Virgin-goddess (*parthenos* = virgin), and built between 447–438 BC, was designed by Ictinus and supervised by Callicrates. The Acropolis, the citadel-hill on which it stands, had been for centuries the site of Athens' sacred shrines; after the Persians in 479 destroyed the old temples and statues, the victorious Athenians, prompted by Pericles, set about rebuilding on a scale calculated to demonstrate Athenian dominance over the other Greek cities. Within the temple stood a forty-foot-high statue of Athene in gold and ivory by Phidias; at the national festival called the Panathenaea, which took place each year and with special pomp every four years, the citizens came in a long procession to present a sacred garment, the *peplos*, to the goddess. Scenes from this great festival, which was a time of rejoicing, celebration and dedication, are portrayed in the sculptured friezes, brilliant examples of Phidian art, which were treated as an integral element of the Parthenon. The two stately figures (right) are among the girls who were traditionally in the vanguard of the procession. Water for libations was carried by young men (far right). The procession included an equestrian cavalcade, of which the two horsemen (below) are leading the way from the city. (2–5)

The Acropolis,
the rocky eminence which towers over Athens now as it did in antiquity (right), bears only relics of the marble holy places built by Pericles, yet even these testify to the harmony of taste, the infallible sense of construction and the majestic conception of the Athenian designers and builders of the fifth century BC. Just in front of the Parthenon is the later small temple, dedicated to the legendary king Erechtheus, Athene and Poseidon, called the Erechtheum (see Plate 14). To the right of the Parthenon are remains of the great entrance and stairway, the Propylaea, which was completed about 431. The last building at the top of the stairs, to the right of the Propylaea, is the Temple of Nike, or Victory, built at about the same time. On the far right of the photograph is the temple dedicated to Hephaestus, the smith-god, which was built at the same time as the Parthenon. (6)

The gods of the Greek myths are naturally personified in the Parthenon friezes. Hera, with an attendant, and Zeus are shown enthroned (below). To the right of them, a priestess of Athene is receiving two cushions from her servants; these were set down as a symbolic invitation to the gods to be present at the ceremony of the sacred *peplos*. The priest at the end of the panel is folding the *peplos* held by a young boy. The reclining figure (below right) from the east pediment of the Parthenon, the sculpture of which was devoted to the birth of Athene, is believed to be Dionysus, god of wine and the inspirer of poets. (7, 8)

Patrician, soldier and statesman, Pericles set his mark on the city of his birth and contributed incalculably to its greatest years of glory. He had, Plutarch tells us, 'greatness of spirit', as well as an uncommon gift for oratory and an adroit sense of politics. Whether or not it is a true likeness, this bust of Pericles (left), a Roman copy of a fifth-century BC bronze original, captures the serenity and poise for which he was well known. (9)

The arts and crafts of Athens were abundantly recorded by contemporary vase-painters. The *krater* by Euphronius, for example (below left), shows a musician and members of the audience. An armourer (opposite left) is evidently burnishing a Corinthian helmet. Two vase-painters are shown in their workroom (opposite right). The school vase by Douris (below right) gives an impression of boys being taught to sing, to play the lyre, to recite poetry and to write with a stylus. (10–13)

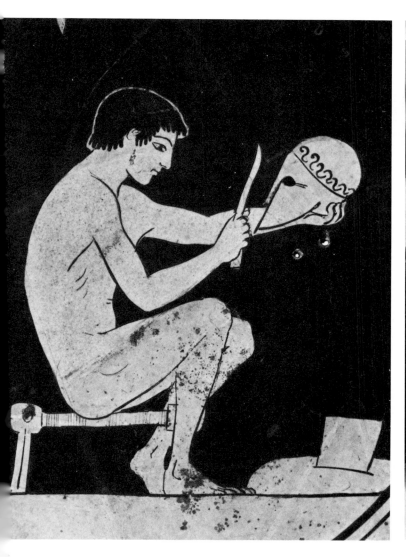
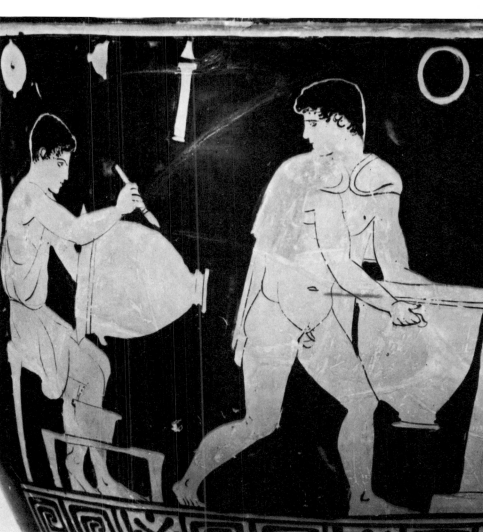

The Erechtheum,

another temple dedicated to the cult of Athene, was the last of the buildings erected on the Acropolis in the fifth century BC (above). Begun in 421 and completed about 406, only two years before Athens capitulated to Sparta, this curiously irregular building, adapted to the slope on which it stands, covers the spot on which Athene is supposed to have gained her victory over Poseidon for patronage of the city. The temple proper consisted of two chambers; there are two porticoes on the east and north sides, and the Porch of the Maidens – with six monumental caryatids in place of columns – on the south. The olive tree within the wall represents the tree Athene produced from the ground at the time of her struggle with Poseidon. (14)

The imperious sea-god, Poseidon, a bronze figure (sometimes identified as Zeus) probably made in Periclean Athens, was found in the sea off Cape Artemiseum in 1926 (presumably it sank while being conveyed to Rome) and is a powerful expression of Athens in its most confident and productive period (detail right). (15)

ATHENS IN THE AGE OF PERICLES

SIR MAURICE BOWRA

It is a commonplace that the modern world owes the most abiding and most valuable elements in its civilization to Mediterranean lands, that what Palestine did for religion and ethics, or Rome for law and government, Greece did for science and the arts. No doubt these remarkable achievements were largely determined by physical conditions. If the first victories of order and organization were won on vast alluvial plains watered by great rivers like the Nile, the Euphrates, the Indus and the Yellow, the equilibrium so established between man and nature was so nicely calculated that life followed a fixed pattern with little call to change or enterprise. The greater difficulties of maintaining life round the Mediterranean gave a sterner challenge and elicited a more vigorous response. In Greece, above all, natural conditions have not made life easy. Barren marble mountains and a thin soil forbid an extensive agriculture; the never too distant sea calls to adventure on and beyond it; violent differences of temperature between summer and winter discourage religions of resignation or philosophies of inaction; continual winds from the north and months of unbroken sunshine make for lively tempers and swift changes of mood; the limpid outlines of mountains and sea-coast sharpen the taste and discipline the intelligence. If civilization was slower to start here than in Mesopotamia or Egypt, yet once it began, it had a more vigorous impetus and a richer variety of experiment and achievement. If most parts of Greece, both mainland and islands, shared in this development, the finest, most dramatic and most influential success was won in Athens, above all in the fifth century BC, which includes the period honoured by posterity as the Periclean age.

An unparalleled achievement

In 510 BC the Athenians expelled their tyrant, Hippias, and the great age began: in 404, broken by a long war, they surrendered to a Spartan general, and something was lost to the world for ever. Much of importance and significance happened before 510, and much was to happen after 404, but between these dates Athens did what it had never done before and was never to do again. In extent and in quality this achievement has almost no parallel in the recorded history of man. A small state, about the size of Yorkshire or Connecticut, with a population of some 200,000 free men, made contributions to thought, literature and the fine arts on an unprecedented scale with so sure a touch that much of it has never been replaced or surpassed. If this was an age of experiment, as it certainly was, there is nothing uncertain or tentative or incomplete in what it did. If politically it ended in disaster, that is after all a tribute to the bold scope of its endeavours and the soaring flight of its vision.

The prodigious outburst of energy which followed the expulsion of the tyrants and turned alike to political action and to the creative arts cannot be explained by any materialistic or economic hypothesis. It was due rather to psychological causes, to the Athenians' discovery of themselves, of their own resources and capacities. They found a new confidence in themselves and sought to express it in many activities both public and private and to create a manner of living worthy of their claims and convictions. The history of Athens in the fifth century BC is largely that of various attempts to find satisfying forms for powerful creative instincts, to reduce to harmony and order ideas which might otherwise be lost in empty discussion, to give a concrete form to the great issues which troubled men's minds and clamoured for solution. The wonder is that in so short a time so much was done and done so well. The transition from tyranny to an almost complete democracy was matched in the arts by the transition from crude and improvised plays to the ripe glories of tragedy and comedy. Despite its taste for experiments and innovations Athens did not waste its energies in futile experiments but seems to have known from the start in what direction to move and what steps to take. The result is that its history has an air of inevitable, predestined development, but this is really the reflection of determined wills and powerful intellects solving problems with decision and with prescience.

Hard conditions

The achievements of this age were based on a very simple economy. Its chief trees are the olive and the vine, its chief animal the goat. While the olive provides the oil which is the basis of all Mediterranean diets, the vine provides the drink which is no less indispensable. The goat gives not only cheese and milk but the staple meat of the country. The remaining chief article of food is fish, which is easy to get in a country which is bounded on three sides by the sea and whose indented coast provides if not good harbours at least adequate anchorage for small craft. Attica grows very little corn, and one of the chief economic problems was its importation from the Black Sea. This simple economy was strengthened in other ways. The mountains give all the marble that any builder could desire. The soil provides a clay which bakes well into pottery and became a notable article of export to places so distant as Etruria, the Crimea, and Egypt. The mines of Laureion produced enough silver for a solid and respected currency. Athenian life was never luxurious, nor by modern standards comfortable. Houses were small and dark; water was scarce in the summer; furniture, if neat and shapely, was spare and simple; horses were the privilege of the rich; the cold of winter was inadequately countered by charcoal fires; agricultural land was full of rocks and stones, had often to be carved in terraces on steep slopes, and was liable to devastation by storms. There must always have been a struggle for existence in most Attic homes, and even the rich never enjoyed the resources of the great magnates of Egypt or Persia. Such conditions called for continual enterprise and improvisation and gave to the Athenian character that toughness and adaptability which were among its salient characteristics.

On the other hand the hardness of life was more than compensated by the unique beauty of the country. Compared with France or Italy, Attica looks at first sight austere and naked. It lacks woods or rivers or lush meadows, and indeed its beauty is perhaps more of

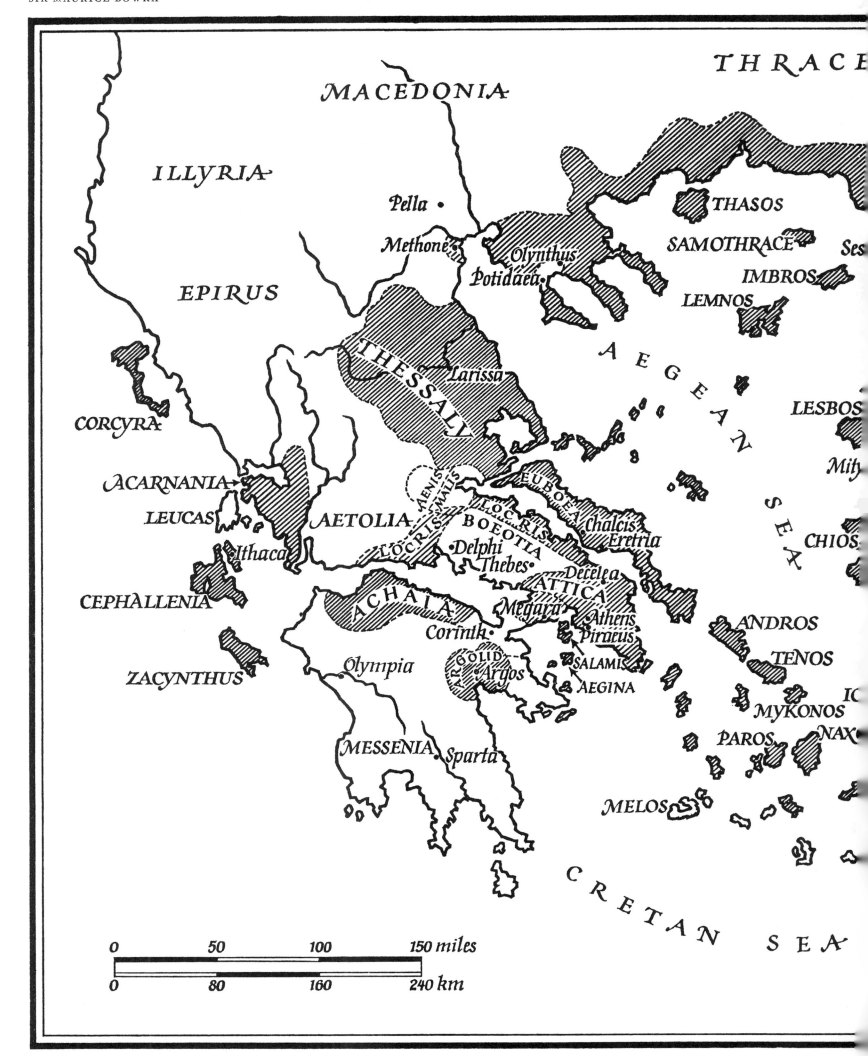

Greece before the Peloponnesian Wars.
The shaded areas indicate states and territories allied to Athens.

line than of colour. At every turn the outlines of mountains etch the sky, while the sea seems always to be lurking behind a corner, if it is not already in full view. But though the first impression is of a grave restraint, the eye soon detects a great range of effects within it. The red-brown earth, the grey-green olive-trees, the honey-coloured marble, the white, pearly sand of coves and beaches, the dark gravity of cypresses and pines, form a subtle and splendid harmony which may be unlike that of western Europe but has its own great variety of tones and shades. The whole scene is held together by an air of an unexampled limpidity, from which every foreign matter seems to have been removed, and in the evening the whole sky changes with bewildering and dramatic swiftness from one dazzling effect to another. Life in such a landscape may be hard, but it can never be dull or deadening. It explains why the Athenians were great both in action and in the arts. Their physical setting was both a challenge and an inspiration, since, while it made them work hard to keep alive, it enriched their life with unparalleled delights to the eye.

This country produced a nation of peasant farmers. Even those who lived in towns and engaged in manufactures or in sea-borne trade were close to the soil and knew its ways. Such men tended to treat one another as equals because they shared common interests and despite differences of income lived in much the same fashion. Living in close contact with one another and knowing their neighbours' intimate secrets and idiosyncrasies they developed a remarkable candour and forthrightness in their social relations. Even if they had some respect for birth and breeding, there seem to have been no such formal restraints between men of different social position as we find in more highly organized societies where specialized pursuits tend to promote isolated groups of people. As in most Mediterranean countries, the centre of social life, at least for men, was not the home but the street or the market-place, where all topics, and especially politics, were discussed with the greatest freedom, eloquence, and even knowledge. If such circumstances allow a reasonable degree of decorum and courtesy, they also allow scurrilous abuse, passionate outbursts, and lewd banter. Hieratic stiffness and commercial servility are alike lacking. Such conditions encourage a lively interest in personal traits and peculiarities, with the result that a man is known as he really is without any delusive disguise conferred by office or pedigree, and, though good manners are usual, they do not prevent him or his neighbours from saying at times what they think of each other.

The true democracy

This social life was the real basis of Athenian democracy and of its two great ideals, equal laws and free speech. Men who knew each other as well as this saw no reason why some should have special privileges or others not be free to say what they thought. All that was needed to make a political reality out of the habits of every day was the enactment of laws which gave the male population a part in governing the country. This was done in a series of stages after 510 BC, and the process was complete before the middle of the century. Henceforth, until defeat in war brought reaction, Athens was in a strict sense of the word a democracy. The people, that is, all free males, were the sovereign power. They took all political decisions, sat on juries, held public office, and had a right to free speech untrammelled by considerations of public security or laws of libel. This democracy was not representative but complete. It did not elect members to some assembly, but the people really met together, discussed, and decided what should be done. If powers were delegated to generals and public officers, it was only for limited periods, usually for a year, though they might be re-eligible. Though the laws by which Athens was governed were published and known, they could be repealed or altered by the decision of the people, and Pericles spoke the truth when he said that a law was whatever the people decided. This in itself was a great revolution from the old view that laws came from the gods and could not be altered. Of course such a system had its perils, which were in due course to reveal themselves, but none the less it made Athenian democracy what it was and was responsible for most of its triumphs.

It is easy to deride this system and to say that it was not truly democratic because it was based on slavery. Yet this defect is perhaps not so great as it seems to modern moralists. Athens differed from many slave-owning societies in the large proportion of free men to

43

slaves. Indeed it has been calculated that this was about two to one. Poor households would not normally own any slaves, a moderately well-to-do one might have as many as twelve, and a rich one fifty. This is nothing like the scale of slavery in imperial Rome or any Oriental empire, and the reason for it is partly the poverty of Athens which could not afford to buy or maintain slaves in large numbers. Slaves were usually employed not on the land, but in mines and quarries and ships, and slave-women were often nurses in rich homes. They were hardly ever Greeks by origin, since Hellenic sentiment seems to have resisted such an exploitation of Greeks by their fellows, but they might be any kind of foreigners or 'barbarians'. Of course, like slaves everywhere, slaves in Athens were at the mercy of their masters, and might suffer from their whims and vices, though no doubt good tempers and common prudence assured that they were usually quite well treated. We cannot doubt that Athenian democracy was able to do what it did because it rested on slavery. This provided the free citizens with leisure to do more than spend their time in finding the means of subsistence. Of course the majority of them still had to work hard, but at least there were times when they could leave their work and give their attention to public affairs. However much we may deplore slavery in any form, we must remember that in Athens the variety of origin in slaves and their relatively small number prevented Attica from developing anything like a 'colonial' economy, or from becoming like Georgia or Mississippi before the American Civil War. The citizens composed the larger part of the population and almost the whole indigenous part of it. And this was indeed democratic in the extent of its powers and its responsibilities.

One large class of persons was excluded from political life. The Athenians did not anticipate the modern world in allowing women to manage public affairs. Indeed their whole treatment of women may rather surprise us. If we are to believe their own statements, women, at least in theory, were confined to an almost Oriental seclusion, and proverbs stress that their right place is the home and that silence is their noblest part. Such statements need not be taken too literally, since they plainly contain an element of wishful thinking and it is hard to imagine women in any Balkan country keeping silent for long. It certainly seems true that women in the Athenian democracy mixed less freely and less easily with men than they do in Homer, but this does not mean that they were locked up. Not only does Attic tragedy give some of its most important parts to women, and in doing this it can hardly have flown altogether in the face of actual experience, but even comedy, which is far more realistic, makes great play with them. A woman is the leading character in Aristophanes' *Lysistrata* and behaves with a remarkable lack of inhibition. No doubt women worked while men talked, and in humble households did much that might have been done by slaves elsewhere, but that need not have prevented them from speaking freely or assuming responsibility in their own sphere. Indeed the evidence of Attic tombstones and funeral vases suggests that the Athenians were just as capable of deep and lasting affection for their wives as any other men. But what was lacking was any conscious or artificial cult of womanhood, such as existed in the Middle Ages, or even any courtly sentiment about them such as has existed in Europe since the Renaissance. In Athens men played the main part and kept their relations with women in the background, as an essential part indeed of their lives but separate from politics and public affairs. Even in their poetry love plays a very small part in comparison with what other poetry leads us to expect, and no conception of Athenian life is right which does not recognize its essentially male character.

The aristocratic heritage of a chosen people

The unusual character of Athenian democracy may be seen in one or two qualities which we do not associate with such a society. In the first place, it inherited an aristocratic tradition of taste and elegance and succeeded in adapting it to a wider circle and in giving it a new strength and solidity. This is clear not only from sculpture and poetry, which show a progressive tendency towards a greater scope and more majestic air until at least the middle of the century, but in the ceremonies and rites of civic or domestic life. The noble art of vase-painting illustrates much of Athenian life to which the written sources do not refer, and on these scenes drawn from the living world we see the Athenians as they saw themselves. In moments of gaiety which the painter has caught there is hardly anything vulgar or unrestrained: style and taste are always dominant, and have an aristocratic distinction, as if they belonged to men who knew almost instinctively how to transform any small occasion with a touch of charm or dignity. Whether it is young men jumping or girls dancing, or graver episodes of adventure and war, the same distinction is always present, and of course the artists have learned it from life around them. Here are the ordinary episodes of every day seen with unspoiled eyes and appreciated at their true worth without exaggeration or rhetoric. Here we can see an 'unbought grace of life' which is entirely natural and unpremeditated and derives its strength from being an accepted part of any household routine.

The respect and taste for the individual, which is so marked a feature of Athenian democracy, was matched and countered by a deep feeling of national unity, by a conviction that all these different men and women were members of a city which made them what they were and was responsible for their most cherished traditions. This was of course patriotism as it exists everywhere, but in Athens it took a special shape. The Athenians boasted that in their long history they had never been conquered, and the fifth century was to confirm this confidence until the tragic end destroyed it. In 490 BC and again in 480–479 they defeated the Persians, who on the first occasion landed on Attic soil at Marathon and on the second burned the sacred buildings of the Acropolis. Athenian patriotism drew a new strength from danger and throve on a faith that the gods loved Athens and protected her. Above all it made a man feel that, however much he might think about his own rights and individuality, he was part of a larger scheme and proud to belong to it. At the great national festival of the Panathenaea, whose religious purpose was to conduct a simple rite of laying a garment on the knees of the image of Athene, the whole population took part, and the scene in all its dignity and harmony can be seen on the frieze of the Parthenon. Young men on horses, young women walking in stately robes, bulls driven to the sacrifice, and the gods watching in pleased detachment show the Athenian ideal of national solidarity. This is the expression of something very dear to the Athenian heart, a harmony of law and liberty, of ceremony and pleasure, of communal strength and individual contributions to it. It is in this same spirit that at the end of Aeschylus' *Eumenides* the chorus sings of Athens:

> Fare ye well, rejoiced with riches' righteous portion, fare ye well,
> Folk that in this city nigh to God's own Virgin Daughter dwell;
> Dear to her as she to Zeus, beloved and loving timely-wise,
> And, beneath her wings abiding, sacred in the Father's eyes.

The Athenians in their own way felt that they were a chosen people, specially loved by the gods, and that this imposed peculiar obligations upon them.

The cause of freedom and the lure of power

This love of country was naturally expressed in war. For a large part of the fifth century Athens was at war with some power or other, usually with Persia or Sparta. War, indeed, was an inevitable ingredient in Hellenic life, and what matters is not that it was so common but that at least in Athens attempts were made to justify it and fit it into a philosophy of life. No Athenian would question that the best thing a man can do is to die for his country, but they liked to ask what this means, what, after all, is the significance of a man's country, and why is he glad to die for it. In answer to such questions they pleaded that Athens had something like a mission and did for others what they were unable to do alone. In the main this mission was to secure political freedom against either foreign conquerors like the Persians or selfish cliques at home, but of course the two aims were easily confused and the conception of liberty was wide and adaptable. This ideal received an enormous impetus from the Persian wars, when Athens took a leading part in repelling the invader, and was sanctified in the following years when Sparta abandoned the military hegemony of Greece and let Athens take it over from her. The spirit of this movement can be seen in Aeschylus' *The Persians*, produced in 472 BC. It is cast in dramatic form but is in spirit a paean of victory for free men over tyrants and slaves. Behind its peals of glory lies that respect for the common man which was the basis of Athenian life and refused to admit any good in tyranny. To die in such a cause was to assert the right of man to be himself and to go his own way, and this passionate conviction gave a special strength to Athenian patriotism.

In the world of affairs this spirit had far-reaching results. When Athens took over from Sparta the leadership of the league against Persia, it was as one free city among others. But by a gradual process this league was transformed into an empire of which Athens was the mistress. Cities that wished to leave the league were compelled by force to stay in it; the money which they paid towards the common costs was taken by Athens as tribute for herself; the democracies established among the allies were kept in power less because they were democracies than because they represented a pro-Athenian element in power. The cause of freedom which Athens had championed for its own sake at the start imperceptibly began to be identified with the cause of Athens and her interests. Once she began to feel the lure of power, she could not resist it, and though it took long for her allies to turn their old trust in her to hatred, in the last quarter of the century the change was complete and Athens, that had begun as the home of liberty, became the tyrant of the Aegean, which might slaughter or enslave a whole male population, as she did at Melos, because it refused to fit in with her plans.

An empire of this kind may be looked at from many angles and is likely to contain many good as well as bad elements. From the practical side Athens certainly did much for Greece, at least in the second quarter of the fifth century. The Persian menace was still real, and Athens countered it, not only on the sea with her excellent navy, but by such far-flung adventures as the invasion of Egypt in support of local rebels against the Persians. This ended in an appalling catastrophe in 454 BC, when 250 ships and a large army were trapped and lost. No one could say that Athens was not prepared to take the leading part and bear the heaviest cost in such undertakings. Equally, it cannot be denied that the democratic régimes which Athens sustained in her allies were probably better equipped for law and liberty than the small aristocratic cliques which opposed them. Even if the payment of tribute to Athens was an indubitable burden, it ensured a degree of safety and order. But to argue in this way is to neglect the other side of the picture – the feelings of the allies themselves and of their friends outside the Athenian sphere who saw Athens in a different and more hostile light. If liberty had made Athens great in spirit, it was a disastrous paradox that she should at times be forced to stifle it elsewhere. The great Athenians were conscious of this and did their best to explain and justify their position.

The finest plea for Athenian imperialism was made by Pericles, who was elected in successive years to the office of general in the years 443–430, and held by virtue of his powerful personality and striking eloquence a special place in the councils and government of Athens. In the speeches which Thucydides ascribes to him and which, though they may not be verbal transcripts of what he said, certainly reflect his views, we see the Athenian justification of imperialism. It is, as we might expect, based on a belief in democracy. He understood with remarkable insight what this meant at Athens and wished Athens to teach it to other cities, regarding her as 'the school of Greece' and claiming with justice that her doors were always open to foreigners. But this task, in his view, had almost inevitably to be carried out through force, and in this he saw a special glory. For him Athenian adventures into distant lands were among their greatest glories, which needed no Homer to sing them since they had their own deathless memorials. He knew that such a conception might, if carried out to the letter, win more enemies than friends, but he was not afraid of that and argued that glory was more important and more than compensated for it. So Pericles turned Athenian imperialism into a mission whose task was to make other cities like Athens and whose reward was an undying memory among men. In this way he justified and explained the new and terrible power which had come to Athens and was still not fully understood either in its use or its results.

The visible expression of Athens' ambition

The imaginative and spiritual side of this ambition was presented in striking visible form in the buildings which Pericles caused to be built on the Acropolis. The rocky hill which dominates Athens and had for centuries been the seat of its sacred shrines became the dazzling and far-seen symbol of Athenian achievement. Since the old temples and works of art had been destroyed by the Persians in 479, the way was clear to building something new and far more striking. In 447 the Parthenon was begun from the plans of Ictinus under the supervision of Callicrates. The cost was defrayed from tribute paid by the allies who thus saw their dependence on Athens in its true reality. Behind the Parthenon and its attendant buildings lay the idea that Athens, guided by her national goddess, Athene, had through the exercise of power found a supreme glory which demanded the highest art to express it. The Parthenon was the temple of the Maiden, Athene, who was also known as 'the Champion' and renowned as a goddess of war. It was therefore appropriate that her statue should stand outside and be visible from land and sea for many miles around as the emblem of her own power and glory, and of the power and glory of Athens whom she inspired and guided. It was no less appropriate that the noble gateway and attendant buildings, the Propylaea, should be built on a scale hardly smaller than the Parthenon, since through it went the ceremonial processions which honoured the national goddess. Both Parthenon and Propylaea were for all purposes completed when war broke out with Sparta in 431, and are the ripest and most revealing monuments of the great age in its ambitions and its grandeur.

The Parthenon was a temple of a goddess in whose reality men believed, and the sculptures which adorned it show what the Athenians thought about themselves. They depict partly struggles against primitive creatures like centaurs, thus illustrating the rise of Athens from uncouth barbarism, partly events of cosmic grandeur which underlie the course of Athenian history. The east pediment shows the birth of Athene on Olympus. A celestial world of dream-like calm is broken by the sudden appearance of a fully grown goddess in the midst of it, and wakes with awe and amazement. The west pediment shows the struggle of Athene and Poseidon for the possession of Attica: two great divinities in conflict, and a fearful sense of power and effort. Each pediment represents a different aspect of the national myth. If the east shows what the emergence of such a power as Athene means even on Olympus, the west shows

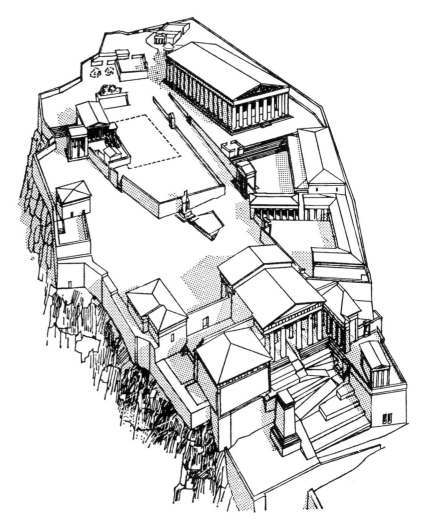

View of the Acropolis as rebuilt in Pericles' time.

what a goddess this must be that even the lord of the sea quails before her. This is not allegory but mythology in the truest sense. The gods in their own sphere display in a pure form what happens to the men who live under their sway. Both scenes are concerned with power, either emerging or in full action, and both present to the eye the unexampled force which the Athenians felt at work in themselves and believed to be divine.

Even in their present ruined state the great buildings of the Acropolis stand as a majestic and compelling memorial to the greatness of Athens. We can see that they were a truly national monument, the expression of what the Athenian people as a whole believed and hoped about itself. If they glorify power, it is not the power of individuals but of a people and its goddess, and the expression of this power is not flaunting or boastful but disciplined by something characteristically Hellenic and Athenian. The Parthenon was indeed richly decorated, and in its unspoiled state, with its gold and ivory statue of Athene, may well have startled and dazzled the eyes, but none the less the decoration is subordinated to an austere and dominating design. The sculptures are confined to the frieze, which is not visible from outside, to the two pediments high in air, and the metopes between the tops of the columns. None of them immediately strikes the beholder, who is captured rather by the plain, magnificent and orderly design of the building with its wonderful proportions, its fine surface of marble turned by sun and rain to a faint colour of gold, and its pillars in their mathematical elegance and harmony. This control is typical of the Athenian genius. However powerful their feelings may have been, whatever ideas and ideals may have stirred them, they reduced them to order, and set them in a design which is at once plain and overwhelmingly majestic. This shows how serious the Athenians were. For all their sense of irony and mockery, for all their outbursts of pride or anger, they felt that their national shrine must conform to the ideal of law which was the foundation of their liberties.

The poet as interpreter and critic

The Acropolis shows the Athenian spirit in its power and glory, but a people with so honest and intelligent a vision of life was not content to rest with this as the only expression of its national life. Parallel to the great development of architecture and sculpture came a no less great development in poetry which was also national and profoundly serious. Because this appealed to a whole people it had a special strength and scope. The poet had no need to defend himself against the Philistine or to justify himself to a society mainly given to other aims; he drew his ideas, his strength, his public from a people of which he was himself a characteristic member and whose outlook he shared. He was not only an interpreter but a critic, not merely a participant in a national experience but a leader of thought about it. It is therefore right that the most powerful literary art of Athens should be drama performed in the open air before a vast audience in the theatre of Dionysus. Drama was in origin a religious rite and never quite lost traces of it. It was usually concerned, sooner or later, with the ways of the gods to men; it was always profoundly thoughtful; it presented great issues through individual stories and related them to current problems of religion and morality; above all it maintained a noble level of poetry, derived in part from hymns to the gods but enriched by imaginative speculation and a keen sense of what divine government means to the conduct of men. It was also a civic rite. The men and women who make their brief appearances on the stage are fundamentally not unlike actual figures of the time; they speak in a rich language, which draws much from the literary past but also owes some of its strength to a close contact with the living word; they take part in grim and tragic stories which seem remote enough from actuality but have none the less an illuminating affinity with it. Greek drama is in every sense a national art just as much as architecture, and serves a parallel purpose. Into it men of remarkable genius put their profound thoughts and imaginative insight, and through their work we get another view into the thoughts of Athenians as their interpreters understood them. In some countries it may be possible to study history without looking at literature, but in Athens it is not, since the poetry of the age provides some of the most important evidence about its character.

Greek tragedy is not always tragedy in the modern sense. It need not and does not always end in disaster. But it is tragic in the Greek sense that it is intended for production at a religious ceremony and has to maintain a high seriousness in its subjects. Through tragedy the Athenians expressed the universal aspects of problems which concerned and perplexed them. Though their themes are nearly always taken from a remote, mythical past, that does not prevent them from being highly contemporary. For instance, in the three plays of his *Oresteia* Aeschylus tells a terrible story of murder and vengeance, of a woman who kills her husband and of a son who has to kill his mother. But though all the horror and excitement of the old story is preserved with a remarkable power, the end comes with all the force of a new discovery. The son, Orestes, is in the end purified of blood-guilt by a law-court, which is none other than the high court of Athens. The introduction of this into the plot reflects a deep social change, of which Aeschylus was fully conscious, from domestic vendetta to the rule of law. The splendid and exalted poetry which closes the third play conveys in an imaginative and compelling form what law meant to a people like the Athenians and is appropriately associated with the guardian goddess, Athene. It was by such means that Athenian dramatists presented their understanding of political events and of the great issues which lay behind them. The audience, trained to listening to tragedy and able to follow its methods, would see what the dramatist meant and come away all the prouder of the institutions of its city.

Tragedy provided something else than this, a kind of national self-examination and inquiry into the universal aspects of its actions. Though it is dangerous to read any reference to passing events in the plays of Sophocles, there is no doubt that he was keenly interested in them and knew of them from the inside, since he was a friend of Pericles and even held office with him as a general in 440. His method is to take some universal problem and to present it in vivid drama with a full sense of its human and moral implications. Above all he seems to have been much concerned with the whole question of power, its motives, its means, and its dangers. In an age of growing imperialism, he was well aware of its character and consequences and did not shrink from a dramatic analysis of its exponents. His *Ajax* turns on the conflict between the old heroic individualism and the new claims of civic power to obedience and respect; his *Antigone* on the discord between the immutable laws of the gods, which lay certain inescapable obligations upon men, and the harsh decrees of a tyrant who is too infatuated with power to know what evil he is doing; *King Oedipus* on the great man, who through no real fault of his own, none the less falls from high position to utter misery because the gods decree that he must; *Electra* on a state of human affairs in which law has ceased to work, and men and women have to undertake ugly duties against which their consciences may rebel but which cannot be shirked. Each play presents in a different shape some issue of power and its limits. The implicit criticism of it is penetrating and deeply disturbing. If Creon in the *Antigone* is a poor thing with delusions of grandeur, Oedipus is a magnificent creature, a true shepherd of his people, who none the less falls disastrously. In two of his last plays, *Philoctetes* and *Oedipus at Colonus*, Sophocles portrays in Odysseus and Creon even more advanced cases of the moral insensibility which power breeds in its victims. His conclusions are unanswerable. Power is fraught with dangers not merely to a man's happiness but to his soul. In its very nature it conceals corruptions of which a man must beware, and the typically Greek conclusion is that he is wise to remember that he is as nothing before the gods. These conclusions are all the more remarkable because Sophocles himself knew about power and office from the inside. But in his art he revealed his real feelings about them. If he stressed the need for moderation and the doctrine of the Mean, it was not because he saw them practised around him but because he felt that something of the kind was vitally necessary if his countrymen were not to destroy themselves by attempting too much.

Unlike tragedy in most ways and yet like it in its criticism of life is Attic comedy, itself also a Dionysiac rite, which with reckless fancy and complete candour approached contemporary questions without any attempt to disguise them in mythical dress. The Attic comedians thought nothing of presenting living characters on the stage or of putting them in the most ridiculous positions. Since the greatest age of comedy seems to have come with Aristophanes in the last twenty or so years of the Athenian empire, it is surprising how vigorous and outspoken it is, how in a time of growing violence it speaks for liberty and peace and common sense. Its dazzling jokes and fantastic situations are in their own way as pertinent a criticism of life as the grave conclusion of the tragedians. It works with different weapons, and of course we cannot always be sure how seriously to take it, but its results are often deadly. If Aristophanes' chief butts are the inferior statesmen who came to power after the death of Pericles, he does not altogether spare Pericles himself, and his whole outlook is a comment, by no means favourable, on Periclean ideals. For him imperial power was hostile to the grace and sweetness of life, and he used his whole armoury of nonsense to press his point home. He believed in Athens with a deep love, but the Athens of his dreams was a quiet, rural town, the home of farmers and small traders, of simple pleasures and graceful decorum. If he accepted facts as he was sometimes compelled to, he was ready with wise and far-seeing suggestions, as when in the *Lysistrata* he urged with powerful eloquence that the empire should be turned into a confederacy of equal states. He was certainly popular, not merely for his jokes; he may well have represented a solid body of public opinion which was frightened of the way taken by events. No doubt, too, he awoke great hostility, but despite a fine or two he was allowed to say what he liked, and until its collapse Athens submitted yearly to this merciless criticism of its favourite personalities and approved designs.

Unpredictable spiritual powers

A city which could allow itself to be criticized in such ways both by tragedy and comedy had an uncommon share of self-confidence and of respect for the truth, and we need ask for no further proof of the extraordinary spirit which carried Athens through her great adventures to her final doom. Yet we may perhaps ask on what ultimate scheme of beliefs this confidence was based, what religious or metaphysical foundation it had. Though it is hard for us to recapture what the Greeks felt about their gods, no consideration of Athens is complete without some attempt to do so. Perhaps we might say that their greatest, most honoured gods were powers of the spirit, forces which they felt at work in themselves but which, not without logic, they believed to exist outside themselves with an independent divine being. Just as Athene was both the adventurous spirit who inspired her subjects and a real power who guided and guarded them, so Dionysus, the god of intoxication, was both the inspiration which poets know in themselves and something even more incalculable which works in the world. Though the essence of such gods was their power, they were not beyond good and evil, and moralists and poets agree that in the end they punish the wicked. None the less there remained something more frightening about them. Being in the last resort beyond understanding, they cannot be explained by human rules of behaviour or expected to conform to common morality. They may always, without warning or apparent

motive, punish or destroy, and a man's task is to be humble and hope to avoid their wrath. Like the sea they allure and amaze and call to action, but also like the sea they are liable to swift changes of mood and often bring death where they seem to have promised success. Greek politics and Greek life were played against this background of glorious, menacing, inscrutable gods. A man might try to resemble them, and even perhaps for a moment succeed, but in the end he was sure to fall. Behind all the reckless activities and the high ambitions of the fifth century lies this uncertainty, and it imparts an almost tragic grandeur to the actors who perform their heroic parts with a full knowledge of what they will cost.

The spirit of inquiry becomes destructive

On the other hand these ancient and half-instinctive beliefs were countered by a searching spirit of inquiry. Just as Greek art and poetry owe much of their indestructible strength to the hard intellectual labour which has gone into them, so in Greek life there was no lack of hard and vigorous thought. How grand this might be can be seen from the searching pages of Thucydides, with their appalling insight into the unchanging ways of political man. Yet we may be sure that he was not alone, that any politician who wished to have his way in public life had to some degree to rely on reasoned argument. The release of Athenian energy meant an enormous impetus for the intelligence, and this process was strengthened by the conditions of life which encouraged talk and forced decisions to be made. When this spirit was combined with the old religious faith, the result was not so precarious as we might expect. Indeed until late in the fifth century the spirit of inquiry served to clarify and give point to much that was already accepted from tradition. In this period Athens was at her greatest. Just as she was able to infuse an aristocratic elegance into a democratic frame, so she was also able to fortify an ancient religion with serious speculations about the worth of man and his place before the gods. In the last years, when victory receded into the distance and self-confidence ebbed, it may be true that this happy balance was shaken and that questions became more deadly and more destructive. The spirit of Euripides and Socrates was perhaps too strong for a war-worn people to accept without danger to itself, and it is not surprising that it turned against both. Most great civilizations fail in the end from the defects of their virtues, and Athens failed mainly from the superabundance of that energy which had made her great, but partly also from placing too great a trust in the intelligence, which turned from the clarifying of great issues to undermining their assumptions. Before these processes were completed, Athens found an equilibrium which allowed the whole human being to work in harmony with itself and to discover the full range of its powers. If in this she made mistakes, they are as nothing in comparison with her successes or with the example and inspiration which these still are for us.

Nereids preparing for a wedding: from an Athenian pyxis, c. 430 BC, by the Eretria Painter.

QUATTROCENTO VENICE

'Ocean's nurseling, Venice',

as Shelley called her, originally the home of poor fishermen and refugees from the barbarian invaders of the Roman Empire, became a leading commercial power as early as the twelfth century. This unique city of water, built upon the mudbanks of the Venetian lagoon, with canals instead of streets, developed into a mighty mercantile republic which served as the entrepôt of Europe's trade with the East. Furs, spices, silks, drugs, gold, dyes and porcelain, transported by sea into the city, gave an exotic glow to its otherwise conservative magnificence. Venetian wealth, Venetian naval power, Venetian stability – the fruit of a complex yet durable republican constitution employing a working aristocracy – were the source of unvarying admiration by foreign visitors.

The Quattrocento was the most striking period of Venetian splendour: a period of prosperity and increasing artistic achievement – but also one of danger. It may be that these new perils provided a new stimulus. Turkish conquests endangered Venice's possessions and markets, and her own conquests on the Italian mainland inevi-

tably drew her into the dogfight of Italian politics. But these also made her subject to new influences, above all that of the Renaissance. Venice adapted Renaissance forms slowly and cautiously; her idiosyncratic traditions and international outlook modified and transformed them (as they had modified and transformed Gothic from the north) and enabled the city to make an important and distinctive contribution to world art.

Gentile Bellini (c. 1429–1507) was among the seminal Venetian painters of the century, and typical in his love of portraying the manners and activities of his native city. In this detail from his large, documentary *Procession of the True Cross* (opposite), Bellini gives an almost photographic impression of the two most important buildings in the city. The setting is the Piazza San Marco. In the left background is the Basilica of St Mark dedicated to Venice's patron saint; it represents the sumptuous Byzantine tradition. On its right, the Doge's Palace, residence of the city-state's elected head, is the outstanding example of Venetian Gothic. (1)

Venetian commercial supremacy depended largely on her naval strength and the seaworthiness of her mercantile marine. The arsenal (built in 1104) in which her galleys were constructed was therefore a vital part of the city. It is shown here (left) in a detail from a woodcut made in about 1500 from drawings by the Venetian artist Jacopo de' Barberi. (2)

Foreign trade bred a cosmopolitan attitude among Venetians: foreigners were a familiar sight in their city. The reception of English ambassadors, for example, in a Venetian setting (above) was used as a detail in one of his St Ursula paintings by Vittore Carpaccio (1486–1525). A Venetian embassy to Cairo is the subject of a painting by the school of Gentile Bellini (detail below). (3, 4)

The Grand Canal, called the 'fairest and best-built street' in the world by a French traveller in 1495, has always been the main thoroughfare of Venice. Along this broad serpentine avenue of water were built the palatial houses in which the aristocracy lived. The photograph at left was taken from a balcony of the Cà d'Oro, one of the most famous and beautiful of these palaces. The use of lions as ornament is typical of Venice; a winged lion is associated with the story of St Mark, and the lion became in time the emblem of the Republic. The building in the background, far right, is the Fondaco de' Tedeschi, which was the German warehouse from the twelfth century. It was rebuilt in 1508, after a fire, and is a fine example of Venetian adaptation of Renaissance styles. (5)

Venetian women, elegantly and colourfully dressed, were much admired by the outside world. Carpaccio, with his eye for descriptive detail, painted two of them seated on a balcony (right). These have traditionally been called courtesans – a judgment based to some degree on their low-cut gowns and their hairdress; but comparison with other contemporary paintings indicates they are indistinguishable from ladies of fashion, with various appurtenances of high Venetian society. (6)

The palaces of Venice were testimony to the city's great wealth and show the gradual shifting of styles in the fifteenth century. The Cà d'Oro (top), built mainly by Matteo de' Raverti between 1422 and 1440, with carved decoration of the façade by Giovanni and Bartolomeo Bon (or Buon), is the perfect example of Venetian Gothic, a combination of the authentic Gothic from northern Europe with borrowings from Byzantium. The Palazzo Vendramin Calergi (left centre), on the other hand, built between 1481 and 1509 to the design of Mauro Coducci and Pietro Lombardo, was the earliest Venetian residence conceived in the Renaissance style that had found its original expression in Florence. Coducci was also the designer of San Michele in Isola (left bottom), the first church in Venice (1469–79) that left Gothic modes behind and followed a distinctly classical composition. (7, 8, 9)

The Doge's Palace, of which the main courtyard is shown right, illustrates magnificently the individual manner in which Venetian designers absorbed and mixed the Gothic and classical. This façade and the so-called Giants' Staircase (named for the statues of Mars and Neptune that stand at the top) are the work of Antonio Rizzo and were built between 1483 and 1498. The Gothic arches of the first-storey gallery are embedded between predominantly Renaissance architectural features; it was the genius of artists working in Venice to blend academically disparate elements. (10)

Gothic and classical, yet each unmistakably Venetian, stand side by side on the Grand Canal (above). The Palazzo Barberi shows, in its ogee arches, the Eastern influence which characterizes so much Venetian architecture; the Palazzo Dario, built around 1487 for the representative of the city of Constantinople, was one of the designs of Pietro Lombardo, who created a number of charming Venetian buildings in this period. The typical chimneys appear also in Carpaccio's painting known as *The Miracle of the Cross at the Rialto* (detail, left). The Rialto Bridge, described by Ruskin as 'a row of shops, sustained on an arch', has long been synonymous with the Venetian market-place. The bridge Ruskin saw was built in 1588 and designed by Antonio da Ponte, but the painting represents the wooden predecessor, with drawbridges in the centre, which existed in the fifteenth century. (11, 12)

57

The development of Venetian sculpture can be studied through various decorative details in the Doge's Palace. The carving of Noah's drunkenness (below left), which was done in the early part of the century and has been attributed to Matteo de' Raverti, has much in common with Gothic sculpture in the north. On the other hand, the graceful and delicate Eve by Antonio Rizzo (below right) is almost entirely a work of the Renaissance, with its reawakened interest in the nude and direct echoes from Greek sculpture. Rizzo was the most gifted and important Venetian sculptor of the later Quattrocento; he and Antonio Bregno, among others, contributed to the statues on the pinnacles above the Foscari Arch in the courtyard of the Doge's Palace (right). The Arch is named for Doge Francesco Foscari (1423–57), who was responsible for much of the rebuilding of the Palace that took place during the fifteenth century. His bust (opposite above) is attributed to Bregno. But the most imposing and expressive statue in Venice was the work of a Florentine master: Verrocchio's symbolic equestrian portrait of the *condottiere* Colleoni (detail, opposite below). (13–17)

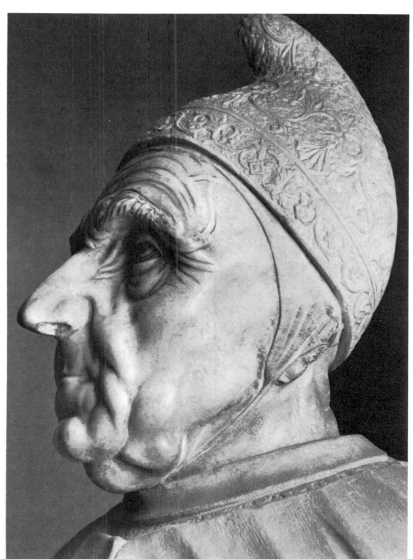

The symbols of Venice, visual and legendary, are combined in Carpaccio's *The Lion of St Mark* (detail), dated 1514. The Gothic façade of the Doge's Palace dominates the background; behind it are the domes of St Mark's Basilica and to its left the Campanile. The winged lion holds open a book on which is written 'Peace unto you, Mark, my Evangelist'. (18)

QUATTROCENTO VENICE

J. R. HALE

THE WORLD has probably known no city where life has been more penetratingly determined by site and governmental structure than Venice. Seen from the air, Venice looks like two molecules trying to bite one another in a drop of water, molecules whose cells, under a still higher magnification, turn out to be rectangles of housing divided by canals. The canals are, of course, what has always made a visit to Venice an exotic experience, but had there been no canals, had Venice been a solid island rather than a mosaic of painfully consolidated mudbanks, the unique character of its economic and political life would have been just the same. The watery streets only add an extra whiff of romance to a story that would have been heady enough without them.

The lone sea-wolf

Islanded in its lagoons, Venice was both part of and separate from the rest of Italy. The extent to which she joined her life to that of the peninsula as a whole was to some extent a matter of choice. Protected by swamp and water, she could not be compelled to join the quarrelsome club of Italian states, though she spoke a dialect form of their common language. Throughout the Middle Ages she remained aloof, her eyes and her business turned east and south, increasing her territory a little to the north, but mainly by the growing deck-space of her shipping. It was not until the Quattrocento, the fifteenth century, that she made up her mind to face west as well and to add a land empire to her maritime one.

It was natural that a city founded by fishermen, a city that became a vast artificial harbour, should produce a race of traders. Their galleys and round ships came to dominate the sea-routes of the Mediterranean. Quattrocento Venice was the greatest market-place in Europe, where goods from the Levant, Persia, India and Africa – silks and spices, dyes and porcelain – were piled beside the ores and cloths of northern and western Europe. The quest for trade concessions and harbours led her into a close relationship with Byzantium, and then, as the Christian empire of the east was prised and chipped from its gorgeous niche by the Turks, into a more hazardous but equally close relationship with them. A lone sea-wolf by force of geography, Venice became a lone wolf diplomatically by force of trade. In 1204 she had cajoled the crusaders whom her fleet was carrying to the Holy Land into sacking Christian Constantinople on the way and obtaining a trading base for her there. When the Turks began to press on the trade-routes of the eastern Mediterranean, Venice negotiated treaties to protect her own interests with one hand, while signing agreements to support new crusades with the other, and she kept in contact with the Muslims while remaining the prime carrier of the pilgrim traffic to Palestine. As the Turks advanced north-westwards across the Balkans, the role of Christianity's spearhead, foisted on Venice by geography, conflicted more and more painfully with the role that geography had chosen for her when the Turks were still beyond her horizon: the role of conveying to Europe the luxuries and, in the case of dyes and spices, necessities of the East.

As a result of this position, Venice was both used and abused by the rest of Europe. The countries who gratefully exchanged goods with her spread bitter rumours of the greed that made her temporize with the Turks and imperil Christendom. And when, as we shall see, Venice turned to accumulating territory on the Italian mainland in the very century that saw the Turks take Salonika and Constantinople and raid the coast of Italy itself, the bitterness became hatred. In 1509 this led to a coalition of hostile powers that stripped her at a blow of all her laboriously won lands on the *terra ferma*.

The site of Venice, then, conditioned the peculiar balance in which she found herself between East and West; it enabled her to be more reticent in aligning herself with the Papacy than were the other Italian states, it made her the most cosmopolitan of European cities, it gave a quite special character, conservative and yet exotic, to her culture. It gave a unique homogeneity of interest to every class, from the noble who planned a trading venture to the worker in the arsenal – it is tempting to write the name of this largest industrial plant in Europe with a capital 'A' – who caulked the seams in the galleys of the state.

'The most triumphant city'

For it was the state, the constitution, the administration of Venice that confirmed the distinction, originating in geography, between this city and the other great cities of the Renaissance world, Venice was a republic. So, for that matter, was Florence, but whereas Quattrocento Florence steadily lost the spirit of republicanism under the Medici and lost even the forms of it in the 1530s, Venice remained a republic, the subject of almost continual admiration, wonder and study throughout the sixteenth and seventeenth centuries. Though the heart gradually went out of her institutions thereafter, she was still a republic when she surrendered to Napoleon in 1797. In contrast to the shifting constitutional forms of the other Italian states, this steady maintenance of her own form was little less than spectacular. In Quattrocento Venice there were no assassinations, no sudden rise of one man or family by intrigue or conquest, no proletarian revolt or threat of one. Florence misliked and distrusted Venice but nevertheless looked to her for lessons when reforming her constitution after the temporary expulsion of the Medici in 1494. We shall have to look more closely at this constitution, which was so stable, and which produced such harmony between classes. For the moment it will suffice to repeat that, together with the island site, this made Venice a state different in kind from any other in Europe.

There is a justification for isolating the Quattrocento from the history of Venice as a whole. In 1405 Venice won her first extensive territories on the mainland and became committed to involvement in the west. Having lost these territories in 1509, she emerged in 1516 from the greatest defeat of her history with her mainland possessions intact but more committed than ever to the vagaries of European power politics. Her markets had been damaged by the Turkish advance in the Mediterranean and the Portuguese opening of an alternative route for the Indian spice trade but, at about the same date, they began a slow but steady recovery. In the arts the Quattrocento begins with a Gothic still vigorous and developing, and ends with the victory of classical forms. It is typical of Venice that in the history of her art, as of her constitution, there are no revolutions. While attracted by the cultural ferment of Florence, which produced in the first half of the fifteenth century works which were both experimental and authoritative, Venice followed the works of Brunelleschi, Masaccio and Donatello with gingerly caution, fertilizing her own soil rather than bringing in new earth from Tuscany. Thus, while Florence experienced the Mannerist revolution, Venetian art steadily matured from Giovanni Bellini through Giorgione and Titian to Veronese and Tintoretto.

In Venice as in Rome the fullness of Renaissance sensuousness and classicism came with the Cinquecento, yet Quattrocento Venice was already considered a marvel, not only for its waterways and swarming gondolas, but for its churches and palaces, its ceremonies and works of art. In 1494, when Pietro Casola arrived to wait for his pilgrim ship, he 'determined to examine carefully the city of Venice, about which so much has been said and written, not only by learned men, but also by great scholars, that it appears to me there is nothing left to say'. Fortunately he was no more daunted by this than are most travel-writers, and went on to say a great deal, even though 'it is impossible to tell or write fully of the beauty, the magnificence, or the wealth of the city of Venice'. And this is not the tribute of a wide-eyed bumpkin. Casola was a distinguished cleric, familiar with Rome and Milan, and his admiration was echoed next year by the French ambassador, Philip de Commines, a man with a still wider experience of great cities. With an escort of five and twenty scarlet-clad gentlemen,

> I was conducted through the principal street, which they call the Grand Canal, and it is so wide that galleys frequently cross one another; indeed I have seen vessels of four hundred tons or more ride at anchor just by the houses. It is the fairest and best-built street, I think, in the world, and goes quite through the city; the houses are very large and lofty, and built of stone; the old ones are all painted; those of about a hundred years standing are faced with white marble from Istria and inlaid with porphyry and serpentine. Within they have, most of them, two chambers at least adorned with gilt ceilings, rich marble chimney-pieces, bedsteads of gold colour, their portals of the same, and most gloriously furnished. In short, it is the most triumphant city that I have ever seen, the most respectful to all ambassadors and strangers, governed with the greatest wisdom, and serving God with the most solemnity.

Visitors exclaimed over the size of the arsenal and the production-belt methods with which the galleys were built and equipped there, the glass works at Murano, the strange and opulent beauty of St Mark's, the profusion of articles for sale, the rich dress and the almost bare breasts of the women, but it was the solemnity of state occasions that impressed them most. They watched the doge setting out to wed the sea in the *Bucentaur*, 'a great ship fashioned like a tabernacle, painted, covered with gilding, shrouded with silken hangings' and propelled by three hundred oars, while cannon roared and trumpets brayed. They watched the processions of civic and ecclesiastical dignitaries, pacing two by two in crimson, scarlet, silver and cloth of gold, gorgeous but grave:

> This is very different [wrote Casola] from the practices I have noted at many courts, both ecclesiastical and secular, where the moment the Prince has passed all go pell-mell and without any order. In Venice, both before and behind the doge, everyone goes in the best order imaginable.

The unchanging face of Venice

The present-day visitor can share the impression made by the city on his Quattrocento predecessors; for, as the engraving of 1500 by Jacopo de' Barbari shows, the general appearance of Venice has changed remarkably little. By the 1420s a population of 190,000, a figure not reached again until the twentieth century, had already jammed the housing into the patterns we see today; only on the Giudecca were there large gardens and leafy spaces, which have since vanished. By 1500 the island of Murano itself had a population of 30,000. Rebuilding has altered the nature of some of the main landmarks – S. Giorgio Maggiore, the Salute, the Rialto bridge – but great churches already stood on these sites, and the Rialto's wooden predecessor crossed the Grand Canal near the Fondaco dei

Tedeschi which, save for the fading away of Giorgione's frescoes, looks now as it did in 1508.

In the Piazza S. Marco at the same date the church, the clock-tower and the campanile were as we see them; the Procuratie Nuove were already half-built, beginning the transformation of a space in part still green with trees and vines, and in part horrid with a much-criticized public latrine, into what Napoleon was to term 'the finest drawing-room in Europe'. The Ducal Palace was as it is now, apart from the statues at the head of the Scala dei Giganti and the court-yard façade facing them. As Commines was rowed past the prede-cessor of the seventeenth-century customs house and up the Grand Canal he would have seen, among the palaces singled out in modern guides: Palazzo Contarini-Fasan, Palazzo Cavalli-Franchetti, Cà Foscari, the nearly finished Palazzo Corner Spinelli and the Cà d'Oro. These, and other familiar buildings like S. Maria dei Miracoli, S. Zaccaria, the Scuola Grande di S. Marco and the main gate of the arsenal, are all works of the Quattrocento. These, and the great earlier churches like SS. Giovanni e Paolo and the Frari, with their piazze – also the fact that there has been no need to drive thorough-fares for cars through the medieval labyrinth – enable us to know Casola's Venice as we cannot know his Rome or Milan.

We can know something, too, of the wealth that produced the Quattrocento palaces and financed the splendid ceremonies of church and state. Just before his death in 1423, Doge Tommaso Mocenigo wrote an account of the riches of Venice as a way of urging his successors not to compromise the city's fortunes by squandering them on mainland wars. The authenticity of the opinions here expressed has been questioned by scholars (the original document is lost), but the statistics have been generally accepted. They are impressive. Venice then had a merchant fleet of 3,000 vessels and 300 warships (galleys were being built at the rate of forty-five a year). The houses of Venice were valued at seven million ducats. A thousand individuals had an annual income of between 700 and 4,000 ducats. Each year the mint struck a million gold and 200,000 silver ducats. An export trade worth ten million ducats a year yielded the city a profit of more than twenty per cent. Mocenigo was sure of his figures because in Venice commerce was not left to the free enterprise of the individual but, as a student of the Venetian economy has put it, 'all the merchant nobles of Venice operated as one large regulated company of which the board of directors was the Senate.' Everything in Venice, from trade to the processions so admired by tourists, was planned and ordered by the state; an understanding of the constitution is therefore essential to an understanding of the city's life and ethos as a whole.

A pyramid of power

The constitution was unabashedly aristocratic. Its base was the Great Council, membership of which was restricted to those whose names were inscribed in the *Libro d'Oro*, the Venetian *Debrett*. In the mid-Quattrocento the register contained 1,300 names, belonging to some-thing like two hundred families. The Great Council's functions were almost purely elective. It chose nearly all the officers of state, from the magistrates who punished blasphemy or were in charge of public health to the doge himself. It also chose, at a series of staggered weekly elections, sixty members to sit in the Senate, the next tier in the pyramid. These sixty sat with another sixty chosen by the out-going Senate every year, and a full meeting of the Senate comprised, in addition to these hundred and twenty members, the doge and his six councillors and the Council of Ten, about whom we shall speak in a moment; also the chief officials concerned with justice, finance and police, and with naval and military affairs. This was the chief legislative body in the constitution.

Above it came the College, or cabinet; the doge, his councillors, and the chief law officers sat here. It also included the five *savii di terra ferma* – the ministers for war, finance, the land forces and state ceremonies, and a minister without portfolio who hurried matters of special urgency through the red tape of Venice's luxuriant bureaucracy. The six *savii grandi* were responsible for maritime affairs and for preparing the business to be discussed by the College before it was passed on for the approval of the Senate: senior in status to the *savii di terra ferma*, they were the prime shapers of Venetian policy. In obedience to precautions taken at every level of the constitutional hierarchy to prevent prolonged or excessive power from falling into the hands of one man, the *savii grandi* took it in weekly turns to introduce the agenda and only retained their office for a period of months (this was true of all offices in Venice except the dogeship itself). There was one other body in the College, the five *savii agli ordini*. This office carried a vote, but not the power to debate measures. Its purpose was to give a political education to young nobles who, in their six months' tenure, could observe the working of the College and prepare themselves for posts of real responsibility. The function of the College was executive. It drafted measures for the Senate to pass into laws, and in due course put the laws into effect. Between the elective Great Council, the legislative Senate, and the executive College there was only one connecting link of real importance – apart from the membership of the Great Council which was common to members of the Senate and the College. This link was the doge and his council, for they alone had the right to initiate business in all three organs of state. Yet in spite of this, and of his lifelong tenure of office, the doge was prevented from exercising real political power. Omnipresent but emasculate, the essential symbol of a state whose will he could not control, the doge, though the cynosure of all eyes, was often propelled, as when he sat in the *Bucentaur*, by forces which faced the other way.

The symmetry of this pyramid was modified by one additional organ, the Council of Ten. The normal process whereby a governmental project became law and was put into effect was slow. To meet moments of crisis, the College passed urgent business to the Ten – business of every sort bearing on the safety of the state. And, as the Quattrocento came to be increasingly a period of crisis, both political and financial, the Ten took over more and more business from the Senate, to which it stood parallel in the hierarchy of the constitution. The speed and secrecy with which the Ten worked caused their influence to be surrounded in the following century with a baleful glamour: they were identified with the midnight summons, with the agony of state prisoners in the *pozzi* beneath the Ducal Palace or in the broiling cells under its roof, with the Bridge of Sighs and with the splash of a heavy object dropped far out in the darkened lagoon. But in the Quattrocento it was accepted respectfully as the organ that added a cutting edge to a constitution that was intrinsically wise and fair. Wise, because it enlisted the service of every member of the aristocracy over twenty-five; fair, because it was designed, through the frequent rotation of offices and through the elaborate methods of election to them, to avoid the accumulation of power in one family or clique.

Dominance of the state

With every noble involved in the ceremony of the state, and likely to take some part in its running, a sense of civic responsibility was diffused through the aristocracy as a whole: it has been rightly said that at the age of twenty-five a Venetian noble ceased to be an individual; thereafter he belonged to the republic. It is no coincidence that the characteristic Venetian portrait of the Renaissance is of a man dressed not in heroic armour or idiosyncratic finery, but in the sombrely generalized magnificence of the senatorial robes. The Venetian noble of the Quattrocento may have been a man of letters or a wealthy and active merchant, but his deepest sense of personal involvement was with the state. St Mark's itself, the most glorious shrine in Venice, was not the cathedral – that was the unimpressive S. Piero di Castello – but the ducal chapel. Its treasury was not so much a collection of pious relics as of brilliant trophies, gifts and loot that bore witness to the city's conquests and prestige. The most characteristic entertainment that the noble attended was not music and dancing in his own palace but the reception of an ambassador or the performance of a political allegory at the Ducal Palace. Sumptuary laws tried, often in vain, to cut down expenditure on private entertaining and dress, but the greatest lavishness was encouraged for official functions. There were fierce penalties for speaking ill of the state and for criticizing it in writing or through caricatures of its members; offenders were punished with the same severity that was used towards those who blasphemed against the Church: loss of a hand, an eye, the tongue or (after suitable torture) life itself.

The role of the state appeared all the more dominant for the extent to which that of the Church was played down. Of all Italian states, Venice paid the least heed to the Papacy, taking no notice of papal censures, electing her own bishops, restricting the amount of

Venetian sea-power required expert knowledge of navigational devices and theories. Above is the frontispiece of the 1537 Venetian edition of Sacroboso's textbook on astronomy, which was the basis of early navigational manuals.

property which monasteries could inherit, depriving the Church of any voice in the Great Council, and taking over the functions of the Inquisition. The Lion of St Mark continually snarled defiance at the keys of St Peter and, at each Venetian territorial advance, the Evangelist's gains were the Apostle's loss.

Venetian nobles felt no aristocratic fastidiousness about going into trade, and here again the state shaped their lives. The fortunes of the state and of the individual merchant were closely identified. The merchant needed the protection of the state along the sea-lanes and mountain-passes; the state depended on the money that the merchants made. Only nobles (together with about one thousand specially privileged *cittadini*) were allowed to engage in foreign trade. The government helped to re-establish nobles who had come near to bankruptcy and, just as young statesmen were trained for administration through the College, so the government created the post of 'bowman of the quarterdeck' to give poor young nobles experience of the galleys. The merchant galleys themselves were built by the government in the arsenal and then rented at auction to individual merchants who, while free to choose what goods they were to deal in and to fix their own prices, were subject to the overall planning of commerce by the state. It was the Senate who determined the routes and times of sailing of the six main trade convoys which left Venice every year for Greece and Constantinople, the Black Sea, Syria, Egypt, the north coast of Africa, and for England and Flanders; the Senate also fixed the freight charges and determined the size and number of vessels in these convoys. In this way private enterprise was combined with state direction, and just as power was kept out of the hands of one family or group within the government, so the trading activities of the nobles were regulated to prevent them being divided into millionaires and paupers. Here again Venice presented a striking contrast to the practice of other states.

The city was thus run by and for a well-defined oligarchy, and such constitutional development as there was in the Quattrocento was designed to restrict the power of the doge. The three doges of the first half of the century, Michele Steno, Tommaso Mocenigo and Francesco Foscari, were all men of strong character, who used their permanency amid a welter of rotating offices to exert a real personal drive towards the policies they preferred. The next elections showed that the oligarchy had learned how to deal with this problem. These three doges had reigned, between them, for fifty-five years; from 1457 to 1486 there were no less than eight doges. Rather than tinker with constitutional forms the Great Council had decided to elect men who were old or infirm. The oligarchy, which presented so homogeneous an aspect to the outside world, did have its domestic jealousies and factions: there was bitter family rivalry, there was indeed rivalry between two whole groups. The 'old' nobles had been prevented from producing a doge since 1382, and their increasing poverty made them resentful of the 'new' nobles. But these differences of interest did not hamper the effective work of policy-making, nor obscure the striking contrast between the stability of Venetian political life and the bloody faction-fights and changes of régime in other Italian states.

A pattern set by trade

Equally remarkable was the general social harmony in Venice. In 1423 the people finally lost their theoretical right to have a say in the election of the doge. Thereafter, no one who was not a noble had any voice in the way in which the government directed his life. But the absence in Venice of a landed military aristocracy, of the sort that had proved so difficult for Florence to absorb in the Middle Ages, not only meant that the nobles shared the interests and values of other citizens, but that Venice did not need a gild-structure to protect tradesmen and artisans from feudal bullying. Vigorous as they were, the gilds of Venice were never forced to demand a voice in government. They were content to accept the rule of merchants whose interests were bound up with their own and whose sharp eye for profit was tempered with a wise paternalism. The gilds were self-governing, with their own meeting-places, chapels and patron saints. Their function was to maintain craft-standards, settle petty disputes and look after members' welfare, both spiritual and physical (they provided sick benefits, dowries and old-age pensions). They were never concerned to bargain about wages, and the reliance of Venice on a varied commerce rather than on large industries meant that she did not experience the sort of slump that can put large numbers of workers in a particular industry out of work and produce a resentful proletariat. The gilds were to some extent organs of state – their chiefs were responsible for seeing that governmental regulations were observed – but this association with the state was a matter of pride, expressed in the patriotic phrasing of their statutes and the gilds' important place in state ceremonies. The chief of one – that of the fishermen of S. Niccolò – was even called 'doge', a title gravely respected by the doge himself.

The key to harmonious class-relations was, above all, a shared interest in trade. During the formative period of Venice's growth, before the city had expanded on to the mainland, trade had set the pattern for all her citizens, from highest to lowest. During the Quattrocento nobles began to buy property on the *terra ferma*, but their main interests remained centred on the Rialto and on the crowded wharves of the Riva degli Schiavoni. From India and the East came gold, drugs and spices; from Germany came metal-work, from Spain silk, wool and leather, from Flanders cloth and tapestry, from Poland and Russia furs. Other cloths were imported from Armenia and Pèrsia, from Cyprus, France and Florence. Goods taken at random from the inventories of one moderately prosperous merchant, Andrea Barbarigo, include: tin, pewter-ware, cotton-thread, slaves, grain, ginger, copper wire, cheese, timber, almonds, olive oil, sugar, building-stone, malmsey wine, wax, cinnamon, cotton and many other materials. Though spices were the most valuable and cloths the most bulky of her commodities, Venice, as the chief European market-place for luxuries, was the centre for expensive, highly finished articles of all sorts, from glass and gloves to church furniture and cosmetic boxes. Visitors exclaimed over

the profusion of goods from East and West piled in her shops and warehouses, and if her citizens dressed principally in the woollens of Spain and England, it has been suggested that the sense of colour shown by her painters was influenced by the richly dyed stuffs that came from the Orient.

The navy and the arsenal

The carriers of this trade included one of history's most famous species of ship – the merchant galley. A cross between a merchantman and a warship, they carried a cargo of up to 250 tons and, with sails for the open sea and oars to work them in and out of harbour, they were able to keep regular and remarkably fast schedules. The voyage from Southampton to Otranto, about 2,500 miles, could take as little as thirty-one days, and their large crews of about two hundred made a redoubtable military force if they were attacked by pirates. The galleys carried the most valuable cargoes, and their high freight-rate was compensated by speed and remarkable safety record. More bulky, less valuable cargoes were carried in 'round' ships, some of which were of great size, up to 1,800 tons, while vessels of 600 tons were common (this was about the size of the British East Indiamen of the seventeenth century). Other types were built to suit the conditions on special routes: lateen-rigged caravels, which plied up and down the Dalmatian coast, *galeoni* for river-traffic, and many more.

> I fatigued myself very much [wrote Casola] by trying to find out if possible – and with the aid of people very familiar with Venice and the surrounding places – the number of all the ships, both large and small, to be found in Venice, beginning with the boats called gondolas, up to the largest *nave* [round ship] and galley in the Grand Canal. I commenced the work; but, although the days were long, because it was the month of May, I found it was no task for me any more than it was for Saint Augustine – as they recount – to write about the Trinity; for the number is infinite.

All war galleys and many merchant galleys were built by the state in the arsenal, which covered sixty acres of land and water and employed something like two thousand workmen. The Quattrocento was a period of frantic activity for the *arsenalotti* for, as the Turks became capable of scouring the Aegean and threatening Venetian trading-posts with fleets of up to four hundred ships, Venice had to increase both the number of her galleys on patrol and those kept in readiness for an emergency. Accordingly the arsenal was first modified, to provide covered dry-dock space for eighty galleys, and then extended by dredging to the north and enclosing a new basin. Emphasis came increasingly to lie on maintaining a reserve of war-ships that could be equipped and sent to sea in the shortest possible time. When mobilization became necessary, the galleys were run down into the water and then towed past a series of equipping points until they were ready to be taken over by their crews. This sophisticated 'direct-line' production method was described as early as 1436 by the Spanish traveller, Pero Tafur:

> As one enters the gate there is a great street on either side with the sea in the middle [i.e. a canal], and on both sides are windows opening out of the houses of the arsenal. Out came a galley towed by a boat, and from the windows they handed out to them, from one the cordage, from another the bread, from another the arms, and from another the balistas and mortars, and so from all sides everything which was required. When the galley had reached the end of the street all the men required were on board, together with the complement of oars, and she was equipped from end to end. In this manner there came out ten galleys, fully armed, between the hours of three and nine.

This fitting-out process became one of the spectacles with which Venice dazzled the eyes of visiting potentates, and it was a shrewd reminder that behind the traditional pageantry of the marriage of the sea lay Europe's largest navy and most advanced industrial expertise.

Conservatism in culture and art

Here is a portrait of a society concentrating in general social harmony on earning a common living, and willingly and proudly admitting the guidance of the state in its religious, political and economic life. It is therefore no surprise that Venice's intellectual life was also conditioned by the special nature of her site and civic atmosphere. The prevailing mood was practical, conservative, rather conformist, cosmopolitan and unfanatical. Venice was not a place where eccentric genius could flourish. The Venetians' characteristic gift was not for bold speculation, in economic or in intellectual affairs; it was for adaptation. They were quick to take up inventions like double-entry book-keeping and decimals, and their ships used the latest navigational instruments. Their printing-presses were, from the late Quattrocento onwards, among the most prolific in Europe, and their maps and charts were in universal demand, but they did not produce notable inventions, or scientific and philosophical theories for others. Venetian culture, as became Europe's greatest middleman, was eclectic. The city had long provided a home for *émigré* Greeks, and it was partly in recognition of this hospitality that Cardinal Bessarion left to the Republic in 1468 his magnificent collection of manuscripts, which constitutes the core of the Marciana Library. In the work of Aldus and his scholarly assistants, the Venetian press identified itself especially with the production of Greek classical authors, confirming a preference for Greek over Latin that marked its culture as a whole during the Quattrocento.

The culture of Venice differed from that of, say, Florence in other ways. The Republic nibbled with great caution at the stream of novelties pouring out of Tuscany, and generalizations about Renaissance Florence must be applied with the greatest hesitation to Venice. Here Aristotle continued to receive more respect than Plato, and Petrarch (who had seen and admired Venice) more than Dante (who had not). Venetians continued, in the Quattrocento, to speak and write in their own dialect, and when they wrote 'pure' Italian they did not try to make it look Tuscan. They produced works of solid learning in preference to poetry. They commissioned works of art that offered sober homage to church and state rather than encouraging work that was whimsical, extravagant, or deeply personal. The schools of Venice used a humanist syllabus to turn out future statesmen and merchants and, when the young noble proceeded to the University at Padua, it was above all to law, rhetoric, mathematics, or medicine that he was drawn. There are no great figures in Quattrocento Venetian literature and, typically, the writings that retain the greatest immediacy and freshness are not the popular songs and plays of Leonardo Giustinian, the most talented creative writer of the period, but the dispatches of ambassadors and the lively and detailed reports they read to the Senate after a tour of duty abroad. These diplomatic documents, which are a basic source for European and Levantine history from the second half of the fifteenth century, are the best clue to the temperament of the senatorial class: full of common sense, observant, confident. But, if Venice did not produce a literature of her own, she multiplied the literatures of others. In the last ten years of the Quattrocento her printers produced 1,491 works, as compared with the 460 of Rome, the 228 of Milan and – here the contrast is especially striking – the 179 of Florence. Amid the wars and crises of the next decade the contrast remained: 536 from Venice, 47 from Florence. And the range of format, as well as of titles, was greatest in Venice: from some of the most beautiful of all large books, like the *Hypnerotomachia Polifili* (1499), to the first pocket classics.

Site and constitution, again, affected the development of the arts. The influence of the Gothic came down strongly through the Alpine trade-routes, and Venice remained a Gothic city until late in the Quattrocento. In Florence, from the beginning of the fifteenth century, a vivid desire to understand the arts of ancient Rome had produced in painting, and still more in sculpture and architecture, a lovingly re-created classical style. Venice, however, showed no more than an objective, scholarly interest in the ancient world. With the Church held firmly in its place, Venetians were not tortured, as were Florentines, by the spectacle of two totally different attitudes to life: the active and the contemplative. Wishing to combat the claims of the cloistered life, Florentines turned for encouragement to the values of the Roman citizen, to the example of Cicero. Plagued by constitutional and class conflicts, they turned to the political experience of the ancient world. Venice did not need this emotional dependence on the past, and thus her approach to antiquity was far more casual, too casual to accept classical art-forms until they had become a familiar and accepted style within the Quattrocento itself. The Cà d'Oro is almost exactly contemporary with Alberti's

Palazzo Rucellai in Florence. Venetians wished to move with the times, they were sensitive to the fact that artistic styles grew out of date; but they waited to test, as it were, the state of the market before they cautiously began buying the classical mode. The first classical church was Mauro Coducci's S. Michele in Isola, finished in 1479; the first 'Florentine' palace was the Palazzo Vendramin, begun in 1481.

Along with Gothic from the north, Venice was exposed to Byzantine influences from the east. Her markets and churches were full of Byzantine works of art, and even after the middle of the Quattrocento Venetian painters were still responding to the formal, flat, unrealistic qualities of eastern art while Florentines were passionately experimenting with the portrayal of anatomy and perspective.

Venice cannot be called insular in her attitude to the arts; Greeks and Germans worked there, and so did many Florentines. But conservative, yes; it took a new style a long time to cross the lagoons. It was certainly not that the work of the great Florentines was unknown: Ghiberti, Uccello, Michelozzo, Alberti and Andrea del Castagno were all in Venice at some time between 1420 and 1440, Filippo Lippi worked at Padua, and Donatello also spent several years there. But while at Padua there was a real fusion of Florentine and Venetian ideas, especially in the work of Mantegna, Venice remained reluctant to seek inspiration by the waters of the Arno, and a progressive-minded painter like Domenico Veneziano was forced to go and work by the banks of that river himself. What new ideas Venice accepted in the first half of the Quattrocento came from the congenial, gaily formal world of International Gothic; her leading painters, Niccolò di Pietro, Jacobello del Fiore and Giambono followed the lead of visitors like Gentile da Fabriano and, even more, of Pisanello, who left Verona to work in the Ducal Palace. Jacopo Bellini, who was more familiar than most of his contemporaries with Florentine work, knew what his Venetian patrons wanted; the drawings he made for his own interest reflect a passion for scientific perspective and classical forms, but his paintings remained quietly conservative.

Illustration from the Hypnerotomachia Polifili, *printed in Venice in 1499, showing Poliphilus and Polia among the nymphs of the fountain of Venus.*

Development of the mature Venetian style

Not until the career of Giovanni Bellini did Venice have a painter who matured steadily into the Florentine inheritance. Thanks to his longevity, this painter was able to absorb the innovations in oil-technique and the treatment of light that were introduced by Antonello da Messina (the most influential visitor to Venice since Pisanello) and to transmit an art – tranquil, exact and poetic – that could be matured still further by Giorgione and Titian. If Venice played no part in discovering the Renaissance style, it also experienced no loss of faith, as did Florence, in its underlying principles. Leadership in the arts in the Cinquecento passed to Venice.

Just as geography did much to determine an artist's style, the tone of life dictated by the Venetian constitution did much to influence his subject-matter. In Venice there were no mythological scenes – until at the very end of Giovanni Bellini's career, when he began work on the *Feast of the Gods*. The staple subjects were religious paintings, processional scenes, and portraits, especially state portraits: Venice was the first state methodically to commemorate its rulers in this way. The large paintings of Gentile Bellini and Carpaccio, which show us in such detail the clothes, the boats, the canals and piazze of the late Quattrocento, not only reflect the Venetian taste for state-organized and state-glorifying pageantry; they also show, in their calm and accurate portrayal of light and space, that the Venetians' increasing interest in recording what they saw about them in a naturalistic manner did not lead them to experiment with theoretical systems which appealed more to the intellect than to the eye. Relying on observation, they slowly produced a natural-looking and popular mode of representation that portrayed the world, not as seen through the eyes of quirkish genius, but as it actually looked to society as a whole. Lack of intellectual passion; the subordination of personal taste; a conviction that in state and Church most things were for the best: in Venice these qualities were transmitted to art, ensuring that, like Church and state themselves, painting in Venice should be *sui generis*.

The same is true of sculpture. In the Middle Ages the mingling of Byzantine formalism with northern Gothic produced in Venice a taste for fusion and an indifference to striking individual personalities that lasted well into the Quattrocento. From 1403 Florentine sculptors were employed on the Ducal Palace, but they were men of the second rank. Only with the work of Bartolomeo Buon on the Porta della Carta (between 1438 and 1442) do we find a strongly marked Venetian talent that used a Tuscan idiom to support a movement which veered well away from the Gothic; and only with Rizzo's marvellous Adam and Eve (after 1483) on the Ducal Palace, and Pietro Lombardo's slightly earlier Marcello monument in SS. Giovanni e Paolo, did Renaissance classicism really become absorbed in Venice. Backed by a growing taste for collecting antique statues, this classicism became an easy mastery in the Vendramin monument (1493) in the same church, which is the work of Pietro's son Tullio. Though the result of an accident, the most famous statue in Venice, Verrocchio's Colleoni monument, is a symbol of the city's reluctance to accept any import without modifying it; the Florentine sculptor died when the model was completed, and the task of casting it was given to the Venetian Alessandro Leopardi, who was thus responsible for its detail and final appearance.

Cautious expansion by land

At the beginning of the Quattrocento, Venice was already established on the Italian mainland. From 1338 she controlled Treviso, immediately to the north, and the districts of Conegliano and Castelfranco, the birth-places of Cima and Giorgione. This conquest, trivial as it was, brought much head-shaking from conservative senators who were unwilling that the city, for so many centuries a sea-creature, should try to become an amphibian. Their opponents had argued that this conquest was for defensive purposes, to guarantee a corn and meat supply to sustain the city in time of war; and the majority of Venetians continued to see their conquests for the next hundred years as defensive operations designed to keep a potential enemy at arm's length, and to control the Alpine passes necessary to their trade. All was done in the name of keeping the Rialto prosperous and the lagoons secure. But Venice's expansion north-east, north and west did not appear in this light to her neighbours. She quickly gained the reputation of being the most greedily aggressive of all the Italian states.

There is little doubt that she came to deserve something of this reputation, not only in effect but in intention. This was not yet true in 1404, when the leaders of the Carrara dynasty were strangled in Venice after a war which put Padua, Vicenza and Verona in the city's hands. The Carrara had aided the city's enemies, especially her

main commercial rival, Genoa. Though the Genoese had been decisively beaten at Chioggia in 1379, the threat remained, and a hostile Padua was too close to be ignored. Nor could Venice be accused of aggressiveness in 1420, when she pushed her frontier up north from Treviso to the Alps and east beyond Aquilea. This was in answer to an invasion from Austria and ensured that future invading armies could not readily debouch into the lowlands north-east of the city. But thereafter she could. In 1423 the ailing Mocenigo pleaded that Venice's mainland buffer was already broad enough to protect her commerce, and that she should turn all her attention to the sea; but Venice already ruled the large territory contained within the Alps, the sea, and the river Adige which flows through Verona before it swings east and runs parallel with the Po towards the Adriatic.

The subject cities were held down with a firmness that appeared to guarantee their loyalty. Venice allowed a certain amount of self-government as a sop to local pride, but Venetian garrisons were sown throughout the mainland towns and castles and in each city there was a Venetian governor, treasurer, and military commander. Civic institutions were retained, but they were presided over by a Venetian senator, and every important issue was referred to Venice itself. The cities were forced to fortify themselves and maintain troops on a scale which was dictated to them, and which involved an expenditure they would not have embarked on of their own free will. In exchange, Venice offered security and trade concessions, and thus bought enough support from the middle class to keep the nobles from revenging themselves for their diminished power. There was resentment, but little danger. Venice could probably have afforded to leave the mainland to itself and to concentrate, as Mocenigo urged, on the sea.

This was not to be, for a variety of reasons. In the first place, what may have been in theory a precautionary girdle of protectorates looked, to outsiders, remarkably like a bid for empire. Almost inevitably Venice was drawn into that subtle, changeable network of alliances and adjustments in Italy that anticipated so closely the diplomatic pattern of Europe as a whole in the Cinquecento. Again, as more and more Venetian nobles bought properties on the mainland, their attitude to it became more possessive. And lastly, the Adige, a thin blue line on the vast Lombard plain, was a well-defined but not easily defensible frontier. As the power of Milan grew, it was tempting not to wait and see, but to cross the river and strike home before it was too late.

This was the temptation which troubled Mocenigo's last years and to which his impetuous successor, Francesco Foscari, succumbed. In 1420, at the very moment when Venice secured her Alpine frontier, the ruler of Milan, Filippo Maria Visconti, succeeded in reorganizing his state, which had fallen into disorder on his father's death. From the Adige frontier he looked menacingly towards Verona, Vicenza and Padua, all of which had been at one time in his father's control. This pressure was disturbing to others besides Venice. Filippo's father, Gian Galeazzo Visconti, had come very near to extinguishing his southern neighbour, Florence, and the Florentines reacted to this new threat by calling for Venetian support. So Mocenigo's call for retrenchment was countered not only by the push of a 'forward' party within Venice but also by the pull of a strong plea from outside. Even, however, when Francesco Foscari became doge in 1423, Venice hesitated. It was not until 1425, when Visconti's great general Carmagnola switched his allegiance and offered his services to Venice, that the Republic allied herself with Florence and went to war.

Venice's reputation at stake

This is not the place to describe in detail the campaigns that followed. Venice took Brescia and Bergamo and pushed her western frontier up to the river Adda, less than twenty miles from Milan itself. She maintained this frontier throughout the Quattrocento, but the land between the rivers was gained at a perilous cost. In the first place, money was needed: Venice relied largely on mercenary troops and she had to pay them by means of heavy taxes levied both on the city and on the *terra ferma*. In the second place, political tension resulted at home: to maintain his 'forward' policy, Foscari kept his party together in a manner that was new to Venice and that brought charges, not without proof, of job-pushing and peculation. He was forced to resign the dogeship – an unprecedented event – in 1457. Finally, Venice's move aroused suspicion and antagonism throughout Italy. In 1432 the Republic, which had become suspicious that Carmagnola was about to betray her as he had betrayed his former employer, executed him between the two columns on the Piazzetta. It was not the drama of the moment itself – he was dressed in crimson velvet, and it took three strokes to get his head off – that aroused startled comment all over Italy, nor the sentence – Venice was able to find other generals to serve her, including Gattamelata and Colleoni, who left the bulk of his estate to the Republic at his death. It was the secrecy in which the proceedings had been veiled that caused the workings of the Council of Ten, who had conducted the inquiry, to be for the first time invested with a mysterious dread. Then in 1481 Venice did something that was not mysterious at all: she declared war on Ferrara and, when she found herself making no headway against that city and its allies – the Pope, the King of Naples, and the Duke of Milan – she tried to persuade Charles VIII of France to invade Naples, and the Duke of Orleans (later Louis XII of France) to occupy Milan. A peace was patched up in 1484, leaving Venetian territory intact but her reputation such as to draw this reprimand, delivered by the Duke of Milan to the Venetian diplomatic agent at his court:

> You Venetians are wrong to disturb the peace of Italy, and not to rest content with the fine state which is now yours. If you knew how everyone hates you, your hair would stand on end and you would let other people alone ... You are alone, and all the world is against you, not merely in Italy but also beyond the Alps. Rest assured that your enemies are not asleep. Take good counsel for, by God, you need it. I know what I am saying.

This warning had all the more force because Venice had become branded as an enemy of Christendom. In 1480 the Turks had established a temporary beachhead on the south Italian mainland, at Otranto. This landing produced more shock and terror among the Italian states than had the fall of Constantinople, and Venice, it was widely believed, was in part responsible.

The attitude of Venice towards the Turks could not be other than equivocal. The eastern Mediterranean was her chief trading area and she had to keep on friendly terms with the dominant power there. On the other hand, the Turks were crusaders for their faith and intent on conquest in Greece and the Balkans. No agreement with them was therefore to be trusted, and the first two-thirds of the Quattrocento were filled with wars, open or undeclared, and with sea-fights and land-battles punctuated by uneasy truces. Meanwhile the Republic, a sword in one hand and a trade agreement in the other, was being pushed further and further west as the Turks occupied one Venetian trading-post after another in the Aegean islands and on the Greek mainland. The pattern of this conflict was immensely confused and many of its details are still far from clear. It was confused by the attitude of the Balkan peoples who now helped Venice, now supported the Turks; by the aid given to the Turks by the Genoese, themselves fighting for a slice of the trade in goods from the Black Sea and the Syrian coast; and by the truces negotiated by the Turks with Christian Hungary, which from time to time allowed them to concentrate on building a fleet to complement their already overwhelmingly superior land forces. Trade, self-protection, and ideology: all these motives underlay the attitudes of both sides, but what the European spectators thought they saw was something much simpler: the richest state in Italy becoming first a fellow-traveller and then an active supporter of Islam. The Otranto landing, following almost immediately after the Venetian-Turkish peace treaty of 1479, seemed to justify their darkest suspicions.

In fact, of course, Venice was not strong enough to oppose the Turks single-handed. In spite of occasional bursts of crusading propaganda among the Christian powers, this was what she was left to do. By 1479 she had lost Scutari, Negroponte and many of her possessions in the Peloponnese and was being forced to pay an onerous annual tribute for the privilege of trading in an area which, at the beginning of the Quattrocento, had been practically her own preserve. The only compensation for this chain of losses was the acquisition of Cyprus, first as a protectorate and then, in 1488, as an outright possession.

The sugar, wine, cotton and grain of Cyprus were eventually to be of great profit to Venice, but not yet. The last years of the Quattrocento and the opening decades of the Cinquecento were dark. The costs of war – against Ferrara and the Turks – had been enormous. On all sides there were signs of financial strain: nobles becoming destitute, interest-payments suspended on government bonds, officials having to accept reductions in their salaries. And, darker still, the spice-routes from the East were being tapped by the Portuguese. A year before Venice's annexation of Cyprus, Bartholomew Dias discovered the Cape of Good Hope. In 1497 Vasco da Gama rounded it and went on to reach the west coast of India. The dismay with which this news was received in Venice was all the more profound because, precisely at the moment when the Republic needed to devote all her energies to the sea, the invasion of Italy by Charles VIII of France in 1494 bound her more firmly than ever to diplomacy and war on the mainland. In 1495 she helped Milan and the Papacy to press the French back north of the Alps; in 1499 she allied herself with the new king of France, Louis XII, against Milan; in 1509 she was herself set upon by France in alliance with her rivals from north and south, the Emperor Maximilian and Pope Julius II, and she lost all her mainland territories after the disastrous defeat of Agnadello. When, after another war with the Turks from 1500 to 1503, she was stripped of yet more trading-posts in the Aegean – Modon, Coron, Lepanto and Durazzo – the humiliation seemed complete, the defeat irreparable.

The splendour to come

Yet the period of greatest splendour – the period of Titian, of Veronese and Tintoretto, of Sansovino and Palladio – was still to come. The secure island site and the stable, shrewd, business-like institutions remained. By 1515 the Republic had taken advantage of dissensions among her enemies to regain her mainland possessions. Patiently she bargained with the Turks and with Portugal and, by the middle of the Cinquecento, she was richer than ever before. She had again become the undisputed centre of Mediterranean trade and – the result of a wise diversification of activity – the leading industrial city in Italy. The main scene of economic activity in Europe as a whole had now shifted, it is true, from the Mediterranean to the Atlantic, to cities like Augsburg, Lisbon and Antwerp; but within her own world, quieter but still thriving, Venice continued to improve her position. Meanwhile her citizens, more cautious now about investing in long voyages through pirate-ridden seas, were increasingly putting their profits into villas, palaces, and works of art. The economic historian may chide an unproductive use of money, but the visitor must feel grateful for this imperishable dividend as he crosses one reason for Venice's greatness, the Lagoon, and enters the other, the Sala del Maggior Consiglio, symbol of the wisest, stablest, and most resilient of Renaissance constitutions.

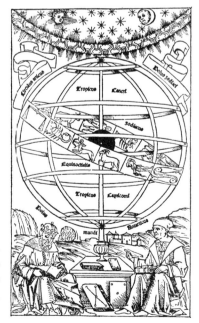

The Epitoma *of Johannes de Montregis was published in Venice in 1496. This woodcut from the book shows Ptolemy on the left, the author on the right, and the Ptolemaic globe above them.*

MEDICEAN FLORENCE

The jewel of Tuscany,
Florence developed in the fifteenth century into the leading city-state of Italy. In a period of relative stability and peace, after absorbing most of its rival cities, such as Arezzo, Pisa and Pistoia, Florence became a focus of commercial, artistic and intellectual activity. Deriving its wealth from trade in woollen and silk cloth, it grew into the primary international banking centre of Europe. In political structure it was a democratic republic, though one family, the Medici, managed to dominate its institutions for nearly a century – a tyranny, but a benevolent one. It was in Florence that the Renaissance, the age of Humanism, had its origins; from there it fanned out to the rest of the Western world.

The 'first modern State in the world', as Burckhardt characterized it, Florence epitomized the reaction against the Middle Ages and the liberation of thought from theological confines. Here, the rediscovery of Greek culture resulted in a new architecture, a new art, a new philosophy and a new view of man. The greatest Renaissance figures,

the pathfinders – Leonardo da Vinci, Machiavelli, Lorenzo de' Medici, Michelangelo – were all Florentines.

A famous example of the new art are the gilded bronze doors of the Baptistery (opposite), which Michelangelo thought worthy to be the Gates of Paradise. They were the work of Lorenzo Ghiberti (1378–1455), one of the key-figures in the transition from the late-Gothic to the early-Renaissance style of art that took place preeminently in the Florence of the Medici. An earlier set of doors which Ghiberti executed between 1403 and 1424 were still in the older tradition, though they reveal that he was aware of antique sculpture and used details from classical architecture. By 1425, however, when he started on this second pair, the new ideas and influences which were the basis of the Renaissance had been more widely disseminated. In these ten framed scenes from the Old Testament, Ghiberti used an entirely different treatment of perspective which gives an uncanny sense of depth and space to each subject. (1)

Architecture in Florence, as it evolved in the fifteenth century, was largely influenced by Filippo Brunelleschi (1377–1446), whose works are often cited as the first in a truly Renaissance style. Versatile as most Florentine artists, Brunelleschi was goldsmith, sculptor and architect. His most famous achievement is the Cathedral's octagonal dome (left top), an ambitious feat of engineering begun in 1420. Classical features appear in the cupola, but are more vividly impressive in the loggia of Brunelleschi's Foundling Hospital (left centre), which derives its structure of columns, round arches and domed bays, as well as its proportions, from Roman antiquity. Many of the same elements are evident in his rebuilding of San Lorenzo (left bottom), the parish church of the Medici family. (2, 3, 4)

The Medici dynasty, whose rule depended ostensibly on democratic election but was in reality maintained by their subtle control of the smaller Gilds, was continued after Cosimo's death by his son Piero 'the Gouty', whose bust, by Mino da Fiesole, is shown above (top). A greater Florentine painter and sculptor, Andrea del Verrocchio, did the likenesses of Piero's sons, Giuliano (above) and Lorenzo 'il Magnifico' (opposite top). The Palazzo Medici (later called Riccardi) was commissioned by Cosimo; its architect was Michelozzo. The interior courtyard (opposite below) appears to have been influenced by the loggia of Brunelleschi's Foundling Hospital, the straight façade of arches being folded to form a square. In the frieze above the arches can be seen the ubiquitous Medici symbol: six balls, representing gold coins, originally the symbol of the Bankers Gild. (5–8)

The **wool trade and banking** were the foundation of the Medici's wealth and power. Two wool merchants are shown (right top) in an illustration from a contemporary treatise on mathematics. The man on the left points to the raw wool in sacks; the man on the right to a length of woven fabric. On the pillar appears the Medici symbol. Banking as a Florentine speciality grew out of the merchants' practice of maintaining branch offices and agencies in foreign cities, which became local clearing-houses. The interior of a bank in Florence itself is shown in a fifteenth-century woodcut (right centre), and the drawing by Filarete (right below) is of the Medici bank in Milan. (9, 10, 11)

The lion of Florence, or 'Marzocco' (below), by Donatello, one of the seminal Renaissance artists, is a civic symbol, which formerly stood in front of the Palazzo Vecchio. The fleur-de-lis on the shield was a Medici heraldic device which the King of France gave Piero the privilege of using in 1465. (12)

The medal-portrait, a detail of a painting by the typically Florentine artist, Botticelli (below), is of Cosimo de' Medici, who ruled the city-state from 1429 until his death in 1464. He came from a family of merchant-princes who had long played a significant part in the city's administration, sometimes in and sometimes out of power. It was in Cosimo's flourishing period of government that the various aspects of the Early Renaissance were crystallized.

The Medici palace (below right), described by Vasari as the first 'in the modern style', based its three-tiered façade and enormous cornice on classical models. A rather naïve rendering of it appears in a fifteenth-century manuscript edition of Virgil (bottom), illustrating the storming of Anchises' palace in the Trojan War. (13, 14, 15)

Love of pageantry was a characteristic of Renaissance Florence. The elegant procession (above) on its way to a wedding was painted on a nuptial-chest belonging to the Adimari family. The rich fabrics are typical of the fine manufacture for which Florence was noted; the Flemish influence on the style of the women's clothing and headdress indicates the cosmopolitan nature of the city.

Pageantry is also an important element in the decoration of the chapel in the Medici palace by Benozzo Gozzoli. One of his frescoes (detail, left) depicts, in terms of the journey of the Three Magi, a council of the Greek and Latin Churches held in Florence in 1439. The figure on horseback is the Byzantine emperor, John Palaeologus, who came to the council. (16, 17)

Public entertainment and celebration of festivals were a particular enthusiasm of Lorenzo de' Medici. Citizens of all classes were delighted by the colourful *Palio*, a traditional horserace which used to take place regularly in Florence as well as Siena (top). The daily games of children in the streets are shown above. (18, 19)

A Florentine banquet is shown (right) in a painting by Jacopo del Sellaio (1442–93), based on the Biblical story of Ahasuerus' feast. The meal takes place in a typical loggia with richly decorated walls. All the individual details of the background and setting give evidence of the Florentine delight in display and fine objects. (20)

Learning, encouraged and subsidized by Cosimo, took a specifically Hellenic bent because of the Greek scholars who came to Florence during the Church Council. So impressed was Cosimo by his gleanings of Platonism that he founded a Platonic Academy in 1459, and put at its head his protégé, Marsilio Ficino, whose translations and commentaries on Plato's works had a pervasive influence on the intellectual development of the Renaissance as a whole. The Academy, like a modern institute of advanced studies, became a thriving centre of Humanist scholarship and speculation. A contemporary woodcut (right above) shows Cristoforo Landino, one of the Academy's translators and theorists, lecturing to scholars. Lorenzo de' Medici was a brilliant product of this intellectual Florentine atmosphere: a cultivated patron and friend of great artists and philosophers, he was himself a poet. The frontispiece of one of his books of songs (right centre) shows masked singers in the street.

The group of four pensive figures in Ghirlandaio's fresco, *Zacharias in the Temple* (detail, right below), are believed to be the Humanist scholars Ficino, Landino, Agnolo Poliziano and Demetrius Chalcondilas.

Cosimo contributed further to the intellectual glory of his city in 1441, by endowing a library for public use, housed in the Convent of San Marco (bottom), which he had Michelozzo rebuild soon after 1434. (21–24)

Portraits of the Medici family
are presumed to be included in the
composition of Botticelli's *Adoration
of the Magi,* painted about 1475. The
figure of King Melchior, kneeling
before the Christ Child, has often been
identified as Cosimo the Elder. Kneeling in the centre foreground is
Cosimo's son, Piero 'the Gouty', who
seems to be engaged in conversation
with his younger brother, Giovanni,
also kneeling and in a white robe.
Piero's two sons are also in the scene:
the haughty young man in the left
foreground bears the features of the
illustrious Lorenzo, and in the group
on the right the dark-haired man
wearing the red-trimmed dark robe is
Giuliano, who was killed in the Pazzi
conspiracy in 1478. The figure in the
far right foreground, looking out of
the painting, is the artist himself. (25)

The sculpture of Florence was profoundly influenced by the reawakened appreciation of classical antiquity, Greek mythology and the new conception of man's place in the universe. Extremely individual in his fascination with the human body in violent action was Antonio Pollaiuolo (*c.* 1432–98), who created for the Medici the small (only 18 inches high) but extremely original and naturalistic *Hercules and Antaeus* in bronze (detail, below). In both its subject and treatment, this is a work which would have been virtually inconceivable in the fourteenth century, before the efflorescence of Humanism had broken down the more rigid patterns of medieval culture.

Like so many Florentine artists, Pollaiuolo's vision was affected by the work of Donatello, whose *David* (right) was the most revolutionary masterpiece of the Early Renaissance. This life-size bronze, which originally stood in the courtyard of the Medici palace, was the first nude cast since the classical age, and must have been viewed with some misgivings as a heathen idol at the time it was made (*c.* 1430–32). (26, 27)

Michelangelo, born in Tuscany in 1475, was the towering figure of the Late Renaissance. As a youth he enjoyed the patronage of Lorenzo de' Medici, and one of his earliest works, the *Battle of the Centaurs* (detail, below), was executed in Florence in 1492, the year of Lorenzo's death. This unfinished marble relief, reminiscent of the sculpture on Roman sarcophagi, is a precocious forecast of the monumental and infinitely expressive work of Michelangelo's maturity, with its emphasis on 'the making of men'. (28)

Fifteenth-century Florence was painted in a bird's-eye view (above) by an unknown contemporary who showed the city's protecting outer wall with its forts and gates. The bridges crossing the Arno made Florence the prosperous midpoint between north–south commerce. In the centre of the city rises the dome of the Cathedral; the square tower in front of it is Giotto's Campanile, and to the left of that the octagonal Baptistery. (29)

Girolamo Savonarola (1452–98), elected prior of the Dominican Convent of San Marco in 1491, proved to be the enemy of all that fifteenth-century Florence stood for. Anti-Medici, anti-Humanist, anti-Pope, Savonarola roused the populace into a frenzy of puritanism and witch-hunting. He was finally hanged and burned for heresy in the great public square of the Piazza della Signoria (below) – but not before he had destroyed the greatest age of Florence. (30)

HAROLD ACTON

CLIMB THE HILL of Etruscan Fiesole north of the river, or the height of San Miniato to the south, and look down over the valley. Let your gaze be leisurely, for this panorama exhales a spirit of civilized leisure. It has an infinite deal to communicate, of human culture, of powerful personalities, and a strong unbroken tradition. Even if you know but little of history, a sense of the past must sweep over you, a past which is polished and alive, not dusty and dead.

All Florence is spread beneath you, cupolas, towers, multitudinous roofs. Without swarming, the city calmly covers the plain. From Fiesole the view is bird's eye, topographical; San Miniato provides a man's eye view, more intimate but equally impressive. Does distance lend further enchantment to what is enchanting? There is no doubt that it accentuates the grandeur of Brunelleschi's Duomo, the bristling height of the battlemented Palazzo Vecchio where the *gonfalonier* and priors used to preside over the republic, the shimmer of the broad Arno winding westward between stone embankments and the walls of mellowed houses. There is no doubt that it often reveals what may be lost in the labyrinth at closer range. The eye may select jewel after jewel, the octagonal casket of the Baptistery and the Campanile of Giotto; it may linger on the venerable Ponte Vecchio; then it may wander to the background of hills, to the nearer slopes meticulously cultivated, chiselled and terraced with sun-steeped villas, almost invariably flanked by slim cypresses and silvery olivegroves, to the remoter Apennines whose summits are often inseparable from cloud. But nothing seems very remote, if the weather be fine, in this crystalline Tuscan air. Every ridge and rill has the sharp outline of a miniature.

It is easy to visualize the city as it was in the fifteenth century. Except that it was then encircled by walls with fifteen gates, protected by forts and bastions, the salient features of Florence have changed little, with due allowance for growth. And the fifteenth was an essentially Florentine century, when Florence was the centre of human culture, second only to Athens in its influence on European civilization. Since the greatest of the Medici then rose to power, it might equally be called the Medicean Age.

Master of central Italy

Even in the previous century the intellectual leadership of Florence was acknowledged throughout Italy. The Italian language itself had come to be known as the 'Tuscan idiom' or the 'Florentine vernacular'. At the Jubilee of 1300 Pope Boniface VIII had observed that all the ambassadors of the Christian powers assembled in Rome were citizens of Florence, and his remark that the Florentines were a 'fifth element' has become proverbial.

This leadership was all the more striking because Florence was no great city by material standards. The boundaries of her state fell between some sixty miles of length and ninety miles of breadth. She owed much to her strategic position on the high road which led from the north to Rome and passed over the Arno bridge.

One by one the thriving cities of Tuscany, Colle di Val d'Elsa, San Gimignano, Prato, Pistoia, Volterra, San Miniato dei Tedeschi, had fallen under her sway – some, like Pisa and Arezzo, after bitter and protracted struggles – until, in the thirteenth century, Florence had become the predominant power in central Italy. In 1421 Leghorn was sold to Florence by the Genoese, thus opening the sea to her merchandise.

Her trade gilds (*Arti*), already well established in the twelfth century, were close-knit microcosms of the republic, each with their own statutes and a similar constitution. Originally there were twelve gilds: seven major, which were engaged in wholesale commerce, and five minor, engaged in retail traffic and internal trade; the latter were eventually increased with variations in number and constitution. The *Signoria* was composed of 'priors of the arts' chosen from the major gilds, who became the chief magistrates of the state under the leadership of a *gonfalonier* or standard-bearer of justice, who held office for two months only.

For a long period the gild of wool dressers and dyers, to which the Albizzi belonged, was the wealthiest and most influential. When the supply of local wool ran short the merchants imported it from France, Flanders, Holland and England. After opening cloth factories abroad they sent the material to Florence to be dressed and dyed. Nowhere else had this process been refined to such a degree; consequently the Florentine product commanded a high price all over Europe, and French or English cloth could be sold again at a profit in the land of its origin. When the manufacture improved in England and Flanders, the Wool Gild continued to make handsome profits by exporting to the East. The Silk Gild waxed when the Wool Gild waned: towards the end of the fifteenth century there were at least eighty-three silk factories in Florence, and Florentine satins, velvets and gold brocades had an unrivalled reputation in Europe.

In all the chief centres of commerce Florentine merchants established agencies which became local clearing-houses, whence the origin of our present system of banking. An extensive system of correspondence was begun, enabling the merchants to make payments on receipt of written orders. The Florentine florin was a harder currency than the dollar is today, and Florentine bankers had a worldwide reputation in the fourteenth and the fifteenth centuries. They made colossal loans to foreign princes, and even when the Bardi and Peruzzi lost the sum of 1,365,000 gold florins to England in 1338 they managed to recover. Philip de Commines asserted that Edward IV of England owed his crown to the financial support of Florentine bankers, and later French enterprise depended upon the support of the Strozzi bank in particular, which had branches in Lyons, Venice and Rome.

Apart from promoting prosperity, the trade gilds had an educational effect which was of considerable political value. The government of each was representative, and as many took part in its administration a great number of citizens were qualified for public life. This helps to explain the advanced political insight and varied forms of human development for which Burckhardt said that Florence 'in this sense deserves the name of the first modern state in the world'.

Constant political reforms had confirmed the democratic character of the government, and every change was described and criticized by its pioneer historians, from Giovanni Villani in 1300 to his more mature and illustrious successors, Machiavelli, Guicciardini, Segni,

Varchi, and others. 'Rome is sinking,' wrote Villani, 'my native city is rising, and ready to achieve great things. Therefore I wish to relate its past history, and hope to continue the story to the present time, and as long as my life shall last.' Already we may note that new sense of historical continuity for which, as H. A. L. Fisher observed, the great school of Florentine historians and publicists was distinguished. Trade and commerce had stimulated economical and political science as well as the fine arts.

The crossing of the Arno at Florence offered unique advantages, as Edward Hutton has pointed out:

> The whole traffic of the peninsula lay north and south and had to cross the Arno immediately before or immediately after crossing the mountains. The traffic lay north and south partly because of the shape and formation of Italy and partly because the south needed the farm produce of the Lombard plain, as the north needed the wool of Latium. Those who held Tuscany were perforce middlemen, traders; and those who held the passage of the Arno were the pre-ordained masters of Tuscany, of central Italy that is.

But this mastery could not have been maintained without a rare combination of characteristics.

Realism and instinct for beauty

Merchants, bankers, lawyers, artisans, business-men who understood the manipulation of money, the hard-headed Florentines were eminently realistic. An exceptional genius might revolt, but however high he soared some part of him clung to Mother Earth and retained her solidity. Boundless curiosity was combined with a talent for exact observation, and the visual arts flowered from a passionate awareness of the tangible, visible world. Like the Greeks, the Florentines were 'guided by some peculiar instinct toward temperance and beauty'. In painting they preferred form to colour, in architecture the most delicate simplicity, in literature the purest narrative. Thus it was to the Greeks that they turned, as to long-lost parents, as soon as they emerged from the muddled Middle Ages. They had never been Gothicized. The rediscovery of Greek culture in the beginning of the fifteenth century became known as humanism, and Florence under the early Medici was the busiest hive of the strenuous humanists: a minority of talented and creative men working in a sensitive and intelligent society.

From a distance the spectacle of the Renaissance may strike one as if the marble statues of antiquity had sprung from the Italian soil and wakened to a new lease of life after centuries of sleep beneath the olives and cypresses. Actually, the transition from the medieval to the modern world was gradual, though in Florence its pace was somewhat accelerated. The contrast between medieval and modern society, however, between an atmosphere hostile to free inquiry and one in which science could thrive, is clearly perceptible.

During the Middle Ages the Church and culture in all its forms were one. Latin was the universal language of the educated, and knowledge had reached a blind alley of theological commentaries. Man was only half-conscious of himself apart from his clan or corporation. Most of his achievements in the fine arts were anonymous. Roger Bacon, Chaucer, Villon and above all Petrarch, were sporadic flashes of a more enlightened future. But in Florence the tradition of humane learning had never been wholly interrupted since the time of Dante, Petrarch and Boccaccio. Conditions had long been favourable to that growth of individual character of which the fifteenth-century humanist was the quintessence. Trade and commerce had boomed during the Crusades, creating a middle class united against feudal disorder. The new humanist who replaced the medieval monk could thus live in an atmosphere of leisure and freedom. Instead of remaining a provincial recluse, he became a citizen of the world.

Rich merchants hoped to win immortality from scholars and artists, who shared the same ardent desire. Vespasiano da Bisticci has left vivid brief biographies of these fifteenth-century scholars, some of whom served as secretaries of the republic or held chairs in the university. Leonardo Bruni, Carlo Marsuppini, Poggio Bracciolini, and Giannozzo Manetti enjoyed immense contemporary fame, and it was largely due to them and to collectors of rare manuscripts, like Niccolò Niccoli, that Florence became an intellectual capital. To us they would seem pedantic, perhaps, with their cold imitations of Cicero, but their contribution to European culture was inestimable. They were orators, poets, scholars, and teachers; and their audiences were responsive and eager to learn. They prepared for the Renaissance by insisting on the individuality of man, by encouraging the adoption of the mother-tongue in literature, by interest in the life and letters of antiquity, and by a close interrogation of nature. The artist went straight to flesh and blood essentials; the human body cast off its cloistral cocoon and leapt into the Arcadian sunlight.

Pilot of the Renaissance

It was under the subtle guidance of a single family that Florence achieved her fame as pilot of the Renaissance. Hysterical historians have attacked the Medici without looking fore or aft. The majority accuse them of crushing republican liberty. But the Florentine republic had never enjoyed much liberty in a modern sense, since both the nobility and the labouring masses had been excluded from the administration. Its early history had been a monotonous tug of war between Guelphs and Ghibellines, between city merchants of Italian stock and feudal barons of Teutonic origin, who pillaged them or levied tolls on their wares. Eventually the merchants won, and their highly organized gilds monopolized the government. The feudal minority was assimilated or banished, and a new aristocracy burgeoned from the trading classes. Towards the fifteenth century a syndicate of wealthy families ruled, and the wealthiest and most ambitious of these were the Medici.

The early Medici were typical Florentines with an extra dose of sagacity and foresight. Their habits of thought, their mode of life, were similar to those of their fellow-citizens, and their interests were identical with those of the dominant merchant class, which they understood thoroughly. They also understood the advantages of a democratic attitude. Though the richest members of the Gild of Bankers and Money-changers, they became the leaders of the opposition. As *gonfalonier*, or chief magistrate of the republic, Salvestro de' Medici had supported the 'little people' during the revolt of the *Ciompi* in 1378 against the oppressive Wool Gild and the extremists of the Guelph oligarchy. The revolt was suppressed and Salvestro was banished, but the influence of his clan continued to increase. The Albizzi family swayed the republic, a fact conveniently forgotten by detractors of the Medici. Maso and Rinaldo degli Albizzi were ruthless in the persecution of political adversaries, and they incurred much hatred by their heavy taxation of the people. Consequently the opposition gathered strength. While the Medici were kept out of office they extended their banking ramifications and gained more partisans by their discreet liberality. Finally the Albizzi were caught napping and Giovanni de' Medici was elected *gonfalonier* in 1421.

The *gonfalonier* was changed every two months, and Giovanni saw that there was little to be gained from his post under actual conditions. The executive was weakened by perpetual interference. Disliking the violent methods of other Italian states, Giovanni decided that the best way to safe predominance was to organize a party strong enough to guarantee the highest offices of the republic to its own adherents over a prolonged period. This became the chief article of his family's political creed. He was credited – some say wrongly – with advocating a new system of taxation known as the *Catasto*, by which every Florentine citizen was required to make a declaration of his property for the regulation of income tax. This proved a boon to the majority and put a stop to the unjust levying of forced loans. Thus, while he secured the financial supremacy of his family in Italian and European markets, he soared steadily on the pinions of democracy, paving the way for his eldest son, Cosimo, who succeeded him in 1429.

Amongst other parting precepts, the dying Giovanni had recommended Cosimo to avoid attracting attention. Cosimo was never to forget this advice. Envy, as he said, is a plant one should never water; and there was plenty of envy in Florence. Frugal in his personal habits, living as a homely citizen among citizens ultra-sensitive to the semblance of equality, he was content with the realities of power: others, like Luca Pitti, could keep the trappings. Instead of showing himself off in the Palace of the Signory, he quietly pulled the strings of government from his private mansion, now Palazzo Riccardi. Instead of building himself a vast edifice like that of the Pitti, he built one of more modest dimensions – modest, that is to say, for one far richer than any contemporary king.

Vasari tells us that Brunelleschi had first designed a palace for Cosimo, but this seemed 'too sumptuous and magnificent, and would attract the envy of his fellow-citizens', so he chose the simpler and less costly design of Michelozzo Michelozzi, the loyal companion of his exile. The building was begun in about 1444, and Vasari said truly that it was 'the first palace built in Florence in the modern style'. It remains a complete example of the Florentine palace in the fifteenth century: that of the Strozzi, which was derived from it, is another. In Rome there are palaces more grand and extensive, but those are less intimate. Cosimo's mansion, as Hawthorne wrote, 'gives the visitor a stately notion of the life of a commercial man in the days when merchants were princes'. The salient features of its façade are the bold projection of the heavy cornice, the irregular rough-hewn blocks of the ground floor, solid as a ledge of granite, the modified relief of the first floor, and the smooth surface of the top storey. Its character is severe and substantial: the building becomes more refined as it approaches the crowning cornice.

The ground floor consists of two courtyards, the first surrounded with a pillared arcade of that cool grey *pietra serena* which is peculiarly Tuscan. Halls, drawing-rooms, waiting-rooms, studies, bakeries, kitchens, and staircases opened on to these courtyards. One of the darkest and smallest rooms is the most sumptuous: this is the chapel covered with frescoes by Benozzo Gozzoli, who must have painted them by lamplight. Here the pageantry of the Medici has been perpetuated in a courtly cavalcade of the Three Kings to Bethlehem. The kings and their attendants are identifiable portraits, and the landscape is that of Tuscany. The Florentines, so frugal in private life, had always been noted for the splendour of their public entertainments, which increased under the Medici. Benozzo's graceful illumination of the Adoration of the Magi also derived inspiration from the General Council for the union of the Greek and Latin Churches, which had been transferred from Ferrara to Florence in 1439. The Greek Patriarch and the Emperor John Palaeologus, who attended the Council, are depicted as the first two kings of the fresco.

The growth of Italian Hellenism

The Council of Florence did more to revive the study of Greek than to unite the Churches: it was one of the three events, as Lord Acton wrote, 'which determined the triumph of the Renaissance'. (The others were the fall of Constantinople and the election of Parentucelli as Pope Nicholas V.) Among the Greek dialecticians present was Gemistos Plethon who devoted his long life – he died a centenarian – to the study of Plato. So captivated was Cosimo by the novelty and force of his arguments that he decided then and there to cultivate this 'new philosophy', with far-reaching effects throughout Europe. Plato was set up in the place of Aristotle, and the Platonic Academy was founded to propagate his doctrines.

With uncommon perspicacity Cosimo selected Marsilio Ficino, the eighteen-year-old son of a doctor from Figline, to become the high priest of Platonism in Florence. 'Thy son', he told the doctor, 'is born to minister to minds, not bodies'; and he took him to live in his palace, as his grandson, Lorenzo, was to take Poliziano and Michelangelo. Henceforward Ficino devoted himself entirely to Plato and the Neo-Platonists, translating their works and writing copious commentaries. One of Cosimo's last letters to Ficino is an eloquent proof that his enthusiasm for Plato was no passing fad:

> Yesterday I came to the villa of Careggi, not to cultivate my fields but my soul. Come to us, Marsilio, as soon as possible. Bring with thee our Plato's book *De Summo Bono*. This, I suppose, you have already translated from the Greek language into Latin as you promised. I desire nothing so much as to know the best road to happiness. Farewell, and do not come without the Orphean lyre.

While other countries were plunged in feudal barbarism, here in Florence was an intellectual atmosphere akin to our own. Here are men we may understand, whose ideas to a certain extent resemble ours, though we may not have time to follow a Ficino through the maze of his metaphysical and theological doctrines. 'The Renaissance of the fifteenth century', wrote Pater, 'was, in many things, greater rather by what it designed than by what it achieved.' Ficino summed up the aspirations of his age. He wished to reconcile Christianity with Platonism, to prove that the one was the consequence of the other. Though a sincere Christian who eventually took orders, he burned a lamp before the bust of Plato and revered him as a saint. His influence on the culture of the age was immense: it permeated Florentine society, inspiring the highest achievements of Florentine art and freeing the human intellect from the last fetters of the Middle Ages. Little wonder that students came from all over Europe to attend his lectures.

Thus Cosimo de' Medici was directly responsible for the growth of Italian Hellenism and stood in the vanguard of the spiritual tend-

Illustration from a book printed in Florence in 1493–4, showing a money-changer with his balance.

encies of the day. Though many of his recorded sayings sound cynical, such as, 'a government cannot be maintained by paternosters', this seeming cynicism is a Florentine veneer not incompatible with piety. He spent many an hour of retreat in the Convent of San Marco, which he had caused to be rebuilt by Michelozzo after his return from exile in 1434. Here the Blessed Fra Angelico began the great work of his life, the decoration of the convent walls; here the prior, Savonarola, was to play his disastrous role at the end of the century. When the insatiable collector of manuscripts, Niccolò Niccoli, died bankrupt in 1437, Cosimo paid all his debts and placed four hundred of his *codices* in the library of San Marco for public use. These were later increased at his own expense, and formed the first public library in Europe. Tommaso Parentucelli, who catalogued this library for Cosimo and noted the books that were necessary to complete it, was to become Pope Nicholas V, and repaid past services by making Cosimo his banker.

Cosimo's power was felt beyond Italy, for he had branch banks or agents in France, England, the Netherlands, and the Levant. He had extended Florentine commerce until 'a blow aimed at the Medici gave a shock to every European market, and hence it was in the interest of foreign princes to protect their credit'. Besides his financial acumen, which was prodigious, he was quick to recognize talent, and he was probably at his best with artists and men of letters. Giovanni Rucellai expressed the feelings of many of his fellow-citizens when he thanked God that he was a native of Florence, 'reputed the noblest and most beautiful city in the world', and that he lived in the age of Cosimo de' Medici.

Digging for spiritual treasure

With the exception of one painter of genius, Masaccio, who died young, humanism bore its earliest fruit in sculpture and architecture. The precursors, Ghiberti, Brunelleschi and Donatello, had appeared at the beginning of the century, but their influence continued far beyond it. They gave visible form to the ideals of the newly awakened intellect. Ghiberti had won the competition for the bronze doors of the Baptistery at the age of twenty, in 1401, a convenient point of departure for the development of Renaissance art. Brunelleschi won the second place in this competition, which was fortunate for architecture. In 1403 he set out for Rome with his friend, Donatello, then aged sixteen. Their interest in the ruins, then infinitely less ruined than today, was incomprehensible to the Romans, who imagined they were digging for treasure, as indeed they were in a spiritual sense. They devoted the next four years to a study of the classical style, a course which was then quite novel. No doubt the completion of the Florentine cathedral was at the back of Brunelleschi's mind. In 1420 his opportunity came: he was appointed to execute the work. His study of the Pantheon helped him to raise the Duomo, on which Michelangelo was to base his design of St Peter's.

The various suggestions at the meeting of master-builders in 1420 explain why Brunelleschi's project – a free dome built with the aid of scaffolding at relatively small cost – seemed incredible to his contemporaries. The most extravagant was that the dome be raised over a huge mound of earth piled on the floor of the cathedral; silver coins were to be mixed with it to encourage the workmen to hasten its removal. In the meantime Brunelleschi had the jealousy of Ghiberti to contend with, and he was often exasperated to the point of resigning. The cupola was not finished till 1436, and it was then the largest in existence, the diameter 138 1/2 feet, and the altitude of the dome itself 133 feet, measured from the cornice of the drum to the eye of the dome. It was the first great achievement of Renaissance architecture. Though the smaller buildings which Brunelleschi completed while the dome was in progress had an influence quite as fruitful. The Pazzi Chapel, built between 1420 and 1430, was in every serene and balanced detail distinctive of the new age; few would disagree with Anderson that it 'was probably the very first ecclesiastical building in Renaissance style, unmatched by any previous building that we know of'. The interior and old sacristy of San Lorenzo, the Badia of Fiesole, Santo Spirito, the loggia of the Spedale degli Innocenti, or Foundling Hospital, the original design of the Pitti Palace – all these masterpieces were due to Brunelleschi, who died in 1446.

Most of Ghiberti's life was dedicated to modelling, casting, and gilding the north and east doors of the Baptistery. They are triumphs of artistic workmanship, and since Michelangelo remarked that they were worthy to be the gates of Paradise there is nothing new to be said in their praise. They have to be seen in all their golden glory. Panel by panel, niche by niche, their influence on painting as well as sculpture has been tremendous. Ghiberti and Donatello did not imitate the antique; they studied it to learn its secrets and apply them to modern sculpture. It was Donatello who persuaded Cosimo to collect antique statues for public exhibition, and these were arranged in the garden of San Marco so as to form an open-air museum and art academy combined. Many a broken statue was repaired by Donatello himself, and the study of the antique was made easier for his successors. With due respect for Ghiberti's doors, Donatello towered above contemporary sculptors. He embodied in sculpture, as his junior Masaccio did in painting, the beauty and dignity of the individual with his peculiarities, of outward life, of physical power and self-reliance. Both selected forms which realized their conception of physical and intellectual ability. Their true interests were those of the humanist.

Cosimo was succeeded by his son, Piero 'the Gouty', aged forty-eight. In spite of chronic ill health Piero continued to control foreign policy, and his correspondence reveals a stoical strength of character. He was also a discriminating art collector and the true organizer of the Medici museum, but his reputation has been overshadowed by his dazzling son, Lorenzo.

Orpheus' three graces

Born in 1449, Lorenzo was only fifteen when Cosimo died, but he was already qualified to step into the public arena. According to Plato, the foundation of government is the education of youth, and Lorenzo had been educated by accomplished Platonists. Gentile Becchi of Urbino, the Greek Argyropoulos, Ficino, and Landino were his tutors; he had associated freely with his father's and grandfather's guests, including statesmen, financiers and ambassadors, at an age when modern children are more concerned with bicycles. He enjoyed riding and open-air sports, and he had a zest for country life which was to give a spontaneous vitality to his poems. Paolo Uccello's romantic *Hunt*, in the Ashmolean Museum at Oxford, may represent Lorenzo hunting near Pisa: it is a superb evocation of the thrill and rhythmic elegance of horsemen and hounds converging upon their quarry in a dark-green forest.

Owing to Piero's gout, Lorenzo and his younger brother, Giuliano, became the social pivots of the Medici party. They shared their youth with the whole of Florence, and the sweet spirit of this fleeting festive season is still vibrant in Lorenzo's carnival songs and in the *Primavera* of Botticelli, whose painting was in perfect harmony with Lorenzo's aesthetic aspirations. Lorenzo was always a poet, and this is what has baffled the historians, who are unaccustomed to the poetic temperament. His complex personality, so sensuous, subtle and impressionable, was a tissue of amazing contradictions. Ficino said that he possessed the three endowments called graces by Orpheus: splendour of intellect, light-heartedness in resolution, and the gift of renewing his youth. He was the new type of Renaissance gentleman, whose portrait was to be idealized by Castiglione in the *Cortegiano*.

Lorenzo inherited little of his parents' caution and sobriety. He had an almost morbid cult of springtime, and he delighted in beautifying the popular festivals which Florence had celebrated since time immemorial, transforming them into splendid spectacles. He personally supervised the pageants for St John the Baptist's day (24 June), the patron saint of the city, choosing the most original artists to design triumphal chariots, and composing special hymns.

The tournaments which Lorenzo organized in the square of Sta Croce have been described minutely in verse. They appear to have been more decorative than dangerous. Each knight entered the lists preceded by an equerry bearing his standard. Some suitable allegory, or the portrait of the lady whose colours he wore, was painted on the latter. For the joust Lorenzo held in honour of his mistress, Lucrezia Donati, on 7 February 1469, no less an artist than Verrocchio painted his standard. Lorenzo rode into the square in a surcoat with a red and white silk cape, and a scarf embroidered with roses, some fresh and some withered, surrounding his motto, *Le Temps Revient*, picked out in pearls. A plume of gold filigree set with diamonds and rubies stood from his black velvet cap, to display a pearl of exceptional value. For the combat he wore a velvet doublet embroidered with

A late-fifteenth-century impression of Florence, in which the Duomo, the Campanile, the Baptistery and the tower of the Signoria can be clearly distinguished.

golden lilies, and a helmet with three blue feathers replaced the jewelled cap. His shield was emblazoned with the three gold lilies of France, the privilege of bearing which had been granted to his father in 1465, and in the centre shone the great Medici diamond. Naturally Lorenzo won the prize, although, as he modestly wrote, 'I was not a very vigorous warrior, nor a hard hitter.'

Piero waived family tradition in finding a bride for Lorenzo outside Florence. A marriage was arranged with Clarice Orsini, of the noble Roman clan whose vast influence and possessions extended from Rome to Naples. Lorenzo's mother, Lucrezia, went to Rome to inspect the bride. Her brother, Giovanni Tornabuoni, was papal treasurer and head of the Medici bank there, but she could only trust her own eyes. Lucrezia was the perfect Florentine matriarch, dignified, intelligent, and cultured: old Cosimo had called her 'the man of the family'. From Rome Lucrezia wrote to her husband describing the bride to be: 'On the whole the girl seems to be far above the average, but she cannot compare with Maria, Lucrezia, and Bianca [her own daughters]. Lorenzo has seen her and you should find out whether she pleases him. Whatever you and he determine will be well done, and I shall be content. Let us leave the issue to God.'

Lorenzo discriminated between passion and policy, and he was satisfied with the choice. His marriage gave further opportunities for celebration, though the festivities did not differ considerably from those of other great Florentine houses. Lorenzo himself refers to the event rather laconically in his diary. But the bride soon won his affection and became a devoted housewife.

Cultural leadership: Florence held in spell

On 2 December 1469, Piero died of rheumatic gout at the age of fifty-three.

> The second day after his death [wrote Lorenzo in his diary], although I was very young, being twenty-one years of age, the principal men of the City and of the State came to our house to condole with us, and to persuade me to take charge of the City and the State, as my father and grandfather had done. I consented to do so, but unwillingly, as considering my youth the responsibility and danger were great, in order to protect our friends and property, since at Florence life is insecure for the wealthy without control of the government.

This candid statement was not hypocritical. The drudgery of administration must have been wearisome to a youth of Lorenzo's temperament, but having inherited the tiger he had to mount it. He rode that wild animal with such skill that it is often forgotten he was much more than a great statesman. His historical importance and, to paraphrase Burckhardt, the spell which he cast over Florence and all his contemporaries, was due less to his political capacity than to his leadership in the culture of the age.

One of Lorenzo's first acts on succeeding to power was to restore the University of Pisa, which had decayed since Florence conquered Pisa early in the century. The university soon became famous throughout Italy, and a Pisan degree was made obligatory for Florentine practitioners of law. In Florence a bevy of distinguished Byzan-

85

tine exiles taught Greek – Argyropoulos, Lascaris, Chalcondilas, Andronicos of Thessalonica among them – so that Poliziano, who translated Homer into Latin, could write truthfully:

> Greek learning, long extinct even in Greece itself, has come to life and lives again in Florence. There Greek literature is taught and studied, so that Athens, root and branch, has been transported to make her abode – not Athens in ruins and in the hands of barbarians, but Athens as she was, with her breathing spirit and her very soul.

Early in the century the humanists had been mainly preoccupied with recovering and interpreting the long-forgotten classics of Greek and Latin literature, and Ghiberti had written of the discovery of antique marbles as rare and wonderful events. Whatever added to knowledge of the ancient world, and thereby to deeper knowledge of themselves, was eagerly collected. At first the admiration for all things classical had been indiscriminate, but the Platonic Academy led to the formation of critical standards. In literature, however, this was not a creative period. Philology and rhetoric had smothered originality, and the growth of vernacular literature was interrupted until the advent of Lorenzo the Magnificent.

Imagine one who combined the functions of a Prime Minister, a banker and business magnate, a Lord Mayor, a director of national galleries and museums, a president of the national academy, and a chancellor of two universities: such was Lorenzo when, without ever losing his dignity, he went out into the streets of Florence and led a masquerade. Far from diminishing his prestige, this proof of his versatility enhanced it.

Il Lasca, who compiled and published Lorenzo's carnival songs in 1559, tells us that some were composed for the olive-oil makers, for the young wives and old husbands, for the gold thread makers, the pastry-cooks, and so forth. The Magnificent Lorenzo's sense of humour was typically Tuscan, and it found literary vent in his rollicking burlesque of *The Divine Comedy*, the *Simposio* or *Beoni*, a forerunner of the satires of Berni and Ariosto. His humour also found expression in outrageous practical jokes, like the hoax on Doctor Manente recounted by Lasca. The sort of conversation he relished on a higher plane has been recorded in Landino's *Disputationes Camaldulenses*, dialogues supposed to have been held by members of the Platonic Academy in the beech woods near the convent of Camaldoli on four summer days in 1468. Virgil was discussed amid Virgilian scenery, and Plato's doctrine of the contemplative life. Leone Battista Alberti argued that the rulers of men should occasionally retire from the world and devote themselves to meditation, for how could anyone reach perfection when he was distracted by material things from developing his spiritual faculties? Lorenzo objected, for what would happen if all the best men withdrew from the duties of government? Would not worse men promptly step into their shoes?

In practice Lorenzo succeeded admirably in leading both the active and the contemplative life. His sonnets and sacred poems show to what a mystical extent this man of the senses could be contemplative, and his *Altercazione* proves that he was steeped in the new Platonism.

Lorenzo as patron

His relations with artists were those of a patron who was never patronizing. Donatello's pupil, Bertoldo, was appointed keeper of his art collection in the gardens of San Marco, with a special commission to assist and instruct young students. The poorer students were supported by bursaries and premiums for proficiency. The *bottega* system of training was thus supplemented, for Lorenzo was not satisfied with the prevalent state of sculpture. Nearly all Florentine artists were trained in some *bottega*, a shop and school combined, which served as a painter's studio, a gold- and silversmith's shop, and a sculptor's and decorator's work-room. There was no division of labour. The pupil or apprentice might have to cast a bronze statuette, paint a merchant's signboard, enlarge his master's sketch for a fresco decoration, or carve a marriage chest. This variety of training helps to explain the remarkable versatility of Florentine artists. Besides frescoes and altar-pieces for churches, Baldovinetti painted household altars for private devotion, panels to decorate bedsteads and furniture, marriage chests and shields painted with arms and

garlands and inscribed with mottoes, gesso frames, mosaics, cartoons for stained glass and inlaid wood. Verrocchio was a goldsmith, sculptor, painter, bronze founder, architect, mechanician and, like his greater pupil Leonardo da Vinci, he also studied mathematics and geometry and became an accomplished musician.

In Lorenzo's time it is probable that Verrocchio's school took the lead in technical training. Verrocchio conducted all kinds of experiments, especially with the novel medium of oil painting; both he and Antonio Pollaiuolo, with their insistence on anatomy, perspective and composition, set the standard for the next generation and established the Florentine school of art as the most scientific in Italy. Pollaiuolo concentrated on the muscular system and emphasized athletic energy; Verrocchio was more concerned with intellectual power. The former excelled in painting, the latter in sculpture: the mantle of Donatello descended on both of them. Their immense contribution to art, which Bernard Berenson has analysed in his indispensable essay on the Florentine painters, was in the rendering of landscape, movement and the naked human body. Verrocchio was chief sculptor to the Medici: his bronze *David* was originally made for the villa of Careggi, so was the buoyant bronze *Putto* with the Dolphin, now in the courtyard of the Palazzo Vecchio. It is significant that in the tombs he designed for Cosimo, Piero and Giovanni de' Medici in San Lorenzo, not an emblem of Christianity is to be found.

Among painters Botticelli stood closest to Lorenzo: he reveals the taste and sentiment of the period more vividly than those whose visions he interpreted. His *Birth of Venus*, his *Primavera*, his *Mars and Venus*, breathe the same atmosphere as the poems of Lorenzo and Poliziano. Here is the Tuscanized Hellas of the Florentine humanists in perpetual flower. For skilled portraits of the same humanists we must visit the frescoes of Ghirlandaio in Sta Maria Novella and Sta Trinità, commissioned by Giovanni Tornabuoni, Lorenzo's uncle, and by Francesco Sassetti, Lorenzo's agent at Lyons. They can be recognized among the guests at Herod's feast, among the crowds who throng the temple, in these thinly-disguised illustrations of public and private life in the Quattrocento.

Lorenzo asked Ghirlandaio to send his most promising pupils to work in the garden of San Marco, where he wished to form a finishing school for sculptors. Among these was Michelangelo, who had already caused his teacher to exclaim, 'This boy knows more than I do.' For the next four years Michelangelo lived in Lorenzo's palace and was treated like a son. Those who were first at table sat next to the host, no matter who came in afterwards, so that Michelangelo was often seated above Lorenzo's sons and other distinguished guests. There he came in frequent contact with Marsilio Ficino, Pico della Mirandola, Luigi Pulci and Poliziano – regarded as the poet laureate of the Laurentian Age. The latter, 'recognizing the lofty spirit of Michelangelo, loved him exceedingly, and little as he needed it, spurred him on in his studies, always explaining things to him and giving him subjects. One day, amongst others he suggested *The Rape of Deianira* and the *Battle of the Centaurs*, telling him in detail the whole of the story.' The resulting high-relief, now in Casa Buonarroti, is the earliest work by Michelangelo to which an exact date, 1492, can be given; and it shows already that 'power over rhythm of line in a crowded composition' which distinguishes his later groups – a prophetic masterpiece all the more extraordinary when we consider his extreme youth.

Savonarola: the wrath to come

A short distance from the garden where Michelangelo was beginning to realize the full aesthetic significance of the naked human body and the ideal grandeur latent in physical expression, Savonarola was preparing for the wrath to come in the Convent of San Marco. In 1491 Savonarola was elected prior of this convent, which had been under the special patronage of the Medici since Cosimo had rebuilt it. Without Lorenzo's favour he could not have been elected, and he did not release his pent-up furies until Lorenzo's death. For a few tormented years the dangerous demagogue from Ferrara was to frighten the Florentines out of their senses, but he could not entirely destroy Lorenzo's achievement.

The large-hearted Lorenzo could not have foreseen this ultimate catastrophe. He had overcome two major calamities, the Pazzi Conspiracy of 1478, when his brother was murdered in the cathedral and he himself narrowly escaped with a wound, and the two years' war with Pope Sixtus IV and King Ferrante of Naples which followed it. The war proved disastrous to Florence, and an outbreak of plague accompanied famine and financial ruin. Lorenzo's courage and diplomacy saved the situation. He sailed quietly to Naples and walked into the lion's den. King Ferrante would not have hesitated to murder him for any possible advantage; fortunately he was amenable to reason and susceptible to Lorenzo's charm. After three tantalizing months, during which Lorenzo had to maintain the role of a lavish and unperturbed Magnifico, the terms of a separate peace-with-honour were concluded. In March 1480 Lorenzo returned to Florence, a popular hero. Botticelli's *Pallas Subduing the Centaur* commemorates this event. Vesuvius and the bay of Naples are seen in the background; in the foreground the Centaur, emblem of war and anarchy, cowers before the victorious goddess of peace and wisdom, wreathed with olive and wearing the interlaced rings of the Medici on her white robe. The anti-Medicean Machiavelli wrote:

> If Lorenzo was great when he left Florence, he returned much greater than ever; and he was received with such joy by the city as his noble qualities and his fresh merits deserved, seeing that he had exposed his own life to restore peace to his country.

On 8 April 1492 Lorenzo died at Careggi of the same disease as Piero and Cosimo, though he was only forty-three. Even before he was forty he had tried various cures which had brought him but slight relief. His wife had died before him at the age of thirty-eight; his eldest son, Piero, had married another Orsini, and his second son, the future Pope Leo X, had been raised to the cardinalate at the age of fourteen. The dynasty seemed secure, and Lorenzo had always identified Florence with his own house.

'The splendour not only of Tuscany, but of all Italy, has disappeared,' wrote the Florentine, Bartolommeo Dei. 'Every day we shall learn more what we have lost. As yet it cannot be calculated, but time will show.' And in Naples his erstwhile enemy, King Ferrante, said, 'This man has lived long enough for his own immortal fame, but not long enough for Italy.'

Under the influence of Savonarola there was a brief and bloodthirsty return to the Middle Ages. It was a tragic end to the most glorious century in Florentine history. Individual liberty was destroyed for the sake of what Savonarola considered a greater liberty: the secrets of the confessional and the privacy of family life were violated, and servants were encouraged to turn informers against their masters. Hideous tortures were devised for such offences as gambling, and costume was made the subject of severe legislation. Fasting became the order of the day; the Burning of Vanities replaced the Medicean festivals. Street urchins were organized into moral police, who trotted from house to house to collect 'luxuries' such as ornaments, mirrors, cosmetics and bric-à-brac, profane writings such as those of Puci and Boccaccio, and, above all, any representation of pagan deities and of the sinful nude for the virtuous bonfire. It was the reign of religious mania and militant puritanism, and again the city was divided as of old. Yet many a historian has been devoted to Savonarola and indulgent to his excesses. The revulsion of the public was ferocious when it came in 1498. 'Prophet! now is the time for a miracle!' shouted the mob, when Savonarola was hanged from the gibbet and a fire was kindled beneath him. In contrast with the yoke he had laid upon poor nature, the so-called tyranny of Lorenzo seemed positively Utopian. For as Guicciardini wrote in the 1530s, 'Florence could not have had a better or a more delightful tyrant.'

Savonarola, the prior of San Marco, is shown in this woodcut of 1495 preaching of sin and punishment to the people of Florence.

GOETHE'S WEIMAR

'Athens on the Ilm'

was a flattering term often applied towards the close of the eighteenth century to the hitherto obscure capital of a petty Duchy in the heart of Germany, one of the many small principalities that preserved their independence well into the second half of the nineteenth century. The tiny city of Weimar probably deserved that title since, for about fifty years, it was a centre of extraordinary intellectual activity and was recognized by all of Europe as a unique spiritual force. Goethe, the greatest of all German poets, who came to live in Weimar by a series of providential accidents, was the presiding genius, the energetic fount and the devoted servant of this remarkable flowering of creativity.

Invited in 1775 by young Karl August, Duke of Saxe-Weimar-Eisenach, the absolute monarch of this miniature realm, Goethe became, in effect, a court official, a member of the four-man Privy Council, and an active power in the government. The year before, he had become the sensation of Germany as the author of *The Sor-*

rows of Young Werther, a novel that set the 'Sturm und Drang' mood which overwhelmed the Continent. But his most penetrating and classical works were written during his mature years in Weimar, a city ever since identified with his name.

After eleven years in the Duke's service, Goethe felt the need for a change of scene and escaped to Italy. For two years he lived in the South, a reviving and liberating experience which, through his enthusiastic appreciation of antiquity, had a decisive effect on his ideas and writings. When he returned from Italy in 1788, he gave most of his time to writing and scientific studies, but as a kind of Minister of Culture and close confidant of the Duke, he continued to live in Weimar until his death in 1832, having brought glory, by his efforts and achievements, to a provincial and backward little state.

During his stay in Rome, Goethe associated mainly with German artists, among them Wilhelm Tischbein, who painted this portrait of the 38-year-old poet in the Campagna (detail opposite). (1)

Goethe's house on the Frauenplan (right) was presented by the Duke to his valued friend and counsellor in 1792. Goethe lived here the rest of his life, having ample space for great scientific and artistic collections. (2)

Weimar's artistic life was promoted by the Duke's mother, Anna Amalia, shown (below left) in a drawing by Tischbein. In 1772, this 'completely human spirit', as Goethe called her, niece of the cultivated Frederick the Great and a sensitive patron of the arts, engaged as tutor for her son Christoph Martin Wieland (below right), an important literary figure who contributed to the transformation of Weimar. The great dramatist, Friedrich Schiller (bottom), was another genius who added to the reputation of Weimar as Germany's cultural capital. During the ten years before his death in 1805 Schiller was a close friend of Goethe and fought as his ally to raise standards in German literature and art. (3, 4, 5)

Karl August (above), eighteen when he became reigning Duke, though a man of strong character and wide practical interests, was not especially talented, and preferred riding and shooting to philosophy; yet he recognized the genius of Goethe, and the two men, so diverse in character, enjoyed a happy and at first riotous companionship. (6)

Weimar's modest architecture, similar to that in most eighteenth-century small capitals in Germany, can be seen not only in Goethe's house but also in the one where Schiller lived (below). The Duke's palace was an attempt at grandeur and occupied about a third of the town. It burned down (bottom) in 1774 and took nineteen years to rebuild, a project in which Goethe took part. (7, 8)

The rebuilt palace and the handsome park of Weimar are represented about 1810 in a painting by F. T. Georgi (above). The redesigning of the park, which extended on both sides of the pastoral Ilm, was one of the many projects undertaken jointly by Goethe and the Duke from as early as 1778. (9)

A garden house near the Ilm was a present to Goethe from Karl August in 1776; the poet used it as his permanent home for six years, and even after he moved to the house in the Frauenplan it remained a refuge for him from the hurly-burly of court life. It is shown here (left), in a watercolour by G. M. Kraus, an artist who came at Goethe's invitation from Frankfurt to Weimar, where he taught drawing and helped to publish a monthly periodical devoted to 'fashion and luxury'. (10)

A company of friends, who typify Weimar's cultural atmosphere, meet for an evening of painting, reading, sewing and discussion. The Dowager Duchess, who formed around her a 'Court of Muses', is the woman with paint-brush in hand in the centre of this water-colour of 1794 by Kraus. Goethe, seen from the back, is identified as the second man from the left; and the figure on the right is Johann Gottlieb Herder, the imposing theologian and writer, one of the leaders of German thought, who had influenced Goethe during the latter's student days at Strassburg and who came to Weimar as the head of the clergy in 1776, invited by the Duke on Goethe's suggestion. (11)

Herder's ideas centred on religion and the history of civilization, Goethe's on poetry and the natural sciences; during the Weimar years, this difference of viewpoint gradually led to a virtual estrangement. Herder preached in the church (above centre) in a square that was later named Herder Place. The house where he lived until his death in 1803 is shown above right. (15, 16)

Late in life, Karl August was drawn visiting the great man through whose reflected glory the Duke's name is remembered at all (right). The last time they were together in Goethe's house was on 28 May 1828. Two weeks later, Karl August died; Goethe, eight years the elder, survived until 1832. (17)

The Court Theatre (top), built in 1780 with a grant from the Duke and managed by Goethe, was the scene of Weimar's theatrical triumphs, performed by a subsidized professional troupe. Until 1783, performances were on an amateur basis and given for a court audience; the most famous of these is the one in which Goethe himself acted the part of Orestes with great success in the prose version of his *Iphigenie* (above) in 1779. Between 1800 and 1805, Schiller was at the height of his powers; the outstanding success of that period was his historical drama, *Wallenstein*. A performance of the first part of this play, *Wallenstein's Camp*, is shown in a contemporary engraving (right). (12, 13, 14)

The aged Goethe,

relieved of his official duties and occupied mainly with the second part of *Faust*, kept to long, regimented workdays. In this painting of 1829–31 he is shown dictating to his secretary. The small and simply furnished study, which he called 'humble quarters', suited his inner creative life. By the time of this portrait Goethe was already a world figure, a man of unique character and abilities who not only had a widespread influence on his own times but also created, as it were, a community of intellect around the petty court of Weimar. (18)

W. H. BRUFORD

THE WEIMAR which achieved fame in the time of Goethe was the capital of a small Saxon duchy about as big as Westmorland or Rhode Island, with a population of just over 100,000, one of the Ernestine Duchies which had resulted from the partition of the Wettin lands in 1485. Its political insignificance towards the end of the eighteenth century may be gathered from the fact that the Habsburg monarchy's territory within the old 'Roman Empire of the German People' was a hundred times, and Brandenburg-Prussia's nearly fifty times, as extensive as Weimar's, and that both these states included twice as much land outside the Empire as within it. Economically, too, the state and the city of Weimar were no more advanced than their small neighbours in the Germany of the pre-industrial age, with her poor communications, unproductive agriculture and very small-scale industry.

Like most German capitals of that day, Weimar revealed itself to the visitor as an extension of the palace of a petty prince, 'not so much a small town as a large château', as it seemed to Mme de Staël. Its population was under 6,000 when Goethe went there in 1775, and about 9,000 at his death in 1832. Its six or seven hundred houses were for most of that time still enclosed by a wall, with four gates for the main roads – a wall useless now for defence, but still important for the collection of excise-duties. Quite a third of the town was taken up by the palace and the buildings which clustered round it and served the purposes of the government and the court. The handsome park which is its chief glory dates back in part to 1778, when Goethe and the Duke began to convert earlier formal gardens into an 'English garden' like that of Dessau, gradually taking in and planting more land on both sides of the river Ilm. A year before Goethe's arrival the main palace had been gutted by a fire which had left only the tower and the outer walls standing, and it was twenty years before the Duke could complete the restoration of this 'Wilhelmsburg' – years during which he and his family had as their town-residence a building intended for office use and quite unsuitable as a palace. The Dowager Duchess was better housed in what had been the residence of the Prime Minister.

It was evident, in fact, in many ways that Weimar was not an affluent state. The narrow winding streets of low thatched houses outside the palace area were little better than those of a village, and the cobbles could not be kept sweet-smelling and clean because of the town's cattle. These were driven out to pasture every morning and back to their owners' yards at night by the communal herdsman, for the benefit of the part-time farmers who cultivated some land outside the gates and kept a few cows. The whole town was so small that the voice of the half-blind watchman who called out the hours all through the night could be heard everywhere. There were two shops for luxury goods in the market-place in the early days, together with an apothecary's and a confectioner's establishments. Country produce of all kinds and craftsmen's small wares could be bought at booths in the open market, and butcher's meat at stalls that stood side by side under the arcades of the sixteenth-century town hall, but tailors, shoemakers, and so forth, received customers in the small houses where they lived and worked, or waited on a client in his home, like the hairdressers so often to be seen in the streets with a wig in each hand.

Weimar looked like what it was – that is, the modest capital of an insignificant state – and it could not be mistaken for a town that owed its importance to industry and trade. There were no buildings in the market-place that expressed the civic pride of an independent community, except for the high-gabled town hall and the Stadthaus (assembly rooms), both about two centuries old.

The fusion of tastes

The way of life at the Weimar court until the last thirty years of the eighteenth century gave as little promise of an 'Athens on the Ilm' as its buildings, or the town which served its needs. 'The metropolis of a little German sovereign', says an English visitor (C. E. Dodd) to the much more splendid court at Darmstadt in 1818, 'has a curious mixture of splendour and insignificance, a sort of miniature elegance which is perfectly novel to an Englishman.' The nearest parallel he could find in England was 'a neat watering-place with its quiet gentility'. 'The inhabitants too', he says, 'show a sort of straitened elegance and economical show.' The aristocracy spent their time in a round of engagements nearly all connected with the court, and all looked to the Prince to provide them with theatrical entertainments, concerts, assemblies, dinners and innumerable card parties. Even after the Napoleonic Wars, the nobility and the middle class did not mix freely, even at a public ball ostensibly organized for this purpose. Dodd found the nobility all together at one end of the room, talking the French which served them as a shibboleth, and which seemed to him 'a part of the court costume, not less indispensable than sword and buckles'. Before the French Revolution, class distinctions were taken as a matter of course, and were strictly observed, in Weimar too. But the remarkable thing that happened there was a genuine exchange between at least some individuals from each class, which brought about a certain fusion of tastes and ideals, so that in time many of the aristocracy came to share the intelligentsia's interest in the things of the mind, and the literary men absorbed some of the traditional values of the gentleman.

Duchess Luise of Weimar, whom Dodd happened to meet at Darmstadt, appears in his description almost as a living symbol of this fusion. She bore herself with great dignity, and her dress had an almost quaker-like simplicity; yet listening to her, you had the impression, not only of the easy self-possession of rank, but of dignity of intellect, and you were aware of the inner resources that had sustained her in her interview with Napoleon, and, one may add, in her unhappy marriage with Karl August. German 'inwardness', an attitude towards experience which can be traced back to medieval mystics like Meister Eckhart, and which had been strengthened in the eighteenth century both by the philosophy of the Enlightenment and by Pietism, became a dominant feature among the élite of Weimar. This proceeded from Christian feeling in some, like the Duchess and Herder, but more commonly from a kind of aesthetic religion such as Goethe's and Schiller's ideal of personal culture, of *Bildung*. This ideal was expressed in *Wilhelm Meister's Apprenticeship* and in Schiller's philosophical essays. Further, this conception of the personal life at its highest became the basis of a social philosophy. 'The harmonious development of those qualities and faculties that characterize our humanity', to quote Coleridge's description of the content of this new humanism or *Humanität*, and not the pursuit of power or wealth or the exploitation of natural forces, was advanced as the true criterion of a nation's civilization. Weimar won its place as the spiritual capital of Germany by providing, within its narrow confines, at least a foretaste of what Coleridge calls a 'civilization grounded in cultivation', both in the life and doctrines of many of its citizens and in the institutions called into being or improved by them with the aim of handing on their insight to others.

Outburst of creativity

Because the external features and the social and administrative structure of Weimar had so little that was remarkable, the interesting question for us is how such a city could so quickly become the centre of an outburst of intellectual and literary activity that was so vigorous and so original. Deliberate patronage by enlightened rulers does not seem to be the answer. The explanation is rather to be found in a series of happy accidents which brought Goethe to Weimar and made him content to stay there; for without Goethe, Weimar would have had comparatively little history worth recording. The first link in the chain was the appointment of C. M. Wieland as tutor to Karl August, Hereditary Prince of Weimar, in 1772 when the Prince was fifteen years old.

Wieland was in many ways a very good choice. Though for a few years he had held a post as professor of philosophy at the University of Erfurt, he was really a literary man, the first translator of Shakespeare into German and the first German novelist to make an appeal to aristocrats who normally read French, as well as to the educated middle class. His philosophy of life, as revealed in his novel *Agathon*, or in the verse tale *Musarion*, which Goethe as a young man knew almost by heart, was the shrewd but kindly epicurean scepticism of a spectator of life, inspired especially by Horace among the ancients and by the third Earl of Shaftesbury, the author of the *Characteristics*, among the moderns. After the success of *Agathon* he had been called to Erfurt to add a little much-needed distinction to its staff, but his duties were light. He had just completed another novel, *The Golden Mirror*. Written in the tradition of *Rasselas* and the *Lettres Persanes*, this was a eulogy in Oriental dress of what we should call benevolent despotism. It was intended in the first place to attract the attention of Joseph II, but failing a response from Vienna Wieland was pleased to obtain a hearing in Weimar. There was nothing novel or substantial in the political philosophy of this work, but it not unnaturally confirmed the favourable personal impression made by Wieland on the Regent, the Duchess Anna Amalia. She was genuinely fond of books, music, and the theatre; like her uncle Frederick the Great she had grown up at a court where such things were counted among the necessities of life. The Rococo flavour of Wieland's work appealed to her, and the two remained good friends for the rest of their lives, though the Duchess soon found that she had over-estimated the good influence that Wieland could have on her son.

Wieland had his own reasons for accepting the post. With his rapidly growing family, what he principally sought was security – a steady income, the prospect of a state pension – and time for his writing. He had not given up all hope of a later appointment in Vienna, and he began to take steps immediately to keep himself in the public eye and to supplement his modest salary by starting a new monthly magazine, modelled on the very popular *Mercure de France*. *Der deutsche Merkur* appeared for the first time in January 1773, four months after Wieland's arrival in Weimar, and it lasted nearly forty years. For the first twenty-three Wieland produced it himself with little help and, unfortunately, with diminishing returns, though in the first year 2,500 copies were printed, a very large number for German conditions. Wieland's 'factory', as he called it, was a thorn in his flesh, but we have it on Goethe's authority that south Germany owed any taste it had for good literature mainly to this periodical. North Germany had a start of about fourteen years with two ventures of Friedrich Nicolai, the Berlin publisher. One of them, launched by Lessing, was concerned mainly with literature, the other mainly with art; both were aimed at the same kind of general public, but their tone was too rationalistic to make much appeal in the south, and communications in Germany were so bad that the range of any publication was limited geographically. It was important for Weimar's future that Wieland came so close behind Nicolai.

Weimar's pre-eminence however, unlike Berlin's, depended almost entirely on the power of words, the activities of professional writers. In the *Merkur*, Wieland made much out of Anna Amalia's engagement of a touring company of actors in Weimar, in which there was really nothing exceptional, and it was in this way that the ruling house of Weimar first came to be acclaimed as patrons of art.

Wieland had been in Weimar for about a year when he was visited by Karl Ludwig von Knebel, who at the age of thirty had just obtained his release from the Regiment of Guards at Potsdam, finding an officer's life in peace-time too empty for his tastes. Knebel had literary leanings, without much talent, and for years he had been trying to keep in touch with leading writers. His visit brought him to the notice of the Duchess and the court, so that, when a tutor with military experience was needed for Karl August's younger brother, Prince Konstantin, Knebel seemed a natural choice. After protracted negotiations he was appointed in October 1774, and two months later he had an opportunity of visiting in Frankfurt another literary celebrity, the author of *Werther*, which had appeared earlier in the year and had caused a sensation. Knebel was one of the party of four that was accompanying the two Weimar princes on their grand tour, to which their mother had now given her consent.

Goethe's initial impact

The travellers were only spending a few hours in Frankfurt on the way to Mainz, but Knebel found Goethe at home, was charmed with him, and took him along to meet the rest of the party. The princes in their turn insisted that Goethe should follow them to Mainz for further conversations, and Goethe spent a couple of days there, much against the wishes of his father. (As a citizen of the Free Town of Frankfurt, a little republic, Goethe's father saw nothing but trouble ahead for his son if he got into the clutches of a prince.) In May of the following year, when Goethe was passing through Karlsruhe on the way to Switzerland with the Stolberg brothers and another young nobleman, he met Karl August again. There was probably some talk of their all visiting Weimar soon after the Duke's accession and marriage to Princess Luise of Hesse-Darmstadt in the autumn. A definite invitation was given to Goethe, and accepted by him, in September when the prince was on his way to be married. While the ducal pair were passing through Frankfurt on their way to Weimar, they promised to send a carriage back from Weimar to fetch him, but he waited for it on the pre-arranged day in vain. At the suggestion of his father, who was now more mistrustful than ever, Goethe had started out for Italy and had spent a day or two in Heidelberg before news of the arrival of a gentleman-in-waiting with the carriage at last reached him. This was not an auspicious beginning of his new relationship with the Duke, and it will be seen that chance had played a considerable part in bringing them together.

Goethe had been looking for an opportunity of escaping from his native Frankfurt, this 'nest', this 'wretched hole', and he particularly welcomed one at that moment, after the breaking-off of his engagement with Lili Schönemann, the banker's daughter. He was curious to see something of life at court, a new world to him, and before long, when he found himself in the position of a favourite of the young Duke, he had visions of using his unexpected chance of 'ruling' to make at least this small corner of the world a better place. 'Favouritism; Self-confidence; Conceit.' – these three words constitute one section of the few notes he made in old age for a continuation, planned but never written, of his autobiography, *Poetry and Truth*, which unfortunately breaks off at his departure for Weimar; and these words show clearly enough what he thought later of the 'Voltairean Huron' with whom he compares his former self in a further note. In Voltaire's story *L'Ingénu*, a handsome and noble Red Indian, suddenly introduced into French provincial society, surprises everyone by his uninhibited opinions and manners, but while the ladies and the younger men take a great fancy to him, older men cannot conceal their disgust and alarm. So too in Weimar, the conventional majority had not a good word to say for their young Duke's new-found friend, but a few, including Anna Amalia, Wieland and Knebel, came completely under his spell. The Duke, for his part, had been greatly attracted by Goethe from what he had seen of him in Frankfurt. Goethe attracted him as a man rather than as a poet. He would bring fresh air, the Duke felt, into the stuffy little court, and what a triumph it would be to capture this brilliant creature for his service! If Goethe had been a nobleman, he would have been offered a post as gentleman-in-waiting immediately, like his friend Fritz von Stolberg. At this stage the Duke probably had no thought of literary patronage: he was only eighteen. As things turned out, Goethe was for long seriously distracted from his writing; after *Stella*, which had been written in Frankfurt and appeared early in 1776, he published nothing but an occasional poem in a magazine or anthology for eleven years.

As the Duke's guest, Goethe accommodated himself to the humours of his host with surprising ease considering the differences between them in age, character and acquired habits. We can perhaps best understand the 'Protean' nature, that disconcerted a philosopher like Fritz Jacobi in Goethe, as part of his equipment as a poet. 'What shocks the virtuous philosopher delights the chameleon poet', Keats wrote to Woodhouse on 27 October 1818. 'The poetical character ... is everything and nothing ... a poet ... has no identity – he is continually in for and filling some other body.'

New roles before him

What delighted Goethe in Weimar, even in the course of the dull duties that he took upon himself, was the variety of new roles, each opening up a new aspect of existence, into which he could slip. In his letters to Frau von Stein from neighbouring courts we can sometimes see the collector of souls at work, and nothing seems too remote to arouse his interest. To contemporaries it seemed a good-natured interest, except when people were not content to be themselves, for then he was often provoked to sharp ridicule. In this spirit he had satirized Wieland's 'Singspiel' *Alceste*, a year before this, but he had immediately apologized to Wieland on hearing from the Weimar visitors in Frankfurt how much annoyance this outburst had caused. When Wieland met him on his arrival, he was won over immediately, in spite of his forebodings, by Goethe's *bonhomie*, his spontaneity and unmistakable genius. Without any suggestion of jealousy he praised Goethe to one correspondent after another, often in extravagant terms, as 'the king of spirits', 'the most amiable, the greatest and best of all the men I have ever seen'.

In early portraits Karl August looks rather sullen and common-place. Field-sports and riding were his passion, and his favourite dogs had to accompany him everywhere, even at table or at court concerts. None of his tutors had aroused in him much interest in books, though Wieland had held his attention with his encyclopaedic course on current affairs, psychology, philosophical theology, the principles of government, etc. (This course was mostly based on summaries of Adam Ferguson's lectures for his class in Edinburgh University, enlivened, no doubt, by good stories.) Wieland was twenty-four years older than Karl August, Goethe only eight. It was quite a different matter to have a constant companion of his own generation, with whom he could talk freely about all their experiences. When they had been out riding, as so frequently happened at first, Karl August to shoot and Goethe to sketch, the talk might be about woods and forestry, the habits of birds and animals, crops, land-drainage and all the practical problems of a landed proprietor; or, if they had been in and about Weimar, it might be about buildings, gardens, and how to plan and pay for improvements to them. People and personal problems would come into all of it, Goethe's intelligence and imagination would find connections everywhere, and questions would suggest themselves on which they needed information – from some Jena professor, from a man of affairs like Goethe's friend Merck, or from a practical man like the English bailiff, Batty. Goethe was learning all the time – he tells us in detail how this happened in botany, for instance – but so was the Duke. 'He used to sit whole evenings with me', Goethe said to Eckermann after the Duke's death, 'deep in conversation about art and nature, serious subjects of all kinds. We often sat up late into the night and sometimes fell asleep side by side on my sofa.' To escape the formality of the Duchess's high table, Goethe and the Duke, with young Herr von Wedel perhaps, his inseparable partner on shooting expeditions, frequently supped together quietly in the Duke's apartments. These three, with Einsiedel, gentleman-in-waiting to the Dowager Duchess, and one or two others, 'kept together, agreed wonderfully, and held the court at arm's length', as Goethe wrote to his mother in February 1776. Six weeks earlier Einsiedel had written some verses about a prince 'who forgets his birth and throne', spending all his

time with a few unconventional companions. They are like brothers together, he writes, and in the name of common sense they banish etiquette, speak from the heart, and do not let the high affairs of state depress them.

Many of the older courtiers, and those younger ones who found themselves neglected in favour of a bourgeois 'upstart', were naturally angry and full of foreboding. Siegmund von Seckendorff, a versatile young man, six years older than Goethe and experienced in court service elsewhere, was secretly discontented, as we know from his correspondence, though his musical talent and skill as an actor and producer found ample scope:

> The prevailing dislike of any kind of court has led the Duke and his entourage [he wrote] to look upon court officials as useless encumbrances ... According to the system of the Duke's advisers there is no such thing as decorum. Our present conventions had their origin in the whims of some man or men, and the head of the state can abolish them.

Contemporary silhouette of Charlotte von Stein, whose close relationship with Goethe developed in Weimar.

Frau von Stein herself, the wife of the Duke's Equerry, a traditionalist herself through and through, but an intelligent and sensitive woman, to whom Goethe had felt himself drawn from their first meeting, confirms Seckendorff's words, but with a fuller understanding of the real situation. In March 1776, she wrote to her friend Zimmermann that the Duke, evidently under the influence of Rousseauistic ideas picked up from Goethe, had just declared to her that people who thought about decorum and good manners could not be called honest men. That, she added, was why he could not bear to have anyone near him now who was not a little uncouth in one way or another. Goethe often annoyed her with his 'Sturm und Drang' ways, his oaths, his coarse expressions, his flirtations. But he was all the same, she said, 'a man with head and heart enough for thousands, who could see everything clearly and without prejudice when he wished, and master any task if he put his mind to it.' The silly things he was said to be doing in the Duke's company, cracking a long whip in the market-place, riding recklessly, bathing in the Ilm, skating, dancing with peasant girls, and so on, seemed to her harmless extravagances, and she was sure he was often just humouring the boy-Duke, 'to gain his confidence and then do good'.

The first effect of the tittle-tattle spread by people like Görtz, the Duke's former tutor, in neighbouring courts and repeated by envious young writers and disapproving seniors, was a *succès de scandale* for the new Weimar. Klopstock, the doyen of German poets, felt himself obliged to send Goethe a reproachful letter, and to try to prevent Fritz von Stolberg from following him to Weimar. By this time, however, Goethe had come to a full sense of his responsibilities, and had resolved to stay on in Weimar for some years. The Duke had decided very soon to try to keep him there, but for some months he could not make him a definite offer. He had first to persuade his experienced Prime Minister, Herr von Fritsch, who did not like the look of things, to remain in office, and then bring him to accept what seemed to Fritsch ill-considered ideas about new appointments. The first of these, that young Herr von Kalb should succeed his father, the retiring head of the Treasury, in office, proved within a few years to have been a great mistake, which led to a serious financial crisis in the state. The second, that Goethe should be made a permanent official with a seat on the Privy Council of four men which governed the state, seemed to Fritsch equally crazy, but in the end, under pressure from the Dowager Duchess too, he agreed to both proposals. The correspondence between the young Duke and his Prime Minister does credit to them both and shows how highly Karl August rated Goethe's integrity, as well as his intelligence. Goethe had of course taken his degree in law at Strassburg and had practised a little, and it was greatly in his favour that he was known to be a man of substance, and not a penniless adventurer. In the end all his own fortune was needed, as well as his salary, to maintain his position in Weimar. Although the arrangements for Herder's appointment had gone through by February 1776, it was June before Goethe's position was regularized and he received his first salary. Until then he looked upon himself and was regarded by others simply as a visitor; he was often hard pressed for money, since at this stage his father was most unwilling to help him. Loans from friends and an occasional present from the Duke saw him through, and in May the Duke also gave him the old cottage in the fields near the Ilm which became his 'Gartenhaus'.

The universal man

At this distance in time the corporate intellectual and artistic achievements of Weimar and Jena seem to us to have been infinitely more lasting in their effect, and to have contributed far more towards Weimar's greatness, than anything that Goethe was able to do through having power thrust upon him. His intentions were good, his intelligence and industry exceptional, he had the deepest sympathy with the class which, as he clearly saw, bore the whole burden under the Old Régime, namely the peasantry. But before he ran away from it all to Italy in 1786, he had discovered that there was no quick and easy way of remedying the ills of society in his day, because all the measures that a benevolent government could take in a small German state were mere palliatives. In old age he reviewed his efforts, first as a member of the Privy Council, which met once or twice a week and had the ultimate say in a bewildering variety of matters, and then as chairman of several of its committees, one to restore the old copper mines at Ilmenau, one to improve roads and waterways and to choose recruits for the militia, and finally one to clear up the mess that Herr von Kalb had left behind him at the Treasury; in retrospect these efforts seemed to him to have been for the most part a waste of time and most frustrating. He did, however, gain experience of the daily life of all classes and of the world of nature; and this nourished his poetic imagination, aroused his interest in science and did more than anything else to make him the 'universal man' that he became.

People who came into contact with Goethe, both in Weimar and outside, soon began to comment on his penetrating judgment as well as on his friendliness. Two years after his arrival, Wieland described him as reserved and serious, absorbed in his work. The change that had taken place in himself and in the Duke by 1784 is vividly conveyed in his poem *Ilmenau*. He had long put behind him the ideas of the time when he had 'foolishly sung of courage and freedom'. Some people now already found in his manner that stiffness of which so many were to complain in his later years. Perhaps this was the result of an over-correction – partly under the influence of Frau von Stein and of life at court – of his 'Sturm und Drang' rejection of the conventions. By the time of the French Revolution, Goethe was a conservative in political and social matters, who urged his countrymen – in *Hermann und Dorothea*, for instance – to hold on to the benefits of a well-established order and not be misled by specious radicals.

Alongside his official duties, Goethe continued for some years to give the court the benefit of his talent as poet and actor. In fact, the first specific task assigned to him (from October 1776) by Karl August was to look after the amateur theatre. For about a year, two groups of amateur players had been putting on plays and operettas, an aristocratic one in French and a middle-class one in German, with the customary separation of the two classes. Each had presented about half a dozen items, with repetitions when these were asked for, but by now their enthusiasm was waning. Goethe had provided two entertainments independently so far. He had produced, and acted in, Cumberland's *West Indian* (in German), and persuaded Anna Amalia to compose new music, orchestrated by Seckendorff,

for the already published short operetta *Erwin und Elmire*. For three or four years longer, Goethe organized fairly frequent performances, all in German now. Then the intervals between them became longer and longer, until in 1783 a troupe of professional actors under Bellomo was called in and given a regular subsidy. Two or three of the plays each year were Goethe's own, either revised versions of older works or lively improvisations full of topical allusions. Goethe acted in these and occasionally took a small part in one or two other productions each year, usually at the more intimate performances at Ettersburg in the summer. The star of the company was Corona Schröter, a professional singer and actress of great charm and cultivation, no longer young, who had been engaged as *Hofsängerin* late in 1776.

She and Goethe took the leading parts in the most famous of all these performances, that of the prose version of Goethe's *Iphigenie* in 1779. The audience were for the most part members of the court, but there was room for a few score of interested townsfolk on benches set out in the gallery, and behind the chairs of the court party in the body of the hall. This had been hastily erected in 1776 by private enterprise, with a little help from the Duke, and it was mainly intended for masked balls. It was replaced by a better one with a permanent stage in 1779; and this served later for Bellomo and, from 1791, for the new Court Theatre.

Cultural entrepreneurs

There was little in all this to distinguish Weimar from other small courts. Amateur theatricals were a favourite form of amusement at them all, as at house-parties at the country seats of the high nobility, and as always most of the fun came from dressing up and from the social intercourse accompanying rehearsals. Together with other activities prompted by Goethe – the drawing school, for instance, and the private court magazine, the *Tiefurt Journal*, which circulated for three years in a dozen handwritten copies – the amateur theatre helped to raise the tone of intellectual life in Weimar, where Goethe found at first, he says, merely a certain 'cheerful mediocrity, with aspirations towards knowledge and culture'; but the theatre can hardly have affected the image of Weimar in Germany as a whole. Until Goethe returned in June 1788 from his journey to Italy, which had lasted nearly two years, the external impact of Weimar was due in the main to other people. One of the most important, though he is seldom given credit for it, was F. J. Bertuch, and the others were Wieland with *Der deutsche Merkur*, as described above, and Herder, whose learned and challenging writings went out from Weimar in a steady stream.

Bertuch was a competent essayist and translator, a Weimar man educated at Jena who was found very useful, on his return to Weimar, by both Wieland and the Duke. He looked after the business side of running the *Merkur* so well that in a few years he was made co-editor. He was Keeper of the Duke's Privy Purse, he produced plays and acted for the middle-class group, and he was in close touch with Goethe and the rest, though always on the fringe of the court circle. His main interest was in making money, and he was shrewd enough to find many ways in which he could profit personally from the concentration of talent in Weimar and from the steady growth of interest in literary and artistic matters in Germany in his time. Bertuch cultivated the acquaintance of creative spirits; and, though many of these looked upon him as a philistine who 'decked himself out in borrowed plumes', as Goethe put it, he served their interests well as a man of practical ideas, a publisher and entrepreneur. He gradually initiated several types of business in Weimar, all connected with the commercial exploitation of the talent assembled there and with the scholarship of Jena.

In the large house which Bertuch built for himself from his literary earnings, particularly from his successful translation of *Don Quixote*, his sister-in-law, from 1782, taught a score of young girls – for whom there was no employment otherwise except in domestic service – how to make artificial flowers in great quantities, to be sold by Bertuch. Christiane Vulpius was employed here before she went to live with Goethe. In 1786 Bertuch started the first German monthly magazine 'for fashion and luxury', with the help of G. M. Kraus, a Frankfurt artist who had been brought to Weimar, through Goethe's good offices, to conduct drawing classes for the court ladies, and later to train promising boys in commercial art. The magazine continued,

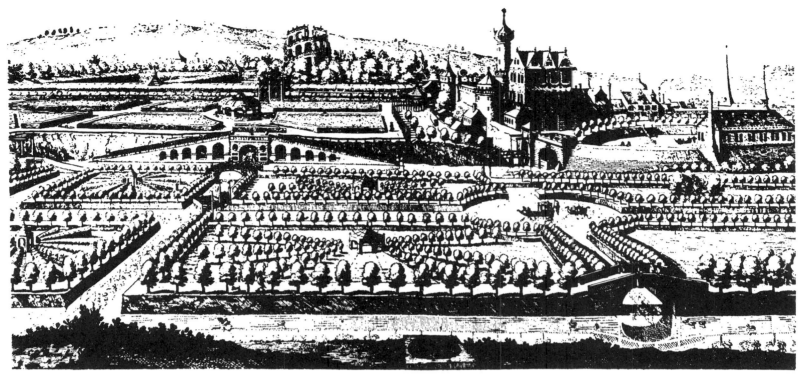

The pleasure gardens of Karl August, Duke of Weimar.
The Residence is in the background.

throughout the troubled times which soon followed, to bring French and English models of elegant living to the notice of the Germans, and to provide customers for the agency associated with it, where they could order foreign luxury goods and see sample products of local arts and crafts. This had developed by 1811 into a group of undertakings employing 450 men, and made Bertuch the richest and one of the most respected citizens of Weimar: a forward-looking democrat and patriot, well known in Germany at large through many popular series of books and periodicals, printed and published by him in Weimar. He went in for safe enterprises like illustrated children's books, geographical and gardening magazines, books of travel and, in war-time, magazines on current affairs and even a newspaper or two. All these played their part in keeping Weimar before the public eye, but the *Allgemeine Literatur-Zeitung*, started by Bertuch and Professor Schütz of Jena in 1785, was a most important instrument for the diffusion of knowledge and the establishment of literary and scholarly standards. It was a general review, much the best of its time in Germany and perhaps in Europe, with scores of well-chosen anonymous contributors, who discussed new books from the whole field of learning and modern literature, including the most important in the chief foreign languages. Four quarto pages appeared six times a week, with a weekly *Advertiser*, and for important reviews like Kant's of Herder's *Ideas* or A.W. Schlegel's of new works by Goethe, there was ample space available.

After Kant's adverse review, Herder had not a good word to say for Bertuch. He felt himself to be in many ways an outsider in Weimar, but before he went there he was already a force in German thought. As a very unorthodox theologian, one of the first to interpret religious ideas as essentially poetic, he fell in Weimar between two stools. In the eyes of Goethe and the Duke, who only went to church when he had to, Herder seemed to cling too closely to the traditional ritual and phraseology, while his colleagues on the Consistory Board could not take seriously a theologian who seemed as much indebted to Spinoza as to Christ, though they had to acknowledge his outstanding gifts as a preacher.

The heritage of creative insight

Herder and Goethe, who never forgot the older man's profound influence on him in Strassburg in his student days, came close to each other again when Herder was writing his greatest book, *Ideas on the Philosophy of the History of Humanity*. Both were intent on spelling out the characters of the sacred book of nature, as Herder puts it – Herder in the effort to understand the beginnings of life on earth, and Goethe under the spur of the profound interest in the

laws of nature, whether in geology, botany or zoology, that had been aroused in him, as an official with an unusually enquiring mind, by the practical problems in his work. They were both ardent admirers of the Greeks as models of true humanity, and they both saw civilized society as one in which the positive creative insight of gifted individuals finds full expression and is handed on in symbolic form for the benefit of future generations. Goethe was more concerned with the genesis of all-round cultivation in the individual, and was busy with the first version of what became *Wilhelm Meister's Apprenticeship*; while Herder was occupied with the great civilizations of the past and how the torch was handed on. For the moment it was only Herder's thought which reached the outer world, where it helped many whose religious beliefs had been shaken by the Enlightenment to find a new meaning in life.

Der deutsche Merkur and Herder's writings, the *Allgemeine Literatur-Zeitung* and the *Modejournal* were followed up by the masterpieces which first appeared in Goethe's *Collected Works* from 1787 onwards, his *Miscellaneous Poems* and the dramas *Iphigenie, Tasso, Egmont* and *Faust, ein Fragment*. After these came the flood of mature works produced in rapid succession by both Goethe and Schiller during the period of their friendship and literary alliance, from 1794 to Schiller's death in 1805. They include Goethe's *Elegies* and many other lyrical poems and ballads, *Hermann und Dorothea, Wilhelm Meister's Apprenticeship*, and several scientific essays; Schiller's aesthetic essays, philosophical poems, ballads, and his five greatest dramas. Schiller's literary periodical, *Die Horen*, achieved a standard that has rarely been approached since, with contributions in the early numbers from all the leading German writers, and his *Musenalmanach* put all earlier verse almanacs in the shade. Writings of this quality still had a limited circle of readers in Germany, but the *Xenien*, the collection of epigrams written by Goethe and Schiller in collaboration and directed against their literary opponents and Philistia in general, evoked such a storm of protest that no reader of a literary journal of any kind could remain ignorant of Weimar and what it stood for.

The Weimar Court Theatre, established in 1791 and managed, at first unwillingly, by Goethe, took some time to reach the standard set by earlier subsidized repertory theatres, but in its best productions it pursued an uncompromising policy of anti-naturalism, though for financial reasons it always had to make concessions to popular taste at a majority of its performances. When its repertoire was enriched by *Wallenstein* and the later plays of Schiller, from 1798 on, it recheda great heights and attracted many visitors. The dramatist himself helped in rehearsals from the end of the next year, when he settled in Weimar. In these same years Goethe tried, without

Title-page of the first issue of Der Deutsche Merkur, *the literary monthly journal founded in Weimar by C. M. Wieland; and the notice of the first performance in Weimar of Schiller's* Wilhelm Tell *on 17 March 1804.*

much success, to lead German painting and sculpture back to classical subjects and to a style inspired by the Greeks, as he and the 'Weimar friends of art' interpreted them in the new art journal, the *Propyläen*. Annual competitions did not evoke the expected response, but they too helped to make contemporaries think of Weimar as a centre for art of every kind.

There is little space to speak of Jena, the university in Weimar territory, which was supported financially by that state in particular and was closely supervised by Goethe, long before he was designated 'Minister of State with the supreme direction of the higher institutions for scholarship and art in Weimar and Jena', as he was when Weimar became a Grand Duchy in 1815. Jena flourished as never before in the last decade of the eighteenth century, when the liberal policy of the state and the opportunities offered by the *Literatur-Zeitung* attracted some of the best university teachers, when Schiller lived there and lectured for a time on history, and when Jena took the lead in philosophy as the stronghold of Kantian thought. Fichte and Schelling went beyond Kant and developed their systems of absolute idealism, while the Schlegels and their friends were starting the German Romantic movement with their periodical the *Athenäum*. There was an activism in Fichte's pupils, a determination not to be mastered by circumstances, which was new in Germany and was to have important consequences when many of the educated class came to be aware of themselves as members of one nation, not only culturally but politically, as a result of the French occupation.

Aesthetic religion: the realm of the ideal

Weimar itself in the age we have been describing, down to the death of Schiller, had no national feeling in the political sense. The educated people there were cosmopolitans and the masses thought of Weimar as their fatherland. The greatness of Weimar was, as we have seen, almost entirely a greatness of thought and imagination and of their embodiment in words. Its writers had little hope of changing their world, and they retreated perhaps too readily to that world of the ideal which Schiller, in his greatest poem, contrasts with real life. The French Revolution was for most of them a warning example; they carried on their work unmoved while Europe was

being reshaped by Napoleon; and, when Weimar itself was occupied after the Battle of Jena, it was of women, the Duchess, for example, and Goethe's Christiane, whom he married at last out of gratitude, that tales of heroism were told.

The everyday life of Weimar remained almost unchanged throughout its great age. It continued to be so different from anything in our experience that to Karl Jaspers, a few years ago, Goethe seemed nearer to Homer than to us. Its system of government was still a paternal absolutism, even when Karl August had granted a new constitution after the wars; and, though the aristocracy and the upper middle class had come closer together, the gap between the educated and the 'people' was greater than ever. Yet there was little discontent, and what there was was seldom expressed, because there was no question yet of education for all. The deepest desire of the Germans, Mme de Staël felt, was to continue for ever as they were, and this old-world atmosphere, as found in Weimar, had a strong appeal for foreigners. The legend of the land of poets and thinkers was chiefly their creation, in books like Mme de Staël's *De l' Allemagne* or Carlyle's *Essays* and *Life of Schiller*, while in Germany itself, as industrialism and power politics made the present hideous, nostalgia threw a rosy glow over this relic of the past. What we call the great age of Weimar was not golden for those who lived in it, and who thought of civilization as a painful advance towards harmony through hard thinking and hard work. But meanwhile they had an unfailing consolation in certain states of mind, not unlike the 'timeless, passionate states of contemplation and communion, not associated with action or achievement' (Keynes, *My Early Beliefs*), which were made into a kind of religion in Cambridge fifty or sixty years ago by G. E. Moore's young disciples. The writings informed by Weimar's aesthetic religion can still bring their 'realm of the ideal' so close to us that we do not dismiss as mere rhetoric Schiller's assertion that:

in *mind* it is the privilege and the duty of the philosopher and the poet to belong to no nation and to no people, but to be in the full sense of the word the contemporary of all times.

That is a measure of the greatness of Goethe's Weimar.

PART TWO
CAPITAL CITIES

ALEXANDRIA

ROME

CHANGAN

CONSTANTINOPLE

CORDOBA

PARIS

MEXICO

ISFAHAN

DELHI-AGRA

ST PETERSBURG

VIENNA

FOREWORD

CAPITAL CITIES, like city-states, are seats of government; but the government that is conducted from a capital city has a wider range than the city itself and the immediately adjoining countryside. The state that is governed from a capital city will include other cities besides the capital and other rural areas besides the one from which the capital draws its food-supply. In other words the government of the state of which a capital city is the seat of government is not identical with the government of the capital itself, and this is the essence of the differences between a capital city and a city-state. The capital city has been made a seat of government for the convenience of a state that is greater than its capital is. A capital is not the master of a state; it is a state's servant, and there have been cases in which the government of a state has withheld even municipal self-government from the capital, in order to make sure that the inhabitants of the capital shall not be able to interfere unduly with the government whose seat happens to be in their city but whose concern is with the country as a whole.

A classic example of this is the local administration of Washington, D.C. This is in the hands, not of the population of the District of Columbia, but of a Commission of Congressmen, appointed by Congress, and representing, not the District itself, but the Union. The position was similar when Alexandria was the capital of Ptolemaic Egypt. At that time, Alexandria was the most populous city in the whole Greek world, and it was also the commercial, industrial, and administrative capital of the whole Greek world, besides being the political capital of the Ptolemaic dynasty's dominions. Yet, just because the Ptolemaic government had made Alexandria its capital, it was chary of granting to this great Greek city the self-government that was the traditional prerogative of any Greek city, however small and insignificant it might be. Since the state of which a capital city is the seat of government covers a far wider area than the capital itself and the countryside that is immediately adjacent to it, the government of the country is faced with a topographical question which does not arise in the case of a city-state. In a state of supra-city-state dimensions, there will be more than one city; and therefore there will be a choice of locations for the seat of government. In selecting the city that is to be its capital, the state's government will have three different desiderata simultaneously in mind. It will want a location that will be convenient for serving as an administrative centre for the whole country; it will want a location within easy reach of abundant sources of food for supplying a large urban population; and it will want a location that will be a good strategic centre for defending the country's frontiers, or at least for defending some particular frontier that is dangerously exposed to attack. In some cases a location has been found that satisfies all three desiderata alike.

In other cases, only two, or only one, of them have been satisfactorily provided for.

The site of Paris is one in which all three desiderata have been met. Paris is both a good administrative centre and a city that can easily be provisioned because it is located at a key point in the basin of the River Seine. The Marne and the Oise make their confluences with the Seine in Paris's neighbourhood. Paris is also relatively close to France's north-east frontier, which is her most dangerous one. The site of Constantinople, again, was ideal for the capital of the fourth-century Roman Empire. Its sea-communications were good for both administration and supply, and it was relatively near to both the Lower Danube and the Upper Euphrates, which, at that time, were the two sectors of the Roman Empire's frontier that were under the heaviest pressure. This accounts for Constantine's transfer of the capital to the new site from Rome, in spite of Rome's historical title to be the capital of the empire that Rome herself had created.

By contrast, the site of Changan was good for defence purposes only. It commanded the western half of China's dangerous northern frontier against the nomadic peoples. But its location in the upper basin of the Yellow River was not convenient for either administration or supply. Changan was remote from the centre of population in eastern China, and it was also difficult to bring food-stuffs, produced on the plains of eastern China, up the Yellow River and its tributary, the Wei River, against the current. It is not surprising that the capital of China should eventually have shifted – as it had shifted, once before, in the age of the Chou dynasty – from a location in the upper basin of the Yellow River to a location in its middle basin. In more recent periods of Chinese history, since the Yangtze basin has been colonized by Chinese peasants and brought under intensive cultivation, the location of the capital has remained in the east, but has oscillated between Nanking ('Southern Capital') and Peking ('Northern Capital'). Nanking is centrally located, and it is easily supplied from the Yangtze-basin rice-bowl; Peking commands the eastern sector of the dangerous northern frontier, but, just for this reason, it is remote, as Changan was, from the centre of population and from the Yangtze-basin source of food-supply. Peking's location did not become more convenient, all things considered, than Nanking's location till the development of China's network of inland waterways had brought Peking into direct and easy communication with the south.

In Egypt the location of the capital has repeatedly shifted in response to changes in the relative strength of the rival pulls of administrative, economic, and strategic considerations. The empire-builders who united Egypt politically in the first instance, and who re-united it again, twice over, after it had twice fallen to pieces, all came from the southern extremity of Egypt. The southern frontier was a dangerous one; the southern marchmen had to see to the defence of it; and this made them militarily superior to the inhabitants of more sheltered regions, lower down-stream. This explains why the southerners were the empire-builders; but, on the first two occasions, the capital did not remain in the south after the country had been united from there. The first two times it shifted to a location at or near the head of the Delta, which is the best location in Egypt for both administration and supply (Cairo, the capital of present-day Egypt, is located here). On the third occasion, the capital did remain in the south, at the empire-building city of Thebes, to begin with. By this time, Thebes was no longer on the extreme southern edge of Egypt, since the Northern Sudan, up-stream from Thebes, had now been incorporated in the Egyptian Empire. However, in the fourteenth century BC, the capital did eventually move away from Thebes, first to Tell el-Amarna (Akhenaton's capital) in Middle Egypt and then to the very opposite extremity of Egypt from Thebes. It shifted now to Tanis, in the north-east corner of the Delta, because the frontier against Asia had become more dangerous than the up-Nile frontier.

After Alexander had incorporated Egypt in the Greek world, the capital of his successors, the Ptolemies, was located at Alexandria at the north-west corner of the Delta. As compared with Cairo or Memphis or Tell el-Amarna, Alexandria is as inconveniently located as Tanis or Thebes or Hieraconpolis is for serving as Egypt's capital. However, when the Ptolemies located the capital of Egypt at Alexandria and kept it there, they were not considering Egypt's convenience. They were thinking of their line of communications with Greece. Alexandria was Egypt's 'window towards Greece', and Greece was the Ptolemies' source of supply for their imports of Greek man-power and Greek culture.

St Petersburg's location and name have the same explanation as Alexandria's. St Petersburg, like Alexandria, was located in the extreme north-west corner of the country of which it was the capital. Its name, like Alexandria's, is a compound of the personal name of an autocrat with a place-name termination in a foreign language. St Petersburg was Russia's 'window towards the West', and Peter was thinking of his policy of Westernizing Russia when he transferred Russia's capital to St Petersburg from Moscow. In our time, Moscow's central location has prevailed over St Petersburg's sea-communications with the Western world. Today, Moscow is once again the capital of the united Russia of which she is the historical nucleus.

ARNOLD TOYNBEE

ALEXANDRIA

UNDER THE PTOLEMIES

The hub of the Hellenistic world,

Alexandria was founded in the winter of 332–331 BC by Alexander the Great, when he was twenty-five years old and in the full flood of conquest. The site on which he instructed his architect Dinocrates to build a city had a number of advantages, being on a strip of land which lay between the Mediterranean and Lake Mareotis, and protected from the open sea by a line of reefs. It could be made into a double port (an advantage much appreciated by the Greeks); its climate was cool and fresh; its economy was securely based on the wheat surplus regularly produced by the Egyptian hinterland. And when, after Alexander's death, his empire was divided, Alexandria became the capital of a powerful state ruled from 323 to 285 BC by one of Alexander's Macedonian generals, Ptolemy I. Under the Ptolemaic dynasty – Cleopatra, the last of the family, died in 30 BC – Alexandria rapidly grew into the largest of all Greek cities, renowned for its fabulous wealth, its artistic and scientific activity, its huge and racially diverse population, and its cosmopolitan outlook. The city never again enjoyed a position of such pre-eminence, though it con-

tinued to flourish under Roman rule, declining only after the Arabs captured it in 640.

The island of Pharos, the most important of the reefs facing the city, gave its name to Alexandria's most famous monument, the commanding lighthouse built by the architect Sostratus, which was one of the 'Seven Wonders of the World' of antiquity, and which E. M. Forster has described as 'the greatest practical achievement of the Alexandrian mind'. So impressive were its size, technical ingenuity and effectiveness that in the ancient world every lighthouse was afterwards called a pharos. A fortress as well as a beacon, the Pharos of Alexandria was completed in about 280 BC, and is said to have been six hundred feet high – an improbable figure and one impossible to check: the lighthouse was partly destroyed in AD 400, and in 1375 an earthquake levelled it completely. The only surviving impressions of it are on Alexandrian coins of the Roman period and on a vase (opposite) of green translucent glass and apparently of Alexandrian manufacture, which was found at Begram in Afghanistan. (1)

Self-proclaimed son of Zeus-Ammon, and thereby rightful successor to the pharaohs, Alexander the Great is represented as wearing the ram's horns of the god bound to his head on this silver coin (below) of Lysimachus of Thrace (286–281 BC). The Ptolemies used similar means to secure the loyalty of their Egyptian subjects, yet remained essentially Greek. (2)

Like other Greek cities, Alexandria was personified by a Tyche, a statue of the goddess of Chance, who is depicted (below) on an Alexandrian coin of Antoninus Pius (AD 138–61). The city was particularly sanctified by possession of Alexander's corpse, which lay in the royal necropolis, outlined in the upper part of a Roman pottery lamp (right). (3, 4)

The Pharos appears on a Roman bronze coin of AD 180–92 (above). The part of the island on which the lighthouse stood has been covered by the sea, but the coin is placed here so that Pharos is shown approximately where it once stood in relation to the aerial photograph (right). (5)

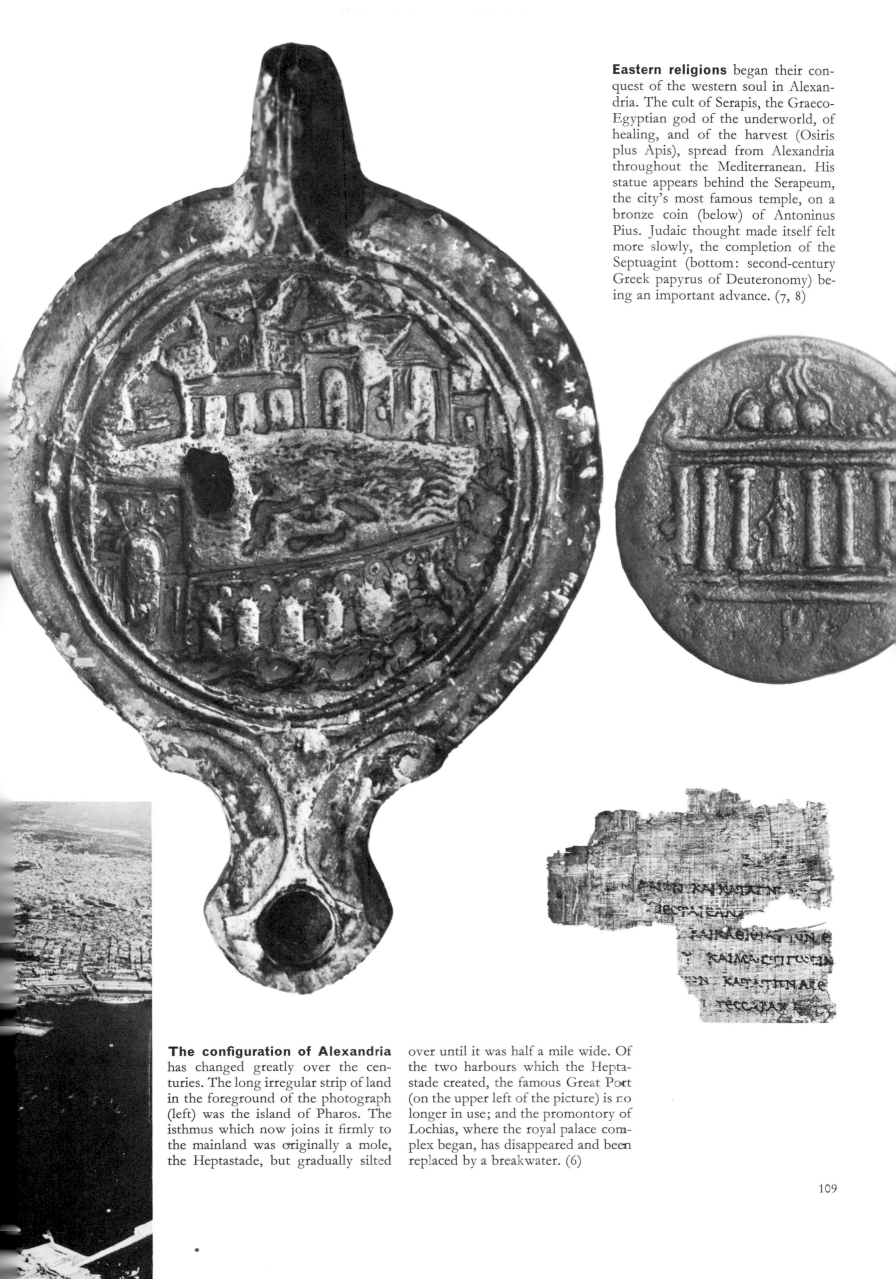

Eastern religions began their conquest of the western soul in Alexandria. The cult of Serapis, the Graeco-Egyptian god of the underworld, of healing, and of the harvest (Osiris plus Apis), spread from Alexandria throughout the Mediterranean. His statue appears behind the Serapeum, the city's most famous temple, on a bronze coin (below) of Antoninus Pius. Judaic thought made itself felt more slowly, the completion of the Septuagint (bottom: second-century Greek papyrus of Deuteronomy) being an important advance. (7, 8)

The configuration of Alexandria has changed greatly over the centuries. The long irregular strip of land in the foreground of the photograph (left) was the island of Pharos. The isthmus which now joins it firmly to the mainland was originally a mole, the Heptastade, but gradually silted over until it was half a mile wide. Of the two harbours which the Heptastade created, the famous Great Port (on the upper left of the picture) is no longer in use; and the promontory of Lochias, where the royal palace complex began, has disappeared and been replaced by a breakwater. (6)

Alexandrian culture was predominantly Greek – however impure in the eyes of other Greeks – though its population was multiracial. The Ptolemies founded many smaller towns on the pattern of the capital, but outside the towns the mass of Egyptians worked on the land and, as in the past, looked to the fertilizing Nile as the source of their prosperity. Visual records of this everyday life are few. By far the best of those that survive is a mosaic of the Delta in flood, part of which is reproduced above. It was found at the Roman town of Praeneste (Palestrina) but is believed to be Hellenistic. In the bottom right-hand corner, the upper portions of a tower villa and a curtained pavilion can be seen; next to the tower is a sacred enclosure, and above the enclosure is a shrine of ibises. But the charm of the mosaic lies in the vivid details of Egyptian life and landscape – the trees, flowers and animals, the native steering his boat – which give a delightful impression of the country in Ptolomaic and Roman times.

By contrast, the mosaic bust (right) – lofty, allegorical, perhaps a little pompous – of Alexandria, garbed as mistress of the seas, is a glorification of the state. It was found at Thmuis, in the Delta, and is late Hellenistic (but probably a copy of an earlier work). It almost certainly celebrates the naval supremacy established by the early Ptolemies. (9, 10)

ALEXANDRIA UNDER THE PTOLEMIES

CLAIRE PRÉAUX

IN THE BIRTH AND DEVELOPMENT of Alexandria there was no geographical predestination whatever. The north coast of Egypt has no natural shelter, and is therefore not favourable to the establishment of ports. Moreover, ancient navigation preferred hugging the coast to long voyages without ports of call, so it was to the east that, in its periods of expansion, Egypt had sought to communicate with the world, and it was Pelusium that was its port.

The coast of the Delta had, too, a bad reputation in Greek legend; a hostile king, the Proteus of the Helen legend, killed all foreigners who touched the shore. Nevertheless, the navigators of the *Odyssey* knew

> an island in the surging sea in front of Egypt, and men call it Pharos, distant as far as a hollow ship runs in a whole day when the shrill wind blows fair behind it. Therein is a harbour with good anchorage, whence men launch the shapely ships into the sea, when they have drawn supplies of black water.

The name given to the island is only the corruption of the Egyptian word for Pharaoh. The error in the distance, which is not a day but some minutes from the coast, may be due to the breakdown of communications between the end of the Minoan navigations and the composition of the *Odyssey*. Perhaps it was on 'Pharoah's' island that the Cretans were established for the purposes of trade when they went, as they did from the time of the Middle Empire, to import their products into Egypt. However, the foundations which undersea explorations have brought to light on the north coast of Pharos do not appear, as was previously thought, to be those of a prehistoric port.

It was in the interior of the Delta that the Greeks founded the port of Naucratis and it was in analogous situations that the Egyptian ports of Sais and of Buto found shelter from pirates and from the sea. There was, however, on the coast itself, at the mouth of the western branch of the Nile, about twelve miles to the east of the site that Alexander chose, the city of Canopus. On Alexander's site the small fishing village of Rhacotis spread out its salting-tubs between Lake Mareotis and the sea.

In this locality a clay ridge runs along the coast between the lake and the sea, and a parallel spine, partly submerged in front of the coastline, forms a line of reefs of which the most important is the island of Pharos. The reefs break the violence of the sea in a way that draws the navigator, once past the narrow and difficult entry, to find calm water and shelter in their protection.

Legends and legacies of Alexander

Let us refrain from trying to explain Alexander's choice by the functions which masters of Egypt conferred on Alexandria at a later time. Of the numerous cities that he founded, many have left no trace and others quickly came to nothing. And perhaps Alexandria also would have miscarried if the premature death of the founder had not brought back towards the Aegean the centre of the world, which

he was preparing to carry into Asia. His biographers say that he loved to read Homer. Could he have been inspired by the knowledge of the island of Pharos that he might have had from the *Odyssey*? So Plutarch thought. Perhaps, too, since he arrived from Tyre, where the siege had delayed him for a long time, he was struck by the semblance of the site to that of the Phoenician port – an island protecting the coast – and had wanted to create in Alexandria the port which would replace Tyre. On the other hand the Greeks themselves loved to found ports in the shelter of an island – at Syracuse or Naxos, for example. The Greeks of Naucratis had, no doubt, an opportunity to advise Alexander, through the intermediation of Cleomenes, and they were in a position to have noticed a configuration which responded to traditional Greek ideas about looking for port facilities. Moreover, the island had only to be joined to the continent by a mole in order to obtain a double port, and this presented the advantage (much sought after by the Greeks) of a specialization of dock basins. Lindos displays a configuration of this type; Rhodes and the Piraeus have three natural bays.

Alexander arrived in Egypt at the end of November 332 BC. He founded Alexandria in the course of the winter 332–331. The accounts of the foundation record prodigies, and the seers' predictions foretold for Alexandria the destiny that Plutarch records: 'the city will be very rich and will nourish men of all races.' But these predictions were, of course, invented retrospectively. The romanticized biography of Alexander that is attributed to Callisthenes dates the foundation of Alexandria after the return from the Oasis of Ammon, where Alexander had received, for his choice of the site, advice and prophecy. The discovery of an ancient sanctuary on the site of the future city, which is reported by pseudo-Callisthenes, is a banal invention designed to consecrate the locality of the foundation.

While it is difficult to discover the motives for the choice of the site, the site itself nevertheless reveals the historical circumstances to which it could respond. Welded as it is on to its port and planted right on the shore, Alexandria testifies that it was founded for the sea. Many Greek cities, even after becoming maritime like Athens, retained an acropolis as a stronghold at a distance of three to six miles from the port. Such cities are, as Thucydides realized, material evidence of the insecurity which reigned at the time of their origins. Alexandria, standing on the seashore, bears witness to the hope of security which animated a founder who had no fear of pirates. Plato, who detested the promiscuousness of port life, had been in favour of keeping the sea eight miles away from his city. It is true that Alexandria too had an *akra*, but this was not the inaccessible acropolis of the cities founded in the troubled times of the Mycenean Age, like Athens, or of the age of the conflicts between the Diadochi, like Pergamon. It was merely the base, at water-level, of the citadel and of the royal palaces.

The city's communications with Egypt, which is separated from it by Lake Mareotis, had to be created artificially by canals which linked it with the Nile. Alexandria was exposed, however, to possible in-

111

vasions coming from the Delta to the east or from the desert to the west, and therefore (*pace* Diodorus) it would have been at the mercy of attacks from the hinterland, if it had not been provided, as early as the planning stage, with the high and strong wall which Diodorus himself mentions. The wall was almost nine miles long, was equipped with towers, and must have resembled the one which can still be seen at Messene in the Peloponnese.

Dinocrates of Rhodes, who accompanied Alexander, was commissioned to lay out the plan of Alexandria; he drew it out from east to west, along the narrow tongue of land which separates the sea from the lake, to a length of about four miles, and laid out, perhaps on the track of an old coastal road, a long street from east to west, Canopus Street. He created another principal street from north to south which crossed this at about its half-way point. These were the axes of a rectangular grid. The papyri have given us the names of some streets dedicated, under different honorary titles, to Arsinoë II. On the south-west flank of the city the old Egyptian town of Rhacotis continued to exist.

A mole three-quarters of a mile in length, the Heptastade, connected the island of Pharos with the mainland. Two openings were left in it which were spanned by bridges. The Heptastade also carried an aqueduct. This mole separated the two ports which it created. The eastern port, the Great Port, is more than three miles wide, and deep enough to take the largest ship. It is well sheltered, but the entry between the eastern point of Pharos island and Cape Lochias, which juts out from the mainland, is infested with reefs and is, for that reason, difficult of access, as Josephus and Strabo note. Strabo gives an account of the harbour entrance and its famous lighthouse:

The extremity of the isle is a rock, which is washed by the sea on all sides and has upon it a tower that is admirably constructed of white marble in many storeys, and bears the same name as the island. This was an offering made by Sostratus of Cnidus, a friend of the kings, for the sailors' safety, as the inscription records; for, since the coast was harbourless and low on either side, and was also beset with reefs and shallows, navigators noting a land-fall here from the open sea needed some lofty and conspicuous mark to enable them to direct their course correctly to the entrance of the harbour.

This monument, which was completed about 280 BC and which was so much admired in the ancient world, is represented on Alexandrian coins of the Roman age, and this enables us to reconstruct what it looked like. Its silhouette is also represented on a fragile and precious glass vase, found at Begram in Afghanistan, which seems to be of Alexandrian origin. The lighthouse was crowned by a statue of Ptolemy I or Ptolemy II, and the corners carried Tritons who gave a warning sound by means of a mechanism that worked by steam. The light from the wood fire that was kept burning at the summit was visible up to a distance of thirty miles, according to Josephus. When Caesar, after his Alexandrian war, had emptied Pharos island of its inhabitants, who had taken the side of the Ptolemies, he left on the wave-beaten rock only a few seamen as caretakers. But the Emperor Claudius allowed the Alexandrians to erect his statue there.

Port and royal city

The vicinity of the port was laid out on a plan, in which the political and religious monuments were grouped in a sort of acropolis. Strabo, who visited Egypt in 24 BC, just after it had come under the rule of Augustus, describes the promontory of Lochias opposite the island and tower of Pharos. On it was a royal palace, and he notes that 'on sailing into the harbour, one comes on the left to the inner royal palaces, which are continuous with those on Lochias, and have groves and numerous lodges painted in various colours'. The difficulty of growing trees in Egypt makes one appreciate the luxury of these groves which overlapped the city walls and gave a Hellenic look to the monotonous landscape of sand and of clay, which here is already so thoroughly African. As a result of a slow subsidence of the soil the promontory of Lochias is now under water and serves as the foundation for a breakwater. But there have been found in its vicinity many shafts of columns and handsome Ionian and Corinthian capitals, which testify to the former presence of palaces here. It was a symbolic and daring decision of the first Ptolemy to abandon Memphis and to install himself on a site commanding a port and the sea.

His choice resembles that of Peter the Great when he abandoned Moscow for St Petersburg, which was in touch with the sea, because he wished to link Russia with a new world.

Below these palaces, says Strabo, lies the hidden artificial harbour which is the private property of the kings. One can picture to oneself the appearance of this little royal port from a mosaic, of Alexandrian inspiration, at Lepcis Magna, which shows *putti* sailing towards a landing-place which is surrounded by a colonnade.

Returning to the south side of the Great Port, as if he were on a boat that was slowly making for land, Strabo says:

Above the artificial harbour lies the theatre; then the Poseidium – an 'elbow' projecting from the 'Emporium' and containing a temple of Poseidon. This elbow of land was extended by Antony along a mole projecting still farther into the middle of the harbour, and on the extremity of that he built a royal lodge which he called the Timonium. This was his last act, when, forsaken by his friends, he sailed off to Alexandria after his disaster at Actium. He had made up his mind to live the life of Timon the misanthrope for the rest of his days, which he intended to spend without the company of all those friends.

One can imagine the beauty of the landscape in which, round the vast bay full of sails and beneath the protection of the great lighthouse, the dwellings of the kings and the gods and the shell-shaped outline of the theatre were concentrated. A painting by a Campanian artist, found at Stabiae, which no doubt represents some part of the Gulf of Naples, can still give some idea of the beauty of the seaside landscape which Alexandria must have presented. Some remains of the theatre have been discovered under the hill on which the Egyptian hospital now stands.

Strabo then enters the western port, the only one which is still in use today, the harbour of Eunostus and, above it, the artificial harbour called 'the Box'. Beyond, there ran a navigable canal which extended to Lake Mareotis. It was by this canal that the port of Eunostus communicated with the port on Lake Mareotis at which there arrived, from all Egypt, the merchandise that was brought there for the provisioning of the city and for export.

Now, beyond the canal, there is still left only a small part of the city; and then one comes to the suburb called Necropolis, in which there are many gardens and graves and halting-places fitted up for the embalming of corpses. On the near side of the canal one comes both to the Serapeum and to other sacred precincts of ancient times, which are now almost abandoned on account of the construction of the new buildings at Nicopolis.

Thus the canal, which certainly ran towards the north-west, traversed the ancient village of Rhacotis, which is dominated by the Serapeum. Among the remains of ancient sanctuaries there extended the cemetery where the dead were embalmed in the Egyptian manner. Cemeteries and gardens announced the limits of the city. It was there, perhaps, that the stadium and the amphitheatre were situated. But the population seems to have abandoned these old western quarters in order to spread out in the direction of Canopus to the east, where the quarter of Nicopolis arose along the sea front. Strabo notes that 'there is an amphitheatre and a stadium at Nicopolis and the quinquennial games are celebrated there, but the ancient buildings have fallen into neglect.' Perhaps this passage should be interpreted as meaning that the public places in the western suburb had become too small, and were therefore reconstructed on a larger scale to the east of the city. The stadium was the starting point of the first procession of the Pentaeterides, a grandiose fête which Ptolemy II celebrated in memory of his parents. It was at the stadium also that the Macedonians proclaimed the young Ptolemy V king in the course of the revolution that put an end to Agothocles' administration. And the amphitheatre, wherever it may have stood, was the point to which the Jews, during the anti-semitic troubles under Nero that Josephus describes, chased the Alexandrian mob and threatened to burn them alive.

But before leading us farther into Nicopolis, drawn by the memories of Caesar and of the death of Cleopatra, Strabo takes us back towards the royal city which opens on to the Great Port.

The city is full of public and sacred buildings, but the most beautiful of them is the Gymnasium, which has porticoes more than a

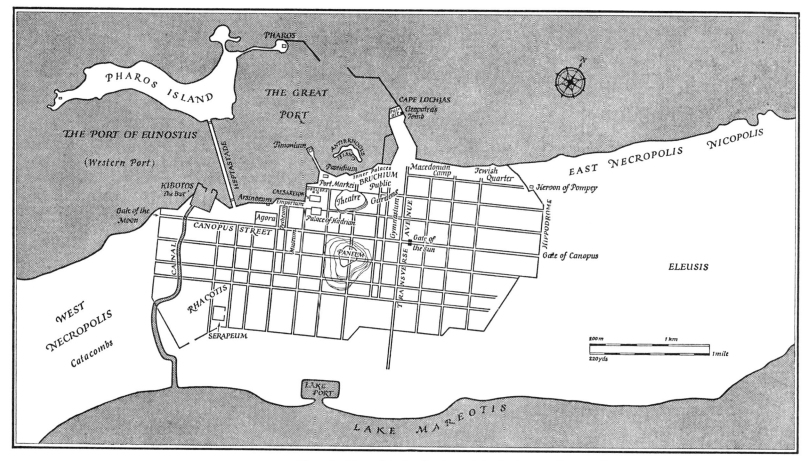

Map of Alexandria in the time of the Ptolemies, showing the curious and advantageous double harbour, Pharos island and the rectangular grid layout of the streets. The Pharos lighthouse dominates the entrance to the Great Port. The Museum, centre of Alexandrian learning and research which radiated out to the rest of the civilized world, was located off the main artery, Canopus Street, and to the left of the Paneum.

stadium [200 yards] in length. And in the middle [of the city] there are both the court of justice and the groves. Here, too, is the Paneum, a man-made eminence; it has the shape of a fir-cone, resembles a rocky hill, and is ascended by a spiral road; and from the summit one can see the whole of the city lying below it on all sides.

This artificial mound may have occupied the actual site of Kom ed Dik. The sanctuary of Pan, which must have recalled the grottoes and rocks that were dear to that god, was at the same time made to fulfil the aesthetic purpose of offering a panoramic view.

Strabo does not mention the political meeting-places which were characteristic of the Hellenistic as well as the classical Greek city: the *bouleuterion*, where the senate met, and the *prytaneion*. But this omission does not prove that there was never a senate in Alexandria, for Strabo is far from mentioning all the monuments of the Alexandria of his time. For instance, he omits the *agora* which, according to Arrian, Alexander had planned to serve as the centre of the city. It was in the *agora* that the oath for legal proceedings was administered, and it was also there, according to Philo, that, after the looting of the Jews' houses, their furniture was sold at auction. What Strabo describes, in effect, is primarily the royal city. Let us retain him as our guide for making our way into the palaces which, on their foundation of reefs, dominated the Great Port.

And the city contains most beautiful public precincts and also the royal palaces, which constitute one-fourth or even one-third of the whole circuit of the city. It was customary for each of the kings, from love of splendour, to add some embellishment to the public monuments; but it was also customary for each of them to endow, at his own expense, a residence for himself, in addition to those already built, so that now, to quote Homer's words, 'there is building upon building'. All, however, are connected with one another and with the harbour, even those that lie outside the harbour. The Museum is also part of the royal palaces; it has a public walk, an exedra with seats, and a large house in which there is the commonroom of the scholars who were fellows of the Museum.

This fraternity is not only the corporate holder of property, it also has a priest, in charge of the Museum, who formerly was appointed by the kings but is now appointed by Caesar.

Science and learning

The Museum was founded at the end of the reign of Ptolemy I. It was the institution in which scientific research was organized, and in the Library which formed a part of it there were assembled the materials of knowledge. Though the museum of Alexandria was unique in the size and scope which it attained, its programme had antecedents in classical Greece. The fraternities of scholars and of philosophers that constituted the Academy, the Lyceum, and later the Garden of Epicurus, may have served as the model for this community that was dedicated to the Muses and that possessed institutions and gardens. The encyclopaedic spirit which animated it went back to Aristotle. Maintained by the king and enjoying an exemption from taxes, this corporate body of scholars is the ancestor of modern royal academies and endowments for scientific research. This community life probably resembled that of a college at Oxford or Cambridge. In addition to other duties persons of high distinction combined those of President or Administrator of the Museum with those of President of the Medical School or of Bursar for the Museum's Fellows.

The principal working instrument of the Museum was the Library. There is a tradition that Demetrius of Phalerum organized the first purchase of books for Ptolemy I. The objective of the Library at Alexandria was to assemble all works of Greek thought in correct texts. This was the origin of the science of philology. The idea was not new; Pisistratus had already undertaken a revised and corrected edition of Homer. But in the development of textual criticism the scope of the programme and the rigour of the method were something quite new. Another of the Library's objectives was to make major works in foreign languages available in translation to Greek readers. For instance, Manetho composed a history of Egypt, of which the surviving fragments provided for a long time the basis for our chronology of the Pharaohs. Berosus did the same for the history of the Chaldaeans. It was also for the benefit of the Library that, according to the *Letter of Aristaeus*, seventy-two scholars of Jerusalem, invited by Ptolemy, translated the Old Testament – though perhaps this translation may have had a single, unrecorded origin in the work of the Greek-speaking Jewish communities of Alexandria. Whatever the truth may be, the Greek text of the Old Testament became – thanks to the triumph of Christianity, whose diffusion was promoted by it – one of the most important of Alexandria's legacies to civilization.

The librarians prepared catalogues of authors and works; we know that Callimachus made one in 120 volumes called the *Tables*, thus organizing the classification of the sciences that had been begun by Aristotle. The Museum and the Library were complementary to each other. It was there that Eratosthenes, assembling the information brought back by the explorers sent into Africa and Arabia, prepared his map of the world. This served as a basis for Ptolemy's map. It was there also that Euclid codified geometry and that Aristarchus of Samos ventured on the conjecture that the Earth moves around the Sun. There, again, anatomy and physiology made new progress, of which the work of Galen, in his polemics against his predecessors, gives us some evidence. In handing over, for purposes of experiment, persons who had been condemned to death, the king made it possible for first steps to be taken towards a scientific understanding of physiology. Herophilus and Erasistratus gained accurate knowledge of the anatomy of the brain, of the heart, and of the eye, and this opened up possibilities of more efficient surgery.

The Museum and the Library were, from the beginning, centres of attraction for the whole Greek world; the scholars and scientists attached to them were rarely of Alexandrian origin; Demetrius came from Phalerum, Zenodotus from Ephesus, Callimachus and Eratosthenes from Cyrene, Herophilus from Chalcedon, Erasistratus from Ceos, and others from Aetolia and from Chalcis.

We must also mention another instrument of scientific research: the zoological garden which hunts and gifts had filled with rare animals. These rhinoceroses, camels, ostriches, gazelles, lions and wild asses figure in the processional display of the royal riches that was organized by Ptolemy II in memory of his parents.

An institution born in the classical Greek city as a child of private enterprise was raised to unprecedented dimensions at Alexandria by the power of the Crown. But the people of Alexandria probably took very little part in the progress of knowledge that was the work of men representing the entire Hellenic world. We know, in fact, that the scholars and scientists were sometimes ridiculed for being so sumptuously lodged and fed.

The grandeur of the Ptolemies

Strabo does not leave the royal quarter without noting the tomb of Alexander: '"the Sema" is also a part of the royal palaces. This was the enclosure which contained the burial places of the kings and that of Alexander.' He explains the *coup de main* by which Ptolemy I snatched Alexander's body from Perdiccas, and continues, 'Alexander's body was carried off by Ptolemy and given burial in Alexandria, where it now still lies – not, however, in the same sarcophagus as originally, for the present one is made of glass, whereas the one in which Ptolemy placed it was made of gold.' The details and steps of this transfer are described, with variations, by many historians. The presence of Alexander's body inside the first of the cities to which he gave his name was essential, because the tomb of the founder gives holiness and protection to a city. By installing the body in the royal quarter the king shared with the city the beneficent power which emanated from the founder's body.

Alexandria was a royal residence, and in the eyes of the Greek world it was the symbol and measure of the power of the Ptolemies. The luxury of the city was the instrument of their propaganda in Greek circles. This wealth of the city is the constant theme of the hundreds of visitors who described it in antiquity. But, if wealth is evidence of the protection of the gods, it is also a form of human insolence and was responsible for the softness of character with which the Alexandrians were reproached. The city was able to enjoy the king's luxury and to take pride in it because the king displayed his wealth to the man in the street. The gates of the palace were opened to the crowd, which jostled to view the costly couch that the queen had decorated with tapestries for Adonis and to hear the

musical recital given at the palace at this god's festival. Innumerable pieces of jewellery, Persian carpets, precious materials, and Negroes bearing ivory, gold and ebony bore witness to the king's power; as did strange animals from India and Ethiopia, slaves and soldiers.

The attraction of wealth was reinforced by that of the climate – something to which the Greeks pay close attention when they describe a city. The north wind, which blows off the sea in summer, is channelled through the north–south streets and keeps them cool. Furthermore, Alexandria enjoyed added freshness thanks to its being situated between two bodies of water. On the other hand the city did not have to fear, in the hot season, the foul air of the marshy borders of the lake, because at that season the lake filled up with water which was brought by the Nile flood.

The ibis, though a nuisance and an eyesore, took care, after a fashion, of the cleaning of the streets of Alexandria. Strabo says: 'Every cross-road in Alexandria is full of them ... the bird is useful because it makes a bee-line for vermin and consumes the refuse of the meat-shops and the bakeries.'

The distribution of water was a difficult problem on a terrain which was at once both marsh and desert. Alexandria was fed by the fresh-water canal which came from the Canopic branch of the Nile. It also rains in the winter on the Egyptian coast, and the rain-water can be collected in cisterns. There is also mention of some fountains; and when Caesar's water-supply was cut off in the fighting at Alexandria, he sank a well and found a water-table of fresh water. The cisterns of Alexandria, which were often reconstructed by the Byzantines and the Arabs, still constituted in the nineteenth century an underground city of thousands of columns and vaults.

Among the dozens of monuments mentioned by the ancient authors and the thousands which actually existed, there is one which gives us an idea of the charm of a royal monument which was placed at the disposal of the public as a playground. It is the Caesareion, which is described by Philo.

There is no other precinct like our so-called Augusteum, the temple of Caesar, the protector of the sailors. It is situated high up, opposite the sheltered harbours, and is very large and conspicuous; it is filled with dedications on a unique scale, and is surrounded on all sides by paintings, statues, and objects of gold and silver. The extensive precinct is furnished with colonnades, libraries, banqueting halls, groves, gateways, open spaces, unroofed enclosures and everything that makes for lavish decoration. It gives hope of safety to sailors when they set out to sea and when they return.

This edifice, which Cleopatra had built for Antony and which Augustus afterwards dedicated to himself, included two obelisks dating from the New Empire, one of which is now in London, the other in New York.

Population and political structure

Alexandria was not, as so many of Alexander's and his successors' foundations were, a military colony designed to guard a strategic position. What struck the ancients first and foremost about Alexandria was the number of its inhabitants. Diodorus claims to have learnt from the officials in charge of the census lists that in his time the population had reached the figure of 300,000 free persons. We do not know whether or not this included women, and this makes it impossible to estimate the total figure. If women were not included – and this depends on the unknown purpose of the lists consulted by Diodorus – the figure would postulate a total population of about 1,000,000 inhabitants. The existence of this list is certain, because as early as the third century BC the 'Revenue Laws' of Ptolemy II estimate the quantities of oil that were to be furnished by the *Nomoi* (departments) of Egypt to Alexandria, which presupposes a knowledge of the number of the inhabitants. Unfortunately too many data are missing, owing to *lacunae* in this papyrus, to allow us to hazard an estimate.

Even if the figure which Diodorus gives is taken as being a maximum, it should be large enough to make it difficult for institutions of the classical type to function. The limit of the effectiveness of these was admirably understood by Aristotle:

Experience shows that it is difficult and perhaps impossible for a city with too large a population to have good constitutional government. There is a proper measure of magnitude for a city as there is for everything else ...

This analysis of Aristotle's explains the problem to which the administration of the city of Alexandria gave rise. Yet one thing that Aristotle had not foreseen is that a dense urban concentration may also be a stimulant and a factor in the progress of mankind.

Another dominant impression that Alexandria made on the ancients was that of the variety in the origins of the population. Greeks from all parts, drawn by the offer of so much work in a city under construction, or in the service of the king – mercenaries, merchants, technicians of all sorts, including philosophers and scientists – all gathered at Alexandria very quickly. The city, to judge from Theocritus' description, was already in full flower only fifty years after its foundation. The necropolises to the east have revealed in their epitaphs the native countries of hundreds of people, and barbarians, for example Gauls or Celts, lie next to Greeks of all origins.

Finally, there was an element called 'Macedonian', composed of soldiers and Jews. If one believes Josephus, who is however suspect, the Jews were installed in Alexandria from the beginning and very quickly overflowed the quarter reserved to them, the Delta, adjoining the royal palaces. They had synagogues in every quarter.

The nucleus of citizens, which constituted at Alexandria the civic body in the classical sense, was no doubt only a small minority of the population. One may guess that this body was limited by a *numerus clausus*, on the lines of the constitution that Ptolemy I granted to Cyrene. The 'Macedonians' appear not to have been citizens. And according to Josephus the Jews, who were assimilated to the Macedonians, had only an equality of civil rights with the Alexandrians. The native Egyptians had scarcely any possibility of becoming full citizens.

This variety of origin is at the opposite pole to the classical ideal of the city, as Plato had conceived of it in the *Republic* and in the *Laws* – an ideal which saw in the homogeneity of race a guarantee of unanimity. This variety of races at Alexandria was also condemned by Polybius, whom Strabo quotes as finding all three classes of Alexandrians – Egyptians, mercenaries and Greeks – in different degrees unfit for civic life. Yet although Polybius reproaches them with being themselves a mixed lot, the Greek citizen-body of Alexandria tolerated scarcely any intrusion of non-Greek elements.

Alexandria must have been given by its founder the characteristic institutions of a Greek city. It claimed to derive its law from Athens, but evidence concerning these institutions is so rare and so ambiguous that it is uncertain whether or not Alexandria had a complete constitution of the classical type. All the same, indications which follow the names of the citizens show that the body politic was divided into 'tribes' which have dynastic names, into demes whose names derived from those of the mythical ancestors of Alexander and the Ptolemies, and into *phratriai* designated by numbers.

As for the assembly of the people, one must distinguish – again the texts are not always sufficiently explicit – between the old Macedonian assembly of armed men who acclaimed and deposed kings, and the true public assembly whose function was to pass decrees and to arrange for embassies that would treat with foreign powers.

The assembly of a Greek city elected colleges of magistrates, the *prytanes*, who took it in turns to be in permanent session. The existence of a *prytaneion* in Alexandria has recently been attested for certain by one of the Oxyrhynchus papyri. The question of the senate of Alexandria is a very controversial problem. Under Augustus it did not exist, and Alexandria was asking the emperor if it could have one. Had it never had one, or had it lost it under the Ptolemies? For the Emperor Claudius this question was evidently an open one. He professed ignorance of what had been customary under the Ptolemies. Yet Septimius Severus granted Alexandria a senate. No decision can be reached on the basis of this evidence, but one may guess that a senate, which was such a characteristic Greek institution, would not have been withheld by Alexander from a city which he had founded himself, considering that he guaranteed the retention of their constitutions to cities that capitulated to him. It is also hard to see how Ptolemy I could have refused a senate to Alexandria when he presented one to Cyrene and to Ptolemaïs. We may, perhaps, con-

Ptolemy II Philadelphus, son of the first Macedonian king of Egypt, reigned from 285 to 246 BC. He is shown here as represented on a gem with his first wife, Arsinoë, daughter of another Macedonian general, Lysimachus.

clude that a senate existed at Alexandria too, from the date of its foundation, but that it was suppressed by some later Ptolemy as a penalty for an excessive display of independence or for refusing to propose to the public assembly the inclusion of some royal decree in the city's laws.

If it is true that a senate had effective power to direct a city's politics, it is also true that an assembly without a senate was a ship without a pilot. If the king became the pilot, from that time onwards the city was left without any real autonomy. But when the king was weak the crowd followed its impulses, and politics were at the mercy of chance, which was dangerous for king and for city alike. Remaining as it did without a senate until the time of Septimius Severus, Alexandria was as turbulent under the Romans as under the kings. The troubles were now no longer the result of dynastic conflicts, but they often arose from anti-semitism. The account of the embassies that Alexandria sent to the emperors reveals a spirit of resistance to Rome which goes to the point of martyrdom, while the account of the pogroms which Philo gives us shows that the mob did not shrink even from committing genocide.

The question of the city's relations with the kings confronts us with the most characteristic problem of Hellenistic cities. The sources of our knowledge of Alexandria's relations with the Ptolemies are fragmentary, but they still give us a glimpse of an evolution in this field. Alexandria certainly obtained its constitution and civic laws from Alexander or from Ptolemy I, and received decrees from the kings, who also installed a military governor there. But from the reign of Ptolemy IV onwards Polybius has thrown light on the growing weakness of the kings and on the greed of the men who had their confidence. From that date onwards it is Alexandria that makes and unmakes kings; it is from the city that the kings hold their sovereignty; it is with the mob that they treat and before whom they justify themselves, without the voice of Egypt outside the city being heard. This is a reversal of roles which was due to the city's economic power.

The multi-racial community

But this Alexandria of the citizens, whose structure we have been attempting to describe, was only a small element in the great cosmopolitan city. The most important of the alien communities was that of the Jews, who insisted on living in accordance with their ancestral laws. That meant the right of practising their own religion, with all the taboos on intermarriage, on cohabitation, and on food which this implies, and which precluded a total assimilation into the life of the city. It also implied the existence of a special civil and criminal law and special tribunals. Greek institutions allowed the existence of a quasi-political form of association, the *politeuma*, with a sort of interior sovereignty of its own, and this answered to the Jews' situation.

But in the cultural and economic life of the city, as well as in its politics, the Jews wished to enjoy the rights of citizens, and certainly they desired to be citizens, although they clearly were not. However, being numerous, active and in many cases rich, they rapidly became Hellenized to the point of wishing, under Claudius, to participate in the games which were the very symbol of the city. Not only did they take part in economic life, they were also admitted to the service of the king as soldiers and administrators, and as tax-farmers too.

The anti-semitism which was to become so violent at Alexandria in the first century of our era makes its first appearance in the work of Manetho who, according to Josephus, offered an anti-semitic explanation of the Exodus. In the conflict between the city and the king under Ptolemy IV the Jews appear to have taken the side of the king. Under the early Roman Empire, the Jews took the side of Rome against the Alexandrians. There followed the ferocious struggles and massacres which Philo records. We catch sight of the economic causes in Claudius' refusal to allow further Jewish immigration into the city.

There must have been other foreign communities at Alexandria with a similar autonomy, and there were also others who were temporary visitors on business; buyers of wheat or speculative lenders of money. To useful foreigners who were Greek in culture besides, Alexandria extended a generous welcome, as it did also to artists, philosophers, and lecturers. She knew that the buyers of the products of Egypt and the East made the fortune of the king and of the city.

Did this multiplicity of racial backgrounds give a specific character to the civilization of Alexandria? Before trying to answer this question, we must remember that almost all our sources are Greek and that we hear only once the voice of Egypt à propos of Alexandria. This is in a prophecy of which several copies exist in Greek translation and which is called *The Potter's Oracle*. This oracle is fearfully hostile. It predicts that 'the city on the sea shore, when its guardian spirit has deserted it, will be no more than a fishing village', and it imagines passers-by saying 'look at the fate of the mother-city where all the races of men came to live'.

We must observe that, in spite of the mutual insulation of the various communities, a mixture of social elements must have been produced by intermarriage, even if this was frowned upon and illegal. The author of the *Bellum Alexandrinum* describes the rapid degeneration

> of the soldiers of Gabinius who had accustomed themselves to Alexandrian life and licence and had unlearnt the name and discipline of the Roman people and had married local wives, by whom many of them had children.

Yet we do not believe that this mixture had gone so far as to create a hybrid culture, except in the field of religion, any more than in the United States, among the European immigrants, the mixing of races has created a mixed culture. Foreigners or Hellenized Egyptians underwent a cultural change, but they did not contribute to a culture that could be called Graeco-Egyptian. But it must be pointed out that even if, in the eyes of Polybius, the Alexandrian Greeks are only 'mongrel Greeks', they did have an exclusively Greek education. And it can probably be shown that whatever is Alexandrian is no more than the logical development of what Greece had already created in the fourth century BC. For instance, the sciences made progress at the Museum by going deeper into problems that, in many cases, had been raised as early as the fifth century (the measurement of the Earth's meridian, for example), and this by employing a rational method that was utterly foreign to the thought of Egypt, which was symbolic, traditionalist, and founded on revelation. Alexandrian literature and art exploited to the full the Greek 'Baroque' elements which had first appeared at the end of the fifth century in the pathos of Euripides. But even though a tincture of Egyptian exoticism appears in the novel and in Hellenistic art, as for instance in the decoration of the pavilion of Ptolemy II or the floating palace of Ptolemy IV, we must remember that the search for the exotic is already present in Aeschylus.

The processional display of the riches of Ptolemy II that Callixenus describes brought together, under the umbrella of a Bacchic theme, objects and animals that came either from Greece or from far away. Scarcely anything came from nearby Egypt. It was from beyond Egypt, from Ethiopia, Persia and India, that the strange objects originated which delighted Alexandria, as they had delighted the first Greek ethnographers even before Herodotus. This sometimes fanciful exoticism shocked the Egyptian Manetho.

In the field of religion, however, a genuine syncretism was at work. This, however, did not affect Egyptian religion; it was of concern to Greek religion only. Isis and Serapis, in their Hellenized form, had more devotees in the Graeco-Roman world than in Egypt, and it was in Greek and for Greeks that the corpus of Hermes Trismegistus offered a fusion of Greek and Egyptian mysticism. Furthermore, the presentation in Greek by Manetho of the history of Egypt, with the religious element that this involves, and the monographs called *Aegyptiaca*, which are now lost, excited a lively interest. This is apparent not only in Josephus, who used these materials for polemical purposes, but also in the authors of Greek novels, in Lucian, in Clement of Alexandria, and above all in Plutarch, in his famous treatise *Isis and Osiris*.

While Alexandria scarcely felt the influence of Egypt it did not, in its turn, have any very profound Hellenizing effect on the Egyptian countryside. In the countryside it is the settlements of military foreigners and the cities that account for nearly all the Greek literary texts that the papyri have given us. The villages of the Fayum have given us much less. And though, in the third century of our era, the Egyptian language came to be written in Greek characters and to admit Greek words into its vocabulary, it remained Egyptian all the same. The Egypt that Alexandria knew and has made known is that which the world demanded of it: it is the Egypt of the Nilotic landscapes, the strange occult Egypt of the magicians and the healers, the Egypt of Isis' religion of salvation; the Egypt in which the Greeks, since Herodotus, had sought to escape from themselves.

The economy: division of functions

Alexandria and Egypt lived in a state of symbiosis based on a division of labour. To the Egyptians belonged what we would call today the 'primary sector' of the economy, and the traditional part of the 'second sector': namely, agriculture, animal husbandry, internal transport, weaving, brewing, the embalming of the dead, the priesthoods of the Egyptian temples; also the professions of scribe and notary in the Egyptian language, and the administration of the royal revenues at the village level. The Greeks monopolized the innovating part of the 'second sector' and the 'third sector': namely, the manufacture of industrial goods of the Greek type, the production of objects of art and luxury, international commerce and maritime navigation, war, higher-level administration and the planning of the economy; also the Greek type of intellectual life, sports, theatre, music, and the priesthoods, of the dynastic cults. It is true that Greek soldiers were endowed with holdings of land and that some of them went to live in the countryside, but they did not always themselves cultivate the land which they held from the king.

So the Greeks kept for themselves those things for which they were technically and mentally equipped. These were all those activities that involved risks that could be estimated by rational prediction. The collection of the archives of the past and of encyclopaedic information in the Library of the Museum served as a basis for all prediction, and it was at Alexandria that this scientific treatment of risk was put into practice.

This division of functions was the basis on which the economy of Alexandria was built. It was different from that of Egypt though it inserted its roots into it. In noting the immense wealth of Ptolemy II, Callixenus writes:

> It is only the Nile, the river truly called gold-flowing, that, with its boundless crops of food, actually washed down unadulterated gold which is harvested with no risk, so that it can supply all men sufficiently.

The Nile was the source of wealth without risk – the wealth of the king, of Alexandria, and of the temples, as it had been under the Pharaohs and still was under the Ptolemies. Callixenus has summed up the economy of Egypt perfectly. And, thanks to the proximity of Egypt, Alexandria realized the ideal of all Greek cities: to have near at hand the wheat on which it lived. This was the old ideal of self-sufficiency, which Athens had fallen away from in provisioning herself with wheat from far-away Russia, Sicily and Egypt – though her rich citizens were already landowners. Some Alexandrians also, as *cleruchs* or as proprietors, did acquire land in Egypt, but it was not mainly by such direct means that Alexandria exploited the countryside.

The commerce of the city was above all directed towards foreign countries. Strabo has described the balance of trade at Alexandria: 'The exports from Alexandria are larger than the imports, as anyone might ascertain if he ... saw the merchant vessels both at their arrival and at their departure.' From the third century BC onwards, in fact, the port of Alexandria exported wheat to other Mediterranean countries. After providing for the needs of the non-productive, namely the cities and the army, Egypt had at her disposal for export an average of 300,000 tons of wheat a year. The king did not hold a monopoly, but he bought on a massive scale and the royal administration organized the transport. In what, as described by Strabo, is an essentially 'mercantilist' economy, Alexandria interposed herself as the obligatory and highly paid intermediary between Egypt and the world. A similar situation existed also in regard to the production of papyrus and cloth.

Alexandria was also an exporter of the products that she received from Africa and the East. Here again, it was the king who organized the necessary machinery: the exploration of routes and of navigable waterways, the establishment of ports and trading-posts. In Africa, posts originally established for the hunting of elephants took on slowly a commercial function, and it was from them that ivory, ebony and panther skins were to come. On the other hand, the trade in spices, medicinal herbs, incense coming from South Arabia, from India, and later even from China, followed either the caravan routes which ended in Syria, or the coastal maritime routes to South Arabia, where the goods were transferred to caravans which finally passed through the hands of the Nabateans at Petra. The political control of these trade-routes was the objective of the Ptolemies' policy, and Roman diplomatic intervention began, even before the Roman conquest, to favour the commerce of Alexandria, which had Rome as its ultimate goal. However, Eratosthenes, knowing that the earth was round, had already envisaged the possibility of reaching India by crossing the Atlantic to the West.

In its export trade Alexandria enhanced the value of the imported raw materials by applying to them the skill of her craftsmen. The aromatic materials became perfumes which were bottled in charming glass and ceramic flasks, the ivory was used for inlaying furniture, raw stones became jewels, gold and silver became the goldsmiths' work which has been found even as far afield as Denmark, medicinal herbs became the drugs and unguents that 'Egyptian' physicians imported to Rome. Finally, the simple sand of the desert became delicate glassware that in the time of the Roman Empire was to be found from China to Gaul, as well as in southern Russia. The stimulus of the Roman demand for the products of the East made Alexandria even more flourishing under Roman rule than it had been under the Ptolemies. And this commerce extended as far as India. To judge by the Roman coins and ceramics found at sites on the trading coasts, it was of great importance.

Succession to Athens' ideals

We can conclude by noting that the maintenance of a great city of about a million people was, for antiquity, a difficult problem. More land was necessary than in our time because of the low yield of wheat, and much more human effort had to be given to transport which was also beset by numerous risks. Only the possession of an empire could assure the city a secure food-supply for its population. Athens and Rome were able to grow and live by such means. The 'empire' of Alexandria was Egypt, and it remained so under the Romans. But the enormous city exploited and impoverished its empire by compelling it to feed her. This was the rule that Alexandria imposed on Egypt, as Rome did on Sicily. And the consequent divorce between the city and country was bound to grow ever more decisive.

While the empire that fed Alexandria was limited to Egypt, the empire of her influence and her commerce was not confined within even the Roman Empire; it extended from the Ganges to Britain and from Russia to the Upper Nile. The possibilities of expansion created by Alexander and the organization of the world undertaken by Rome enabled Alexandria to take up again, on a larger scale, the ambitions that had been entertained by Athens. In a world that was still bowed to the earth she aimed at a life dedicated to the things of the mind and to beauty.

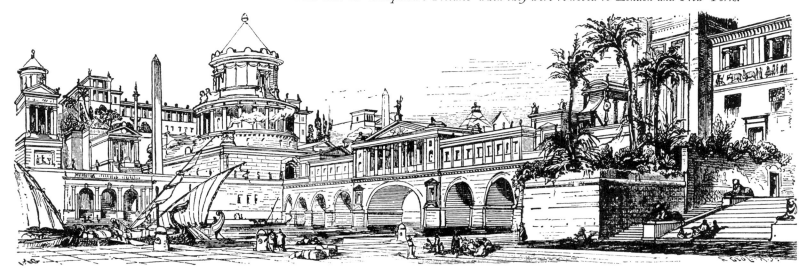

A reconstruction of Alexandria as it is believed to have looked in imperial times. These are the royal palaces, built along the Great Port; and the two obelisks are presumably those which became known much later as 'Cleopatra's Needles' when they were removed to London and New York.

THE ROME
OF THE ANTONINES

City of cities, city of the world,
the Rome of the Antonines was a sophisticated metropolis and the
nerve-centre of a global empire. With justification Martial could
salute her as 'Rome, whom nothing equals and nothing rivals'. Standing on her seven hills, she looked out over a world which she had
subdued, and one which acknowledged, to a greater or lesser degree,
her ascendancy. By the end of Trajan's reign in AD 117, Rome's
period of expansionism was over – the empire had reached its greatest
extent. Now Romans settled down to enjoy the experience of their
unique position.

The Antonine emperors governed with absolute power, guided by
virtue and wisdom. Gibbon, the great historian, claimed that this was
the time in the history of the world when the condition of the human
race was most happy and prosperous. The situation was precarious,
however, since one individual wielded absolute power, and men were
not free. Yet few doubted the excellence of the emperor, or the fact
that Rome would continue forever in her position of overweening
eminence. The population of the metropolis increased rapidly during
the second century, and Rome became the greatest consumer power
on earth.

With vast spoils from the Dacian campaigns at his disposal, Trajan
commissioned his architect, Apollodorus of Damascus, to build a
forum in Rome. The immense undertaking was completed in 114. A
column celebrating the victories formed an integral part in its design,
and stood in a colonnaded court flanked by two libraries, one Greek
and one Latin. Its height was fixed at 125 feet to indicate the amount
scarped from the Quirinal hill in building the forum.

The magnificent reliefs (opposite) are a close-up view of the lower
part of Trajan's column. Wound about the column spiral-fashion, the
reliefs are a superb visual narrative of the campaigns. In the absence
of any written history of the Dacian wars they are an extremely important historical record, quite apart from their aesthetic value. The
2,500 individual figures are carved with consummate artistry from
Parian marble, and were once coloured and adorned with metal
accessories. Details of the sculpture were easily viewed from the two
libraries.

Trajan's ashes, and those of his wife Plotina, were placed in the
base of the column. At first, the column was crowned with an eagle,
but later a statue of Trajan surmounted it. (1)

Multi-storey apartment houses, called 'islands' (*insulae*), were the places where most Romans lived. These houses were usually built of baked brick like the one in Ostia (above), whose lower two floors are all that remain today. The owner of a tenement or a rich tenant would occupy the ground floor, enjoying central heating, running water and sanitation, while those who lived on the upper floors had to rely on public facilities such as the lavatory (above right), also in Ostia. Waste disposal was effected by a system of sewers running into the Tiber. (2, 3)

Rome's bustling harbour, Ostia, catered to the needs of the mother city, gathering her imports from the shores of the far-flung empire. The detail from a mosaic in a shipping office in Ostia's 'Corporation Square' (below) shows a consignment being transferred from an ocean-going vessel to a barge on its way up the Tiber to Rome. The representation of a dolphin on the right-hand vessel suggests open seas. Often, however, imports were stored in Ostia in vast warehouses built for the purpose, like the one opposite (far right) with its imposing doorway. (5, 6)

Annona Sancta, the deified provision of Rome with food, involved financial transactions which were international in scope. A money-changer is depicted on the relief below. (4)

The Colosseum (far left) is considered by many to be Rome's supreme achievement in architecture and structural engineering and has become a popular symbol of the city. It was begun by Vespasian, but inaugurated by Titus in 80, and was built to house extravagant spectacles of public entertainment. Under the Antonines, Romans worked no more than seven hours a day in summer and six in winter, and were thus free to flock to the Colosseum in the afternoons to watch the brutal entertainments staged by the emperor. Details of the mosaic below, from a rich man's house in Zliten, North Africa, show some of the commoner scenes that a visitor to the amphitheatre was likely to see. Prisoners secured to stakes are being torn to pieces by panthers, animals are hunted by a man with dogs, and a dwarf seems to be entertaining the crowd with his tame boar. (7, 8)

Trajan's market (left) comprised a hundred and fifty individual shops (*tabernae*) and, among other facilities, a great two-storeyed hall, water tanks for liquid goods and live fish, and administration offices. Streets on three levels provided access to the buildings. Staples like corn, wine and oil were brought here from Ostia, and there was a steady commerce in expensive delicacies too; hams, peaches, lemons, plums, dates, and spices were imported as a matter of course from the gardens of the world. The Public Assistance Board organized the free issue of corn to the urban proletariat, so that no Roman citizen need ever die of hunger. (9)

Trajan (98–117) is seen in the right foreground of a stone-relief (top left), accompanied by senators in an imperial procession probably attending a sacrifice. He had made himself, through his second Dacian conquest in 107, the master of milliards of sesterces, and was thus able to rain down plenty on a world that had never before known such abundance. Rome boasted twenty-six individual libraries; the imposing semicircular wall (above) is from the library which Trajan incorporated in his great public bath-house. (10, 11)

Corn supply was carefully regulated under the *Annona* (see Plate 4), and corn-speculation was a serious offence. In the mosaic at left, an official supervises the measuring out of corn, while the relief (left centre) depicts farmers in cloaks with characteristic hoods, paying tribute money. With the enormous quantity of cash at his command, and with no danger of inflation, Trajan – and also his successor Hadrian – could institute far-reaching financial reforms. In 118, Hadrian remitted all tax debts of the previous sixteen years. The ceremonial burning of the tax records, which took place in Trajan's forum, is portrayed in the relief (bottom left). (12, 13, 14)

Most perfect example of the circular Roman temples, which were common under the empire, is the Pantheon or 'Most Sacred Place' (opposite), dedicated to the gods of the seven planets. It was begun by Agrippa in 27 BC, but completely rebuilt by Hadrian (AD 120–4), whose portrait appears on the coin below (*c.* 132). Although the exterior of the Pantheon has been criticized for lack of harmony, it was as an interior that the building was conceived. Indeed, the exquisitely proportioned dome, 144 feet in diameter, is a masterpiece. Having served continuously as a place of worship through the ages, the Pantheon is well preserved, and indeed probably appears today much as it did in the days of its enlightened builder. (15, 16)

Hadrian (117–38), Spanish-born and deeply inspired by the ideal of classical Greece, was one of Rome's most capable and accomplished emperors. Devoting all his great talents to the interests of the state, he tried to remove distinctions between the provinces and the capital and instituted humane reforms in Rome itself. He was a great builder. His own elaborate mausoleum (right) – whose construction he supervised personally – was intended for himself, his family, and his successors. The Antonine emperors down to Commodus were buried there. Hadrian also built this graceful bridge, the Pons Aelius, leading to the mausoleum; it was called after his surname Aelius. (17)

Antoninus Pius (138–61), like Trajan and Hadrian before him, was an adoptive emperor. Hadrian, who had no heir, adopted him on condition that he, in turn, name Marcus Aurelius as his own successor. Antoninus begged the senate in person to decree divine honours on Hadrian – thereby earning himself the name Pius. His reign continued the just, careful rule associated with Hadrian, and, according to most historians, marked the apogee of the Roman Empire. The emperor is depicted on a relief (below) with his wife Faustina; below right is the Temple of Antoninus and Faustina erected by the emperor in honour of his deceased wife. After his death the senate dedicated it also to his memory. (18, 19)

Marcus Aurelius (161–80) was a practising, if not strictly orthodox, Stoic throughout his life. Ironically, war dominated the reign of this philosopher-emperor, and he was obliged to spend much of it defending the empire against attacks from all sides. He did not flinch from the harsh military life he was forced to lead, and his *Meditations*, written as occasion permitted – often on the eve of battles with the empire at stake – indicate that he was a practical moralist, a man who aimed not at happiness, but at tranquillity or equanimity. The fine bronze equestrian statue (above right) probably survived destruction because it was thought to represent the first Christian emperor, Constantine. Below right: a detail from the column erected to commemorate Marcus Aurelius' victories over the Marcomanni and the Sarmatians on the Danube frontier. It is obviously modelled on Trajan's column, with which it has much in common, telling its story in the continuous style of spiral relief. (20, 21)

Shops in Rome were generally 'holes in the wall' – one-room concerns opening on to the street. The street (top left) which became known in medieval times as Via Biberatica – a corruption of the Latin for Pepper Street – was actually on the third storey of Trajan's market (see Plate 9). In the relief (top right) a man at a wine-stall holds his flask in position so that the woman attendant can decant a measure of liquid through the funnel. Note the drip-trays on the step above the man's feet and the graded measuring jugs hanging from a rack at the top. Vegetables are being sold from a low trestle table (centre left), and the relief (above) shows an animated scene in a poulterer's shop. One customer is buying fruit or bread (possibly even eggs) from the woman, and another haggles with the salesman over poultry. Dressed poultry is hanging from a beam, and chickens' heads protrude from between the upright bars of their coop. Monkeys, hares and serpents were common pets in Rome; hence, perhaps, the presence in this relief of a pair of monkeys and hares. (22–5)

The ancient ramp to the Pons Aelius is revealed in a historic photograph (left) taken in 1891. When the course of the Tiber was being altered and new embankments built, the two Hadrianic ramps to the bridge were uncovered. These were destroyed to make way for drastic alterations to the bridge, but the three centre arches (see Plate 17) are original. (26)

More elegant shops catered to the tastes of rich Roman citizens. Left: a couple of well-dressed customers sit on a bench, attended by their slaves, as two young assistants display what appears to be a cushion in an open box. The shop owner is seen hovering behind his slaves. The type of merchandise on display and the aristocratic bearing of the figures in this relief are in marked distinction to the other shop scenes portrayed here; and the shop itself, graced with Corinthian columns and a tiled roof, is obviously of a higher class. (27)

Weighing instruments were invented far back in antiquity. The balance – two pans equidistant from a point of suspension – was used by the Minoans, and possibly even before them by other peoples. Only in Roman times, however, did the steelyard begin to appear. Due to its greater convenience it quickly grew in popularity. The object to be weighed is suspended from the shorter arm, and a weight moved along the graduated longer arm until the arms balance. Two examples are illustrated in the reliefs below. In the butcher shop on the left, a steelyard is seen suspended from a beam. The butcher's implements closely resemble those used today. On the right, a man is shown actually sliding the weight along the graduated arm. The large bale would probably contain wool. (28, 29)

An ancient sky-scraper has been partially reconstructed in this model (right) of a five-storey Roman *insula*. The actual dwelling-house was built in the first half of the second century AD. On ground-level, there was a row of shops (compare the shop fronts with those illustrated opposite). The second storey – which had double and triple window openings – had a projecting balcony; although this feature is not incorporated in the model, it was common among the *insulae* of Rome and Ostia. The orientation of the façade of the building was on to an exterior court. (30)

A child's lot in antiquity was cruel if he was born in dire poverty as so many were. Down to the third century BC in Athens, new-born babies were still often abandoned at cross-roads to the slave-trader or dog-pack. Antonine Rome instituted a system of *alimenta* – funds for poor children – being the interest on land mortgaged by farmers. The funds were increased by Hadrian and Marcus Aurelius, but Rome, like Athens before it, did not go so far as to proscribe the abandonment of children. In this detail of a sarcophagus-frieze (above), three stages in the early life of a more fortunate boy are shown, although he, too, died pathetically young. (31)

Domestic furniture was scant in Roman houses, but beds were an indispensable item. They were often made of sculptured bronze or more exotic materials like cedarwood or ebony, inlaid with gold and ivory, and were of various types: the common day bed, the double marriage bed and a treble dining bed. Romans, influenced by the conquered East, preferred reclining to sitting, even at meals, so that chairs, benches, stools and large tables were hardly used. Room furnishings, however, were profuse: mosaic-floors, wall-paintings and -hangings, tapestries and screens. The love-scene (left), from a small mosaic found near Rome, offers a contemporary impression of a first-century Roman interior. (32)

JÉRÔME CARCOPINO

IN THE FIRST TWO-THIRDS of the second century of the Christian era, Rome was at the height of her greatness and her prosperity. The pulse of an empire beat in her heart: an empire then at its greatest extent, enjoying an atmosphere of unparalleled serenity and a vitality that drew effortlessly upon the wealth of her provinces and her vassal kingdoms. Both the rich and the poor in the countries that she ruled or protected looked towards her and accepted her sway: the former with the object of confirming their ascendancy; the latter in order to attain the standard of living to which she had raised her own proletariat. Virgil had long since lauded her as the city that dominated all others just as the lofty cypress overtops the rowans:

> Verum haec tantum alias inter caput extulit urbes
> Quantum lenta solent inter viburna cupressi.

Now she was established as *Urbs Orbis: Urbs* – the city of cities, capital of the world, glowing with a beauty that through the genius of her rulers was a reflection of the perfect beauty of the heavenly sphere – *orbis*. She had herself become the goddess whom Martial invoked as 'Goddess of continents and nations, Rome, whom nothing equals and nothing rivals':

> Terrarum dea gentiumque, Roma,
> Cui par est nihil et nihil secundum.

A century earlier Augustus had put an end to civil war but had lost the legions of Varus; a century later Rome was to tremble before barbarian invasions; but in the second century of our era she enjoyed freedom from fear.

Trajan had enriched her with fresh conquests and fruitful spheres of influence: Dacia, Arabia, Mesopotamia. His successors, Hadrian (117–38) and Antoninus Pius (138–61), avoided the necessity of waging glorious but exhausting campaigns by relying on the strength of their defences, the wisdom of their administration, and the skill of their diplomacy. Their military activity was limited to reviews and manœuvres and more or less summary police action against local insurrections in remote provinces – Cyrenaica, Judaea and Mauretania. During their reigns Rome enjoyed the most profound and lasting peace that she had ever known: civil peace, social peace, peace at home and abroad. It was the golden age of her history.

It was a clear sign of Rome's prosperity and of her magnetic attraction that she has hardly ever been more populous. During the last century of the Republic (150–50 BC) the population of the *urbs* had grown slowly and steadily from 322,000 in 147 to 463,000 in 85 and to 486,000 in 57. Since then the increase had become so rapid that in the second century there were more than a million inhabitants. The figure is only approximate, for St Jerome's statistics come to an end too soon to state it exactly; but the figure is unquestionably of this order. It is confirmed alike by the topographical measurements of G. Lugli, the consumption of rationed corn studied by Oates, and the lists of houses which I have myself investigated.

The architecture of a populous city

In population alone Rome was three or four times the size of the capital cities of Asia and Africa that most nearly approached her: Alexandria, Carthage and Antioch, and was thus comparable with the cities of today. The latest census of Buenos Aires, Rio de Janeiro, Berlin, Paris, Moscow, New York or London may record two, three, four, or eight times as many inhabitants as Rome held in the age of the Antonines, but a hundred years ago none of these cities was more populous than she was in the second century.

An increasing influx of inhabitants drove the Roman architects, as it has ours, to find, in the words of Vitruvius, 'an answer to overpopulation in the height of their buildings'. We too often think of the houses of Rome in terms of the villas of Pompeii or of the House of Augustus (called that of Livia) on the Palatine. These are horizontally developed with state apartments and reception rooms, *atria, triclinia,* and *tablina*. The glorified villas built on the Esquiline or the Pincian, in the middle of large grounds that in their turn enshrined gardens as exquisite and varied as those of Japan, exemplify the *domus*, the private house that offered a measure of isolation to a single family. In the time of the Antonines such houses could no longer be built, except for princes and the great men of the court, who were wealthy enough not to care how much land they occupied. Few men were still rich enough to be so wasteful of space. The very name of *domus* was now used to dignify the best flat on the ground floor of an apartment house, or *insula*, in which the owner of the whole occupied only a single floor and let the rest. In the fourth-century lists of the wards of the city there are only 1,797 private houses as against 46,602 blocks of flats, and this striking preponderance is certainly much older than the drawing up of the relatively late documents which reveal it. Whereas the *domus* was an exception, especially in the recently developed quarters, the *insula* was everywhere the rule. As more and more apartment houses were built, so was their height increased. The ruins of Roman houses at the foot of the Capitol, near the Porta Tiburtina, under the Palatine along the Via Nova, above all in the little suburban town of Ostia, fifteen miles from Rome, redeveloped under Hadrian, all show that they once had two or three or more storeys. Such a block as the Insula Felicles was a veritable skyscraper; its enormous size had won it universal fame by the end of the second century, and made Tertullian as giddy as the ascension into heaven of the false angels of the Valentinian heresy would have done. The ruling powers were conscious of the danger and the want of elegance of such inordinately tall buildings. An edict of Trajan strengthened previous legislation by setting a limit of sixty feet to the height of private buildings. It goes without saying that cupidity impelled the builders to accept this maximum as a minimum, very much as the architects of Paris did fifty years ago.

It was another sign of prosperity that these buildings were resplendent with luxurious decoration. Mosaic floors were a commonplace, some with geometrical designs (*opus tessellatum*), others depicting flowers, animals, men and gods (*opus vermiculatum*), forming a gay and glittering pattern in the white ground, or glowing richly from one of black, as in the house of the Via dei Cerchi. The houses were solidly built, sometimes of blocks of ashlar, tufa, or travertine (*opus quadratum*), most often with baked brick (*opus latericium*) laid in regular courses to link and define with their red stripes the no less regular sections of lozenged brown tufa (*opus reticulatum*). The exterior was sometimes coated with fine-grained white roughcast (*opus tectorium*) or faced with thin sheets of marble (*opus sectile marmoreum*), but such additions were not essential, and it was not long before brickwork itself was decoratively exploited, in the same fashion as it was later to be in the Versailles of Louis XIII.

The inside walls were covered with delicate stucco work or with frescoes, either of landscape in Alexandrian style, of scenes of ordinary life, or of mythological subjects. They were all treated with considerable freedom of movement and charm of colour, whether they adorned a commonplace house like that which lies below the Church of SS. Giovanni e Paolo or the successive *domus, transitoria* and *aurea* of the extravagant Nero.

The splendid furnishings were in harmony with the decoration of the rooms they adorned. Furniture, however, was relatively scanty. The Romans, influenced by the customs of the conquered East, preferred to recline rather than to sit, even at meals, and left benches and stools to inns and workrooms and shops. The use of high-backed chairs was the privilege of ruler or judge at his official work, of priests at their rites, and of teachers lecturing *ex cathedra*. Apart from these, their use was the mark of scholars such as the younger Pliny, who liked to give a professorial air to their casual conversation, and of a few affected great ladies who loved comfort.

Large tables were little used; chests, *guéridons*, variously mounted shelves, and tripods took their place. The most important pieces of furniture were beds: little single day-beds which were found everywhere; double marriage-beds for bedrooms; and dining-beds for three people (*triclinia*). The finest were made of sculptured bronze or rare woods, for example thuya inlaid with shell and ivory; on them and round them was scattered a profusion of covers, carpets, quilts, cushions, hangings and screens of a kind that can be reconstructed from the finds at Herculaneum.

The table-services were magnificent. Even lesser men would have been ashamed not to eat off silver, and the rich had their plate parcel-gilt or set with precious stones. Poor men made do with pottery and truckle beds in the miserable attics for which they paid 500 *denarii* a year, a twentieth or thirtieth part of the rent of the *piano nobile*.

Ancient chaos and modern peace

All the same the poor men of Antonine Rome grumbled less about their lot than do their successors in England or France today. For one thing, a depressing lodging is more easily borne in a sunny country, in which the tenant passes the brightest hours out of doors; for another, the fourteen districts of the *urbs* did not offer that sharp contrast between working-class and wealthy districts which may be seen in modern capitals, and there was the same kind of accidental egalitarianism in the Rome of the Caesars as there was later to be in the Rome of the Popes, with wretched apartment houses and magnificent palaces built next door to each other, and millionaires and men of modest means living on different floors under the same roof. Furthermore, and more significantly, the poor men of Antonine Rome endured a poverty less harsh than that of today, for the very poorest could always escape into the aristocratic peace of parks and gardens, or to the Roman countryside.

Though Roman houses equalled those of our own day in height and size, they were set without formal alignment along streets as narrow and winding as those of the Middle Ages. Under an edict of Julius Caesar that was still in force, carriages were forbidden to use these streets by day, since it was found that there was not room in them for both wheeled vehicles and pedestrians. Even the disastrous fire of AD 64 had not given the town-planners space enough to provide their metropolis with the regularity and ease of communications which Hippodamos of Miletus had been able to bestow on Piraeus and Thurii as early as the fifth century BC. The planners succeeded in imposing their plans only on such limited sites as Ostia, where it seems that Apollodorus of Damascus, or at least one of his imitators, was at work at the time when Hadrian decided to build it anew.

The Roman planners were therefore reduced to dealing indirectly with their problem; but they succeeded, if not in solving it, at least in making it less acute. They prevented the increase of winding streets and bottle-necked lanes, the dark entanglement of *viae* and *vici*, though they could not altogether transform them. They devoted their ingenuity to seeing that they did not spread their tentacles over

empty spaces; they surrounded them with open esplanades, and intersected them by wide avenues of light and air. They beautified the Campus Martius, from which dwellings were excluded. They maintained the gardens with which great men had surrounded their private houses, and which, one after another, had been incorporated into the imperial demesne and opened to the public. Thus it was that Antonine Rome offered at first sight the contrast between the red of tiles and bricks, the white of marble, and the greenery which dotted and surrounded the built-up areas. The occurrence of these 'green belts' was indeed most striking. On the Esquiline the gardens of Maecenas were continued in those of Aelius Lamia, of Statilius Taurus, of Pallas, and of Epaphroditus. In Trastevere the gardens of Julius Caesar lay beside those of Mark Antony. On the Vatican the gardens of Nero adjoined those of Domitia. On the Pincian there was no boundary between those of the Pincii, the Anicii, the Acilii, which the financial administration had taken over together with the *horti* of Lucullus, and – perhaps the most beautiful of all – the Horti Sallustiani. The presence of these gardens at the centre as at the periphery of the *urbs* gave it a double aspect. There were two Romes in one: the first was still involved in its ancient past, archaic and inchoate, stifled and twisted, and deafened at night by the rattle of chariots; during the day it was besieged by an army of busy walkers, casual Praetorians, rough muleteers and by haughty and aristocratic litters borne on the shoulders of eight porters. This was a Rome of which the hubbub and colour and stench and crowds and hurly-burly can now be seen only in some Eastern souk or in the Medina of Fez. The other Rome, which the emperors had tried to purge and modernize, encroached upon and surrounded the first with its *horti* – airy, peaceful and verdurous as the squares and parks of London.

Nor was this all. The Romans of the second century were the proud possessors of sanitary arrangements of which the inconvenience and the rudimentary efficiency would make us, now, smile or groan; but to them they seemed new and wonderful.

To escape from the constriction of their alleys, they multiplied the many kinds of balconies that projected from their long façades, and pierced their walls with windows of which the size astonishes the modern visitor to Ostia. The spectator forgets that, in default of transparent glass, the Romans covered these wide openings with curtains or shutters which not only protected the rooms from curiosity, rain and cold, but also shut out daylight. At night oil-lamps (*lucernae*), candelabra and wax candles (*cerei*) were equally inefficient in lighting town houses. Those who went out after dark lighted their path with the lanterns they carried, like villagers going to a midnight Mass; and this black-out encouraged highwaymen and gangsters of every sort. The imperial administration did its best to suppress them, and redoubled the activity of the police. Thus Hadrian enforced the beats walked by the watchmen – *vigiles* – with unexpected inspections by his secret police.

The Caesars of the second century occupied themselves not only with the security of their capital, but also with its sanitation. They kept up the magnificent network of sewers that Agrippa had established under the city, first on the line of the ancient *cloaca maxima* from the Capitol to the Velabrum, then on the cross-line from the Circus Maximus, and finally from the Pincian to the Pons Fabricius. Since their engineers could only apply their sewage system to the ground floors of the houses it served, they supplemented it for those who lived in the upper floors by the construction of numerous public conveniences, promiscuous enough, but furnished with marble seats, and – to judge by the remains of those near the Forum Julium – with suitable heating systems.

Moreover they completed the provision of spring water to a Rome that still enchants us by the melodious murmur of her innumerable fountains. Trajan alone raised the daily output of the Anio Novus to 177,000 cubic metres, and built the aqueduct for Trastevere that still bears his name and feeds the roaring cascades of the Aqua Paola on the Janiculum. This cool, pure water, which spouted in the public squares and at the crossroads, was not carried to the upper floors of the houses, and the benefit of running water – like that of main drainage and central heating – was economically reserved for the inhabitants of the ground-floor apartments. The Romans of the second century tried to counter the cold, not by building chimneys (which came into use later, and only in the northern provinces of their empire), but by installing under their floors the heating system

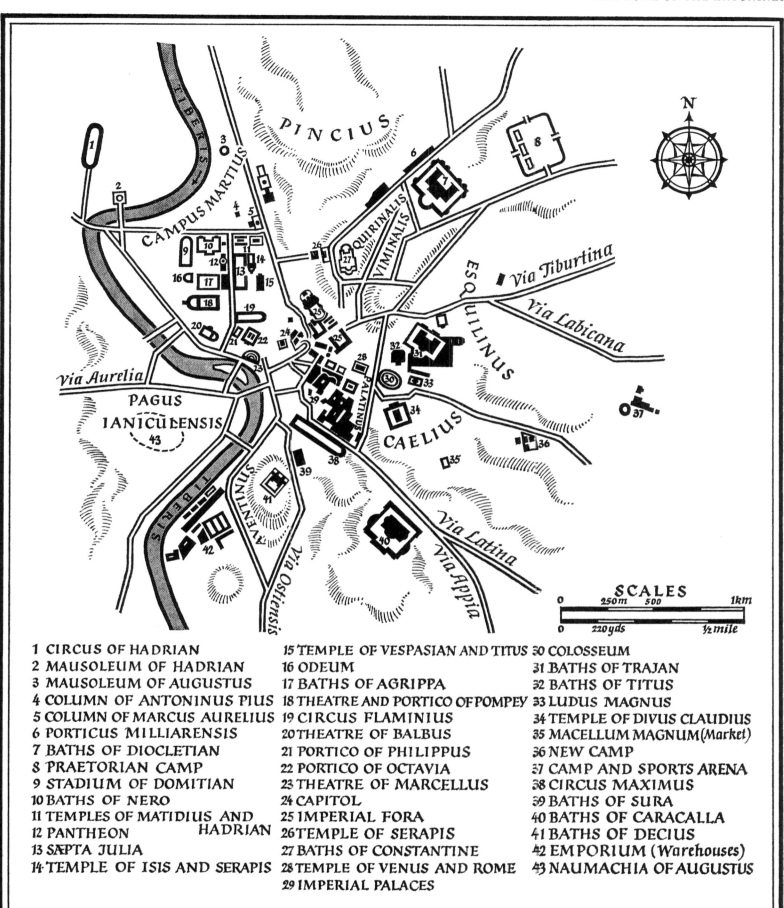

1 CIRCUS OF HADRIAN
2 MAUSOLEUM OF HADRIAN
3 MAUSOLEUM OF AUGUSTUS
4 COLUMN OF ANTONINUS PIUS
5 COLUMN OF MARCUS AURELIUS
6 PORTICUS MILLIARENSIS
7 BATHS OF DIOCLETIAN
8 PRAETORIAN CAMP
9 STADIUM OF DOMITIAN
10 BATHS OF NERO
11 TEMPLES OF MATIDIUS AND HADRIAN
12 PANTHEON
13 SÆPTA JULIA
14 TEMPLE OF ISIS AND SERAPIS

15 TEMPLE OF VESPASIAN AND TITUS
16 ODEUM
17 BATHS OF AGRIPPA
18 THEATRE AND PORTICO OF POMPEY
19 CIRCUS FLAMINIUS
20 THEATRE OF BALBUS
21 PORTICO OF PHILIPPUS
22 PORTICO OF OCTAVIA
23 THEATRE OF MARCELLUS
24 CAPITOL
25 IMPERIAL FORA
26 TEMPLE OF SERAPIS
27 BATHS OF CONSTANTINE
28 TEMPLE OF VENUS AND ROME
29 IMPERIAL PALACES

30 COLOSSEUM
31 BATHS OF TRAJAN
32 BATHS OF TITUS
33 LUDUS MAGNUS
34 TEMPLE OF DIVUS CLAUDIUS
35 MACELLUM MAGNUM (Market)
36 NEW CAMP
37 CAMP AND SPORTS ARENA
38 CIRCUS MAXIMUS
39 BATHS OF SURA
40 BATHS OF CARACALLA
41 BATHS OF DECIUS
42 EMPORIUM (Warehouses)
43 NAUMACHIA OF AUGUSTUS

Plan of Antonine Rome

which C. Sergius Orata had invented fifty years before Christ. A furnace was built to take a fire of faggots and dry weeds, which sent its heat, smoke and soot between the piers of brick on which the pavement rested and up the conduits made in the lower walls. This rudimentary central heating, however, was confined to the basement and to the rooms immediately above it. The ordinary Roman who lived in a flat on the upper floors not only had to go into the street to use the nearest public latrine and to buy his drinking water from the water sellers under his window (as indeed the citizens of Paris did under Louis-Philippe and Napoleon), but had also to face the cold (which admittedly was rarely severe) with the sole aid of smoky and unhealthy braziers, and to cook his stew over a chafing-dish. He could console himself for these inconveniences, to which he had become inured, by the good smell of the excellent food with which he was provided by the foresight and generosity of his emperor.

Wealth in abundance

Never, indeed, had so many people been comfortably off in a city in which even poverty had lost its sting. Peace, of which the atmosphere is as necessary to a healthy economy as fresh air is to a healthy body,

133

seemed eternally assured. Trajan's last great conquest, that of Dacia in 107, had enabled him to divert to Rome a Pactolian stream in the form of gold from Transylvania and treasure from the vanquished. At one blow the emperor found himself master of milliards of sesterces, which permitted him to rain down plenty on a world that had never before known such abundance. A series of measures, easily financed by a treasury that commanded what seemed an inexhaustible source of wealth, benefited every part of the empire and especially its mistress, Rome. Trajan was able to diminish taxation and to increase the national income. By recoining the *aurei*, making them of a fixed weight, and establishing a constant relation between the respective values of gold, silver, and copper coins, he was able to cut out large monetary inflation for two generations, and to arm the Romans with the monetary stability, at least of silver, that is the best weapon against speculation and rising costs of living. Then, since he had an enormous quantity of cash at his command, he could, disinterestedly but without sacrifice, provisionally renounce those dues of which the temporary suspension would attract labourers to the parts of his domains that were lying fallow or neglected, to exploit them and ultimately give back to him a part of their harvest. Further, he invested large sums in loans which he granted to the landed proprietors of Italy who were short of capital: loans which were in fact hidden subsidies of agriculture. Finally, he dedicated yet larger sums to great undertakings likely to stimulate production because they offered producers an easy market for their goods.

One would have said that the imperial machine was geared only to soften the material conditions of life and that the emperor had no other duty than the amelioration of the human lot. So, indeed, declared the ministers of Hadrian, with rather pompous flattery, in a resolution of which the writer discovered the text in Tunisia sixty years ago:

Caesar pro infatigabili sua cura, per quam adsidue humanis utilitatibus excubat.

Thus the interests of the masters of the world were identified with those of their subjects. The provinces furnished Rome with the fruit of their earth and their labours; and Rome, by giving them riches in return, linked them to the general prosperity. The 'Corporation Square' at Ostia, of which the plan and decoration date from this time, bears witness to this wonderful collaboration. In the middle rise the ruins of the temple of Annona Auguste, the Annona Sancta of the Roman people: that is, the deified provision of the people of Rome with food. The terrace that surrounds it is closed to the south by the back wall of the stage of the theatre and on the other three sides by sixty-one rooms each about sixteen metres square, with a portico before each and a mosaic floor which shows by its figures and inscriptions to which corporation the room belonged. Each one of these professional associations had a direct part to play in the service of Annona: ship-builders of Carthage, Alexandria, Cagliari, Narbonne and Mauretania; fullers of cloth, ropemakers, skinners, timber merchants, inspectors of weights and measures, and the rest. As one treads the pavement used by these merchants and sailors and craftsmen, one seems to see them sailing and rowing in from all the shores of the Mediterranean to meet the needs of the mother city and to shower upon her the products of their countries; and looking at the mosaics on which their corporations have proudly set their canting badges, one realizes that their burdens were lightened by their fidelity to Annona Auguste, and that the satisfaction they felt in serving the needs of Rome was heightened by a religious enthusiasm.

It was thanks to such corporations as these that Rome enjoyed regular imports of corn from Africa and Egypt, wine from the Greek islands, oil from Spain, hams from Gaul, and of peaches from Persia; also lemons from Media, plums from Damascus, dates from the oases, and silphium from Cyrene. Spices from the Far East reached her from India by the caravan route through newly conquered Arabia and vassal Palmyra, or directly by sea from the depths of the Persian Gulf via the Ptolemaic ports of the Red Sea, Myos Hormos and Berenike, each now with its garrison of legionaries. There was so much trade in ginger, cinnamon and pepper at this time, when the armies of Trajan had reached as far as the Shatt el Arab, that a whole floor of Trajan's market was assigned to it. Long afterwards, when the market had been given up and its halls used for other purposes, the medieval tenements of the street still bore the name of Via Biberatica, a clear deformation of Via Piperatica, the 'Pepper Street' of ancient Rome.

Archaeological and literary evidence combine to indicate the delicacies that the ingenuity of gourmets invented at this time, and the junketings which the masses were every day invited to enjoy. No citizen of Rome need then die of hunger. As M. Denis van Berchem has shown, the entire urban proletariat - that is to say, all Romans who were neither senators nor knights - were listed on the rolls of the Public Assistance Board. This gave them the right not only to draw every month a free ration of five pecks or *modii* of corn, but also permitted them on festival occasions, in which the emperor wished his people to share, to draw cash gratuities – 75 *denarii* in 99 and 102; 500 *denarii* in 107; 800 under Antoninus Pius, 850 under Marcus Aurelius. These were so many windfalls and gave them some of the feelings of the workman who has won the big prize in the pools. On the other hand the emperor, whose immense fortune spread its tentacles everywhere, and whose tithes from provincial taxpayers filled the warehouses, could at any moment control current prices by his monopolies and effectively oppose any increase in the price of food. The lofts and cellars of Rome overflowed with provisions and wine was cheap.

Civic order in a vast social perspective

This fact, far more than the presence of impressive police forces – Praetorian Guards, *vigiles*, city cohorts – explains the civic order which in the second century reigned in the overcrowded city, and the maintenance of untroubled peace in spite of devastating social inequalities. At the bottom of the ladder were the slaves whom their masters had fallen into the habit of paying, and who saved, *sesterce* by *sesterce*, the money to purchase their freedom. Then came the *plebs*, citizens with little or no capital, living from hand to mouth, but with no cause to take thought for the morrow, since victuals were cheap and each and all could count on the free issue of rations and on the uncovenanted mercies of gratuitous *congiaria*. Above the *plebs* came the two orders of chivalry: first the bourgeoisie of the Equestrian Order, and above them the nobility of the Senatorial Order. The burgess rights of the knight could only be obtained by those who owned at least 400,000 *sesterces*. Promotion to the nobility presupposed an annual income of a million *sesterces*; but this was merely an administrative minimum and senators thought themselves only moderately well off if, like the younger Pliny, they left only twenty millions. Finally, far above even the most fortunate nobles, there sat in superhuman glory the golden majesty of the emperor, the multi-millionaire on whom the revenues of the treasury and his immense properties throughout Italy and the provinces, not to mention his overlordship of the land of Egypt, conferred the prestige of an incomparable way of living and an almost unlimited sphere of action.

It is frightening to see the vast social perspective that stretched between him and the poor men of the *plebs* and the domestic slaves; and, as if there were not classes enough for him to dominate, in the first half of the second century the emperor introduced yet more divisions into society. While the *honestiores*, who owned at least a clerkship or else a property, came to be distinguished more and more clearly among the plebeians from the *humiliores* who had not so much, Hadrian detached from the bulk of the knightly class – who were content to call themselves men of distinction, *viri egregii* – an élite of men eligible for the prefecture to whom he granted the title of *viri perfectissimi*; and a yet higher class, from which he drew the commanders of his guard, the highest officers of his general staff, who received the title of eminence, *viri eminentissimi*: a title that passed from them to the cardinals of the Roman Church.

Yet in spite of these social divisions which divided them more drastically into classes than before, the citizens of Rome lived together on an admirably friendly footing. There was no sedition among the proletariat, there were no revolts among the slaves. The slaves, indeed, were treated more humanely than they had been in the past. Both Hadrian and Antoninus forbade their masters, under severe penalties, from prostituting or mutilating them or from putting them to death; and Arrian, a senator who was governor of Cappadocia between 131 and 137, had no hesitation in publishing his conversations with Epictetus, a former slave from Phrygia, who had made himself the greatest teacher of his time of Stoic asceticism.

The emperors commonly allowed freedmen entry to public careers and the right to wear the gold ring that marked them as knights. Slaves and freedmen could elbow free men as brothers in the sanctuaries where social distinctions were forgotten, at the Corporate feasts, and in the religious and funeral gilds – as in the college of Diana and Antoninus at Lanuvium in 133.

The balance of work and leisure

It would be a great mistake, in my opinion, to take too seriously Rostovtsev's epigram that imperial Rome was a city of *rentiers* since she held within her walls 400,000 people who received the free issue of corn. It would be as true to assume that the millions of people covered by health and unemployment insurance in London and New York and Paris spent their lives with their arms idly folded. Rome, in fact, was in the second century a city humming with activity, with the business of her merchants, the trade of her shops, and the work of her craftsmen. The vastness of her population ensured constant activity in victualling, clothing and housing them. In a classic book Waltzing has listed all the corporations necessary to her life: gilds of those who had to build or repair the houses; of the bakers, pastrycooks, confectioners, butchers, fishmongers, vintners and wine merchants; of those who dressed and shod and washed and scented the citizens; of boatmen, hauliers, drivers, vanmen and porters. Moreover her pre-eminent position as mistress of the world brought within her walls the offices of the central government, the Bullion Exchange that regulated the money market, and the supreme courts that judged the most important or the most delicate cases. In consequence there were vast numbers of civil servants, bankers, money-changers, lawyers, law-clerks and scribes. Finally, her wonted luxury, which set a standard for all other great cities, was maintained by a host of decorative industries, in textiles, fine woods, ivory and jewels. The Romans were thus far from idle; and with a little energy and *savoir-vivre* a man could save enough for the slave to purchase his emancipation, the freedman to push his clever sons into the knightly order or the civil service, the knight to gain senatorial rank. The time was as yet distant when military reverses would affect the recruitment of slaves, and first retard and then stop this social climbing. The sky was still clear and seemed to promise a future even more brilliant than a present that was already eminently satisfactory for anyone willing to work.

Industry was already organized in such a way that although very different from that of our own day, it made even the hardest kind of labour bearable. While our own aim is to give equal opportunities to both sexes, the Romans permitted women only exceptionally to enter professions other than those indicated for them by decency or aptitude – as that of dressmaker (*sarcinatrix*), hairdresser (*ornatrix*), midwife (*obstetrix*) and wet-nurse (*nutrix*). Apart from these, women in second-century Rome were seldom admitted to any profession. They did not go out to market; they stayed at home and occupied themselves with the ordering of their households and the comfort of their husbands – unless great riches, by freeing them of every material care, left them with nothing to do but to dress fashionably and amuse themselves.

Most modern nations have limited by law the number of working hours and working days in a week. The forty or forty-eight-hour week, the week-end and bank holiday have become a part of our everyday life by enactment. By force of habit the Romans of the second century had achieved the same result. Apart from the Senate, whose members might be called upon to sit without respite from dawn to dusk, and apart from certain trades, such as those of the barbers, keepers of eating houses, warders of exhibitions, sports ground attendants, and the staff of the public baths, who were busiest when other men were at leisure, one may say that normally they worked every day; but that they only worked from dawn until about midday. After the fifth hour – which ended at 10.45 a.m. at the winter solstice and at 11.15 a.m. at midsummer – the more easy-going employers let their workmen go. One of the parasites whom Martial satirizes comes to his host a little before he is asked; the sixth hour is not over, and it is not yet midday, but he has already on his way met a troop of slaves whose master had let them go and who were heading for the baths. In any case, after one o'clock in the afternoon there was not a shopman that did not make ready to close his shutters, nor a manufacturer that did not shut his gates.

Martial, again, is our informant: 'Rome prolongs her activities until the fifth hour; the sixth hour brings rest to the weary; the seventh is the end for all.'

> In quintam varios extendit Roma labores
> Sexta quies lassos septima finis erit.

Thus at a quarter-to-one in winter, and a quarter-past in summer, work was over until the next morning in every section of the city's economy. If one considers, as one should, the Roman winter hour as equal to forty-five minutes, that implies that in Martial's day, in the second century, the working day was seven astronomical hours long in summer and less than six in winter. The forty-hour week was ordinarily worked only in winter, but in every season the twenty-four-hour day included seventeen or eighteen of complete liberty. Indeed citizens enjoyed so many hours of leisure that they would not have known what to do with them if the injunctions of the calendar and the generosities of the ruling powers had not helped to fill the void. The calendar still transmitted the traditions of an older paganism, at least in its feasts, and lengthened as their list was by the addition of new festivals in honour of the imperial cult, it ended by indicating a festival every two days.

Feasts, pageants and gladiators' blood

The government, through the munificence of the emperors and the highest officers of state, met the greater part of the cost that these endless holidays entailed. There were religious feasts for every taste. Some recalled the peasant origins of the great city, like the fishing competition of the 8 June that was linked with the ancient cults of Vulcan and the Tiber; others of this kind were the sack races of the Robigalia on 25 August, the foot races and mule races of the Consualia on 21 August and 15 December; the horse races of the Equus October on 15 October, and the Ludi Martiales on 1 August. Since the end of the first century the gaieties of Saturnalia, when slaves might joke with their masters if not against them, and eat at their table and even make them wait upon their own servants, had been extended over a whole week, from 17 to 25 December.

There were two series of *ludi* – the official games, pageants and chariot races, which had been established by the devotion of the pious in the last centuries of the Caesars in honour of the imperial divinity or to commemorate their victories; they now lasted for six, seven, thirteen, or fifteen consecutive days. Furthermore there were the sporadic and frequent *munera*, combats between gladiators which horrify us now but which were then shockingly popular. Under Trajan they once lasted uninterruptedly for a hundred and seventeen days, from 7 July to 1 November 109; in these three months 4,912 pairs of gladiators spilt their blood to satisfy the cruel frenzy of pitiless crowds of spectators.

On the days when there were no state-supported spectacles, the Romans could find other pastimes: gild meetings, ward festivals held round the shrines of the Lares at crossroads; and a host of more individual amusements. Connoisseurs could dawdle round the exhibitions of works of art in the Campus Martius; the intelligentsia could attend public lectures, or ensconce themselves in one of the two libraries, Greek and Latin, that Trajan had established by his triumphal column. The pleasure seekers could haunt the *cauponae* of more or less dubious reputation or pub-crawl round the bars of the *thermopolia*; the lazy could loiter under the porticoes and in the basilicas whose pavements still show the wear from their tread, and the marks of draught-boards and shuffle-boards that they traced upon them. Finally men of every social class could meet and every taste be satisfied in the monumental baths which the emperors designed as real people's palaces. Entry to them was free or nominal (the quarter of a brass *as*) and every pastime and recreation was to be found under their roof: swimming pools and Turkish baths, gymnasia, walks under covered porticoes, bars and restaurants in their annexes, and even libraries and a museum of works of art.

It is noteworthy that the use of leisure was governed by the Roman working day, in which a free afternoon followed on a morning's labour. Two examples will suffice to show this. If the *munera* sometimes lasted all day, the programme was planned as if their organizers were anxious to hide the more shameful exhibitions from the great crowds. The most horrible items, when naked men and women and girls were thrown to the wild beasts, or men fought a fight that was no fight but simply the massacre of an unarmed man by a gladiator armed to the teeth, who in the next round was the unarmed man, were of set purpose staged in the morning hours when ordinary men were at work. They were played to empty benches, or rather to benches that held only a few sadists and psychotics drawn from their *dolce far niente* by the scent of blood, as the dregs of our population used to be drawn to a place of execution. The *munus* itself only began after midday, and comprised equally matched combats between gladiators in which victory, and life with it, went to the strongest and bravest. It might end with the *venatio* that, to judge by Roman inscriptions, crowned the proceedings not only in Rome but also at Alba Fucens in the Abruzzi, at Pisaurum on the Adriatic, and at Pompeii: a lively battle in which gladiators with lassos, boar-spears and swords, fought with bulls and wild beasts and re-enacted for the spectators the excitement and noble traditions of the chase. Thus the majority of the onlookers saw only the sporting half of the *munus*; the shameless and abject turns were unseen by the multitude.

Public pastime and imperial generosity

This tendency to adapt the times of amusements to the leisure hours of workers is still more evident in the police regulations established by Hadrian for the public baths. For the first time, to translate literally the phrase of his biographer, he divided the baths according to sex: '*lavacra, pro sexibus, separavit*'. The division was made not by any partition of space, but by a separation of time. At Rome the sixth and seventh hours were reserved for women, who, having little employment outside their homes, could come at any hour. The eighth and subsequent hours were kept for men, of whom the busiest would only be free after the seventh hour.

The emperors were in a particularly strong position to regulate their subjects' employment of leisure, since they met the cost. To have some idea of their prodigality in this respect, it is enough to consider some of the most impressive ruins in Rome. Of the Circus Maximus, where a hundred and fifty thousand spectators could view the chariot races, nothing remains but the outline of its immense ellipse; it was rebuilt after the fire of 64, and was only finished forty years later, under Trajan. The theatre of Marcellus, however, restored at the end of the first century, still stands in the imposing symmetry of its travertine arches and the monumental variety of the three orders of its columns. If we can forget the nature of the spectacles that it witnessed, the Colosseum itself must fill us with admiration for its size, the honest solidity of its building, and the perfection of its plan. Finally, though the colossal mass of the Baths of Caracalla (211–17) did not rise between the Appian Way and the Aventine until the second century had elapsed, the reign of Trajan yet saw the erection of the baths that bore his name on the site of the Domus Aurea – baths adorned with such sculptures as the *Laocoon* – and of those called after his most intimate friend, the vice-emperor, Licinius Sura. The Baths of Agrippa, which had been destroyed in the fire of 80, were rebuilt, enlarged and beautified, under Hadrian.

These varied constructions, destined only for the pastimes of the people, cost many millions, and their magnificence sheds a significant light on the importance attached to leisure by imperial policy. Juvenal might well grow indignant that his contemporaries no longer felt strongly about anything but bread and circuses:

> ... duas tantum res anxius optet
> panem et circenses.

Less than a century later, the senator, Dio Cassius, far from sharing in the poet's indignation, was to honour the memory of Trajan for the skill which he had shown in exploiting the strongest forces at the emperor's disposal.

> The wisdom of Trajan [he declared] never failed to pay attention to the stars of stage, circus, and arena. He well knew that the excellence of a government is shown as clearly in its anxious watch over amusements as in its dealings with serious matters, and that even if the distribution of coin and money satisfy the individual, there must also be spectacles to satisfy the people as a whole.

Dictators, indeed, whatever the ideology of their absolutism, are bound to come to the demagogic view that, after bread, amusement

is a people's first need. The French revolutionary, Danton, was to declare that it was education; and it was because they had not given enough heed to this salutary truth, because they had been too timid in fulfilling the educative mission that under their system of government was incumbent on the ruler, that the Caesars of the second century allowed an intellectual rust to spread over their age of gold, which was ultimately to cause its decay.

We must not, however, exaggerate. There was danger in the tensions of a mixed population, the inequality of fortunes, the rapidity with which some men became rich, and the insolence of a luxury that was on the way to becoming dissolute. Likewise the temptations to idleness, debauchery and wastefulness which were inherent in the distribution of *congiaria*, and the baseness and savagery of some of the spectacles enjoyed by crowded audiences, created conditions that were favourable to a negligent *laisser-aller*. They encouraged selfishness and the propagation of vice rather than the virtues in which had lain the strength of Rome: virtues which should have endured to justify Roman supremacy for a long time to come. Yet, in spite of these causes of internal decline, the greater part of the population remained healthy-minded. Even if the Caesars of the second century did not effect the drastic reforms which the changing climate of society and the implications of their conquests demanded, they none the less tried to prevent, by legislation and example, the lowering of the standards of feeling and thinking which, if it was not checked, might bring about the collapse of the empire.

A healthy imperial stock

The Antonines – the brute Commodus alone excepted – were better men than their predecessors. With a slight modification of Albertini's striking phrase, it could be said that they brought into being the best world which was possible in antiquity. Coming of provincial stock – Gaulish in Antoninus, Spanish in the others – they brought to their accession a wider political vision, extending to the farthest limits of the *orbis Romanus*, and a fresher energy, derived from a family unspoilt by the hereditary enjoyment of supreme power. They had a high conception of their functions, the higher because none of them had been born to the purple; and all of them, even those who were in later generations predestined to the throne by birth, seemed to attain sovereignty by their merit alone. Antoninus, surnamed Pius, was a man of wisdom; Marcus Aurelius, who was called Antoninus the Philosopher, was a saint. Trajan was granted by popular acclaim the title of *Optimus*, 'the Best', and it was voted to him as a surname by the Senate. Trajan, Hadrian, Marcus Aurelius – the first two with cheerful optimism, the third with serene resignation – all endured without flinching the rough life of the camp, sleeping in tents, eating the same stew and fat bacon, drinking the same sour wine as their soldiers, indifferent to danger, which in time of peace they sought in the chase.

People might whisper that Trajan drank too much, but it must be admitted that he hid his weakness remarkably well, and that he used to astonish the guests whom he liked to invite to his castle of Centumcellae by the frugality of his table and the general dignity of his manners. As to Hadrian, his biographer accuses him of many adulteries, and he was cynic enough to try to transfer the empire to his favourite bastard. But to mask his intention, he never called his son anything but *Verus*, 'the True'; he did not reveal his purpose until his wife, Sabina, was dead, and he did not fail in her lifetime to shower upon her the outward marks of the deepest respect, whether at court or on the journeys they undertook together. He punished remorselessly any allusion to their domestic differences, and brutally disgraced his official historian, Suetonius, for a want of consideration to the empress. Even when they did not practise it, the Antonines always preached virtue.

Moreover they tried to make their subjects virtuous. So far as lay in their power, they tried to purify the use of the leisure accorded by their princely generosity. The regulations for the baths made by Hadrian re-established decency, their enlargement helped to develop sports and physical culture. If the Ludi Scaenici had degenerated to a point when tragedy and comedy were the exception and the usual level of programme was that of the music-hall, Trajan, although he himself enjoyed variety turns, none the less tried to restrain indecency, especially in the actors' gestures, by forbidding certain sorts of pantomime. Inscriptions scattered as far afield as Leptis Magna show that there existed at Rome an imperial *Conservatorium* for the training of mimes: one might almost say an imperial School of Ballet. As to gladiatorial combats, Marcus Aurelius had the courage to discourage their shameful popularity, and not only set a ceiling cost to municipal *munera*, but also wished to substitute harmless representations, *lusiones*, for the homicidal duels fashionable in Rome.

These various reforms prove that the Antonines, even if they did not find the solution of the problem, had at least given attention to the education of the masses.

With them the Roman state for the first time came to the aid of unfortunate children. Ever since the principate of Nerva (96–8), in spite of the financial difficulties of a treasury exhausted by the wild extravagances of Domitian, grants – *alimenta* – had been made towards the maintenance of young children, boys and girls, legitimate and illegitimate. By an ingenious system of compensatory transfers Trajan collected the money from the interest on the loans he had made to land-owners to help them to clear land and increase its production. In their turn Hadrian and Marcus Aurelius increased the amount of the *alimenta*. If none of these emperors went so far as to proscribe the abandonment of babies, an ineffaceable stain on the societies of antiquity, at least they tried to mitigate its results.

Education for all

One of them, Hadrian, became an enthusiast for the kind of enlightenment that the eighteenth century called '*la diffusion des lumières*'. A skilled man of letters, he was himself an occasional poet in Greek as well as Latin, with a tireless curiosity. This remarkable emperor, who enjoyed the pleasures of learned controversy with grammarians, geometers, rhetoricians, and philosophers such as Favorinus – his favourite companion in argument – organized in Rome a system of higher education. It was based on the rudimentary beginnings that Vespasian had instituted forty-five years before, for the benefit of Quintilian. Hadrian showered benefits on the professors, whose lectures he supervised in person; if he judged them not to be up to their work he sent them home, laden with riches and honour. Although his biographer is silent on the subject, he was no less interested in elementary schools. We have a decisive proof of this interest in the fact that when his procurators had to draw up regulations for the various professions to be allowed to settle in a mining district of Lusitania that belonged to him, the only person they exempted from tax in the town of Vipasca was the schoolmaster: '*ludi magistros immunis esse placet*'. Elementary education might not yet be compulsory and free, but it was already general even in the depths of the remoter provinces because of its cheapness and the encouragement given to teachers.

There is thus no cause for surprise in the fact that in the second century education was more widespread than ever before. For a long time illiteracy had been identified with barbarism in Rome and the Italian cities, and those who could not read or write were an insignificant minority. At the end of the second century such men were only to be found in backward provinces. Quintilian came across them only among the village boors: '*rusticus illiteratusque*'. In a fashionable town like Pompeii everyone could read and write, which is the reason why its walls are covered with a rash of electoral posters and *graffiti*. In the second century even slaves were literate; those of Lanuvium were able to collaborate in the drawing up of the statutes of their gild. It was not rare to discover humble servants, in the households of great men, who had pursued their studies beyond the level of the elementary school: men such as the freedman mentioned in a conceit of the younger Pliny's, who not only knew his letters but was even literate: '*libertus est mihi non illiteratus*'. Most men of some standing, engaged in the civil service of either half of a bilingual empire, knew Greek as well as Latin, and prided themselves on their knowledge to a point when out of intellectual snobbery they would choose to listen at Rome to the lecture of a man speaking in Greek. Favorinus, a Gallo-Roman born at Arles, was in the habit of lecturing in Greek; and Lucian, a Greek of Samosate, collected a fortune on his lecture tours in the West. May not this progressive Hellenization even have been one of the causes of the decline of Latin literature? Who would wish to cultivate the mother tongue when even the emperor disdained the language of his ancestors, and Marcus Aurelius drew up the spiritual testament which he bequeathed to posterity in Greek?

In the first half of the second century Greek had not yet won this pre-eminence. Already, however, the literary inflation that derives from a passion for public lectures was visible. Soon the seeking after effect and applause, inseparable from these performances before a *cénacle*, of which every member is familiar with the author's personality, corrupted the general taste with preciosity and artifice, and an avalanche of petty and conventional talent overwhelmed the spontaneous creative power of the greater men. In about the year AD 120, however, there was a happy change for the better, and the glory of Rome was uplifted in poetry by the epic furies of Juvenal and in prose by the genius – the most pictorial and the most modern of antiquity – of Tacitus.

In the sphere of morals it would be a mistake to take the epigrams and satires of the time literally. They show us the wrong side of the tapestry in a distorting mirror. The structure of society still held firm, and the level of morals was such that their bitterest censors were best-sellers. Naturally there were in Rome gangsters and spivs, gluttons and drunkards, pimps and debauchees, pederasts and lesbians. But the Romans of the old school tried to believe that these unfortunate specimens of humanity were usually of exotic origin, and the indignation they directed against them testifies as much to their innate decency as to their xenophobia. In fact, Stoic austerity had never more adherents than at this time. Not so long before, under the Flavians, it had been persecuted; now it was admitted both privately and publicly in court. The opposition had been converted into its supporters. Trajan used the homilies of Dio of Prusa both to oppose sedition among his legions and to support his own bold agrarian policy. According to the *Historia Augusta*, Hadrian enjoyed the conversations of Epictetus. Finally Marcus Aurelius, himself an adept, preached the Stoic doctrine; and the alliance with his dynasty of a school of philosophy of which he had become the propagandist explains both the ascendancy of the Antonines over their contemporaries and their prestige in history.

Religion's new spontaneous force

At the same time as this lofty philosophy was fashionable a new religious fervour did much to uplift men's hearts and minds. The devout were no longer satisfied with abstract deities, mechanically performed rituals, and fossilized creeds. They tried to introduce into the state religion the aspirations of their spiritual life, the spontaneity of their private prayers, and the force of their hopes of an after-life; and when their attempts failed they turned away from the dry formalism of the official cults and sought spiritual food elsewhere. Most of them were initiated into the Oriental mysteries which, for all their irregular and orgiastic side, were not lacking in spirituality; they became the devotees of gods who were not local and impassive, but divinities of universal power, undergoing suffering and rebirth, jealous and protecting, capable of balancing the merits of a man in this world against the rewards due to him in the world to come. Already a few of them lent ear to the evangel that reached them, in Greek, from Aramaic Palestine: the gospel that had circulated freely in Rome ever since Trajan, initiating a rule of religious toleration that was to survive until the end of the century, had forbidden the persecution of the followers of Christ and declared he wished only to punish those who offered them provocation. The Church of Christ the Saviour, the Son of the Only God, was thenceforward established in the city. The catacombs where the Christians honoured their dead, the halls in private houses where they celebrated their Eucharists, were filled with unheard-of promises of peace and love; and a Christianity hardly yet born illumined the golden age of Rome with its dayspring.

Only a century later the Romans saw their property ravaged, their creations ruined, and the evils which they had thought to have suppressed forever once more coming to life: *coups d'état*, insurrections, secessions, plagues, famines, defeats in the east, invasions in the west. Their material advantages were born of effort, and they had allowed themselves to relax. The moral progress that at first had accompanied these advantages had lost its highest inspiration. They no longer possessed that spirit of abnegation and that collective will to action without which societies, numbed into an insidious inaction, and states, undermined by widespread selfishness, are disarmed by the fear of making sacrifices. Soon, for all their brilliant appearance, they become no more than majestic idols with feet of clay.

CHANGAN

A vanished capital of China,
on the site of modern Sian, was perhaps the greatest city in the world from the seventh to tenth centuries AD. Like Constantinople – its only contemporary rival for that distinction – Changan was a thriving imperial centre of commerce, administration, religion and cultural splendour. The new capital rose, beginning in 582, in a fertile plain with strategic advantages of armed defence, where the capital of the ancient Han dynasty had once stood.

Between AD 220, when the Han disintegrated, and the founding of the Sui dynasty in 581, China had been disunited under a succession of short-lived dynasties. The first Sui Emperor set about subduing rival powers and uniting China under one rule; his new capital, with its deliberate reference back to Han glory, was planned to symbolize the country's reunification. Wen Ti, the founder of the Sui dynasty (ruled 581–604), is shown opposite, flanked by two courtiers, in a detail from the *Portraits of the Emperors*, a scroll painted

on silk and attributed to the artist Yen Li-pên (d. 673). Wen Ti entered his capital, while it was still only a skeleton of what it was to become, in April 583.

The great development of Changan took place under the Sui's successors, the T'ang dynasty, who ruled from 618 to 906 – the golden age of China; and at the height of its power there was a population of one million within the city walls, with another million around it. Residing in the cosmopolitan city were courtiers, prosperous merchants, foreign traders, soldiers, artists, entertainers, priests of many faiths and a numerous bureaucracy.

Beginning in 775, the T'ang suffered reverses at the hands of rebellious war-lords, Tibetans and Turkish tribes; and the power of the dynasty began to ebb. The end came in the first decade of the tenth century when the T'ang finally lost even the semblance of power. The dynasty fell and the capital city was abandoned. (1)

During the period of T'ang power, China experienced an impressive flowering in architecture, painting, sculpture and the design of fine glazed pottery. The founder of the T'ang, though he was in fact the second Emperor of the dynasty, was T'ai Tsung (ruled 626–49). This deep relief panel (above) at the tomb built for T'ai Tsung in 637 shows the Emperor's saffron yellow charger and a groom. The pottery figures of a camel (right) and bullock cart (opposite left) represent two forms of Chinese transport and commerce. The camel was used for domestic transport as well as for the trading caravans between Changan and the West. The merchant holding a wine-skin vessel (opposite right), a West Asiatic type with his beak nose and beard, would have been a familiar figure in the Changan market. (2–5)

Among tomb figures found in Changan are this Persian (above), a type that might have been seen anywhere in the capital, but most often in the West City and the vicinity of the West Market. The seated woman (above centre) may have been a court lady. The T'ang official (above right) would have been one of Changan's many bureaucrats, possibly a member of the Emperor's retinue. (6–8)

Pageantry in religious life is illustrated in these paintings of a Buddhist deity in a chariot, with attendants dressed as officials (below left), and a high dignitary – probably one of the donors – visiting a Buddhist shrine (below right). (9, 10)

The religions of T'ang China included Confucianism and Taoism, apart from Buddhism, which came to China from India and became the most popular of all faiths. Evidence has also been found in Changan of a Nestorian Christian population in that city. The stone image (above) is of a Taoist god, T'ien Tsun; it comes from Sian and is dated AD 709. (11)

Ancient precepts on the planning of capital cities were based on a cosmology which pervaded many other aspects of Chinese life, among them religion, magic, art and this T'ang dynasty magic mirror back (right). The compass was invented in China, and mirror backs, especially the early ones of the Han dynasty, were often just simple forms of the customary design on a compass dial. In the Chinese scheme one faces south (not north, as Westerners do), since that is the most beneficial quarter; hence south is at the top of the mirror. (14)

Luxury items of intricate grace and beauty were to be found in the great houses of T'ang Changan. On the jade comb-top (below) are carved a dancer with musicians. The cup (below centre) is silver-gilt and extremely sophisticated in its shape, handle and engraved decoration. The ewer (below right) bespeaks the many cultural influences on T'ang pottery: Sassanian Persian in shape, Hellenistic in decoration, and Indian in the figure wearing a dhoti. (15, 16, 17)

The great temples and pagodas that were once the pride of Changan are almost entirely destroyed. This construction scene (above left) is from a copy of a cave wall-painting; the frame of the building is wood, the base is faced with mud brick, and the roof is tiled. Bricks were occasionally used in the construction of religious buildings, such as the Wild Goose Pagoda (above right), one of the two structures that remain from T'ang Changan. This pagoda was begun in 652, at the instigation of the Chinese Buddhist pilgrim Hsüan-tsang who spent some years in India and translated the Sutras. Though several times extensively restored, the building is considered to be close to the T'ang original. (12, 13)

Changan
Forbidden Park
Ta Ming Palace
Palace City
Administrative City
Hing-Ching Palace
West Market
East Market
Serpentine Park

CHANGAN

ARTHUR F. WRIGHT

SEVENTEEN YEARS after the death of Justinian in his splendid capital on the Bosphorus, plans were being made at the other end of Eurasia for a city which for the next three centuries was to be a magnificent centre of power and of culture. This was Changan, founded by the short-lived Sui dynasty (581–617) and developed as its capital by the great T'ang (618–906). During these centuries Changan was perhaps the world's greatest city – the political hub of a vast empire, the epicentre of Chinese civilization in an age of brilliant creativity, a cosmopolis which attracted merchants and travellers from distant lands, a model for the city-builders of neighbouring states.

A site famed in history

The site of the city was an alluvial plain some 1,400 feet in altitude located near the western borders of the ancient Chinese culture area. The plain, known in history as Kuanchung, was surrounded by mountains and hills and was watered by the Wei River, which flowed eastward to join the Yellow River at its great bend. Fertile and easily defended, the Kuanchung plain was dotted with monuments to its great role in China's history. Here were the tombs of the Chou kings who, in the eleventh century BC, had led their armies eastward to overwhelm the Shang kingdom and found a new political order. Here was the awesome tumulus of the man who had forcibly unified the Chinese culture area and proclaimed himself First Sovereign Emperor. And here was the city that had served as the first capital of the great Han (206 BC–AD 220), the dynasty that shaped the imperial institutions and extended its power through all of eastern Asia.

The founder of the Sui dynasty, who rose to power in this plain, was aware of its strategic advantages and of its symbolic links with a glorious past. But herculean efforts were required before a capital in this plain would once again dominate China and its neighbouring peoples. After the collapse of the Han empire, China had entered upon a long period of political partition and far-reaching cultural change. Non-Chinese peoples had controlled the north – the heartland of Chinese civilization – while weak Chinese dynasties succeeded one another in control of the Yangtze valley and its meagrely developed hinterland. In north and south, different political orders had developed; Buddhism had everywhere transformed the life of people of all classes and races; varied sub-cultures and sub-societies had proliferated. For three and a half centuries, in north and south alike, leaders had talked of the restoration of a unified empire, but all their plans and campaigns had come to naught. The Sui founder and the ambitious men around him proposed to succeed where others had failed. The first of their tasks was the consolidation of their hold on north China; the second was the conquest of the 'legitimate' Chinese dynasty in the south, the third was the long and arduous work of reintegrating vast areas that had long evolved along divergent lines.

The mood of these men – their high hopes and vast plans – is reflected in their decision to build a new capital at a moment when their hold on north China was not yet consolidated. Little more than a year after the establishment of the Sui dynasty, the emperor and his advisers began discussing the building of a new capital. It was

argued that the old Han city – repeatedly sacked and burned in the centuries of disunion – was cramped and depressing, that its water-supply was foul, and that it was haunted by the ghosts of murdered men. The decision was for a new capital, and in the summer of 582 commissions were appointed for planning and construction. Work was pushed through with masses of forced labour, and building was far enough advanced for the emperor to ride into his new capital on 15 April 583. Much further building and embellishment was to be done before the city attained its full grandeur, but later monarchs made only minor changes in the basic plan developed by the Sui. This plan marked a watershed in the history of Chinese city-planning; the outline of the plan and the provenance of some of its features will suggest the balance that was struck between tradition and innovation.

The planning of the city

The outer walls of the city formed a rectangle which ran 5.92 miles east and west and 5.27 miles north and south. The walls were made of pounded earth faced with sun-dried bricks; they were probably about 18 feet high, and were from 15 to 30 feet thick at the base. The walls thickened near the openings of the eleven outer gates, each of which was eventually surmounted by a watch-tower. The usual gate had three ports, but the main gate of the city – the 'Gate of Brilliant Virtue', centred in the south wall – was some 150 feet broad and had five ports. The area within these walls was divided into three precincts. The outer city was divided by eleven north–south and fourteen east–west avenues into 106 wards and two markets. Each of these units was walled, and the wards generally had four gates giving on to the broad tree-lined avenues. An east–west and a north–south street divided most of the wards into four sections. Lanes and alleys provided additional access to houses, shops or temples within the wards. The administrative city (*huang-ch'eng*) was set off from the outer city by walls through which gates opened on to seven north–south and five east–west streets. Along these streets were ranged the bureaux of the central government, store-houses, barracks and other official buildings. To the north of this was the walled enclosure of the palace city whose imposing south gate led into the forecourt of the great audience hall known as the 'Hall of the Supreme Ultimate' (*T'ai-chi tien*). To the north of the ceremonial buildings was a complex of audience halls, palaces and pavilions for the use of the imperial family and its entourage. North of this and beyond the north wall of the palace – which was also the outer city wall – was a large park-like area dotted with orchards, gardens, lakes and pavilions and containing some surviving buildings of the earlier Han capital; this was reserved for the pleasure of the court and was known as the 'Forbidden Park' (*Chin-yüan*).

The men who planned this city drew ideas and inspiration from two main sources: the canons and traditions of Chinese city-building, and their experience with the cities of north China built in the period of disunion by various non-Chinese dynasties. The Sui founder and his empress were of mixed descent, and so were all the key-figures in the planning and construction of the city. Some were descended from fairly recent immigrants from central Asia; one had a Zoroastrian personal name. All had come to maturity in the polyglot society of north China. With such a background and in the expansive mood of the moment, they felt free to innovate and to take only what they pleased from ancient Chinese prescriptions and practices. Let us note some features of the city plan that reflect the two sources of its architects' ideas.

The scale of the city was itself unprecedented, for the capitals of even the most prosperous earlier dynasties had not been planned to cover such a large area. This would seem to be a reflection of the expansive plans of the Sui dynasty's founder and his advisers. They were determined to build an empire that would be more extensive and more centralized than any of their predecessors' dominions. On the other hand, the orientation of the city to the four points of the compass (with great exactness, according to recent archaeological evidence) is prescribed in the earliest Chinese writings on capital-planning. So too is the grid street plan, with the principal avenues determining the location of the outer gates. Earlier cities, too, had been divided into wards, but the new city carried this system to a new level of symmetry and rationality. Ancient texts had prescribed a separate quarter for commerce, but had prescribed for it a location 'behind (i.e., north of) the prince's palace'. In Changan the markets were indeed separate but were located pragmatically where they could best serve the needs of the city's population. In earlier cities, government bureaux had been scattered, as they are in Paris, throughout the city. In this new capital they were concentrated in the administrative city adjoining the palace city. This appears to be a Sui innovation based perhaps on the planners' observation of the most highly developed previous capital, that of the northern Wei at Loyang. Residential wards in Changan lay in the U-shaped outer city, whereas canonical prescription allowed them only to the east and the west of the prince's palace. Here again the planners had probably based themselves on observations of recent northern capitals where the area south of the power-centre had naturally developed – in defiance of the canons – as a prime residential district. Although the altar of Earth and the imperial ancestral temple were located canonically to the west and to the east of the central north–south axis, there was nothing in the canon to provide for the official metropolitan temples of the two great religions which had come, during the period of disunion, to command the loyalties of millions: Buddhism and religious Taoism. The Sui planners placed these centres to the east and to the west of the central north–south avenue that bisected the outer city. These illustrations may serve to show the pragmatic, eclectic and innovative spirit which governed the planning of the city.

The hub of empire

When the Sui dynasty's founder moved into his new capital in 583, it was little more than the skeleton of a city. Open fields filled much of the area within the hurriedly built walls. More than a century was to pass before the city became in fact the brilliant and prosperous pivot of a great empire, the centre of a new social and political order. The rise of the city was intimately linked, first with the military and political success of its masters, and second with the successive building of institutions that centred in the capital of the new imperial order.

The founder succeeded in 589 in crushing the last of the Chinese dynasties in the south. This was followed by the establishment of a structure of provincial and county administration staffed and controlled from the capital. The staffing of a centralized bureaucracy on a larger scale than that of the long-vanished Han required sweeping innovations. The founder had initially to depend for his officialdom on established families of the north-western area. He soon took the first steps to organize an empire-wide system of recruitment by examination. Under his son, this effectively brought into government service more and more people from the eastern plains and from the increasingly populous south. The T'ang continued and developed the system. Thus the élite of the capital came to be drawn from all the provinces of the empire; the capital was the focus of ambition for the sons of upper-class families everywhere, for it was the place where the highest civil service examinations were held and the political arena in which the successful candidates would struggle for power and preferment.

The success of such a system of centralized power depended on the development of a network of routes that would provide easy communication between the capital and provincial centres and at the same time ensure a steady flow of tax-goods from the provinces to the capital. The Sui first built a canal running parallel to the Wei River (which was navigable only seasonally) to facilitate access to the north China plain. Then, under the second Sui emperor, various old waterways were reconstructed and linked together by the first of the grand canals. This crossed the rich plains watered by the Yellow and Huai Rivers, then the Yangtze at Yangchow, whence it led south to the head of Hangchow bay. A second canal, connected with this system at Loyang, led north to the strategically important area of the modern Peking. The T'ang dynasty inherited this system and worked steadily to improve it. Granaries for tax-grain were built; the administration and handling of grain-shipments were improved; and repeated efforts were made to solve the problem of the San Men rapids of the Yellow River – the most hazardous and costly link in the system.

The canals were supplemented by a system of imperial roads that radiated from the capital. Along these roads, as they passed through mountains and valleys and across innumerable rivers by ferry, ford and bridge, were post stations and inns for official travellers, and private hostelries for merchants or for pilgrims on their way to one of the holy places of Buddhism or Taoism. On the roads to the capital one might also see tribute-bearing missions from satellite states – a line of carts and bearers or a camel-train laden with presents for the Son of Heaven. Changan at its height was thus the hub of two complementary communication-systems by which the capital made its power felt in the provinces and drew in the taxes and tribute of the empire. More than this, the two systems radiated out to the terminal points of the sea-routes and caravan-routes that linked China to the rest of the world. From thriving ports and bustling landward entrepôts, T'ang China drew in the world's ideas and products. It was this that made Changan a great cosmopolis.

The empire and its capital were sustained by a complex system of taxes, state monopolies, and forced-labour imposts. Although much of the tax-income was used by local officials for local purposes, the proportion of taxes in grain and cloth transported to and disbursed from the capital was high indeed. One estimate for the prosperous period 742–56 indicates that close to forty per cent of an annual grain-revenue of 25,000,000 bushels (shih), and forty-eight per cent of an annual textile-revenue of 27,000,000 units, were disbursed by the Department of Public Revenue in Changan. Tax-income paid out in official salaries, gifts, military pay and wages was the economic life-blood of the capital. To this was added the income which wealthy families living in the capital drew from their landed estates. Changan was indeed what Max Weber called a 'consumer city'. It prospered when state revenues were abundant and well administered; it languished when war or maladministration reduced those revenues.

While the T'ang dynasty was perfecting the institutions of government, and as the systems of recruitment, administration, communication and taxation took shape, the city attracted an ever-growing official population. And the power and wealth of officialdom, plus a more and more elaborate court, in turn drew in vast numbers of merchants, clerks, artisans, clerics and labourers to service the needs of the élite. By the eighth century, Changan had a population of a million within the walls, with perhaps another million in the metropolitan area. At times, population-growth had outpaced improvements in the supply system, and during much of the seventh century – despite frequent bumper harvests in the irrigated Kuanchung plain – court and officialdom were obliged by shortages to move for long periods to the eastern capital at Loyang. Early in the eighth century these problems were solved, and Changan entered on the period of its greatest prosperity. Let us consider some aspects of the progressive development and embellishment of the city in its rise to greatness.

Builder and buildings

One of the most colourful features of Changan was provided by the temples and pagodas of the dominant religion of Buddhism. Temple-building had begun in Sui times, with the encouragement and patronage of the emperors. By 722 there were, in Changan, ninety-one Buddhist establishments, some of them occupying all or most of a ward; at the same time there were sixteen establishments of religious Taoism, two Nestorian Christian and four Zoroastrian temples. The numbers increased in the prosperous decades that followed. Buddhist temple-buildings were typically laid out in a series of interconnected courtyards, with tile-roofed galleries running along the inside of the courtyard walls. The main halls of worship, tile-roofed, brightly painted and housing a central image of a Buddha or Buddhist saint, were often of great magnificence. Near by were other buildings: bell-towers, libraries of sacred books, meditation halls, private chapels, dormitories and refectories for the monks or nuns. From the street one might glimpse the brightly painted roof-structure and tiled roofs of the main buildings, but what most attracted the eye were the pagoda reliquaries – some of them of great height – with multiple roofs topped by gilded metal finials. Here is a contemporary description of a temple that evokes the colour and splendour of Buddhist architecture:

Here were dragon purlins indeed, spanning the empty void, here rainbow girders crossing and returning again. Here were red pillars to outdazzle the Sun, and green jade pendants lengthening to the breeze. Though it was not spring, yet were there flowers opening out in the coffers; though it was not night, yet the piled-up eaves were shrouded as if in mist ... The marvels of sculptured ridge and painted brackets exhausted Creation's patterns ...

The notables of the Sui and early T'ang generally lived in rather modest dwellings. But as the power and prosperity of the T'ang increased, the great officials, landed aristocrats and imperial kinsmen began building mansions of ever-increasing splendour in the capital. Lavish courtyards were set in fantastically landscaped grounds containing pleasure pavilions, ball-fields and ornamental lakes. One

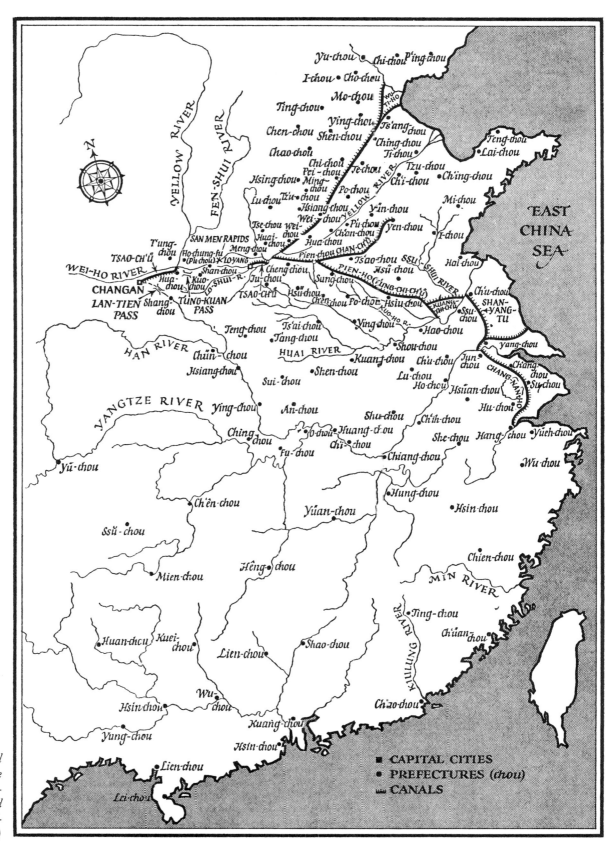

Map of T'ang China, showing the canal system, the capital city Changan, the former capital Loyang, and the important administrative centres. (Adapted from D. C. Twitchett, 'Financial Administration under the T'ang Dynasty'.)

great minister had a household staff of three thousand, and the wealth flowing from the establishment is said to have enriched all the residents of the ward. Competition in embellishing and furnishing their houses and gardens – in 'conspicuous consumption', in fact – was characteristic of the life of the T'ang élite. We read of doors and windows ornamented with semi-precious stones, of gilded or) golden) door-fittings, of carved marble balustrades, of the use of rare woods and the building of fanciful towers and terraces. One high official built a 'self-raining pavilion' air-conditioned by fountains playing on its roof; a contemporary remarked that on hot summer days it was as cool inside as a day in autumn. The mansion-building of the great became so lavish that 'the lower classes were roused to much discontent' and sumptuary decrees had to be issued restricting the scale and ornamentation of private mansions. The lower classes, we might add, lived crowded together in one-storey houses which were mostly concentrated in the western, particularly the south-western, section of the outer city.

The greatest builders in the history of Changan were of course the emperors, and we should mention some of their projects. The greatest of these was the Ta-ming palace complex on 'Dragon's Head Rise', north of the city wall. It had been begun modestly in 634 as a summer retreat. A subsequent emperor decided to build on a larger scale. To finance the construction, he pre-empted one month's salary from all imperial officials and took over the tax-revenues of fifteen prefectures. Recent archaeology provides abundant detail on the layout of this palace. Its outer walls were some four and three quarter miles in circumference. A splendid approach to its great main gate was carved out of residential wards in the north-east city. Within the palace walls were two lakes fed by stone-lined watercourses. There were three rows of sumptuous palace buildings. Adjoining these were other buildings for work and pleasure: administrative offices, guards' headquarters, storehouses, an archery hall, pleasure pavilions set in their own parks. One of the great halls, where an imperial feast was once served to two hundred guests, has been excavated. Its pounded earth foundations measure approximately 425 by 235 feet, and its high roof-structure was supported by seventeen rows of huge columns running north and south and ten running east and west. The great Ta-ming palace complex, when completed, replaced the palace city as the regular residence of the imperial family and the centre of government.

A third major palace was developed in the eastern part of the outer city by the Emperor Hsüan-tsung, who came to the throne in 713. This was the Hsing-ch'ing Palace. The palace compound first took in an entire ward and gradually was extended to take in parts of four other wards and a corner of the East Market; the palace had a park-like atmosphere, complete with an ornamental lake, and it was less formal than the other palaces. The location of the new palace in a residential and business district created problems, for a Son of Heaven could not move about freely on public ways. The solution was to build a raised covered road inside and running parallel to the east wall of the city. It first connected the Ta-ming Palace with the new Hsing-ch'ing Palace. Later it was extended south, so that Hsüan-tsung could visit the lovely park and Serpentine Lake at the south-east corner of the city – Changan's most renowned beauty spot.

The history of the building of Changan calls attention to certain characteristics of its architecture and its culture. The standard building consisted of a complex of wooden columns supporting an elaborate network of brackets, beams and rafters, which in turn supported the tile roof. The columns, often with stone or bronze pediments, generally rested on a pounded earth base (often paved and faced with tile or stone), and the walls were not bearing but 'filler' walls – usually of plastered brick. Such buildings could be, and often were, moved; the wooden portions of an old building were frequently re-used for new structures. These buildings could be built in a short time (one emperor ordered a reception-hall to be built for a favourite minister, and it was completed in five days); but they required frequent repairs and were also easily destroyed by fire. All these things give to the architecture of Changan an ephemeral quality. Except for masonry pagodas there were few 'historic' buildings that survived more than a century. Houses lived in by the same family for more than three generations were unusual. Ancestral halls and memorial temples remained only so long as the interested families

continued to be wealthy and powerful; when they ceased to be, the buildings were converted to other uses or razed to make way for a new building. Chinese anthropocentrism did not encourage building for the ages or for eternity, and Buddhism – with its illusionist strain – perhaps reinforced this disposition. One should also note that no buildings in Changan were built from what we call 'civic pride'. Building and rebuilding were first of all at the initiative of the imperial family, which commanded the resources and could confiscate and reallocate property at will. Secondly, building projects were acts of piety: the construction or embellishment of a Buddhist or Taoist temple or, less universally, the building of an ancestral hall. Officials in their public role would frequently petition for funds to build or remodel a particular bureau or to dig a canal. But they argued for these projects in terms of improving the efficiency of imperial administration, not in terms of civic pride or 'civic improvement'. Although we read much of the parks and pleasances of the great, of their ball-fields and archery halls, there is no mention of any such facilities for the populace. Philanthropy expressed itself through the Buddhist temples with their charitable functions, but the 'bread and circuses' of Rome and Constantinople are not to be found. Nor is there anything comparable to the forums, public baths and arcades built by the Roman emperors for the pleasure and convenience of the citizenry.

The emperor's heavy hand

The residents of the city were not 'citizens' but the emperor's subjects. This is reflected in the layout of the city, in its administration and in its functioning. The city was administered by two separate county governments, with the great north–south street dividing their jurisdictions. Above these was a high-ranking metropolitan governor. There was neither mayor nor city council, and there was no charter. The city and its populace were controlled by the throne through officials of the imperial bureaucracy. During much of the T'ang period, the regulation of city life was severe. No one was allowed to have a house facing one of the main avenues (variances were ultimately granted to those of high rank); the ward gates were closed at sundown, and no one was allowed out on the avenues until the official drums were beaten at dawn the next day. Mounted soldiers patrolled the streets and called out the watches of the night. The law ordained that any commoner who crossed the wall of a ward, market or official compound without authorization was to be punished with seventy lashes. The east and west markets were also strictly controlled; their gates were opened at noon, closed at sundown. Imperial market-officials supervised trade and prices; when grain was in short supply and the price rose, the government moved grain supplies into the market. Merchants in the same trades were grouped into gilds to facilitate government control.

Religious life and the temples of all the faiths were strictly controlled by imperial bureaus. Wine-shops were officially licensed, pawnshops and brothels were under government supervision; hospitals and free dispensaries were contracted by the state to the Buddhist clergy; the monks received a bonus if less than twenty per cent of their patients died. Defence and the policing of the city were the duty of the metropolitan troops and the imperial guards. The average number of military personnel in the city was about 100,000, and we have records of the usual conflicts between the soldiers and the civilian population, some of which were adjudicated by the emperor himself. One might quote any one of thousands of ordinances to show the direct, paternalistic and pervasive control of the city by the state. Here is one by way of illustration – an edict of the summer of 731:

> The two capitals of Changan and Loyang are pre-eminently the Mansions of the Emperor; the streets and thoroughfares, the wards and markets must be kept in good repair. Within the city walls it is forbidden to excavate kilns and to fire bricks and tiles. When public or private construction is going on, it is forbidden to dig holes in the streets or lanes to remove earth.

The necessity for countless orders of this kind, and much other evidence, suggests that the bustling life of the city was never fully controlled by the state apparatus, omnipresent though this was. Creative energies, economic enterprise, religious zeal, the pursuit of pleasure, the drive for wealth and power, love of beauty and luxury combined to give the city its great colour and vitality. Let us turn to some features of the life of the city in its days of prosperity. We shall concentrate on the period from 700 to 750, but drawing illustrations, when necessary, from other periods. We shall begin from the top of the power pyramid – the emperor and his court – and proceed to the city's élite and then to other groups.

The life of the emperor and his entourage was shaped by three simultaneous cycles of activity: ceremonial duties, political-administrative obligations, the pursuit of pleasure. These cycles, though centred in the palaces, governed the life of the capital's élite and gave both colour and rhythm to the general life of the city. The T'ang emperors inherited the ideology of Chinese kingship and, with it, the great complex of rituals which symbolized the many roles of the Son of Heaven: cosmic pivot, first farmer of an agricultural empire, ceremonial head of the ruling house, guardian and exemplar of the state ideology of Confucianism. By T'ang times he was also expected to be patron and devotee of the popular religions of Buddhism and Taoism.

Imperial ceremonies marked each phase of the agricultural year. State ritualists, guided by ancient codes and precedents, planned these observances in meticulous detail, for ill-timed or unorthodox rites might impair the balance that the Son of Heaven was to maintain between the forces of nature and the world of men. One of the most important of these many ceremonies was that which occurred in the first lunar month and symbolized the opening of the agricultural year. Long before dawn on the appointed day the emperor – having prepared himself by a period of abstinence – left his palace in a special six-horse chariot, on which was mounted a ceremonial plough. Accompanied by soldiers, guards and a numerous retinue, he moved in stately procession to a ceremonial area outside the south wall of the city. There, assisted by ranking nobles, officials from the office of agriculture, by musicians, ritualists and other functionaries, he solemnly took the plough and proceeded to cultivate a furrow to signal the opening of the new season. He was followed by other dignitaries who took their turns at the plough. At the close of the solemn ceremony, the emperor would often take further steps to symbolize the harmonious concord that he desired for the land and the people. Often he would proclaim an empire-wide amnesty, sometimes confer gifts upon his officials and sometimes change the era-name to suggest the opening of a new and auspicious period of his reign. The emperors' ceremonial duties were numerous and heavy. Some could be assigned to the crown prince or other members of the ruling house. The empresses had their part in the cycle of observances symbolizing the close links between the dynasty and the crops that supported the empire; they officiated at ceremonies, usually in the third lunar month, to the primordial silkworm – rituals carried out at a special altar in the Forbidden Park north of the main city-wall.

As head of the imperial clan, the emperor participated in another cycle of ceremonies. Among the more important of these were funerals and burial rites for the imperial dead, usually in the 'Hall of the Two Forces' (Liang-i Tien) in the palace city; solemn memorial services for the clan's honoured dead in the imperial ancestral hall (T'ai-miao); and burials and visits of commemoration at the imperial tombs scattered widely through the mountains across the Wei River. The emperors took a leading part in the ceremonies surrounding the elevation or coming of age of a crown prince, the marriages of the imperial princesses, and the ceremonies celebrating the conferment of new ranks and titles on imperial kinsmen, both living and dead. The birthday of the reigning emperor was often marked by an official holiday, by the ceremonial presentation of congratulatory messages and gifts (to which the emperor would respond with appropriate munificence), and by a great reception for ranking officials, sometimes in one of the palaces, sometimes in the Serpentine Park at the south-east corner of the city.

Buddhism, as the dominant religion of the capital and the empire, made its ceremonial demands upon the emperors. Some emperors were devout Buddhists, and the first Sui emperor and his empress held daily services at the palace, which they required their courtiers to attend. T'ang emperors, whether Buddhist or inclined towards Taoism, were obliged to symbolize in rituals their patronage of the dominant faith. There were masses ordered for the welfare of the realm and the ruling house, ceremonies for the presentation of im-

perially written name-plaques to new temples, and dedication ceremonies for a new temple or reliquary; also imperially sponsored services, lecture series and vegetarian feasts – sometimes for clergy and laity alike – in the temples of the capital. Buddhist monks held memorial services for past emperors and empresses on the official anniversaries of their deaths. These ceremonies at officially designated temples were usually followed by a vegetarian feast for the clergy, often numbering several thousand and drawn from many temples. On these occasions, Taoist monks and nuns participated along with the Buddhist clergy. The celebration of the emperor's birthday was often marked by Buddhist as well as secular observances. Emperors would invite the Buddhist and Taoist clergy to a vegetarian feast in one of the great halls of the Ta-ming Palace and would order representatives of the two orders to hold doctrinal disputations. Here is a description of an imperial birthday ceremony held in 675 in the monumental Lin-te Hall of the Ta-ming Palace:

> The emperor set up a place of worship in the Triple Hall. He had members of the palace-staff play the part of Bodhisattva images, and ornamented them with precious things. Soldiers from the north gate of the palace took the part of the mighty Guardian Kings. Bedecked in multi-coloured robes, wearing armour and holding lances, they stood impressively at attention at the corners of the throne. There was burning of incense and chanting of hymns of praise. The great ministers and the attendant officials formed a surrounding circle as they made their obeisances. Then the maigre feast was served and music was played ...

The administrative-political cycle of imperial activities brought all the problems of a vast empire to the attention of the Son of Heaven for his decisions. Here too the weight of traditional pomp, of ritual procedures and taboos, was considerable. One of the regular features of this cycle was the great audience customarily held on the first and fifteenth of the lunar month. Well before dawn the ministers and ranking civil and military officers began arriving on horseback or in palanquins outside the great south gate of the Ta-ming Palace. Each wore the robes and insignia appropriate to his rank and was accompanied by his allotted number of attendants. When the clepsydra's bell chimed, the gates swung open, and all filed in to their appropriate places in the court and audience chamber of the Hsüan-cheng Hall. When all were in their places and the guards of honour, recorders, and chamberlains had taken their assigned positions, the emperor entered from the side of the hall and crossed to his throne. Newly appointed officials were presented to the throne. Policy matters were presented orally by the appropriate officials for discussion and for imperial decision. When the audience ended, the officials withdrew to their various bureaux, and the organs charged with drafting edicts and other state papers began their work. More restricted dawn audiences were held almost daily, and these were supplemented by less formal 'discussions of state affairs', at which the emperor sometimes met with his high-ranking ministers. The atmosphere of a regular imperial audience in one of the halls of the Ta-ming Palace is evoked in this poem by Tu Fu dating from 758:

> Outside the inner doors, the two court ladies with flowing
>   purple sleeves
> Now turn to the throne to lead the procession from the
>   audience chamber
> The spring wind blows the swirling smoke of incense
>   in the hall
> The sunlight plays across the dazzling robes of the
>   thousand officials
> We hear the striking of the hour from the clepsydra
>   in the high tower
> As a servitor standing near, I note that the Heavenly
>   Countenance is joyful ...

The audiences were but a small part of the administrative and political activities of the emperor. He gave frequent feasts to ranking officials and in honour of tribute-missions from the satellite states; these were customarily held in one of the great halls of the Ta-ming Palace. In wartime, besides taking part in strategy conferences and the issuing of orders and commissions, the emperor sometimes joined in the ceremonies reporting victories held in the imperial ancestral hall, or came to one of the gates of the Ta-ming Palace to acknowledge the presentation of war-captives by his military leaders.

In war and peace the volume of documents that the emperor had to deal with was staggering. To handle this flow of paper, well-staffed offices and personal secretariats were established within the palace walls, and some of these functioned around the clock. Eunuchs in the emperor's personal service busied themselves with administrative affairs (in spite of the continuous protests of officialdom) and in the management of the palaces, the harems, the privy treasury, etc.

The Son of Heaven commanded vast resources for his pleasure and the pleasure of the imperial family and court. The imperial harem was filled with beautiful and accomplished women, imperial academies for music and drama supplied skilled entertainers, the imperial stud had the finest horses in Asia, which the emperor might use for pleasure riding, hunting or polo. The ball-fields and archery halls in the palace precincts were well kept and well staffed, and the vast lands of the Forbidden Park were available for picnics, boating expeditions on artificial lakes and seasonal outings which sometimes included a sentimental visit to the ruins of the Han palaces. The more literate emperors enjoyed their poetry meetings with the great T'ang poets, who were usually officials. Those with artistic or architectural interests could commission at will new buildings, new gardens, new wall-paintings, and could surround themselves with rare objects from the whole world.

The tasks and fortunes of officialdom

The life of the capital's élite was keyed to the rhythm of imperial activities. For many, attendance at audiences was obligatory, and the pre-dawn journey in bad weather through streets thick with mud was wearisome indeed. The poet-official Po Chü-i evokes this for us:

> At Ch'ang-an – a full foot of snow;
> A levee at dawn – to bestow congratulations on the Emperor.
> Just as I was nearing the Gate of the Silver Terrace,
> After I had left the suburb of Hsin-ch'ang
> On the high causeway my horse's foot slipped;
> In the middle of the journey my lantern suddenly went out.
> Ten leagues riding, always facing to the North;
> The cold wind almost blew off my ears.
> I waited for the bell outside the Five Gates;
> I waited for the summons within the Triple Hall.
> My hair and beard were frozen and covered with icicles;
> My coat and robe – chilly like water ...

Whatever the discomfort, it was as well to appear, for those who failed to attend without an approved excuse could be docked a month's pay, be demoted, or – worst of all – might incur His Majesty's displeasure. Of those who attended the audience, some went on to spend a working day in their offices, while others returned to their homes. In some offices time off was equal to time worked, so that ranking officials would put in seventy-two hours on duty and then have a like period off. Lesser officials worked 240 hours over the course of a lunar month and then had a month off. In these cases, officials on duty slept and had their meals at their offices. The T'ang calendar was generous in official holidays, which were sometimes as many as fifty-three a year. Government officials were also granted leaves with pay for family events, plus two fifteen-day holidays a year.

Surviving collections of documents testify to the volume of paper-work that was the daily lot of the capital's official élite. Proposals generated at the local or provincial level or in one of the six principal boards moved up, through approved channels, to be reviewed by higher officials, who then rejected them, returned them for redrafting or ordered them to be prepared for imperial attention. If action was favourable, then the appropriate boards would draft the implementing decrees to be issued in the emperor's name and to be despatched by courier to provincial or local governments. Religious and ceremonial decrees, amnesty proclamations, documents enfeoffing tributary rulers, treaties, judicial decrees, orders of appointment, promotion or demotion – these are but a sample of the flood of paper which the official élite of the capital had to deal with.

If routine bureaucratic operations consumed much of their time and energies, it was the political arena that absorbed their attention. Who was rising in imperial favour? How long would the old chief minister last, and who would succeed him? Would the so-and-so clique survive the disgrace of their leader? Would the in-coming

group reverse the policies of their predecessors? The ebb and flow of power was dramatized in the streets and wards of the capital. Once proud and wealthy families would be dispossessed, and their survivors would be seen weeping in the streets and carrying a few treasures as they were turned out of their houses. Or one might see a procession of officials and eunuchs escorting some rising political figure to a new mansion, perhaps conferred upon him by the emperor himself. Then would come a display of imperial gifts – fine textiles, silver vessels – with musicians from the imperial academy coming to play for the house-warming banquet. Even more colourful was the marriage of an imperial princess to the son of an official family. Elaborate and costly ceremonies were invariably followed by the installation of the newly-weds in a mansion – perhaps recently confiscated – newly refurbished and stocked with valuable furniture. The families which flourished by official success, by fortunate marriages and by alliances with rising power-groups were a source of pride in the streets and lanes around their mansions. Imperial messengers came and went, the fine horses, the grooms and attendants of the great crowded around the gate; more than this, what such families spent for provisions, entertainment and services enriched the whole neighbourhood. As one account put it, 'The small pedlars of the ward and the alleys rose to the status of be-hairpinned and be-tasselled gentlemen ...' Perhaps in another part of the same ward a widowed imperial princess was converting her mansion into a nunnery and taking the tonsure, or a family of noted lineage was being forced by mortgage foreclosure or political pressure to cede part of its property to a newly powerful neighbour.

The rank and file of the official élite sometimes had no regular houses in the capital, but when posted there lodged in Buddhist temples, stayed with friends or relatives, or rented modest houses, often at an inconveniently great distance from the audience halls of the Ta-ming Palace. Their hours of work were longer, and their pleasures were relatively simple: walks with friends in the Serpentine Park, outings to the Buddhist temples in the Chung-nan mountains south of the plain, flower-viewing at the appropriate seasons, chess-games with friends, poetry parties and visits to simple cabarets to sip wine served by pretty girls. Yet, if we can judge from their poems, men of the middle and lower official ranks always hoped that something might bring them to the attention of authority and give them a chance of high office. They longed for a chance to pay their debts and improve their status and style of living, but there was also in many a genuine yearning for self-fulfilment, which, so their Confucian studies had taught them, was only to be found in helping the emperor to 'govern the state and put the world in order'.

Life among all the élite of the capital was marked, as we have seen, by the constantly changing fortunes of families and individuals. This atmosphere of perpetual change was reinforced by the arrival in the capital each year of five to seven thousand young men who came from the provinces to take the state examinations. Some were rich and brought their own personal servants, horses and grooms; others were poor; but all aspired to success in the examinations and to a notable official career. They settled in hostels and lodgings, mostly in the Ch'ung-jen ward between the bustling East Market and the examination-halls in the south-east sector of the administrative city. When they tired of cramming for the examinations, they took their pleasure in the P'ing-k'ang ward just to the south, with its three streets of wine-shops and brothels.

For these young men the great moment of the year was the posting of the examination results on a wall of the south compound of the Board of Rites. For the successful candidates a magnificent official banquet was given in the Serpentine Park. After the banquet, the new graduates went to the nearby Buddhist temple of Tzu-en Ssu and inscribed their names on the walls of its pagoda. This was the time for young men of promise to choose a wife, and the parks were filled with the horses and carriages of officials with marriageable daughters. The girls walked or rode about, and many an alliance was negotiated after these meetings. With luck and influence, new graduates might be assigned to a bureau in the capital and thus continue to enjoy the pleasures of the city. But the majority necessarily were assigned to provincial posts. The farewell parties and the poems on the occasion of seeing a fellow-graduate off to the provinces speak eloquently of the strong bonds among graduates of a single year and also of the magnetism of the great capital, which was left behind with reluctance and sorrow. Young officials worked hard at their provincial posts in the hope of making a name and being transferred to one of the organs of the central government in Changan, where, if they were lucky, they might rise to great office, power and wealth.

Monks, merchants, festivals

The monks and nuns of the city's temples had renounced all such worldly ambitions. Living lives of study, meditation, prayer and charitable works, they nevertheless participated in a cycle of public observances that added greatly to the colour of the city's life. The Buddha's birthday was celebrated with splendour throughout the city on the eighth day of the fourth moon. The feast of all souls was another seasonal festival. There were also numerous special ceremonies: the placing of a holy relic in a new pagoda, dedication ceremonies for new temples or for scriptures newly translated into Chinese, the installation of abbots and abbesses. Sometimes, when a noted artist had completed a religious wall painting, there was a special ceremony of dedication. The clergy were drawn into many aspects of the capital's life. They operated free dispensaries and hospitals, ran pawnshops and offered lodgings to examination candidates and other laymen. And, as we have seen, they had their part in the cycle of imperial ceremonies; they offered masses for rain and a good harvest, masses for the imperial dead, and prayers for victory in war; they gave sermons or carried on disputations in the palaces. When, on such occasions, they moved through the city, it was a splendid spectacle: the clerics in magnificent robes, accompanied by numerous attendants, carried the costly impedimenta of their faith, waved censers and chanted sutras to the accompaniment of drums and gongs.

Of the life of the merchants and the market-place we know relatively little. T'ang tales speak often of pedlars carrying their wares from house to house, and of specialty shops in some of the wards. The official East Market had some 220 business firms, and dealing was heavy in horses, harness, grain, timber and other goods, largely of domestic origin. The West Market was altogether different. To it came the camel-trains from central and western Asia, and there one could discover all manner of exotic wares. Edward Schafer has described the spirit of the place:

> ... a busy, raucous, and multi-lingual cluster of bazaars and warehouses, whose visitors were also entertained by prestidigitators and illusionists of every nationality, not to mention story-tellers, actors and acrobats. Here one sought for the precious symbols of exotic mystery, magic and luxury. For instance, the market contained the Persian Bazaar, where, among other vendors of miracles, were to be found the famous Iranian connoisseurs of pearls, both magical and otherwise.

It seems clear that foreign merchants of the West Market often became rich and built fine houses nearby, and near the temples of their Zoroastrian and Manichaean faiths. There are reports of Chinese merchants of great wealth building magnificent mansions, but T'ang law hedged the merchant about with restrictions and disabilities (his sons, for example, were barred from taking the examinations), and official historians gave the merchant class scant and grudging attention. Little as we know of their mode of life, we may assume that merchants had a notable role in the commerce and the financial transactions which were essential to the complex life of the city.

For the common people life was, for the most part, rather grey and constricted. Small shopkeepers, pedlars, artisans, gardeners, grooms, sweepers – all those who did thousands of menial jobs – were strictly taxed and controlled. Their working hours were long, and they had much less security, leisure and free entertainment than the plebeians of Antonine Rome. Police regulations kept them confined to their wards from sundown to sun-up, and they were subject to the harsh exactions of landlords, of the bullying military and of the tax collectors. The winters were long, dark and cold, and it is not surprising that the approach of spring was celebrated with universal rejoicing. The lunar New Year brought a series of official holidays; offices were closed, the gates were allowed to remain open all night, and all the people of the great city could stroll about, visit the famous temples and beauty spots or take outings beyond the city walls. The fifteenth of the first lunar month was the occasion

for a gala festival – the feast of lanterns. In 713 this was celebrated with a great display. The Emperor Hsüan-tsung, celebrating his first New Year on the throne, had a tall structure known as a lantern-wheel built outside the south-east corner of the palace city. The wheel was 150 feet high, and on it were 50,000 lanterns. While the beauties of the city, clad in colourful costumes, danced and sang in the lantern-light, the spectators thronged about, and the emperor and his father watched the festivities from the wall of the palace city.

That New Year's celebration ushered in almost half a century of prosperity and peace – perhaps the most glorious years of the T'ang dynasty and its capital. Thereafter the great T'ang order gradually weakened, first from the disruptions of the insurrection of An Lu-shan and then, over many years, from the steady growth of provincial and regional satrapies. Changan remained, through the second half of the eighth and most of the ninth century, by far the greatest city in Asia, but it gradually lost control of the systems of power, transport and tax collection that had made it great. There was little new construction; palaces and public buildings fell into disrepair or were destroyed by fire. In the years 841–5 a combination of xenophobia and fiscal desperation led the government to a wholesale destruction of the temples of Buddhism and the other non-Chinese religions. This is not the place to recount the melancholy history of the city's downfall. A poet evokes for us, through the eyes of a high-born lady, the tragedy and terror of the city's end – its sack at the hands of the Huang Ch'ao rebels:

I had just shut the golden bird-cage after giving a lesson to
        my parrot,
And was looking sidelong in my phoenix mirror as I lazily
        combed my hair,
Idly leaning the while on the carved balustrade in silent thought,
When suddenly I beheld a cloud of red dust rising outside
        the gates,
And men appeared in the streets beating metal drums.
The citizens rush out of doors half-dazed with terror,
Meanwhile government troops are entering the city from the west,
And propose to meet the emergency by marching to the
        T'ung pass ...
Yet a little while, and my husband gallops up on horseback;
Dismounting, he enters the gate; stupefied he stands, like
        a drunken man.
Even now he had met the Purple Canopy departing into exile,
And had seen the white banners advancing from all parts of
        the country ...
Supporting the infirm and leading children by the hand,
        fugitives are calling to one another
        in the turmoil;
Some clamber on to roofs, others scale walls, and all is in
        disorder.
Neighbours in the south run into hiding with neighbours in
        the north,
And those in the east make for shelter with those in the west ...
Boom, boom! – Heaven and earth shake with the rumbling of
        chariot wheels,
And the thunder of ten thousand horses' hoofs re-echoes
        from the ground.
Fires burst out, sending golden sparks high up into the
        firmament,
And the twelve official thoroughfares are soon seething with
        smoke and flame.
The Sun's orb sinks in the west, giving place to the cold pale
        light of the Moon ...
Every home now runs with bubbling fountains of blood,
Every place rings with a victim's shrieks, shrieks that cause
        the very Earth to quake.
Dancing and singing girls must all undergo secret outrage;
Infants and tender maidens are torn living from their parent's arms.
Our eastern neighbour had a daughter, whose eyebrows were
        but newly painted:
A beauty above all price, to overthrow a city or a state;
Between tall spears she is escorted into a warrior's chariot,
Turning to gaze back at her fragrant boudoir, while her
        handkerchief is soaked with tears ...

CHRISTIAN
CONSTANTINOPLE

The greatest city in Christendom

and for more than a thousand years the capital of a vast empire, first expanding and later dwindling to within its own walls, Constantinople is an example of extraordinary endurance in world history. Facing both east and west, and frequently threatened from both directions, the city founded by the Emperor Constantine in 352 was, for most of its existence as the centre of the Byzantine Empire, a cultural, political and commercial force of the first magnitude. Ravaged by religious divisions, and being forced periodically to defend its dominions against Persians, eastern European tribes, the forces of Islam and even the Christian powers of the West, Constantinople nevertheless exerted an incalculable influence far beyond its borders.

In choosing the site of an old Greek settlement, Byzantium, surrounded on three sides by water, with excellent harbour facilities and easy to defend from land or sea attack, Constantine displayed a wis-

dom for which the people of Constantinople, centuries later, had reason to be thankful. At the time of its greatest power, creativity and wealth – the tenth and eleventh centuries – the metropolis contained about a million people, as well as artistic and religious treasures which were the wonder of the civilized world. The diminution of the empire was gradual and the city itself seemed impregnable; yet it fell twice – first in 1204, when it succumbed to the Franks, and finally in 1453, when the Turks put an end to Christian Byzantium.

Constantine was the first Roman emperor to opt for Christianity, thereby decisively affecting not only the destinies of millions of people but also the cultural development of Europe. He is represented in a famous late-tenth-century mosaic in Hagia Sophia in Constantinople (detail opposite). In his hands is a model of the city which he is presenting to the Virgin. (1)

The oldest known map of Constantinople was drawn in 1420 by Buondelmonte (left). Though crude and fanciful, the map does make clear the situation of the city, with the Sea of Marmora at the bottom, and the inlet of the Golden Horn in the centre. The two lines of city walls evidently indicate those built originally under Constantine and the later ones erected in the reign of Theodosius II. The U-shaped walls below the domed building (presumably Hagia Sophia) apparently indicate the Hippodrome, site of games, circuses and triumphs. On a pedestal made for an ancient Egyptian obelisk placed in the Hippodrome in 390 (bottom left) is a carving of the court of Theodosius I, showing the enthroned emperor himself, his wife and two sons, receiving homage from defeated enemies. (2, 3)

Tragic actors and Amazons (below), and a circus scene with audience (below right), are details of an ivory diptych carved in Constantinople in 517. (11, 12)

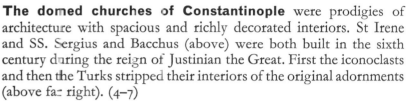

The stout city walls of Theodosius II, built in 413 (below far left), withstood potential invaders for many centuries. The marble ceremonial entrance to the city, now a ruin (below centre), was built around 390 and was known as the Golden Gate. Fragments of the once splendid Imperial Palace (below) are still standing on the wall facing the Sea of Marmora. (8, 9, 10)

The domed churches of Constantinople were prodigies of architecture with spacious and richly decorated interiors. St Irene and SS. Sergius and Bacchus (above) were both built in the sixth century during the reign of Justinian the Great. First the iconoclasts and then the Turks stripped their interiors of the original adornments (above far right). (4–7)

The civic improvements of the Roman Empire were continued in Constantinople by the early Byzantine emperors. This underground cistern (below) was constructed in the time of Justinian; a system of pipes and aqueducts brought water here from higher land outside the city. The chamber was supported by 336 pillars. (13)

The great Justinian (527–65), who ruled during a period of imperial expansion, was responsible for an intensive embellishment of the capital. He shares a position of greatest honour with Constantine in the Hagia Sophia mosaic (see Plate 1); he is presenting a model of the great church to the Virgin (right). Mosaics of the Justinian era from a courtyard pavement of the Great Palace near Hagia Sophia have recently been excavated, among them a young girl carrying water (below left) and a water mill (below right). (14, 15, 16)

Hagia Sophia (above), rebuilt in 537 after the fifth-century cathedral of the same name had burnt down, is Justinian's greatest monument. It was a marvel of conception as well as construction, a feat which in its day seemed almost superhuman. Procopius said of the great dome (opposite) that it appeared 'to cover the space as though suspended by a golden chain from heaven'. (18, 19)

Under the Comnenus dynasty in the twelfth century there was a revival of splendour after some fifty years of decline. One of the rare remnants of that period are the walls of Tekfur Saray, the Imperial Palace built during the reign of Manuel Comnenus (left). (17)

The rise of Islam was one of the principal factors in the eventual disintegration and collapse of the Byzantine Empire. Relations between the emperors and the Muslims were mainly bellicose, but these miniatures (above) from a thirteenth-fourteenth-century manuscript depict an embassy from the East to the imperial court in Constantinople. The ambassador is first shown borne upon a litter; then he and his retinue present gifts first to the empress and then to the emperor. (20, 21, 22)

Byzantine works of art, mostly religious in conception, are examples of remarkable craftsmanship in a variety of media. The elaborate ivory Harbaville Triptych, which shows on the back of the central panel (above left) a cross in the Garden of Paradise, was made in the tenth century. Metalwork and enamelling were also among the specialities of Byzantine artists. This chalice (above centre), of about 1070, made of gold and semiprecious stone, and decorated with plaques of cloisonné enamel, was among the booty brought back to Venice after the sack of Constantinople in 1204. The statuette of Virgin and Child (above right) is one of the most impressive examples of tenth-century ivory carving. (The Child's head is a restoration.) (23, 24, 25)

Imperial claims to divine sanction appear as a continuing theme in Byzantine art. Constantine VII Porphyrogenitus (913–59), for example, is shown being crowned by Christ in this ivory carving of about 944 (left). The inscription reads, 'Constantine, through God, Autocrator, King of the Romans'. A magnificent crown presumably presented in the eleventh century to the Hungarians bears enamelled portraits of Empress Zoe and Emperor Constantine Monomachus (above). (26, 27)

Silk weaving of great delicacy and beauty was another Byzantine accomplishment, introduced from Persia. The Auxerre shroud of St Eusebius (right) shows the sophisticated textile work of late-tenth-century Constantinople. (28)

The five-domed church in this detail of a twelfth-century miniature is believed to represent the Church of the Holy Apostles, built by Justinian, who pulled down an earlier church of Constantine's, which was damaged by an earthquake. This church, which did not long survive the Turkish occupation of the city, was the model for St Mark's in Venice. (29)

The Church of the Chora, converted to a mosque by the Turks and renamed Kariye Cami, is a product of the late flowering of Constantinople after the Latins were expelled in 1260. In the early fourteenth century, Theodore Metochites, a wealthy humanist and bureaucrat, underwrote the restoration of the church's mosaics and additional ornamentation. He is depicted (left), in a mosaic from Kariye Cami, holding the church which enjoyed his patronage as it was before being converted by the Turks. (30)

CHRISTIAN CONSTANTINOPLE

SIR STEVEN RUNCIMAN

As the roman empire passed into decadence, harassed by barbarian invaders from over the frontiers and worried by constitutional and economic problems beyond the understanding of its government, the city of Rome became unsuited to be the imperial capital. It was far from the border-lands where the emperors now spent most of their days; it was placed in an impoverished province, away from the sea, and all its food had to be imported; it was the home of the senatorial families, with their traditional dislike of the autocracy, and of the Praetorian Guard, with its ambition to make and unmake emperors. Few of the third-century emperors had resided there for long; and at the end of the century Diocletian planned definitely to move the seat of government to the east, nearer to the Asiatic frontier, where the rival power of Persia provided a perpetual menace, and the Danube frontier, along which the threat of barbarian invasion seemed most urgent. His choice of Nicomedia, at the eastern extremity of the Sea of Marmora, was ephemeral; but the greatest of his successors, Constantine, revived the plan. Constantine is one of the most important statesmen in history. It is due to his work that the Roman empire was able to survive the collapse of the West. He reformed the administration. His monetary policy gave the empire a currency that kept its value for more than seven centuries. His conversion and his recognition of Christianity provided a spiritual binding-force for the Roman world. And he founded a great city to be the capital of the new Christian empire, the city still commonly called after him: Constantinople.

Constantine's superb choice of site

The site was chosen with care. Constantine had considered the sentimental claims of his birthplace, Nish, and the romantic claims of Troy before his choice fell upon the old Greek colony of Byzantium. Byzantium was set at the end of a small peninsula on the European coast, where the narrow strait of the Bosphorus comes out into the Sea of Marmora. The peninsula was triangular, with curved sides. The twelfth-century French chronicler, Odo of Déols, compared it to a three-cornered sail bellying in the wind. At the eastern end its apex curved northwards, looking up the Bosphorus towards the Black Sea. The southern shore, along the Marmora, was convex at first, then slanted south-west. The concave northern shore ran along a splendid bay known to the Greeks and their Turkish successors from its shape as the Horn, and to the west from its riches as the Golden Horn. Along the peninsula there were, as at Rome, seven hills; and on these seven hills Constantine built the city that he named New Rome.

It was a superb situation, quite apart from its natural beauty. It commanded the easiest land-route from Europe into Asia and the sea-passage between the Black Sea and the Mediterranean. The huge land-locked harbour of the Golden Horn could accommodate a vast armada; and if sailing ships had difficulty in rounding the point into the harbour against the prevalent north wind and the currents of the Bosphorus, there were snug little anchorages along the southern shore. The wooded hills outside the city were well endowed with springs, and the neighbouring provinces, Thrace in Europe and Bithynia across in Asia, were rich in corn-fields and pasture-lands. The site was easy to defend, with its two longer sides protected by the sea. Only on the third were strong fortifications required.

The town of Byzantium was swallowed up in the new capital. Constantine's land-wall that was to limit the city left the Golden Horn about a mile and a half west of the apex of the city and curved in a generous arc to reach the Marmora nearly a mile farther west. At the apex, on the old Acropolis of Byzantium, he built a citadel to be the main arsenal of the empire. Just to the south, on the site of the chief pagan temples of the old town, he laid the foundations of a church dedicated to Hagia Sophia, the Holy Wisdom of God. Sloping down from Hagia Sophia to the Marmora was the area reserved for the imperial palace, the residence of the emperors and the seat of the government. It was bounded on the west by the Hippodrome, enlarged from the old Hippodrome of Byzantium, built by the Emperor Severus, to suit the needs of a capital. From the palace gate the main street of the city, the Mese or Middle Street, ran westward, through the Forum of Constantine, where his statue looked down from a tall column on his city, and the later Forum of Theodosius. Just before it reached Constantine's land-wall it passed the second great Christian shrine founded by Constantine, the Church of the Holy Apostles, which was to be the mausoleum of the Christian emperors.

To fill his city, Constantine encouraged immigration from all parts of the empire. Before his death, large numbers of noblemen, merchants, and artisans had gathered there, to be near to the imperial court. Constantine's immediate successors seldom lived at the new capital, but the immigration continued; and when the emperors of the Theodosian dynasty definitely established themselves there, it became apparent that the founder had miscalculated. Early in the fifth century, during the minority of the Emperor Theodosius II, the regent, the Prefect Anthemius, built a new line of land-walls, about a mile to the west of the walls of Constantine, so as to include within the city an area over half as large as Constantine's original area, in order to provide room for the growing population. Apart from a slight extension at the northern end, these walls marked the official limits of the city throughout the Byzantine period.

History soon justified the foundation of the new capital. After the death of Theodosius I in 395 the empire was divided into two halves; and not many decades passed before the western half disintegrated.

There were various reasons for its collapse and the survival of the eastern half, but one of the most useful assets of the east was this prosperous and impregnable administrative centre. There was nothing to compare with it in the west.

During the reign of Justinian, in the mid-sixth century, the population of Constantinople rose to be about a million. Plague later in the century may have caused a temporary reduction; but it never fell far below the million-mark till the Frankish capture of the city in 1204. Justinian himself greatly embellished his capital, especially after the great fire that accompanied the riots of 532. To his builders we owe the present structure of Hagia Sophia, as well as the Church of the Holy Apostles that survived till the Ottoman conquest and served as a model for St Mark's at Venice. The disasters of the seventh century, the long Persian war and the subsequent loss of Syria and Egypt to the Arabs, helped rather than hindered the growth of the city, in spite of anxious moments during its siege first by the Persians then twice by the Arabs. The great rival metropolises of Alexandria and Antioch passed into infidel hands and declined in prosperity, while refugees from the lost provinces crowded to seek safety in the capital. There was a certain economic depression till the middle of the ninth century, when both political security returned and foreign trade improved. Thenceforward for three and a half centuries Constantinople was without doubt the greatest city in Christendom and probably the richest city in the world.

Initial impact on the visitor

It was her riches, even more than her size, that impressed the medieval traveller, whether he came from the east or from the west. Indeed, the Christian westerner found the civilization of Constantinople, the civilization known in history as Byzantine, stranger to him than did the Muslim from east; for the Arabs, like the Byzantines, had retained the urban civilization of the Roman empire and were accustomed to great cities, whereas western Europe in the early Middle Ages followed a self-sufficient rural economy, and its cities were small provincial market-towns. The accounts that survive of western travellers who visited the great capital all show a regard that is sometimes envious, sometimes frankly hostile, but always awe-struck. During the late tenth and early eleventh centuries, when Byzantine civilization was at its zenith, there were many such travellers; for the pilgrimage to Jerusalem was now highly popular, and Constantinople lay on the route.

The land-traveller followed the coast of the Marmora for the last lap of his journey. From Rhegium onwards, some fifteen miles from the city, he passed through a succession of suburbs, mostly fishing-villages, smartened by villas and hunting-boxes belonging to the aristocracy. At last the huge walls of the city appeared, first a foss that could be flooded in times of siege, then a lower wall, and behind it the high wall of Anthemius with its crenellations and its regularly spaced towers. The road led straight up to the Golden Gate, the ceremonial entrance to the city, made of honey-coloured marble and ornamented with sculpture and with plaques of bronze. After entering through the gate the traveller followed the Triumphal Way of the Emperors, which passed through the busy quarters by the Marmora to join the Middle Street about a mile from the imperial palace.

The traveller by sea, unless he were a crowned head and could disembark at the private harbour of the palace, did not make such an impressive entry into the city; but he was compensated by the superb view of Constantinople rising out of the sea. The skyline was not, as now, interrupted by tapering minarets; it was lower, but more congruous. It was dominated on the right by the great dome of Hagia Sophia, with the walls of the citadel behind and in front the varied domes and roofs of the imperial palace. To the left the high curved end of the Hippodrome towered over the Church of St Sergius and St Bacchus, and beyond there were other domes on the skyline, and houses covering the slopes down to the walls that ran along the sea-front. Trees and patches of garden appeared in between the buildings, which stretched away for nearly four miles south-westward to the towers of the land-walls and to the suburbs beyond.

When he had entered the city the pilgrim had to find himself accommodation in one of the hostels reserved for the use of foreigners. To facilitate police control, the Byzantine authorities liked

a visitor to inhabit quarters definitely assigned to people of his same provenance. Russian merchants, for instance, were lodged in specially reserved houses in the suburb of St Mamas, just outside the walls; and if they were registered traders they did not have to pay for their lodging and were in addition allowed one bath a week free of charge. In the eleventh century, pilgrims from the West usually stayed in a great inn known as the Hospice of Samson, in the heart of the city, not far from the site still occupied by the Great Bazaar. The management of the hostelry apparently had to report the visitor's arrival to the police; but, so long as he behaved himself, he was otherwise left unmolested during his visit.

To the Christian pilgrim the main attraction of Constantinople lay in its tremendous collections of Christian relics. The most famous were kept in the chapels attached to the imperial palace; and piety as well as a natural curiosity would make a visit to the palace the chief objective of the pilgrimage. If he made a friend amongst the palace officials such a visit was easily achieved; but it seems that there were also occasional escorted tours for humbler pilgrims. To reach the palace the pilgrim passed down the Middle Street through the arcade of the Golden Milestone into the great square of the Augusteum. Opposite him, on the east side of the square, was the low but dignified building of the Senate House. On the north towered Hagia Sophia. In the centre of the square was a great column surmounted by an equestrian statue of the Emperor Justinian and other statues stood round the sides of the open space. On the

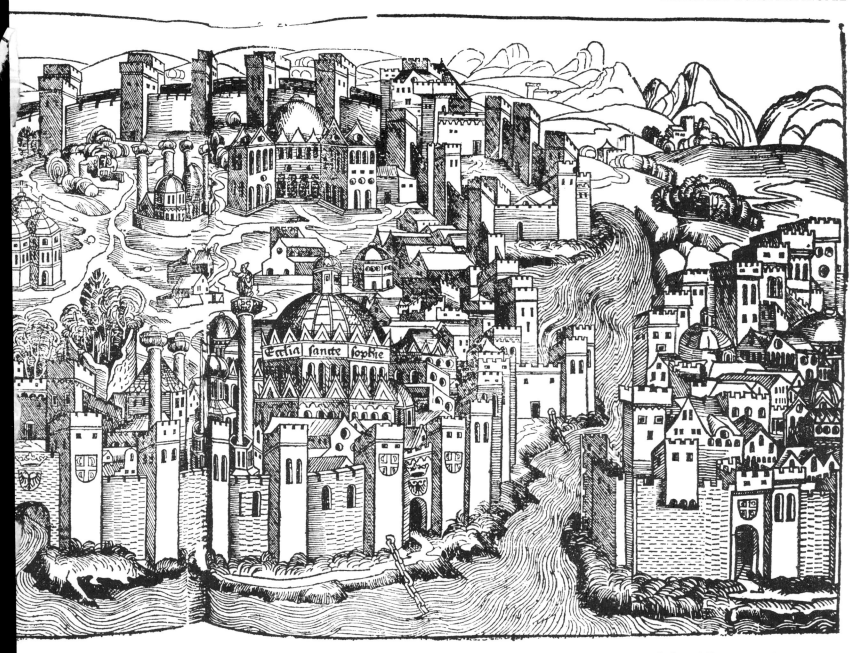

A view of Constantinople, from Hart-mann Schedel's Liber Chronicarum, *published in Nuremberg about 1479.*

south the main entrance to the Hippodrome abutted on to the Golden Milestone, while on the square itself was the Great Gate of the Palace, with a huge icon of Christ set amongst polychrome marbles over the entrance.

Temporal and spiritual glories

The palace area was surrounded by a strong wall and carefully guarded. For whoever held the palace held Constantinople and the empire. Within this area there was not one large single building, like a royal palace of today, but a series of halls and pavilions, dwelling-houses and baths, churches and libraries, offices and barracks, a prison and a textile factory, all set amongst gardens and orchards, with shady streams and lakelets, and terraces skilfully laid out to catch the sunshine and the view. The palace was not only the residence of the emperors; it was the seat of the imperial secretariat and the chief ministries of state. The treasure of the empire was kept in its vaults, from which was extracted the salary of every imperial official. Down on the eastern slopes was the factory where women operatives wove the famous imperial brocades destined for the ceremonial wear of the court and occasionally as gifts to specially favoured foreign potentates. The visitor passed first through the vestibule of the Chalce, built by Justinian. Long arcades permitted him to go on under shelter to the other ceremonial halls. There was the Chrysotriclinium, a throne-room lined with gold mosaic, built by the Emperor Justin II. There was the later throne-room of the Triconchus, built in the ninth century by Theophilus and modelled on the fashionable architecture of Baghdad. It was here, now, that foreign envoys were received in audience, with all the fantastic accompaniments that Byzantine ingenuity could devise. While the ambassador bowed down before the Presence, his forehead touching the ground, the throne would slowly rise, and he would lift his eyes again to find the emperor seated high above him; and at the same moment the golden lions that flanked the throne would roar and wave their tails, and the jewelled birds that sat on the gold and silver trees round the chamber would open their beaks and sing. Round the Triconchus, set in formal gardens, were some elegant pavilions where the emperor could receive his friends informally. Official banquets took place usually in the halls of the Caenurgium, the palace built by Basil I close to the Chrysotriclinium. For their actual residence the emperors preferred buildings farther down the slope towards the Marmora, where their official suites were grouped round a series of courts. There, too, was the Gynaeceum, the buildings reserved for the empress and her ladies. There the empress was complete mistress, and no man, except eunuchs, could enter without her express permission. But neither she nor the ladies of the court led the secluded lives of Muslim women. They emerged as frequently as they wished, to take part in the court ceremonies or to pay visits to the outside world. But the emperor and empress usually preferred to inhabit some quieter villa within the palace precincts. In the later tenth century Nicephorus Phocas refitted the small but magnificently decorated palace which is sometimes called the House of Justinian, on the edge of the sea, for the use of himself and his empress, Theophano; and there it was, on a December night in 969, that she brought in her lover to murder him. Beside this palace was the imperial harbour of Bucoleon, so named from the statue of a bull fighting a lion that stood on the harbour wall. Here the emperor and empress would land when they crossed the straits from Asia, and here a few favoured foreign potentates were allowed to disembark. There were many chapels and oratories dotted about within the palace area. The largest and most recent was the New Basilica, built by Basil I, according to the latest principles of Byzantine architecture; but the chapel that attracted most attention stood on a hill behind the Bucoleon next to a lighthouse that served to guide shipping round the point into the Bosphorus. In this shrine of Our Lady of the Lighthouse were kept the holiest relics of Christendom, the objects connected with the Passion of Our Lord. You could see the Crown of Thorns, the Lance, the Seamless Coat as well as the chief portion of the Wood of the Cross and a phial of the Holy Blood. Every pilgrim sought to pay worship here.

After emerging from the palace the visitor might cross the square into the Church of Hagia Sophia. This was the Cathedral of Constantinople, where the patriarch conducted the service on feast-days and where the emperor traditionally was crowned. This huge edifice, built for Justinian by Anthemius of Tralles and Isidore of Miletus, enclosing an open floor space, unrivalled for size till modern times, under a dome so delicately poised that, as Procopius said, you would think it suspended by golden chains from heaven, with splendid side-aisles and galleries, has never failed to impress all that see it. Now it has the chill of a museum; but the visitor of the late tenth century could see it at the height of its living glory. The columns were of porphyry and *verd-antique*; the lower walls were covered with plaques of many-coloured marble. Above them was gold mosaic, patterned with grey and blue. Great figure-mosaics shone in the apse and on the pendentives of the dome. The altar-screen was of marble and of gold, and the thrones of the emperor and the patriarch blazed with jewels. An earthquake in 989 caused a crack to appear in the dome. After its immediate repair, by an Armenian specialist, further figure-mosaics were added to increase the richness of the upper walls. It was all dazzling enough if you visited the shrine by day; but during the great services that took place after dark the effect was still more dazzling. In the bright, tremulous light of a thousand lamps and candles, with clouds of incense floating upwards, the mosaics glowed with a rhythm that was almost hypnotic. It was small wonder that the ambassadors of Vladimir of Russia believed that they had seen angels descending from the dome.

There were magnificent buildings round the cathedral. Its Baptistery shone with mosaics showing the life of John the Forerunner. The Patriarchal Palace was a splendid edifice, and behind were the rich churches of St Irene and the Virgin Chalcoprateia, the latter containing Our Lady's own girdle. Entrance to the Acropolis was doubtless forbidden to foreigners; but they might visit the Church of St George near by, to see the relics of the saint.

No visitor of enterprise would fail to attend a spectacle at the Hippodrome, to watch the chariot-races that were the chief entertainment of the people of the city. Forty thousand spectators could be contained within its walls; and on special holidays the emperor and empress in person witnessed the scene from the imperial box, where they were received with a tremendous formal ritual. The passionate quarrels between the circus-factions of the Blues and Greens, that in earlier centuries had often led to riot and bloodshed, had now been stilled; the factions only kept a formal entity for ceremonial purposes. The Hippodrome was also used after a triumphant war, to parade the prisoners that had been taken.

City of contrasts

Starting from the Golden Milestone, the Middle Street led straight into the chief commercial quarters of the city. It followed the central ridge of the city, in a slight curve; for the Byzantines preferred to avoid straight streets that served as funnels for the wind; and it was lined with arcades, on to which opened the more important shops, arranged in groups according to their wares. Nearest to the palace were the goldsmiths and the silversmiths, and behind them, towards the Great Bazaar of modern times, was the building known as the

House of Lights because its windows were lit up by night. This was the silk bazaar. After passing the imperial law-courts and the offices of the Prefect of the City you came to the Forum of Constantine and on to the clothiers' and the furniture-makers' shops. The bakers' market lay behind to the north; and the whole area down to the Golden Horn was mainly given over to commerce. The Middle Street led on to the huge Forum of Theodosius and the Church of the Holy Apostles, where the bodies of past emperors and empresses lay in sarcophagi of porphyry and of basalt. As you moved farther towards the land-walls and the Charisian Gate, or down the Triumphal Way to the Golden Gate, the districts became less specialized and the city became, rather, a conglomeration of townships, each complete in itself and joined to its neighbours by orchards and gardens. In the valley of the little river Lycus, which flowed down from beyond the walls into the Sea of Marmora, there were even a few small corn-fields. But on the whole the gaps between the built-up areas were very small, till after the thirteenth century when the population began rapidly to decline.

There was no smart residential district. In every quarter palaces and monasteries, shops and slums had grown up side by side. The older houses of the rich were built in the Roman manner, two storeys high, presenting a blank exterior and facing inward round a courtyard which was often roofed over and was usually adorned with a fountain. Later, three-storeyed palaces were built, to look outward over a terrace commanding one of the splendid views for which the city was renowned. Sometimes monasteries would be converted into palaces, or palaces into monasteries. The houses of the middle classes were built with their upper storey jutting out over the street or else with balconies. They had almost all been built by private enterprise; but a law of the fifth century attempted to introduce some control. Where thoroughfares already in existence were less than twenty-two feet wide new buildings were not allowed windows for prospect but only gratings for ventilation. Side streets must be at least twelve feet wide, and balconies must not extend to within ten feet of the opposite wall. Outside staircases on the street were forbidden. This law remained in force throughout the history of the empire; but it was impossible to control the wooden shacks in which many of the poor were living. Drainage was carefully regulated. All the drains led into the sea; and no one but an imperial personage might be buried within the city. Water was brought to the city by magnificent aqueducts, of which most foreign visitors spoke with admiration; and it was stored in innumerable cisterns. There were big underground cisterns near the palace and the Acropolis and still larger open cisterns nearer to the walls. In addition, most monasteries and private houses had their own cisterns, which, it seems, could be filled in winter from the aqueducts. Even in times of siege the city was never short of water. There were many public baths, kept up by the municipality; and there were hospitals and orphanages attached to many of the monasteries. Such charters dealing with their foundation as survive show that careful attention was paid to hygiene. There was only one authorized brothel in the city, in the Zeugma quarter by the Golden Horn. It was marked by a statue of the pagan goddess Aphrodite.

In spite of all these regulations many of the poorer quarters, especially by the Golden Horn and in the districts towards the walls, were horribly filthy. In the tanners' quarter the stench was notorious, for the water used for tanning would be thrown out afterwards carelessly on to the street. Constantinople was a city of contrasts. The main streets, with their handsome buildings and their arcades, the squares ornamented by memorial columns and many of the finest statues of antiquity, the well-kept public gardens and all the splendid public edifices gave little hint of the squalor of the poorer alleys behind. Even amongst the slums you would find some famous church. The pious pilgrim would certainly wish to visit the ancient monastery of Studium, in Psamathia towards the Golden Gate, to admire the Church of St John. Still more, he would hurry to see the Church of Our Lady of Blachernae, where was housed the portrait of the Virgin painted by St Luke himself. It lay at the extremity of the city, where the land-walls came down to the Golden Horn; and nearby, right up against the wall, which they reconstructed for the purpose, the emperors of the twelfth century made themselves a new palace, smaller than the Great Palace but less diffuse and even richer in its decoration. The whole history of the empire was said to be depicted in its mosaics and frescoes. They were great huntsmen; and it suited them to be able, when the pressure of business was relaxed, to slip out through the walls to the countryside. To the earlier emperors, obliged to ride through four miles of city streets or else to take a boat to a suburban harbour, this recreation was impossible unless they moved with their household to some country seat; and it was seldom that they could take so long a holiday.

Even the various suburbs of the city were each of them comparable with a great town of the west. A bridge led across the Golden Horn near Blachernae to Pegae and Galata on the northern bank. Fishing-villages and market-gardens alternated with palaces and monasteries along both shores of the Bosphorus. The sheltered Asiatic coast of the Marmora was a favourite resort of the wealthy; and there, too, were grown early fruits and vegetables for the city markets. Small boats plied incessantly across the straits to bring passengers and goods to and fro. Though Baghdad and Cairo may each at times have held a larger population than Constantinople itself, there was nowhere in the medieval world so large a conglomeration of people as in the area round the imperial capital.

The interior of the houses was equally surprising to the pilgrim from the west. Furniture was finely carved and often encrusted with metal or mother-of-pearl, very different from the crude carpentry to which he was used. Instead of rushes on the floor he saw patterned marble or exquisitely woven carpets; there were rugs even in the poorer houses. He was unused to window-panes of glass or of thinly cut alabaster, or to curtains of brocade. Table and toilet utensils were mostly of metalware, though there were many factories making pottery.

Human diversity and international exchange

Next to the size of the city and the splendour of its public buildings the visitor was struck by the diversity of human types that he saw in the streets. Its commercial activity made Constantinople a cosmopolitan centre. There were always foreign merchants in the city. As you passed through the bazaars you might meet a company of Russian traders, come to sell furs and wax and slaves, wandering with a police escort – for one could not trust such barbarians' behaviour – or you might see Arab merchants treated with the deference that members of a sister-civilization deserved; or slick Italians, from Venice or Amalfi, fraternizing with the citizens but viewed always with a certain suspicion. Occasionally you might come across a group of Persians or slant-eyed men from Central Asia, or might watch members of the small Jewish colony welcome co-religionists from the Caspian or from Spain. In the main streets you might at any moment be pushed aside to allow the passage of some foreign ambassador and his train, come from Egypt or from Germany to present his credentials to the emperor; or it might be a vassal-prince from the Caucasus riding by in state. And in his hostelry or at the sacred shrines the pilgrim would almost always find some of his own compatriots.

To a traveller coming from lands where strangers were seldom seen, this international activity was particularly impressive; it was the aspect of Constantinopolitan life with which he naturally came into contact and one which he could easily appreciate. It was not so easy for him to understand the lives of the citizens themselves. The wearisome and squalid lives of the poor have always been much the same all the world over; but to the medieval westerner, unused to the sight of urban slums, the poverty that he could see in Constantinople seemed more alien and shocking than it would appear to us. But the lives of the bourgeoisie and the nobility were quite incomprehensible to him. At his home everyone wore woollen garments; and the ladies and gentlemen of Constantinople in their silks and linens seemed to him decadent and immoral. It was distressingly effeminate, too, to eat your food with knives and forks instead of the fingers given you by God for that purpose. He could not sympathize on the one hand with the taste for personal cleanliness or for intellectual discussions that characterized the Byzantines, nor, on the other hand, with their deplorable delight in intrigue and in sharp business dealings. Even the magnificent Byzantine army did not display the qualities that he admired. Individual knightly prowess was discouraged there; for Byzantine strategists, like the best generals of today, believed in discipline and in only risking a battle when victory was assured. The various military disasters that had

befallen the empire had almost all been due to some rash hero neglecting proper caution. Nor was the Church that the westerner found in Constantinople familiar to him. It used a language and a ritual different from his own. Priests, monks and nuns all wore strange clothes. To the more ignorant pilgrim it sometimes seemed questionable whether they were really Christians, and he resented their guardianship of so many sacred relics.

The Byzantines returned his contempt, and with better cause. They had inherited the old Greek arrogance towards the barbarian. But it was a cultural and not a racial feeling. The Byzantines themselves were of very diverse origins. Greek and Roman blood had long since been mixed with the blood of the indigenous stock of Asia Minor and the Balkans and was constantly enriched by the immigration of Armenians, Syrians and Slavs, Arabs and Turks, and even Franks from the west. Spaniards, Syrians, and Armenians had all reigned as emperors, and there had been empresses of Slav and Frankish and even Turkish descent. The bond was supplied by membership of the Orthodox Church and by the belief that every citizen belonged to the one true Christian empire, whose emperor was God's viceroy on earth. Had you asked a Byzantine what was his nationality he would have answered 'Roman'; for he considered his empire to be the direct continuation of the supranational empire of Rome, hallowed by the adoption of the Christian faith. He even called the Greek language, which was now the official language of the empire, by the name of Roman or Romanic. Anyone who would conform to the Orthodox Church and admit the sovereignty of the emperor was welcomed within the empire, whatever his origin. The barbarians were the ignorant folk who would not conform; and for them the Byzantine felt no real friendship nor much regard, merely a certain curiosity. Of such foreigners he preferred the Muslim to the Frank; for Muslim civilization, despite its heterodox religion, had some resemblance to his own. He felt far more at home in Cairo or Baghdad than in the primitive little towns of the west. Yet for all his exclusiveness the Byzantine was very ready to adopt foreign fashions, so long as they could be moulded, like foreign immigrants, to fit into his way of life.

The emperor: source and subject of the law

Byzantine life pivoted round the emperor. He was the autocrat, the source of law and the head of the Church. But he was not an irresponsible despot. Though he might make and amend laws, the Law was considered to be above him; he could not go against its principles. He might appoint the Patriarch; but the Patriarch represented a moral force that he could not defy with impunity. He was the crowned emperor; yet if he lost the favour of his subjects they had

Plan of Christian Constantinople, showing the location of its most important buildings.

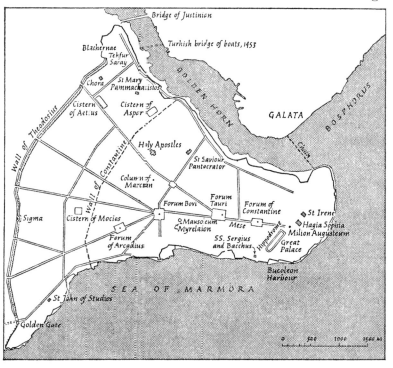

no hesitation in rioting to secure his fall. Tradition and public opinion alike limited his power. His job was no sinecure. He was in charge of the government; and much of his day was spent in administrative routine. On every feast-day there was some ceremony in which he played the leading role as representative of the Christian Commonwealth. He was commander-in-chief of the armed forces; and many emperors spent long months campaigning on the frontiers, governing the empire from their tents. At such times everything depended on the presence of loyal and efficient ministers at Constantinople; and it says much for the Byzantine civil service that there was so seldom trouble at home when the emperor was away at the wars. Other emperors, like the tenth-century Constantine VII, spent their spare time in literary activities, no doubt with the help of a host of secretaries. But an emperor bent on a life of pleasure seldom held the throne for long. There was no hereditary succession to the empire. Nominally the army, the Senate, and the people elected their ruler; but an emperor could co-opt a junior colleague, who on his death succeeded to the full power and who in the meantime could take over some of the ceremonial duties. A visitor to Constantinople about the year 1000 would probably never have seen the great warrior-Emperor Basil II in person. During his many absences, on the Bulgarian or the Armenian front, his place in the court ritual was taken by his younger brother, the co-Emperor Constantine VIII.

The empress led almost as busy a life. Part of the palace was under her control. She had large estates and revenues to manage, and innumerable ceremonies to perform. There were several highly efficient empresses-regent in Byzantine history, in complete control of the government. There had been already an empress-regnant, Irene, who fell from power more from her own ill-health than from incompetence or from any dislike of her sex. For a few months in the eleventh century the visitor would have seen the remarkable spectacle of two old ladies sitting side by side on the throne of the Caesars; and one of them died some years later as the sole depository of the imperial power. The empress was not necessarily the emperor's wife. She had to be specially crowned; and it was part of her imperial right that in the absence of a crowned emperor she could nominate a successor.

Round the emperor and empress were grouped the officials of the court, arranged in strict precedence. No title was acquired by birth, except that of Porphyrogennete, reserved for children of the empress born in the Purple Chamber of the Palace. Other members of the imperial family had specially to be appointed to their rank. Many of the titles were purely honorary but commanded a salary. They could be bought, and thus represented a form of gilt-edged security, very useful in the days before banking. The offices of state all had their traditional names. But the conception of the Byzantine civil hierarchy as a rigid, inelastic affair is wholly misleading. As in England old titles survived but were given new functions to suit the needs of the day. It provided an efficient machinery; and particular regard was paid to finance. The imperial treasury was in ultimate control. Except in certain unruly districts where the governors lived on the taxes that they managed to collect, the provincial administration was paid from Constantinople, though the governors were given wide administrative and military powers. But they were continually visited by inspectors from the capital.

Sections of society and their status

The nobility was not, as in the feudal West, necessarily a hereditary affair. There were great families in Byzantium, though few arose before the late ninth century when at last it became safe to invest money in land. But throughout Byzantine history, as in eighteenth-century England, a successful financier or general, often of humble origin, might buy or be granted estates, and henceforward would take his place amongst the aristocracy. He might himself be despised if his accent was rough or his education deficient; but his sons and daughters, if they conformed in culture and manners, could mix and intermarry with the oldest families. It was not an idle aristocracy. Its members went into the army or the court or the civil service; they were not above commercial affairs. But almost all of them loved pomp and luxury and modelled their palaces on the emperor's. By the middle of the tenth century they were beginning to grow ominously powerful, particularly in the provinces.

The Church was drawn from all ranks of society. The parish priest was then, as now in Orthodox countries, a simple villager, only a little better educated than his parishioners; and he had to be a married man. But the regular clergy, from whom the ranks of the hierarchy were drawn, contained peasants' sons as well as noblemen's and merchants'. An imperial prince might be succeeded by the child of an artisan on the patriarchal throne. The episcopate was open to all comers, though influence certainly might be useful; and nearly all the great hierarchs of Byzantine history were men of character and high intellectual gifts. Their influence was tremendous; and though the emperor had the last word in any quarrel with the patriarch, for he could convene and put pressure on the synod of bishops, yet he would seldom go to such lengths unless he had a considerable backing from public opinion. Even more powerful than the Church hierarchy were the monasteries, who by gifts and legacies and good management had acquired enormous estates throughout the empire. Many emperors tried vainly to curb their power; for they represented a force of opinion that was not always helpful to the government, while the growing numbers of monks deprived it of many potential soldiers and cultivators. Yet the monasteries performed many useful tasks. They ran hospitals and orphanages, and they acted as almshouses and homes for the aged. Thousands of men and women, rich and poor alike, would, when their active lives were over, retire to some monastic establishment where they could prepare themselves in peace for the hereafter, thus ridding their families or the state charities of the burden of their upkeep. The eastern monk's life is given more to prayer and less to work than the western; but the monasteries indulged in several useful intellectual labours. There were learned monastic authors, historians and biographers as well as theologians; and many manuscripts were copied and stored in their libraries.

The visitor would be struck by the high general level of education. Only the poorest classes were illiterate. The mother of the historian, Psellus, who belonged to the lower bourgeoisie, considered it a grievance that she had not been taught her letters adequately. She educated herself in later life in order to direct the studies of her brilliant young son. At that time – the very beginning of the eleventh century – illiteracy was rare in her class. In the wealthier classes boys and girls alike were given a sound general education, based on the *Trivium* and *Quadrivium* of Roman times, which included grammar, rhetoric and philosophy, arithmetic, geometry, music and astronomy. This education was given either by private tutors or in schools run by the Church. At this time, about the year 1000, the State University was in abeyance. The Emperor Basil II was an austere man who did not have much faith in the value of higher education. He would have agreed with the old soldier, Cecaumenus, who had served under him and who held that a study of the Scriptures and a little training in theoretical reasoning was all that anyone required. But the average Byzantine felt otherwise. He admired a cultured mind; he would be ashamed not to recognize a quotation from Homer or a reference to Plato's *Dialogues*. It was a matter of general satisfaction when the Emperor Constantine IX reopened the university in 1045, chiefly because the lack of authorized law-schools was damaging the quality of work in the law-courts. In particular the study of Latin had been neglected.

Soldiers were not much in evidence in the streets of the city. The visitor might notice the tall, magnificent Scandinavians who formed the Varangian Guard, attached to the emperor's person. But the main army was kept away from the capital, in barracks along the high roads of Thrace or Bithynia. The men could thence be more easily moved to the front; and meanwhile they were beyond the reach of scheming politicians in Constantinople. Each province also had its own local regiment. But the imperial fleet might be seen anchored in the Golden Horn, or, more usually, in one of the nearby Asiatic harbours.

The western visitor was sometimes surprised by the position of women in Byzantium. The women in the poorer and middle classes led much the same lives as their sisters in other lands, running their houses, bringing up their children, sewing for their families, and gossiping in the market-place. But the high-born lady of Constantinople seemed strange to him. She seldom emerged without a train of servants, and was probably carried in a litter. She wore a veil to protect her complexion, which anyhow was protected by a shockingly thick layer of cosmetics. Her clothes were usually of silk; her hair was braided with jewels. She had her own exclusive quarters in her house. She seemed at first sight as restricted as any Muslim lady and certainly quite incapable of supporting the hard, robust life led by a western noblewoman. But in fact, though fashion and convention required her to appear fragile and retiring, the Byzantine lady moved freely in society and made her influence felt. She might never, like a western chatelaine, be called upon to defend her castle, unless, perhaps, she lived close to the frontier. War never came near her; and it was anyhow to the Byzantine an unpleasant job which was left to professional soldiers. Instead, she expended her energy on passionate political intrigue; and if her plots failed, her sex did not protect her from punishment. She was the heiress of the Roman empresses and the Hellenistic princesses, not a passive ornament in a harem. Or she might be a lady of letters; a poetess like Casia, whose pert repartee lost her an imperial husband, or a historian like Anna Comnena, herself an incorrigible intriguer. Or she might run a great business concern, like the widow, Danelis, who owned most of the western Peloponnese and would occasionally visit Constantinople with all the pomp due to a millionairess who had once befriended an emperor. There were women doctors to attend ladies who were too modest to endure attention from a man. There were even women saints; but they were rather rare. Yet, despite the luxury with which Byzantine ladies surrounded themselves, their private lives were not markedly immoral. They were so seldom left unattended that adultery could not pass unnoticed.

Repugnant features and fabled splendour

There were two aspects of life in Constantinople that the average westerner found definitely repugnant. First was the presence everywhere of eunuchs. Eunuchs had been introduced into Roman life by the Emperor Diocletian, in his desire to copy the ritual of the Persian court. Soon every great household had its eunuchs as servants who could wait upon the ladies without scandal. Eunuch secretaries and eunuch medical attendants appeared, and were equally appreciated by the ladies that they served. Before long the emperor began to find amongst the eunuchs his most faithful and useful ministers; for eunuchs had no children whom they sought to enrich, and a rigid convention kept them from aspiring to the imperial throne. There were eminent eunuch soldiers, like Justinian's great general, Narses; there were eunuch patriarchs, and innumerable eunuchs amongst the high officers of state. In the tenth-century tables of precedence the eunuchs figured at the head of each titular category. Parents considered it no disgrace to castrate one of their sons and so help him to advancement in the Household or in the civil service. But to western eyes these strange creatures were unnatural and rather horrible; and later in Byzantine history, when occidental fashions grew more popular, the eunuch became far rarer, to be reintroduced into Constantinople by the Ottoman Turk.

The second repellent sight was the number of mutilated men to be seen in the streets. Byzantine justice was on the whole fair, but the punishment given to convicted criminals was severe. The Byzantines disliked the death penalty. Though murders were not infrequent, and though when the temper of the crowd was roused human life was of little account, in their calmer moments the Byzantines felt that it was wrong to kill. Their strictest theologians even held that to slay an enemy in battle was canonically murder, however patriotically desirable. For political crimes such as treason the punishment was often nothing worse than relegation to a monastery, where the criminal could repent and save his soul far removed from the temptations of active life. But, though there were prisons in Constantinople, the authorities found it cheaper and simpler to punish offenders by extracting fines or confiscating property; and for the many criminals whose possessions were too few for such punishment a rough system of mutilation was evolved. Serious crimes were punished by the loss of sight or of the right arm, lesser offences by the loss of an ear or by branding. The maimed beggars that resulted from this method were not a pleasant spectacle.

It is possible that these horrors merely threw greater emphasis on the splendour of the city. For its glory and magnificence were always the main theme of every traveller's tale. Its conquest had long been the aim of every Muslim chieftain. Every Slav potentate dreamed of reigning in Tsarigrad, the city of the emperors. Merchants from west and east brought home stories of its luxury and beauty.

Warrior princes set sail from Norway and Iceland to have the honour of serving in the Emperor's Guard at Micklegarth; and thither, to join them, came Anglo-Saxon adventurers dispossessed by William the Conqueror. Pilgrims, too, could not withhold their admiration, though many, from jealousy or from genuine disapproval, murmured of Babylon and the burden of cities whose pride is an offence to God. We may question whether all this luxury was in fact so tremendous as visitors made out. In the old Roman empire there had been cities quite as wealthy, Alexandria or Antioch or Rome herself; and the coming Renaissance was to bring an equal splendour to the cities of Italy, though not perhaps on so large a scale. The extraordinary impression made by Constantinople on its foreign contemporaries was due to their own comparative poverty and simplicity of life.

Transitory pleasures and their doom

Byzantium was at the height of its power in the first years of the eleventh century. Before the century was over disasters had befallen it. Its internal organization, perfected as an instrument of defence against a hostile world, broke down in the face of prosperity. Its hegemony over the Mediterranean Sea was lost with the Norman conquest of southern Italy and the simultaneous growth of the Italian merchant-cities. Worse still, the plains of Asia Minor, its main source of manpower and of food, were irretrievably lost to the Turks. During the twelfth century the splendour of Constantinople seemed still undiminished. The imperial army, with its scientific armaments, its well-run commissariat and medical services, was still a formidable factor in world-politics. But the emperors were living on accumulated reserves. Many wealthy provinces had been lost; and trade was passing into Italian hands. When disaster struck again and the great army perished in a ghastly and unnecessary battle against the Turks, there was no chance of recovery. The horrors of the Fourth Crusade, when western adventurers, pledged to fight against the infidel, joined the Venetians in an attack on the great Christian city, which they captured and sacked and burnt, left Constantinople a desolation. During the half century of the so-called Latin empire its population went down by some two-thirds. Large areas fell into ruin; the Great Palace became uninhabitable and was deserted. The great relic-collections were dispersed. The return of the Byzantine emperors brought an ephemeral return to prosperity; but money was scarce, and commerce had crossed the Golden Horn to the Italian colony at Galata. Travellers to the city in the thirteenth and early fourteenth centuries told of vast areas within the walls where you saw the remains of former houses lying in open fields. The city seemed to have become a series of disconnected villages. Yet they still all admired the gracious lives led by the court and the nobility. They still saw Hagia Sophia in all its glory; and though many older churches were in decay, others had arisen, such as the monastery-church of the Chora with its gay mosaic decoration. But an element of sadness hung over it all. Christian Constantinople was doomed. The end came on 29 May 1453, when the last of the emperors fell fighting at the breach in the walls, and the Turkish soldiery passed in over his body. The centre of Christian civilization had moved long since to the West; and though Constantinople was soon again one of the world's great cities, it was the capital not of Christendom but of Islam.

It was as the Byzantines always had foreseen. In the melancholy climate of the Bosphorus, with its sudden changes from heat to chill, with its bitter north wind and its sultry south wind, its constant rain and the mist from the sea, the Greek temperament lost much of its natural gaiety. For all its wealth, for all its wise statesmen and efficient institutions, the empire was haunted by insecurity and fear. Countless prophecies warned the citizens that their glory would come to a finish, that the number of emperors was fixed and that their heritage would in the end pass to the infidel. The emperor might be God's vicercy on earth, and the splendour of his court a reflection of the splendour of the Courts of Heaven. But, with the barbarians growing in strength around them, his subjects had no faith in human progress, no confidence that their empire would endure. They knew that the pomps and pleasures of this world are transitory things, and that the eleven centuries of their imperial destiny were as nothing in the eyes of God, whose Kingdom alone is eternal.

MUSLIM CORDOBA

The capital of Muslim Spain

endured for some five hundred years, from its capture in 711 until 1236, when Ferdinand III of Castile finally drove the Moors out of the city. Its period of greatest power and prosperity, however, was the tenth century, when it was an opulent city – with a population of about half a million Muslims, Christians and Jews who lived in harmony – of palaces, mosques, libraries and gardens. Of Cordoba's Moorish achievement, almost nothing remains. The splendours which shamed a Europe emerging from the Dark Ages were ravaged by Berbers in 1013, and the city which Hroswitha had called 'the ornament of the world' never properly recovered. The contending fanaticisms of Moor, Berber and Christian did the rest: the books (estimated to number about 400,000) were burned, the manufactures ruined, the buildings destroyed.

One great monument remains: the Cathedral Mosque (La Mezquita Aljama), built by Abdurrahman I in 785. At the height of Cordoban culture and supremacy it was the seat of a university of international repute; converted into a cathedral by the Spanish Christians, it was and is the largest of all churches except St Peter's in Rome. The Mosque was the first example of the distinctively Spanish-Arab style of architecture. Even so, it did not long remain free from Christian insertions and replacements – moving so fervent a Catholic as Emperor Charles V to remark that 'You have built here what you or anyone might have built anywhere else, but you have destroyed what is unique in the world'. If the structure as a whole has been marred, individual parts like these decorated multifoil archways (opposite) remain moving and impressive. (1)

The most notable innovation of Spanish-Arab architecture were the double horseshoe arches of the Mosque (below, the crypt), with their voussoirs in contrasting colours and materials. They were necessary to offset the shortness of the pillars – 850 marble, porphyry and jasper columns of various sizes, taken from Roman and Visigothic buildings – and to provide adequate roof space. The larger columns had to be sunk into pits in the ground; the smaller were topped with capitals of appropriate size. The result has a singular and striking beauty.

The Moorish relief decoration of this dome (right), built over an antechamber (961–66) by al-Hakam II, is more restrained than that of the east front (right, below) which is suggestive of Syrian or Persian influence in its profusion and exuberance. (2, 3, 4)

The palace-city of az-Zahra' was built by Abdurrahman III (ruled 912–61), at the instigation of a concubine, with the money left by one of her predecessors. Az-Zahra' was the administrative centre of al-Andalus (the Moorish name for Spain), as well as Abdurrahman's court, and contained 14,000 domestics alone. The walls were lined with coloured marble, the ceilings were gilded, the doors inlaid with precious stones, and the windows made of translucent alabaster. Even the envoys of Byzantium were awed by this magnificence. The ruins have been excavated (above), but the grandeur and activity of az-Zahra' can no longer be seen. On the other hand, the adroit selectivity of the photograph below captures something of the spirit of Muslim Cordoba: the water-wheel and bridge over the Guadalquivir must have looked much the same a thousand years ago. (5, 6)

Ivory-working was an important craft in tenth-century Cordoba, and Cordoban ivory was exported as far as central Asia and India. These objects sometimes contain depictions of human figures – otherwise rare in Muslim art – and preserve something of the cultured and leisured life of the city. A fine example is the detailed work on the casket (above right) carved by the artist Khalaf in 968; the central figure is playing a lute, which the Moors introduced into Spain from Persia. More to the taste of an active official, perhaps, were travelling in state on an elephant (right) and hawking (far right); the figure portrayed is Ziyad ibn Aflah, Prefect of Police, and the scenes appear on a casket made for him in 969–70. (8, 9, 10)

170

MUSLIM CORDOBA

A. J. ARBERRY

THE GOLDEN AGE of Cordoba, present-day regional capital of Andalusia, may be dated to the tenth century of Christian, the fourth
century of Muhammadan reckoning: from the reign of Abdurrahman III (912–61) – who called himself an-Nasir li-Din Allah ('Defender of Allah's Religion'), to that of his grandson Hisham II's
powerful minister-regent al-Mansur (d. 1002).

An ancient city, ideally sited

A township of importance has probably stood on the banks of the
Guadalquivir, overlooked by the Sierra Morena to the north, since
Phoenician times. The Romans found a flourishing settlement there
when they mastered Spain two centuries before Christ, and under
their rule Corduba, capital of Hispania Ulterior, produced such notables as the Senecas, as well as the emperors Trajan and Hadrian.
The Visigoths in their turn found Kordhoba conveniently sited to
serve as an administrative centre of their Christian kingdom; and
when the city was captured in 711 by a handful of Arab and Berber
invaders, a very rich harvest of holy spoils was gathered in. Thereafter Cordoba became a Muslim capital, at first of a province ruled
by a governor who acknowledged the supremacy of the distant
caliph of Islam, then of a belated, semi-independent Umayyad prince-
dom, and finally of a realm whose absolute monarch styled himself
Commander of the Faithful in defiance of degenerate Baghdad. The
successors of an-Nasir lacked the resolution and shrewdness which
had qualified him to be the greatest sovereign of his time, and Cordoba never recovered from the Berber sackings and subsequent
chaos of the early eleventh century.

Cordoba was indeed ideally sited to serve as a capital city in those
days. The Guadalquivir has already broadened out, by the time it
debouches into its wide plain, to such an extent that the great bridge,
first constructed (so report says) by order of Augustus Caesar, supported on sixteen arches, spans no less than 223 metres; from there
down to the salt-swamps of Las Marismas and the Bay of Cadiz, it
runs through fertile country over a hundred miles, passing Seville
on its way. The approaches to Cordoba are readily defensible by
resolute troops; to the south and south-east the city is protected by
mountain-ranges soaring to the snow-peaked Sierra Nevada; its
northern gates are guarded by the heights of the Sierra Morena. Only
in times of insurrection and civil war was the capital exposed to successful attack, with a fifth column ready to open its gates; so long
as a firm hand held the reins of power tightly, the city prospered in
serene impregnability.

The broad expanse of flat land surrounding the core of the city
provided the physical means of rapid growth; the increasing population was readily sustained by the produce of the fertile plains. The
heart of Cordoba was the *madina*, an ancient walled city whose ramparts measured about four kilometres; it was shaped roughly as a
rectangle whose shorter southern side rested on the river-front,
bisected by the Via Augusta leading northwards to Toledo and
Saragossa, southwards over the bridge to Algeciras. Close against
the river stood the two massive edifices of Alcazar, the royal palace,
and the Cathedral Mosque, La Mezquita Aljama. Outside this central
madina, densely packed with old mansions, offices and markets, an
ever-extending series of suburbs (*rabad*) sprang up. The ancient
Secunda (Shaqunda) across the bridge, held within the semicircular
turn of the river, had been razed in 818 by command of al-Hakam I
and left in ruins to form a huge necropolis. Large lateral extensions
on the right bank of the Guadalquivir absorbed the overspill of
population; these terminated in the west at an-Nasir's new palace
az-Zahra' and in the east at az-Zahira, the residence of Hisham II's
regent. The conurbation at its greatest extent is said by one Arab
author, not noted for hyperbole, to have comprised 471 mosques,
213,077 houses of the working and middle classes, 60,300 residences
of officials and aristocrats, and 80,455 shops – figures which, if true,
point to a population of at least a million. Modern scholars, looking
askance at these soaring statistics, offer calculations ranging between
100,000 and 500,000.

A multi-racial society

The population of medieval Cordoba, and of Muslim Spain in
general, was extremely mixed, an instructive prototype of a multiracial society with fairly rigid stratification. The topmost layer of
the pyramid was occupied by the descendants of the original invaders,
reinforced by subsequent immigrants from Syria and Arabia; these
occupied the most fertile lands, erected the finest residences, and
formed the aristocracy of al-Andalus. The highest nobility were those
who could successfully claim clan-kinship with the ruling Umayyad
house. When the 'Abbasids storming out of Khorasan seized the
caliphate, a grandson of the Umayyad Hisham escaped the general
slaughter of the Marwanid princes and found his way from the
Euphrates to the Guadalquivir, his rallying supporters capturing
Cordoba for him in 756 This founder of the Umayyad Amirate in
Spain is known to history as 'the Falcon of Quraish', Abdurrahman I.
By the tenth century the original Arab blood of the Umayyads had
in fact run somewhat thin. Circumstances had constrained them from
the beginning to take as wives and concubines local women, whose
physical (to say nothing of mental) attributes in any case attracted
them. Thus the Cordoban theologian Ibn Hazm (994–1064) writes
in *The Ring of the Dove*, that charming manual of the *ars amatoria*,
and a social document of the first importance:

All the caliphs of the Banu Marwan (God have mercy on their
souls!), and especially the sons of an-Nasir, were without variation
or exception disposed by nature to prefer blondes. I have myself
seen them, and known others who had seen their forebears, from
the days of an-Nasir's reign down to the present day; everyone of
them has been fair-haired, taking after their mothers, so that this
has become a hereditary trait with them; all but Sulaiman az-Zafir
(God have mercy on him!), whom I remember to have had black
ringlets and a black beard. As for an-Nasir and al-Hakam al-Mus-

171

tansir (may God be pleased with them!), I have been informed by my late father, the vizier, as well as by others, that both of them were blond and blue-eyed. The same is true of Hisham al-Mu'aiyad, Muhammad al-Mahdi, and Abdurrahman al-Murtada (may God be merciful to them all!); I saw them myself many times, and had the honour of being received by them, and I remarked that they all had fair hair and blue eyes. Their sons, their brothers, and all their near kinsmen possessed the selfsame characteristics.

The royal preference naturally set a fashion which the courtiers were eager to follow. Ibn Hazm, himself sprung originally of local Christian stock, defended his predilection in verses which suggest clearly enough that this mingling of races was not effected without opposition:

> They blame the girl of whom I'm fond
> Because her lovely hair is blond;
> 'But that's exactly', I reply,
> 'What makes her pretty, to my eye!'
>
> They criticize the colour bright
> Of glittering gold, and shimmering light,
> And they are crazy so to do,
> And stupid, and erroneous, too.
>
> Is there just cause to crab, think you,
> The tender-sweet narcissus' hue,
> Or is the twinkle of a star
> So hateful to behold afar?
>
> Of all God's creatures, I declare
> That man of wisdom has least share
> Who chooses, in his darkened soul,
> To love a body black as coal.
>
> Black is the hue, the Scriptures tell,
> Of the inhabitants of Hell;
> Black is the robe the mourner dons
> And mothers who have lost their sons.
>
> Moreover, since from Khorasan
> The black Abbasid banners ran,
> The souls of men know, to their cost,
> The cause of righteousness is lost.

Ibn Hazm belonged to the upper middle classes, that numerous segment of Andalusian society known as *muwallads*. These were descendants of local families who had accepted conversion to Islam, whether from conviction, convenience or necessity; the circumstances of their attachment to the triumphant religion were well remembered, so that the volunteer converts – or at all events those who made the best showing of sincerity – enjoyed a privileged status and certain tax-exemptions not conceded to more recalcitrant believers. The next layer of the social pyramid was filled by the Mozarabes, the 'Arabizers': these Goths had remained faithful Christians, and were bilingual in Romance and Arabic; their Mozarabite liturgy was composed in Arabic, and after the Reconquista they continued for some time to employ the Arabic alphabet in writing Spanish. Like 'people of the Book' throughout the empire of Islam, they were called upon to pay heavily enough in dues and taxes for the 'protection' of the régime under which they lived. In the same boat with them were the Jews who kept to the faith of their fathers, and – in all justice let it be said – were far freer from persecution and vexatious discrimination than their forebears had been under the Christian Visigoths. Christians and Jews alike were broadly scattered through the countryside as share-cropping peasants; concentrated in the towns, in their own segregated quarters, they served in the main as craftsmen, petty shopkeepers and clerks. Their status was frequently that of serfs, a condition which they shared with the poorer *muwallads*, Berbers and liberated slaves. Slaves unredeemed inhabited the bottom layer of the pyramid; upon their backs the whole economy eventually rested.

Rewards of slavery

The foregoing scheme adumbrates a rigidity of class-differentiation which was broadly factual, but to which exceptions were always possible. To take the lowest group first: it was of slaves that the caliph's numerous personal bodyguard was composed, and by virtue of their employment these defenders of the Defender of the Faith enjoyed considerable privileges denied to the great majority of free citizens. Virtuous slaves might also look forward to being liberated by their masters as a reward for conspicuous merit, and were then admissible to clientship of the noble families who had owned them. The position of female slaves could be even more enviable. Purchased speculatively as young girls out of the spoils of war or freebooting, if they showed promise of unusual beauty or exceptional talent they were delicately nurtured and expensively educated by their owners, so that their natural gifts stood every chance of maturing to the full. Taken as concubines, by bearing sons they earned manumission, and acquired a very favoured place in aristocratic households. To cite a famous instance, it was a concubine of Abdurrahman III who caused the palace city of az-Zahra' to be built; dying young, she left a large fortune at first intended for the ransom of Muslims held in Christian prisons. These being very few at that time, her successor in caliphal favour, a concubine named az-Zahra', proposed that the legacy should be expended instead upon bricks and mortar, or rather marble and mosaic, now that the ancient Alcazar had become too cramped for the enlarged royal establishment.

The pages of Ibn Hazm abound in surprising testimony to the chivalrous attitude of enlightened Cordoban masters to their female possessions. One passage must suffice to illustrate, not only this particular point, but also the urbane luxury of the prosperous Moorish household:

I can tell you with regard to myself, that in my youth I enjoyed the loving friendship of a certain slave-girl who grew up in our house, and who at the time of my story was sixteen years of age. She had an extremely pretty face, and was moreover intelligent, chaste, pure, shy, and of the sweetest disposition; she was not given to jesting, and most sparing of her favours; she had a wonderful complexion, which she always kept closely veiled; innocent of every vice, and of very few words, she kept her eyes modestly cast down. Moreover she was extremely cautious, and guiltless of all faults, ever maintaining a serious mien; charming in her withdrawal, she was naturally reserved, and most graceful in repelling unwelcome advances. She seated herself with becoming dignity, and was most sedate in her behaviour; the way she fled from masculine attentions like a startled bird was delightful to behold. No hopes of easy conquest were to be entertained so far as she was concerned; none could look to succeed in his ambitions if these were aimed in her direction; eager expectation found no resting-place in her. Her lovely face attracted all hearts, but her manner kept at arm's length all who came seeking her; she was far more glamorous in her refusals and rejections than those other girls, who rely upon easy compliance and the ready lavishing of their favours to make them interesting to men. In short, she was dedicated to earnestness in all matters, and had no desire for amusement of any kind; for all that she played the lute most beautifully. I found myself irresistibly drawn towards her, and loved her with all the violent passion of my youthful heart. For two years or thereabouts I laboured to the utmost of my powers to win one syllable of response from her, to hear from her lips a single word, other than the usual kind of banalities that may be heard by everyone; but all my efforts proved in vain.

Now I remember a party that was held in our residence, on one of those occasions that are commonly made the excuse for such festivities in the houses of persons of rank. The ladies of our household and of my brother's also (God have mercy on his soul!) were assembled together, as well as the womenfolk of our retainers and faithful servants, all thoroughly nice and jolly folk. The ladies remained in the house for the earlier part of the day, and then betook themselves to a belvedere that was attached to our mansion, overlooking the garden and giving a magnificent view of the whole of Cordoba; the bays were constructed with large open windows. They passed their time enjoying the panorama through the lattice openings, myself being among them. I recall that I was endeavouring to reach the bay where she was standing, to enjoy her proximity and to sidle close up to her. But no sooner did she observe me in the offing, than she left that bay and sought another, moving with consummate grace. I endeavoured to come to the

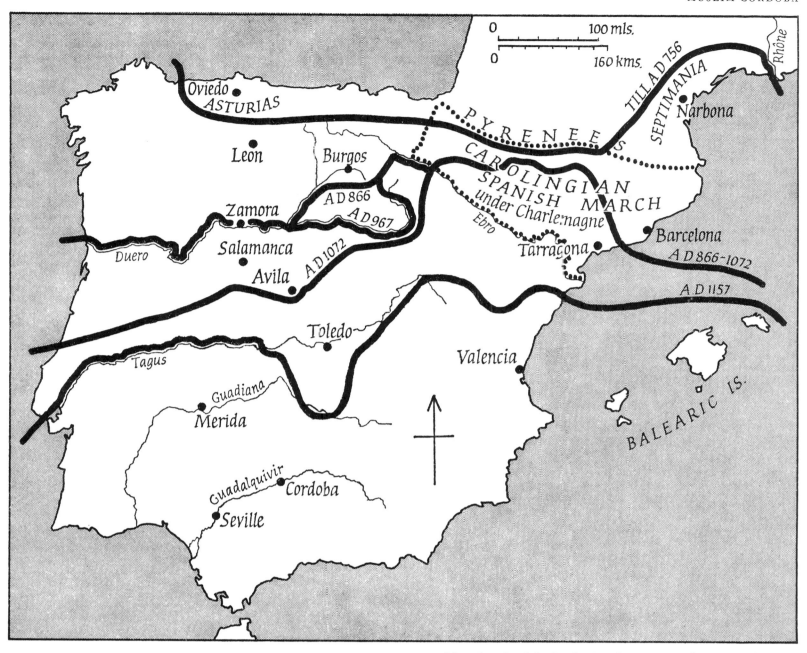

Map of medieval Spain, showing the progressive diminution of Muslim domination between 756 and 1157.

bay to which she had departed, and she repeated her performance and passed on to another. She was well aware of my infatuation, while the other ladies were entirely unconscious of what was passing between us; for there was a large company of them, and they were all the time moving from one alcove to another to enjoy the variety of prospects, each bay affording a different view from the rest. You must realize, my friend, that women have keener eyes to detect admiration in a man's heart, than any benighted traveller has to discover a track in the desert. Well, at last the ladies went down into the garden; and the dowagers and duchesses among them entreated the mistress of the girl to let them hear her sing. She commanded her to do so; and she thereupon took up her lute, and tuned it with a pretty shyness and modesty the like of which I had never seen; though it is true of course that things are doubly beautiful in the eyes of their admirers. Then she began to sing those famous verses of al-Abbas ibn al-Ahnaf:

> My heart leaped up, when I espied
> A sun sink slowly in the west,
> Its beauty in that bower to hide
> Where lovely ladies lie at rest:
>
> A sun embodied in the guise
> Of a sweet maiden of delight,
> The ripple of her rounded thighs
> A scroll of parchment, soft and white.

> No creature she of human kind,
> Though human fair and beautiful,
> And neither sprite, although designed
> In faery grace ineffable.
>
> Her body was a jasmine rare,
> Her perfume sweet as amber scent,
> Her face a pearl beyond compare,
> Her all, pure light's embodiment.
>
> All shrouded in her pettigown
> I watched her delicately pass,
> Stepping as light as thistledown
> That dances on a crystal glass.

And, by my life, it was as though her plectrum was plucking at the strings of my heart. I have never forgotten that day, nor shall forget it until the time comes for me to leave this transient world. That was the most I was ever given to see her, or to hear her voice.

Slaves in Muslim Spain, then, could well console themselves – if they were fortunate in their masters and their natural endowments – for the loss of the most precious gift of freedom. They usually converted to Islam, and when set at liberty felt small yearning to return to their homeland.

173

Opportunities for the middle classes

As for the Mozarabes, from the earliest days of the occupation the able amongst them, as elsewhere throughout the empire, were welcomed into the newly evolving society, whether as experienced administrators, cunning financiers, skilled physicians, artists or mastercraftsmen. Though the history of the Church under the Moors is at best fragmentary, it is certain that bishops and priests, monks and nuns were left unmolested except, as sometimes happened, when they deliberately courted martyrdom and were reluctantly obliged. In the beginning the conquerors of Cordoba appropriated one-half of the Church of St Vincent for their Muslim worship, in imitation of what had been done at first in the east under the caliph Omar; it was only when the congregation outgrew these modest bounds that they negotiated the purchase of the remainder, to serve as the foundations on which was erected in due course the majestic Cathedral Mosque. The Jews too, who had good reason to welcome the change of régime, resumed in peace their community life and worshipped in their synagogues; Cordoba in the tenth century became a leading centre of Talmudic studies.

The eminent Jewish physician, scholar and statesman Hasday ibn Shaprut enjoyed the special confidence of Abdurrahman III, and of al-Hakam after him. He was entrusted with diplomatic missions to Ordoño IV of León, and Queen Tota of Navarre. When Constantine Porphyrogenitus of Byzantium sent an embassy to Cordoba, carrying amongst other gifts the Greek text of Dioscorides, Hasday ibn Shaprut presided over its translation into Arabic out of a Latin version made by the monk Nicolas.

An Arab historian has painted for us an impressive picture of the reception accorded to Constantine's embassy. Landing at Pechina, the legates were greeted one stage without the gates of Cordoba with a military parade; two gigantic eunuch-officers of the caliphal guard escorted them to their guest-lodgings in Munyat Nusair, where they were kept incommunicado. On a chosen Saturday the caliph proceeded from his new palace of az-Zahra' to Alcazar, there to receive the deputation. The great hall was richly carpeted and hung with precious silks. Abdurrahman, seated on his golden throne, was flanked to right and left by his sons and nearest kinsmen, whilst the ministers and other high dignitaries took up their appropriate stations. Dazzled by such a display of majesty and wealth, the Byzantine envoys delivered their message, inscribed in gold Greek characters on blue vellum, encased in a golden box and sealed with a seal bearing on one side the effigy of Christ and on the other Constantine's portrait. In the exchanges which followed, the orator chosen to speak for the caliph was overcome by the splendour of the scene, and his place was taken at shortest notice by an eminent visitor from Baghdad, the author Abu Ali al-Qali. An alternative version of the story is that al-Qali was the man appointed, and that when he stammered into silence the day was saved by a local product.

The Mozarabe community was organized under the headship of a *comes*, who acted as spokesman for all the Christians of Cordoba in their dealings with the government; we know the name of this official in 970 – Muawiya ibn Lope. Their private differences were subject to the arbitration of a special judge, the 'cadi of the Christians'; presumably he administered the Visigothic law. The Bishop of Cordoba at the same date was a certain Isa ibn Mansur. The most prominent Christian under Abdurrahman III was Rabi' ibn Zaid, baptized Recemundo, whom the caliph was pleased to send on embassies to Otto I of Germany, and later to Byzantium and Syria to procure works of art for the furnishing of az-Zahra'.

Andalusia's finest stock

We have noticed that Ibn Hazm, that notable *muwallad* who was perhaps the greatest all-round Muslim scholar al-Andalus produced, described his father as 'the late vizier'. No office indeed, save that of headship of the state, was barred to these descendants of local converts; for all that snobbery often enough induced them to claim Persian or other foreign origin, and to enhance their names with the aid of forged genealogies. On the other hand, we find eminent Cordobans boasting of their ancestors Princess Sara and Count Julian. Nomenclature provides a clue to Spanish blood, as in the ending '-un' to Arab personal names. The celebrated poet Ibn Zaidun, who vainly courted that grand lady the Princess Wallada, thereby revealed

himself a *muwallad*. Other similar forms, declaring Visigothic descent, are the names of Ibn Hafsun, the colourful leader of a revolt which shook the foundations of Umayyad rule in Spain in the closing years of the ninth century; Ibn Badrun, the poet and statesman of Almoravid times; and not least Ibn Khaldun, though to be sure that illustrious historian traced his ancestry to a Yemeni emigrant to Spain. It would be scarcely an exaggeration to attribute to the *muwallads*, whose blood was so freely mingled with that of the Arab conquerors, almost all that was finest and most creative in the civilization and culture of al-Andalus. Formally, their Arabization was complete; they used the language of the Koran with absolute mastery, and followed assiduously the literary traditions of the Arab East; yet they contrived to impose their own cachet on the highly conventional pattern. Andalusia under Abdurrahman III felt itself to be a nation (in the medieval sense of the term) with its own national character, prepared in its literature and art to challenge comparison with Egypt, Syria and Iraq.

Not less comprehensive was the Islamization of the *muwallads*, and the rigorously puritan standards of belief and ritual to which they, along with the Umayyad aristocracy, rigidly adhered. Cordoba in the tenth century was a bulwark of Sunnite orthodoxy, when the extremist Shi'ite sect embodied in the Fatimid movement threatened to capture the heart and body of Islam. Four schools of canon law had developed within Sunni Islam; it was the strictest and most conservative of these rites, the Maliki, which prevailed in Muslim Spain. The spirit of extreme conservatism reveals itself even in the style of calligraphy employed by Andalusian scribes; at a time when the ancient Kufic writing had given place in the East to a more fluent

hand known as *naskh*, in Spain as throughout the Maghrib the squarer 'monumental' characters still found favour, a difference reflected down to the present day. And whereas paper was rapidly displacing parchment from Egypt to India, in the West vellum continued to be preferred for fine and sacred books even after the manufacture of paper had been introduced into Spain. The intellectual ferment set up in Baghdad by the translations of Greek philosophy and science spread to all parts of the Muslim world, but in the West its effects were more narrowly controlled. Nevertheless, tenth-century Cordoba knew something of the contention of jarring sects; Mu'tazilism and Sufi theosophy did not lack for adherents, until the inevitable reaction of the diehards set in with a disastrous burning of books and banishment of scholars.

Lovers of books and learning

Manuscripts ranked as prized possessions in the golden age of Cordoba. The caliph al-Hakam II, a veritable Maecenas of literature and learning, is reported to have assembled in the Alcazar a library of 400,000 volumes; the careful catalogue itself ran to forty-four registers each of fifty leaves; the collection must have easily rivalled that famous library of the Samanids in Bokhara which the young Avicenna was so excited to explore, and which not so many years later perished in flames lit by Mahmud of Ghazna's soldiery. Private citizens also took pride in collecting books. 'Cordoba', reported Ibn Sa'id on his father's authority,

held more books than any other city of al-Andalus, and its inhabitants were the most enthusiastic in caring for their libraries;

such collections were regarded by them as symbols of status and social leadership. Men who had no knowledge whatsoever would make it their business to have a library in their houses; they would be selective in their acquisitions, so that they might boast of possessing unica, or copies in the handwriting of a particular calligrapher.

Ibn Futais, vizier and cadi under al-Hakam II, loved nothing better than to retire to his library, which he had decorated entirely in green; he employed six full-time scribes; declining to lend his own precious volumes even to his best friends, he preferred to present them with copies made on request in his scriptorium. When his grandson was constrained by circumstances to sell the collection, the library fetched 40,000 dinars. Of those huge accumulations, which must have included many thousands of masterpieces of calligraphy and illumination, sumptuously bound, not a trace has survived the repeated destruction of libraries, motivated for the most part by religious intolerance.

Elementary education was perfectly general throughout al-Andalus, save in the poorest households. The majority of boys and girls attended the local primary school, where for a modest salary the master taught his pupils reading, writing and the recitation of the Koran before passing them on to learn a trade. The well-to-do engaged private tutors for their children, paying them a stipend fixed by contract and enhanced by bonuses at the great feasts. As we learn from a number of sources, women shared equally with men in the work of pedagogy; not a few became accomplished scholars. Ibn Hazm provides us as usual with first-hand evidence:

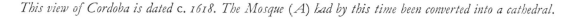

This view of Cordoba is dated c. 1618. The Mosque (A) had by this time been converted into a cathedral.

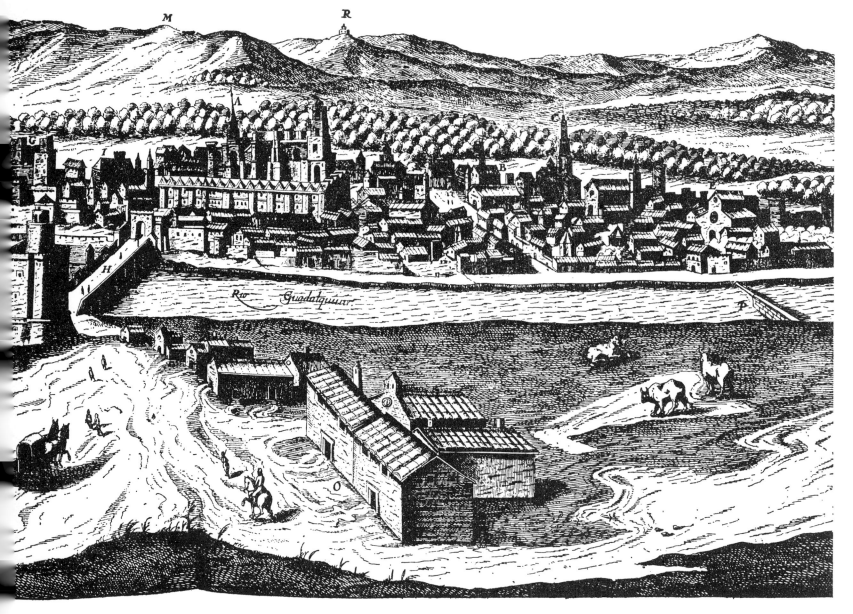

I have myself observed women, and got to know their secrets to an extent almost unparalleled; for I was reared in their bosoms, and brought up amongst them, not knowing any other society. I never sat with men until I was already a youth, and my beard had begun to sprout. Women taught me the Koran, they recited to me much poetry, they trained me in calligraphy.

The elements mastered, those youths who were destined for careers in the administration or the professions passed on to mosque schools and colleges. Each quarter of Cordoba was liberally provided with mosques, maintained out of special public funds and private benefactions; individual mosques enjoyed prestige according to the reputed scholars who elected to teach in them. The Cathedral Mosque in the old *madina* naturally attracted the ablest professors, both from home and abroad, and by the middle of the tenth century had acquired (by medieval standards) university status. Cordoba's Mezquita became an international centre of higher learning earlier than Cairo's al-Azhar and Baghdad's Nizamiya, drawing to its spacious courts students, Christian as well as Muslim, from many lands. Here instruction was offered in all branches of contemporary learning. Pride of place naturally belonged to the traditional 'sciences' of Koranic exegesis, the study of the Traditions of the Prophet, and the principles and applications of Muslim jurisprudence. These were followed by advanced grammar and syntax, Arabic philology, the elucidation of the old poetry, and the evaluation of serious literature. The syllabus included logic, mathematics, astronomy, those parts of the natural sciences available at the time, and apparently medicine as well. The method of teaching was by lecture courses, either free dissertations or expositions of set books, seminar-fashion. Students were expected to bring and annotate their own copies; at the conclusion of a course the professor would enter into successful pupils' manuscripts a certificate (*ijaza*) giving licence to teach that text on his chain of authority.

Ibn Hazm tells us how he put his university studies of old poetry to a sufficiently curious use:

I myself experienced in my youth a breaking-off in my relations with a very intimate friend. The rupture soon healed, but then it returned. When this happened frequently, I extemporized a poem as a sort of joke, inserting after each couplet of my original composition a couplet taken from the beginning stanzas of the *Suspended Ode* of Tarafa ibn al-'Abd, which I had studied with commentary at the feet of Abu Sa'id al-Fata al-Ja'fari, transmitting from Abu Bakr al-Muqri' and from Abu Ja'far an-Nahhas (God have mercy on their souls!) in the Cathedral Mosque of Cordoba:

I called to mind the love I bore
For her, my heart's adored of yore,
That seems like Khaula's traces now
Wind-swept on Thahmad's rocky brow.

My memory of that firm bond
She pledged with me (and I so fond)
Still lasts as clear as the blue band
Tattooed upon an Arab's hand.

And there I paused, not knowing true
If she would come to me anew,
Yet not despairing, and I wept
Until the morn, nor ever slept.

Then long my kinsfolk chided me
And made reproach abundantly;
'Nay, perish not of grief', they cried,
'But be with courage fortified.'

The divers moods and rages of
That fickle lady whom I love
Are like the wrecks of schooners spread
Along Dad's rocky torrent-bed.

Those alternations of repulse
And union, which my heart convulse,
Are as a ship some helmsman veers
To catch the wind, then forward steers.

First she was pleased a little while,
Then turned away in anger vile;
So children playing in the sands
Divide the parcels with their hands.

Here lips were smiling graciously,
But in her heart she raged at me –
A double necklace, fashioned with
Gay pearls, and sombre chrysolith.

A splendour with secure foundations

The brilliance of Cordoba's social life, the splendour of its public monuments and private residences, and the general prosperity and tranquillity enjoyed by its teeming population – these were secured by the strong hand at the helm and the loyalty and devotion of his officers and ministers whose personal interest it was that the régime should be stable (for some had invested huge fortunes in buying promotion); also by the energetic exploitation of the natural resources of a land endowed with fertile, well-irrigated estates and a variety of mineral wealth. Further assets were skilled artisans taking pride in the products of their hands, and the regular gathering, by whatever tortuous devices, of revenues and taxes. The frontiers had been stabilized, and were held secure by strong and fanatical garrison outposts; every summer, to the accompaniment of a May day parade in the capital of armed might, expeditions were despatched northwards to keep alive the sacred tradition of the *jihad* and to discourage any Christian prince who might be ambitious to transgress the boundaries of Islam. A well-ordered justiciary, with courts presided over by learned judges interpreting to the best of their understanding the revealed ordinances of Allah, kept the faithful content. Malefactors and conspirators were restrained by the severity of the sentences meted out to those who broke the law; rows of heads kept

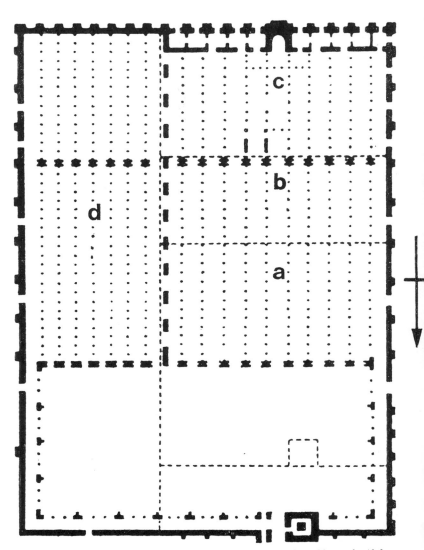

Various stages of Cordoba's Mosque: (a) the original building of Abdurrahman I, plus the additions of Abdurrahman II (b), al-Hakam II (c) and al-Mansur (d).

impaled in public places long after execution proved a powerful disincentive. The streets, narrow and winding as many of them might be, were well paved, well lighted and clean; save in years of drought, water flowed abundantly, and baths might be had by all. The daily markets were filled with a wide variety of goods and produce at reasonable prices; weights and measures were subject to close inspection to safeguard against defrauding.

Cordoba was particularly renowned for the excellence of its leatherware, commemorated in the word cordwainer. It was in Cordoba, in the ninth century, that the process of manufacturing crystal was discovered. Other fine products included gold ornaments of every kind, jewellery, inlaid copper, ivories, marquetry, woollen and silken cloths and brocades. These products were exported as far afield as India and central Asia; a brisk import trade added to the stock of available amenities and the soundness of the economy. The royal mint struck large issues of gold and silver coins which were acceptable currency even in the northern states of Europe. The various crafts and trades were localized in particular market-quarters, as may be seen still today in the ancient *madinas* of Fez and Marrakesh; their nomenclature has survived in modern Cordoba, in streets called after butchers, shoemakers, booksellers, weavers.

Intellectual decline

The intellectual adventure of tenth-century Cordoba came to a brusque end after the death of al-Hakam II. His successor on the caliphal throne was a boy of twelve, Hisham II, who reigned from 976 to 1009 in the shadow of his chamberlain Ibn Abi 'Amir, calling himself al-Mansur.

As soon as he became master of the empire [the Andalusian historian Sa'id informs us] he proceeded to the library of al-Hakam, Hisham's father, caused all the writings therein contained to be brought forth in the presence of a number of theologians, and ordered these latter to put on one side, with the exception of medical texts and treatises on arithmetic, all those books dealing with the sciences of the ancients: logic, astronomy and other sciences cultivated by the Greeks. When these had been separated from all the books relating to lexicography, grammar, poetry, history, medicine, jurisprudence, traditions, in short those sciences recognized by the Andalusians, Ibn Abi 'Amir commanded that the works treating of the ancient sciences should be burned. Some were in fact committed to the flames; others were flung into the palace moats, or buried, or destroyed in some other manner. Ibn Abi 'Amir acted in this fashion in order to ingratiate himself with the people of al-Andalus and to discredit in their eyes the principles followed by al-Hakam. Indeed these sciences were ill regarded by the older generation, and criticized by the leading men. The majority of those then engaged in the study of philosophy lost their ardour, and kept secret what they knew of these sciences, only cultivating openly the branches permitted them, such as arithmetic, the rules governing the partition of inheritances, medicine and the like.

The days of Avempace and Averroes were yet to come, but here we have the twilight before the dark night; the splendid noon was long over.

The kingdom soon fell apart after the death of the strong and sagacious al-Mansur. His son and successor as regent, al-Muzaffar, was poisoned by his brother in 1008; the latter, having announced himself heir-designate to the caliphate, was promptly assassinated. Andalusia was rent to pieces by a series of insurrections, the horror of which culminated in 1013 when Berber rebels seized and sacked Cordoba. The sumptuous palace of al-Mansur, az-Zahira, was utterly destroyed. Of az-Zahra' at least the ruins have been excavated, to bear melancholy witness to the times when Cordoba was, in the famous phrase of the Saxon poetess Hroswitha, 'the ornament of the world'. Only the Cathedral Mosque was spared, in later days to be reconverted into a Christian church.

Elegiac voices

Neither the sumptuous Christian fabric that today rises in the midst of those countless columns, nor all the treasures of art lavished upon it by the celebrated artists of the sixteenth century who erected it, nor that interminable series of chapels of every epoch which, resting against the walls of the Mosque, disfigure it; nor the clumsy angels that seem to suspend their flight to shed glory over the divine service, nor the words of the Evangelist sounding from the seat of the Holy Spirit, can dispel or banish in the slightest degree the majesty of those wandering shades, that in vain seek in the sanctuary the sacred volume whose leaves, according to tradition, were enamelled with the blood of the caliph Othman, martyr to the faith. A world of souvenirs here enthralls the mind of the traveller as he gazes with a feeling of sorrow upon these profanations – works dictated by the intolerant yet sincere faith of our ancestors, impelled by the desire of banishing for ever from that spot consecrated to the law of Jesus, the spirit of Mohammed and the ghosts of his slaves that haunt it, and will for ever haunt it while it exists. For, in spite of the mutilations it has endured, and of the changes it has undergone, there is impressed upon it, by a superior ineradicable law, the seal of the art that inspired it, and the character of the people by whom it was planned and erected.

Elegies on the former glory of Cordoba have been composed by many authors, besides Amados de los Rios; it is a familiar nostalgic theme of Muslim poets today. Of all that has been written in ancient or modern times, nothing evokes the memory of lost beauty and the ghost of gracious living with such poignant eloquence as the lines penned in exile by her erstwhile citizen, Ibn Hazm:

A visitor from Cordoba informed me, when I asked him for news of that city, that he had seen our mansion in Balat Mughith, on the western side of the metropolis; its traces were well-nigh obliterated, its waymarks effaced; vanished were its spacious patios. All had been changed by decay; the joyous pleasaunces were converted to barren deserts and howling wildernesses; its beauty lay in shattered ruins. Where peace once reigned, fearful chasms yawned; wolves resorted there, ghosts frolicked, demons sported. Wild beasts now lurked where men like lions, abounding in wealth and every luxury, once paid court to statuesque maidens; who were all now scattered and dispersed to the four corners of the earth. Those gracious halls, those richly ornamented boudoirs, that once shone like the sun, the loveliness of their panorama lifting all cares from the mind, being now entirely overwhelmed by desolation and utter destruction seemed rather like the gaping mouths of savage beasts, proclaiming the end that awaits this mortal world, and revealing the final destiny of those who dwell therein, the ultimate fate of those you now see abiding here below; so that you would be moved, after so long reluctance to abandon the world, henceforth eagerly to renounce it.

Then I remembered the days that I had passed in that fair mansion, the joys I had known there, the months of my ardent youth spent in the company of blooming virgins, very apt to awaken desire in the heart of the most sedate young man. I pictured those maidens now lying beneath the dust, or dispersed to distant parts and far regions, scattered by the hand of exile, torn to pieces by the fingers of expatriation. I saw in my mind's eye the ruin of that noble house, which I had once known as beautiful and thriving, and in the shadow of whose well-ordered establishment I had passed my childhood; empty were those courts once so densely thronged. I seemed to hear the voices of owls hooting and screeching over those passages, astir of old with the busy concourse of people in whose midst I grew to manly estate. Then night followed day with the selfsame bustle, the selfsame coming and going of countless feet; but now day followed night there, and all was forever hushed and desolate.

These sad reflections filled my eyes with tears and my heart with anguish; my soul was shattered as if by a jagged rock, and the misery in my mind waxed ever greater. So I took refuge in poetry, and uttered the following stanza.

If now our throats are parched and dry,
Yet long its waters slaked our thirst;
If evil now has done its worst,
Our happiness was slow to die.

THE PARIS
OF ABELARD AND ST LOUIS

The Monarchy, the Church, the University

(*Imperium, Sacerdotium, Studium*): these were the corner-stones of medieval Paris. Their combined influence during the period between the accession of Philip Augustus in 1180 and the death of Louis IX in 1270 made Paris a singularly favoured city, the capital of European civilization.

Hugh Capet founded the royal dynasty at the end of the tenth century in his own city on the Seine, Lutetia. The withered remains of this former seat of the Roman administration grew, under successive kings, into the Paris of medieval maturity. Philip Augustus, a successor to the Capetian throne, was the city's real builder and the first effective king of 'France'. During his reign, Paris became a walled city – a circumscribed civic unit.

Just as the Church had kept learning alive during the Dark Ages, so it preserved the continuous life of Paris during that period. Now, however, the kings of the house of Capet gave new life in turn to the Church. Ecclesiastical architecture rose throughout the city; a fresh 'Gothic' impulse inspired the age. Work on the Cathedral of Notre-Dame was begun in 1160 by Maurice de Sully, bishop of Paris, and continued by his successors until its virtual completion three-quarters of a century later. Notre-Dame appears opposite in a detail from

a miniature painted by Fouquet in the fifteenth century: the area depicted has been greatly enlarged so as to illustrate familiar features of the cathedral's façade. One of the last stages in the work of construction, the façade is divided by plain buttresses into three large recessed portals, all clearly visible here, and featuring in the centre the famous rose-window. The two stunted spires of Notre-Dame can also be seen.

Neither the monarchy nor the Church would of themselves have ensured for Paris its unique position at the centre of medieval Europe. But Paris, alone among the cities of Europe, possessed a university, the prototype of nearly all the later universities of northern Europe. The University of Paris had grown around the figure of Abelard, in response to the awakened curiosity of the age. It attracted an intellectual élite from many lands, who transformed Paris into a vibrant, cosmopolitan centre.

The city's vigorous bourgeoisie, active as it was in providing for an urban population which has been estimated at 150,000 in the mid-fourteenth century, nevertheless did not achieve the degree of pre-eminence enjoyed by the three cardinal institutions of medieval Paris. (1)

178

Aspects of student life

in the University of Paris – the earliest and greatest of the European universities founded during the Middle Ages – are illustrated from contemporary reliefs. The first (above left) shows four students taking their revenge on a harlot – her crime is unspecified – who is being punished on the 'bishop's ladder'. Set up on the parvis of Notre-Dame, this served a similar function to the stocks. The students hurl mud and filth while two law-enforcement officers stand by.

Above right: Three students place their hands on an open Bible to take the oath being administered by an ecclesiastic. Students had to swear to obey each new regulation, and also, before each examination, not to bribe the examiner. The couple on the right of this relief may be publishing their banns.

A medieval seminar is shown opposite, centre left. The inscription on the scroll is no longer legible, so the subject being discussed must remain conjectural. The fourth relief (opposite, centre right) shows students attending a lecture. The lecturer is identified by his elevated central position and by his cape and biretta. The students seem to be attending closely, although they take no notes.

The university's struggle for independence, supported by royal power against the civic authorities, sometimes erupted into violence. An Austin friar – on whose tomb the relief (far right) was carved – was murdered by three constables in 1440. The assailants, seen kneeling, were punished and are offering 'l'amende honorable', i.e. making a humble apology to the university authorities. (3, 5, 6, 9, 10)

Abbot Suger (opposite, top left) was a monk-statesman, an exceptionally talented man who combined ecclesiastic and secular enthusiasms. He embellished his abbey, St-Denis, and since Denis was the patron saint of the monarchy as well as of the abbey, Suger became friend and counsellor to Louis VI and VII. Suger, in fact, was the effective ruler of the kingdom while Louis VII was abroad on the second crusade. (2)

Maurice de Sully (opposite, top right), bishop of Paris from 1160 to 1196, founded the Cathedral of Notre-Dame and baptized King Philip Augustus there. (4)

'University' derives from the Latin word *universitas* ('association') and was originally used for associations of the various trades. From the early association of teachers and scholars in the Latin Quarter grew the University of Paris. Its spiritual foundation and present location are due to Abelard (right), the greatest and most popular teacher of the age, who migrated with a swarm of students from Notre-Dame, which had been the traditional centre of education. Bottom left: seal, dated 1292, of the University of Paris. (7, 8)

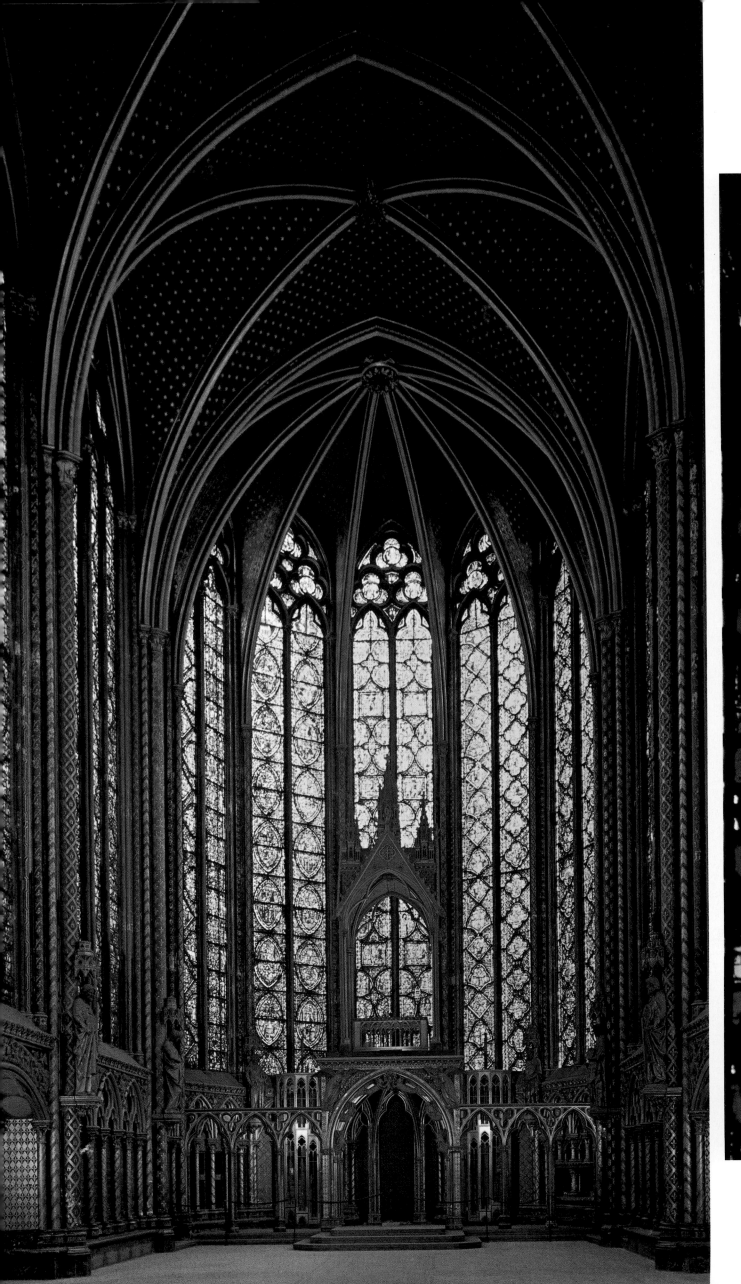

St Louis' shrine, the Sainte-Chapelle, thanks to judicious restoration, remains today almost as it was when completed in 1258. It typifies the resurgent energy of medieval Paris during a spate of architectural activity. St Louis had been inspired to create this exquisite private chapel as a worthy repository for the holy relics he had acquired from the sacred treasury in Constantinople. A stained-glass window in the Sainte-Chapelle (below) depicts St Louis and his brothers themselves bearing the Crown of Thorns. This was the most coveted of the relics, all of which were believed to have played a part in the crucifixion. The royal party took eight days to carry it barefoot from Sens to Paris where it was placed in the chapel in the Cité to await completion of the Sainte-Chapelle. (11, 12)

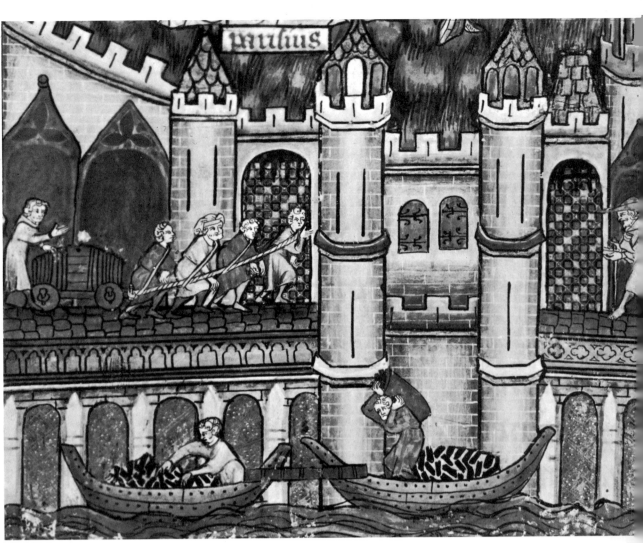

The real builder of medieval Paris was Philip Augustus, who
first surrounded the city with a rampart. The wall survives today in
fragments (left). He also engineered Paris' first water supply, and,
overcome by the pestilential stench of her streets, decreed that they
should be paved with stone. Cobbles can be seen (top) in one of the
fourteenth-century illuminations which capture vividly the daily life
of the time. They are scenes on the Grand-Pont, a bridge which was
bordered with houses and shops, and was the city's commercial centre.
Four men drag a barrel loaded on a trolley across the bridge; a barefoot pilgrim enters at right, and two coal-barges float on the river.
Above: A flour mill with its waterwheels set between the arches of
the Grand-Pont. Opposite, top left: A loaded passenger carriage enters the covered section of the bridge. Barges on the river contain
barrels of wine, on which a toll is being paid. A metal-working establishment is shown opposite, bottom left. (13–17)

Philip Augustus, who ruled between 1180 and 1223, is presumed to be the subject of a statue (detail, top right) in Reims Cathedral. (18)

The Bishop of Paris (right) gives his blessing at the Lendit Fair. This annual Parisian trade fair, like many others of the Middle Ages, began early in the twelfth century as a religious festival. (19)

The Ile de la Cité as it appeared in a painting for the Duc de Berry's early fifteenth-century Book of Hours *Très Riches Heures*. Prominent are palace buildings and – on the right – the Sainte-Chapelle with a view of the rose-window. The French kings had always had a modest chapel in their palace in the Cité, but when St Louis built the Sainte-Chapelle he bestowed on it such a degree of magnificence (see Plates 11, 12) as to guarantee it wide and permanent renown. (20)

The Louvre was originally built by Philip Augustus as a royal residence outside the city walls. The donjon – or keep – served as royal treasury and state prison, and a deep dungeon, dug there during Philip's time, still exists today. The château was embellished by Charles V (1364–80), who transformed it into a completely self-contained community by accommodating within its walls representatives of every craft and trade. The painting of the Louvre (below) is another illustration from *Très Riches Heures*. (21)

THE PARIS OF ABELARD AND ST LOUIS

DAVID DOUGLAS

THERE ARE MEN who in their time seem so to bestride their generation as almost to stand outside it. So also is it with cities which likewise possess their own inherent life. Yet in the one case as in the other, it is often the pre-eminent which best represents the generality, and no town has ever better reflected the civilization of which it formed a part than did medieval Paris. Its early growth was intimately connected with that of the medieval social order; the transformations which later came upon it exhibited the changes which were in due course to disrupt the medieval world; and in the resplendent interval of its medieval maturity, Paris between 1150 and 1300 took its place, as of right, as the most characteristic city of western Europe. It was, in this sense, the heir after a long interval of Antonine Rome. It was also in some respects the heir of that newer Rome on the banks of the Bosphorus which had helped to preserve the legacy of Mediterranean culture for the benefit of western men. In so far as the cultural achievement of the Middle Ages was based upon a classical tradition modified by the teaching of the Church, to this extent may medieval Paris be said to have represented that civilization at the climax of its development.

The past and the present

If, therefore, medieval Paris is best to be surveyed as it was in the thirteenth century, it was none the less the product of a long growth which itself accurately reflected some seven hundred years of European history. Certainly, no visitor to Paris in the time of St Louis could fail to be conscious of an intimate blend therein between the past and the present. At his first impression, for instance, he would have perceived the town to be dominated by the Christian Cathedral of Notre-Dame set on the island of the Cité, which is the heart of Paris and which had been the seat of the first Roman administration. To the south, on the hill of Sainte-Geneviève – which is even now the Latin Quarter – he would have found the most famous university of Europe, and there he would have discovered men concerned above all with questions of divinity, but speaking Latin as the language of learning, and studying Aristotle as a guide to Christian theology. In such ways were the ancient sources of medieval civilization displayed in thirteenth-century Paris, and its very streets might have served yet further to impress the traveller with the continuity of western culture. It was a Roman road (now the Rue Saint-Jacques) which could lead him from the Christian cathedral through the academic home of secular and ecclesiastical learning. It was likewise a Roman road (now represented in the Rue Saint-Martin) which could take him from the same essential starting-point northward through the merchant quarter of the Halles. Even today there is perhaps no spot in all northern Europe better suited than the Parvis in front of Notre-Dame to impress the modern observer with that subtle medieval achievement whereby the long pathway of the Latin genius was merged almost imperceptibly into the *Via Sacra* of the Cross.

Yet during the twelfth and thirteenth centuries Paris might also have been regarded as a new city pregnant with the impulses of a new life. Our visitor would have found established there the greatest of the new monarchies which were giving secular order to Europe, a monarchy which had its first home in the Cité, and which had but recently created the fortress of the Louvre outside the walls. The merchants of the Halles would have told him of new privileges recently won, and new economic ventures recently undertaken. Passing to the Left Bank, he would have met a multitudinous student body which had but lately been set all afire with a new curiosity. A fine wind of hopeful endeavour was in fact already blowing through the narrow alleys of this thirteenth-century city whose stench impelled Philip Augustus to his plan of paving the Paris streets. Men were living adventurously in the present, although so conscious of the past, and the urgent quality of their immediate enterprise was plentifully exhibited in their town. Most clearly of all was it to be discerned in the new ecclesiastical architecture that was everywhere arising. Massive Romanesque arches, redolent with age, could still be seen in the abbey of Saint-Germain-des-Prés, but it was a fresh 'Gothic' impulse that was now giving expression to the most lively inspiration of the age. Notre-Dame was still in this sense new, but newer still was the lovely shrine which Louis IX had just erected. The Sainte-Chapelle remains today almost as it was when it was completed in 1258 after three years' labour, and it typifies the resurgent energy of medieval Paris at the height of its constructive endeavour.

This city was at once intensely individual and widely representative, and if today every instructed traveller can find in Paris a cosmopolitan as well as a French town, and is conscious that here the two qualities are in harmony, that is due in large measure to a legacy from the Middle Ages. The golden age of medieval Paris lasted for little more than a century, but it enshrined, between 1150 and 1300, very much of the European past, and it held much of the European future in its keeping. So active, however, was its own contemporary life that this may be studied for itself: in the men who then dominated the city, in the buildings they erected, and in the labours they undertook.

This was the Paris of Philip Augustus and Louis the Saint, the greatest of the medieval kings of France. This was also the Paris of the great churches, of the earliest Halles, of the first Louvre, and of the first walls. This was, finally, the Paris of Abelard and the rising university. Nor is the bare recital of these famous names itself without significance to an explanation of the greatness of medieval Paris, or of its influence upon Europe. Medieval Paris was royal; it was ecclesiastical; it was (though to a lesser extent) mercantile; and it was above all the centre of European learning. By combining together these essential characteristics Paris became in the thirteenth century a unique city, and only thus was she then enabled to mirror the civilization of the age.

Civilization's darkest hour

It was the royal house of Capet which was primarily responsible for the rise of medieval Paris, but the kings of that dynasty none the less here built upon foundations which were already old. The importance of the site of Paris was in fact clearly indicated by geography. The three islands in the Seine, chief of which is the present Cité, commanded the most important reach of the greatest waterway of northern France, and dominated the plain that controlled the confluence of the Seine with the Oise and Marne, the one leading to Picardy and the other making an avenue from the east. With their strong sense of actuality, the Romans had, therefore, recognized the importance of this site, making Lutetia (as it was then called) the centre of a road system. They erected a temple on the Cité and also administrative buildings, whilst on the hill to the south, which they termed Mons Lucotitius, an urban settlement grew up. There was a forum near the present Luxembourg gardens and an amphitheatre where now runs the Rue Monge. With the breakdown of the Roman administration, however, this flourishing settlement slowly declined; and continuity was, here as elsewhere, only maintained through the permanence of the ecclesiastical organization which inherited so much of the Roman political system. St Denis, bishop of Paris in the fourth century, had his successors, and it was these men and their followers who were enabled, albeit with difficulty, to preserve the Parisian identity. From the fifth century to the eighth the chief persons in the history of Paris are thus the saints who were in due course to give their names to Parisian churches: Marcellus and Germanus the bishops, and Geneviève, from Mont Valérien. All else save the Church was in decay. The Roman buildings crumbled; over the baths and edifices of Mons Lucotitius vegetation spread; the Cité remained intact but deserted; and no secular ruler came to revive the splendour of the Roman past. Paris was but one – and not the most important – of the seats of Merovingian government; Charlemagne looked rather to Rome and Aachen; and his successors in Gaul reigned not from Paris but from Laon. Not until the last quarter of the ninth century did the fundamental importance of medieval Paris begin to be foreshadowed in connection with a new dynasty.

Western civilization was in greater danger between 850 and 950 than ever it was in the sixth century, and it was in the work of preserving this civilization in its darkest hour that Paris emerged into the European consciousness as in a true sense a capital of the west. The wave of Scandinavian expansion which formed Normandy, and transformed England, all but submerged western Christendom under a pagan tide. That it did not do so was due largely to the work of the West Saxon monarchy in England, and also to the achievement of a family of magnates in northern France whose home was by the Seine, and who took the title of Counts of Paris. The successful defence of Paris against the pagan 'Northmen' between 885 and 887 was one of the turning-points in the history of Europe, and neither the city nor its secular rulers ever lost the prestige which they then won. Later, when a successor of these early Counts of Paris, by name Hugh Capet, in 987 established a new royalty in France, he centred this in his own town by the Seine. From henceforth every advance in Capetian power was reflected in the city, and it was from these beginnings that the royal Paris of the Middle Ages arose.

It is well to observe, however, how much these early Capetians had here to do. The ancient town which Hugh Capet chose for his royal seat had shrunk to scarcely more than the Cité with some few buildings on each of the adjoining banks of the river. Grass grew where the Roman forum had stood on Mons Lucotitius, and there were still marshes between the river and Saint-Paul. Around the central settlement there was thus the desolation of ancient decay, but farther out (though still by modern standards very close) there remained the great monasteries which during the long centuries of decline had stood like rocks in a receding tide: Saint-Germain-des-Prés and Saint-Germain-l'Auxerrois faced each other across the river; Sainte-Geneviève was on the southern hill; Saint-Marcel stood near the modern boulevard of that name; and towards the north there was Saint-Merry near the present Halles. These great churches, all situated in what is now the midst of Paris, had in the past been each the centre of a small hamlet, and at the beginning of the eleventh century these hamlets still remained distinct from the central Paris of the Cité. The first growth of medieval Paris under royal tutelage was, so to speak, to enclose them. Slowly did the new monarchy grow under the first four Capetian kings (987–1108): equally slow was the concurrent growth of their capital. Nor were the two movements ever unconnected. There is an account of Philip Augustus at a later date sitting in the palace that had been built on Roman foundations at the western extremity of the Cité; he is described as gazing at the turbid waters of the river and brooding over the town which lay around him; and that picture is symptomatic of the origins and early growth of medieval Paris.

The royal city transformed

Thus did the eleventh century come and pass, and before its close there was everywhere the stirring of a new life. The Normans set out on their triumphant career of conquest. The Crusades were about to start. Hildebrand at Rome was presiding over an ecclesiastical revival. The 'Twelfth-Century Renaissance' was at hand. In all this Paris and its kings shared, and all this likewise they helped to promote. In the early twelfth century there were in Paris, at one and the same time, Abelard representing the revival of learning, and Suger, the great minister, developing the royal government. If they ever met they would have had much to say to each other about their related, though distinct, interests, and about the city in which they dwelt. For Paris was responding to such stimuli more rapidly than ever before. It is reported to have doubled its size during the reign of Louis VI (1108–38). The 'suburb' of Saint-Merry was already absorbed, and there were now scattered dwellings where stands today the Church of Saint-Eustache. Eager students were beginning to move southward from the Cité into the Latin Quarter. The Mons Lucotitius had become the famous 'Mount' of Sainte-Geneviève. Paris was still small but it contained within itself all the germs of a great expansion. Already, too, it had become the special home of most of what was most productive in medieval civilization.

With Philip Augustus, who succeeded in 1180, the profitable results of this close connection between the Capetians and their capital reached their climax. This king became, more truly than any of his predecessors, king of 'France', and his reign was marked, as if inevitably, by something of a transformation of the royal city. He began to pave the streets with stone, and he built the first walls, so that medieval Paris was for the first time circumscribed and can be watched as an entity. The walls of Philip Augustus have only survived in fragments but their course was reconstructed by the careful scholarship of M. Halphen, and they are worth contemplating in that they girdled what had become the most important city of transalpine Europe. Perhaps, however, it is the smallness of the area which they marked out which may be of most surprise to the modern observer. For the Paris thus walled by its great king did not stretch so far as the Louvre on the west, or east beyond the present Rue Saint-Paul. The northern circuit of the walls did not extend beyond the streets north of Saint-Eustache, and the southern circuit which started on the east at the Quai de la Tournelle did not go farther than to include the site of the modern Pantheon, and then swept back along the line of the Rue des Fossés-Saint-Jacques, past the present École de Médecine, to regain the river at a spot near the present Institut de France. In this restricted area so much of primary importance to Europe was already enclosed! Not until the middle of the fourteenth century were the northern ramparts of Paris to be constructed along the line now made familiar by the Grands Boulevards.

The Paris of Philip Augustus and Louis the Saint was, however, far larger than any town which had previously existed on this site, and it possessed a unity which it had not exhibited since Roman times. Of ancient lineage, it had, moreover, been so transformed that physically it must then have appeared white and new. For this was not only the capital of a rising monarchy, it was also an ecclesiastical capital whose importance was reflected in the number and character of its churches. To this phase in the history of Paris must for instance be assigned the familiar outline of Notre-Dame which in its present form was begun by Maurice de Sully, bishop of Paris from 1160 to 1196, and continued by his successors until its virtual completion in 1235. What was later to be added, was, so to speak, in the nature of an elaboration of a design which had been conceived and brought to perfection during the most brilliant years in the history of medieval Paris. Elsewhere, too, similar, if smaller, churches were arising, sometimes freshly built, though more often created by an adaptation of older Romanesque edifices. By the middle of the thirteenth century

*Commemorative seal of the University of
Paris, designed in 1896 (see p.181).*

*The reverse of the seal shows the emblem of
the city of Paris, a ship on a rough sea.*

Paris was in fact studded with churches, some old and some new, but
all giving an impression of recent construction, and all testifying to
the ecclesiastical influence which pulsated through the royal city.

The twelfth-century Renaissance

The Church had preserved the continuous life of Paris through the
Dark Ages. The kings of the house of Capet gave it a new life. But
neither the Church nor the monarchy could of themselves have provided for Paris its unique position in the medieval social order. Alone
among the great capital cities of medieval Europe, Paris possessed a
university, and the University of Paris was in turn to serve as the
prototype of nearly all the universities of northern Europe. Moreover, although the University of Paris was at different times to be
styled 'the eldest daughter of the King of France', and also 'the first
school of the Church', it possessed always its own inherent life. It
sprang in some sense from the two chief forces which combined to
make Paris great, but if it derived from Paris it gave to that city as
much as it received. Like Paris itself, of which during the Middle
Ages it was the mind, and in part the soul, this university was a force
of European significance. Perhaps more than any other institution in
the West it reflected the special quality of medieval culture. The
university as an instrument of learning was, it should be remembered,
a creation of the Middle Ages. The University of Paris was the
greatest of all the European universities and is the parent of most of
them. Its birth in the city of Louis the Saint was, therefore, an
event of European importance, and one which of itself would have
made medieval Paris the worthy representative of a golden age in
European culture.

The beginning of the University of Paris – and indeed the prime
cause of its activity – must be found in that great stirring of the
European mind which is often termed 'The Twelfth-century Renaissance' – a revival which in its manifold products must be reckoned
as one of the most important factors in the growth of western civilization. The pervasive manifestations of this movement could be
watched in many directions. It was marked, for instance, by a revival
of legal studies which in due course were to find their special home
in Bologna. It was marked also by the fine humanistic learning which
spread over the West from centres such as Chartres. It found expression, again, in the new developments in ecclesiastical architecture
which were characteristic of that age. Best of all, perhaps, it might be
detected in the spread among humble people of an ever-extending

curiosity. There has been much sentimental eulogy about the wandering scholars of this period, but it is none the less a phenomenon
of great significance to the historian of European culture that at this
time the roads of western Europe became alive with the figures of
men and boys constantly travelling, eager to learn, to inquire, to
argue, and to teach. They moved from place to place to sit at the
feet of the master of their choice. They were often shabby, frequently
disrespectful, sometimes unworthy of their high profession. But they
formed, so to speak, the seed-bed from which sprang the flowering
scholarship of the age. And where they came, and where they most
settled, there were to arise the great universities of medieval Europe.

That Paris was to become the chief of such centres is now a commonplace of knowledge. But at the beginning of the twelfth century
there was as yet little to indicate that such a development would take
place. There were, however, in Paris at that time schools established
at the monasteries of Sainte-Geneviève, Saint-Victor, and Saint-Germain-des-Prés, and at the Cathedral of Notre-Dame; and these,
though not specifically distinguished, were made to serve as the basis
of the new movement. One of the great educational changes of the
period was to be a transference of general teaching from the monks
to the secular clergy, so that in one sense the rise to predominance
within Paris of the cathedral school of Notre-Dame might be regarded as the first movement towards the later formation of the university. But by itself this would have meant little, for as yet even the
school of Notre-Dame had not begun to rival the more notable
schools established elsewhere, as at Chartres and Rheims. It was, in
short, not through any administrative action but owing to an astonishing wave of popular enthusiasm that the schools of Paris rose
to leadership in Europe. The University of Paris was not to be
created. It grew. And the beginning of its growth is to be dated from
the coming to the Cité of one of the most famous teachers of his age.
It was from the presence of Abelard in Paris in the middle of the
twelfth century, from the disputes he stimulated, and above all from
the crowds of pupils he attracted that the University of Paris took its
origin, in spirit, if not in form.

To estimate the place of Abelard in the history of European
thought is no part of the purpose of this essay, but he is certainly to
be regarded as one of the makers of medieval Paris. For it was he
who first gave to the Capetian capital its position as a centre of
European learning. As an exponent of a new Nominalism he brought
into opposition against himself many of the most notable scholars of

the age, and the debates between them attracted an ever-increasing audience. The neighbourhood of Notre-Dame began to swarm with an ardent, tumultuous and disrespectful student body, and Abelard's own conflicts with the ecclesiastical authorities led him and his followers to desire a position of greater independence from the officials of the cathedral. The abbot of Sainte-Geneviève on the Mount was thought by some to offer a suitable counterpoise to these, and partly for this reason Abelard migrated for a time from the Cité, and his followers began to establish themselves in what has ever since been known as the Latin Quarter – a district which has from that time remained unique in the world. This community, which was rapidly becoming self-conscious, was still, however, completely unorganized, and not until after Abelard's stormy and unhappy life did any university exist in Paris in the modern sense of the term. The intellectual and social ferment which had been engendered can, none the less, be regarded as the true mainspring of the University of Paris which at a later date was to achieve a distinct and independent existence.

A pattern for higher education

The evolution by the University of Paris of a constitution proper to itself is, none the less, itself of considerable interest, because it concerns the formal establishment of what has ever since been regarded as the best medium for the higher education of Europe, and because university organization everywhere still tends to reproduce with suitable modifications the forms which were first crystallized in Paris during the twelfth and thirteenth centuries. The original schools at Paris were (like those of Chartres and elsewhere) under the control of the bishop's chancellor, and as has been seen it was from these schools that the university grew. The chancellor therefore always remained an extremely important figure in the government of the university. But the beginnings of a more distinct type of organization can be seen in the development of a gild of teaching masters which was gradually to become self-conscious and to vindicate its right to a considerable measure of independence. A charter of Philip Augustus suggests that this Gild was already of importance in 1170, but for a long time after this the Masters' Gild had still to struggle for its autonomy against the bishop and his chancellor. The claim of the teaching masters could in fact best be watched in relation to what was called 'Inception' – that is to say the ceremony through which the Masters of Paris insisted that a newcomer should pass before he was admitted to their fellowship. And so far were they successful in this that before the end of the twelfth century, two things had become necessary before a man was permitted to teach in Paris: firstly he must have obtained the permission of the bishop's chancellor, and secondly he must have been made free of the Masters' Gild by the ceremony of 'Inception'. And the authority of the Gild became predominant when after a long struggle it was recognized that the chancellor's licence must be given gratuitously to anyone who had formally been made a member of the Masters' Gild. Soon, too, the corporate character of this Gild was to be more formally recognized when it was allowed to plead by means of a proctor, to elect common officers, and to use a common seal. By these steps medieval Paris was brought to give to the world the idea of the university as a learned corporation possessed of its own independence and informed with its own individual life.

The Gild of Masters was thus in Paris the core of the nascent university, but in respect of the control of teaching it had to contend with a formidable rival. From the first the two great Orders of Friars had been closely connected with the learned movement in medieval Paris. In 1221 the Dominicans established themselves by the banks of the Seine, and speedily developed what has been described as a separate and exclusive school of orthodox theology. Within the next few years the Franciscans followed, and even before the death of St Francis, the learned Franciscan, Alexander of Hales, was lecturing on the Mount. From this time forward, throughout the Middle Ages, many of the greatest scholars in the university were to be friars, and a mention of even a few of their names would indicate the magnitude of their achievement. Bonaventura the theologian and Roger Bacon the scientist were both Franciscans, whilst in the work of the Dominican Thomas Aquinas, who likewise studied and taught on the Mount, the medieval theological system achieved its formal perfection. Such men, and many more like them, gave to the Uni-

versity of Paris a distinction it would never otherwise have possessed, but the coming of the friars none the less created a difficult institutional problem. The friars wished to occupy university chairs without submitting to the discipline of the Masters' Gild, whilst the Gild strove to exclude them altogether from the university. After a long struggle, which culminated between 1251 and 1257, a compromise was reached. The Gild was compelled to recognize the claims of Mendicant teachers of theology, though the Masters of Arts managed to exclude them from their faculty. On the other hand the friars undertook to observe the oath of teaching masters and to abide by the university statutes.

As a result of these conflicts, the medieval University of Paris perfected its organization – an organization which was to be followed in whole or in part by nearly all the universities of northern Europe, and to give us the academic terms with which we are familiar today. For by the end of the thirteenth century the Masters' Gild had itself become elaborately organized. It was divided into four 'faculties' – Theology, Law, Medicine and Arts. And the Faculty of Arts was divided into four 'Nations': France, Normandy, Picardy and England. The faculties other than Arts were each presided over by a 'Dean'; and each of the 'Nations' in the Faculty of Arts by a 'Proctor'. The whole Gild was under the rule of its 'Rector'.

This organization, with its elaborate regulations as to membership and duties, on the whole worked well since it provided at least one of the most vital necessities of university life: the free interchange of thought among an independent and qualified professoriate. But it carried within it certain defects which needed remedy. In the first place it made no pecuniary provision for teaching, since there were no salaries, and since every doctor, master, or professor (the terms in the thirteenth century were almost synonymous) had the right to teach for whatever fees he could extract from such students as he could persuade to come to his lectures. Secondly, the Gild of Masters tended to be out of touch with the student body as a whole, which was frequently undisciplined and could itself provide no assistance to its poorer members. It was largely to meet these two needs that a college system early came into existence in medieval Paris. The colleges were at first only unofficial lodging-houses for students, but they later came to be officially recognized, and became more and more a part of the university organization, making themselves responsible both for the teaching and for the good conduct of those they housed. The earliest of these Paris colleges was a small house for poor students set up in the Cité in 1180 and known as the Collège des Dix-Huit, but during the next century more important colleges were established on the Mount. It was in 1257 that the Collège de la Sorbonne was founded, and some twenty-five years later the Collège d'Harcourt. Even more lavish in their early endowments were the Collège du Cardinal Lemoine, and the Collège de Navarre founded respectively in 1301 and 1304. Many of these medieval colleges were to have a long and distinguished history, and that of the Sorbonne was finally to give its name to the University of Paris itself. They have left abundant traces in the street names of the Latin Quarter today.

Great teachers and awakened curiosity

The developing form of the University of Paris supplied the whole of north-western Europe with a pattern of academic organization. Thus before the twelfth century had closed, Oxford had started its career as a university modelled upon Paris, and during the thirteenth century the movement spread throughout the West. Its amazingly rapid growth is not, however, to be explained solely, or even chiefly, by reference either to administrative skill or to lavish endowments. The beginnings of the movement in Paris derived directly from an awakened curiosity stimulated by the presence of great teachers filled with ardour, and from the enthusiasm of a multitudinous student body eager to learn. It was this tradition carried out without interruption from the time of Abelard which gave to medieval Paris an undisputed hegemony in the republic of European learning. To write the history of the University of Paris would in fact necessitate a survey of almost the whole of medieval scholarship. Law might find a special home in Bologna. Some of the older humane studies characteristic of twelfth-century Chartres may have been lost. But philosophy and theology, and later law also and medicine, were prosecuted at Paris to an extent unparalleled elsewhere. Between

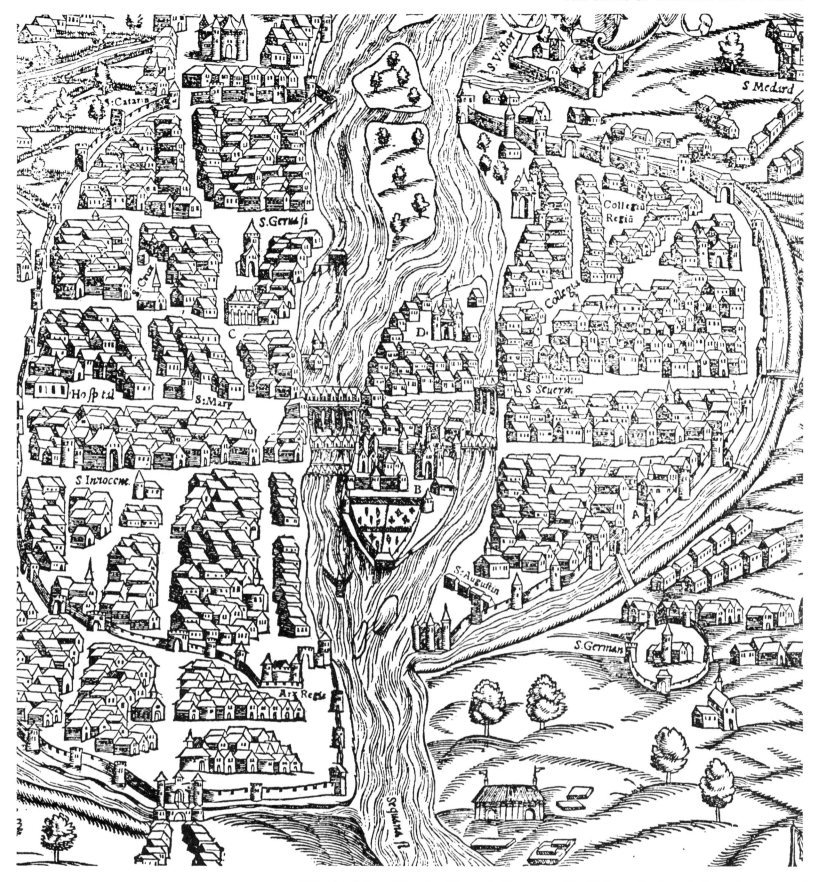

This detail from Sebastian Munster's Cosmographia Universalis *(1550) shows the extent and principal features of twelfth-thirteenth-century Paris. The inner wall was the one built during the reign of Philip Augustus. On the Ile de la Cité appears a conventionalized symbol of Notre-Dame (D), as well as the royal palace and Sainte-Chapelle (B). The University colleges are across the river from Notre-Dame, and St-Germain (lower right corner) is in the fields outside the walls.*

1150 and 1350 there was hardly a single notable scholar in western Europe who did not at some time in his career either study or teach in Paris. To such an extent did the pervasive influence of the Parisian university inform the mind of western Europe in the Middle Ages.

The great masters in the University of Paris during this period were not only notable scholars themselves: they were also great teachers developing the older educational system of the Trivium and

Quadrivium to impart an instruction to their pupils which might stand comparison with that of any age. And the student body which surrounded them was equally remarkable. Constantly changing, it can seldom during the thirteenth century have numbered less than six thousand persons at any one time. And it was cosmopolitan in character. The teachers at Paris were not invariably or even usually Frenchmen, and their pupils came from all over Europe. They thus gave to the Parisian population a special quality. They were, more-over, the future clerics in an ecumenical Church, and having been welcomed on the banks of the Seine, they carried the influence of Paris throughout the West. It was not only through the medium of professed scholars, but also at the hands of popes and prelates, that the teaching learnt at Paris became the affair of all Europe. Indeed, it is doubtful whether the independence of the University of Paris could ever have been achieved apart from the support given to the Masters' Gild by popes such as Innocent III, who could recall the years of their youth spent on the Mount. The teachers and students of Paris in the thirteenth century were conscious of forming an intellectual élite, a scholarly leaven in European society.

It is hardly surprising, therefore, that the dominance exercised by this cosmopolitan society should have conferred a unique prestige on the city in which it was established. There seem indeed to have been hardly any limits to the respect and affection which Paris could excite in those who had passed through its university. 'Paris!' exclaimed one of these, 'Paris! Queen among cities! Moon among stars! On that island Philosophy has her ancient seat, who with Study her sole comrade, holds the eternal citadel of light!' 'Happy city!' declared another, 'where the students are so numerous that their multitude almost surpasses that of the lay inhabitants!' No scholar could feel a foreigner in Paris, remarked John of Salisbury, the great English humanist of the twelfth century; and in the fourteenth century, Richard of Bury, Bishop of Durham, could still enlarge on the 'mighty stream of pleasure which made glad his heart' whenever he had leisure to revisit the city. Such declarations are constant, and their significance to the position occupied by Paris in the medieval world can well be seen in the contemporary description given by a thirteenth-century chronicler:

> In that time letters flourished in Paris. Never before at any time, or in any part of the world, whether in Athens or Egypt, had there been such a multitude of students. The reason for this must be sought not only in the beauty of Paris itself, but also in the special privileges which King Philip and his father before him had conferred upon the scholars. In this great city the study of the trivium and the quadrivium, of canon and civil law, as also of medicine, was held in high esteem. But the crowd pressed with a special zeal around the professorial Chairs where Holy Scripture was taught or where problems of theology were resolved.

Such sentiments are not to be dismissed as empty phrases. They are among the important factors of history. Certainly, they go far to explain the special function discharged by medieval Paris in the history of Europe. Christian in its scholarship, ecumenical in its interests and membership, the University of Paris in the thirteenth century reflected all that was best and most characteristic in the culture of the age.

Teeming mercantile life

Medieval Paris achieved its pre-eminence in Europe as a royal city, and as the home of the greatest university in western Christendom. It thus owed its position to political and cultural causes, and no view of the historical process which is based upon an exclusively economic interpretation of the past will suffice to explain the importance of Paris in the medieval world, or the influence it then exercised over the minds and imaginations of European men. Its commercial development was also notable, but always secondary in significance, for medieval Paris developed no 'heavy industries', and if its crafts were distinguished they were not peculiar to itself. The Parisian bourgeoisie, vigorous and active as it was, had its counterpart in most of the great cities of the West. Nevertheless, no sketch of medieval Paris, even as it reflected to a special degree the civilization of the age, can omit to mention, however briefly, the merchants and traders who served this great capital, who met the needs of the court and the aristocracy gathered in it, and who ministered to the crowd of scholars who lived and wrangled on the Mount. For the city, which had acquired such prestige, steadily grew in size. By the middle of the fourteenth century it had come to comprise a population of not less than 150,000 persons. Even the latest walls to the north, running along the line of the Grands Boulevards, were now insufficient to contain it.

This population needed to be fed and clothed. In its midst therefore were a multitude engaged in retail trade, and within it great mercantile houses arose. The small traders of medieval Paris have formed an attractive subject for detailed study, and they are worthy of it. Among them were the dealers in meat, fish and wine, and of a wider importance the *marchands à l'eau* developing the ancient river trade, and carrying their enterprise up and down the Seine from Burgundy to Rouen. The drapers and merchants in cloth already famous in the thirteenth century formed early connections with the wool merchants in England, and with the cloth manufacturers of the Flemish towns. The mercers, who were among the richest of the Paris merchants, dealt not only in ordinary apparel, but also in silks from the Levant and in furs from the north. All these had their place in the teeming mercantile life of medieval Paris, and luxury trades also developed and in their turn ministered to the arts. Gold and silver ornaments were made and the decoration of manuscripts played such a large part in Parisian commerce that Dante was constrained to give it a special mention in his *Divine Comedy*. Banking in its turn developed, attracting to Paris the Lombard manipulators of the money market, and a large Jewish community which had its first home in the Cité, but which later moved, under compulsion, to the Rive Droite. Here in truth was the reproduction on a large scale of the economic life of any great medieval town.

Typical also was the organization of that life. The thirteenth century was the golden age of the craft gilds, and those of Paris were notable and distinguished. All the familiar features of that system were developed, for each craft in Paris as elsewhere had its separate organization which fostered the welfare of its members, regulated its production, and supervised its relations with the world outside. These gilds controlled their several crafts, forbidding participation in them to those who were not members of the gild, insisting on a high standard of professional competence by means of the apprenticeship system, regulating wages, and to a certain extent attempting also to regulate prices. Such a system of corporations was in fact characteristic of the age of St Louis, and only after his time did it begin everywhere to break down, with the rise of a new class of capitalist traders who obtained an ever-increasing control of industry, and with the consequent creation of a proletariat of workers who could themselves never hope to become masters. There was, of course, in this tendency towards oligarchy nothing that was peculiar to Paris, but it helps to explain why the municipal history of Paris in the later Middle Ages was to be a stormy one. For a more perfect social equilibrium among the trading classes in Paris it is necessary to turn rather to the condition of the earlier thirteenth century. Never after that time was there the same balance between a large body of independent craftsmen organized in their gilds, and on the other hand a smaller body of wealthier merchants whose activities stretched throughout Europe and beyond. Such a harmony could hardly be expected to endure when trade became less local in its scope. But so long as it lasted it provided a life of self-respect for a large class of small traders, while at the same time it gave to the wealthier members of the mercantile community a political opportunity to impart a sense of communal self-consciousness to the city they aspired to rule.

The special interest attaching to the Parisian bourgeoisie at this period derived, however, not so much from its share in an economic activity that was common to western Europe, but rather from its close association with the monarchy. Paris was the royal town, and as the power of the Capets grew, so also did the importance of the citizens of the capital. From the first, there can be seen a connection between the two interests. Very early royal charters protected the Lendit Fair on the road to Saint-Denis, and established the Halles on the site that the modern building now occupies. Soon, too, an even more remarkable association was to be disclosed. In 1190, when the king was about to depart on the Crusade, among those whom he appointed as regents during his absence were six burgesses of Paris who were entrusted with the custody of the royal seal, and given a key to the royal treasure in the Temple. Subsequently (after the king's return), the names of Parisian burgesses are frequently to be found as witnesses to the royal charters, and when in 1226 the young Louis IX entered Paris against some opposition, he put himself under the protection of a guard of the citizens. From this time, indeed, dates the notion that the citizens of Paris had their own special part to play in the government of France. This claim was to be voiced again and again in French history, and to find its most spectacular expression through the mouth of Danton during the French Revolution.

Harmony and a common purpose

The primary factor in promoting the greatness of Paris during the period of its finest medieval achievement was, in fact, the close harmony which then prevailed among the dominant forces which were there displayed in exceptional strength. The four cardinal institutions which contributed to the making of this city – the monarchy, the Church, the university, the bourgeoisie – seemed here for a brief period to be able to co-operate with a wholly remarkable felicity. Philip Augustus may have constructed his fortress of the Louvre outside his walls in order to be able if necessary to dominate the city, but he never needed to use the stronghold for this purpose, and he is to be remembered rather as the friend of the citizens, the first paver of the Paris streets, and the first man to girdle the capital with ramparts. Similarly, both he and his greater son consistently stood friends to the rising university; and the debt was repaid with affection and support as when men out of all countries sallied forth from the Mount in 1213 to acclaim the king on his return from Bouvines, victor over his conquered enemies. In its turn, the influence of the Church impregnated every Parisian activity at this time. The Church fostered the craft gilds which were religious as well as trading organizations. It supported from Rome the Masters' Gild in the university. It inspired the scholarship and art of the town and it gave a special sanction to the monarchy. Thus were the multifarious activities of this city united in relation to a common purpose. Could the spirit of medieval Paris in its golden age be better discerned in the university where theology was the Queen of Sciences, or in the Sainte-Chapelle which St Louis, as king, constructed as a casket of stone to receive the Crown of Thorns?

The Church, secular government, and the university – *Sacerdotium, Imperium, Studium* – these, according to a medieval writer, were the three powers which guarded the health of Christendom, and it was precisely these three which by their combined action on a single favoured city made medieval Paris the capital of European civilization. When these powers weakened in their influence, and ceased in this place to work in harmony, the unique position of Paris in the medieval world at once began to be less assured. Set like a jewel in Parisian history, is, therefore, the brief period which elapsed between the accession of Philip Augustus in 1180 and the death of Louis IX in 1270. Afterwards there was to be much notable achievement but never again such confident equilibrium. It is not to be forgotten that the fourteenth century in Paris began with the mysterious scandal of the Templars, or that the suppression of this ecclesiastical Order was effected by a French king by means of the most savage brutality. It was a grandson of St Louis who brought the papacy to humiliation at Anagni, and during the same century the activities of Parisian citizens were usually associated with revolt or disorder. The harmonious balance of cultural forces which in the early thirteenth century had made Paris so representative of medieval civilization was itself coming to an end.

Degeneration and the call of new voices

Each of the dominant powers within the medieval social order seemed now to be entering upon a period of strain, and the results were speedily to be seen within Paris. The French monarchy was never stronger than under Philip IV, but it was already displaying a tyrannical lack of moderation. Soon the disasters of the Hundred Years War would fall upon it, and the long Valois tragedy would begin, with calamitous results for Paris. The University of Paris grew in size during the fourteenth century, but its pristine vigour waned, and the philosophical studies which were its pride, though never without importance, seemed often to be degenerating into a war of words. The bourgeoisie increased in wealth, but became more sundered between rich and poor. Étienne Marcel might rouse for a time a municipal patriotism which found expression in the first Hôtel de Ville, but he brought violence to Paris, and he died murdered; and when at the beginning of the fifteenth century the early democratic movement of the 'Cabochins' gave Paris for a time into the hands of the butchers, tripe-sellers, and skinners of the Halles, the atrocities of their rule shocked the conscience even of a brutal age. Finally, the Church, whose influence was pervasive through every institution in medieval Paris, itself entered upon an epoch of difficulty. It continued of course to produce great scholars and great saints; and notable artists were still devoted to its service. But in the increasing ornamentation of the Parisian buildings, and in the growing subtleties of Scholastic theology may perhaps be detected the curse of cleverness which is the symptom of fatigue. The papacy underwent its schism. There were scandals and revolts.

It is, of course, misleading to compare the dominant figures of one century with the lesser men of another, and it is easy to over-emphasize a general tendency to which there were plentiful exceptions. But concentrating the gaze more exclusively upon Paris, it is difficult not to make the contrast between the king whom Joinville praised, and the men whom Villon knew. Nor (if the comparison be held unfair) would it be difficult to press it elsewhere. Between 1350 and 1450 Paris suffered many disasters which were not of her making, but within the city itself there were none the less signs of an inherent *malaise* that was exhibited alike in the growing isolation of the rich, in the breakdown of secular order, and in the degeneration of learning from a hard discipline into a soft diversion. Even in the more strictly political sphere something of the same transformation might be watched. Paris shared to the full in the French misfortunes during the Hundred Years War, but perhaps she reacted to them with less than the former vigour which had once for three hard years held the Cité against the pagans. Henry V of England might ride in triumph out of a flaming countryside to pass down the ancient Rue Saint-Martin, pausing only to kiss the relics which were successively offered for his veneration, but, in the full waning of the Middle Ages, it was not the men of Paris, but a girl from Lorraine, who saved France.

The golden age of medieval Paris had passed. Men were beginning to listen to new voices – voices which came from over the Alps and which would soon be heard with especial clarity in Medicean Florence and Borgian Rome. They spoke of a renaissance very different from that of the twelfth century, though perhaps no greater. Soon in Paris would be seen in Louis XI a king spinning over Europe a web of other texture than that woven by Louis the Saint, and in the boisterous scorn of Rabelais would in due course be found the solvent of former enthusiasms which had at last grown cold. Yet the earlier achievement was none the less to endure, and it left its abiding mark upon Europe.

Medieval Paris may be seen today in many edifices, and more particularly in adapted buildings which still stand on the sites originally chosen for them in the twelfth century. It survives also in the tradition of secular government there propounded, and sometimes put into practice, by the greatest of the French kings. Most particularly does it survive in the spirit which still broods over the university hill of Sainte-Geneviève. These things are all a legacy from the Middle Ages, but separately they represent only part of the inheritance. Medieval Paris represented Europe by being itself, and it bequeathed to the future its own intense personality. It was the microcosm of western Christendom which ever since has been a reality, though often in mortal danger. And for that reason, no one conscious of being part of western civilization, has, since the Middle Ages, ever been able to enter Paris wholly as a stranger. He comes conscious of a fundamental debt, and confident of recapturing an ancient inspiration. Even as a man in age may revisit a lover of his youth, or an exile after long wandering return to a second home.

MEXICO-TENOCHTITLAN

The greatest city in Middle America,

Mexico-Tenochtitlan, was founded between 1325 and 1345 by the Aztecs, a warlike nomad tribe of extraordinary beliefs, creativeness and genius. In less than two hundred years they rose from insignificance and poverty, and established an empire with a capital city whose magnificence and artistic splendour astonished the Spanish conquerors who captured it in 1519. Seven thousand feet above sea-level, Tenochtitlan was built on an island in a large shallow lake, and was connected with the mainland by a series of stone causeways. A city of huge pyramidal temples, palaces, dwellings and canals, it was an animated, densely populated centre of commercial activity.

The Aztecs had a special interest in the sun. This pitiless deity, who, according to their highly developed and symbolic religion, had to be fed continually with human blood, was their own tribal god, Huitzilopochtli: their guide in the wilderness and the founder of their city.

In this detail from the *Codex Borbonicus*, a pre-Conquest ritual calendar painted by Aztec artists for use in the priestly seminary, Huitzilopochtli is shown (upper right corner) in the aspect of Paynal, the fleet-footed 'Mercury' of the Mexican pantheon. He brandishes his sacred weapon, the turquoise fire serpent (turquoise symbolizes fire), while the New Fire is carried to his temple by runners from the sacred mountain, where it has been kindled with a fire-drill in the gaping chest-cavity of a human sacrifice. This ceremony took place at the end of a calendar cycle, and was intended to forestall the possible end of the world. In the centre are four priests who clutch mysterious turquoise-coloured quadrupeds and feed the flames with bundles of sticks. The sacred number four is repeated in the crosses on their faces and in the bundles of sticks carried by gods (perhaps impersonated by their priests) who march to join in the ceremony. They are led by Quetzalcoatl, 'feathered serpent', the god who symbolized for the Aztecs the traditions of a thousand years of civilized life which was capped by their own culture. He is followed by Totchtin, the rabbit god of *pulque* (cactus wine); Tezcatlipoca, the sorcerer god of the smoking mirror; Totec, 'our lord'; Ixtlilton, 'little black face', god of medicine; and Centeotl, the maize god. Bringing up the rear is Tlazolteotl, 'dirt goddess', one of the numerous earth-goddesses of Aztec religion. The glyph at the top of the illustration represents the year Two Reed, which recurred every fifty-two years. (1)

en tie Rodino the g sclupia de d

g un g un caci que s a dos se on ag re s a van to dos

pas s las cerimonyus y Ritos g en ello venan

The whole edifice of the Aztec state was maintained by a policy of wars of conquest which provided a large income from both trade and tribute. The interests of religion coincided with those of the state. War provided the gods with their food: the hearts and blood of sacrificed captives. At the re-dedication of the great pyramid in Tenochtitlan, the emperor Ahuitzotl sacrificed 20,000 men in four days. In the contemporary painting below, a captive's heart is cut out in the customary way and offered to Huitzilopochtli. (2)

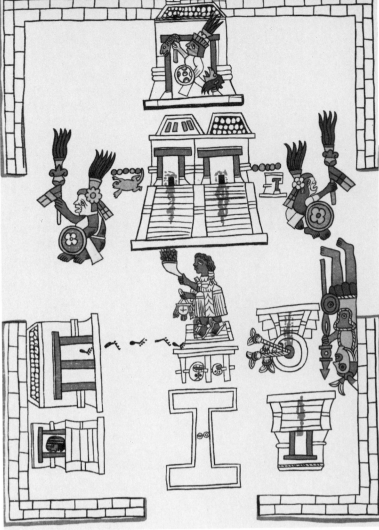

Tenochtitlan grew from a marsh village into an immense imperial metropolis. At its heart remained the four-part clan division of the Aztec tribe and the sanctuary of the tribal god. The Great Temple precinct, over a quarter of a mile square (reconstruction left), was dominated on its eastern side by an immense double pyramid sacred to Huitzilopochtli and Tlaloc, the rain god. The precinct, enclosed by a crenellated 'serpent wall', also included in the centre a stone disc (*temalecatl*), to which a captive warrior was tethered to fight for his life with a blunted sword; a cylindrical temple of Quetzalcoatl; and a ritual ball court (on the right). In the background is the pyramid of Tezcatlipoca. The sixteenth-century plan of the same area (above) shows the H-shaped ball court and a priest emerging from the seminary (*calmecac*). To his right is the stone disc, above him the great temple with its blood-stained stairways, and on top another temple where Huitzilopochtli stands wielding his turquoise fire serpent. (3, 4)

Relative calm and efficiency reigned in the vast market of Tlatelolco (below) with its neatly arranged wares, its chattering vendors and its strutting turkeys. (5)

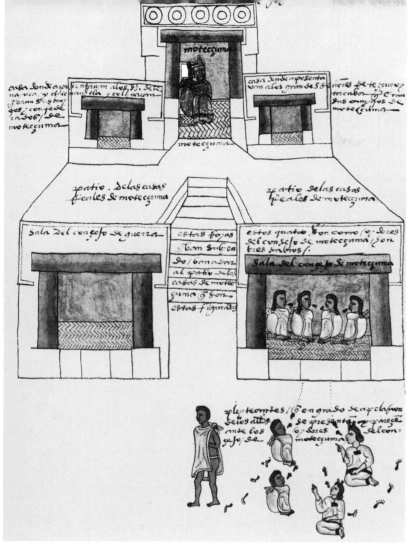

'Those at the feet' of the emperor were the learned judges of his Supreme Court (*Tlacxitlan*). As a native manuscript painting shows (above), this was on the ground floor of the imperial palace, underneath the raised patio where Moctezuma II (1502–20) sits in state between separate apartments set aside for the allied monarchs of Texcoco and Tacuba. The emperor's glory was reflected not only in huge palaces but also in religious monuments and the arts. The twenty-ton Calendar Stone (right top), which was made at Moctezuma II's command, represents the 'Earthquake Sun', the sun which illuminates and will destroy the present (fifth) creation of the world. The 'St Andrew's Cross' in the centre is the earthquake glyph, and the sun's tongue hangs out for blood. (8, 9)

The emperor Tizoc (1481–6) has immortalized his name on the Stone of Tizoc (right), a monolith over eight feet in diameter which was probably used as a vessel for sacrificial blood. (10)

Costume and symbols showed a man's place in Aztec society. The more prosperous peasant and his wife (opposite, bottom centre) wore simple colourful garments, suitable to the climate, and sandals. The three warriors (below left) carry shields marked with the insignia of their clans. (6, 7, 11)

The emperor was transported by litter (below), attended by musicians who played conch-shells, tortoise-shells, flutes, or wooden drums like illustrated (below right): the two-toned log drum (*teponaztli*) and the skin-covered *huehuetl*, with the carving of a solar eagle. (12, 13, 14)

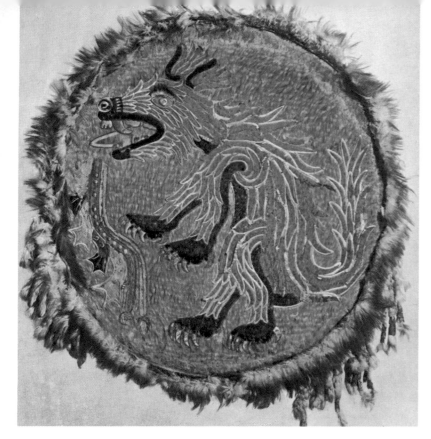

Brightly coloured objects were most highly prized by the Aztecs. Tiny pieces of precious feathers were woven into cloth on the loom to produce magnificent feather mosaics, presumably used as decorative shields (above, and opposite, bottom right). Mosaics of turquoise and shell on a wood base, especially ritual objects, were also manufactured, as they had been from the beginnings of civilized life in Mexico. The eagle warrior on the handle of a sacrificial knife (below) wears the uniform of an order dedicated to Huitzilopochtli, the sun. The blade, made of flint, was designed to sever the aorta, superior vena cava and pulmonary vessels of a living victim so that the heart could be pulled out by the officiating priest. As is often true of the Aztecs, the technique is sophisticated, the tools those of the Stone Age, and the rationale is worked out with impeccable logic from false premises. (15, 17, 20)

'Our lord the flayed one', Xipe Totec, god of springtime, was honoured every March by priests who put on new skins, taken from sacrificial victims, as a symbol of the renewal of nature (right). (16)

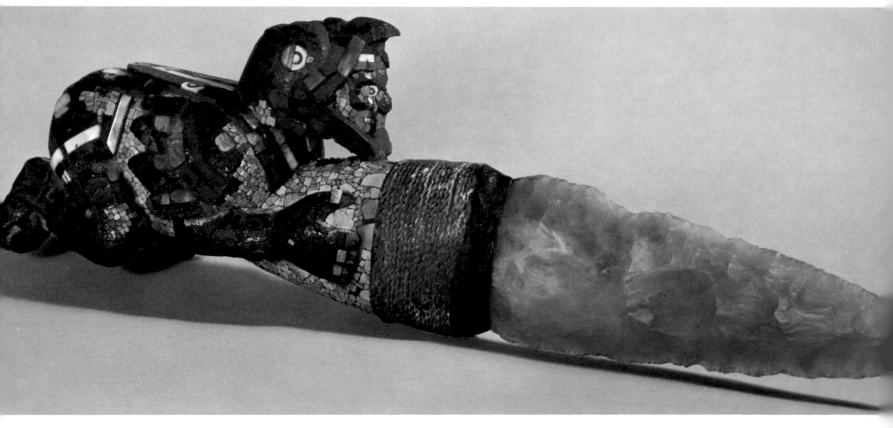

The treasure of the Aztec Empire has nearly all been destroyed. Objects of gold and turquoise alike were treated by the conquerors as mere raw material, and great quantities of treasure were lost on the so-called 'Sad Night' (10 July 1520) when Cortes and his men fled from Tenochtitlan after the death of Moctezuma II. Among the rare and priceless survivals of Aztec art are a mosaic mask (right), consisting of two entwined turquoise fire serpents – the emblem of the sun's fiery course, borne by Huitzilopochtli – and a tiny gold statuette (below) representing the emperor Tizoc in his coronation decorations: feather diadem, greenstone nose and ear ornaments, gold bracelets and belled anklets. The back of the figure bears Tizoc's name ('bloodletter', represented by a picture of a bleeding leg), and the date of his accession, Two House (1481). The statuette turned up mysteriously in the nineteenth century at Texcoco, once the ally of Tenochtitlan and second city of the empire, which under Prince Ixtlilxochitl joined the Spaniards to defeat the Aztecs, only to be crushed in its turn. The statuette may have been sent to Texcoco as a gift from Tizoc, whose short reign was marked by the beginning of the last and most spectacular rebuilding of the great pyramid of Huitzilopochtli and Tlaloc. (18, 19)

Aztec sculpture seems to have reached its apogee in the late fifteenth century, when astounding examples of both religious and realistic art were produced. The stupendous figure of Coatlicue, the earth mother (left), is an awesome symbol of death in life. The eight-foot figure wears a skirt of snakes; her clawed feet are wide-eyed monsters; her necklace is made of hands, hearts and skulls; and her face, two serpent faces combined into a single fork-tongued mask, represents the life-giving jets of blood that spurt from the severed neck of a woman sacrificed in her name. The coyote and rattlesnake (below) are decorative symbols rather than idols – the coyote a warrior totem animal and the snake a fertility symbol. The rabbit (bottom) represents a god of the moon and *pulque*. He appears to be giving birth to an eagle knight, or more probably wearing one on his belt (as Coatlicue wears a skull over hers). (21–24)

The masterpiece of Aztec realism is the head of an eagle knight (above left), perhaps a more successful evocation of military virtues than most European portraits of medieval knights. The beautiful seated figure (left) is probably that of Xochipilli, the flower god, one of the few deities to inspire no terror in his votaries; hence his profoundly human aspect. But the human figure in Aztec art is never free of a certain fate-ridden intensity, as in the statue of a *macehual* (above), one of the plebeians who were the only section of Aztec society to preserve anything of their former way of life through the harsh colonial years. (25, 26, 27)

The foundation of Tenochtitlan is depicted in a page (left) from the most beautiful of Aztec history books, the *Codex Mendoza*, a post-Conquest copy by an Aztec painter-scribe. The national emblem is shown at the intersection of four creeks, recalling the four-part division which was retained well into post-Conquest times. Huitzilopochtli's eagle is perched on a prickly pear (*nochtli*) growing on a rock (*tetl*) – the portent through which the god showed his people where to found their city. 'Prickly Pear on the Rock' (*Tenoch*) is also the name (and emblem) of the first Aztec leader; a similar emblem appears on the coat-of-arms of the present-day United States of Mexico. Tenoch is seen, left of the prickly pear, with his captains, his house, his skull-rack and the blue reeds and green sedge of the marshes. A shield emblem (seven or eight eagle-down feathers) is borne by the Aztec warriors who conquer the cities of Culhuacan and Tenayuca at the foot of the page. The fall of each town is denoted by a glyph showing a temple crashing in flames.

Round the border are the year signs of Tenoch's reign, from Two House (1325) to Thirteen Reed (1373). The year Two Reed (1351) is marked with a fire-drill to show that this was when the New Fire was kindled (see Plate 1). (28)

The plan of Mexico City after the Conquest (below) shows the cruciform layout of the centre of the city. To the north, at right, is the great market-place of Tlatelolco, and the Spanish church of Santiago which was built on the ruins of the temple pyramid of Tlatelolco, with the proceeds of the treasure buried in its foundations. The great causeways and the five lakes are also indicated. The artist has followed the native convention of showing the city nearly as large as Lake Texcoco itself (see map on p. 209). (29)

MEXICO-TENOCHTITLAN

IGNACIO BERNAL

*Temple of Huitzilopochtli
and Tlaloc in Tenochtitlan.*

THE VAST BODY of water that once partly covered the 3,000 square miles of the Valley of Mexico has been, in our century, entirely drained by man. Long before, most of the forest in the surrounding mountains had also disappeared. Only the snowclad peaks of the two great extinct volcanoes have remained free from man's destructive hand and still tower above the wonderful scenery. In Aztec times the shallow waters were divided by nature into five lakes: the two on the south emptied their fresh water into brackish Lake Texcoco, which occupied the centre of the valley, while two more lay to the north. This sheet of water was dotted with many small islands.

Two of these islands – later called Tenochtitlan and Tlatelolco – formed part of an archipelago in the unpotable waters of Lake Texcoco. Perhaps because of the brackishness of the water surrounding them, they had been almost deserted until the beginning of the fourteenth century of the Christian era, though each possessed at least one fresh water spring. The islands in the other lakes had been inhabited since civilization had spread to the valley, more than two millennia before. Although the unoccupied islands were formed in part by rocks, they consisted mainly of sand, rushes, and aquatic plants. Many years of hard work were needed in order to enlarge the islands, to join them and to make them one. Thus they became the great city of Tenochtitlan, the imperial capital that amazed the Spanish conqueror Cortes and his companions in 1519.

The creators of this transformation were the Mexica, generally known as the Aztecs. They were the last arrivals in that series of immigrants who had descended, like an avalanche, from different regions in the north, and who had destroyed the Toltec Empire and established themselves on its ruins. When the Aztecs arrived in the Valley of Mexico in the second half of the thirteenth century, all the land was already occupied, partly by the semi-barbarian immigrants and partly by the survivors of older civilizations which had been destroyed. Thus the Aztecs found – living side by side – states of the old Toltec tradition and kingdoms formed by new people who were called, collectively, Chichimecs (a synonym for barbarian). At this time the Aztecs, although civilized, were a small and extremely poor tribe. 'Their clothing and their breechclouts were of palm fibre, their sandals of woven straw, likewise the strings of their bows and their carrying bags'.

In 1276 they settled at Chapultepec, which had a fine strategic position; as late as 1847 Chapultepec was Mexico's last bastion of defence during the war between Mexico and the United States. The Aztecs remained there for many years, until they lost a battle and became subjects of their neighbours, the Toltecs of Culhuacan. The victors, however, preferred not to live side by side with the vanquished, so they gave them land in nearby Tizapan. They hoped that the enormous quantity of snakes that infested the place would destroy the Aztecs, but, says a chronicle, 'the Mexica were delighted when they saw the snakes and cooked them and ate them' – a typical irony of Mexica history.

The god's command

Not content with having eliminated the serpents, the Aztecs, by order of their god, killed with appalling cruelty the daughter of the king of Culhuacan. Enraged, the father threw them out of his dominions, as he knew that no other nearby tribe would let them settle on its lands, so that they would have to move on again to farther regions. At this juncture their god Huitzilopochtli, whose oracles had led them in their wanderings, spoke again and through the priests ordered his people to settle on one of the abandoned islands, among the reeds and the rushes.

> There will be our city: Mexico-Tenochtitlan; the place where the eagle screams, opens its wings, and eats; the place where the fish swim; the place where the serpent is torn asunder: Mexico-Tenochtitlan.

The foundation has always been thought to have taken place in 1325, but it is quite possible that it occurred as late as 1345. Tenoch, the Aztec leader at that time, gave his name to the new city, which he also called Mexico in honour of Mexictli, another name for Huitzilopochtli. The neighbouring island of Tlatelolco was occupied twelve years afterwards by a late-arriving group of Mexica. When once the city had been founded, the Mexica's pilgrimage was at an end. The Aztecs' first act was to build a humble altar, which, over the years, was to become the magnificent temple in which the satisfied god was to rest.

That this forlorn island became the site of their capital is proof enough of the faith, courage, and tenacity of the Aztecs. The choice is also an indication of practical intelligence and political skill, for here the Mexica had land that was so poor that nobody, not even its legal owner, the Tecpanec king of Aztcapotzalco (then the principal power in the Valley) cared to dispute their possession of it. Its geographical position also allowed them a certain amount of liberty and assured them at least the beginnings of independence.

At the time of the foundation of Mexico-Tenochtitlan, the Aztec tribe was still organized in clans (*calpulli* in the Nahuatl language) which combined a personal tie with the collective possession of land. It was therefore to a considerable extent a classless society, and in this it was typical of the backward groups from northern Mexico. This would change greatly in time, as the proverbial poverty of the tribe was overcome. So the first years were spent in austere labour and endurance, while the Aztecs' *calpulli* evolved into a small kingdom. By 1376 the Aztecs had obtained a real monarch, Acamapichtli, of the royal blood of the Toltecs, thereby establishing a hereditary pretension to the great empire whose prestige was still immense, notwithstanding its collapse. The new ruler swiftly led his people to their first conquests on the mainland.

The career of empire

This was the beginning of the Aztecs' astonishing career of empire. The next king, Huitzilihuitl, broke through Morelos in conquests that were constantly victorious and that raised the conquerors' standard of living. The first books appeared at about this time. It is believed that the Aztecs, in a later day, destroyed their historical chronicles, because they wanted to obliterate the memory of their humble origins when, after Itzcoatl's reign, they saw a brilliant future ahead.

All this time and until 1428 the Aztecs were partly subject to the Tecpanecs and had fought as their mercenaries. But their strength was now such that their fourth king, Itzcoatl (1427-49), by joining forces with the exiled king Nezahualcoyotl of Texcoco, was able to overthrow the Tecpanec empire. The victors and a group of the defeated Tecpanecs founded the Triple Alliance: an association in which Texcoco represented the earlier wave of Chichimecs, and Tacuba the remnant of the Tecpanecs, while Tenochtitlan was so clever as to represent not only the humble Aztecs, but also the heritage of the Toltecs, with all its prestige. From its inception the alliance set out to conquer the remaining independent towns of the Valley. War led to the rapid development of a large group of military leaders who, together with the small ancient nobility, considered themselves to be superior to their fellows. This put an end to the more democratic tribal régime, and transformed Aztec society into a state with a clear class stratification.

The empire was founded about 1433, but its real maker was Itzcoatl's successor, Moctezuma I (1440-69), a man of outstanding talents. His victorious campaigns into what is today Central Veracruz and into Mixtec territory brought him wealth and prestige; his method of making war became the model for the whole of Middle America. The method was to take the enemy by surprise through quick raids during which their main temple was set on fire, as many men as possible were taken prisoner, and tribute was imposed on the conquered people. Tenochtitlan usually appointed a member of the vanquished dynasty as head of the local government.

But Moctezuma was not only a great conqueror. He was also an organizer of the nascent state, a builder and a patron of the arts. Skilled architects from Chalco and the famous goldsmiths of the Mixteca region were brought to Tenochtitlan, and the city grew rapidly. Large stone edifices were constructed and permanent houses replaced the previous huts. A vast botanical garden, which is said to have contained every known plant, was created for Moctezuma in Morelos. When he died, his three sons were elected emperors one after the other, Axayacatl (1469-81), Tizoc, and Ahuitzotl. During their reigns, Tlatelolco, which was uncomfortably near, was annexed by force, many lands were conquered, and the empire was extended as far as the present frontier between Mexico and Guatemala. These three imperial brothers were also great builders. During their reigns, temples and palaces were erected or enlarged and the greatest part of extant Aztec sculpture was carved.

In 1502, when Moctezuma II was elected emperor, he could be proud of the achievements of his family and of his people. In fifteen generations the miserable unwanted tribe had become the head of the Valley of Mexico, or Anahuac – 'the circle of the world between the seas'. He knew that all this was the gift of the mighty god Huitzilopochtli, and the fulfilment of the god's very old but unforgotten promise: 'And so, verily I say unto you that I shall make you lords, kings of whatever exists throughout the world, and, when you are kings, you shall have countless, never-ending and infinite vassals to pay you tribute ...' Thus his belief in his god could not be shaken, because Moctezuma ruled an empire that was about the size of modern Italy, embraced the most varied regions and climates, and was inhabited by many peoples speaking scores of languages. Yet Aztec trade and influence reached an even wider area. In many ways Moctezuma was also a great ruler; but fate was harsh with him, for in his reign Cortes arrived. On 13 August 1521, the capital fell, and this was the end of the great empire.

An American Venice

Against this historical and geographical background we can visualize the city of Tenochtitlan as we know it best, on the eve of its fall. Descriptions by some of the conquerors, and other documents, together with what has been recovered by archaeology, present a fascinating though incomplete view of the last indigenous capital, which was the culmination of two thousand years of urban life in Middle America.

Actually, a complete city plan could not have been worked out in Tenochtitlan's short life if this had not been inherited from the Toltecs, who, in turn, had taken it from Teotihuacan. This, the largest of all ancient cities in Middle America, had come into existence in the last centuries before the beginning of the Christian era. It created an urban civilization that became, with great vicissitudes, the predominant type of life and of political and social organization in the central valleys of Middle America. From then on there is a continuity not only in spirit but even in style.

While we know that Tenochtitlan-Tlatelolco – which we shall refer to only as Tenochtitlan – had enlarged the original islands to about five square miles in 1521, it is very difficult to estimate its population. Still, by calculating the available land-surface and the amount of tribute collected from the empire, we believe that it must have had about 80,000 inhabitants. This number, which seems so low today, is greater than that of the majority of contemporary European cities, since only four of these – Paris, Naples, Venice, and Milan – had more than 100,000 inhabitants. The largest Spanish city, Seville, had only 45,000 in 1530. Therefore it is not strange, not an exaggeration on the part of the conquerors, that they should have described Tenochtitlan as enormous.

Whatever its size, the American Venice was certainly impressive. Its pyramidal profile was symbolic of its inner life, since the Great Temple – rising above and dominating all others – was both the axis of the city and its crowning point. Around this, in diminishing heights, were grouped the countless pyramids with their shrines, the palaces, and the private houses; then came the huts and the gardens, down to the shores of the lake, where the marginal evergreen carpet of the *chinampas* (artificial islands made of rafts covered with silt from the lake bottom) was covered with flowers and vegetables. Surrounding Tenochtitlan were the water and other islands, and on solid land many cities formed a crown around the capital.

And when we saw so many cities and villages built in the water and other great towns on dry land and that straight and level causeway going towards Mexico, we were amazed and said that it was like the enchantments they tell of in the legend of Amadis, on account of the great towers and temples and buildings rising from the water, and all built of masonry. And some of our soldiers even asked whether the things that we saw were not a dream. It is not to be wondered at that I here write it down in this manner, for there is so much to think over that I do not know how to describe it, seeing, as we did, things that had never been heard of or seen before, nor even dreamed about ... Gazing on such wonderful sights, we did not know what to say, or whether what appeared before us was real, for on one side, on the land, there were great cities, and in the lake ever so many more, and the lake itself was crowded with canoes, and in the Causeway were many bridges at intervals, and in front of us stood the great City of Mexico.

Later, continues Bernal Diaz, on the top of the temple of Tlatelolco, Moctezuma took Cortes' hand and

told him to look at his great city and all the other cities that were standing in the water, and the many other towns on the land round the lake, and that, if he had not yet seen the great market-place well, from where they were they could see it better ... From it [the temple] one could see over everything very well, and we saw the three causeways which led into Mexico ... and the fresh water that comes from Chapultepec ... and the bridges ... and a great multitude of canoes ... and we saw that from every house of that great city and of all the other cities that were built in the water it was impossible to pass from house to house, except by drawbridges ... and we saw in those cities temples and oratories like towers and fortresses and all gleaming white, and it was a wonderful thing to behold; then the houses with flat roofs ... After having examined and considered all that we had seen we turned to look at the great market-place ... Some of the soldiers among us who had been in many parts of the world, in Constantinople and all over Italy, and in Rome, said that so large a market-place and so full of people, and so well regulated and arranged, they had never beheld before.

If Tlatelolco merged fully into the life of Tenochtitlan when it was annexed, it never formed a whole, organically, with the plan of the

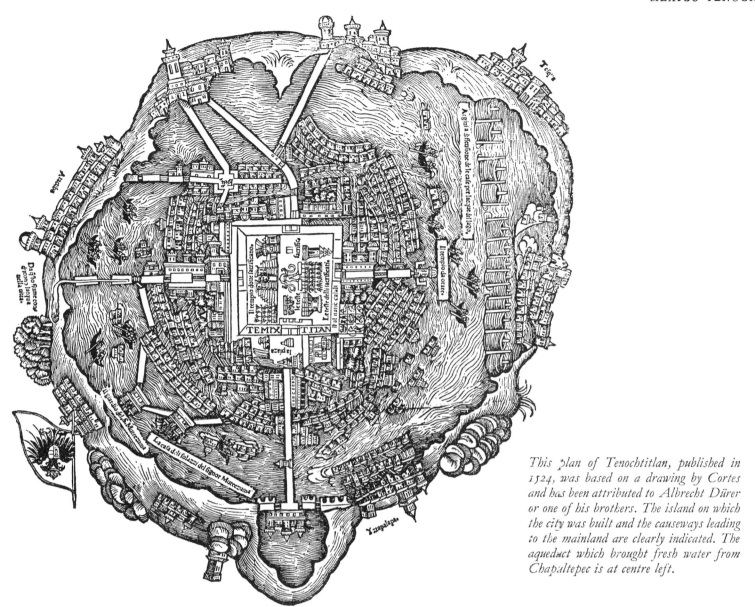

This plan of Tenochtitlan, published in 1524, was based on a drawing by Cortes and has been attributed to Albrecht Dürer or one of his brothers. The island on which the city was built and the causeways leading to the mainland are clearly indicated. The aqueduct which brought fresh water from Chapultepec is at centre left.

city, whose original area had been divided previously into four symmetrical parts corresponding to one of the four great wards or *calpulli* (four was Middle America's magic number). Each *calpulli* contained a variable number of subdivisions, remnants of an older organization, based on clans, on which the imperial state had been superimposed. The boundaries of the four original *calpulli* met at a central point, which was the area occupied by the Great Temple, the imperial palaces, and the homes of some of the lords. From each of the four gates of the enclosure of the Great Temple, there ran a street that marked one of the boundaries of the wards. Three of these streets became causeways built of stone and supported by rows of stakes driven into the lake bottom, and thus they crossed the water to the mainland. To the north went an avenue that ran the whole length of what is now Argentina Street and reached the site of the present-day Shrine of Guadalupe. The southern road, which began at the gate of the Eagle, went to Ixtapalapa; from it a branch turned off to Coyoacan. This was the road followed by Cortes in his first entry into Tenochtitlan. To the west, by the gate of the Palace of Axayacatl, the highway to Tacuba began; it is the only one that still bears its original name. This road divided, one branch going to Chapultepec. A fourth street, running to the east, reached only as far as the shore, at the point where there was the dock for canoes that crossed Lake Texcoco, since the lake was very wide in this direction. Cortes built his shipyard here. The site corresponds to the present-day San Lazaro railway station.

Tenochtitlan was, then, a very orderly city, laid out on a quadrangular plan, which was also the basis of the Spanish planning that it was to have later on. Even the natural irregularity of the island's shores had been modified by rectangular *chinampas* which were built little by little and had thus enlarged the dry surface. Evidently Tenochtitlan did not grow by chance but was planned with care. There was even a public official, the Calmimilolcatl, whose work consisted in seeing that the houses were duly aligned along the streets or canals, so that these would be straight, with well-defined boundaries. Traffic was by canoe, since many of the streets were canals, although in places paths for pedestrians ran alongside them. Wherever canals crossed a road, they were spanned by bridges made of strong planks that could be removed easily in case of danger. These bridges were responsible for Cortes' defeat on the 'Sad Night'.

Tenochtitlan was a perpetual victim of floods when the lake waters rose. To avoid these, great walls or dykes were built, not only to contain the lake waters, but to separate fresh water from salt. Nezahualcoyotl, who was a great king, a poet, and also an architect, directed the principal hydraulic works and managed to prevent major inundations. Officials, like the Acolnahuacatl, kept a continuous watch on the shores of the island, to see that the water which filtered into new *chinampas* did not destroy them, for, if this were allowed to happen, land that had been so difficult to redeem would be lost and the likelihood of floods would be greater. The problem was so enormous that it was never completely solved, either in Aztec times or during the three centuries of the colonial period. The recent draining of the lakes has diminished inundations but has created other problems that are just as serious.

As water from Lake Texcoco was not fit for drinking, fresh water had to be brought to Tenochtitlan by building two great aqueducts. One, built during Moctezuma I's reign, came from Chapultepec; the other, from Coyoacan, which was built by Ahuizotl, had two channels in order to avoid interruption of service during repairs. The aqueducts ended in reservoirs from which water was distributed to the houses by canoe. In this manner, as long as Tenochtitlan controlled the springs, the city was assured of the drinking-water that was needed by its constantly increasing inhabitants.

When Cortes first came to Tenochtitlan with four hundred Spanish soldiers, he was lodged in the palace of Axayacatl, 'some large houses where there were apartments for all of us ... where there were great halls and chambers canopied with the cloth of the country for our

Captain, and for everyone of us beds of matting with canopies above, and no better bed is given, however great the chief may be, for they are not used. And all these palaces were coated with shining cement and swept and garlanded'. 'A very large and very beautiful house', Cortes called it. Situated to the west of the enclosure of the Great Temple, this edifice was followed on the same side of the avenue by the palaces of Moctezuma I and the Cihuacoatl ('Snake Woman' – the grand vizier). All the property behind these three buildings had been turned into a complex of pools, gardens, and special houses for birds and for animals. On the south of the square to the south of the Great Temple were the homes of nobles; on the east side, the palace of Moctezuma II occupied the same ground that the National Palace occupies today. Also, behind this to the east were the emperor's gardens and zoos. 'It seemed to me almost impossible to describe their excellence and grandeur', wrote Cortes. This ceremonial section, consisting of temples and palaces, which formed the heart of the city, must have occupied about 125 acres. According to Ixtlilxochitl, Nezahualcoyotl's palace in Texcoco, with three hundred rooms and numerous gardens and annexes, was as large as Tenochtitlan's centre, but Ixtlilxochitl tends to exaggerate the greatness of his ancestors. Cuauhtemoc lived to the north of Axayacatl's palace, along the avenue that led to Tlatelolco (outside the principal enclosure), in the residence that had once belonged to his father Ahuizotl. The dwellings of the numerous nobles were dispersed over the rest of the city.

As happens in our modern cities, the buildings were probably crowded close together in the core of Tenochtitlan, although not of course inside the Temple enclosure. But, as the houses spread out towards the outskirts, the homes of the lower classes were separated from each other by their small private gardens, which were filled with edible plants and with flowers, which the Aztecs so loved and tended. These poor dwellings had adobe walls built on stone foundations, with beams supporting the flat roofs. One rectangular room was enough to house the family. The kitchen, the granary, or the steam bath were built as out-houses on the garden plot.

The houses of the noble and the powerful were quite different. They had one or more square courtyards surrounded by high rectangular rooms; some, we are told, ran to as many as fifty rooms. These were lighted only by the doors giving access to the patios, since windows were unknown and, no matter what dimensions a dwelling might have, there was never more than one entrance from the street. The family shrine for private devotions rose in the centre of the main courtyard. A practical drainage-system cleared the water away, even during the heavy rainy season.

Stone and lime were used for building these wealthier homes. In contrast to the peaked roofs of the temples, the roofs of these houses were flat, so that they could be used as terraces. These roofs were made of large wooden beams, crossed by narrow round ones, and then by reeds, which filled all the gaps, so that earth or light pumice could be placed over them on an imperceptible incline, to allow rain-water to run off. Purely decorative merlons frequently ran round the edge. Here the hours of leisure could be spent, to watch the setting sun or the stars on the rare warm nights of the high plateau. In accordance with the Middle American tradition, houses consisted of only one floor, but some had rooms above, which opened on to the terraces.

The whole house was covered with stucco to make it waterproof, and walls as well as floors were painted with strong colours, mainly white and red. The ancient tradition of frescoes covering the inside walls of important dwellings, with brightly painted subjects, seems to have disappeared in Tenochtitlan or at least not to have been prevalent. One must remember, of course, that not a single house remained standing after 1521, and that the archaeologist of today cannot do any extensive digging under the modern metropolis. So our information is most incomplete.

As is still usual today in Indian dwellings, houses were sparsely furnished. Occasionally a stuccoed bench, used to sleep on or to sit on, oriental fashion, stood at the shorter end of a room. There were wooden chairs and benches, mats and coverings for sleeping, chests for clothing and other objects. It was only in the great homes that the walls and roofs were tapestried with woven cotton-cloth, painted or embroidered in many colours. In the most luxurious households, deer or jaguar skins covered the floors.

Just as no North American home of today is complete without a motor car, no Aztec house was complete without a canoe. This was indispensable for transportation in the network of canals and for crossing the lake. Some were plain – for instance, those used for fishing or carrying merchandise – but the elegant craft were often quite large, with many oars and carved prows. Canoes were so much a part of life that they were used for the most unexpected purposes. Since the Aztecs were a very clean people (they took a bath daily), human excrement had to be disposed of somehow: large canoes collected this refuse and it was then sold for fertilizer.

Almost all works of art were dedicated to the temples. There were many of these in Tenochtitlan, but the main ones were the Great Temple in the centre of the city and the one in Tlatelolco. According to Sahagun, the Great Temple included seventy-eight buildings surrounded by a wall decorated with serpents, the *coatepantli*. The highest pyramid supported the shrines dedicated to the gods Tlaloc and Huitzilopochtli. This pyramid, like other structures, was enlarged in different periods. These reconstructions were required not only by the growing importance of the city but also by the necessity of repairing buildings, which sank rapidly into the swampy earth; what is left of Tlatelolco and of the Great Temple stands many feet below the present level of the city. Collapse caused by the settling of buildings must have occurred fairly frequently, as happened in the time of Tizoc, when part of the Great Temple caved in. Even today, Mexico City daily suffers damage caused by the nature of the mire on which it is built. The choice of site made by Huitzilopochtli continues to present dangers that neither the ancient god nor modern technique are able to parry.

The economy: agriculture and tributes

While the success of the Aztec capital is to be explained by a combination of various factors, economics played a particularly important role. The economy of Middle America was based on agriculture. In the Valley of Mexico there was a fair quantity of fertile land, but not enough of it to sustain the Aztecs and all the other inhabitants of the Valley (these were even more numerous than the Aztecs). The increase in population, which accounts for the growth of the city, made it necessary to import products from outside the Valley. A series of conquests, yielding tribute, was the inevitable result.

By 1519, conquered peoples sent annually a tribute of 10,000 tons of corn, 7,800 of beans, 6,000 of *chia* (a small seed), and 3,000 of *huauhtli* or amaranth (both *chia* and amaranth were used for making cakes). If we add to these some smaller quantities of cacao beans, chili, honey, and salt, this gives us approximately the total of the imperial budget in the form of food. Probably this was enough to maintain 53,000 persons permanently. But not all of this tribute found its way to Tenochtitlan, since it was required – though perhaps only theoretically – to be shared with Texcoco and Tacuba. It is possible that Tlatelolco also received other goods not entered in Moctezuma's book of accounts. According to information dating from 1554, it can be calculated that the total sum of tribute in foodstuffs and in all sorts of other natural or manufactured products was equivalent to twenty million Spanish silver *reales*.

To these food supplies should be added: the products of the Tenochca *calpulli*; revenue from the land of the nobles, of the king, and of the temples; other tributes or rents received by the nobility, by the priesthood, and by the emperor himself; as well as the produce of domestic animals, hunting and considerable fishing (even mosquitoes from the lake were harvested). We have no means of calculating the grand total.

It is evident that any deficit was made good by trade, both with nearby groups and by way of mercantile expeditions to far-off lands. Luxury articles were imported from the latter, but food was brought from towns on the lake's shores.

Tenochtitlan – probably following a precedent set by other empires that had preceded it in ruling the plateau – established markets far and wide. This was done with the aim of satisfying demands for all kinds of products – demands that were constantly increasing. These demands were both consequence and cause. In order to trade, it is necessary to have something to give in exchange and someone who is disposed or forced to serve as the other trading party. Since exchange was impossible (for Tenochtitlan hardly produced anything), the only way for the Aztecs to obtain the raw materials necessary for manufacturing the products which formed the basis of their commerce was to secure control, by means of conquest, over the producers, and then to impose tribute and open up communications. Documents of great importance, which fortunately have been preserved, tell step by step the story of the commercial and imperial growth of Tenochtitlan and show how each conquest was reflected in the market by an increase not only in the variety but in the quality of the objects of trade. At the end of the fourteenth century the market offered only feathers of inferior class and clothing of maguey fibre, but at the beginning of the fifteenth century small pieces of jade and turquoise and cotton clothing for men appear. This was a result of the conquests in Morelos made by Huitzilihuitl. The great culmination was reached from 1430 onwards, and was the result of the victory over Azcapotzalco. From that time on, many goods became available: feathers of the splendid quetzal bird and of other rare birds, jaguar skins, jade and turquoise, and goldsmiths' work. Towards the middle of the century these products abound and embroidered mantles, adorned with feathers for great lords, also appear. Women could then acquire embroidered skirts and *huipils* or blouses. Extraordinary luxury made its appearance at that time. One example of it was a chocolate drink made from cacao beans; the beans also served as the equivalent of money.

Luxury in the market-place

Even after the conquest of Tlatelolco by Tenochtitlan, the great market continued there. The wars of the Emperor Ahuitzotl brought new luxury products: great head-dresses of quetzal feathers, insignia made of feather mosaic, skins of many kinds of animals, shields of turquoise mosaic; also mantles of increasingly elaborate style, embroidered or dyed with the colours that were the most difficult to obtain, and sometimes adorned as well with strips of paper and rabbit-hair. In their hands they carried large fans made of macaw feathers, with handles of gold. Now they no longer drank their chocolate in simple gourds – these were lacquered, and wooden spoons were replaced by others made of tortoise shell.

Apart from these goods, that were available only for the Tenochca nobility, ordinary people could acquire in the Tlatelolco market innumerable objects obtained by tribute or brought by merchants. There was a wide variety of clothing (mantles and breechclouts for men, wrap-around skirts and tunic-like blouses for women, sandals for everyone). There were household supplies: ordinary pottery or very fine and highly esteemed ceramics from Cholula, baskets and mats, furniture cheap or fine (the latter well finished and covered with feathers or with jaguar skin). There were also canoes, plain or with carved prows, charcoal and firewood for the kitchen, articles for personal adornment, blades for shaving, and dyes for painting the body and face or for dyeing cloth. Perfumes, liquidamber, *copal* incense, sea-shells, copper implements, bone needles and rubber

balls were some of the other items available. One part of the market sold both offensive and defensive weapons. In another part there were beams, boards, and lime for building. The Tenochca, like people in modern Mexican markets, had a choice, for eating, of tamales, tortillas, *mole* (a turkey dish), sauces made of many kinds of *chili*, beans, and many other dishes.

It is not strange that this great market should have constituted a very special attraction and that people should have come from all the villages surrounding the lake to buy, sell, eat, or just to amuse themselves. They did their business, made offerings to their gods, learnt the news of the day, and greeted friends. This immense beehive – it is said that 60,000 persons gathered here daily – which so greatly impressed the conquerors, gave a decisive commercial predominance to Tenochtitlan.

Money, as we understand it, was lacking, but certain objects served as substitutes for it. For instance, a piece of cloth was worth between sixty-five and a hundred cacao beans according to its size and quality; a good slave could be worth forty *mantas* or pieces of cloth, although only thirty were paid for an inferior slave. This explains the apparently fantastic and useless quantity of *mantas* demanded of conquered towns by the lords of Tenochtitlan; they were actually demanding the equivalent of money. Cacao was difficult to obtain, as it was produced only in limited and distant regions.

In a world without wheels or beasts of burden, there were great advantages in living on an island, where everything could be transported easily in canoes. It was not an accident that the great market was situated near the lake, next to a place called La Lagunilla (Little Lake), where today there is still an important market. The insular situation of Tenochtitlan contributed to the development of its commerce and its arts, and gave an international character to the city, where groups of different origins came to live, and languages other than Nahuatl were spoken.

The city was also a centre for artisans, whose raw material, brought by tribute or by commerce, came from many different regions. Goldsmiths, originally from the Mixteca region, received gold-nuggets which they transformed into those magnificent jewels that so excited Dürer's admiration. Tanned skins went to the leather-worker or to the scribe in charge of painting the hieroglyphic books. Plumage of rare birds enabled the feather-worker to make the shields, head-dresses, and rich clothing. Other artisans spun cotton, and still others received rods with which to make arrows or spear throwers. Turquoise plaques and precious stones were inlaid in knife handles, in warriors' helmets, and in many other objects that were decorated with mosaics.

The merchants were the centre of all this activity: not the humble tradesmen who sold in the market, but the organized mercantile lords who directed caravans which went to 'the ends of the earth', taking and bringing back merchandise. These formed the material soul of Tenochtitlan and ranked as minor nobility; but their importance steadily grew; Ahuitzotl even allowed them to wear insignia

A meeting between Moctezuma and Cortes was drawn by an Aztec artist about 1560, some forty years after the event. Behind Cortes stands an interpreter, and behind Moctezuma three of his generals.

reserved for the military aristocracy at great festivals. These *pochteca* or merchants possessed considerable wealth, but 'they did not wish to be considered rich or grand on this account ... they went around with a torn mantle'. They acted in this way more from caution than from modesty, for, as history shows to have happened in many places, the emperor at times 'lost his love for them ... and sustained his own luxuries and pomp with their estates'!

The *pochteca* was not only a merchant. As in that other great lake city, Venice, he also played the parts of soldier, ambassador, spy, and informant about distant regions. He was sent under the pretext of commerce to provinces not yet conquered, and he returned with precise information regarding the situation of the land, its economic assets, its military strength, and the best approaches for invading it. In some cases the *pochteca* was unmasked and was killed, and this gave the ruler of Mexico, who was indignant but also delighted, 'just cause' for war. In order to avenge his merchant-ambassadors, he would send his troops against that state and destroy it, as was the fate of Coixtlahuaca in the Mixteca region in the time of Moctezuma I.

Life in Mexica society

Tenochtitlan was so young that many traces of the tribal background were still visible, especially in the life of the common man or *macehual*. These people were born and lived within some particular ward. Individually they worked plots of the collective land of the ward, but these did not belong to them (a clear antecedent of the modern Mexican *ejido*). Since the small amount of land belonging to the original wards was not sufficient for the inhabitants of the city in the sixteenth century, they were constantly augmenting their *chinampas* and taking new tracts from the lake shores.

Each ward had its own local authorities, its school, its temple, and its god. Ward members went to war together. The life of the Tenochca *macehual* guaranteed security. It was organized within a framework of routine and was limited in scope. This may have made it boring at times, but apart from wars, in which young men were offered possibilities of bettering their position at the risk of danger to their persons, Tenochtitlan provided constant entertainment. News of victories won in regions each time farther away not only created a festive atmosphere but also diminished the risk of enemy attack. These victories also brought a constant increase in food-stuffs, goods of many kinds, and riches.

But, above all, there were the very frequent religious festivals held in public or in private. These have left their mark on modern Mexico, which still preserves the tradition of *fiestas*. In Tenochtitlan, festivals were bloody; prisoners or slaves were sacrificed, or a captive soldier had to defend himself without weapons against well-armed soldiers, with the inevitable end. But there were dances, music, and processions, too; there was the continuous social life provided by the market; and there were games of chance that were very popular. All this made daily life in the city less monotonous.

The small original *pilli* (noble) group had increased continually in size and power until now it owned private estates, held all the important positions, and possessed many rights not enjoyed by the common man. The rise of the aristocracy inevitably diminished the importance of the *calpulli*, and in a few more generations the gap between the nobles and common people would have become complete. The *pilli* was not bound by tribal rule, he paid for his liberty and his honours with other obligations and with a life full of risks. He could choose between two professions which actually did not exclude each other: the army and the priesthood. The emperor himself, who was both high priest and military leader, gave, by this double activity, the keynote for the Aztec state: theocratic militarism. If the warrior is the arm and perhaps the head, the priest is the soul.

Warriors who gained important positions won glory, shared in the loot from victories, could employ the nationals of conquered states to work their lands and to provide for them different products, and enjoyed prestige. But the priests had the most important weapon: they were the representatives of the gods on earth. Just as the empire had been superimposed on the *calpulli*, so the priesthood was no longer a group of tribal magicians but had become an organized body of professional clerics, with a hierarchy of ranks and strictly defined attributes. Those in charge of the Great Temple were in the ranks of the imperial society and received rents from conquered lands – besides the offerings of the faithful. Each god had his own priests

and many acolytes and assistants, who took charge of the cult and of the frequent ceremonies.

Another basic source of priestly power was knowledge: medicine, astronomy, calendar calculations, writing, history, literature and philosophy. In the school for nobles, the *calmecac* – an annex to the Great Temple – the priests taught all these things, as well as law, government, and the art of war. Thanks to higher studies carried out in this *calmecac*, the alumnus became qualified to fill elevated positions that were out of reach of the *macehual*, with his minimum amount of culture acquired in the tribal schools.

High above all his people stood the emperor. He was the indisputable ruler, high priest of Huitzilopochtli, and first military leader. His position was not hereditary but elective. Since Acamapichtli's time, however, the election had always been confined to members of one family, a situation which reminds one of the structure of the Holy Roman Empire. By the time of Moctezuma II – and especially since the death of Nezahualcoyotl of Texcoco – the political skill of Tenochtitlan had imperceptibly placed the lord of Mexico above the other two kings of the Triple Alliance, who by then hardly pretended to be his equals and hardly presumed to oppose his candidates for the thrones of Texcoco and Tacuba.

Descriptions of the life of this man who had everything his world could offer are astonishing. He had many wives, although only one was 'legitimate'; he had people to serve him, games, dwarfs, and hunchbacks to amuse him, poets, actors, and music to entertain him. Riches, and above all the veneration of his subjects, made him almost a god. A court ceremonial that rivalled Asiatic splendour and despotism was established, so that nobody could doubt the greatness of the Lord of the Toltecs. Yet this excessive well-being had not made the imperial family either effeminate or degenerate. Moctezuma II had proved himself brave in the battlefield and austere and penitent in the temple but, unlike his predecessors who had been mostly men of action, he was essentially a man of thought – a quality that he had perhaps inherited from Nezahualcoyotl, his illustrious grandfather. The civilized attitude of this handsome and humorous Moctezuma at fifty-two – his refinement, his generosity, and his fatalism – caused his downfall in the indecision and weakness that he showed in the face of Cortes. His most noble qualities were fatal to himself and to his empire.

The Aztec achievement in art

Just as Tenochtitlan could not in its short span of life have evolved an urban civilization, which it had taken over from Tula and from Tula's predecessors in the dominion of the Valley, there was also no time for a distinctive architectural style to have evolved. Thus, when the Aztecs were ready to erect their first important monuments, they borrowed the Toltec style directly, mainly as this was reproduced at Tenayuca. Actually this city is the direct antecedent of Aztec architecture. But both Tenayuca and Tula were themselves imitators of the long-dead colossal wreck lying at the northern end of the Valley, on that site whose name was forgotten but which the Aztecs, in their admiration, called Teotihuacan, 'the city where the gods are born'. If we compare an Aztec temple and a temple at Teotihuacan, it is easy to see that there are only minor differences between them. In other words, the whole civilized history of the High Valley saw, in its two thousand years, only one basic style of architecture – a standard of permanence that reminds one of Egypt and of those other first-generation civilizations of the Old World that are the morphological contemporaries of ancient Mexico. This may explain why, like the divinities Huitzilopochtli and Minerva, Aztec architecture was already full-grown on the day of its birth.

But the other arts of Tenochtitlan can be traced elsewhere. Rather primitive forms were probably brought by the Aztecs from their distant place of origin, while the intricate and refined style of the feather or turquoise mosaics, or the fine design and composition of the pictographic manuscripts, certainly came from the Mixteca-Puebla region.

However, the Aztecs' monumental sculpture goes beyond all these antecedents. It is in this art that they were really great. Curiously enough, the Olmecs at the beginning of civilized history and the Aztecs in the epilogue of indigenous evolution were – though two thousand years apart – the two indigenous creators of sculpture. Both cultures lived on islands where there was no stone with which to execute their masterpieces.

Aztec sculpture seems to follow, step by step, the development of the city which produced it. It is a local art created in Tenochtitlan, eminently representative of the city, and nourished in its essence by the religious psychosis of the Aztecs. It is a triumphant, urban style of carving, powerful and heavy with religious symbolism. It has no softness, no frail delicacy, no lyrical lust, but displays tense drama, admirable restraint and force, with perfect proportions and balance. It was made not to charm but to impress.

Some objects are not religious but civil and imperial, such as the bas-reliefs portraying the victories of the emperor Tizoc or the portraits – now vanished – of the emperors, carved on the living rock at Chapultepec. A few smaller sculptures, mainly of animals and plants, suggest that only here was beauty alone sought – and found. If this is true, these are unique examples of Aztec art for art's sake.

It is impossible to understand the success of Tenochtitlan without reference to the messianic mission of the Aztecs. This mission seems to have marked them out as being different from the peoples who surrounded them, since in other things – environment, race, language, economic and socio-political organization, and the ceremonialism which was the very soul of Middle America – the Middle American peoples were all very similar to each other. The challenge had been the same for all, but the Aztecs responded in a different way because the others lacked that single but important trait: the mystique of a revelation assuring them that they were the chosen people who would obtain not only the promised land but also the empire over all. Huitzilopochtli's promise, at the very roots of an obscure past, had been sustained all through the Aztecs' migrations. When the god was reborn as a fully clad warrior, brandishing in his hand the divine weapon – the *xiuhcoatl*, serpent of fire – he became the Sun itself; from then on not only did his importance grow, but slowly his promises were fulfilled in the course of history. In the days of their misery the Aztecs had to pay for this glorious promised future with continuous hardships; in the days of their triumph they

had to pay for it by supporting the terrible burden of keeping the god – the Sun – alive. Every evening it went down behind the mountains in the west, but who could tell if, after the darkness, it would ever rise again? It had to be strong to fight its nocturnal enemies, and the Sun could be made strong only by drinking human blood. In logic, therefore, blood was indispensable for the world's survival; but the most elementary considerations of self-preservation and the most elementary egotism counselled the Aztecs to procure the blood, not by sacrificing Aztecs, but by sacrificing other people. After all, they were helping not only themselves but the whole world. Therefore war became necessary in order to bring prisoners to the feet of Huitzilopochtli. With time, and the increasing conquests and victories, Huitzilopochtli could be satisfied with torrents of foreign blood shed in his honour. By then he had become so powerful and his temple was so high that he only exacted reverence, no longer gave counsel. But the divinity was represented by an enormous statue that still held in its right hand the *xiuhcoatl*, the divine weapon that would forever ensure victory to Aztec armies. Thus in the last days of the siege of Tenochtitlan by the Spaniards, when everything seemed lost, Cuauhtemoc, the last emperor, made use of the last invincible resource. Huitzilopochtli's weapon was given to a warrior in order to annihilate the Spanish invaders. When this failed the war ended. Then the Spaniards and their allies

ascended the pyramid and cast down many idols, especially in the main shrine where Huitzilopochtli stood. Cortes and Ixtlilxochitl arrived at the same time, and together they assaulted the idol. Cortes took hold of the golden mask from the face of the image and Ixtlilxochitl cut off the head of him whom until recently he had adored as his god

The death of Huitzilopochtli symbolizes the death of his city. It also marks the birth of the Spanish city which is today the capital of Mexico.

Tenochtitlan and its surroundings as it is believed, in the light of most recent archaeological findings, to have been situated at the time of Cortes' conquest. In an earlier age the lakes were much larger and intercommunicating; in more recent times they have almost disappeared.

SHAH ABBAS'S
ISFAHAN

The splendours of Isfahan

are mainly due to the seventeenth-century ruler of Persia, Shah Abbas I, a strong, nationalist leader who came to the throne in 1587, upon his father's abdication, when he was only a boy of sixteen. At that time the capital city was Qazvin, about 260 miles north-north-west of Isfahan, and there the young Shah maintained his official residence for ten years, while he gradually reorganized his diffuse country into a united and formidable military power, capable of challenging the Turkish and Özbeg forces that occupied parts of the land. By the end of his reign in 1629, his army had regained the lost territories. Through his dynamic innovations, administrative and economic as well as military, Shah Abbas the Great made Persia a country of international importance, in communication with Western governments who considered her a valuable ally in the struggle against a common enemy, Ottoman Turkey. This intercourse with the West also helped Persia to expand her trade and, consequently, her prosperity.

In 1598, Shah Abbas decided to move his capital from Qazvin to Isfahan, more suitably situated in the centre of the country. Isfahan was merely a provincial town, with a population of about 40,000, but it was set in a beautiful green valley within a mountainous desert. Instead of enlarging and adapting the modest town that already existed, Shah Abbas set about creating a new town centre in what

was then an outlying district. Over a period of some thirty years, he supervised both the plans and the buildings for his new capital, which was erected in various stages. Envoys and visitors from Jacobean England and other Western countries found it a remarkable and opulent city, full of dazzling buildings and unexpected elegance.

One of the first buildings completed was the Shah's palace, Ali Qapu (opposite, below); it was actually a thoroughgoing reconstruction of an old pavilion, to which additional storeys and the large covered balcony were added. Abbas already visualized the great square, called Maidan-i-Shah, which was to be laid out just to the east of Ali Qapu, and his balcony provided a perfect location from which to look out over that active and handsome area. During the years he lived here, while a series of palaces were being built near by, he often gave audiences on this balcony.

Another of Shah Abbas's early buildings was a small mosque, Masjid-i-Sadr, in honour of Shaikh Lutfullah, his father-in-law, across the open space from Ali Qapu. The photograph (opposite, top) shows the Lutfullah Mosque, as it came to be known, as Abbas would have seen it from the balcony of his residence. The tiled dome, with its delicate colouring, is one of the great monuments of Shah Abbas's city. In the background are the parched mountains that surround Isfahan. (1, 2)

Shah Abbas the Great as a young man was idealized in the contemporary miniature (right) by an unknown Mughal painter. Though a vital and progressive force in his country, he was also, like most monarchs of his epoch, arbitrary in his use of power and cruel in his treatment of enemies and offenders. (4)

The Maidan-i-Shah (the Shah's Square) was Abbas's most impressive creation. Begun in 1611–12, it is not in fact a square at all but a huge rectangle, 1674 by 540 feet (bottom). On the west, or left, side is *Ali Qapu*, the Shah's palace, and on the right the Lutfullah Mosque; both of these had already been built by the time the whole *Maidan* was laid out. In the centre of the north end is the gateway of the *Qasaiyeh* (Royal Bazaar), which leads to the Royal Caravanserai and the main parts of the bazaar. A seventeenth-century engraving of the *Maidan* from the reverse end (below) shows the Shah's Mosque which takes up the whole southern expanse of the *Maidan*. The Square was a public gathering-place where traders' booths were set up, polo was played (below right) and coffee drunk. At night, in Abbas's time, the buildings were all illuminated with striking effect. (3, 5, 9)

'The Champs-Elysées of Isfahan', a wide thoroughfare or promenade called *Chahar-Bagh* (above left), was one of Abbas's early designs for the city. Lined on both sides with trees and the palatial residences of courtiers and men of wealth, it crosses Isfahan's river on 'The Bridge of 33 Arches', built by the Shah's Commander-in-Chief, Allahverdi Khan. This distinctive structure is seen in a contemporary engraving (top) and as it appears, unaltered, today (above right). (6, 7, 8)

The Mosque of the Shah, *Masjid-i-Shah* (above left), was begun in 1612–13, across the *Maïdan* from the Royal Bazaar gateway. Abbas feared that this magnificent edifice might not be completed before his death, and sought to hasten its construction in various ways. The dome (above) was finished in tile-mosaics, like those used on the smaller Lutfullah Mosque. But in other parts of the building, painted tiles were used, as they could be set more quickly.

The Mosque, which covers an extensive area and has a religious college connected to it, comprises a number of arcaded courtyards decorated with painted tiles (far left). The large central court (left) surrounds a pool, and the covered areas have floors of blue tiles which give the impression of water and make the interiors seem cooler (left centre). (10–14)

215

Foreigners were welcomed by the Shah to his new capital. In 1615, he authorized the English East India Company to trade in Persia. Two years later the Company started a 'factory' in Isfahan near both the bazaar and the palace; nothing remains of those buildings, but the site is shown in the photograph at left top. The Dutch East India Company, following suit, also opened a factory and residence in the city, somewhat less advantageously placed; it was represented in a seventeenth-century engraving (left centre). (15, 16)

Religious tolerance was a characteristic of Isfahan in Abbas's time. Augustinian, Carmelite and Capuchin missions were established there, and a Jewish quarter grew up in the northeastern part of the city. The largest minority, however, were the Christian Armenians, who built a fine suburb called Julfa and prospered in business. Above: an Armenian woman of the period is shown in a contemporary engraving. (18)

Chihil Sutun, meaning 'Forty Columns' (left bottom), was the name given to a royal building erected towards the end of Abbas's reign. Situated in a large garden near the northern end of the *Maidan*, it was an open porch, looking out over a rectangular pool; the Shah often entertained foreign ambassadors there. (17)

Isfahanis at home or at their labours were the subjects of many contemporary drawings. The Persian lady dressing her hair (left) is a study by an unknown Isfahani artist. A calligrapher with his implements (far left) was painted by Aqa Riza, the leading artist of the period; at the lower right-hand corner of the painting is the royal seal of Abbas the Great. Aqa Riza was also responsible for the painting showing a groom brushing down a royal horse (left centre). A camel being loaded with some exertion by three turbaned men (left bottom) appears in the stylized brush drawing by an early seventeenth-century artist. (19–22)

Jahangir, ruler of Persia's neighbour, India, is shown with Shah Abbas I in a painting by a Mughal artist (below). There is no evidence that such a meeting ever took place, but it was not unusual for Indian court artists to paint idealized ceremonial occasions. Abbas is much more realistically portrayed here than in Plate 4. (23)

The hunting scene (left) is part of a wall painting in the Hall of Forty Columns. The European is in Jacobean costume. Below: a painted tile-panel from a royal garden pavilion; the noble Persian woman holding a wine-bottle is attended by her servant. (24, 25)

LAURENCE LOCKHART

IT IS THE PROUD boast of the people of Isfahan that their city is 'half the World' (*Isfahan nisf-i-Jahan*). The fact that there is an ample basis for their civic pride is due in no small measure to Shah Abbas I or Shah Abbas the Great as he is often called. Isfahan, however, was no creation of his, for it had been a great city long before his reign; it had, moreover, been at times the capital of the country. Its position far from any frontier, its temperate climate, its excellent water supply and its fertile and agreeable surroundings have all combined to make Isfahan a place of importance since very early times. Nevertheless, although much had been done before to embellish the city, notably in the Seljuq era, there can be no question that it was Shah Abbas who, far more than any other person, was responsible for the greater part of what we now admire and enjoy there at the present time. It was he who made Isfahan not only the foremost city in Persia, but also one of the great cities of the world.

The young ruler's precarious heritage

When, in 1587, Shah Abbas, then no more than a youth, was placed on the Persian throne in place of his weak father Shah Muhammad Khudabanda, few if any would have been bold enough to foretell the great changes which he was to bring about not only in Isfahan, but also in the country as a whole. His heritage seemed, in fact, to be most precarious at the outset of his reign. With the Ottoman Turks in possession of most of the north-west provinces and the hardly less formidable Özbegs threatening and often overrunning the north-east, Persia was being held in a hostile pincer-grip. Moreover, the internal position was far from reassuring, since the powerful Turcoman tribal chiefs held a monopoly of military power in the country. More often than not, they used this power not for the defence of their country and their sovereign overlord, but merely for the purpose of warring among themselves. It is beyond the scope of this chapter to describe how Shah Abbas, by building up a new and highly efficient army, paid by, and faithful only to himself, was able not only to restore national unity, but also to drive the Turkish and Özbeg intruders from Persian soil. Under him, Persia became a great military power. It was for this reason and because of the Shah's well-known antipathy to the Turks that the European powers, when hard-pressed as they often were by that militant people, endeavoured to make an alliance with Persia against the common foe. This fact was responsible for a number of diplomatic missions from the European powers, some members of which, such as Don García de Silva y Figueroa and Sir Thomas Herbert, spread knowledge of the Persian court and of the splendours of Isfahan when they returned to their respective countries. The Shah, for his part, was equally anxious to find Western allies against the Turks, and from time to time would send his envoys to Europe in the endeavour to achieve common action against them.

Other useful sources of information on the Isfahan of those days are the letters and records of the Carmelite friars and the members of other religious orders whom the tolerant Shah allowed to settle in Isfahan and its suburb of Julfa. We are also indebted to the agents and factors of the English and Dutch East India Companies for additional data of a contemporary nature. Individual travellers, such as the intelligent, observant, but decidedly prolix Italian Pietro della Valle, have also provided much interesting information. Last, but by no means least, we have the long and very detailed description of Isfahan that is contained in the *Voyages* of Sir John (Jean) Chardin, the French Huguenot jeweller, who spent in all ten years there. Although he wrote some forty years after Shah Abbas's death, conditions in Isfahan had changed but little during the intervening period. In addition to these and other Western sources, we have the *Ta'rikh-i-ʿAlam-Ara-yi-ʿAbbasi*, a detailed contemporary account of Shah Abbas's reign by Iskandar Beg, his historiographer; a well-edited and printed edition of this important work was published in Tehran in 1955.

His choice of capital

At Shah Abbas's accession the capital of Persia was Qazvin, a city which lies 260 miles to the north-north-west of Isfahan. The original capital city of the Safavids had been Tabriz, but in 1548 Shah Tahmasp I had moved his court to Qazvin because, being much farther from the north-west frontier, it was less exposed to attack by the Ottoman Turks. It was in the spring of 1598 that Shah Abbas decided to make Isfahan his capital in place of Qazvin; his main reason for so doing was probably the fact that it was far more centrally situated. He had already, in 1590, celebrated *Nau Ruz* (the Persian New Year, which falls on 21 March) in Isfahan, and may well have realized its potentialities then.

Having taken this decision, the Shah felt it essential to carry out drastic changes in Isfahan in order to make it a fitting metropolis. In his town-planning he showed himself to be a man endowed with wisdom and good taste. He decided not to reconstruct the existing city except in minor respects; the main feature of his scheme was the moving of the central point of the city a mile or so to the south and the construction of magnificent new buildings around it, and also in the still open country which lay beyond. However, as Shah Abbas doubtless realized from the outset, it is one thing to make a plan and often quite another to carry it out, especially if the plan is an ambitious one. Such a scheme as he envisaged would obviously take a good many years to carry out in full; it would, moreover, involve great expense and need close supervision. Such was the Shah's interest in his scheme that he determined to do much of the supervision himself. Situated as Persia then was with powerful enemies to the north-west and north-east and with the internal situation far from settled, it was obvious that he could not carry out his aims to the full under such unfavourable conditions. He therefore decided to implement his plan in two phases. He would begin with a minor one and then, when the situation had sufficiently improved, carry out the principal and concluding one.

Hardly were the New Year celebrations over in 1598 when Shah Abbas had to muster his forces and march north-eastwards against the Özbegs. In the brief campaign which followed the Shah was completely victorious, and the Özbegs ceased for some time to be a menace. It still remained for him, however, to reorganize his army and then, with its aid, to curb the power and influence of the Turcoman chiefs; it would then be necessary to drive the Turks from Persian soil and thereafter to keep them at bay.

When the Shah reached Qazvin after his brief campaign in the north-east, he found awaiting him there a mission from the Earl of Essex headed by Sir Anthony Sherley. Sir Anthony was accompanied by his brother Sir Robert and a number of attendants. (It is to be noted that Shah Abbas by no means abandoned Qazvin when it ceased to be the capital. He frequently held his court there subsequently, sometimes for months at a time.) This mission had two objects. The first was to induce the Shah to join with the Christian powers in an onslaught on the Turks, while the second was to endeavour to improve trading relations between Persia and England. After a stay in Qazvin, the Shah, accompanied by Sir Anthony and his suite, went to Isfahan. Abel Pinçon, the ambassador's French steward, described Isfahan as a very large city (it had then a population of some 80,000); he added that it had no beautiful palaces and that there was no fortress or citadel there. (On this latter point Pinçon was wrong, as the old citadel called Tabarak was then in existence; it was, in fact, demolished only recently. This fortress, which dated from the fourteenth century, consisted of a number of buildings surrounding a parade ground; it was protected by a high and thick wall of mud-brick.)

The Shah, after listening attentively to Sir Anthony's proposals for an alliance, sent him back to Europe as his own envoy in order to arrange matters with the Christian powers. He also promised to grant privileges to any English merchants who might visit his realm. This attempt to arrange for joint action by Persia and the Western powers failed, like other attempts both before and after, because, with a hostile Turkey lying in between, communications between Persia and the West were both devious and hazardous.

It is not without interest to quote Pinçon's description of Shah Abbas as he was then. He was, said Pinçon, about thirty years of age (this was a good guess, as Shah Abbas was then twenty-eight). Although small in stature, he was well proportioned, with an agile body and a strong and active mind. He was very gracious to strangers, especially Christians. Pinçon and his companions found in Isfahan an old French clock-maker whom the Shah continued to maintain although he was, through age and infirmity, unable any longer to practise his profession. On the other hand, the Shah could, he said, be terribly cruel, even to members of his own family and to his subjects. (This was only too true. The Shah deprived his own father, Muhammad Khudabanda, of what little sight he had; he put one of his own sons to death, and he blinded each of the two remaining ones.)

When Sir Anthony Sherley left Persia to undertake his mission, his brother Sir Robert remained behind for a number of years. Being a trained and experienced soldier, he was of great practical help to the Shah in the reorganization of the army.

A grand design for the 'Sketch of the World'

It was at this juncture that Shah Abbas began to put into effect the first or preliminary part of his plan for Isfahan. He possessed in that city a park called the Naqsh-i-Jahan ('Plan – or Sketch – of the World') in which was a pavilion dating from the Timurid era. The Shah ordered the reconstruction of this pavilion, making it into a four-storeyed building. At the ground level he had a gateway constructed right through the building in order to give access from an open space in front to the farther (west) side where the palaces and gardens were to be situated. In front, above the arched entrance, he had built a large *talar* or covered balcony overlooking the open space to the east where markets were then often held. Behind this balcony was a small audience chamber, the walls of which were (and

still are) richly decorated. The two storeys above contained a number of rooms, most of which were charmingly ornamented with floral patterns and paintings. Until the main palace buildings were completed some years later, the Shah always resided, when in Isfahan, in the Ali Qapu ('The Lofty Gate'), as this building was appropriately called. He also often used the *talar* for giving audiences.

Simultaneously with the reconstruction of the Ali Qapu the Shah put in hand the making of the great and noble thoroughfare called the Chahar-Bagh ('Four Gardens'); it was so called because the Shah had to rent four vineyards in order to construct it. He was determined that his capital should have a worthy approach. The alignment was from north to south, and it was sited so as to pass some six hundred yards to the west of the Ali Qapu. The Shah did not wish this thoroughfare to enter the open space in front of the Ali Qapu, as he had already envisaged the creation of the great Maidan-i-Shah ('Square of the Shah') there, with a magnificent mosque occupying the entire southern end of it.

The Chahar-Bagh was designed more as a promenade than as a thoroughfare. Streets or lanes were designed to lead off it at right angles on either side. A stream, with basins in which fountains played, ran down the centre, bordered on each side by a promenade and an avenue of trees. Such was the Shah's zeal that he is said to have supervised personally the planting of each tree. Most of the Chahar-Bagh passed through what was at first open country. Shah Abbas put strong pressure on his wealthier courtiers and nobles to vie with each other in building splendid residences, complete with elaborate gardens, on each side of the Chahar-Bagh. He also induced Allahverdi Khan, the Governor-General of the great province of Fars and the Commander-in-Chief of his forces, to build the magnificent bridge over the Zayandeh-Rud ('The Life-Giving River') which is still called by his name. This bridge, which stands unaltered at the present time, is 968 feet long and 45 feet wide; it rests upon 33 arches (hence it is often referred to as the 'Bridge of 33 Arches'). This splendid bridge carried the Chahar-Bagh over the river, enabling it to continue in the same alignment on the south bank.

Sir Thomas Herbert, who was a member of Sir Dodmore Cotton's mission to Persia in 1628, thus described the Chahar-Bagh in his book entitled *Some Yeares Travels into Divers Parts of Asia and Afrique*, the first edition of which was published in London in 1638:

> If you go from the Medan [i.e. the Maidan-i-Shah], you passe by Cherbaugh, through an even delicate Street two miles long at the least, most of the way wall'd on both sides, bestrew'd with Moholls or Summer Houses, but more remarkable in that abundance of greene, broad spreading Chenore trees [i.e. chenar trees, the Persian plane-tree], yeelding shade and incomparable order and beauty.

Later in the seventeenth century, Dr John Fryer, another English visitor to Isfahan, gave the following account of the Chahar-Bagh as it was at nightfall:

> Now all the Pride of Spahaun was met in the Chaurbaug, and the Grandees were airing themselves, prancing with their numerous Trains, striving to outvie each other in Pride and Generosity.

Pierre Loti, writing some sixty years ago, aptly styled the Chahar-Bagh the Champs-Élysées of Isfahan.

In those days the southern part of the Chahar-Bagh led to the famous Hazar Jarib ('Thousand Acre') garden. This garden was planted with an abundance of trees of many kinds. Situated as it was on ground rising up from the river, it had a number of terraces, each some six feet in height. There were, it was said, no less than five hundred fountains in it. Herbert, who visited this garden, stated that it measured one thousand of his paces from north to south, and seven hundred from east to west. The water for this garden was brought by a canal from a point on the Zayandeh-Rud some thirty miles upstream. This canal, the course of which can still be easily traced, has long since ceased to function, as there are numerous breaches in its banks; consequently, the site of the Hazar Jarib garden is now brown and sterile.

The provision of sufficient water not only for this garden, but also for the many others in the city, to say nothing of the rapidly growing populace, posed a problem for Shah Abbas. The Zayandeh-Rud, when swollen with the flood water from the lofty Zagros range to the west in the spring, provided sufficient water for all possible requirements. However, as the year went on, the stream dwindled progressively until it became a mere trickle. Shah Abbas therefore revived a project which Shah Tahmasp I had attempted to carry out in the previous century. The Zayandeh-Rud has its main source on the eastern flank of the Kuhrang mountain, a lofty peak of the Zagros. Only a mile or so to the west, but on the other side of this mountain, is one of the sources of the Karun River. Shah Tahmasp attempted by means of a tunnel through the mountain to tap this source, but lack of ventilation brought the operations to a standstill. Shah Abbas sought to achieve the same end by making an immense cutting round the mountain. Although a multitude of men were employed on this undertaking, it also failed because, owing to the altitude, the work could only be carried on for three months every year, when the area concerned was free of snow. (It is of some interest to note that the waters of the Karun were successfully tapped and added to those of the Zayandeh-Rud by means of a tunnel over a mile in length some years ago; the work was carried out under the supervision of a British engineering firm.)

While the Chahar-Bagh was under construction, Shah Abbas decreed the building of a small but really superb mosque on the farther side of the open space to the east of the Ali Qapu. This mosque, which the Shah intended to use for his private devotions, was sited immediately opposite that building; Shah Abbas constructed it in honour of his saintly father-in-law, Shaikh Lutfullah, by whose name it is generally known; it used sometimes to be known as the Masjid-i-Sadr (the Sadr was the supreme judge of the religious law in Persia). The mosque has a beautiful tiled dome of a *café au lait* colour, with blue and white arabesques. The interior is richly decorated with blue tile-mosaic; it also has inscriptions in the same material written by Ali Riza Abbasi, the greatest calligrapher of that time. The construction of this really lovely mosque formed part of Shah Abbas's scheme for the creation of his majestic Maidan-i-Shah ('Royal Square'), of which more will be said later.

City of many faiths

A most interesting development in the early years of the seventeenth century was the creation of the Armenian suburb of Julfa on the south bank of the Zayandeh-Rud opposite Isfahan. Shah Abbas was fully conscious of the need to foster industry and commerce in or near Isfahan. For this reason he decided to transport, by force if necessary, a large number of Armenians from the town of Julfa on the river Araxes, in northern Persia. The country round Julfa had suffered severely in the course of the fighting between the Persians and the Turks, and the Shah deliberately had it still further ravaged in pursuance of a 'scorched earth' policy designed to make invasion by the Turks through that region more difficult. In consequence, many of the Armenians there were ready and, indeed, anxious, to move elsewhere, and responded gladly to the Shah's order to settle in the suburb to be created immediately south of Isfahan. There were some Armenians, however, who were loath to leave their homes in the north; the Shah thereupon took the drastic step of cutting their irrigation canals, thus making it impossible for them to continue to cultivate their lands; they were therefore compelled to follow their more willing compatriots to the south. In quite a short time, such was the zeal of the Armenians, the suburb of New Julfa came into being, with well-built houses and, in due course, fine gardens. As the Shah allowed the Armenians complete freedom of worship, they were also able to build their own churches, including

The tree-lined promenade called Chahar-Bagh, built in the time of Shah Abbas, as depicted by Cornelius de Bruin in 1698.

All Saviour's Cathedral (the existing building of that name was erected in 1655 on the site of the original edifice, which dated from 1605). At one time there were as many as twenty-four churches in Julfa, though not all of these were constructed in Shah Abbas's time; of these churches, thirteen now remain. Most of the inhabitants of Julfa were (as they still are) of the Gregorian faith, but there was always a Catholic minority. Besides allowing the Armenians of Julfa liberty of worship, the Shah gave them leave to have their own mayor or headman; in addition, he granted them loans free of interest in order to encourage the establishment and development of their industries and businesses. In consequence of these concessions and privileges, and the energy and zeal of the inhabitants, Julfa (the epithet 'new' was increasingly little used as time went on and was finally dropped altogether) soon became extremely prosperous.

Herbert thus described Julfa as it was in 1628:

> Ielphey is the last part wee propos'd concerning this great Citie; the scite resembles Pera to Constantinople, or Southwark to London, the river Syndery [Zayandeh-Rud] interposing. 'Tis call'd a Suburb as be Gower-abaut [Gabrabad, the Zoroastrian quarter, which then lay to the east of Julfa, on the further side of the Chahar-Bagh]. Ielphey is govern'd by a peculiar Podestate [i.e. *podestà*], an Armenian Prince, Hodge Nazar [Khwaja Nazar] by name, indeed a Christian merchant. Hee and his enjoy freedom of conscience, but for many matters are at the disposition of the avaritious King. In Ielphea (nam'd from another of that name in Armenia) the people are numbered ten thousand. The Jelphelyns are habited like the Persians, but differ in face; most of these and the Georgians have brighter haire, but more modest eyes than the Mahometans. They are generally Merchants.

It was not only to the Armenian Christians that the Shah showed favour. When the Portuguese Augustinian Antonio de Gouvea and two other members of that Order reached Isfahan in 1602 on a mission from Goa, they were kindly received by the Shah. He allowed them to erect a convent and chapel in the north of the city and himself defrayed part of the cost of decorating the buildings. Here it must be pointed out that Western Christians were not usually allowed to reside in Isfahan unless they were missionaries or (as will be shown later) members of the English and Dutch East India Companies.

The Shah also extended a cordial welcome to the Carmelite Fr. Juan Taddeo who, together with two other Carmelites, reached Isfahan late in 1607 as envoys from Pope Clement VIII. At that time the Shah looked upon the Pope as being, of all the European potentates, the one who most hated the Turks and who might therefore use his great influence with the other Western rulers to induce them to take concerted action with Persia against the common foe. When the Carmelites asked for a residence in Isfahan, the Shah gave them the choice of several. They happened to choose a house which had become vacant because of a tragedy which had occurred there not long before. This house had belonged to an irascible army commander who had three beautiful daughters. He was almost insanely anxious to prevent any male eyes other than his own from being cast upon them. It was, as elsewhere in Persia, the custom for the occupants of houses in Isfahan to sleep upon their roofs in the hot weather. It so happened that, from time to time, a male occupant of a neighbouring house would mount to his roof to sleep. Immediately he appeared, the eunuchs in charge of the three girls would shoot at him and kill him. After quite a number of male neighbours had perished in this way, strong complaints were made to the Shah, who gave peremptory orders to the father of the girls to keep them night and day in the harem, where they would be safe from being seen by unauthorized eyes. The father of the girls paid no attention to this order. When one of the Shah's officers took a house near by and went up one night to sleep on his roof, he also was shot at and killed by the zealous eunuchs. An immediate complaint was made to the Shah who, in a fury, had the father, his three daughters and all the other occupants of the house put to death. The Shah then confiscated the house and later placed it at the disposal of the Carmelites.

Towards the end of Shah Abbas's reign the Capuchins also set up a mission in Isfahan. Their advent was due more to political than to religious motives. Père Joseph de Paris, the celebrated 'Éminence grise', and Cardinal Richelieu, being aware of the preponderance of Italians and Spaniards in the Carmelite missions in Persia and of the exclusively Portuguese nationality of the Augustinians, sent the Capuchin Père Pacifique de Provins to Persia, where he arrived in 1628. He was well received by the Shah, who allowed him to establish a mission in the capital. As Père Pacifique de Provins had travelled to Persia as an ambassador, he and his successors were for many years looked upon as representatives of the King of France.

The Shah, like many of his people, was much interested in theological discussions. In 1618 he requested the Carmelite Fr. Juan Taddeo to have the Gospels translated into Persian, as well as the Hebrew Psalms. For the translation of the Psalms, Juan Taddeo had to obtain the services of a rabbi who was resident in the Jewish quarter of Isfahan.

The Jewish quarter was situated (as it still is) in the north-eastern part of the city known as Yahudiyeh. It is believed that the Jews were first settled there by Queen Shushan Dukht, the Jewish consort of the Sassanian monarch Yezdigird I, early in the fifth century AD. The Jews in Isfahan were relatively prosperous during most of Shah Abbas's reign. They were engaged in many crafts and trades. Late in that reign, however, a renegade Jew took to the authorities a fragment of a cabalistic book and alleged that the Jews of the city were using sorcery against the Shah. This absurd allegation was taken seriously, with the result that a very severe persecution of the Jews in Isfahan took place; they were forcibly converted to Islam and all their Hebrew books were seized and thrown into the Zayandeh-Rud. Furthermore, just at the close of the reign, a law of apostasy was promulgated which decreed that any Jew or Christian who became a Muslim could claim the property of his relatives. Though the Pope and the Christian powers protested against this iniquitous law, no one came forward to defend the rights of the Jews in this respect.

The 'Shah's Square' and its great mosque

The second or major phase of the Shah's plan for beautifying and expanding his capital was begun in 1611–12, when work started in earnest on the Maidan-i-Shah, 'the Shah's Square'. (Actually, it is not a square, but a rectangle, as it measures 1,674 feet from north to south and 540 feet from east to west.) On opposite sides, facing each other, the Ali Qapu and the Lutfullah mosque were already in position, although much work had yet to be done to complete the elaborate decoration of the latter building. Simultaneously, orders were issued for the erection of the portal of the Qaisariyeh ('Royal Bazaar') in the middle of the northern side of the Maidan. This portal is set back a little, in a recess; it is decorated with enamel mosaic representing Sagittarius. The galleries flanking this portal are called the Naqqareh Khaneh ('Drum-House'), where music, cacophonous to Western ears, was played at dusk and again in the small hours whenever the Shah was in Isfahan. Beyond this portal is the main portion of the bazaar; other parts of it extend a long way to the north and also to the north-east. In the bazaar each trade or craft had its own particular area assigned to it, as is still largely the case. Also dating from this time is the Royal Caravanserai, which is on the west side of the main alleyway leading from the portal. It consists of two-storeyed buildings facing on to an octagonal courtyard.

The whole of the southern end of the Maidan was taken up by the great Masjid-i-Shah, the construction of which began in 1612–13. So anxious was the Shah to see this great building take shape that he ordered his chief architect and superintendent of works to proceed with the walls before the foundations had had sufficient time to settle. In vain the architect pointed out that the safety of the building would be jeopardized if such action were taken. Finally the architect, after taking careful measurements by means of a length of chain, went into hiding, as he knew that the work could not continue without his expert guidance. Search was made for him everywhere, but without success. When the man deemed that sufficient time had elapsed for the foundations to settle, he emerged from his hiding place. Taking his chain with him, he took further measurements and found that the foundations had sunk to an appreciable extent. He thereupon went to the Shah, explained fully what he had done, and was forgiven. Work on the structure was then resumed. So much time was taken up by the making of the tile-mosaic for the entrance fronting on to the Maidan that the Shah decreed that most of the rest of the building was to be decorated instead with painted tiles.

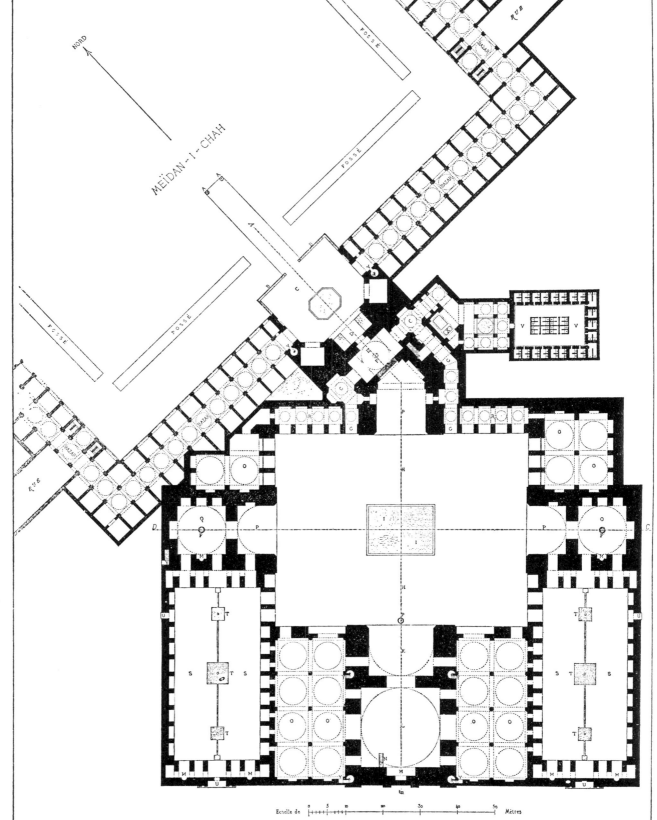

This ground-plan of the great Mosque of the Shah, at the southern end of the Maidan, shows the complex structure and organization of Abbas's most magnificent creation. Courtyards, fountains, pools, prayer-rooms, porticoes are all integrated with extraordinary architectural finesse. The sanctuary is at the bottom under the main dome marked L.

He was also rendered impatient by the lack of suitable marble slabs which were needed for certain parts of the building. He thereupon gave orders for a number of such slabs to be taken from the old Masjid-i-Jami' or Cathedral Mosque, an action which, if carried out, would have almost irreparably damaged that splendid structure. The mullas of the Masjid-i-Jami' went down on their knees before the Shah and begged him to desist. They pointed out that marble of the kind required could be obtained from quarries near Ardistan, an old town 62 miles to the north-east of the capital. The Shah thereupon acceded to their pleading and issued orders for the marble to be quarried and brought from there. Unfortunately for the Shah, he died before these slabs could be placed in position, and it was not until some years after his death (he died in January 1629) that the mosque was at last completed. Professor Pope has described the Masjid-i-Shah as marking in a real sense the culmination of Persian architecture. The entrance, as already stated, is decorated with tile-mosaic; on the roof, fronting on to the Maidan, are twin minarets.

The great dome, which rises on the farther side of a large courtyard, is covered with beautiful painted tiles; in front of the dome are twin minarets of similar type to those over the entrance. It has been estimated that no less than eighteen million bricks and nearly half a million tiles were used for the construction of the mosque.

The intervals between the Masjid-i-Shah, the Ali Qapu, and the other great buildings of the Maidan were filled by two-storeyed buildings of uniform design and height; each house had two recessed arches, one above the other, with a balcony over the lower arch. The Italian traveller Pietro della Valle much admired the symmetry of these houses, stating that though those in the Piazza Navona in his native Rome were higher and more magnificent, he had to award the palm to the Persian houses when taken in conjunction with the other beauties of the Maidan.

Shah Abbas took particular delight in having all the buildings surrounding the Maidan illuminated at night. It is said that no less than 50,000 small lamps were used for this purpose. The Spanish

Ambassador Don García de Silva y Figueroa and Pietro della Valle were both much struck by this spectacle.

Polo and coffee-houses

The Maidan itself was used for a variety of purposes. Merchants would set up their booths there on certain days; on others polo would be played (the original goal-posts can still be seen at each end of the Maidan). Sometimes fights between wild beasts would be staged. At other times a high pole would be erected in the centre; on top of this pole an apple or a melon would be placed; on special occasions a golden cup would be substituted. Riders would then go at full gallop towards this pole; as they passed they would, in Parthian fashion, turn in their saddles and discharge their arrows at the mark. Shah Abbas would frequently play polo or shoot at the mark; on other occasions he would watch what was going on from his great balcony on the Ali Qapu; foreign ambassadors would sometimes be invited to sit there and watch these spectacles in his company.

Pietro della Valle was not the only visitor to Isfahan to admire the Maidan. Herbert described it as:

> ... without doubt the most spacious, pleasant and Aromatic Market in the Universe; a thousand paces from North to South, the other way above two hundred, resembling our Exchange or the Place Royale in Paris, but six times larger.

Another building that was included in the second part of Shah Abbas's plan was the Chihil Sutun ('Forty Columns'). It stands in a spacious garden of its own between the northern end of the Maidan and the Chahar-Bagh. It is in the form of an open porch; it faces east, overlooking a large rectangular basin of water. The roof is supported by twenty columns, two of which are in the throne recess at the back. These columns, which are made from the trunks of chenar (plane) trees, are encased in wooden panels; the four columns in the centre rest upon stone bases representing lions. The usual explanation of the name 'Forty Columns' when there are only twenty is that, when the building is viewed from the other side of the tank in front, the total, after taking into account the reflections in the water, amounts to forty. On the other hand, the word *chihil* in Persia, meaning 'forty', is also often used to denote any rather considerable number. How much of the building dates from Shah Abbas's reign is difficult to estimate, as it was badly damaged by fire in 1712 and the portion destroyed was later restored.

Like the *talar* on the Ali Qapu, the Chihil Sutun was often used by the Shah for giving audiences to foreign envoys, of whom there was a considerable coming and going in the latter part of the reign. These envoys were mainly concerned with the perennial question of the alliance against the Turks, and also to some extent with commercial matters. The mission of Don García de Silva y Figueroa, the envoy of Philip III of Spain, had as one of its objects the welfare of the Portuguese settlements in the Persian Gulf, regarding which there was much apprehension in Portugal and Spain. Don García's outward journey had been much retarded by the Portuguese at Goa and elsewhere because they were annoyed that a Spaniard and not a Portuguese had been sent. Though the intensely nationalist-minded Shah had strong feelings regarding the Portuguese possession of the island of Hormuz at the entrance to the Persian Gulf, and no agreement could be reached with Don García regarding the matter, he always treated the Ambassador courteously. Shortly before Don García's departure, the Shah took him and some other envoys to drink coffee (which was then a novelty to most Europeans) at the Royal Caravanserai. Don García described 'cahua' as a black and bitter liquid which the Persians made from certain herbs.

Coffee was then drunk in Isfahan and elsewhere in Persia in coffee-houses (*qahveh-khaneh*), a term still in use in Persia, though it now has usually the meaning of 'tea-house'). These establishments were situated as a rule in the best parts of the city; they were spacious and lofty, and often had a basin of water, with a small fountain playing, in the centre. The citizens would gather in these buildings to sip their coffee, smoke tobacco, gossip or listen to the news or to poets reciting their verses. Games such as draughts, chess, and hopscotch were often played in them. Sometimes a mulla would stand up and preach to those present, but it was not considered obligatory for them to give up their games or conversations and listen attentively to these discourses.

An important feature of Isfahan – as it still is – was the *hammam* or bath. Thomas Herbert described the Isfahan baths as follows:

> The Hummums or Sudatories in this Citie are many and very beautifull; quadrated some, but most be globous. The stone is white, polisht, made narrow; the glass is thick, anneald and darkling; the top or covering, round. The inside of these hot houses are [*sic*] divided into many cells or camerations, some for delight, others for sweating in, all are for use, of pure stone all, all pav'd with jetty Marble; men use them commonly in the mornings, women towards night; the price is small, but so generously us'd as makes the gaine aburdant.

Privileged merchants

In 1615 the English East India Company sent two of its factors, John Crowther and Edward Connock, to Isfahan to see what steps could be taken to establish a foothold in Persia, since the Company was then having difficulty in disposing of all its stocks of cloth in India. Shah Abbas received the two factors kindly and granted the Company a *farman* or royal order enjoining his subjects 'to kindly receive and entertain the English Frankes and Nation who might present themselves'. The Company followed up this development by sending Connock on a further mission to Persia. Connock, who travelled by sea, took with him a cargo of cloth. Despite an attempt by the Portuguese to intercept the ship, Connock landed his cargo safely and travelled again to Isfahan. There, after a long delay caused by the Shah's absence on a campaign against the Turks, he eventually obtained from the Shah a further *farman* enabling the Company to trade freely anywhere in Persia and to appoint an agent at Isfahan who, besides carrying out his business for the Company, was to be the representative of the English crown. In consequence of these developments, the Company, inter alia, opened a factory in Isfahan in 1617. This building and its garden, all traces of which have disappeared, were situated to the north of the Royal Caravanserai, at the end of a narrow alleyway running westwards from the main thoroughfare of the bazaar. The open space where this factory stood is still called the Timcheh-yi-Firangiha or 'Little Caravanserai of the Franks'. This factory occupied an advantageous position, as it was situated in the best part of the bazaar area; it was, moreover, not far from the Ali Qapu. The building had been constructed at the end of the fifteenth century by the chief of the town-criers; this man, having been disgraced by the Shah for some offence, was not only dismissed from his post, but had his house and other belongings confiscated by the monarch. This establishment was quite an elaborate one, and there the Agent of the Company could on occasion entertain his guests on a fitting scale. After Sir Dodmore Cotton and his suite had arrived in Isfahan in April 1628, William Burt, the Company's representative, in Herbert's words:

> ... banqueted our Lord Ambassador, and showed us a rich and hearty welcome; to agrandize [*sic*] it, at night a Tanck of water was beset with lighted Tapers, artificially uniting the two Contrary Elements; squibs also and other fireworks that made all the Citie gape and wonder.

Eight years earlier, there had been a decidedly less distinguished, but perhaps even more convivial entertainment at the factory when the Company's door-keeper 'and two Runaways from the Fleet' met together there and drank so much that one of them, 'whom Wine deprived of ffootmanship', had to be borne to his quarters by his slightly less inebriated companions.

The Shah showed much favour to the English East India Company, partly because he wished to stimulate trade, particularly the silk trade, but also because he wished to enlist its aid against the Portuguese at Hormuz. Mention has already been made of the critical situation in regard to this island at the time of Don García de Silva y Figueroa's visit. Much though the Shah resented the Portuguese hold on Hormuz and other places in the Gulf, he could do nothing against them without ships. He put strong pressure on the East India Company, and made it agree, though with reluctance, to lend several of its ships and for these to co-operate with his land forces in an assault on Hormuz in 1622. This operation was carried out with complete success.

The Dutch East India Company, following in the wake of the English, also set up a factory in Isfahan. Their establishment was situated some little distance to the north-north-east of the English factory; it was not in such an advantageous position, being outside the bazaar quarter and a good deal farther from the court than the English factory was.

It must have been a great relief to the employees of the English and Dutch East India Companies to go up to Isfahan from the hot and unhealthy town of Gombroon (Bandar Abbas) and elsewhere on the coast and enjoy the cool and shady gardens surrounding their establishments there.

A king 'after his own will'

Although Shah Abbas wrought such a transformation in Isfahan, a large part, especially in the north and north-east, remained unchanged. There were many unpaved and frequently ill-kept lanes which were thick with dust in dry weather and deep in mud after rain or snow. These lanes were generally very narrow and tortuous, with high mud-brick walls on either side. However, hidden behind such forbidding walls would often be pleasant houses and charming gardens. The houses were usually of one storey only, with flat roofs; they had often a central courtyard, with a pool in the middle.

Security in the streets of Isfahan was good, as indeed it was elsewhere in Iran at that time, since the Shah dealt very severely with robbers and other malefactors. He would frequently emerge from his palace unaccompanied and incognito, and wander at will through the streets and bazaars, coversing freely with all and sundry. If he happened on such occasions to hear any criticism of himself, he usually took no notice. If, on the other hand, he heard of any misbehaviour by his ministers or officials, he would afterwards see that justice was done. One day, when walking through the streets in company with two Augustinian friars, he turned to them and said: 'How does what I am now doing seem to you? I am a king after my own will, and to go about in this manner is to be a king, but not like yours, who is always sitting indoors.'

In general, as has been shown, Shah Abbas enforced law and order with severity, but, acting apparently on the principle of 'divide and rule', he authorized or inspired the formation of two artificially antagonized parties, called the Haidari and the Ni'matillahi, in Isfahan and other towns. The members of these two parties, like those of the Blues and Greens in Constantinople or the Guelphs and Ghibellines in medieval Italy, would attack each other with the utmost fury. They were denied swords or muskets, but used sticks and stones instead.

Something must be said in conclusion respecting the area and population of Isfahan at the close of Shah Abbas's reign. The area was certainly a large one, but much of it was taken up by gardens. When viewed from a distance one saw a great mass of green, with the dome or minaret of a mosque showing here and there above the trees. The walls were some twenty miles in circumference, but they were not well maintained. Herbert scornfully remarked that they would be 'of no use against the confounding vomit of the flaming Cannon', but he admitted that they might stand up to attack by 'horse and shock of Launces'. In those days there were twelve gates, but four of them had been blocked up.

Pietro della Valle estimated the population of Isfahan at half a million, as did Adam Olearius, writing of the city as it was some sixteen years later. Herbert, on the other hand, put the total at only 200,000, a figure which seems far too low. In Chardin's time, nearly fifty years later, it was equally difficult to arrive at a reliable figure. The estimates then ranged from 600,000 to 1,100,000. It would perhaps be fairly safe to suggest that, by the end of Shah Abbas's reign, the population was between 400,000 and half a million.

Isfahan still contains many buildings dating from the time of Shah Abbas, and his layout of the city has, in the main, been preserved. One can still gaze in admiration at the buildings facing on to the Maidan-i-Shah. Except for the fact that the Masjid-i-Shah has long since been completed and that in quite recent years a garden was made to cover the greater part of the Maidan, it has remained practically unchanged since Shah Abbas's time. If one had to find a suitable epitaph for Shah Abbas, there could be none better than the one written for Sir Christopher Wren, 'Si monumentum requiris, circumspice'.

Nineteenth-century impression of the Royal Bazaar at the north end of the Maidan-i-Shah. This centre of trade, which formed part of Shah Abbas's plan for his new capital, has changed little since the time it was constructed.

MUGHAL
DELHI AND AGRA

'If there is a Paradise on earth

it is this', proclaims an inscription in the Red Fort at Delhi. And in the two cities of Delhi and Agra, over a hundred miles apart on the Jumna River in northern India, the Mughals carried out their design for a world of order and beauty.

When the first Mughals arrived from the central Asian steppes in the early sixteenth century – their name is a variant of 'Mongol' – they were merely the latest of a series of invaders stretching back to Indian prehistory: Mughal Delhi was established on or near the ruins of possibly twelve previous cities. But the Mughal invention was to develop two cities together, one controlling the north and one the centre of India, dividing all possible enemies. Thus from the first these strategic cities were court-oriented, and their large populations (Delhi had up to two million people and fifty-two bazaars) were drawn by the court itself: merchants and farmers, scientists, artists and builders.

Nomadic Turks by race, rulers by profession, and Persians by cultural adoption, the Mughals combined these elements into a unified attitude to life. The great emperor, Akbar (1542–1605), even tried to develop a hybrid religion. Though this failed, it was characteristic of the eclectic nature of Mughal civilization.

After the accession of Aurangzeb in 1658, the cities began to lose their vigour: a convinced Muslim, Aurangzeb, disturbed the cultural balance Akbar had so carefully established, and spent his life warring in the Deccan. After him there was little public building, and though

Delhi became the capital, its population gradually declined to some 150,000 by the early nineteenth century, when the exhausted Mughals gave way to the British Empire. The twin cities have continued in use, and though the British, like the conquerors before them, built their New Delhi adjacent to the Old, the Mughal town plans have become blurred and the buildings – virtually unchanged and highly evocative – are surrounded by a clutter of more recent houses and bazaars.

What the Mughals tried to achieve is clearest at Fatehpur Sikri a city near Agra, deserted and untouched for almost four hundred years. Built in the late sixteenth century by the emperor Akbar around the shrine of a Muslim saint, it contains the shrine-mosque, palaces for the emperor, his wives, and his nobles, and also an elephant tank and pit for wild animals; there is even a pavement laid out as a gaming-board where the emperor could play *pacheesi* with dancing-girls as movable pawns. The shrine of the saint is surrounded by screens of pure white marble (opposite), cut into delicate Islamic patterns by local Hindu craftsmen. Used throughout palaces, these screens let in air and muted light in a climate of intolerable summer heat.

Delhi and Agra were the seats of power: Delhi has remained so. But as a town Fatehpur Sikri more clearly suggests the spirit of the Mughals, their power and magnificence, their love of order and beauty, their nomadic temperament and their transitoriness. (1)

227

The first Mughal, Babur, found Hindustan inhospitable – though redeemed by 'an abundance of gold and silver' – and when he arrived at Agra in 1526 his first act was to lay out a garden in the Persian style (far left). (2)

It was a man's world: women rarely went out, and when they did their brilliant clothes and make-up were hidden under tent-like *burqas* or behind the screens of palanquins. A very few, in the royal family, were highly educated and made their mark within the world of the women's quarters. One exceeded all the others: Nur Jahan, wife of the early-seventeenth-century emperor Jahangir (they are seen together on the left), went so far as to have coins minted in her name, and is said to have advised her husband from behind a screen during audiences. (3)

The hub of each city was its imperial Red Fort. The one in Delhi (left) was entered from the town through the gates in the distance. In the farther courtyard with its central tank all but the most privileged had to dismount; but all men were free to pass through the gate to the Hall of Public Audience (its roof visible in the centre, surrounded by coloured tenting and a fence), where they would be heard by the emperor. Between this Hall and the river were the emperor's private apartments, with the completely enclosed *zenana* of the chief sultana and the other wives on the left. On the right is the Hall of Private Audience, which the emperor, sheltered by a broad fan, is seen entering. Farthest from the town, the marble-screened apartments were closest to the river and its cooling breezes. Like a town in miniature the Fort has its mosque, at the far right, and was dotted with gardens and crossed by a network of water flowing in marble channels. The illustration is a Mughal artist's rendering; while not wholly accurate, it gives a true general impression. (4)

Akbar made Agra his capital, building the Red Fort on the edge of the Jumna River. In a miniature (right) he is seen leaving Agra, visible at the top, by a water-gate and setting out for Delhi. The court travels with him, nobles in his boat, a falconer and an elephant-driver with his goad in the boat on the left; on the right are military men, one of them a Hindu Rajput who holds a long gun. At the bottom worried grooms try to calm the emperor's Arab horses. Horses were so highly valued that their tails were used – here on the boat prows – as a sign of royalty. (5)

Cosmopolitan Delhi at its height was one of the largest cities in the world. In its crowded streets Indians of all religions mingled with traders, priests and embassies from the major powers. Ambassadors from Persia were received by Shah Jahan – whose name means 'ruler of the world' – in the Hall of Public Audience (left). The leader, in an embroidered silk coat and large plumed turban, salutes the Mughal high above on a carved marble dais, while his gift-bearing followers wait at the far left. Europeans who visited the Mughal cities brought back descriptions of their organization and splendour; they left, among other gifts, works of art which the Mughals seized on and copied, as in the frieze above Shah Jahan's throne. With a specialization of labour unheard of then in Europe, the cities were the industrial workshops of the world: rice, dyes and spices were exported, and crafts were organized into factories to produce luxury goods and hand-woven cloth sold as far away as Japan and the east coast of Africa. (7)

Tents of stone were the setting of life in Delhi and Agra. Originally nomads, the Mughals continued to live in canvas cities during campaigns: Humayun is shown (left) enthroned in a tent with open flaps, surrounded by a wall of canvas, and when over a hundred years later Shah Jahan rebuilt the Hall of Public Audience in Agra Fort (far left) it was still reminiscent of a tent, with marble columns instead of posts, edged when in use with a coloured awning, its courtyard fenced in by an arcade of stone. Even the great congregational mosque in Delhi, the Jami Masjid (below), is basically an open tent in stone for the prayer-leader and the eminent, with a walled courtyard to contain the multitude. To this tent pattern the Mughals added Persian domes and minarets, from which the faithful were called to prayer. The great court with its central fountain for ritual washing will hold some 10,000 people; while important men were sheltered in its arcaded east end, women were allowed no farther than the western entrance. (6, 8, 9)

The private apartments of the rich became interior gardens: in a pavilion in Delhi Fort (right) water rippled over a marble fall amid flowers of coloured stones, and even the columns have become leaves and buds. (10)

Thousands of builders worked on the mosques, tombs and palaces (left: Agra Fort). Under the eye of the foreman on the right, low-caste men and women bring stones, carry sand and rubble, and attend to laden bullocks. Craftsmen of higher status, both Hindus and Muslims, work with dressed stone and build the dome. At the top Akbar arrives to inspect the progress of his building. (11)

The gates still stand at Agra Fort (above) – of the same red sandstone in banded layers, panelled, crenellated, and with some bright decoration; but their actual size and mass dwarf human beings. (12)

For his favourite wife, Mumtaz Mahal – who died in 1631 bearing his fifteenth child –, Shah Jahan built the last great masterpiece of Mughal architecture. The Taj Mahal at Agra (right) rises above a reflecting pool, in a formal Persian garden planted with flowering trees and cypresses. The tomb took twenty years to build: the white marble is inlaid with glittering coloured patterns of semi-precious stones, there were silver doors, and the monument within was enclosed by a grille of gold. Next to it Shah Jahan had planned a tomb for himself, entirely of black marble, but it was never built. (13)

Rich and beautiful objects were the delight of the ruling classes. Most of the day was spent in administration, interrupted by times of prayer, but the high points of court life were such ceremonies as that shown at right, in which the emperor Jahangir weighs his son against gold. Brilliant carpets have been laid in a courtyard and, in addition to the sacks of gold on the balance, gifts lie on trays in the foreground: fine silks, daggers of steel with jewelled hilts, jewelled scabbards, necklaces, and small vessels of crystal inlaid with gold, emeralds and rubies. (14)

A world of artists grew up in the cities, under the patronage of the emperors and the great Hindu nobles. Some came from as far as Persia and France to work on imperial projects. At public contests, rival poets improvised in Persian, and a factory was set up at Agra to meet the demand for illustrated manuscripts. Manohar, who drew himself as a young man with the calligrapher Husain Zarin (below), became one of Jahangir's favourite artists, painting for his albums pictures of birds, animals and people who had attracted the emperor's curiosity. (15)

A united India, in which Hindus and Muslims would willingly co-operate, was a goal of Mughal rule, and for a time this was achieved in the cities. Merchants and bankers were almost all Hindus, and Rajput generals mingled freely with the Mughals (below right: Muslims tied their coats on the right, Hindus on the left), even intermarrying. Christians, Buddhists and Jains were tolerated, and in the eighteenth century, Muslim rulers still patronized Hindu religious festivals. The well-run empire was in the hands of a largely Hindu civil service. The Indo-Persian civilization developed in Delhi and Agra failed in the end to engage the masses, but at its best it is an experiment for modern India to study. (16)

PERCIVAL SPEAR

IT IS CHARACTERISTIC of the Mughal empire in India that its capital did not stay fixed permanently in a single place, but kept on shifting. When the imperial Mughals are mentioned it is usual to connect imperial Delhi with them. Or, to reverse the order, the mention of Delhi conjures up a vision of the great Mughals. Agra is the city of the Taj, not otherwise thought of as memorable. Yet, while it was from Delhi that the last of the Mughals departed to a British-imposed exile, it was to Agra that the first of the Mughals went after his victory at Panipat, and there that he stayed till his death. This dichotomy in fact continued throughout the Mughal period. The second Mughal, Humayun, returned to Delhi, but his famous son Akbar lived longer in Agra than in Delhi and in addition spent fifteen years in a capital of his own devising, Fatehpur Sikri. Jahangir spent more of his time in Lahore, Ajmir, and the Deccan than either at Delhi or Agra. His magnificent son built the present 'old Delhi' or Shahjahanabad, but in fact spent the first half of his reign in Agra, where he not only built the Taj Mahal, but also rebuilt most of Akbar's palace within the Fort. He was at Agra in 1658 when he met disaster on the defeat of his favourite son and intended heir Dara Shekoh by his younger son Aurangzeb, and it was there that he spent the last eight years of his life as a state prisoner.

Aurangzeb, or Alamgir, to give him his correct imperial title, divided the first twenty-two years of his reign between the two cities. But this period was interspersed by long journeys to the north occupied in visiting Kashmir and settling the affairs of the Afghans. If it was of the court of Delhi that François Bernier gave his famous description, it was at Agra that Aurangzeb gave the equally famous interview to the Maratha chief Sivaji. From 1681 to his death in 1707 at the age of eighty-eight Aurangzeb deserted both cities and spent his years moving in camp in the Deccan, overthrowing the Muslim kingdoms of the south and wrestling with the obstinate and evasive Marathas. Here we meet a third feature of the Mughal capital. The capital is a camp.

Aurangzeb's son Bahadur Shah, in his brief reign of five years, was always on the move. He ranged from Kabul to Hyderabad in the Deccan; never set foot in either of the twin cities, and arrived at last in Lahore to die. It was in fact only with the later and less admirable emperors, up to the murder of Alamgir II in 1759, that Delhi became the permanent imperial residence. There followed an interregnum of thirteen years while Alamgir's son Shah Alam wandered from place to place until he settled at Allahabad with British support. From 1772 to 1858 the emperors were again continuously in residence. But only for about the first thirteen years could Delhi seriously be called a capital, and then only of the small 'kingdom' of Delhi rather than of an all-Indian dominion. For the rest of the time the emperors were pensionaries, first of the Marathas under Sindia and then of the British, and in the end, after less than five months of nominal power during 1857, they became the prisoners of their supplanters.

It is thus clear that we cannot consider Delhi to be the sole or even the major capital of the Mughals. The less powerful the emperors became, the more prominent was Delhi in their lives. They were concerned, in fact, in their great days, in almost equal measure with Delhi and with Agra, and in addition they spent a good part of their time in neither, but in camp. It seems right, therefore, to consider Delhi and Agra as the twin capitals of the Mughals and to treat them as a joint imperial city.

The invaders' paths

Delhi and Agra are not physically contiguous like Buda and Pest in Hungary or Minneapolis and St Paul in America. They are, in fact, about a hundred and twenty miles apart, and can only claim a common river on which they stand and a common plain through which the river Jumna flows. How comes it, then, that they were linked imperially? And why were those particular sites chosen and no others? The first answer to these questions is geographical and the second strategic. India has always been open to invasion from the north-west, both because passes from the Iranian tableland exist to give access, and because there have been populations which, suitably motivated and organized, could march through them. Once through the passes and over the Indus, invaders of India have found themselves in a land that shapes itself into two corridors of riverine plain, bounded on either side by mountains or deserts. One of these is the Indus valley, which runs south to the Arabian sea and, with its eastward barriers of the Thar desert and the marshes of Kutch, has formed an invader's *cul-de-sac*. The other runs roughly south-eastwards between Kashmir and the Himalayas to the north and the Rajasthan desert to the south. It is when it reaches the line of the river Jumna that this corridor diversifies itself. One route continues down the flat and fertile Ganges valley to the sea in the Bay of Bengal. The other turns south and, following the Jumna to Agra, provides thence easy routes to central and western India and to the key of Rajasthan, Ajmir. The line of the Jumna from near Ambala is thus of great strategical importance. Its control enables touch to be maintained with the north-west and pressure to be exerted on that traditional seat of Indian power and wealth, the Ganges plain or valley, on the region to the south and west, with its access to the sea at Surat in Gujarat, and on the citadel of last-ditch resistance, the arid plains and hills of Rajasthan. It is for these reasons that successive invaders have placed their headquarters on this line. The Indo-Aryans themselves had a capital named Indraprastha whose site is traditionally associated with Delhi. It was only later that, as they penetrated deeper and became more at home in the country, they moved their capitals eastward to Ayodhya and Pataliputra (Patna). The natural base for an invading power is thus the Jumna valley, while the natural headquarters for an indigenous north Indian power is down country at Allahabad or Patna.

Granted that the centre for an invader's empire should be on the line of the Jumna, the questions remain: why Delhi and Agra, and why both together? The two together possessed more advantages than those possessed by any other site on this line, such as Mathura or Baghpat. Both possessed fords, an important consideration during seven or eight months of the year in a region where river-beds are so wide that they have been bridged only within the last century. For centuries before that, Delhi's only access to the east had been a bridge of boats in the cold weather and barges in the rains. Another consideration was river-transport. In the absence of good roads, the rivers were of great value; the Jumna–Ganges system provided a thousand miles of waterway down to the Bay of Bengal. Today so much water is taken by irrigation that the Jumna is not navigable in the cold weather much above Agra. But formerly, river-boats regularly plied to Delhi, which received much of its supplies that way. Delhi was the most northerly point to which navigation was really practicable, while Agra, in addition to its fording facilities, lay at the point where the river veered from south to south-east. With the river Chambal flowing forty miles to the south, and the Rajput centres, Jaipur and Ajmir, almost due east, Agra was well placed for watching the Rajput strongholds, for advancing south into Malwa, or for defending the north from southerly attack. On the other hand, from Agra the north-west could not be watched, nor the Gangetic plain be controlled so easily. The two cities therefore formed a geo-political pair. Together they provided a base from which the whole of north and central India could be controlled; and they neatly divided possible foes in Rajasthan, central India, and the Ganges valley, who could be defeated in detail before they could unite.

We can therefore regard Delhi and Agra as the natural twin centres for a northerly power controlling most of northern India. But Delhi and to a lesser extent Agra are notable for the number of their sites. Delhi is said to have had seven cities before New Delhi became the eighth. But the true number is nearer fourteen, and even Agra has had at least three. A reason for this is that Delhi and Agra were more important as military and political than as commercial or agrarian centres. They were not natural centres of agrarian tracts which might acquire importance in their own right and thus continuity and perhaps reverence. Their importance was political; it was the courts which attracted the merchants and farmers, not the grain and commerce which attracted the rulers. Thus we hear little of Delhi between the days of Indraprastha in about 1000 BC, when the Indo-Aryans moved their centres of power farther east, and the time of the Turkish invasion in AD 1192. The city then existing was a dependent of the Rajput Chauhan kingdom of Ajmir, and its only known predecessor was little more than a rocky fastness in stony hills.

Mughal wanderlust

The political nature of these cities brings into question the personal predilections of kings, and it is these which mainly account for the changes which have occurred. New dynasties, especially conquering ones, were inclined to celebrate their victory and impress the world by building new capitals. To this Delhi owes the three city sites at Mahrauli and the famous Qutab Minar there, conceived as a tower of victory. Different rulers of the same dynasty might also build cities, or palaces to which cities accrued, for reasons of strategy or prestige. Thus Muhammad Tughlak, in the fourteenth century, moved altogether from Delhi because he wanted to control the south of India. His successor Firuz Shah made a break with an unpopular past by building Firozabad to the south of the present city of Shahjahanabad. The rule has usually been for two cities to be current, as it were, at the same time. One attracted the hangers-on of the court, political and economic, while the other was where the merchants resided for so long as they could live there without loss. Each city in turn became a quarry for the next but one, and this explains why in most of the cities few traces today are found of houses, shops, or streets. Thus the old city at the Qutab continued to exist long after Firozabad had been built; for a time in the early fifteenth century rival kings reigned in each city. Firozabad continued alongside the next city, and this joint complex survived, with Shahjahanabad, until the late eighteenth century.

We can now trace the Mughal contribution to this politico-architectural kaleidoscope. When Babur defeated Ibrahim Lodi at Panipat in 1526, he went straight to Agra, the Lodi capital, where his first act was to lay out a garden in the Persian style. He lived only four years more, so it was left to his son Humayun to express in stone the Mughal image. He chose a rocky eminence near the Jumna for his fortress-palace, where its striking walls still survive. But before he could complete it he was ousted by the Afghan Sher Shah, who gave his name to the mosque and the surviving pavilion within. Humayun returned for a few months after Sher Shah's death, and

Akbar followed him. Akbar lived there for the first few years of his reign – leaving, it is suggested, on account of an attempt to assassinate him in the city. In view of his later history, it is not difficult to detect also the desire of a young, successful, and ambitious ruler to have a city of his own. Humayun's city was only half-Mughal, for it had been completed by Sher Shah and so was overshadowed by the Mughal's humiliation of being defeated by the Afghans and having to flee to Persia.

The dream-city deserted

Akbar's choice was Agra, where the second Lodi king had given his name to a capital now perpetuated as a suburb of Agra and as the site of Akbar's own mausoleum. Akbar took over the eminence commanding the ford of the Jumna, surrounded it with a massive wall, and filled the interior space with original and delicate architecture in the local red sandstone. Some ten years later his restless spirit produced a new city, the dream-creation of Fatehpur Sikri. The spot was twenty-three miles from Agra, close to the site of Babur's victory over the Rajputs. There lived the Muslim saint Salim Shah Chishti, whose prayers were effective, so Akbar believed, in providing him with three sons, the first of whom was named Salim in the saint's honour. In this spot, on a hill rising from a plain, Akbar designed an immense mosque, with the most lofty gateway in India. Hard by he built his palace, and surrounded the hill with a wall to enclose his city. The adjacent plain was flooded to make a pleasure lake, and also, one suspects, to provide a sufficient supply of water. Here Akbar passed the most critical years of his life and reign, when he abandoned orthodox Islam for eclecticism, developed his cult of imperial sanctity, and defeated the only large-scale rebellion (by the orthodox party) in his reign of forty-nine years. But after about twelve years' residence at Fatehpur Sikri he returned to Agra. The reason is obscure, but was possibly connected with the supply of water, which was brackish, and the climate, which was sultry and feverish. Akbar preferred Agra to Delhi in his later years because of his increasing absorption in Deccan conquests. When he went north, it was to Lahore, and when eastward, it was to Allahabad. Fatehpur Sikri has remained untenanted and deserted apart from occasional visits by passing emperors who used the buildings as a standing set of stone tents. The climate has preserved the buildings, the presence of a mosque and a saint's shrine and the lack of treasure have restrained plunderers. The palace therefore stands virtually complete in its glory of colour and craftsmanship. Here, more than anywhere else, one can sense the spirit of the Mughals, their power and magnificence, their love of order and beauty, their nomadic proclivities and their transitoriness.

Akbar's son Jahangir retained Agra as his capital, for he too was much involved in Deccan campaigns. But he also possessed the Mughal wanderlust in spite of his love of good living. He spent much time in Lahore, where he adorned the Fort and was finally buried; he stayed at Ajmir in Rajputana where he built a marble pavilion by the lake, and then at Burhanpur in central India where the English ambassador, the pertinacious Sir Thomas Roe, followed him in search of a trade treaty, complaining of the discomforts of travel.

With Jahangir's son Shah Jahan (1627–58), a new period begins. Akbar, as befitted such a wide-ranging mind, expressed himself in thought and in all forms of art. Jahangir had a special feeling for painting: he was one of the most discriminating art-patrons the world has seen. Shah Jahan had the same feeling for buildings. He was a master-patron of architecture, who not only gave orders to build but inspired and guided his architects. For about twenty years he lived on in Agra, where he rebuilt most of Akbar's palace in marble instead of red Agra stone. His reconstruction included a special tower for viewing the Taj Mahal, which he had built in memory of Mumtaz Mahal, his principal wife (the *Padshah Begam*).

Shah Jahan loved Agra; he was there at the time of his fall in 1658, and spent the last eight years of his life as a state prisoner in the palace. But it is said that the lack of a processional way in the city irked him, and that the citizens' refusal to demolish enough property to make one disgusted him. Also the memory of Akbar could not be completely banished from the palace: was not the city called Akbarabad? The result was Shah Jahan's construction of a complete new palace and city at Delhi. The palace fort had one processional

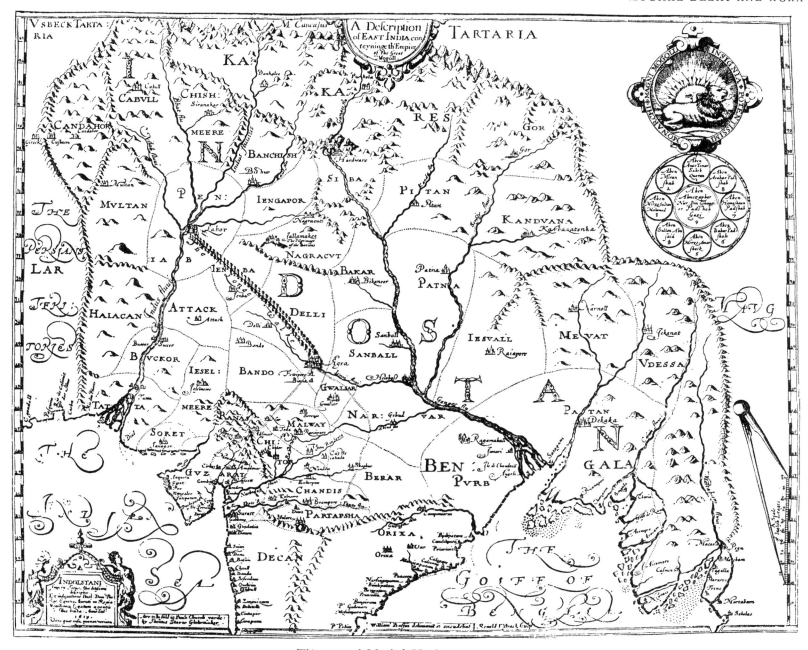

This map of Mughal Hindustan was drawn in 1619 on the basis of information from the English ambassador to the Mughal court. Agra, in the centre, is given more significance than Delhi, north-west of the centre.

way to the 'great mosque' or Jami Masjid, Shah Jahan's finest creation after the Taj and the Moti Masjid at Agra, and another a mile long through the centre of the city. The palace, like that of Agra, overlooked the river to catch the cooling breezes; the city walls were four and a half miles round. This Shahjahanabad, built to balance the Akbarabad at Agra, is the crowded 'Old Delhi' of today.

Delhi: from seat of power to a Mughal Weimar

Shah Jahan's son and supplanter, Aurangzeb or Alamgir, brought a change. Aurangzeb expressed himself through theology and ethics rather than the arts. His aim was to be the orthodox Islamic ruler of India – to turn the Mughal empire into a Muslim empire – and his private leaning was towards the puritan strain in Islamic ethics. The age of great buildings came to an end, and such as were erected were the result of private effort. The reign of Aurangzeb divides into two almost equal halves. During the first twenty-two years (to 1680) his headquarters was at Delhi, which at this time reached its apogee as the imperial city of the Mughal empire at its zenith. There were excursions to Agra, to Lahore, to Kashmir, and to Peshawar to pacify the north-west, but Delhi was the seat of power. From 1680 to his death in 1707, Aurangzeb spent his years in the Deccan, dealing with Rajputs, southern Muslims, and Marathas. He was a wanderer too, and only stumbled back to Ahmadnagar in 1706 to die. Agra was never again the capital, while Delhi lay fallow until the appearance of Aurangzeb's ne'er-do-well grandson, Jahandar Shah, in 1712. Delhi's second great age, an age of pomp

in decline, lasted until the waves of Persian, Afghan, and Maratha invasion rolled over it, to culminate in the battle of Panipat in 1761. During those years the court was fixed, with nothing more than an occasional excursion a few miles out. With their nomadism, the virtue of the Mughals departed. Delhi saw another English embassy under Surman, more modest but no less successful than Roe's: it saw the famous shoesellers' riot; it saw the Persian Nadir Shah's invasion and his sack of the city in 1739; it saw a civil war between rival ministers in 1752, the murder of four emperors in palace revolutions, and finally successive occupations by Afghans and Marathas. In these tumults imperial Delhi went down, to reappear later as a kind of Indian Mughal Weimar. Two of the last three emperors were minor poets of some merit, and they gathered round them a philosophizing group. In Aurangzeb's time the city was estimated to have two million inhabitants and fifty-two bazaars and wholesale markets. Between 1712 and 1750 the actual figures were probably not far short of these, but, by the time of the British occupation in the early nineteenth century, only about 150,000 inhabitants remained.

The nomadic court and its tents of stone

The story of the dealings of the emperors with Delhi and Agra provides the first characteristic of the Mughal capital in its great days; the Mughal's life was semi-nomadic. The heart of the Mughal capital was the Mughal court, a semi-permanent abode like a beehive, with the palace itself serving as the cocoon for the queen-bee and her attendants. Nor was this surprising in view of the Mughal

237

emperors' antecedents. They had started as nomads in the central Asian steppes, and until their last days they never forgot their origin. The first four generations spoke Turkish, with Persian as the language of culture, as nineteenth-century Russians spoke French. The body of the Mughal emperor's followers was the horde or *urdu*, and this word became a synonym for camp, the place where the horde rested in its wanderings. The palace itself was named the *Urdu-i mu'alla* or exalted camp, and it was only in the Mughals' latter days that the first word was exchanged for *mahal* or palace. The architecture of the palace reflected the nomadic mind, which thinks in terms of tents. The groundwork was a series of courtyards, more or less spacious, surrounded by low colonnades, which in the steppes would have been canvas walls. These led up to the two great pavilions of public and private audience, of which every Mughal palace has a set. The pavilions consisted of dignified and beautifully proportioned rectangular colonnades, open on three sides to the air and punctuated in the centre of the long side by a platform which served for a throne. The sun was excluded by movable and colourful screens, while carpets were laid and removed as required. This was, in fact, no audience chamber or throne-room in the European sense; it was a tent or *shamiana* frozen into stone. Only the higher nobles could get under cover; the main body of courtiers stood in the open court outside, which was also used for the nomadic recreations of inspecting horse and camel flesh. If it is thought that this was a natural reaction to the nature of the north Indian climate, it should be remembered that both the heat of high summer and the winter chill of January and February make some sort of shelter very desirable. This style of building was, in fact, a nomadic reaction to sedentariness. The materials depended on Mughal prosperity. So these buildings pass from brick or local stone through red sandstone to marble and back to brick again.

The nomadic heritage was most apparent in buildings, such as palaces, which concerned the Mughals most personally. But it also appears in others like mosques. In many parts of the Islamic world the mosque is covered to give the worshippers shelter. But the Mughal mosque is always first an enclosure to contain the bulk of the congregation, leading to a platform on which stands an open-arched building of three, five, or seven sections, containing the *mihrab* or prayer recess and usually a simple stone pulpit. Only the very faithful can get shelter even in the Jami Masjid at Delhi, whose courtyard will hold ten thousand worshippers. The Mughal mosque is, in fact, an open tent (in stone) for the *Imam* or prayer-leader and the eminent, with space for the multitude fenced off from the steppe outside. It also has, however, two non-nomadic features which spring from Persian influence yet to be discussed. These are the domes which surmount them and the minarets which flank them.

Nomadic influence is also apparent in Mughal ceremonial. Horses played an important part. Favoured nobles were allowed to ride into the courtyard of the Dewan-i-'Amm, the equivalent of the outer audience chamber of a European palace; they were often inspected there. Horses' tails were an emblem of royalty, and so were yaks' tails. The fish standard was one of the principal Mughal emblems. White horse tails were also used as fly-whisks.

Infiltration of Persian culture

After nomadic influence, the strongest was Persian. The Mughals were nomadic Turks by race, kings by profession, and Persians by cultural adoption. After the first flush of Mongol destruction under Chinghiz Khan it was to Persian culture, as well as the Islamic religion, that his followers turned. The supplanting Turks, Taimur and his successors, did the same. So the mosques with which Taimur adorned Samarkand were Persian in style, while the coloured tiles with which their domes glow were Persian in craftsmanship. Babur spoke and wrote his memoirs and poetry in Turkish, but his conscious culture was Persian. So it was with his successors. It was not until the reign of Muhammad Shah (1719–48), no longer a nomad, that Urdu, which is a hybrid of Persian and Hindi, was admitted as a court language, and even then many poets continued to compose in Persian. Muhammad Iqbal, the intellectual parent of Pakistan, composed more freely and copiously in Persian than in Urdu.

The Mughal capital was a Persianized city. But its culture was not wholly exotic; it was not just a museum of Turkish survivals and a factory of Persian couplets. The Persian influence combined with

local Indian elements to produce an Indo-Persian culture which was something distinctive in itself, neither imitative Persian nor hybrid Hindu. It spread from Delhi and Agra through the whole of north India, and traces of it are to be found throughout the subcontinent. It may even be ranked as an 'abortive civilization' – a civilization in that it developed a unified attitude to life which expressed itself in art, architecture, and manners, and abortive in the sense that it failed to win the permanent allegiance of either Muslim or Hindu masses.

Four civilizations or cultures bordered on the central Asian steppes: the Chinese, the Tibetan, the Persian, and the Russo-Byzantine. There seems to be no doubt that in the sixteenth and seven-

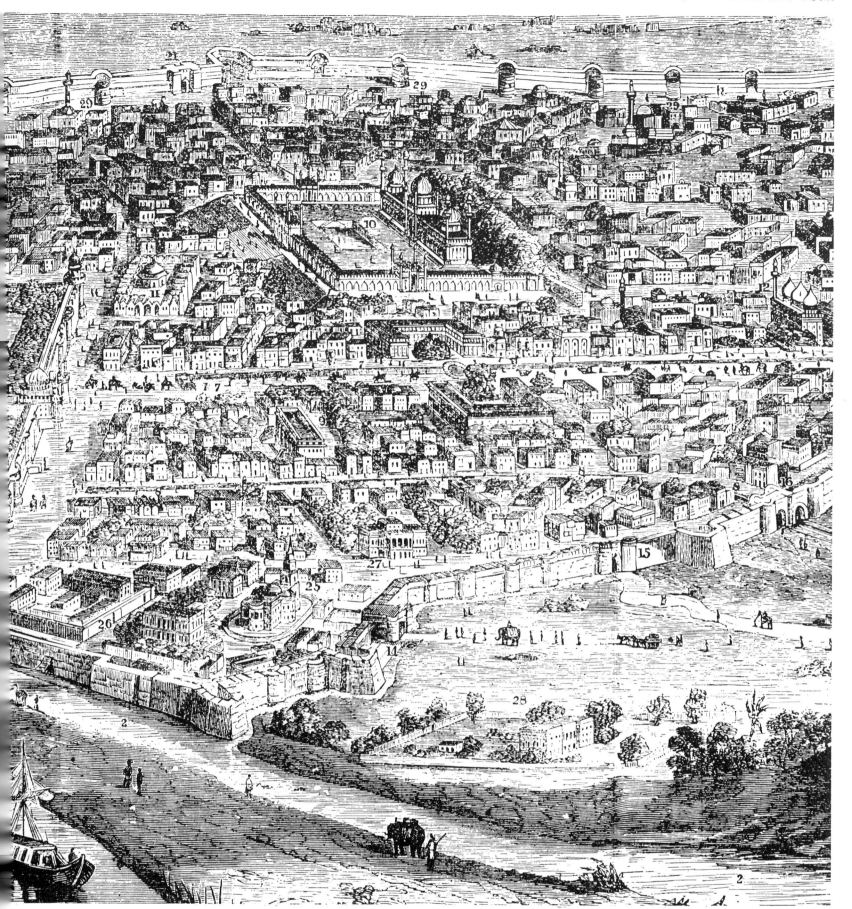

The walled city of Delhi in 1858, when it was hardly changed from the Mughal period.

teenth centuries the Persian was the most magnetic of the four. The Mughals not only adopted Persian culture, they revelled in it. It is perhaps not without significance that the Mughals' vigour began to fade when Persian culture itself lost its inspiration. We see the Mughals as the standard-bearers of this culture all over India, and we also see them combining local elements with it.

The process is worth tracing in a little more detail. The first element was the Persian language with its Indian child, Urdu. Persian was the official language of the Mughal Empire and of its successor the British administration down to 1835. Thereafter Persian had no value for careers or for commerce, but poets continued to write in it

and students to study it as a cultural exercise, down to the Second World War. India became a literary province of the Persian cultural empire, and some of its poets, like Faizi, were accepted into the corpus of standard Persian literature. In prose there was a long line of distinguished writers, from Abu'l Fazl, the encyclopaedist of Akbar's reign, to Sayyid Ghulam Husain Khan, the Indian historian of the Mughal decline and the East India Company's rise. Through the influence of Persian, Urdu not only grew out of Hindi but became a literary language in its own right. Literature played an important part in social life. Songs and poems, recitations and declamations, were essentials in all entertainment. The most characteristic feature of all was the *mushaira* or public poetical contest, where rival poets would improvise on a previously chosen couplet and the audience would indicate its feelings with shouts of *wah, wah,* or groans of disapproval.

The Persian influence on Mughal culture is next apparent in Mughal art. Here the mingling with Indian themes was quicker and more complete than in language, so that by the seventeenth century pure Persian art was no longer to be seen. In the field of painting the Mughals brought their painters with them, and the work of the first half of the sixteenth century was strongly Persian in tone. In the second half of the century Akbar revolutionized the art by giving a training in Persian techniques to the local artists of the Hindu tradition. Thus arose the Mughal school of painting, which was neither Persian nor Hindi but was certainly Indian. Akbar and his son Jahangir were the virtual directors of this school over more than sixty years, prescribing subjects and rewarding merit with remarkable acumen. The paintings were miniatures in form and began as illustrations to classical Persian works, such as Firdausi's *Shah Nama*. But they soon went beyond this to depict all kinds of court scenes, domestic as well as public. The art thus became an epitome of court or aristocratic life. Jahangir, who always carried some painters with him, added scenes of natural beauty and exquisite studies of wild life. The more formal Shah Jahan encouraged portraiture and has left us a gallery of portraits of grandees. No noble was without his illustrated Persian classics or albums of paintings.

A city of tombs and gardens

In architecture the first buildings, such as Humayun's Tomb (Delhi, 1560) with the semicircular dome, brilliant glazed tiles and the six-pointed star, were Persian in style. Here again Akbar, with his free employment of Hindu craftsmen, wrought a revolution. Fatehpur Sikri was almost wholly Hindu in execution, but the architects learnt to combine the Hindu transom with the Mughal arch, Hindu detail like the temple bell and the lotus with Islamic geometrical patterns, to produce a characteristic Mughal style, which here again was neither Persian nor Hindu but certainly Indian. It is seen in its developed form in Shah Jahan's Agra and his Shahjahanabad or Delhi, and its masterpieces are the Taj, the Moti Masjid in Agra Fort, and the Jami Masjid at Delhi, three works that any capital might be proud to own. We may perhaps describe the Persian contribution to this style of architecture as the dome, the *dalan* and the *darwaza*. The dome developed from the semicircle of Humayun's Tomb into the bulbous forms of the eighteenth century, with a graceful half-way house in the seventeenth. The *dalan* was a domestic building with open arches on one side, really a tent with the flaps folded back. The *darwaza* was the great archway, leading to a smaller entrance, that is found to perfection in the great Mughal tombs and that culminates in the Buland Darwaza or great gate of the mosque at Fatehpur Sikri. Apart from the palaces and mosques, which have already been mentioned, there were tombs and *sarais*, or travellers' rest-houses, in profusion. Delhi is a city of great tombs. The idea of the monumental tomb came from Persia, but their profusion was due to local conditions. The Mughals had an official nobility, holding office and relying for their wealth on official appointments. Their salaries were large, to enable them to maintain stipulated forces, and, as they were always short of cash, the state treasury made them advances. At death, their property was sealed for the recovery of the advance, a process which in practice amounted to a death-duty of a hundred per cent. So the lords or *omrah* spent in display and magnificence the funds they could not pass on to their heirs. The building of large tombs was a form of personal advertisement, while the building of mosques and *sarais* was charitable work, acceptable to God and so admirable also to man.

One more Persian gift to Mughal India was the Persian garden. With its hills and its heat, its running water and its love of order, Persia produced the formal garden at several levels, divided into squares for fruit-trees or flowers and channelled by water-courses rippling over waterfalls. The pavilion or summer-house completed the scene. Ideally there were seven levels, to represent the seven stages of paradise. The Mughals brought this concept with them to the dusty plains of Hindustan. In the plains the levels sank to three, and in the hands of the emperors the gardens spread to the great Shalimars of Delhi (now in ruins), Lahore and Kashmir. The

Hindus adopted them, as at the Jat garden at Dig and the Sikh garden at Pinjaur. They were of all sizes, from the grounds of what were virtually summer-palaces to small enclosures. The garden concept was carried over to the tomb, which gave the garden a convenient centre, or for which it formed a natural and dignified setting. The enclosures of the Taj and of the tombs of Humayun and Safdar Jung are examples. Gardens were attached to palaces like the Hayat Baksh and Mehtab (moonlight) gardens in the Delhi Fort; even if there was no pavilion, no tomb, and no palace, gardens would still be found in enclosures irrigated by wells. The Indian Mughal garden thus became something quite beyond the original Persian. Once more, the Mughals created something that was neither Persian nor Hindu, but certainly Indian. Its characteristics were regularity and order, formal cultivation, water, and repose.

Symmetry, embellishment, and novelty

The last Persian gift which the Mughals brought to India was the love of order and symmetry. Here again the original concept was transformed by Mughal minds into something characteristic of themselves. Babur, on his arrival, lamented not only the poverty but also the confusion of north India. In the capital cities this love of order was first manifested in the symmetry with which the palaces were laid out. Whatever the shape of the site, however irregular the contour of the walls, all was geometrical regularity within. Shah Jahan extended this from his palace to his city, so that his Shahjahanabad, with its processional ways, became the first example of town-planning in modern India. From Delhi the Rajput Jai Singh adopted, in the eighteenth century, the idea of moving his capital from picturesque Amber to Jaipur. This sense of order also appeared in the court ceremonial, which was noted for its solemnity and strict order, its sense of decorum and regulated etiquette. Sivaji scandalized the court and Aurangzeb when he talked angrily in his place because he thought that he had not received his due from the emperor. The same feeling can be observed in Abu'l Fazl's masterpiece, the '*Ain-i-Akbari* or 'Acts of Akbar', with its minute descriptions, analyses and dissections of the whole palace routine and imperial administration. Here order reigned, whatever the tumult in the streets; it was this sense of it, and their capacity for arrangement, that distinguished the Mughal régime from its more haphazard predecessors and made possible the development of their work by the British.

The Mughals loved embellishments as symbols of their glory. This trait was responsible for the range and extent of their public works. In view of the precarious nature of official wealth mentioned above we can understand the great range and variety of private works as well. Besides the royal palaces, mosques and gardens (like the Roshanara, where cricket is now played, and the Qudsia) the streets were filled, in the great age of Delhi, with graceful mosques erected privately. The city was studded with *sarais*, the river bank was lined with gardens and country palaces, and the environs were dotted with enclosures and garden tombs, whose prospective occupants enjoyed the garden meanwhile.

To this love of embellishment the Mughals added a passion for novelties. Unlike the Deccan kings, who thought that anything foreign derogated from their own greatness, the Mughals welcomed foreign adventurers, artists, artisans, and objects; their ability to summon these from afar was, for them, evidence of their greatness. Thus an Italian was employed to embellish the Taj and a Frenchman, Austin de Bordeaux, to execute inlay work on the throne platform of the Delhi palace. This included an Orpheus playing on his lute, with a lion, a leopard, and a hare lying charmed at his feet. Foreigners were freely employed in all kinds of situations, the most famous European being perhaps the French doctor François Bernier, who served the Mughal official Danishmand Khan as his physician for nine years and wrote reports of Aurangzeb's Delhi to the French minister Colbert. So great was this love of the novel and the unfamiliar that it often developed into an undignified scramble with little regard for decorum. Sir Thomas Roe has recorded the avidity with which Shah Jahan (when heir-apparent) seized on goods sent from England intended as presents before they reached the ambassador, appropriating for himself articles intended for others and for the emperor himself. With these foreign influences and this love of the strange, Mughal Delhi and Agra were cosmopolitan cities in every sense of the term.

A masculine world

And what of the people who, as we are told, thronged the streets, making Indian metropolitan cities seem more populous than they really were? They were the followers of the various nobles, part of whose mystique was to have as many retainers as possible, as well as the most imposing palaces.We have noted that the Mughal capital was essentially a court, or even a camp fixed at a semi-permanent site. It was the court which determined the site of the city and drew people to it, not the place which attracted the court. The city revolved round the court and, if the court was absent for any length of time, it sank to the level of a provincial town. The first thing that a modern observer would have noted about it, after the crowds in the streets and the numbers of public buildings and gardens, was that it was a man's world. In the bazaars, in the open spaces, in the mosques, were men of all kinds. There were shopkeepers, soldiers, retainers, manual workers in tattered clothes; the Pathan stalking through, a king in his own right; the discreet Brahmin, and the great lords on their elephants or in palanquins surrounded by parasites. But few women were evident. Only working women from the country, of low caste, such as are seen on building-sites today, showed their faces above colourful bodices and heavy swinging skirts. Others were be shrouded in the shapeless and dingy *burqa*, but they were few in number except at festival times, when they visited shrines and gardens with their families. Others were concealed behind the screens of palanquins or the humbler *dhuli*, hurrying on their way from palace or house. Great Mughal ladies, it is true, played a part in the life of the period, but it was all behind the purdah screen or curtain. For several generations they were highly educated, many becoming sophisticated and determined personalities, but this could not be said of most of the nobles and certainly not of other Muslims. Babur's sister, Gulbadan Begam, wrote her memoirs, and Zebun-Nissa, Aurangzeb's daughter, was a poetess who produced a *diwan* of her own. Two daughters of Shah Jahan, Jahanara and Roshanara, backed rival brothers for the throne. The most famous woman of them all, Nur Jahan the consort of Jahangir, had coins minted in her name and was said to have advised her husband from behind a screen when he was holding an audience. But though these great ladies gave their name to gardens and tombs their faces were not seen. The world of women was invisible and secluded and, except for a very few, a dreary one. In this the Hindus followed the Muslims; it was only in the south that the sexes mixed more freely.

The classes and their characteristics

The nobles were naturally the most conspicuous of the inhabitants. Their life revolved round the court and their mansions within the city and the camps and gardens without. They went about in great trains, preceded by heralds with silver maces, pronouncing their titles and merits and ready to thrust those in their path roughly aside. Brawls between the followers of rivals were frequent and sometimes became great riots. Go-betweens were innumerable and mischief-making was a fine art. Delhi would have been a paradise for Iago. In the court the rule of conduct was decorum and sycophancy in public, pride and generosity in the mansion:

> If at noon the King should say it's night,
> The court replies: behold the moon shines bright.

In their own mansions their pride was proverbial, to make up per-haps for their humiliation at court, but so also was their hospitality. They commonly kept open house, and would feed all comers without question as Hindus fed Brahmins. Their amusements were hunting and hawking, kite and pigeon flying out of doors, and music and song, poetry and wine within. For the Mughals were no puritan Muslims. The imperial family itself produced many drunkards, in-cluding two sons of Akbar as well as Jahangir and one son of Shah Jahan. These things were regularly denounced, but rather in the manner of the moralist who would rather see his style praised than his views.

Among the nobility must be noted the Hindu Rajputs, who during the great century of the Mughals, were treated as partners in the empire. This was the work of Akbar, who first defeated and then made alliances with them. These alliances were cemented by matri-mony so that Jahangir was half Rajput, and Shah Jahan three parts. The Rajputs held high office; their commanders enjoyed special privileges in the Mughal capital; their fidelity provided an effective insurance against Muslim revolt. This policy of Akbar was the political side of the grand Mughal attempt to produce an organic Indo-Persian society.

After the nobles came the ministerial class – the men of business, the secretaries and the clerks, who kept the great machine moving. They were mainly Hindu and their core was the interesting Kayastha community. They are to be found in all the chief cities of the north, prominent today as administrators, professional men, and public figures. The second prime minister of India, Mr Shastri, was a Ka-yastha. This group may be called the Mughal Hindus, for they were in such close contact with the rulers that they imbibed some of their characteristics, even in the matter of social custom. They were pro-ficient in Persian, the language from which they earned their daily bread; they were capable and conscientious administrators and sec-retaries, with an Indian loyalty to their masters, whoever these might be. They were prominent in the process of fusion, for they were the carriers of Urdu amongst the Hindus. This process of fusion can be seen in their own society: down to the present day some are vege-tarian, while others are not. Their attitude to wine was never as strictly abstinent as that of other high castes.

Beyond the ministerial world lay the mercantile and banking worlds. These, extending from high finance through wholesalers and dealers in luxury goods to petty shopkeepers and street vendors, were predominantly Hindu. The money-lenders in particular were Hindu and orthodox. Though their services were essential and their loans had to be bargained for at high rates of interest, they enjoyed little respect and no status. Caste – and in this case Muslims adopted Hindu attitudes – was the bar to the purchase of position by cash.

These classes were the essential components of Mughal Delhi and Agra, but they were of course only a minority of the population as a whole. Below them were the artisans and craftsmen, who often lived in their own quarters. They were both Hindu and Muslim and many, such as the Hindu shoemakers and leatherworkers, were outcastes. The silversmiths, for example, lived in the main street and the adjoining Dariba; the Muslim shoesellers near the Jami Masjid. Still further down the scale came the sweepers, performing their humble, necessary, and often odious tasks with a minimum of re-quital. But even they could not be wholly disregarded, for they were corporately organized with their own headmen, and if maltreated too much would decamp, leaving the city to stink.

These might be called the regular inhabitants of Delhi. There was also a large floating population of domestic servants, retainers and hangers-on, adventurers, day-labourers and beggars. As the emperor was fair game for the nobles, the nobles were fair game for the rest. As much as possible must be done while the fleeting moment lasted, for all was precarious, from the emperor downwards. The glitter of the court concealed the grim struggle for betterment or mere sur-vival.

The great failure which prepared the way

Delhi and Agra may be said to epitomize the Mughal achievement. It is a story of 'very nearly but not quite'. Previous Muslim régimes in India had been little more than armies of occupation or centres of exotic culture, relying on foreign troops and Hindu inertia to main-tain themselves. The Mughals attempted to fuse themselves with the country and to do this through the medium of Persian culture. So we see the imported Persian architecture and painting developed into genuine Indo-Mughal styles, which nearly but not quite cap-tured the Indian artistic imagination. There is Akbar's Rajput policy, which nearly but not quite solved the problem of political unity; also his religious policy of making the emperor a semi-divinity, which just failed to make the emperor the focus of Indian authority. We see the development of Urdu, which so nearly provided India with a *lingua franca*. Delhi and Agra were, in fact, the *milieu* of one of the great failures of history: the attempt to unite Hindus and Muslims organically and willingly, not merely to control one by the superior force of the other. When the experiment broke down, the two cities lost their significance. Perhaps, after all, the real signif-icance of the Mughals – apart from their undeniable artistic legacies – was to prepare India by their sense of order for the more intricate organization to come, and to reconcile Indians, by their strangeness, to the still greater strangeness of their successors from overseas.

EIGHTEENTH-CENTURY
ST PETERSBURG

Nationalism, strategy and commerce

were the governing factors behind Peter the Great's campaign, beginning in 1700, to drive the Swedes from the Neva River delta and the province surrounding it. After twenty-one years of war, Peter achieved his aim, ending more than a century of foreign occupation. In 1721, thanks to his ruthless determination and vision, the Neva was fully protected against invasion from abroad, and Russia now had free access to the Baltic Sea, so vital to the expansion of trade. Expulsion of the Swedes was a primary historical event, for it ratified Russia's claims as a major European power.

Following his first hard-won military successes as early as 1703, Peter began the work of fortifying the Neva estuary against counterattack. For this purpose he chose, from various possible locations, the small island called *Liust Eland;* the fortress built there, starting on 16 May 1703, was the nucleus from which grew the idea of the future capital city, Peter's 'window on Europe'.

The site, marshy and water-logged, was unpromising; all buildings had to be constructed on piles. Nevertheless, the position was right for a westward-looking port, and Peter had no qualms about using hordes of forced labour, prisoners and peasants from all parts of the country, to get it built in the course of surprisingly few years.

St Petersburg was not one of those cities, like Paris or London, that grew into a national capital through centuries of accretion and tradition; on the contrary, it was a *planned* capital, like Washington, D.C. Its arrangement was laid down in Peter's time and has hardly changed since. Impressed by eighteenth-century ideas of rational order, and set on bringing his country up to the 'modern' standards of Western Europe, Peter imported foreign architects not only to design and supervise buildings, but to draw up a precise city-plan. In the beginning he thought of the large island called Vasilievski Ostrov as the ideal centre of the projected city, and the different classes of society were to be provided for in different parts of the city-complex, but in fact the most important part of St Petersburg was eventually situated on the southern bank of the Neva.

The founder and creator of St Petersburg is himself seen opposite in a portrait painted by Godfrey Kneller in 1698, while the young Tsar was visiting England during a tour of the West. (1)

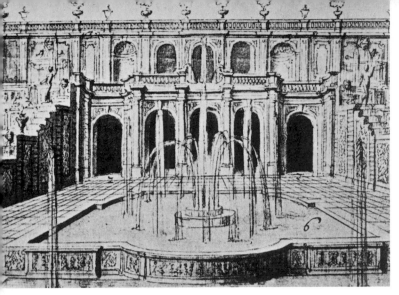

Peterhof originated as a halfway house for Peter the Great between the fortified island of Kronstadt, in the Gulf of Finland, and St Petersburg, but its utilitarian purpose was soon submerged in Peter's grandiose plans for a country palace, fountains, formal gardens and charming vistas: a Russian Versailles fit for an eighteenth-century Tsar. The most distinctive feature of Peterhof, built between 1712 and 1724, is the Great Cascade (below left); it was already implicit in one of the sketches made by Peter himself (left). Peter's original 'cottage' by the sea (below) was called 'Mon Plaisir'; from here he could observe naval exercises between the city and Kronstadt. After Peter's death, his successors undertook many changes and extensions to Peterhof. The imposing façade (bottom) was reconstructed and lengthened between 1747 and 1752 during the reign of Peter's daughter, Elizabeth, to the designs of her favourite architect, the Italian Bartolommeo Rastrelli. (2–5)

Peter's wife, Catherine, had the palace known as Tsarskoe Selo built in secret, only a few miles south of St Petersburg, as a present for her husband in 1714. The town that grew round the palace park is now called Pushkin, in memory of the great nineteenth-century poet who spent his schooldays there. The building of imperial palaces near the new capital, as well as the mansions commissioned in the city itself by the nobility and people of wealth, signified Peter's determination to transfer both the central administration and the trappings of power and rank from Moscow. As at Peterhof, Tsarskoe Selo was extensively remodelled and enlarged by Elizabeth and later by Catherine the Great; as a whole, the final product ranks as one of Rastrelli's most brilliant achievements. An impression of the Great Palace and forecourt, as they appeared in 1753, can be gathered from the engraving of Mikhail Makhaev (top). Rastrelli's façade, which retained the structure of the much smaller original, is 978 feet long, and provides a notable example of a restrained Rococo style, imported to Russia from the West. The extraordinary expanse of repeated elements – windows and columns – was animated by the use of vivid colours (right above). At right is shown one of the ornamented side gates to the Great Court. (6, 7, 8)

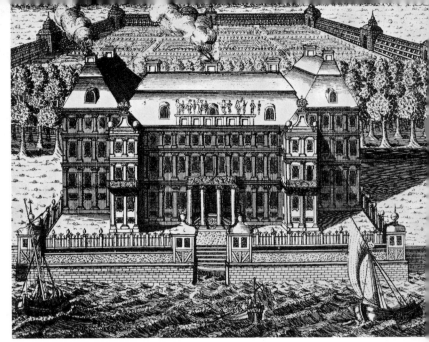

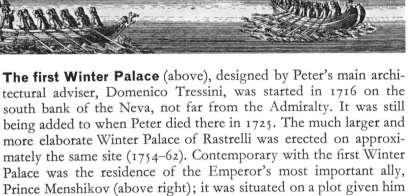

The first Winter Palace (above), designed by Peter's main architectural adviser, Domenico Tressini, was started in 1716 on the south bank of the Neva, not far from the Admiralty. It was still being added to when Peter died there in 1725. The much larger and more elaborate Winter Palace of Rastrelli was erected on approximately the same site (1754–62). Contemporary with the first Winter Palace was the residence of the Emperor's most important ally, Prince Menshikov (above right); it was situated on a plot given him by Peter on Vasilievski Island. (9, 10)

The population of the city was about 40,000 when Peter died, and grew to over 200,000 by 1800. Varieties of quayside activity can be seen in a detail of an engraving (right) done by Le Bas in 1778. The view is from the south bank, and in the left background are the warehouses on Vasilievski Island as well as the government offices, designed by Tressini and built in 1722, known as the Twelve Colleges. In the right background is the fortress of SS. Peter and Paul, from which rises the cathedral tower. A busy wharf at the east end of Vasilievski Island is shown in Makhaev's 1753 engraving (below). On the mainland a series of canals were dug according to the early plans, giving St Petersburg a slight resemblance to Amsterdam; another of Makhaev's engravings shows the meeting of the Moika Canal with the Neva and the drawbridge which crossed it (below right). (11, 12, 13)

A memorial statue of Peter was commissioned from the French sculptor, Etienne Falconet, by Catherine the Great; its unveiling in 1782 was treated as a civic event (opposite, bottom). This monument is the subject of Pushkin's poem, *The Bronze Horseman*. (15)

The Kunstkamera, or Cabinet of Curios, was designed for Peter by the architect Mattarnovi and built between 1718 and 1725. On the Vasilievski Island embankment across the river from the Admiralty, it was used to house the Tsar's varied collections (right) and appropriately became the nucleus of St Petersburg's Academy of Sciences. (14)

The Academy of Sciences is the building on the left of this view of Vasilievski Island (right). It is one of the works of Giacomo Quarenghi, the leading architect in Catherine the Great's reign. To its right is the earlier Kunstkamera. This eastern tip of the island, known as the 'Strelka', entirely devoted to institutional buildings, has been called the cradle of Russian science. The granite embankments, constructed along all the river-fronts, were one of Catherine's major contributions to the city. Above is the reverse view, showing the centenary celebrations that took place in 1803. The temporary bridge of boats leads directly to the Falconet statue of Peter and the Cathedral of St Isaac; on the far left is the Admiralty spire. (16, 17)

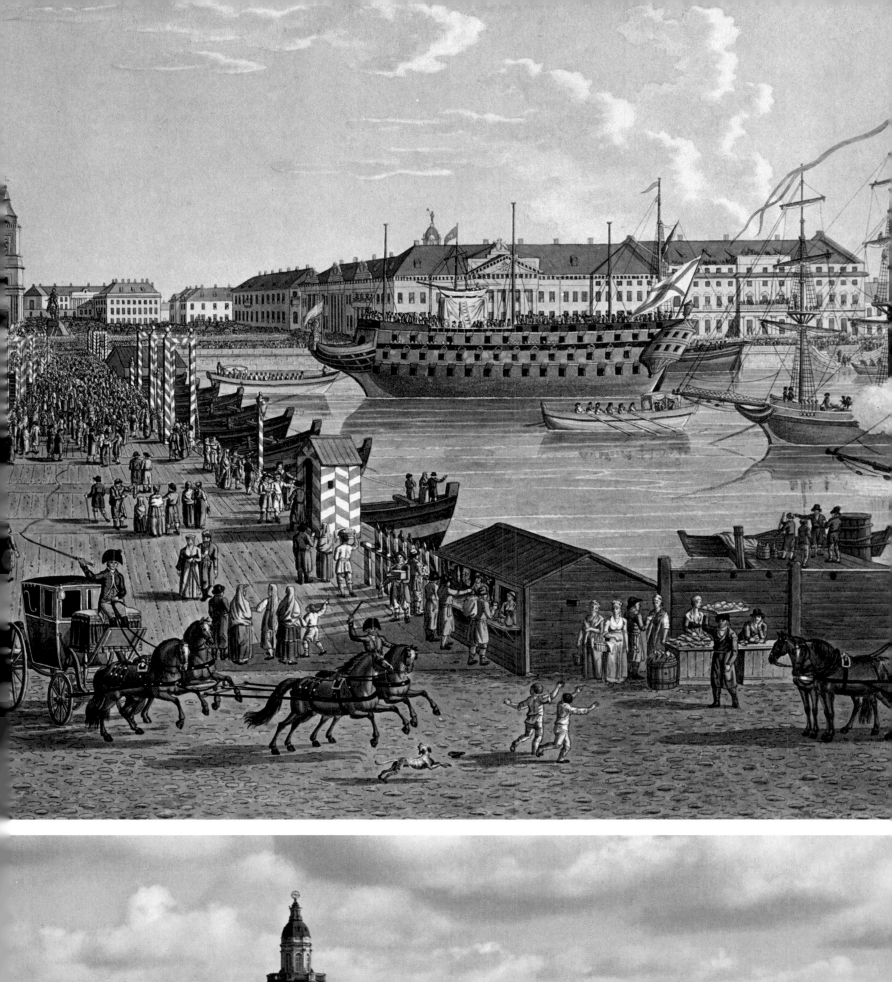

Russian monarchs who embellished Peter's original outline for a capital and left their own distinctive marks on St Petersburg were Elizabeth I (centre), Catherine the Great (far left) and Alexander I (left). Each favoured and enjoyed a different architectural style, but managed not to destroy the simplicity and restraint of Peter's project. The most spectacular relic of the eighteenth-century city is Rastrelli's Winter Palace (below), which was the Tsars' official residence until 1917, and now houses the Hermitage art collection. (18–21)

TAMARA TALBOT RICE

As RIVERS GO, the Neva, though majestic, is not old. It began as a strait; then, 4,000 years or so ago, it altered its character. The Swedes noted the change and spoke of the river as the Nien, meaning new – a word which the Russians eventually transformed into Neva. By early Christian times Ingrian tribesmen had settled on its southern bank and, by the eighth century, at least one of the major trade-routes linking Scandinavia with Central Asia, Persia and the Orient passed through their territory. Its establishment did not affect the Ingrians in any noticeable way, for the majority continued to depend upon agriculture, fishing, boat-building and navigation for their daily needs. In contrast, their southern neighbours, the Novgorodians, soon became interested in the new commercial outlets and their desire to participate, and if possible to control, this north-eastern trade route led them to adopt a policy which, in the course of the ninth century, brought Ingria within their borders. A great deal of evidence exists to attest to the increase in trade which resulted from this union, as well as to its international character, but perhaps none more evocatively than the large horde of ninth- and tenth-century Arabian coins discovered during the building of St Petersburg in the district of the town known as the Vasilievski Ostrov (Basil's Island).

The struggle for Baltic access

The Neva's lucrative trade soon attracted the covetous eyes of the Swedes, Livonians and Teutonic Knights, but it was the Swedes who, from the eleventh century onwards, proved most anxious to wrest Ingria and the Neva from the Novgorodians. In 1240, when it appeared as though the Mongols had brought Russia to the verge of extinction, they invaded Ingria and marched on Novgorod. They had, however, misjudged the patriotism of the Novgorodians. Though in the east the Mongols were threatening their very existence, they rallied round their prince Alexander to defend their western boundaries. The Novgorodians gave battle to the Swedes on the banks of the Izhora, a tributary of the Neva. Alexander's skilful leadership and the fighting qualities of his men carried the day. Their success ensured the independence of Novgorod and Alexander became a national hero. His people bestowed upon him the appellation of Nevski, meaning of the Neva; he was sanctified by the church and, in due course, Russia's greatest tsar proclaimed him the patron saint of the town he loved above all Russia's cities.

Autonomous Novgorod considered Ingria her most valuable outpost. To safeguard it from the Swedes, Novgorod's parliament in 1323 built on one of the islets at the head of the Neva the fortress of Oreshek, which the Swedes were to re-name Noteburg. At the same time the Novgorodians were able to enforce upon Sweden a boundary line which Europe as a whole accepted as valid till the end of the sixteenth century. When, in 1478, Moscow annexed Novgorod, this boundary became a national frontier. By its very existence it gave substance to Ivan III's (1462–1505) dream of acquiring a port having free access to the Baltic. The economic need for one had even then made itself clearly felt, but it became increasingly pressing with the passing years. However, it was not until 1496 that the tsar attempted to capture the Swedish stronghold of Vyborg. The com-

plete failure of his efforts to do so encouraged the Swedes in their turn to encroach upon Muscovy, with the result that the possession of Ingria was fiercely contested throughout the sixteenth century. Then, in 1590, the Swedes won definite superiority, wresting the Neva from the Muscovites and penetrating so deep into Russia that they captured Novgorod. They held the city for twenty-seven years, and even after they had relinquished it, they retained possession of the whole of the Neva, thereby depriving the Russians of access to the sea. The latter could not accept the loss of a region which, in addition to its economic importance, also ranked as an integral part of their homeland, and the Swedes, realizing this, fortified the Neva's delta. They therefore had little difficulty in successfully resisting Russian onslaughts in 1656–8, and again in 1676 and 1686. Yet the Russians could not reconcile themselves to the loss of Ingria and still persisted in their determination to regain it. It was largely with this object in view that Peter I declared war upon Sweden on 9 August 1700.

Peter the Great and the war with Sweden

At the outset Peter suffered so disastrous a defeat at Narva that it might well have cost him the war, but two years later the course of events changed and on 11 October 1702 – an anniversary which he never omitted to celebrate – Peter captured the former Novgorodian fortress of Oreshek. Pinning its key to its western bastion Peter re-named the stronghold Schlüsselburg, for he realized that it held the answer both to the Neva's future and to the outcome of the war. 'By the grace of God', he wrote to announce its fall to a friend, 'our native fortress has been restored to us after ninety-two years of alien rule.' Its return was, he felt, worthy of commemoration, and he gave orders for a bronze medal to be struck and inscribed with the words: 'I was in enemy hands for ninety years.'

Possession of Schlüsselburg made it easier for Peter to move troops down the Neva, and he was thus able to install a shipyard on the river Svir, close to its entry into Lake Ladoga. To ensure its safety, on 8 April 1703 he attacked the Swedish fortress of Nyenskantz, situated at the juncture of the Okhta and the Neva. Within two days it was in his hands and had been re-named Slotburg. This victory was again celebrated by the issue of a bronze medal. Then, just two days later, Peter won his first naval victory, capturing two Swedish men-of-war off what is now the Vasilievski Ostrov. Though trivial in itself it was considered a good omen for the future. Peter was enchanted, celebrating his success by firing frequent salvoes from his batteries. Indeed, he had every reason to be satisfied, for Ingria had been re-conquered even though the Northern War was still far from being won.

There could be no denying that the effect of the Russian army's shattering defeat at Narva some three years earlier still represented a threat to the country's security, rendering it imperative to continue the war even though its main objective had been achieved. Yet if the war was to be pursued on other fronts, Ingria's retention had to be ensured. This could hardly be accomplished without the aid of a strong fortress at the mouth of the Neva and a navy to help in defending the river. Peter began to survey its complicated estuary in order to choose the most suitable spot for its fortification. After considering Slotburg on the Okhta as a likely stronghold he discarded it in favour of the tiny island of Liust ('Gay') Eland, situated opposite to the Vasilievski Ostrov, at the point where the Small Neva joins the main stream. The islet had the advantage of being surrounded on its west, south and east sides by deep water with only a narrow, moat-like channel on the north to separate it from the large island which later became known as the Petersburg or Gorodskaya ('Town'). Liust Eland had the additional merit of being precisely the same size as the fortress Peter had in mind, so that, once built on, no areas would be left outside the fortifications to serve as tempting landing grounds for an invading force.

In Ingria's climate only the spring and summer months were suitable for building and warfare. With the enemy within such easy striking reach the construction of the fortress therefore became a matter of extreme urgency. Some 20,000 men were hurriedly rounded up from all parts of Russia and sent to assist the soldiers who had been detailed to build the fortress, as well as the base and provisioning port which were to be situated on the adjacent island. Work was put in hand on 16 May 1703. Peter was present at break of day to name the fortress St Petersburg after his patron saint and a bronze medal was issued bearing the date of the foundation.

In the rush and confusion no steps had been taken to provide the workmen herded into the area with shelter or provisions. The men were obliged to fend for themselves; they scavenged for food and erected what shelters they could close to their work. A cottage of pine was run up in two days (24–26 May) for the tsar's use. It was built on traditional lines and contained two rooms separated by a kitchen and hall, but it is not perhaps without significance that its walls were painted to simulate brick and its roof to resemble tiles. During the next eight years Peter spent all the time he could spare there, supervising the construction of his defences. A cathedral was quickly set up near his cottage. Like all the buildings constructed in St Petersburg prior to 1710, it was built of wood; this was the country's traditional building material, and was easily obtainable from the neighbouring Berezovyj ('Birch') Island. The cathedral was dedicated to the Trinity and the square in front of it was called Troitza ('Trinity'). The base and port were situated to the west of the square whilst the stock exchange and Gostinnyj Dvor – the Russian equivalent of a covered market or bazaar – rose on its northern side. Towards the end of the century Catherine the Great was piously to enclose Peter's cottage in a stone shell to ensure its survival.

Peter was determined to incorporate the most up-to-date ideas and devices in the new fortress. Partly for this reason, partly too because of the marshy nature of the soil, he invited the Italian architect Domenico Tressini to come to Russia. He wanted him to act principally as a technical adviser, for Tressini had spent some years in Copenhagen where he had gained valuable experience in sinking foundations in boggy subsoils. Ustinov was appointed architect in charge of the fortress, and carpenters, master builders and artisans were sent from Novgorod to assist him. To speed the work Peter decided himself to supervise the construction of the first of its six bastions, instructing five of his most trusted adjutants – Aleksasha Menshikov, Feodor Golovin, Nikita Zotov, Juri Trubetskoi and Kiril Razumovski – each to take charge of one of the others. By 30 June, SS. Peter and Paul's day, the fort's wooden chapel had been completed. It was dedicated to the two saints on the same day. Almost immediately their names were used not only in connection with the chapel, but also to designate the fortress, whereupon the townlet which had grown up on the adjacent island, and which had until then served merely as a base, appropriated the original name of St Petersburg.

Peter's daring rewarded

Work on the fortress and its supporting installations was carried out in frenzied haste. Men continued to be drafted to the island from every corner of Russia, till there were soon some 40,000 toiling on its sodden, uncultivated ground. Nothing but potatoes and turnips seemed able to grow on it, and food had to be brought from so far afield that supplies were often inadequate and always expensive. Thousands of workmen died from hunger, disease and exhaustion; others from the cold of the icy water and swamps in which they

were obliged to sink the foundations required to support the buildings; many were drowned in the first of a long series of disastrous floods. To make matters worse, Swedish troops were massing on the river Sestra. Peter decided to forestall a full-scale offensive by attacking first. With much at stake he advanced against them on 7 July 1703, using a force of 8000 men. Following the recurrent pattern of Russian history, courage brought its reward. The enemy ranks gave way under the impetus of the Russian onslaught and the Swedes withdrew to Vyborg, to spend the winter in preparing a counter-attack timed for the spring.

Peter realized that he had won little more than a brief respite and determined to make full use of it. Skilled men remained his prime need, but even rough labour had become scarce. The whole of Russia was combed to meet Peter's requirements; even so, his demands never slackened. By 23 September he was crying out for 'several thousand thieves, and, in fact, if possible for two thousand men by the spring'. He followed this request by issuing orders that all criminals who had been sentenced to exile in Siberia were to be drafted to the Neva. These frantic efforts, though often ill thought out and badly applied, bore fruit, and by the early winter the fortress was nearing completion. Regardless of this the Swedes recalled their flotillas to their winter moorings at Vyborg without attacking.

They had underestimated Peter's industry as they were to misjudge his daring. Disregarding the ice which had begun to form on the Neva, the tsar's tiny navy crept out in the wake of the Swedes, slipped into the Gulf of Finland and captured the small island of Kotlin, lying eight miles beyond the Neva's mouth, at a point from which the entry of enemy ships into the Neva's delta could be effectively controlled. Peter had soundings made round the island's shores without loss of time, and throughout the bitterly cold winter months that followed Russians toiled ceaselessly at fortifying this valuable addition to their defences. Peter called the island Kronstadt, and ever since its name has remained prominent in Russia's history.

When in the spring of 1704 the Swedes emerged from their winter quarters to attack St Petersburg by land and sea Peter was able to repel them. His success gave him confidence, and on 28 September, with the summer safely behind him, he made the only allusion on record to the possibility of St Petersburg's one day superseding Moscow for, in a letter to Menshikov, he called it, perhaps inadvertently, his capital. At any rate it was in the following spring that he started to build Strelna, the first of his country residences.

The Swedes attacked anew in the summer of 1705. The outcome of the campaign hung in the balance for a time, but eventually they were repulsed, though not so effectively that the possibility of a future attack could be discarded. Peter therefore gave orders for the wooden bastions of the SS. Peter and Paul fortress and the defences of Kronstadt to be replaced by brick ones. The first of these tasks soon ceased to be of military significance, and as a result it was not completed till 1740; work on Kronstadt on the other hand continued to occupy Peter's attention for many years to come. By the early summer he felt the need for a half-way house between St Petersburg and Kronstadt, to serve as an over-night resting place; he chose to build it at what was soon to be known as Peterhof. He amused himself in his spare time in making sketches for the palace and the grounds he hoped one day to lay out there.

Peter is one of the greatest of the world's unrecognized architects. With his love of the unostentatious yet grand he developed a straightforward yet arresting style, which reflects a characteristically eighteenth-century delight in vistas and perspectives. Thus, for the main features of Peterhof he decided upon a wide cascade – the Great Cascade of later times – to link with the sea a small palace situated on the rising ground. To balance this he created two vistas, one leading from what was to become his cottage of Mon Plaisir to the Checker Board Cascade, the other from the future pavilion of Marli to the Golden Cascade. Work on these lines was begun in 1712, and so far as Peter's plans were concerned, completed in 1724, though Rastrelli the younger was later to transform and enlarge the palace for the empress Elizabeth.

The critical summers of 1706 and 1707 passed peacefully enough, and it was not until 1708 that the Swedes resumed their offensive. Again they were unable to effect a breakthrough. Indeed, time had ceased to be their ally, for in 1709 Peter smashed their main army at Poltava, and in the following year he captured Vyborg. These

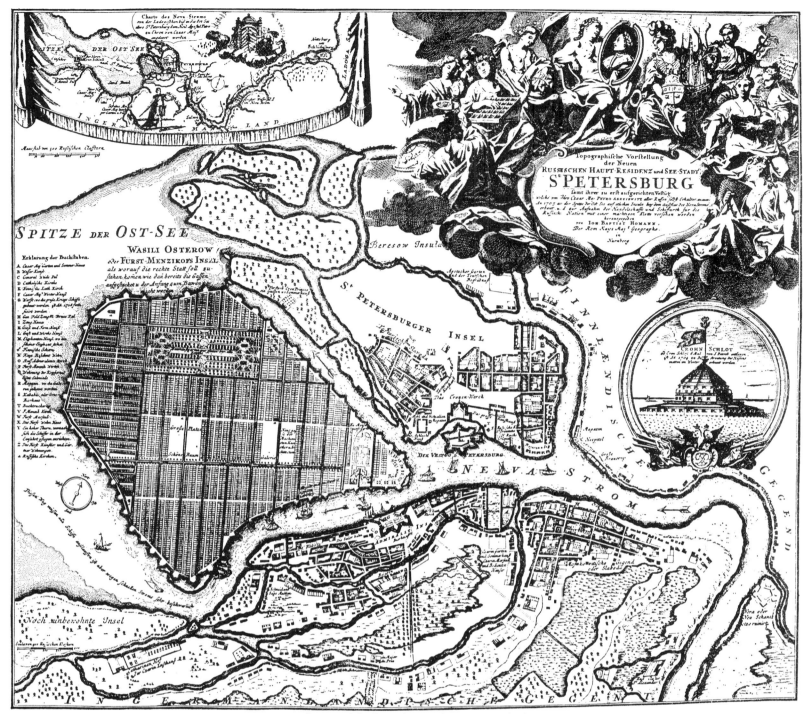

A map of St Petersburg, 'the new capital of Russia', drawn by J. P. Homann about 1720. At this time it was still thought that the main part of the city would be established on the large island called Vasilievski Ostrov.

victories not only ensured the safety of St Petersburg and its hinterland, but also marked the end of a phase in the Northern War and, with it, of Sweden's aspirations in Ingria. Peter had regained a long-lost province, won possession of the Neva with its outlet to the sea, and had in addition raised Russia to the rank of a major European power. He was at last in a position to pause in order to take stock of his gains, to assess their political and economic implications, and to decide upon the future role and character of the townlet he had established on the shores of the Neva.

The city and its single-minded creator

The site on which his town had grown was indeed a bleak one. Water-logged and often fog-bound, it had little beyond its strategic position to commend it. Yet, quite apart from the historic ties which endeared its soil to its countrymen, on a sunlit day it possessed the unspectacular, essentially Russian type of beauty which, once perceived, continues to exercise a compelling and permanent appeal. However, few of those who were living huddled in hovels amidst its bogs and maze of waterways were at the time in a condition to appreciate this. Peter alone had from the start found solace and inspiration in this tender landscape and, from as early as 1704, had often headed letters to his intimate friends 'From Paradise, alias Sanct Pietersburkh'. In that year he made his first request for shrubs

and plants, especially aromatic ones, to be sent to him there. And today, whenever the air around his city is heavy with the scent of lilacs and lilies of the valley, it is the gentler, visionary side of Peter's character that is as vividly evoked as its more sinister aspects are in Pushkin's verses.

Basically St Petersburg is wholly Peter's creation, for none of his followers ever altered its structure; until the middle of the nineteenth century they confined their activities to adorning its framework by filling in the gaps left in its streets, adding final touches to unfinished works or enlarging buildings that had become too small for their purpose. As a result the city reveals at every turn the duality of its founder's personality and the imprint left upon it by eighteenth-century taste and thought. Thus, not only does St Petersburg's layout illustrate the importance which the eighteenth century attached to the intellectual approach but, together with its architecture, it also reflects Peter's personal clarity of vision and singleness of purpose. Its very individual culture – for Petersburgian culture was to become, like that of Alexandria, Constantinople or Venice in their heyday, very much its own yet representative of the country as a whole – embodied all that was best in Peter's aspirations. At the same time the truly odious living conditions of its less fortunate inhabitants mirror Peter's harsh disregard of others. Yet, paradoxically, it is precisely because Peter strove to teach Petersburgians to think clearly and to pursue their aims with unshakeable determination that the latter were among the first Russians to become aware of the existing social evils and to attempt to set them right, even to the extent of sponsoring revolutionary outbreaks.

In 1706 Peter created a Chancery of Building under the directorship of Tressini and Siniavin, and in the following year he asked Tressini to lay out the Summer Gardens for him. Four years later Peter replaced the Chancery by a Building Committee. Tressini remained in charge of it, with Ivan Matveev and Feodor Vasiliev assisting him, but Peter continued himself to act as prompter and supreme authority in all architectural matters. It was then that it was made illegal to use any material other than masonry for building purposes in the heart of St Petersburg; elsewhere only the use of wood was allowed.

In fact, 1710 heralded a new era in Russia, yet for a time Peter and Tressini, thinking on established lines, continued to regard the Vasilievski Ostrov district, on account of its defensive advantages, as the one best suited to serve as the town's main residential area. To attract courtiers to the island Peter gave Menshikov a large plot on which to build a palace and park. The royal favourite engaged Fontana as his architect. At Menshikov's fall from grace the palace reverted to the Crown and Catherine the Great altered its interior in order to use it as the school of the famous Corps des Pages. Even Menshikov's presence on the island failed to tempt others to settle there – most preferred the Petersburg Island or the Neva's southern bank, where Peter had himself built his Admiralty, choosing for it much the same site as that occupied by the Admiralty of today. Peter's first Admiralty was modest enough, consisting of a row of workshops and offices with side wings running down to the river to enclose a row of slip-ways. On the landward side it was fortified by bastions and a vallum, and faced on to a vast glacis, part of which Rossi was to incorporate a hundred years or so later into the Winter Palace Circus. As a concession to romance Peter erected a tall, narrow iron spire at the centre of its main block. This addition quickly came to be regarded as a symbol and beacon; as such it became an integral element of Peter's conception of an admiralty and was permanently retained, to serve both as an emblem and as the pivot for the area's ultimate layout.

Though Peter is often described as irreligious, he nevertheless built many churches and founded, in the spring of 1707, St Petersburg's first monastery. He happened one day to be inspecting the point where the river Chornaya joined the Neva and was suddenly overwhelmed by the beauty of the place. It seemed to him to be ideally suited for a monastery. The thought instantly became an act, and by 1711 a wooden church had been erected there; temporary cells were completed by 1713 and the foundation was then dedicated to the Trinity and St Alexander Nevski. Although the saint's relics were not transferred thither till 1723, the very existence of the monastery did much towards establishing St Petersburg in Russian eyes.

It had for some years been realized that St Petersburg might one day replace Moscow as the country's capital. However, Peter never made any official pronouncement to that effect, and the transfer therefore took place gradually; in certain respects it was not in fact completed till the reign of Catherine the Great. Thus, although the Admiralty and the Ministries of War and Foreign Affairs were soon set up in St Petersburg, other departments, notably those of Manufacture and Finance, remained in Moscow till late in the century. Even the Senate, though generally thought of as an essentially Petersburgian institution, was in fact founded in Moscow in 1711, and assembled there for two years. The court as a whole did not move to St Petersburg till 1712, the diplomatic corps did not complete its transfer till 1718 and the judiciary followed only in 1723. Till the end all Russia's tsars continued to be crowned in Moscow. Thus, in spite of the concentration of political life on the banks of the Neva, Moscow acted as the country's administrative centre for practically the whole of Peter's life.

Peter's decisions were often made too hurriedly and inopportunely, yet this distribution of power was the result of much thought. It was as carefully conceived as was Peter's habit of appointing Russians to act as advisers and assistants to foreigners holding positions of trust in his service. Both measures were devised for a similar purpose, for the first was to enable Peter personally to mould the mentality of St Petersburg's society, the other to ensure that the new culture, though culling all that was best and most enlightened from the Western world, should at the same time retain its native character and flavour.

Buildings inspired by victory

Even though Russia was to remain at war till almost the end of Peter's life, the victories of Poltava and Vyborg brought a sense of peace and security to Petersburgians. This expressed itself in a surge of inspired building. Tressini remained Peter's favourite architect, and was indeed to spend the remaining years of Peter's life working for him in his capital. In 1710 he started to build the Summer Palace to serve as the tsar's first official residence. A year later he abandoned it to build the first Winter Palace, but in 1716 this was scrapped in favour of the second palace of that name which was erected on part of the ground now covered by Rastrelli's masterpiece. By 1725 this second Winter Palace had become too small, and workmen were actually engaged in enlarging it as the tsar lay dying within. From 1712 onwards Tressini also devoted a great deal of time to improving the fortress of SS. Peter and Paul, building its lovely main entrance gate and replacing its wooden cathedral by a stone one. However, it was Peter who suggested the form of its belfry and who insisted that the latter should be surmounted by the tall, thin spire which still today contributes so much to the beauty of Leningrad.

It also fell to Tressini to supply the designs for the three standard types of houses Peter thought would suffice for the homes respectively of the noble, the well-to-do, and the lowly inhabitants of the capital. Each type was to differ in size, height, external plan and degree of ornateness of its façades, but the interior arrangements were to be left to the individuals to establish. It was also possible for people to build to their own designs provided that their plans received the approval of the Building Committee. Nor was Peter content merely to prescribe the types of houses Petersburgians were to inhabit; in addition he proceeded to specify the districts in which each class of the town's population was to reside. Thus noblemen, merchants and pedlars were directed to the Vasilievski Ostrov, soldiers and artisans to the Petersburg Island and workmen to settlements in the neighbourhood of the factories and workshops appropriate to their particular trades. Even before these measures had been announced people had shown little desire to abandon a cosy, easy-going life in a well-loved town to settle in St Petersburg, under the all-seeing eye of a monarch who was by then widely dreaded, and who expected all inhabitants to assemble in the Troitza Square at the sound of a drum beat, to listen to the edicts which emanated in a well-nigh ceaseless flow from his active brain. Even fewer of Peter's subjects were prepared to live in particular districts at their ruler's wish. Peter was, however, profoundly annoyed by their refusal to comply with his instructions. In 1714 he ordered nine hundred families to be selected from the nobility, merchant and artisan classes; they were to build themselves homes in the course of the summer in the districts allocated to them and to move into them in the autumn. Nevertheless people still refused to live in the areas chosen for them by the tsar and in 1718, and again in 1725, many were punished for their obstinacy by forcible eviction or by seeing the roofs torn off the houses they had so recently built.

Peter's longing to create an ordered town and society is understandable enough, and in 1716 he instructed Tressini to prepare a plan for the town's future development. Tressini's proposals were made on the assumption that the Vasilievski Ostrov would remain the town's centre. He visualized the island as a walled area intersected from east to west by wide canals, with narrower ones cutting across them at right angles. Though Peter accepted these proposals he took no steps to implement them, and at the same time laid out on the river's opposite bank the street known as the Nevski Prospekt, which led in a straight line from the base of the Admiralty's spire to a position on the road which had for centuries connected Novgorod to Moscow. To his delight he was also able to secure the services of the eminent French architect Leblond, who was on his arrival in 1717 appointed Director General of the Building Committee. Peter invested him with complete authority and asked him in turn to suggest a layout for the town.

When Leblond submitted his plan it proved however to be no more than an academic exercise based on the eighteenth-century conception of an ideal city. Shaped as a large oval, his proposed boundary embraced the fortress of SS. Peter and Paul and the Admiralty, but it took no account of existing buildings and depended for its success on the destruction of the Crown works of the fortress. The area within the oval was divided into three districts, each of which contained a network of straight, intersecting streets and canals, whose monotony was relieved only by the inclusion of a number of squares, parks and water reservoirs. Peter, for all his high hopes, felt unable to agree to this plan, and at Leblond's death in 1719 he instructed Eropkin to produce yet another layout for the town. Eropkin appreciated the numerous advantages to be derived from placing the centre of the town on the mainland and managed to persuade the tsar to agree to this radical change of outlook. As a first step to carrying out Eropkin's recommendations, a series of straight streets were cut to balance the Nevski Prospekt; all were disposed in a ray-like formation, with the Admiralty's spire serving as their apex. Later Rastrelli's Winter Palace was to block the vista of the most northerly one.

However, the Vasilievski Ostrov never quite lost its attraction for Peter, and in 1718 he instructed Mattarnovi to build his Kunstkamera or Cabinet of Curios on its southern bank, facing the Admiralty. The building was to be used to house Peter's collections, but it was also to contain a large and up-to-date anatomical theatre and an observatory; many years later it became the home of the Russian Academy of Sciences. Again in 1722, the new government offices were built by Tressini on the Vasilievski Ostrov, on a site adjacent to Menshikov's palace. These probably represent Tressini's masterpiece; they took the form of a long three-storied building known as that of the Twelve Colleges.

Whilst these developments were taking place in the heart of the town, work was also in progress in its outskirts. In 1710 Menshikov had been the first to build a summer palace at Oranienbaum, employing Fontana as his architect. In 1712 Peter followed this up by building a retreat for his second wife, Catherine, on an island bounded by the Fontanka and the Mojka; it was called Ekaterinenhof in her honour. Two years later, knowing that nothing gave Peter greater pleasure than a new building, Catherine in her turn surprised him with the present of a palace which she had built for him in secret at Tsarskoe. Peter was enchanted by the gift and changed the name to Tsarskoe Selo (Royal Village); but meanwhile he had himself been engaged in building, with van Zwieten as architect, the palace of Podzornoe, on an island in the Fontanka's delta. All these residences were laid out on the open, rectilinear plan rendered fashionable in the Western world by a supremely self-confident society, a series of pencil-straight alleys and walks drawing attention to their vast forecourts and glass-studded façades. Complexes such as these were, however, beyond the reach of the bulk of Peter's courtiers, for it was only in the time of Catherine the Great that noblemen became wealthy enough to compete in magnificence with their sovereign. In Peter's day they were generally content to adapt one of Tressini's standard designs for the villas they had begun to build on the Fontanka's right bank.

The transformation of society

Although Peter devoted a great deal of thought both to Petersburg's architectural development and to military affairs, these occupied but part of his time, for his main efforts were largely directed at transforming Russia from a medieval country into a modern state. Some of the measures to which he resorted to achieve this ambition, such as the remodelling of his administration on the lines of Sweden's collegiate system, caused no great concern. Others evoked deep resentment. The first of these, introduced by him on his return from Europe in 1698, forbade the wearing of beards. Since beards were an accepted symbol of Orthodoxy their removal was so firmly resisted that Peter was unable to enforce their prohibition; instead he imposed a heavy tax on all members of the upper classes who persisted in wearing a beard and exacted a toll from peasants passing through the gates of a town, the money thus raised being used to help in financing the country's wars. The edict of 1701 imposing Western dress on all excepting the clergy and peasantry, though resented at first, was accepted by 1705, at any rate in St Petersburg, and so too was the law of 1718 obliging the well-to-do classes to entertain in their homes in the Western style, with ladies in attendance. However, Peter's decision to alter the existing structure of society aroused intense ill-feeling. The measure was made legal in 1722 in a document entitled *The Table of Ranks*; its effect was to dispossess the old feudal aristocracy of many of its hereditary privileges whilst bringing these within the reach of all civil servants and members of the services who, as a result of new conditions of service to the state, could acquire land and titles as a reward for ability and signal usefulness. This measure, taken in conjunction with the imposition of serfdom and the abolition of the patriarchate, alienated all but the merchant classes. But the use Peter made of the secret police and his cruel ruthlessness did even more to increase the number of his enemies. There were many among the gentry, lesser clergy and peasantry who regarded him as the devil incarnate, the Antichrist upon earth.

Among his intimates and the rising generation of intellectuals there were, however, not a few who were beginning to appreciate Peter's ceaseless efforts to provide Russia with an army as outstanding as Austria's, a navy and a school of painting as admirable as the Dutch, with industries as efficient and highly developed as the German and with a general culture and school of architecture that could equal those of Italy and France. Yet in the anxiety that nothing should be overlooked a lack of method was everywhere apparent; whilst music was being encouraged and a botanic garden and zoo were being established, sanitary conditions remained rudimentary and workers continued to be badly housed, forced to live in squalor and want. St Petersburg must have seemed a very curious place to the innumerable foreigners who arrived almost daily in the town to seek advancement and wealth in the emperor's service. Though its basic layout had by then been firmly established, though many of its buildings were already of singular quality, living conditions were in general still very uncomfortable and many of the more elementary refinements of civilized life were totally lacking. Even the Russians,

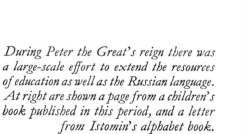

During Peter the Great's reign there was a large-scale effort to extend the resources of education as well as the Russian language. At right are shown a page from a children's book published in this period, and a letter from Istomin's alphabet book.

the majority of whom had been forcibly transplanted from towns containing many amenities, were puzzled and unsettled by the repudiation of their ancient comforts and traditions.

Nevertheless, Peter had achieved some quite astonishing results. Shipbuilding on a large scale was well established in the Admiralty's wharves and on the upper reaches of the Neva. Factories, founded originally to meet the pressing need for building material and military equipment, had begun to produce luxuries such as stockings, silks, or velvets, even tapestries and glass. The mineral wealth of the Urals had been surveyed and a College of Mining and Industry had been established in 1717.

Peter as publisher and educationist

In the educational field Peter's reforms were already well advanced in their task of transforming Russian thought. The Academy of Mathematics and Navigation had been founded by Peter in Moscow as early as 1701. It was Russia's first secular school, but following upon its transfer to St Petersburg twelve years later, two additional academies, one of Engineering and one of Artillery, opened their doors in the capital to children of landowners. By 1714 elementary education had become available for the middle classes. Peter adored books and had collected them throughout his life. The reform of the alphabet in 1707 was due to him and reflects his fondness for reading. The new alphabet was to prove of inestimable value in furthering education. It made it possible for Peter to found a newspaper in both Moscow and St Petersburg, and to sponsor the publication of some seven hundred books, over three hundred of them of secular character, during the eighteen remaining years of his life. To be seen in their true perspective these figures must be compared with the 374 works, only nineteen of them secular, published in the course of the entire seventeenth century.

Pending the founding of the Academy of Sciences Peter held the Holy Synod responsible for the printing of these books, but he took a personal interest in their production, insisting that a copy of each work be sent to him on the day of publication. He was constantly on the look-out for works suitable for translation or for stories likely to appeal to children and country-folk. He insisted that the language used should be the 'simple, direct, Russian tongue and not high-flown Slavonic words' – a condition which was superbly fulfilled a century later by Pushkin.

In 1724, shortly before his death, Peter founded the Academy of Sciences. Many thought this premature, especially as, in order to function at all, the Academy was obliged to rely at first on the services not only of foreign teachers, but also of students. Peter's reply to their criticisms may serve as a fitting tribute to his work:

I have great crops to harvest, but I have no mill; and there is insufficient water within reach for a water mill; yet there is plenty of water further afield, but I shall not have time to make a canal, for the length of my life is uncertain. I am therefore building a mill first and making a track for the canal which will serve my successors in bringing water to my mill.

These were inspired words, for within only a few decades Mikhail Lomonosov, a boy born to a White Sea fisherman in 1711, was to unlock the flood-gates of Russia's modern culture using a key which Peter had provided. Of all the tributes paid to Peter after his death the two which would surely have pleased him most were the transfer in 1729 of his library – it was ultimately to form the nucleus of the Academy of Sciences' magnificent collection – to the Cabinet of Curios, where it became available to the public, and the holding of an exhibition of his collection of antiquities in 1736. It included Peter's rare Oriental coins, his superb examples of Asian art ranging from the gold and silver buckles fashioned by Siberian nomads in pre-Christian times to magnificent Graeco-Bactrian vessels of silver and gold, Achaemenid jewellery of great beauty, and curious examples of Oriental arms and armour.

Peter's life had hardly drawn to a close when arguments broke out round his death-bed. The old aristocracy wished the tsar to be interred in Moscow and the seat of government to be re-established there. Whilst the popular presses Peter had established were deriding the dead sovereign by printing and distributing Russia's first cartoons, his closest friends, more especially Theofan Prokopovich,

Archbishop of Pskov, and Counsellor Peter Tolstoy, fiercely opposed these demands. Their devotion to the late tsar was unshakeable and they were determined that his body should lie in the Cathedral of SS. Peter and Paul, within the walls of the fortress he had toiled to build. Their views prevailed, and Peter's burial there created a precedent which was adhered to by all those who succeeded him on the throne of the Romanovs.

Restless years and elegance under Elizabeth

It was in an atmosphere of scandals, social unrest and political dissensions that Peter's wife Catherine succeeded to his throne, but it was not she so much as Peter's henchman Menshikov who in fact ruled Russia. At her death two years later her successor, Peter II, was but twelve years old. Leaders of the old hereditary nobility took advantage of his youth to form themselves into a Privy Council. With power vested in their hands they hastened to banish Menshikov and to arrange for the court's return to Moscow early in 1728. This, inevitably, had an adverse effect on St Petersburg's economy, for although many of Peter's friends refused to leave the town, some factories closed down almost at once. Conditions worsened when the Privy Council thought fit to repeal a law introduced by Peter, which sought to establish the town's foreign trade in preference to that of Archangel by forbidding imports to enter any other such northern port. The working classes were thereby reduced to poverty more dire than ever before.

In 1730 Moscow was overflowing with guests who had assembled there to attend their young sovereign's wedding when the tsar suddenly fell ill with smallpox and died within a few days. The Privy Councillors acted quickly amidst the general consternation and contrived to raise Peter the Great's niece, the widowed Anne of Courland, to the throne. However, their attempt to persuade her to delegate some of an autocrat's sovereign powers to the Privy Council was prevented by Peter the Great's loyal supporters who saw in the move a first step towards the ultimate repudiation of all that Peter I had stood for. Led by men such as Theofan Prokopovich and the enlightened satirist, Prince Antioch Kantemir, they called for a return to Peter the Great's policy; the Guards supported them, in their turn clamouring that 'things should be as they were under Peter'. Their joint insistence obliged the court and government to return to St Petersburg in 1732; in tsarist times they were never again wholly to abandon it.

Peter the Great's youngest daughter, Elizabeth, ascended the throne in 1741. Though she inherited many of her father's gifts, she lacked his sense of urgency. The dangerous, unhappy years of her youth had made her selfish and pleasure-loving, leaving her with little time to spare for the unfortunate. Yet, like her father, she was a born statesman and a dedicated ruler, and she shared to the full his preoccupation and delight in the arts and sciences. Under her control, life in St Petersburg acquired, at any rate for the privileged, a savour, elegance and zest that were wholly new to Russia. She cherished the visual arts, and particularly architecture, which her protégé, Rastrelli the younger, invested with a quality that was not surpassed at the time anywhere in western Europe. In St Petersburg itself, as well as in the country palaces of Peterhof and Tsarskoe Selo, the exuberant, ornate, vital magnificence of his immense façades were created to balance and enhance the sobriety of the earlier buildings. In the capital the Winter Palace and Smolny Cathedral displayed all the compulsive force of great masterpieces but in no way disturbed the basic character or exquisite harmony of Peter's town. Nor, amidst the pomp and gaiety of court life under Elizabeth were the conveniences of everyday existence overlooked. Basic amenities were brought within the reach of many; street lighting was provided on an adequate scale, numerous charitable institutions were founded and entertainments to suit a variety of tastes and purses were made available. The medical services were among those which received particular attention. They were expanded and, under Catherine the Great, came to include vaccination against smallpox.

The Athens of the North

Some of Catherine's major monuments are the Hermitage Theatre, the entrance to Peter's New Holland wharves, the Gostinnyj Dvor, the public library, the Academies of Sciences and Fine Arts, and the palaces Catherine built for her favourites, such as the Marble Palace

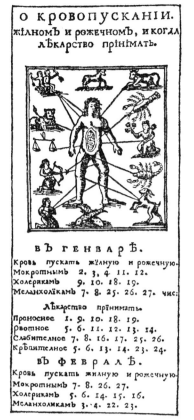

At far left is the front page of a newspaper Vedomosti *published in St Petersburg as early as 1711. The illustration appears to be a scene of the Neva with the fortress of SS. Peter and Paul in the left background. The page at left, showing the signs of the zodiac, is from a Russian almanac of 1721.*

for Gregory Orlov and the Tauride for Prince Potemkin. But her finest architectural achievements are to be sought outside the capital, in country palaces such as Tsarskoe Selo, which she was especially attached to, or Pavlovsk, which epitomizes her taste. In the main, in so far as the capital was concerned, Catherine appears to have set herself the task of putting the finishing touches to Peter's unfinished works. Whilst her noblemen were adorning many a side street with palatial mansions designed according to their personal wishes Catherine was adding missing details. She was commissioning the Summer Gardens' magnificent iron gates and railings from Felten, facing the walls of the fortress of SS. Peter and Paul with granite, confining the Neva's often turbulent waters within their superb granite quays and spanning their great expanses with permanent stone bridges. She increased the number of existing charitable institutions and schools, and widened their scope; she transformed Elizabeth's modest school of dancing into the Academy which was later to win world renown; she created the Academy of Fine Arts and saw to it that it was fittingly housed; she founded the Smolny Institute on the lines of Madame de Maintenon's St Cyr to become a famous boarding school for girls of noble birth. Catherine collected works of art of every kind, acquiring for Russia some of the greatest masterpieces of European painting; she encouraged craftsmen and actors, even to the extent of herself designing pieces of metal work and writing plays for production in her private theatre at the Hermitage. Indeed, her genius lay not so much in innovation as in using all the various strands set up in Peter's loom to increase the intricacy of his pattern. She handled them with such skill that she won for St Petersburg the title of the Athens of the North. She was doubtless fully aware of the value of her contribution to Peter's handiwork since, in 1782, when arranging for Falconet's magnificent bronze equestrian statue of the monarch to be set up on a vast Finnish granite monolith in what was then known as the Petrian Square, the words she chose to have inscribed upon it read: *Petro Primo Catherina Secunda.*

Poor mad Paul revived the terrors which had lain dormant in the hearts of Petersburgians since the death of Peter the Great. His rule was despotic and he set about transforming Russia into a vast barracks, even obliging the inhabitants of the capital to retire to bed, rise and go out at prescribed times. In the architectural field he was able to introduce, by means of the Mikhailovski Castle (1787–1800) – later, as now, the College of Engineering – a touch of the fantastic into the city's sky-line, and to imbue the building itself with something of those sinister forebodings and 'Gothic horrors' fashionable at the time in English literature; nor did this malignant element

entirely belie fate, for Paul was to be murdered in the castle within a year of its completion. Documents discovered within recent years show that it was Bazhenov – the most gifted of Russia's many talented eighteenth-century architects – who designed it, but as he was too ill by 1797 to supervise its construction Paul replaced him by Brenna. Brenna probably made many changes in Bazhenov's designs, but the castle's rounded, turret-shaped corners, tall spire and the dome supporting its flag-staff are typical of Bazhenov's style.

At Paul's death a century had elapsed since the founding of St Petersburg. In that time Russia had grown into a major European power; her way of life and outlook had altered radically, her economy had been brought up to date and her young capital had come to rank with Europe's loveliest and most stimulating cities. Its population, which had numbered 40,000 at the death of Peter the Great, had risen to over 200,000 by the end of the century, a figure which was to double itself in the course of the next twenty-five years. Those two and a half decades were also to witness the final phase of the capital's architectural history, for Alexander I, Napoleon's conqueror and the young visionary who had hoped to end war by binding Europe into a sort of League of Nations, was to be the last great builder of the Romanov dynasty. He made the Empire style his own and, with Rossi acting as his chief architect, contrived to blend it with the styles of his predecessors. Indeed the unity which, for all the diversity of architectural formulae, binds the heart of St Petersburg into a single artistic entity is largely to be attributed to Alexander's wisdom in continuing to build on the same grand scale as that adopted by Elizabeth and Rastrelli whilst adhering to the logical principles Peter had so closely followed. Rossi's brilliant scheme for providing the Winter Palace with a great circus by means of two immensely long, curved buildings joined at the centre by a monumental archway, though shortening the vista of the Nevski Prospekt, provided a really magnificent and much needed terminal point; Zakharov's reconstruction of Peter's and Eropkin's Admiralty deserves to rank with the masterpieces of the age – it served to counterbalance the Winter Palace Circus; Thomas de Thomon's Stock Exchange completed the Neva's panorama whilst Rossi's Theatre Street and Mikhailovski Palace (now the Russian Museum) are beautiful in themselves and add interest and distinction to their neighbourhoods. In the country, Elagin, the palace built by Rossi (1812–22) for the tsar's mother, completed the belt of royal residences encircling the capital. In its original state it was no less delightful than Pavlovsk, and its grounds, with their network of lakes and streams, had an idyllic quality of its own; it seemed to owe something of its poetry to the charm and glamour associated with Alexander in his youth.

VIENNA
UNDER METTERNICH

'The wonderful, inexhaustibly enchanting city',
as Hugo von Hofmannsthal described Vienna, came into full bloom as an imperial capital and a leading centre of international importance only after the Congress of 1814–15. The years between the Congress and the revolution of 1848 – a period of peace, relative calm, economic stability and industrial progress – were those in which Vienna, at the height of its power, went through the happiest phase in its history. The capital of an extensive empire, comprising German, Slav, Magyar and Italian nationalities, and the seat of the Habsburgs, that enduring dynasty which had had such widespread and diverse effects on European history, Vienna was the cultural, commercial and administrative focus of central Europe.

The medieval walled city on the Danube, transformed during the eighteenth century into a ravishing Baroque museum, impressed visitors during Francis I's reign with its self-confident, civilized charm. The Viennese themselves, a mixed and sophisticated population, were known for their ceremony, their good-natured gaiety, their universal love of music and their light-hearted enjoyment of life. This Biedermeier period, as it has been called, was one of great creativity – but more noted for its quantity than its lasting quality. Beethoven and Schubert were probably the only authentic artistic geniuses of Vienna in the period, but the elder Johann Strauss was more typical and more popular.

The characteristics of post-Congress Vienna were nourished by the policies of the Emperor and his remarkable Chancellor, Prince Metternich (shown opposite in a portrait by Sir Thomas Lawrence). It was Metternich who persuaded the powers that had defeated Napoleon to revise the map of Europe in Vienna. 'The history of the world', he said proudly, 'has never before witnessed a similar gathering of emperors, kings, princes and statesmen.' Metternich was also a strong supporter of the Holy Alliance, which governed international diplomatic relations for so many years after the Congress. At the same time, he was responsible, along with his Emperor, for the measures of censorship and internal security which sought to isolate Vienna from the 'dangerous' ideas of nationalism, constitutional monarchism, democracy, socialism and revolution which were infecting the rest of Europe. Francis's 'enlightened despotism' and Metternich's authoritarian administration, until the Emperor's death in 1835, relieved the Viennese of the basic cares of life and provided a joyful, though static, hiatus between a long war and a shattering revolution. (1)

Metternich (1773–1859), though born in Germany, followed his father's example in devoting his life to the service of Austria. Minister of Foreign Affairs from 1809 until his death, and Chancellor after the Congress, he was a highly skilful diplomatist and an aristocrat of great personal attractiveness, who strove to hold back the social changes which were eventually to overtake all of Europe. His work-room at the Hofkanzlei is shown at left. (2)

Francis of Austria (until 1806 Francis II of the Holy Roman Empire) was painted with a gathering of his many relations in 1834, the year before his death (right, engraving after the painting). In a period when absolute monarchy might almost be called an anachronism, his attitude towards his subjects was that of a stern father who managed a well-regulated family. (6)

Outside the walls of the inner city was a ring of green suburbs where the overflow of the city lived and many of the nobility had their summer-houses and palaces. Later in the nineteenth century, when the walls were finally demolished, the suburbs and the old city became the whole of modern Vienna. Below is an engraving of about 1816, which gives a view of the suburbs Alservorstadt, Rossau and Lichtental (where Schubert was born and died). (3)

By the 1820s Vienna had not only recovered from the near-bankruptcy caused by the Napoleonic Wars, but was experiencing a tide of unusual prosperity. In 1815 the Rothschilds had opened a branch in the capital, which soon became a notable banking centre. The Börse, scene of international financial transactions, is shown in a contemporary lithograph (left). (4)

The Hofburg, Francis I's official residence, which Adalbert Stifter called 'a little city in itself', was a vast complex of buildings and stately courtyards. One of the latter, Josefsplatz, is shown at right. The Imperial Guard was composed of fifty Hungarian nobles with the rank of First Lieutenant. An English visitor in 1828 thought this 'the most magnificent bodyguard in the world'. A portrait painted in 1823 by Peter Krafft, one of the first Austrian classicists, shows the famous red Hussar uniform, the tiger-skin mantle, the sable hat topped with white egrets (far right). (7, 8)

The Fiakers of Vienna and the equipages of the nobility (below and opposite) were a familiar sight as they drove to and from the Prater, the extensive park and pleasure-garden which lay between the inner city and the Danube. (5, 9)

The military Mass (below), which took place by the Outer Burgtor in the western suburbs of the city, was painted in 1826 by Peter Fendi, a Vienna-born *genre* artist. (11)

The hills around Vienna were so close to the city that the population could easily drive out for a day's excursion into a pastoral setting, drink the local wine at one of the many inns scattered throughout the countryside, or roam in the Vienna woods. The watercolour above left shows picnickers and strollers on Gallizinberg. (10)

Dominated by the tower of St Stephen's Cathedral and surrounded by the walls on which people can be seen promenading, Vienna is shown as it appeared until the fortifications were removed in 1858–60. 'Those born in Vienna', wrote Stifter, 'are sore at heart when they can no longer see St Stephen's tower.' (12)

Schönbrunn Palace, once a hunting-lodge, destroyed by the Turks and rebuilt between 1696 and 1700 in a grander style by Leopold I, was one of the summer residences of the Austrian Habsburgs. Rudolf von Alt, a contemporary master of watercolour, gives an impression of part of the palace and grounds in 1845 (below). (13)

The public pleasures of Vienna were many and varied. Coffee-houses, such as the 'Jünglings Caféhaus' (right), originated during the Turkish siege of 1683 and became a characteristic feature of the city. Public festivals, like the Brigittenkirchtag (right centre), which took place in a large park outside the city wall on the Sunday after the full moon in July, were enthusiastically celebrated by the whole population. The more intimate and quiet diversions of the Viennese are portrayed by a native Romantic artist, Moritz von Schwind (below). (14, 15, 16)

Theatre and music were among the special Viennese delights. The Kärntnertortheater – the old opera house – is shown opposite, top left. The so-called 'Dreimäderlhaus' (opposite, top right) was the setting of a later operetta about a fictitious incident in Schubert's life and based on his music. Beethoven's funeral on 29 March 1827 was attended by an estimated throng of 20,000. The procession in front of the Minorite Church is shown in this watercolour by Franz Stöber (opposite centre). (19, 20, 21)

Contemporary artists have left a record of many of the personalities identified with Metternich's Vienna. Sophie Schröder, a leading actress, was painted (right) by Moritz Michael Daffinger, a portraitist in miniature. The playwright and actor, Johann Nestroy, is the figure at left in a scene from his comedy, *Lumpazivagabundus* (far right). Gathered round the cashier of the Silberne Kaffeehaus are a number of men in the arts, including Johann Strauss II, the playwright Ferdinand Raimund and the actor Ignaz Schuster (opposite left). Schubert plays the piano (opposite right) for such friends as Schwind, the Fröhlich sisters and the playwright Grillparzer. (17, 18, 22, 23)

The Emperor's arrival at the Kärtnertor, where he and his victory over Napoleon were acclaimed by a joyous populace on 16 June 1814, marked the beginning of an era which lasted about thirty years. During this time Vienna managed to shut its eyes and ears to the outside world. The coming of the railway (below, painted in 1847) was one of various irresistible changes – technical, economic and social – which brought the era to its end. The particular flavour of Biedermeier Vienna, with its unambitious and *bourgeois* contentedness, was altered by the revolutions of 1848, and the capital became larger, more serious and less secure. (24, 25)

ALAN PRYCE-JONES

LET US IMAGINE a traveller coming from the west. Driving down from the low hilly woods, and cursing at the abominable state of the roads, he would arrive, beyond the suburbs, at a short avenue leading to the cream-coloured façade of Schönbrunn. Here, if the court were not in residence, he might turn aside to visit the state-rooms, to stare into a world of gilding and porcelain and crimson silk, and out again beyond the high windows to the long pleached alleys which conduct a population of statues towards the pillared hill at the end of the formal gardens. But if the court were out of residence it was probably late autumn or early spring, and then there was little temptation to linger in the splendid melancholy rooms, warmed at best by a stove more delicate than cordial, and never forgetful of the white months in which the snow piled against the plinths of Mercury and Neptune and scurried against the hill-side in front of a searching wind.

For Schönbrunn was a summer palace. It needed to be seen when the citizens crowded along the lime walks and admired the Hungarian Guard, in red and silver and a tiger-skin at the shoulders, riding across the courtyard with Prince Esterhazy at their head. It needed the familiar presence of the emperor and the archdukes walking among the collection of Alpine plants or joining the imperial ladies at the Tyrolean chalet; it needed the double warmth which went with the summer light – and that, in central Europe at least, is as brilliant as ever – and with the paternal presence of the emperor himself, a simple, friendly figure who was perfectly ready to be stopped in his daily walks by anyone with a grievance or request.

Our traveller, then, would not linger long. He would press forward into the suburbs, holding his passport ready, and prepared for exactly the questions which harass his descendants today. Had he any tobacco? Any foreign goods? And, above all, any undesirable literature? For, paternal though it might be, the emperor's government, under the cautious guidance of Prince Metternich, kept a watchful eye on the arrival in the country of new, and so possibly subversive, ideas; and therefore travellers were advised to jettison all books and papers so as to be on the safe side. The public libraries of Vienna, they would find, were plentifully supplied with wholesome or consoling reading matter.

But already, from the suburbs, a sight appeared which made the tiresome behaviour of the local officials seem inconsequent: the high polychrome roof of the cathedral, topped by an immense fretted spire, gathered the wandering roof-lines of the city to a single point; and when, after a mile or two, the outline of Vienna proper could be seen, pressed behind high brick walls in front of which lay a straggle of garden, palace, and dusty plantation, the traveller, keenly expectant of the comforts awaiting him at the Erzherzog Karl, or, better still, the Kaiserin von Österreich, anticipated as well the pleasures of a city second only, if second at all, to Paris itself.

He would drive in by the Josefstadt Gate. And then, in the centre of the city, he would find a Vienna which was to change surprisingly little in the next hundred and twenty years. Locked behind their walls, the inhabitants congregated into a maze of small streets and squares. The light and air came no lower than the attic windows; below, a thrusting, excitable, polyglot throng pattered over the cobbles, or drew back to the wall while some princely carriage rumbled by, preceded by a liveried runner with a silver-topped stick in his hand. In these years – the years of Metternich's greatness – Vienna played something of the part of modern New York: it set a pace, it stamped with its own pattern the different nationalities which came to it because it lay at the centre of a civilization; and yet it remained a small city in spite of its wealth and its influence; not many more than 300,000 souls lived in centre and suburb together, and of these seven-eighths in the suburbs.

Because all the activities of the court, the government, and the world of industry, as well as the palaces of the nobles, were crowded behind walls, the city, at first sight, seemed rather cramped and disappointing. The shops were small, the houses towered high, all the families of a vast cousinage were crammed into edifices which one visitor describes as resembling inns of court rather than private dwellings. The imperial palace itself was the reverse of cheerful; the state apartments had not been redecorated since the time of Maria Theresa, and the private rooms were dank and threadbare. Nevertheless, an extraordinary animation was in the air. The coachmen in the streets were famous for their skill and dexterity, and in the crowded hours – from midday to one and from six to seven – the press was so thick that slow-going foreigners were liable to be bowled over into the gutter.

A sense of purpose

Where, then, did the attraction of Vienna lie? It was not at all like the Vienna of Johann Strauss. It frowned upon unnecessary levity. It was cautious, subtle, rather dull. Music-making, conversation, and cards filled a great part of the time; every evening the streets were deserted by eleven. Over the whole city an extraordinary attention to rules could be observed. Not only to minor rules, such as that against smoking in the streets, but to iron conventions of social behaviour, some of them handed down from medieval times. It was, to say the least, unexpected that it should be the emperor's duty to attend every fire, yet it was a duty punctually observed by Francis I in his capacity of chief citizen. And, in matters of daily conduct, the strictest laws of precedence were maintained, so that from the imperial family down to the slavey each place was known and kept, and every lifetime regulated in a series of concentric circles between which close communication was almost impossible.

And yet the fact remained: Vienna, on closer inspection, spread a snare so alluring that each traveller was caught in turn. It was not the *tourbillon irrésistible de plaisirs continus* – in La Garde-Chambonas' phrase – to which foreigners succumbed; such gaieties had been a temporary by-product of the Congress and died with it. But they had left something in the air: something, moreover, which had combined with a high sense of purpose. In a word, it soon became apparent to the sympathetic observer that the Austrians believed themselves to be set upon a business both important and enjoyable.

For consider: to the archduchy of Austria came north Italian noblemen and Triestine merchants; Jewish bagmen from Galicia and legendary magnates from the Hungarian plain; Moravian Brothers from Reichenberg and subtle Greeks from the Adriatic provinces; Unitarians from Transylvania and monarchist refugees from all over Europe. The local capitals played their part: Buda and Prague and Venice and Milan kept their own state and often their own counsel as well; but at the higher level at which all those conflicting interests had to be reconciled and smoothed into a single policy Vienna stood as the single imperial centre.

Furthermore, while the different provinces of the empire looked to Vienna for guidance, the whole German-speaking world observed it with very different, but not less attentive, eyes. That world, spreading from Poland to the Rhine, across a multitude of kingdoms, principalities, grand-duchies, free cities, might turn up its nose at the absurd peoples upon whom the emperor wasted so much of his time: the incomprehensible Magyars, slavish Bohemians, facile Lombards, the clowns and Shylocks and rogues who ought to be put in their places and kept there. It might turn up its nose at such, but not at the Austrians themselves. For whatever the kings of Prussia and Saxony might say, it was the emperor of Austria, not they, who held the inheritance of Charlemagne; and, on a lower plane, it was not Sans-Souci, or Karlsberg, or Ludwigslust which set the tone of German society – that indefinable tone which sounded in music and poetry and subtle talk – it was not they but the Hofburg and Schönbrunn. The Prussians might grumble at Austrian delicacy; the Bavarians might vaunt a greater purity of race. But the emperor could still afford to smile at such presumptions. He alone stood at the still centre of the axis round which all Germany revolved.

This accounted in part for the special relation in which he stood towards his peoples. It gave his power that paternal kindness which touched every aspect of government. Government could be arbitrary, certainly; it could be narrow-minded, overcautious, old-fashioned; but those are all paternal qualities, and qualities evoked by a family growing up untidily, its members strongly individual in character and divided by wide differences of age. And always, above government itself, stood the figure of the emperor. It could not be said that Francis was a very lively monarch. He was not clever, or brilliant, or dashing. His favourite reply to any concrete suggestion, 'Let's sleep upon it', reflects the embarrassed and pernickety caution which was so intelligently exploited by Metternich. But at least he accepted his position at the head of the German-speaking world. And so, during his reign, a constant attractive power was exerted upon it by his capital.

For this, no doubt, the Congress of 1815 was partly responsible. If the Congress splendours were only temporary they at least revived a forgotten standard among classes of society each of which had been exhausted by a whole generation of high political and economic tension.

It had long been the fashion, for example, among the nobles to visit Vienna as little as possible. Now, however, the influx of distinguished visitors brought with it a fresh taste for the city. Neglected palaces were refurbished, and not only the nobles but plain citizens as well obtained such a reputation for civilized living that a marked industrial revival took place – a revival which attracted the ambitious and the forceful from abroad, especially from south Germany, and gave Vienna that air of fabulous promise which clothes the greater American cities today.

Metternich: servant of the emperor

It is necessary to remember that Metternich himself had obeyed this attraction. Born in Coblenz fifteen years before the French Revolution, he had become a servant of the emperor as a result of the revolutionary upheaval which deprived his family of its Rhineland property. It is natural enough, therefore, that he should have looked to his master chiefly as an upholder of order. During the years between his first appointment as imperial representative at The Hague and his final accession to power after the disaster of Wagram, the old Europe had been swept away – or so we can now perceive. Yet at the time it cannot have seemed quite so certain. Revolutionary zeal had been stemmed; through the marriage of Napoleon to Marie-Louise two contradictory orders had been united in the fragile person of the King of Rome; the future – to one of Metternich's temperament – held a tantalizing balance between hope and fear: hope

of an internal concord from which all threats to the imperial house could be progressively scotched, and fear of the strain and ferment which were still to be felt throughout Europe. 'The true character of our age', he told Guizot many years later, 'is that of an age of transition ... I made myself a conservative socialist.' And if Metternich's idea of socialism is remote indeed from the concept which gradually formed after 1848, the statement shows at least that his mind was neither inelastic nor conventional. Not surprisingly, therefore, he felt a particular sympathy for English institutions; not surprisingly, at the end of his life, Disraeli turned to him in affectionate admiration. And there can be no doubt that in the years of his power this intense (and sometimes blind) desire for order, tempered by a lively interest in the thought, the art, the applied sciences of his time, was the chief factor in the renaissance of Austria.

For under his rule a remarkable change occurred. Goethe's friend, Varnhagen von Ense, summed the matter up in the early 1830s: 'The whole aspect of the city and its surroundings', he wrote of Vienna, 'has something rich, pleasurable, and gay of heart about it. People here seem healthier and happier than elsewhere; the dark spirits which dog mankind, which harass us unremittingly, find it hard to breathe in this air, and seldom have tried to lodge here. Such an appearance has something uncommonly agreeable; it exerts a power for peace on every temperament, every humour, and promotes the feeling that thus should it be for every man among us; for everybody such an atmosphere is the right and natural one. And even if it is only an appearance, the appearance is not in vain.'

A breathing-space in history

It was, indeed, only an appearance – linked to the wave of prosperity which broke upon the city during the 1820s. A few years later, when the July Revolution in France had touched off minor insurrections throughout Europe and thus alarmed the Austrian government into redoubling a policy of rigid isolation from all liberal currents of thought, the dream was broken. But in the 1820s a youthful spirit of enterprise was abroad; and although the life of the city was quiet enough, a runnel of open good humour spread through a populace tired of war and poverty. The court, the nobles, the government officials, might oppose levity; but among the middle classes that spirit was now forming which later made the gaiety of Vienna a commonplace. Dancing suddenly became the fashion. In the Apollosaal, in the 'Schwarze Bock', above all in Dommayer's Casino not far from Schönbrunn, the sound of the waltz broke delightfully over the crowded tables; at Dommayer's, Josef Lanner himself, and the elder Strauss, began their years of fame; and it was not long before the mild pleasures of a Viennese evening became celebrated throughout Europe.

To what did they amount? Certainly not to excess. The emperor, like the middle classes, dined at the old-fashioned hour of two; receptions at the court were rare; and even though the nobler families might dine at four or five, they had little to look forward to except a reception which began at ten and ended soon after midnight. The opera and the theatres started at seven; a little whist or an hour of music closed the day well in time for early rising except during Carnival and in a short season of ball-giving after Easter. There was, in fact, not much in the Vienna of 1830 to support a legend of high living. But there was something better: an extraordinary diffusion of kindly temper, of ease, of mutual confidence.

That, perhaps, was the great contribution of Vienna to European civilization. It provided, in the Biedermeier period, a momentary suspension of history – a breathing-space before the great industrial struggle of the mid-century, in which men and women of different classes, religions, nations, showed themselves perfectly at home in a strictly hierarchical society, perfectly disposed to innocent amusements, and singularly free from the warping rancours which disfigured the more liberal countries of western Europe.

Innocent pleasures and gaiety

Perhaps it was a little stuffy, a little acquiescent, yet it is hard not to be touched by the crowds sitting under the trees at Nussdorf and Döbling, listening to the *Harfenisten* – musicians who, in earlier times, had sung comic songs to the music of a harp, but now played violin or clarinet, zither or guitar, under the nut-trees among the wooden benches; or again, hard to watch without affection the popular festivals, such as that in the Prater on 1 May, or at the Brigitten-au on the first Sunday in July.

The Prater, it must be added, played its part every Sunday in the year. The *Ausflug* – the Sunday excursion – was already a settled habit among the Viennese, who flocked out, on any auspicious day, into the welcoming landscape which surrounded their city. But the Prater, because the nearest, was also the most animated of meeting-places. There, on a sunny day under the trees, a microcosm of Vienna assembled. The long shady avenues kept the heat away; in countless low buildings, each set in its garden, the tables were spread for a midday breakfast. The Papagei, the Eisvogel, the Tracteur competed for custom (for fashion, among these friendly little restaurants, was both absolute and changeable); and in the afternoon, after admiring the view from the Lusthaus, and watching the boats on the sweeping Danube, the traveller would plunge among the coffee-house tables, among the coloured shacks, crammed with young people singing and dancing, spilling out under the avenues, clapping the little trios which accompanied a singer, admiring the musician who blew a trumpet fixed to his violin and worked the drums with his feet, or gathering round a story-teller in the shade, while a Turkish band did its best to distract the kite-flyers, the exponents of optical illusions, the pigeon-shooters, the sausage-sellers at every corner.

Tired of these lowly pleasures, he might walk into the Haupt-allee – a triple avenue devoted to elegant display. There, on Sunday afternoons, the fashionable rode or walked; and in the middle avenue three to four thousand coaches followed slowly behind the bowing figures of the imperial family in an open carriage. If he were lucky enough to be present on 1 May, he would certainly (after watching the well-dressed display their spring gowns in the Augarten) stay to see the traditional race between the runners of the princely houses. These runners, in rich and brilliant uniforms, casqued in feathers, were maintained in the first instance to run ahead of the family coaches, two and two, torch in hand, both to light the road and to clear a way. Later they were cherished as objects of family pride, not unlike race-horses; and each 1 May an immense crowd gathered to watch a dozen or so of the best show off their paces. High wagers were laid, and tribunes were built to accommodate the families whose runners took part in the race. Excitement was immense. 'Bravo, Kinsky!' the crowd cried; 'Faster, Karoly! Keep to it, Auersperg!' And finally the winner was rewarded with a purse of gold.

The July festival on the Brigittenau was still more animated. There, on a quiet site occupied only by a chapel and a hunting lodge, a whole city of tents was built for the day, between which a kind of Feast of Unreason took place. All social distinctions were banished (although the leaders of society, it must be admitted, did not arrive till the evening), and until night fell the peculiar unity of the city was fully manifest, whereby the prince and the goose-girl, the magnate and the kitchen-maid, shared their pleasures without embarrassment.

Among these pleasures the theatre stood high; and in order to catch the flavour of the times nothing is more evocative than the pieces of Raimund and Nestroy. How can they be described? To what can they be compared? To the Keystone comedies? The Aldwych farces? Scarcely: for, though they may not seem very amusing today, they represent a kind of popular art which was solely Viennese. Its merits can be glimpsed through Nestroy's *Lumpazivaga-bundus*: merits of a strongly local, heady order, and meant for display by an author who was also a beloved comic actor. Dialect, verbal humour, imaginative fantasy – such are the ingredients. And there can be little doubt that it was largely by means of the Vorstadttheater – the light comedy stage, as it were – that the ebullience and the ironical *bravura* of the Viennese character were formed.

In part, no doubt, these traits can be attributed to the Italian strain in the Austrian nation, in part to the Slav. It is only necessary to look as far as Munich or Dresden to perceive how marked a difference lies between the popular world of Vienna and of any German city outside the empire. But the Viennese spirit did not show itself only in trivialities. At this distance it is very easy to feel too sentimental an affection for the frank merriment of the Brigittenkirchtag, for the open, humorous temper of the city populace. We see a Teniers without grossness – foreign observers were much struck by the fact that the Viennese so seldom became drunk – a Boucher without preten-

sion. But the same mixture of blood which gave the Viennese so marked a taste for simple pleasures also gave them a quick appreciation of sensuous or evocative themes at however high a pitch. Thus the performance of Sophie Schröder in Grillparzer's *Sappho* became legendary; and the very presence in the city of such men as Beethoven, Schubert, or the painter Daffinger was felt to be a measurable honour even by those to whom their works made no special appeal.

The character of Biedermeier

Indeed, to an art-loving people, the time was wonderfully propitious. Yet it contained a paradox implicit in the very name, Biedermeier. Biedermeier was originally a comic personage, the symbol of a truth as penetrating as that hidden in Colonel Blimp or in Marius. Biedermeier was the comfortable bourgeois, the timid, convention-ridden, respectful little citizen. And as the years of Metternich's rule succeeded one another the role of Biedermeier became more emphatic. He was the supreme counter-revolutionary, the exactest of adherents to church and state. And yet the civilization of which he was representative nourished such unexpected ardours as the quartets of Beethoven and the great simplicities of Grillparzer.

Perhaps the dwelling-houses of the Viennese exemplify best the Biedermeier character. The palaces of the Herrengasse and the Wallnerstrasse are not representative. Kinskys, Czernins, Lobkowitzes, Wilczeks and the innumerable consanguinity of the *Almanach de Gotha* stood apart. Their vast houses usually dated from the eighteenth century; all round them, however, were the modest villas of plainer folk, many of which have survived almost as they were built.

Their elevations were classical: in Hietzing, in Nussdorf, at Lainz, the sober milk-coloured façades still stand, their double windows bolstered against winter cold, or hidden from the July sun. The rooms inside were plain. No carpets hid the complex pattern of the parquet floors, and the sofas were the reverse of comfortable. Under elaborate pelmets the winter curtains retained the warmth of a porcelain stove, shaped like a vast inkstand and set in one corner; in summer the muslin draperies floated on a calculated draught from the garden brilliant with phlox and geranium. Commodity, not splendour, was required. But the furniture (unless modelled on French originals) was light and cheerful. Pearwood and cherry, Hungarian ash and mahogany, were set sparely round the walls; treasures from an earlier generation, imported or copied from abroad, had been replaced by a half-rustic simplicity; instead of the Georgian display which reigned in London, or the cosy elaboration of French contemporary taste, an Austrian household wore rather a conventual air. Plain living and plain thinking (so far as he could impose them) were Metternich's ideals for the subjects of the emperor.

In such settings the question of human happiness became all-important. For if the Viennese were not happy they were nothing. The paternalism of the state took away much of their responsibility for their own welfare, the barriers established by a strict censorship between Austria and the rest of the world (not least the rest of Germany) gave them an unusual intellectual self-sufficiency. The empire could feed, amuse, and (between economic slumps) employ them. They lived, therefore, in almost a private world, moved by internal stresses but secured, for a whole generation, from the disturbing touch of the unexpected.

No doubt it was rather dull; no doubt the peaceful well-being of the Biedermeier years chafed the more restless spirits of the time to provoke the irascible temper of 1848; but the dullness had its charms while it lasted. It can be compared to the dullness of Adalbert Stifter, among the greatest and most unjustly neglected of Austrian writers – dull because static, careful, prosy, but at the same time drenched in warm sunlight and nourished on clear, bright air. Both aspects were reflected in the appearance of the people themselves. 'I certainly', wrote Mrs Trollope of 1836, 'never saw the elements of what in most other cities would have constituted a mob, so decently clothed, so generally clean and *well-to-do* in appearance, and, in the midst of great gaiety and good-humour, so perfectly quiet and orderly.' 'A most happy and enjoying people', another traveller of the same period, Peter Turnbull, calls them. 'With all their apathy and slowness ... a very gay, junketing nation', Lady Londonderry wrote in 1840. And before dismissing Metternich's government as a reactionary tyranny it is worth examining in some detail exactly how it worked upon the daily life of the Austrians.

Government and happiness

First, as to religion: although Catholicism prevailed, clerical power was sternly curbed, and equality of right was given to other denominations. The Archduke Joseph, Palatine of Hungary and brother of Francis I, was married in succession to a member of the Greek Church, a Calvinist, and a Lutheran; and when the Lutheran wife of his brother Charles died, her funeral rites were celebrated in St Stephen's, at the emperor's orders, as a Protestant ceremony. Not surprisingly, the archbishop complained, with the support of the nuncio, that it was unfitting to use a Catholic cathedral for a Protestant rite. 'Tell the nuncio', the emperor merely replied, 'that this is no affair of his.' And on every occasion (following the precedents established in the 1770s by Joseph II), he took care to assert the supremacy of the civil power, as vested in the throne, over the ecclesiastical – to the extent that no Austrian subject could be excommunicated without imperial consent, or, more striking still, that army marriages contracted without the permission of a superior officer were declared in every case invalid.

The emperor thus became, in his own domains, effectively head of the Church; even the monastic communities were removed from the authority of Rome; and an equal jurisdiction was exercised over other religions, which were classified under four heads, as Greeks, Lutherans, Calvinists, and Jews. Each community maintained its own independence; disabilities upon the Jews had been cancelled progressively, until they could fill any office in state or army; unauthorized sects could only meet in public by licence; in fact, the religious life of the country was used as a channel of communication between the emperor and his subjects to an extent perhaps unparalleled in history. For although he did not much care to which religion they adhered, the emperor insisted on each of them being registered as belonging to one or the other, in order (it can be surmised) to attach to the civil government the most intimate of all principles of order.

Not unexpectedly, the educational processes of Austria developed the same theory. To quote Turnbull once more:

> Aiming at the gradual and peaceful amelioration of her internal condition, the equalization of rights before the law, and the general development of the national resources, Austria views education in its larger sense, as a mighty engine to mould the public mind; to cement it together in a bond of cordial union with her existing institutions; to excite and to regulate its energies, so that it shall be neither a drag on the state machine by its ignorance and grossness, nor a spur to unsafe speed by its crude theoretical fancies. She strives at the creation of a happy, not a brilliant people ...

Thus, again, the ideal of happiness is put forward. And again happiness is bound up with a sense of security. This may sound heavily pedestrian, yet its ideals must be measured against the uncertain and often violently changing background of the preceding generation throughout Europe. The French Revolution inevitably produced extremes of licence or restriction, and the foreign examples open to the Austrian government after the fall of Napoleon were not reassuring. In Germany the Romantics had impressed a surface of passionate, often of anarchic, feeling upon a habit of mind either military (as in Prussia) or casuistical; in France an uneasy compromise had been struck between the libertarianism of the Revolution and the cautious respectability of a restored monarchy; in southern Europe every branch of education was under rigid clerical control. The Austrian authorities tried, therefore, to avoid the obvious pitfalls. Education was in the hands of the state, but it was closely bound to the five official religious denominations. Without testimonials from the religious body with which each pupil was registered, no educational advance could be made, but, under the supervision of rabbi, priest, or pastor (who were severally forbidden to proselytize), schools were free, varied in character, and universal. If education was not compulsory, the absence of a certificate made later employment, except as a labourer, illegal; and under Francis a coherent attempt was made to weld the whole empire together by means of a uniform system.

It will be seen that the government was playing safe. Contentment was its chosen virtue, and anything which might disturb contentment or foster ambitious inquiry was banished from the schools.

From this distance that sounds a comforting principle, if unexhilarating. The difficulty which arose, however, was that it weakened the Austrians in that faculty in which they were already weakest – the faculty of independent judgment. By making their formative years so snug, it gave them no defence against the outside world, it confined their intelligence to practical skills, and it required of their rulers a constant vigilance against the importation of vigorous ideas.

This vigilance, more than anything else, has darkened the reputation of Metternich as a wise ruler. It was not alarming – indeed, all contemporary travellers agree that police activities were less in evidence in Austria than anywhere else in Europe – but it had the disadvantage of cramping opinion within narrow bounds. True, the rules were languidly applied. The censors fussed, and then forgot. But, in a negative way, the police supervision worked a good deal of harm – by eliminating almost all home news from the newspapers, and by forbidding travel abroad except to the very important or to the professional classes who had a specific reason for leaving the country. Bad habits might be picked up abroad, and so it was wiser to be on the safe side.

But within the country itself there was no terrorism of any kind. Nor was the law in itself severe. Even the convicted criminal – and there were surprisingly few of them – only felt the paternal hand of a state which was more than a century ahead of the rest of Europe in matters of criminal jurisprudence. To begin with, the death sentence was extremely rare, and had in all cases to be ratified personally by the emperor. Otherwise the extent of the fault was measured by the extent of the public disturbance caused, except in cases of treason, first-degree murder, or forgery of currency notes. In every case, however, all possible excuses were allowed to diminish the crime; full responsibility was only admitted at the age of fourteen, and liability to the death sentence only at eighteen; and at a time when English children were being executed for insignificant thefts, the young Viennese were treated as unfortunates in need of care rather than punishment – indeed, the punishment, if exacted at all, often fell (and severely) upon their parents.

Faults in the system

From the vantage-ground of modern England it is fascinating, and perhaps sobering, to see how nearly the Austria of the 1830s resembles the ideal of the Welfare State. A uniform education gave equal opportunity to all, and a vast civil service found place for all who did sufficiently well in their examinations. Then, a fatherly interest was taken in the citizen by his government. Better mechanism to deal with ill-health, old age, and unemployment existed in Austria than elsewhere in Europe, and the exchequer was permanently out of funds owing to the responsibilities shouldered by the state towards its citizens. The result should have been a paradise; in fact, however, it sustained the faults of the Austrian character at the expense of its virtues. By giving a paramount importance to peace of mind, it cramped initiative, and, as might have been foreseen, gave an exaggerated influence to those who refused to conform. For so long as all went well within the state, and above all, so long as contact with the outside world was kept to a minimum, the Viennese enjoyed, in no spirit of fervour or inquiry, their privileges as the citizens of a capital city.

They developed the scheme of life which played a considerable part in wrecking any possibility of unity within the empire. Under this, it was assumed that the hard work would be done by the Slav and Magyar populations, while administration was perfected by the Germans; or, worse, that it would be safe to tolerate the disparities of a feudal system as practised outside Austria proper, so as to make sure of the loyalty of the nobles.

Not that the Viennese administrators were wholly blind. They saw (or some saw) quite clearly the social changes which would have to be made in order to fuse together the different parts of a state not only sharply divided by variations of tradition and language but ranged between high urban fashion and the most primitive simplicity. They saw that the nineteenth century was married, within their frontiers, to the Middle Ages, and that the marriage was not going too well. Yet somehow the moment for introducing a change never seemed quite to come. 'Let's sleep upon it', the Emperor Francis had said; and they slept, until the pressure of the outside world became too great, and with the coming of the railway round about 1840 it was found impossible to keep dangerous ideas at bay any longer.

The climax, after years of mounting unrest, brought about the fall of Metternich and the revolution of 1848. But the sleep, while it lasted, had been wonderfully pleasant – a light sleep, moreover, enlivened by exhilarating dreams. Was it really impossible to combine the best of the old world and the new? Round that question turned the brightest of Metternich's visions. Was it so hard to make people see that violent changes were of their nature impermanent? That out of order alone progress could grow? It is not odd that an instinctive friendship and respect should have grown between Metternich and Disraeli. Both perceived very clearly the problem of the nineteenth century: how to guide a state through the coming industrial revolution without its breaking under the centrifugal pressure of rival economies, policies, societies; how to use the revolution as a creative, not a convulsive, force. But Metternich, who had known the eighteenth century, was the warier man. Too wary, no doubt. By knowing what had been good for the past he conceived that he could prescribe for the future. Ease of spirit, security from want, a quiet life: to these his own period, like that in which we live, attached a perhaps exaggerated importance. In such a scheme there was not much scope for the nobler virtues, but plenty of room for holidays, light music, cheerful conversation. There was room, too, for judicious experiment.

Technical schools, for example, were warmly supported by the government. In Vienna itself a Polytechnic Institute had been founded in 1816; and beneath the foundation-stone laid by the emperor was a roll which dedicated the building above all to 'die gemeinnützige Ausbildung meines lieben und getreuen Bürgerstandes' – to the intellectual enlargement for the common good of the faithful middle classes. The phrase sums up an official attitude of mind in the Biedermeier period. Things had to be gemeinnützig – for the common good – and the middle classes were to be given as much attention as possible, whether they liked it or not.

The arts: pleasure without genius

Certain things, however, though in themselves desirable, are not particularly designed for the common good. The arts, for example. And since a generation is chiefly recorded by the books, the pictures, and the music it leaves behind, it must be regretted that Metternich's personal pleasure in the arts offered so meagre an encouragement to the Austrians. It is usual to praise their extreme musicality; and so far as sheer volume of music-making goes it is right to do so. But already the vitiating flaw in Viennese musical life was apparent. The bad drowned the good; and the good too often included whatever it cost an intellectual effort to comprehend. Fascinated by brilliance, and easily captured by charm, the Viennese knew no standard to maintain except that of immediate pleasure. Furthermore, they were fickle. And if Beethoven was in high reputation at the time of the Congress, it needed his death, eleven years later, to make him once again the object of public interest. In the intervening years Rossini had become fashionable. The Italian opera outbid the German upon its own stage. In brief, it is easy to overpraise the musicianship of early-nineteenth-century Vienna, in spite of its exceptional executants – Czerny, Thalberg, Moscheles, the young Liszt, among pianists alone – and of a small number of devoted amateurs who supported the quartets of Schuppanzigh and Mayseder.

In the other arts an absence of vitality was much more apparent. Among painters there was the romantic Moritz von Schwind, whose art has been compared, without much reason, to that of Schubert; but the general run of competent painting can be deduced from the fact that Daffinger – one of the most agreeable of portrait painters but no more – owed much of his fame to the albums of celebrities which he compiled for Princess Metternich's drawing-room table in the 1830s.

As for the writers, they were most skilfully discouraged by an oppressive censorship. Some, like the Count Auersperg who wrote under the name of Anastasius Grün, took refuge in satire at a safe distance; others, like Grillparzer, wore themselves out in alternations of bad temper and attempts to please the authorities. In general, however, Turnbull's verdict on the period stands: 'In point of daring original genius, it is rare to see a work of literature, art, or science, proceed from an Austrian.'

And yet ... should one forget the wide diffusion of simple and pleasurable art throughout Vienna in his time? Should one overlook Fanny Elssler the dancer, or be deaf to the haunting street-music under the trees on summer evenings, or turn away from the processional side of daily life inside the city walls? Suppose one were to catch sight of Prince Colloredo on his way to pay respects at the imperial palace. First, we are told, came four mounted guards in dark-green uniforms heavily embroidered in gold lace; next, two running footmen, carrying silver batons, in short jackets and tight pantaloons of scarlet and silver; next, half a score of liveries, striding through the mud in white stockings; then a fool; followed by the prince himself in a state chariot drawn by six black horses; and finally a troop of mounted guards to bring up the rear. Such sights were to be seen every day. Every day the German Guard, in black and gold and scarlet, or the white aigrettes of the Hungarian Hussars, might turn the corner into view; and it is arguable that the senses of this tranquil people were satisfied by the colour and vivacity of daily life, enhanced by a climate of extremes in which the world lay for weeks under a glittering cover of snow, or breathed, even on the verges of the city, the warm flowers and fresh-cut wood of the hills beyond the Danube.

Metternich would have argued thus. He would have preferred to see his people amused than stimulated. So much better for them, he would have said, so much less agitating. Let them leave the books alone and dance instead under the lindens. And there can be no doubt that the chancellor's caution, over a long generation, was the chief element which formed the character of his people. For it is to Metternich that all inquiries into the state of Vienna during the Biedermeier period eventually lead: to Metternich who shared with the emperor himself for over thirty years the status of universal father-figure to the subjects of the empire.

Metternich's failure

His reputation has not taken the turn he expected. He looked for fame to posterity, and posterity has rewarded him instead with an almost unqualified dismissal. Perhaps that comes partly from exasperation. Metternich was prolix, confident, and scornful. He declined to have doubts, but at the same time refused to hope. He foresaw, with rare clarity, the chaos of modern Europe, but in his search for a palliative he erected a rigid system of political conduct which was quite incompatible with the world before him. And so it is not entirely surprising that posterity should have taken an easy revenge by setting the failure of Austria in the nineteenth century too directly to his account.

He possessed, moreover, that quality which brings discredit to any statesman unlucky enough to possess it: he pleased. He pleased by his manner, by his looks, his conversation; he pleased by his variety of interests – by having read so widely, cultivated the sciences so elegantly, trained so well a musical ear and an eye habituated to whatever was best among pictures, furniture, flowers. He entertained so splendidly, got into debt so negligently, built up his estates in Bohemia and on the Rhine with so princely an intermittence; he loved so widely, he flattered so discreetly, that it was natural to accept a stern view of his character as soon as the presence of his charm was removed. 'He believes', said Lord Liverpool, 'that politics consists in finesse and tricks.' It would be truer to say that he believed in Metternich. But such conviction, sustained to the point of fatuity and adorned with all the graces of a civilized mind, could hardly fail to irritate. Finesse and tricks – that was what it came to in the end. And perhaps Sir Charles Webster's verdict goes as far as anyone is likely to go in making amends to his shade a century later: 'In diagnosis Metternich was without an equal in Europe. But no one would trust him to prescribe a remedy.'

His diagnosis was more or less thus: After the French Revolution two main forces were abroad in Europe – the continuing spirit of the revolution and an anxious desire for social order. Metternich rejected the revolution out of hand; he saw, however, that social order was not to be defined once for all, and so he came to conceive a state of equilibrium between conflicting forces, an equilibrium which would allow necessary changes to be introduced into the national order by a series of minimal steps calmly undertaken.

But he had a logical mind. He saw also that there was an essential connection between the individuals within a state, and the state itself viewed as one member of a family of nations. In a multi-national state like the Austrian empire this connection needed no underlining, and it impelled Metternich to press his theory of a desirable equilibrium into international affairs. 'Political bodies', he wrote, 'have an independent existence as little as the individuals who make up society.' In his own mind, therefore, the nations of Europe bore at least some degree of responsibility for each other's well-being, as a condition of the well-being of their own peoples. How could this responsibility be maintained? Only by a strong personal rule. Monarch must speak to monarch as brother to brother. Throughout all Europe subversive ideas must be extirpated so that in tranquillity the brotherhood of kings might guide the ease and enlarge the privileges of their obedient subjects.

The concept was noble. But it was not compatible with two ideas held by Metternich with equal tenacity. One of them was the pre-eminence of Vienna among European capitals, the other a fastidious dislike of the middle classes. Metternich, let it be remembered, had come to Vienna as a servant of the emperor. His loyalties were closely bound, therefore, to the reigning house, and he was firm in his aim of making Vienna the centre of a European concert. The city lay, after all, at the physical heart of the Continent; why should it not become its spiritual heart as well? The fact that the power of the empire had declined once for all, the fact that its internal administration, however good in separate parts, was hopelessly cumbrous as a whole, the fact that to pacify the Hungarians and the Italians alone was almost beyond the resources of the centralized government – none of this weighed with him. And as for the middle classes, were they not the most obvious centre of disaffection everywhere? The poor knew their place; the nobles governed; it was from the intermediate class that revolution sprang. And his prevision that the dominance of that intermediate class was to be the prime event of the century filled Metternich with a kind of obstinate horror. At least they should not have their way in Austria. It is symbolic that although the upper classes mixed freely with the people at the fêtes in the Prater and the Augarten, they should have maintained a chilly distance whenever it came to mixing with their immediate inferiors. For example, during the Carnival of 1835, as the price of attending a public ball, Princess Metternich (the chancellor's third wife) insisted on a roped enclosure being erected in the middle of the ballroom so that the noble visitors present might not come into contact with the bourgeois. And on another occasion, dining with a banker who had largely financed her husband, she prompted one of her attendants to bring her own gold plate and lay it on the table before her.

As the years went by – and especially after the upheavals which shook all Europe in 1830 – the position of Metternich became harder. While Francis lived, he could at least count on the sympathy of his master. It was a sympathy offered on terms, no doubt: so long as Metternich agreed with the emperor on matters of principle, the emperor would give him the negative support of a benevolent inertia. He would at any rate keep rivals away. But Francis was succeeded in 1835 by the feeble-minded Emperor Ferdinand, and almost at once Metternich's absolute power within the state was limited by

the creation of a Staatskonferenz – a committee of three, in which Metternich was given charge of foreign affairs while the internal conduct of the state fell to an enemy of long standing, Count Kolowrat.

Perhaps it was already too late. Metternich was sixty-two years old. His plans for Austria and for Europe might gain conviction with the passing of time; they could not develop. Now, however, after holding the reins of state in his hands for a generation, he found himself abruptly diminished. And not only that: he found himself vulnerable to the hostility of his colleagues. His health was declining, his optimism sinking. And during the twelve years which ended with the upheavals of 1848, the current of public opinion set finally against him. A new life was stirring throughout Europe. Ideas which could not be repressed by a censorship, however harsh, were crossing from frontier to frontier. And when the end came, during a hurried flight from Vienna, his wife wrote of him in her diary, 'This man whose daily habits and pleasures were the object of constant preoccupation, in aid of whose comfort I was trying up to yesterday to avoid draughts and chills, now, at 75, found himself shelterless and with no knowledge of where he might be the next day. ... He had seen in the space of 24 hours the collapse of all he had built up in a lifetime of work.'

That, no doubt, is what it looked like at the time. And during the liberal century which followed 1848 it was natural to associate the defeat of Metternich's ideas with a notion of their impropriety. At this distance, however, we can see that Metternich was both wiser and more valuable as an example than he is commonly admitted to be. He saw clearly that the older Europe had been swept away, and that a period of deadlock must ensue before a new Europe came into being. His fault lay in the assumption that a weakened Austria could be the instrument of that new order, and that it would suffice to ensure internal and external calm for a replenished and harmonious concert of nations to be formed under the inspiration of Vienna.

The nineteenth century rejected him, certainly (indeed, the rejection was mutual). But he would have been perfectly at home in the world of President Wilson, and still more in that of Franklin D. Roosevelt. A concept like the United Nations would have been exactly what he liked most – an orderly, schematic ideal with plenty of scope for manœuvre. And a world which has seen the mounting tyrannies of the last thirty years might, paradoxically, have reversed the judgment of his contemporaries and regretted, not his conservatism, but his lack of an effective national power during the crucial years which ended in 1835.

As it is, we cannot deny that the price paid by Austria for her generation of tranquillity was in the long run ruinous. Yet at the same time, it is easy to allow some feeling of envy to rise. Periods in which history seems to be suspended are the most dangerous of all. Beneath the quiet surface, cracks are forming through which the angry forces of nature will one day burst. But at least we can say of the Viennese – as we might say of the Parisians in the 1880s or of the Edwardian Londoners – that they were happy while it lasted. And no architect of an age can ask more than that.

Etching by Moritz von Schwind, from the title-page of a collection of Viennese dances.

PART THREE
MEGALOPOLIS

LONDON

THE AMERICAN CITY

NEW YORK

ECUMENOPOLIS

FOREWORD

THE GREAT AGES of some of the world's historic cities that have been surveyed in the first two parts of this book are not 'ancient history'. They are preludes and pointers to a new age on which we are now just entering; and this is the sense in which these cities are 'cities of destiny'. During the 9,000 years or so, reckoning back to the earliest stratum at Jericho, during which there have been such things as cities, these have been relatively small and few and far between. The vast majority of the human race has continued to live in the way in which it had begun to live when agriculture was invented and when animals were domesticated. It has continued to live in the open country and to make its living from crops and livestock, not from trade and industry. But in the near future, the vast majority of the people of the world are not going to be country-folk any longer; they are going to be city-dwellers. Country life, not city life, is going to become the exception, while city life will become the rule. All the once separate cities on the face of the earth are going to coalesce into a single continuous world-city with patches of agricultural land enveloped in it here and there. This has already happened in Japan, and present-day urbanized Japan gives us a pre-view of what the whole world is soon going to be like. Urban trade and industry are going to become predominant over rural production. In terms of productivity, the remnant of the countryside is going to become parasitic on the world-city, in contrast to the past relation between town and country, in which the town has been parasitic on the countryside.

This social revolution that is now taking place before our eyes is being produced by two causes. In the first place the application of scientific technology to agriculture and to animal husbandry is already resulting, in economically advanced countries, in a greater production per acre with a smaller number of hands; and this development is going eventually to spread all over the world. In the second place the reduction of the rate of premature deaths through improvements in public health is increasing the world's population by leaps and bounds. By AD 2000 it is likely to be two or three times its present size; and the great majority of this vastly increased population will be living in the world-city.

Here we have what is going to be mankind's principal problem if and when we succeed in eliminating the present danger of mass-suicide through atomic warfare. This problem of world-wide urbanization is now rushing to meet us. It is examined in the present part of this book, and the two preceding parts lead up to it and throw light on it.

The subjects of the following four chapters have been chosen to illustrate the gathering mass, momentum and speed of mankind's headlong rush into Megalopolis. This is a flying leap out of a traditional rural life which, by comparison with the current onset of urbanism, has been static and stable since our Neolithic ancestor made the last previous major revolution in the conditions of human life by domesticating a few of the plants and animals that are our fellow living creatures. In the race towards Megalopolis, London was a pioneer, but, unfortunately, not a pilot. New York is the nucleus of the North American ganglion of Megalopolis. The rise and growth of the American city are indexes of the speed with which life is changing in our time. The chapter on the coming world-city shows man striving, at the eleventh hour, to save himself from the fate of the Gadarene Swine.

Mr Fulford's Victorian London is a gipsy's magic mirror of a Wellsian 'shape of things to come'. My own family has been living through the London phase of urbanization during the last three generations. My grandfather was a farmer's son who became the first consultant aurist in London. He was already gravely concerned about the slums. My father was an officer of the Charity Organization Society, and his job was to do what could be done, strictly within the limits of private enterprise, to bind up the cruel wounds that urbanism was now inflicting on human life. On the staircase in our tall (four storeys tall!) London house, there hung the original ink-and-colour-wash sketch of a cartoon by George Cruickshank (given to my grandfather by the cartoonist, who was a friend of his). The title of the picture was *London Going out of Town*. An affluent minority was already 'going out of town' to find holiday relief from the horrors of the budding Megalopolis; but Victorian London was following close on the heels of these refugees. The picture shows the vandal city attacking and overwhelming a farm. London on the war-path is uprooting the trees, polluting the brooks, driving off the cattle with a pitchfork, and burying barns and fields under a cascade of bricks and a pall of smoke. My grandfather's own way of life illustrates the transition. He was a commuter between his town consulting-room and his suburban home, but, at the suburban rail-head of the local branch of the Metropolitan Railway, he was met by his horse, and he covered the last lap of his journey on that horse's back, as if he were still living in rural Lincolnshire.

However, the symptoms that had first appeared in London were soon duplicated in New York, and this on a scale that made the difference one of kind, and not just of degree. Cruickshank might have been hard put to it to devise a cartoon that would have been an adequate picture of New York's physical rush and roar, and it would hardly have been possible to portray visually the psychic restlessness that has been both a cause and an effect of those terrific physical phenomena. The problem of Megalopolis that New York illustrates is the moral one. How are we to salvage rural man when he has been trapped in an urban environment to which he is failing to adapt himself yet from which he has no escape? This is the problem of Harlem; and, in human terms, it is the problem of the Negroes and the Puerto Ricans. I once hovered over the middle of the island of Puerto Rico in a helicopter, and was able to peer down at the tiny isolated cottages, each set in its own miniature clearing in the midst of the insulating bush. Pick up one of those cottagers, detach him from his family and from his ancestral way of life, and dump him on the East Side of New York. How can you imagine that this stunning change of life is not going to knock him silly?

And then there is the speed of the process, which is the theme of Mr Nevins' chapter on the American city. The United States had barely given herself time to become a country of settled farmers instead of vagrant pioneers when she began to make herself over once again. The country of stable farmers now began to turn itself into a country of vagrant slum-dwellers and suburban commuters. Even as recently as the time of the Second World War, a majority of the American soldiers whom I met in London were country-bred boys who had never before seen a city of this size. Today, only twenty years later, we are told that the food-supply of the United States is being produced by not more than five per cent of her population. But Americans, like the rest of us, are subject to the limitations and necessities of human nature; and no human being can run forever at top speed; he must pause occasionally to take breath. In its rush towards Megalopolis the American people has not been allowing itself time to pause, and it is now sweeping the rest of mankind along with it, galloping at the intolerable American pace. What New York is today, Baghdad and Bombay and Caracas are going to be tomorrow.

This third part of the book is the concluding part, but it is not the conclusion of the story. The reader will have noticed that the first three chapters in this part all break out of the past and present into the future; and the fourth chapter is concerned with the future entirely. Mr Doxiadis is like some benevolent technician who has fitted a telescopic sight to a racing motorist's car. The technician hopes that the speeder will make use of this safety-device now that he has been equipped with it. If he neglects it, he is likely, before long, to wreck his car and break his own neck. The subject of this chapter is the problem of how to make human life livable in Megalopolis when Megalopolis has grown to its titanic future stature. This is one of the current problems that are challenges to mankind's capacity for survival. The problem of Megalopolis ranks, in importance, urgency, and difficulty, with the problems of atomic power and population. If and when these two other major current problems have been solved, Megalopolis will still be with us and with our descendants. We shall still be wrestling with it for as long as our feeble human faculty for prescience allows us to see ahead into the future.

Arnold Toynbee

275

VICTORIAN AND EDWARDIAN LONDON

The capital of the British Empire,

London at the turn of the twentieth century was the greatest city in the world, both in size and sphere of influence. The sprawling conurbation, spilling over its borders and swallowing up the surrounding countryside, had a population of four and a half million. Victoria, Queen of the United Kingdom of Great Britain and Ireland, Empress of India, for over sixty years between 1837 and 1901, sat on a throne to which a significant proportion of mankind, living in all continents of the world, owed allegiance.

London's prodigious growth – its population increased fivefold between 1800 and 1900 – was principally due to the Industrial Revolution and foreign trade. London was Britain's main port and warehouse, and along its vital artery, the Thames, raw materials flowed in one direction and finished goods, bound for the markets of the world, in the other. Within the boundary of the square mile known as the City, beat the golden heart of the empire. The great god was gold; here were situated the banks, the exchanges and all the involved commercial apparatus controlling the nation's financial destiny.

The gracious living of the aristocratic class and the ostentation of the *nouveaux riches* offset, to a large extent, the squalid conditions in which one-third of the population had to live. Yet the 'rookeries' of Victorian London, as slum-dwellings were called, were reminiscent of the meanest *insulae* in the capital of the greatest empire before Britain's, Rome. There was a social conscience, however, which manifested itself periodically in substantial acts of philanthropy, such as

George Peabody's gift of half a million pounds for the housing of London's poor; many of these 'Buildings' still exist.

It was an age of self-assurance and unbounded faith in the future. Building boomed and the face of London was transformed. New bridges were thrust across the Thames, the Embankment was created, the docks enlarged. Markets, hospitals, hotels, museums sprang up. The railways proliferated and London's underground transport system was born. The majority of public buildings in use today – and a considerable proportion of domestic buildings too – were constructed during this period.

The old Palace of Westminster, part of which went back to Norman times, was rebuilt to Charles Barry's design after it burnt down in 1834. The magnificent new buildings, Gothic in style, and a worthy home for the 'mother of parliaments', were opened in 1852 by Queen Victoria who then knighted the architect. The photograph opposite was taken from an adjacent public park, looking towards the House of Lords. (The House of Commons and Big Ben are not visible from this vantage.) Victoria Tower – 336 feet high and the tallest square tower in the world – rising majestically in the background, is the sovereign's entrance for the ceremonial opening of Parliament. Featured in the foreground is a drinking-fountain, typical, though perhaps more than usually florid, of others to be seen in London; it was erected in 1865, according to the inscription, 'in commemoration of the emancipation of slaves 1834'. (1)

Billingsgate has been London's fish market since at least the end of the seventeenth century, although the building shown in the old photograph (left, *c.* 1892) dates from only 1877. To 'talk Billingsgate' has, for many hundreds of years, meant to use uncouth language. The author of a Victorian guidebook, who advised his readers that the best time to visit Billingsgate was at five o'clock in the morning, forewarned them, not about the rough talk, but about the 'ancient and fish-like smell'. (2)

London Bridge for five hundred years, from early in the twelfth century to 1750, was the only bridge to the south bank of the Thames. The present bridge, shown in a photograph of about 1909 (right), was completed in 1831 and widened in 1904. The crowd had gathered on this occasion to watch squadrons of the fleet on the river below. (4)

The heart of the City

and, by extension, of Britain and the empire, was the area shown in the photograph on the left, taken in about 1907. This open space, bounded on the left by the Bank of England, 'the old lady of Threadneedle Street' as it was affectionately called, and in the centre by the Royal Exchange, was – indeed still remains – the focal point of London's venerable financial institutions. The Royal Exchange was designed by William Tite in the classical style. Queen Victoria opened it with great ceremony in 1844; the Duke of Wellington was present, and saw his own statue (visible in front of the façade) being unveiled.

At about the same time that the photographer recorded this active street scene, a prescient social commentator was writing: 'The motor car, which is gradually beginning to appear in the streets, may possibly supersede all other vehicles ... [it] would require nothing but a little cleaning ... [but] it must be worked without jar and without the smell of oil.' (3)

Half the world's coal supply, until 1870, was mined in Britain. It was vital to metallurgy and shipping, two of the mainstays of Britain's industrial pre-eminence. Above: the revolutionary iron-and-glass dome surmounting the Coal Exchange, opened in 1849. (5)

'The workshop of the world' was not an aspiration, but a statement of fact. England imported raw materials and exported finished goods. Above: St Katharine's Docks, opened in 1828 and still in use, were built on the site of the old royal and collegiate chapel of St Katharine by the Tower. (8)

The advantages of steel and the Victorian *penchant* for ornate embellishment were combined in Tower Bridge, completed in 1894. The detail on the left shows riveting arranged with an ornamental effect and the cast-iron tracery of the balustrade. (6)

Smithfield Market was the world's largest cattle-market in the mid-nineteenth century. At that time it had accommodation for 4,000 head of cattle and 24,000 head of sheep. As there were slaughter-houses in the vicinity, local inhabitants pressed the Corporation of the City of London to remove what was to them a constant nuisance. This was eventually done. The live market was transferred to north London and the Italianate-style building, shown above in a contemporary coloured lithograph, was opened in 1868, dealing in meat and, later, poultry. (7)

'Safe as the Bank of England'. Since the late 1700s, when the Bank was attacked by rioters, a military guard has been in attendance each night. The Bank was originally established in 1694 by Royal Charter. During the nineteenth century, members of the public who had invested in government securities would present themselves at the Bank on the appointed day each year to collect their dividends. Right: a detail from the painting *Dividend Day, 1850* by G. E. Hicks shows a cross-section of the Bank's clients. (9)

London County Council was created in 1888 by special Act of Parliament to administer the complicated affairs of the capital. The opening meeting of the Council (above) was held in 1889 in the Guildhall. Lord Rosebery was in the chair. (16)

The underprivileged Londoner had a harsh and dismal life. Grinding poverty and squalor were the backdrop against which the elegance of the upper classes has to be seen. Destitute men, 'dossers', who mostly slept rough, were to be found all along the Embankment. At about midnight Salvation Army workers issued free meal tickets (left above). Three young children – street urchins – are shown (left below) gazing into the window of a small shop. Barefoot children were a common sight in Victorian times, even in the depths of the London winter. Flower sellers (one is portrayed on the right) used the steps of the fountain in Piccadilly Circus as their base, but dispersed to other areas where trade looked promising. The streets of the City, where gentlemen considered a fresh *boutonnière* to be a necessary item of dress, provided a good market. (14, 15, 17)

Ornamental lettering in wrought iron was typical of Victorian and Edwardian taste; the example shown below is on a building that still exists. (19)

Victorian architecture is characterized by the imitation of past styles, the most popular revival having been the Gothic. St Pancras Station and Hotel, like a vast medieval cathedral, dominate the skyline in John O'Connor's *Pentonville Road* (above), painted in 1881. The general aspect remains little changed today; the tall spires still present a similar picture when viewed from Pentonville Road. Sir Gilbert Scott's terminal hotel almost completely hides the train shed designed by William Barlow. The shed, with its 243-foot span of cast-iron and glass (just visible to the right of the spires), had – and retained for a century – the distinction of possessing the largest roof in the world without internal support. The arched entrance to the station (above left) is a compendium of Gothic details.

A modern critic has written of this building-complex: 'It stands as a monument to the great age of steam power and mid-Victorian self-confidence, when Britain was top nation in the world.' (18, 20)

The Royal Courts of Justice were built when the Gothic Revival was at its height; of the six architects invited to compete for the project, five submitted plans in the Gothic style. The competition aroused great public interest and the eventual winner was G. E. Street, whose building in the Strand is often mistaken by the casual visitor for an authentic medieval structure. Thirty-five million bricks and a million cubic feet of stone were used. The architect, perhaps exhausted by his monumental labours, died before the new law courts were opened in 1882. (21)

'Eros', the fountain (left) in Piccadilly Circus which commemorates the philanthropic Lord Shaftesbury (d. 1885), is a landmark of London's theatreland. Sir Henry Irving (above) – seen with Ellen Terry – was the most accomplished actor of the age. (22, 23)

'Bubbles', a portrait of his own grandson, was painted in 1886 by Sir John Millais, a leading pre-Raphaelite and president of the Royal Academy. Bought by a soap company to advertise its product, 'Bubbles' became the best-known poster of its time. (24)

Varied aesthetic tastes were catered for in London's places of entertainment. Apart from the theatres there were the music-halls; the Alhambra (left), photographed in 1899, was one of the most popular. The 'Gaiety Girls' (right) were a spectacularly successful music-hall turn towards the end of the century. Covent Garden Theatre, photographed in 1896 (above), is still the home of grand opera in London. (25, 26, 27)

Polite society descended upon Burlington House for the occasion which was generally held to mark the annual opening of the London social season: the private view at the Royal Academy. In the above painting of this event (1881), William Powell Frith, RA, included portraits of leading personalities on the late-Victorian scene. Among many others, the young Oscar Wilde, wearing his green carnation, is prominent towards the right of the picture. (28)

In their heyday, there were about 500 music-halls in London. Walter Sickert, whose *Old Bedford* in Camden Town (1907) is shown below left, found inspiration in them for some of his most appealing work. Below: *The Café Royal* (1911), by Charles Ginner, gives an impression of the restaurant founded in 1865. Providing an atmosphere until then known only in Paris, it attracted the more theatrical talents of London at the turn of the century. (29, 30)

Albert, the Prince Consort, died in 1861; for Queen Victoria there remained thirty-nine years of widowhood. Albert had a special interest in promoting science and art, and especially the application of science to industry. He instigated the Great Exhibition of 1851, and its overwhelming success was largely his own. He is commemorated by the Albert Memorial (right), a remarkable example of over-elaborated neo-Gothic erected in Kensington Gardens in 1876. It consists of a colossal gun-metal statue of the seated Prince under a resplendent spire surmounted by a cross. (31)

'The Lungs of London' – thus the elder Pitt described Hyde Park. In 1536, during the reign of Henry VIII, the park, formerly an ancient manor, passed into the possession of the crown as a royal hunting-ground. By 1637 it had become a public park. *A Summer Day in Hyde Park* (below) was painted in 1858 by John Ritchie in the style of Frith. The scene is on the Serpentine looking towards Marble Arch, which can be seen on the horizon, just to the left of the coachman's head. To the right of Marble Arch is Park Lane, at that time the most fashionable address in London, studded with the great town mansions of the nobility. (32)

ROGER FULFORD

As THE NINETEENTH century drew to its close, London was easily the largest city in the world. With a population of four and a half million, it exceeded the population of New York by one million, of Paris by two million, and of Vienna by three million. Anyone who had known eighteenth-century London – that thriving, self-reliant, and compact city admirably described for us in the pages of Boswell's *Life of Johnson* – would have been astounded by this colossal expansion, which had been experienced by the capital in the short space of a century. The two principal causes of this were the growth of foreign trade and the application of numerous inventions to home manufactures which brought about the Industrial Revolution. But the natural energy and ingenuity of Londoners, which is one of their abiding characteristics, also has its place in any estimate of the reasons for the phenomenal growth of London. For more than anything else it was the prosperity of London which revealed that 'the nation of shopkeepers' (as Napoleon had once described England) had been transformed into 'the workshop of the world' – a phrase coined by Disraeli.

The workshop of the world

The following facts illustrate the truth of this point. Until 1870 Great Britain raised more than half the whole coal supply of the world. In that year the combined trade of the United Kingdom and the British empire was greater than that of France, Germany, Italy and the United States put together. The abandonment of the old Protectionist system of trade in the 1840s gave a great impetus to British shipping and magnified the significance of London as a port. In 1800 the tonnage of ships coming into the docks of London was nearly 800,000; by 1880 the figure had reached nearly 8,000,000. The fact that London was first and foremost a market and not the centre of a manufacturing district is shown by the value of the imports into London being more than double that of the exports. But the history of London during these years is but a reflection of what was going on throughout Europe at this time. The old courtly, traditional civilization, based on agriculture and petty manufactures, was being pushed on one side by the emergence of commercial nations, devoting their skill and endurance to the capture of markets. Of this London was the pioneer and on this her rise to pre-eminence was founded.

The first impression of any visitor to London during these years would have been of the vast dimensions of the town. This is illustrated by some comments made in his diary by a member of the United States Legation in England. Looking over the capital from some high ground to the south on a lovely evening in May in the 1860s, he was astounded by what he called 'the magnitude of London'; in attempting to describe his impression he used the simple but effective phrase 'London is illimitable'. The great town stretched in an almost unbroken mass of bricks and mortar and stone to the hills of Hampstead and Highgate in the north, past the densely crowded poor quarter of the East End to the flats of Essex, and through a great diversity of prosperous villas to the chalk and conifers of Surrey in the south, and to those historic fields in the west through which flowed the Thames and where Runnymede lay.

Financial solidity

The size of London showed at once that it was both the capital and a great commercial town, for this dual aspect is the true explanation of its size and power. Yet of these twin foundations the surest and the most important was London's long-standing pre-eminence in both commerce and finance. For that reason the curious observer was invariably anxious to see the City – because there, and in the docks which adjoined it, were congregated all the bustle and activity of money and of commerce. In the heart of the City, exuding confidence, respectability and tradition was the Bank of England which had stood supreme among the banking houses of the world for two centuries. Possibly the best indication of what the Bank stood for in the life of London was to be seen on 'Dividend Day'. In the twentieth century the majority of people who own British government securities have dividends sent through the post; at the end of the nineteenth century, when the number of these investors was infinitely smaller than today, it was usual for many of them to go to the Bank and collect the dividends themselves. 'Dividend Day' at the Bank in the closing days of the nineteenth century afforded a fascinating study in human nature – the rich, of course, predominating but yet varied by shabby-looking individuals of miserly habit, who owned perhaps thousands of pounds in gilt-edged stock, or nervous-looking widows clutching possibly their sole resources for the year. And out of sight lay all the glittering expressions of the wealth and might of London and England – the great ingots of gold and the sovereigns and half-sovereigns with the beautifully designed head of the widowed Queen Victoria and, on the reverse side, the proudly capering figure of St George. Nothing seemed to emphasize the financial dominance of London so effectively as this solidity of the Bank of England. Lying close to the Bank were the headquarters of the financial institutions of the empire – joint-stock and foreign banks, shipping and insurance companies, stockbroking firms and trust companies. All these great financial and commercial houses, no less than the streets which surrounded them, were an exclusively male preserve. Like the Houses of Parliament and like all government offices at that time, the City of London was kept inviolate from the advances of women. At the end of the century one or two progressive firms admitted women to work the recently invented typewriting machines but broadly speaking all was masculine – top-hats were everywhere and even the humblest City clerks aped the subfusc clothes and formal attire of the financier.

Within the boundaries of the City was to be found the proof that the greatness of London and the survival of England depended on the flow of foreign trade, for in the establishment of London's supremacy trade played a part for which, in the history of Europe, Venice alone provides a counterpart. At the eastern end of the City were the great marts where goods were exchanged – corn in Mark Lane, rubber and tea in Mincing Lane, coal in Lower Thames Street, wool in Coleman Street, and diamonds and precious stones in Hatton Garden. Outside the City, on the other side of the Thames, were the exchanges for hops, butter and bacon. Behind these exchanges were the docks – the arteries through which flowed the life and prosperity of London. Many years ago it was well said that England was

Possibility of a career for woman in business: advertisement for a Female School of Typewriting, c. 1879.

balanced on the end of a collier's pick-axe, meaning that coal was the commodity by which the nation paid for its food and raw materials, and it was not less true to say that the life of London depended on the muscle and brawn of the dockers at the waterfront. The way in which the fortunes of the capital were bound up with the dockers was forcibly illustrated by the great dock strike in 1889. In the summer of that year almost all the dockers in London came out on strike with the demand that they should be paid at the flat rate of 6d. an hour. The dock companies obstinately held out against this scale of pay, but public opinion, perhaps conscious of how much turned on the dockers, was largely against the employers. When two of the strike leaders came to negotiate with representatives of the companies in the City, they had the heartening but extraordinary experience of being loudly cheered by a group of businessmen in this stronghold of respectability. This is an example of that underlying humanity of London which was a powerful influence in moulding its history at this time.

Aristocratic splendour

Yet in spite of the fact that London was essentially a commercial city, life at the summit was conducted with a splendour which has not been exceeded in history. King Leopold I of the Belgians, who was familiar from boyhood with the courts and capitals of Europe, decided after staying at Buckingham Palace that there was no country 'where such magnificence exists' as in England. The public functions of the English court at Buckingham Palace or St James's Palace – such as a Drawing Room, a Levee, or a Presentation – were conducted in a style which was exacting but not finicky, awe-inspiring but not absurd. The richness and variety of the ladies' clothes on these occasions – the costly, silken trains of brilliant colours – amber, sky-blue, or deep green – were a reminder of the solid foundations of wealth of which the English court was to some extent the expression. An American who attended one of these functions confessed that his eyes ached with the quantity and richness of the spectacle.

The English aristocracy was quite distinct from its counterpart on the continent of Europe; there *la haute aristocratie* was an exclusive section of the community – possibly poor, but proud and slightly forbidding; but in England it was constantly recruited and refreshed by intermarriage with the manufacturing and City classes. One consequence of this merging of the classes was that the jealousy of the aristocracy, which often marked other European countries, was not conspicuous in London at this time. Indeed the feelings of most people ran rather to imitation of their social superiors than to envy. Therefore the organization of the top strata of London life had something in common with the kind of commercial oligarchy which flourished in Venice at its prime.

The solid dignity of the wealthy classes, which was marked both in the aristocracy and in those on the fringe of society, was obvious to all, and it made itself felt in many of the activities of the capital. At Westminster – in the House of Commons and the House of

Lords – the government of the country was conducted against an unchanging background of formality and tradition. Members of both Houses invariably appeared in the standard uniform of frock-coat and silk hat, and when in 1892 the first Labour Member of Parliament was elected, Victorian London was scandalized not so much by his election as by his appearing at Westminster in a tweed coat and a cloth cap. For their relaxation Members of Parliament belonged to clubs, chosen according to their political bias, where the surroundings and the countless liveried men-servants matched the splendours of the homes of the nobility slightly farther to the west. The chief professions in London then were the Church and the Bar, and these were both marked by a high style of personal comfort and even by profusion. A garden-party at Lambeth or at Fulham Palace (the homes respectively of the Archbishop of Canterbury and the Bishop of London) was one of the outstanding features of the London social season. But even the most successful professional man never lost sight of the value of money; once when the Lord Chancellor (and in those days his princely salary of £10,000 a year amounted to a very substantial private fortune) was driving in Piccadilly, his horses bolted and he was heard shouting out of the window to his coachmen, 'For God's sake drive into something cheap.'

The same solid and dignified standards governed those who carried on their business within the golden square mile of the City of London; they likewise had their maxims based on success and integrity and they were the first to despise fortunes made from unorthodoxy or from lucky speculations. They remained at the end of Queen Victoria's reign very much as they have been drawn for us by Charles Dickens in the middle years of the century. They were perhaps a trifle vulgar, indifferent to the arts and culture and too partial to the fleshly joys of eating and drinking, but with it all sound, dependable, and guided by certain rules of what could and could not be done. All these classes – the aristocratic, the parliamentary, the professional, and the commercial, with a huge retinue of shop-assistants, servants, and clerks ministering to them and copying them – provided the main-spring which regulated the mechanism which governed the great community of London.

The other side of the coin

Certainly in any account of London at this time it is essential to emphasize that if there was great prosperity and if there were great prizes to be won these went hand in hand with deplorable poverty and desperate disillusion. The squalor and degradation of life in some quarters of the East End were scarcely to be credited. To working-class audiences, Radical speakers were fond of pointing the contrast between the glories of empire and the horrors of life at its heart. A favourite question was this: 'What is the good of belonging to an empire on which the sun never sets if you live in a court on which it never rises?' Nothing perhaps brought home more vividly how precarious life was for thousands of honest Londoners than the scene at a busy pawnbroker's on a Saturday night. Furniture, trinkets, and even the tools of a man's trade were marched off to one of these brightly lit emporiums, with their swinging emblems of the three brass balls, in an effort to exist over Sunday with the hope that the new week might bring better times and regular work. The nicely balanced economic mechanism of London was kept in place by what was unquestionably the curse of the day – casual labour. Any visitor to London was quickly struck by the sudden appearance of an abject, dishevelled figure – seeming to spring up from nowhere – eager to earn a copper by holding a horse, by sweeping a path across the street clear of dung and mud, or by fetching a cab. Similarly anyone who was astir in the morning would have been immediately aware of the sprinkling of casuals, waiting in the hope that the sickness of a regular worker – even an omnibus driver or conductor – might lead to a day's employment. Another illustration of the dire poverty which existed just below the surface is afforded by the aftermath of the famous Tooley Street fire. A huge storehouse, filled with butter, close to the docks, caught fire and burned for several days. Streams of melting butter were carried away by the Thames, and where it was deposited by the tides, urchins scooped it up and found a ready market for their mixture of burned butter and river mud.

Yet London at this time had a strong social conscience and was in this respect outstanding and remarkable among the capitals of Europe. Gone were the days when poverty was a crime; the point of view satirized by Bernard Shaw in *Major Barbara* that 'our first duty is not to be poor' would have found small currency among intelligent citizens of London at the end of the nineteenth century. This is an important point because it was something new: in past centuries great prosperity had gone hand in hand with complete indifference to the fate of those who, in the economic struggle, went to the wall. In London the man who crystallized attention on this subject was Charles Booth, whose scientific investigations into conditions in London were published in the 1890s. His researches were collected under the omnibus title of *Life and Labour of the People of London*; they were based largely on the reports of school visitors and on information amassed by various charitable bodies.

Simultaneously with this attempt to analyse the problem of poverty went a real effort to ameliorate it. To give two examples: unorthodox religion formed the Salvation Army which was founded in Whitechapel in 1865, and the stalwarts of the Army combined a trumpet call to repentance with the tangible earthly blessing of shelter and food. While it was easy to laugh at the Salvation Army (as the author of *The Belle of New York* found) such laughter, on closer acquaintance, was apt to become respectful and affectionate. More conventional religion provided Oxford House, Toynbee Hall, and Mansfield Hall, where university and public-school youths could live in the East End and bring to its denizens some savour of a larger and nobler existence. This social conscience also manifested itself in substantial acts of private benevolence. The money which individual members of the Rothschild family distributed in charity for the benefit of Londoners was astounding. At Christmas each year Lord Rothschild gave a brace of pheasants to all the omnibus drivers and many of the cabbies plying in central London. The more grateful ones used to tie their benefactor's racing colours to their whips.

From the harsh countries of eastern Europe, driven out by terrors, purges and privations, immigrants drifted to London in the certainty that they would be free from persecution and in the hope that they might be able to scratch together a livelihood. The majority of these were Russians, Poles, and Rumanians; for the most part they found work as 'sweaters' in the tailoring or boot trades. But here again London showed that even for such people (whose claim on its solicitude was only slender) the capital would not tolerate gross abuses, and their conditions were the subject of special inquiry by a committee of the House of Lords at the end of the century. Many of them were, of course, Jews – by the end of Queen Victoria's reign the Jewish colony in London numbered at least 100,000 – and they were to a large extent cared for by various philanthropic organizations run by members of their own race.

The great god gold

It should not for a moment be supposed that the wealth of London was apparent only to those who moved in the charmed circle of the court, the aristocracy, or the well-to-do business community. As the traveller from the provinces or visitor from abroad stepped out from one of the termini he was at once conscious of the thriving and bustling prosperity in which he was moving. In a passage in one of his letters Charles Lamb gives expression to his idea of the richness of London life. He writes: 'O her lamps of a night! Her rich goldsmiths, print-shops, toy-shops, mercers, hardwaremen, pastry cooks ... These are thy Gods O London!' But what would Lamb's language have been if he could have seen seventy years ahead and looked into the shop-windows in Piccadilly, Regent Street, Bond Street, and Oxford Street in all their glory in the 1890s? Any visitor to London had but to stroll along those streets, gazing at the wonderfully dressed shop-windows to his right and left, to realize the full force of worldly temptation and to see how easy it would be to fall down and worship the great god gold. In the twentieth century London shoppers are accustomed to windows, which may be arresting but which too often prove on examination to be grimly bare. At the end of the nineteenth century, profusion was essential in order to catch the eye of the passer-by. 'Everything into the shop-window' was the ideal. The drapers' shops, for instance, were dazzling and tempting – huge rolls of silks, satins and velvets, carpets, dress-materials and woollens, linen, art-needlework and hosiery, lace gloves and mantles were all grouped and blended in a blaze of colour.

The prominence of business, of commerce, and of shopping would have been the most constant impression which any foreign visitor to London would have taken away with him. He would have felt that he had been a part of a community which was essentially money-making. Naturally this concentration on commerce was not without its influence on art and letters. Victorian London was certainly not completely dead to the importance of art, but to some degree art was smothered by the prevailing commercial characteristics of the time. Huge prices were paid to successful painters, and with the proceeds they bought or built unwieldy palaces in which they gave conventional parties for people who, like themselves, had achieved distinction in society. Lord Leighton, Millais, and Sir Lawrence Alma-Tadema, who were all prominent Royal Academicians (the first two being Presidents) all lived in substantial style in the inner suburbs – each a witness to the prosperity of Victorian art. The Private View Day at the Royal Academy – which, ironically enough, was generally held to mark the beginning of the social season in London – was an annual rendezvous for all the leaders of English society, politics and the professions. The traffic in Piccadilly was disjointed for hours and the paintings hung somewhat neglected on the walls while the building rang with laughter, chat, and social courtesy.

In London there was no art quarter, and students, unlike their counterparts in Paris or Munich, had few chances of easily meeting together outside the art classroom. In spite of this somewhat unpropitious climate Victorian London yet succeeded in producing some fine pictures and buildings – the St Pancras railway station is a case in point – which were not wholly unworthy of a great city at its prime. But in London, as indeed throughout the whole country at this time, there was a preoccupation with worldly success and an indifference to culture which even the warmest admirer of the Victorian age has to admit and regret. Ruskin once expressed this feeling in an outburst of characteristic vigour. He wrote: 'This yelping,

Headquarters of William Booth's Christian Mission, which was renamed the Salvation Army in 1876.

carnivorous crowd mad for money and lust, tearing each other to pieces and starving each other to death, and leaving heaps of their dung and pools of their spittle on every palace floor and altar stone.' Though to some extent this language might seem exaggerated, it drew attention to that streak of the Philistine in Victorian England which left a decided mark on the life of London. People found that it was only too easy to worship comfort and call it civilization.

Yet these strictures would have to be qualified by the admission that, at any rate on the religious side, Victorian London devoted its energies to something which was not commercial and which was not Philistine. In the fashionable and residential parts of London, the Sunday morning parade was virtually compulsory and the crowds thronged the churches in the 1890s in much the same way that their grandchildren later filled the cinemas. On a Sunday evening it was possible to be sure of a seat in Westminster Abbey only by getting there at least half an hour before the service began. One consequence of this attention to religion was that the clergy were very influential in London. A large part of the feelings aroused over the conditions of the poor sprang from knowledge obtained by the clergy and church workers in the course of their parochial visiting. The politicians – even the Socialists – really worked on facts provided for them by the churches. It was not chance that the Bishop of London and the Cardinal-Archbishop of Westminster were the two men largely instrumental in settling the dock strike in 1889.

Variety, noise and gaiety

A visitor coming to London at the end of the nineteenth century would have searched in vain for those obvious and spectacular glories of architecture which had distinguished the cities of Italy, or for the preoccupation with learning and philosophy which had been a characteristic of many of the large towns of Germany. To some extent these things did exist but they were not obvious – not the essence of London. And perhaps after the impression of wealth, the predominant picture left on the mind of a foreigner would have been of the immense variety of London. Coupled with this and clearly perceptible through all the noise and bustle were the gaiety and vitality of the town. There perhaps lay the secret of London's individual character: there certainly lay its difference from many of the other capitals of Europe. For the overriding impression of London was of human beings, not of bricks and mortar. Again it is Charles Lamb who, in a telling phrase, puts into words this aspect of the life of London. He wrote: 'All the streets and pavements are pure gold, I warrant you. At least I know an alchemy that turns her mud into that metal – a mind that loves to be at home in crowds.'

Nor would it be any exaggeration to suggest that it was the streets which focused the attention of the stranger on the gay variety of London life. They were far noisier than is often supposed by people whose only acquaintance with horse-drawn traffic is through hearing it mimicked by an agreeable 'clop-clop' produced behind the scenes at a theatre or cinema. At night an uneasy sleeper could hear the noise of a single, quick-moving cart or carriage from a quarter of a mile away as it rattled over the uneven granite setts with which the majority of streets were paved. Many people wrongly suppose that the roar of traffic is something which began with tram, motor-bus and motor-car, but that is not so. It was Tennyson who wrote as far back as 1852 of 'streaming London's central roar'. Although to the elderly and neurotic noise is doubtless highly offensive, it is not scientifically untrue to say that it leads to an increase of energy in human beings, and it was (and is) undoubtedly an element in the generally stimulating effect of being in London.

The spectacle of the traffic in those days was memorably gay. Although the pillar-box red of the modern motor-bus is fine and striking, it is uniform. Sixty years ago the streets were bright with buses and trams of varying colours. They might be blue, green, white, yellow, brown, chocolate, black, or red, and they were set off by the sober hues of the private carriages and the distinctly shabby look of cabs or 'growlers'. The craftsmanship which went into the building and painting of London vehicles was something of which the metropolis was rightly proud for they helped to give a general effect which was striking and elegant. This was enhanced by the hansom-cab, with its glistening body and burnished metal, and with its pair of large wheels generally picked out in yellow or scarlet paint. Cabs were latterly fitted with rubber wheels and to give warning of their approach they had a jingle of bells attached to the horses' necks. Characteristic of that attention to trifles, which marked the Cockney at that time, was the careful arrangement of a gay little bunch of flowers inside the cab. The driver, perched high at the top of his vehicle, had a wonderful command of the streets and his comments on the passing pageant, relayed to his passengers through a trap-door in the roof, was an education in that quickness of wit which was developed by life in the capital. It was Disraeli who summed up the excitement and romance of a journey by hansom-cab when he called it 'the gondola of London'.

The vigour and liveliness of the streets spread to the pavements. Among the pavement *habitués* the most conspicuous were possibly the large army of shoe-shiners. The streets were less efficiently cleaned than in a modern city – partly owing to the horse-dung – and there was in consequence a big demand for shoes to be cleaned. The most successful of the fraternity offered their clients a comfortable chair, with a plentiful supply of periodicals, and really regarded themselves as being equal in importance with the hairdresser. They introduced an agreeable splash of colour with their jackets: red was the most common but it varied according to the district – blue in the East End, white at Marylebone, and brown at King's Cross. Like the hansom-cab driver they beguiled their patron's leisure with plenty of pungent chat. One consequence of the rapid tempo of London life on those born and nurtured there was illustrated by the speed and eel-like quality of the boys who acted as street orderlies. Armed with a hand-brush and scoop, and wearing a jacket of conspicuous red, they darted among the traffic whisking up the dung from among the *mêlée* of the horses' hooves. This process was not without danger, and if the boys were injured they were entitled to a pension of 10s. a week for life.

The struggle beneath the surface

But if the streets were gay with life and movement, they could also remind the observer of the struggle to live which was never far below the surface in London. The crossing sweeper, shabby and dishevelled, his broom often worn down to the wood, hoped to earn a copper by cleaning the path in front of some wealthy pedestrian. A dry wind and a burst of sunshine would probably convert him into a match-seller. In addition to these recognized classes the pavement was thronged with typical Cockneys eager for business. Here were paraded for sale the most astounding mechanical toys ranging

from a clockwork hansom-cab to a poodle which barked. Besides toys almost everything could be bought on the kerbstones, from walking-sticks to groundsel for the canary, from shirt-studs to comic songs. Everything was sold to the accompaniment of an arresting but unceasing patter. Many of the salesmen were abjectly poor, and the purchaser of some trifle often had the feeling that his or her copper might make all the difference between a night in the open on the Embankment or a tolerably comfortable bed in a lodging-house. There were in London alone at this time over a thousand of these doss-houses – some for women, some for married couples, but mostly for men. For 4 d. a night a man could be assured of warmth and a good night's rest, but the very number of these places illustrated the uncertainties confronting labour. An analysis of these street vendors, holding their goods in meek silence or to the accompaniment of a rather reproachful whine, showed that many of them – here and there they were educated and had even in happier times owned their own small businesses – were the weakest who, in the economic struggle, had gone to the wall.

Drink: degradation and comradeship

No picture of London at this time would be complete which did not give some account of life in the public-house and of the part it played in the entertainment of those living there. While it is perfectly true that both the theatre and the music-hall had never been so prosperous and successful as they were in these years, they catered to some extent for a migrant public – visitors and those who came up to London for a conventional night out. In those days before cinemas, wireless, the general spread of libraries, and working-men's clubs, public-houses provided the permanent residents of the city with their sole means of communal recreation. In singling out the undoubted attractions of the public-house, we should keep the picture in proportion by remembering the colossal abuses of alcohol at this time. The various social workers, investigating conditions in the poorest parts of London, were unanimous in condemning drink as the principal cause – often the only cause – of squalor, degradation and poverty. The hours in which drink could be bought were virtually unlimited, and it was not uncommon to see workmen hurrying into the public-house for a tot of gin on their way to work at six o'clock in the morning. Many enlightened people, especially in the Radical section of the Liberal Party, felt that if the scourge of drunkenness was firmly tackled half the programmes of social reform to which politicians were committed would be unnecessary.

None the less the picture of the drink trade was not wholly black, and the fairer side was shown in the comradeship and cheerfulness of the London 'pub'. An intelligent foreigner once observed, after a prolonged study of the destination boards on London buses, that the omnibus system of London must have been designed to take the hard-drinking citizens from one public-house to another. This was understandable enough when it is remembered that the commonest termini of buses were *The Angel* at Islington, *The Crown* at Cricklewood, *The Elephant and Castle* at Newington, *The Welsh Harp* at Hendon, *The Manor House* at Finsbury, or *The Swiss Cottage* in Finchley Road. But these were the great renowned houses of London and it was perhaps in the smaller, more secluded establishments that the essence of Cockney friendliness seemed enshrined. Such a place was well described by W.W. Jacobs when he wrote, 'A little pub in the turning off the Mile End Road – clean as a new pin, and as quiet and

respectable as a front parlour. Everybody calling the landlady "Ma", and the landlady calling most of them by their Christian names, and asking after their families There were two poll parrots in cages, with not a bad word between them – except once when a man played the cornet outside – and a canary that almost sang its heart out.' In these places (as in so much of London) the best things – the company, the glowing coal fire, the highly polished mugs and glasses, the cosy nooks – were thrown in free. The *habitués* of the public-house have been well described by a survivor from those days:

> We met simply to be ourselves for a short time, to throw off the trappings that we had to wear in civilized society, to discuss affairs of the day, sometimes to be rude to one another, and for a time we all glowed in the fascinating light of human individuality.

Exploding population and drastic change

Nothing illustrates more clearly the sudden spectacular leap forward during the nineteenth century than the figures of population. In 1800 there were only 800,000 people in London. In 1820 there were 1,200,000, in 1840 there were 1,800,000, and in 1860 there were 2,800,000; in 1880 there were 3,000,000, and by the end of the century the number had reached the figure quoted at the beginning of this chapter. Men of eighty at the end of the century, who had passed their lives in the capital, had seen the face of London change beyond recognition. With the exception of Waterloo Bridge, they would have seen the building or rebuilding of every bridge across the Thames. Such people could also remember the building of the Houses of Parliament, the British Museum, the great markets for meat, fish and fruit, nearly all the hospitals, the banks, the hotels, the General Post Office, the theatres, Trafalgar Square with its awe-inspiring monument to British naval greatness, Northumberland Avenue, Kingsway, Piccadilly Circus, Holborn Viaduct, Victoria Street and the Embankment along the Thames. In addition such people could have watched the creation of most of the docks, all the tramways, the underground railways and the railway termini. Moreover they would have seen whole tracts of farming land turned into residential areas.

Although emphasis in this chapter has been placed on the distresses and dire misfortunes of poverty, it is also right to stress the great efforts which were made during this period to improve the lot of the unfortunate. Some thoughtful observers might argue that these efforts were not less worthy of admiration than the more obvious structural embellishments of the time. Anyone recalling those filthy streets and alley-ways described by Dickens, and then looking forward to the housing improvements at the end of the century, would at once be conscious of what this advance meant in the amelioration of human suffering. One of the men in the van of the movement to improve the housing conditions of London was an American, George Peabody, who gave half a million for the re-housing of the London poor. In his huge blocks of flats known as Peabody Buildings working men were given homes with baths and laundries attached. The first was built in Spitalfields but others quickly followed in the inner suburbs – Islington, Bermondsey and Chelsea.

Equally impressive was the expansion of schools during these years. Apart from the Board Schools which, after the introduction of compulsory education in 1870, multiplied with great rapidity, the growth of schools for the middle classes and of establishments for adult education was striking.

Workers' dwellings. Designs of Rowland Plumbe for a housing estate at Hornsey. The terrace at far left consisted of 'first-class' houses. The other terrace was described as 'second-class'.

Perhaps, therefore, the most striking and most remarkable achievement of London at its zenith lay in what was done to improve the well-being of the race. Certainly it was to that aspect of their life that Londoners themselves would have pointed as their most considerable triumph for, like all who lived in nineteenth-century England, they believed above all else in progress and improvement. The genius who adorned the City of London in the seventeenth century – Sir Christopher Wren – is buried in St Paul's Cathedral and on his tomb are inscribed proud words of advice to posterity – *Circumspice, si Monumentum requiris*. So might it have been said to one wandering through the streets of London in search of a trophy to the pioneer work in social reform achieved by the British people in the nineteenth century. Writing at the time of his retirement from politics, Mr Gladstone expressed his opinion that the half-century from 1840 to 1890 would be known as the 'half-century of emancipation'. In that work – and it might well be argued that this was the greatest contribution made by the genius of the British people to the civilization of Europe – London played a part which was conspicuous and illustrious.

A city possessed by the crowd

Many years before this period, in the placid calm of the eighteenth century, Dr Johnson agreed in conversation with a friend that Fleet Street was full of life, and then he added, 'But I think the full tide of human existence is at Charing Cross.' Perhaps by the end of the nineteenth century the tide of which he spoke had shifted a trifle farther west and was situated at Piccadilly Circus. This concentration of humanity helps to explain what was to the foreigner one of the most incomprehensible things about London – the way in which the personality of the city was expressed through the crowd. Anyone privileged to see the great Jubilee processions at the end of Queen Victoria's reign would have realized the truth of this. It was not the pageantry of soldiers, not the foreign princes bobbing up and down, not even the queen herself which made the Jubilee: it was the people of London. Queen Victoria, describing her drive through London on the occasion of the Golden Jubilee in 1887 (and no one had a keener perception of what was striking or important), wrote in her diary, 'Everyone seemed to be in such a good humour.'

This kind of ebullient good humour in the citizens of London often broke out with little warning or prompting. For instance, in May 1900, the news of the relief of Mafeking inspired one of the most astonishing spectacles which even London has seen. The news did not reach the city until nine o'clock at night so there was no possibility of any celebration being arranged or premeditated. The crowd literally seemed to spring from the pavements. Surging and cheering, they took possession of the town as they had done in 1887 and in 1897. They seemed to illustrate the essence of London's history during those days – which was, as has already been explained, that London was symbolized rather by human beings than by buildings.

But with the closing years of the century came clear signs that the commercial supremacy of England, which had grown and expanded since Waterloo, was being seriously challenged. Years before, Disraeli (with remarkable foresight) had said that the continent of Europe would never allow England to remain the workshop of the world. The full truth of this was abundantly plain, for both the United States and Germany were making great advances and were capturing markets where Great Britain had long been supreme – although even at the end of the nineteenth century British trade was still double that of any other nation. In particular the development of coal-mining in Germany and eastern Europe was a mortal blow. These were the clouds – admittedly small but yet lowering – which smudged the sky. Men looking to the future might have said with the most characteristic of the Victorian poets, Browning:

> ... the glimmer of twilight,
> Never glad, confident morning again.

In addition there were clear signs, which became much more obvious as the twentieth century began, that Englishmen were more concerned with welfare and social justice at home than with maintaining pre-eminence in the markets of the world. Those portents of misfortune moved at a vastly accelerated pace during and after the War of 1914.

When the First World War began, the people of London called attention to the hour by marching amid scenes of the greatest enthusiasm along the Mall to Buckingham Palace. But the harsh events, ushered in by that August evening, were to prove unfavourable to the geniality and kindliness on which so much of the strength of London depended. Henceforward the history of the capital was to be less smooth and the observer was to be less conscious of the surging vitality of the town. One who watched that momentous August evening in London has well summed up the truth when he wrote: 'And I heard the great crowd roar for its own death.' For certainly the War of 1914, which changed the face of Europe, swept away the pre-eminence of London.

The transition to Megalopolis

But if the pre-eminence of London vanished with the War of 1914, the ramification of the town emerged more patently. Though outstripped industrially and commercially by other capitals, the London of the twentieth century continued to grow. One question remains to be answered. Were the energy and high spirits of the Londoner symptoms of the wealth and pre-eminence of the Londoner or were they some inherent characteristic which survives (though in more muted form) in a London which has become larger but less splendid, more European but less imperial?

Victorian and Edwardian London could be regarded as the prelude to Megalopolis. Now, in the middle of the twentieth century, the prelude is over, and has given place to the main work – thunderous, alarming and carrying the hearer almost beyond the realm of imagination. For, as figures prove, London has become Megalopolis. In 1961 the population of London in the area roughly corresponding with that administered by the Greater London Council was rather more than eight million. This shows that in sixty years the figure had almost doubled. Yet that is by no means the whole story. For an even wider area than that embraced by the Greater London Council must be now accounted a part of London. The complete London region stretches from Royston in the north almost to Brighton in the south: from Basingstoke and Aylesbury in the west to Southend and Chelmsford in the east. Indeed it is in this outer ring that the great increase in population has taken place. In the ten years before 1961 the population of the old suburban parts of London – the inner ring – slightly declined; on the other hand the numbers in the outer ring increased by almost a million people. As figures sometimes tend to confuse the mind rather than convince it, the total enlargement of London can be vividly and succinctly described as the addition to it every ten years of a town the size of Brighton. On to the problems created by this phenomenal growth politicians, statisticians, economists and sociologists have fastened with delight – comparable with that of a bluebottle attacking a round of beef. But all their patient and faithful labours, their admirable schemes, their wise provisions have not served to staunch or divert the flow of London. This lies before us – the one clear fact in a confusion of comment and conjecture.

The inundation is not something just haphazard, comparable with the easy path taken by a languid stream: its strength derives from something strong and deep in the twentieth-century progress of mankind, which has been defined by Professor Toynbee as the progress of technology. This underlying strength is implied by two facts. The first is the ease with which the current has moved after crossing the Green Belt. It is true that the Green Belt was not devised as a barrier against the spread of the town: it could not be compared with the barrier against the Great Fire created by the deliberate destruction of streets. As first conceived by the London County Council thirty years ago, the Belt was at most a line of demarcation. But the point is that neither created boundaries nor geographical features have seriously impeded the advance. Even health, that mighty god of the twentieth century, has had little effect: supposedly 'unhealthy places' have given no pause. Southend, as the great authoress of Regency England reminded her readers in *Emma*, was famous for agues and fevers. Already more than a quarter of a century ago there were more than 10,000 London season-ticket holders there.

The other fact proving the force behind the spread of London was more paradoxical. Although the German Heinkels and 'V' weapons scattered the population of the capital during periods of the Second

World War, they returned and multiplied because, throughout all that time of danger, London remained a magnet drawing to itself new industries and new workers.

The dangers in this vast agglomeration in a small country are obvious for all to see. Here the most considerable may be stressed. There is first the intricate confusion – now impossible to disentangle – of homes and factories. This was the principal planning failure to which Sir Patrick Abercrombie drew attention in his famous London plan drawn up for the L.C.C. in 1943: 'An industrial survey has revealed a veritable peppering of whole districts with factories ... which have insinuated themselves into real residential areas.'

He also pointed out the accumulating factors leading to the fantastic increase of traffic – especially the siting of trading estates far from the homes of those employed there. This fight to move along the streets has – as was said long ago by one of the commissioners of police – 'reached battle-level'.

Possibly worst of all is what the advancing tide leaves behind it. 'Leave this', commanded the London Underground poster of 1924, 'and move to Edgware'. 'This' was portrayed as a slum in winter. Today as the more prosperous, affluent workers move farther out they leave behind them houses (too often the worst examples of Victorian racketeer building) ready prepared, with vacant possession, for conversion into slumdom. This is Lord Jellicoe's description of some of these houses in our own day: 'Basement areas used as common refuse dumps, roofs used for garbage disposal, entrance halls bearing the marks, if I may use the term, of a common pissoir, with contraceptives strewn on the rickety Dickensian staircases, often with the plaster peeled off and the bare lattice boards exposed; broken window panes, exposed and dangerous electric fittings, and common lavatories and bathrooms of almost indescribable sordidness.'

A less sordid but no less real danger in the growth of Megalopolis lies in the well-intentioned but hopelessly extravagant use of land which accords to many a pleasant suburban home a surround of lawn and garden resembling the policies round a Victorian manse.

Some see in Megalopolis more mortal dangers. There are the ominous words of Sir Patrick Abercrombie, at the beginning of his report, quoting the opinion of some sociologists and technicians, that 'Megalopolis must end in necropolis, killed by its own hypertrophy'. Some psychologists, at work on the consequences of overcrowding, consider that the urban dweller is exceeding the level of 'density tolerance' and that the endless companionship of too many human beings is a more real danger than the bomb. Can it be that the high spirits of existence – so conspicuously fostered in Victorian and Edwardian London – are doomed to be squeezed out of human

beings by the pressures which they themselves unwittingly create? Is it impossible that the sturdy individualism of London communities – the phrase is Abercrombie's – could continue on the vastly extended canvas which the twentieth century is using?

Surviving distinctions

Gloom comes easily enough in trying to answer those questions. Yet it could be that the traditions of suburban life and their history through Victorian and Edwardian times offer a ray of hope. Traditionally the suburbs of London were distinctive entities, connected with the centre by the silk-hatted gentleman, whose wife's warning to the single, domestic helper reveals the life as it was: 'Get up and see to Master's breakfast, otherwise he will be late for the City and goodness knows what will happen then.' The City, where Master worked, was a completely unknown terrain to those whose lives were bounded by the complete communities of Finchley or Richmond. Mr Peter Hall gives us a glimpse of the obliteration of all this in *London 2000*. The 'suburban' family is living 61 miles from London and daily discharges itself from the home – the father to work in London, the mother to work in Canterbury, the son to a college of technology and the daughter to a local biscuit factory. But when this family returns for the evening or for the leisurely Friday to Monday (which will presumably be the general rule) we cannot picture them as quite divorced from the community around which they cluster. Nor can we picture their part of Megalopolis as exactly identical with other parts. There are cherished distinctions even today round the centre of London. Lord Snowdon has pointed out that there are still local types to be found in Victoria, in Chelsea, in Portobello Road, in Stepney and Rotherhithe: they are guarded in their talk with strangers from outside the district. An Edwardian lady once remarked that the charm of St John's Wood lay in the gardens 'where you can wash your feet without being seen'. Such idiosyncratic delights may be less in the middle of the century, but the component parts of London are certainly not all of a piece.

The hopeful may clutch at one further straw. As London grows it spreads over many a historic town and village – a totally different advance from the Megalopolis of the United States which chiefly devours unoccupied land. As London spreads, it dilutes but does not destroy the traditional life in its path. May we not legitimately hope that although the millions may belong to London, the component thousands within them may be influenced by the character and habit of the smaller town or village in which they settle and say – as was said by the same distinguished resident of St John's Wood long years ago: 'You have to be worthy of living here'?

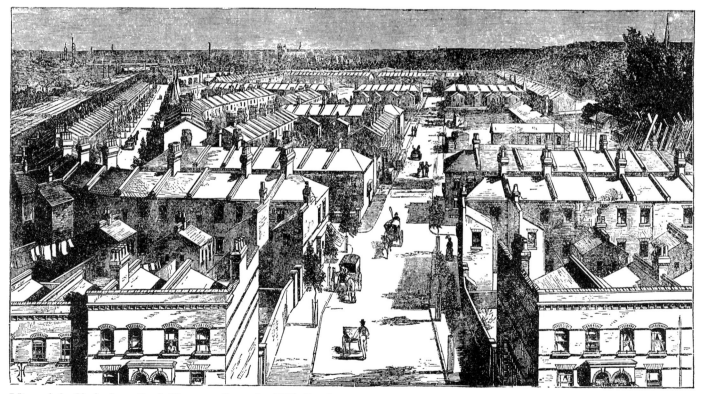

View of the Shaftesbury Park Estate at Lavender Hill, London. These rows of identical houses were intended for working men.

THE AMERICAN CITY

IN HISTORY

Speed of growth

has been the hallmark of American cities. Whereas most of the important cities in other parts of the world developed through centuries of gradual accretion, the process was telescoped in the United States, so that within a space of twenty to fifty years a clearing in the woods, a trading post, an outlying fort or a Spanish mission became an estimable city with a life and character of its own. The rapidity with which the United States changed from a vast, unkempt wilderness into the most highly organized industrial nation, dotted with huge sprawling cities and criss-crossed by superhighways, is phenomenal. In the period of most intensive growth, between 1860 and 1910, the face of the country was violently altered. As the population and the correlative demand for consumer goods increased, as the development of inventions, processes of production, distribution and sales was speeded up, the essentially rural, agricultural mode of life was overtaken by the thick concentration of cities.

In 1900, New York had a population of three and a half million, Chicago a million and a half. By the middle of the twentieth century, these figures had more than doubled, and at the same time other cities, formerly of lesser significance, began to gather steam and to rival the two giants. As populations swelled, cities inexorably expanded, attracting the satellites of suburbia and increasing year by year the distance between country and city.

The price that had to be paid for this rapid, headlong expansion can be seen in the slums that emerged and now linger in most American cities. The cities could not keep pace with the growth of population, which was largely caused by foreign immigration. Of the masses who arrived in New York or Philadelphia, moved to the Middle West and even went on to the Pacific Coast, many failed in their search for work, or were underpaid, and were caught in the crowded tenements and streets of the cities. As these grew in size and wealth, building great centres of culture and education, so the slums – often encouraged by corrupt city governments and real-estate profiteers – also grew, spreading to once decent neighbourhoods and causing the epidemic 'flight from the city' which has made so many downtown areas, as they are called, desolate and deserted reminders of the thriving commercial ganglions they used to be.

Responsible city governments are aware of the problem and have been attempting to rehabilitate their cities, particularly the faded downtown centres. These efforts are most conspicuous in Philadelphia, Pittsburgh, Boston, St Louis and San Francisco, where specific building programmes have been undertaken to replace the slums and revive the city-cores. Yet the pace remains too slow to meet the demand, and lower-income housing is clearly one of the nation's most pressing problems.

Chicago, which sometimes resents being called 'The Second City', has been for a hundred years the queen of the Middle West. Its situation mid-way between East and West, its proximity to the great plains where most of the country's grain and livestock are produced, and its excellent port on Lake Michigan, were all bound to give it predominance in its part of the country. It has always been a progressive and experimental city. The skyscraper began in Chicago, and it was Chicago that produced one of American's most significant architects – Louis Sullivan – in whose office Frank Lloyd Wright learned his craft. Like most American cities, Chicago is constantly in flux, constantly seeking to rejuvenate itself. The circular towers of Marina City (opposite) are among the most recent experiments. This sculptural apartment building, on the narrow Chicago River next to the city's central 'Loop', provides a large area for the parking of cars as well as living quarters on the upper storeys. (1)

The future great cities were nourished by the flow of Europeans who left a life of deprivation behind them in hopes of a fresh beginning (below left). **Cincinnati,** shown above with the neighbouring towns of Covington and Newport about 1855, was settled in 1790 – during the first big drive into the uninhabited hinterland after the War of Independence – and became a city in 1819. Lying on the Ohio River, it had easy access to raw materials and grew quickly into a major manufacturing centre. Cincinnatti attracted such great numbers of German immigrants that for a time German and English were recognized as equal official languages.

Salt Lake City (early view, opposite above) was established in Utah – at that time Mexican territory – in 1847 by a large band of Mormons under the leadership of Brigham Young. A religious farm-

ing community, planned entirely round the Mormon Temple, it led an autonomous existence until the general trek to the West eventually absorbed it within the federal system.

Occasional treasured relics, such as Louisburg Square in **Boston** (below centre), manage to withstand the tides of urban expansion and change. Once the Otis Brothers perfected their father's invention (below right) and real-estate investors appreciated its potentialities, there was nothing to prevent the construction of skyscrapers, serried as on Exchange Place in lower Manhattan (opposite left). (2–7)

The city as backdrop: Los Angeles at night seen from a bubble-like glass house designed by Bernard Judge in the Hollywood Hills (opposite below right). (8)

Philadelphia, founded in 1682 by the English Quaker, William Penn, was a flourishing commercial city by the mid-eighteenth century. Its choice as the venue of the first and second Continental Congresses indicates its standing as the virtual capital of the thirteen colonies. The painting of about 1810 by John Lewis Krimmel (right) shows the celebration of Independence Day, the Fourth of July, in the city where the Declaration of Independence had been drafted and signed. At the beginning of the nineteenth century, Philadelphia ranked as the most progressive city in the country, with the best public water-supply system, the most salubrious parks and the handsomest houses.

It was its favourable site on the navigable Delaware River that made Philadelphia one of the great ports of the East Coast, but the Schuylkill, seen above in a photograph of 1859, is its own, more intimate river, now lined on both banks by speedways which are intended to facilitate communications to and from the wide belt of suburbs. (9, 10)

The great cities of the West Coast emerged in the second half of the nineteenth century, a development much hastened by the discovery of gold in California and the coming of the railroad. Their swift growth can be appreciated from the contemporary lithograph of Seattle in about 1876 (left top) and the drawing of San Francisco in 1847 (left centre), the year before gold was found in the Sacramento River (see Plate 40). Immigration also had its impact on the West Coast – but from the Orient. San Francisco's Grant Avenue (left bottom) is the main street of Chinatown, an enclave which is not merely a tourist attraction, but a specific ingredient in the texture of the city. (11, 12, 13)

Washington, D.C., the federal capital since 1800 (above), was one of the few American cities built to plan. The design of Major L'Enfant was superbly rational and elegant (see p. 316), but Washington has long outgrown it. Dulles International Airport (right) is located in Virginia but serves the needs of the capital, which now has a population approaching two million. (14, 15)

New Orleans, at the mouth of the Mississippi, was a Spanish and a French city before it became an American one (below). Degas' *The Cotton Exchange in New Orleans* (1873, right) illustrates the chief source of its wealth. (17, 18)

The Mississippi, that great division between East and West, became a commercial highway after the invention of the steamboat. The restored riverboat (above) is a nostalgic reminder of Huckleberry Finn's world and the traffic which used to ply the river. It was the French who first explored the Mississippi, and St Louis, perhaps the most important city on its banks, was first settled by Frenchmen in 1764. After the Louisiana Purchase in 1803, it became the governmental seat of the territory; in 1822 it was incorporated as a city. The nineteenth-century engraving at left shows St Louis as an established solid community. Its greatest period of growth took place after the Civil War; as river traffic declined, the city became a leading railroad centre. (16, 19)

The frontier has always been a symbol in the American way of life, even after there were no more physical frontiers to conquer. The push to the West – an extension of the pioneering spirit which established the original colonies – is illustrated in a Currier and Ives print of 1867 (below). The log-cabin, which could be built quickly from the trees that had to be felled to make a clearing in the forest, was adapted from the Swedes. (20)

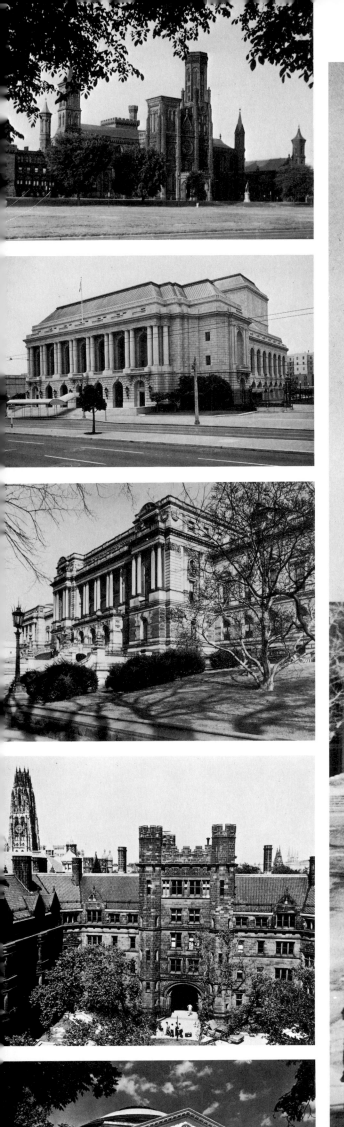

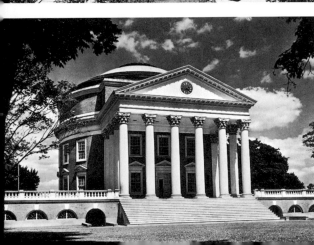

The universities, museums, libraries and other cultural institutions of American cities are the outward signs of an earnest and aspiring society. The Smithsonian Institution (far left top), founded in Washington, D.C., in 1846 through a bequest of an Englishman, James Smithson, has become a huge storehouse for the most diverse scientific, technical, historical and artistic collections. Far left, second photograph: San Francisco's Opera House adds to the cosmopolitanism of that city. The Library of Congress, when established in 1800, was what its name implies; because of its prodigious growth it was moved in 1897 from the Capitol to the building shown at far left (third photograph) and, in 1939, a modern annex of Georgian white marble was added.

The Boston area has one of the largest concentrations of colleges and universities in the world; Harvard, founded in Cambridge in 1636, is the best-known and the oldest university in the country. The Yard with its Colonial chapel is shown at left. The Massachusetts Institute of Technology is a neighbour of Harvard's in Cambridge; its Kresge Auditorium (below) was designed by Saarinen. Right: A recent building designed by Paul Rudolph for Wellesley College in the same state. Yale University, in New Haven, Connecticut (far left, fourth photograph), was chartered in 1701. Its present name was first used in 1718, after Elihu Yale, one of the earliest donors to the school. The University of Virginia in Charlottesville (far left bottom) was based on a plan of Thomas Jefferson's; building began in 1817. (21–28)

The opening of the West.

Drawn by the gold first discovered in California in 1848, Americans and foreigners sold their homes, farms or businesses, equipped themselves with food, horses, guns and wagons, and started the long trek along the trails that crossed the prairies and mountains and led towards the Pacific Ocean. Great fortunes were made, not only by the lucky prospectors, but by those who came along to service them with tools, drink, entertainment and bank-loans. This Currier and Ives print of the 1860s (detail above) shows a wagon train at South Pass, Wyoming, where the California Trail branched off from the route to Oregon.

The wagon-makers at home also made fortunes out of the Westward flow. Clement Studebaker (1831–1901) and an elder brother founded a blacksmith and wagon shop in South Bend, Indiana (below), which prospered in the years when the West was being settled. In time it grew into one of the largest coach and wagon manufacturing firms in the world, and by 1911 the Studebaker Corporation was producing automobiles. (29, 30)

The railroad, along with the invention of automatic farming equipment, such as the reaper and thresher, had the most far-reaching consequences in the development of the West. It was in 1869 that the United States was finally linked from East to West Coast. The idealized Currier and Ives print (below) shows the 'Through Line, New York – San Francisco', which seems to stretch across the plain into infinity. The railroad was the beginning of numerous cities, which started as junctions or watering-stops; it enriched the speculators who were helped by lavish land-grants from the federal government; and it also hastened the inevitable defeat of the Indians. Between them, the railroad and the automobile made horses and carriages obsolete in cities. The hitching-posts that still exist in New Orleans (left) are retained only as antiques. (31, 32)

Particular industries

have accounted for the growth and prominence of many American cities. The meat-packing industry which brought wealth to **Chicago** is illustrated by the famous stockyards (far left above). From the vast and fertile prairies of Minnesota came the wheat which is still milled in **Minneapolis,** on the northern part of the Mississippi (left above). **Houston** (far left below) is located 50 miles inland from the Gulf of Mexico, but it is a thriving port city and the petroleum-processing centre of Texas. **Toledo,** Ohio, astride the Maumee River at the western end of Lake Erie, is a major Great Lakes port, clearing grain, iron ore and oil. Grain storage elevators and two of the city's nine bridges can be seen at left centre.

Pittsburgh is the 'Steel City', close to the coal-mining areas of Pennsylvania, where Andrew Carnegie and his associates laid the foundations of the mammoth United States Steel Corporation. At the confluence of the Allegheny and Monongahela is Pittsburgh's 'Golden Triangle' (left bottom), a post-war urban renewal scheme. **Mystic,** Connecticut, was once an important whaling port; now that the flood of commerce has passed it by, it remains a charming reminder of the American past (above). **Detroit** is pre-eminently the centre of the automobile industry. Right: exterior of the General Motors research establishment in that city. (33–39)

Still growing most rapidly in population, power and wealth are the cities of the West Coast – the youngest part of the country. California has finally overtaken New York as the most populous of the fifty states, and the Westward movement of both people and industry shows no signs of ebb. The two most important cities in California are San Francisco and Los Angeles, neither of them the seat of government but sharing the majority of the state's financial, commercial and industrial potential. San Francisco (left), with one of the most beautiful harbours in the world and built on a number of forbidding hills, is the more traditional, the more worldly, of the two. Los Angeles is perhaps the more vital. Its extraordinary freeways (below) are part of the nightmare of the twentieth-century Megalopolis, in which the effective boundaries grow farther and farther away from the city-core. Indeed, Los Angeles might be called a city without a core; it is a centrifugal cluster of cities, diverse, disjointed and lacking in basic identity. (40, 41)

ALLAN NEVINS

WE MUST NOT BE MISLED by the frequently repeated statement that when the American Revolution began Philadelphia was the second largest city in the British Empire. This statement is true; but London was a very old and populous city, while Philadelphia was young and small. The distinctive features of American cities derive largely from their comparative youth, and the speed with which they have risen to great size and power.

The immediacy of the forest

Historically, American life has to be described in four aspects: the life of the pioneer settler, the life of the farm, plantation, or ranch, the life of the small town, and the life of the city. Pioneer life differed from later country life chiefly in its primitiveness, and in the fact that the pioneer east of the Mississippi clung to the woods, while the farmer and planter needed open fields. The era of the pioneer hunters and trappers merged rapidly into the era of the first-generation tillers of the soil, as anyone can perceive by reading that classic of Wisconsin in its wild early days, John Muir's *The Story of My Boyhood and Youth*, or John Burroughs's equally graphic account of his early years in the Catskills, *My Boyhood*. When we recall that Burroughs had a grandfather who served at Valley Forge under George Washington, and himself lived to become a close friend of Theodore Roosevelt and Henry Ford, we can better realize the rapidity with which social change has taken place in the United States.

It was the woods, the pioneer clearing, and the newly made farm which gave American life its special traits throughout all of the eighteenth and most of the nineteenth centuries. Towns were few, cities almost non-existent. A poetic atmosphere invested the woods even as the settlers swiftly levelled them; so, at least, it seemed in later memories:

> When I was a boy [writes the noted theologian Morris Schaff, who was born in Ohio three years after Victoria became queen] three fourths of Etna Township was covered by a noble primeval forest. And now, as I recall the stately grandeur of the red and white oaks, many of them six feet and more in diameter, towering up royally fifty and sixty feet without a limb; the shellbark hickories and the glowing maples, both with tops far aloft; the mild and moss-covered ash trees, some of them over four feet through; the elms and sturdy beeches, the great black walnuts and the ghostly robed sycamores, huge in body and limb, along the creek bottoms, I consider it fortunate that I was reared among them and walked beneath them ... Nature has many moods, but she was in her grandest when she ordered the woods of Ohio to rise up.

Thus multitudes recalled the forest.

Such memories stand with others of the pioneer time: the rivers black with swimming herds of buffalo, the groves bending under vast flocks of passenger pigeons, the sky red with the awesome glare of prairie fires. The flavour of the frontier still permeates the national character, in ways which Frederick Jackson Turner has described. We do not have to go far back in time to reach Lincoln splitting his hickory rails in an Illinois innocent of city ways, and the poetry of Robert Frost yet holds the bucolic flavour of old-time New England. Rural and semi-rural life was dominant in the United States until late in the last century, a fact which still affects the city. It knit into the American mind a belief that the virtues bred by the forest and farm were sturdier and finer than the virtues created by the street and the factory; and it gave countless Americans a suspicion and jealousy of the big city that remains widespread. In few of the old thickly settled lands of Europe is the psychological gulf between country and city quite so wide.

As for the small town, who is not familiar with Emerson's Concord, Lincoln's Springfield, and Eisenhower's Abilene, to name fairly typical small towns of three different generations? When Lincoln went to Springfield in 1837 it was hardly more than an overgrown village. That could be said of Galena when U.S. Grant took up his residence in the little mining centre in 1860. The small town and the surrounding countryside have furnished the early background for most Presidents from the Adamses to Wilson, Coolidge, Hoover, and Harry Truman. Urban ways and institutions cannot be comprehended except in the light of their recent origin. Not until 1820 did New York have 100,000 people, and in 1860 Chicago had only 110,000. Perhaps the best chapter in Harriet Martineau's book on the United States of the period when Andrew Jackson reigned is that entitled *Villages*, for it best captures the spirit of the land. Not until after the Civil War did the nation begin to create the gigantic city that Britain, France, and other countries had known long before. At no time has it had, or desired, a metropolis in the European sense.

In the last quarter of the nineteenth century and the first of the twentieth, however, great cities became a striking feature of the national scene, and American culture grew to be predominantly urban in character. By 1900 New York had three and a half million people, and Chicago one and a half million. James Bryce quoted Seth Low, who became mayor of New York at the turn of the century, as saying: 'The problem in America has been to make a great city in a few years out of nothing.' In solving that problem by hurried growth the country conspicuously failed to give its greatest cities honest and efficient governments. Indeed, Bryce thought the political bossism and corruption of municipalities the grossest single blot on the shield of the republic, and illustrated that judgment by chapters on the Tweed Ring in New York and the Philadelphia Gas Ring. But in other respects the cities were signally successful, and their swift rise conferred inestimable benefits upon the nation. They did much, particularly in the fields of sports, amusements, and theatrical and musical pursuits, to break up that 'uniformity of American life' which Bryce found particularly depressing. The best of them, including Boston, Cincinnati, and San Francisco, emulated within a few decades the cultural achievements which cities of like size in Europe had taken centuries to attain.

Planning comes into its own

The problem of which Seth Low spoke to Bryce was not solved, and the power of the new urban era was not consolidated, without a fairly creditable amount of planning. William Penn had devised a plan for Philadelphia, very rectangular but roomy and handsome,

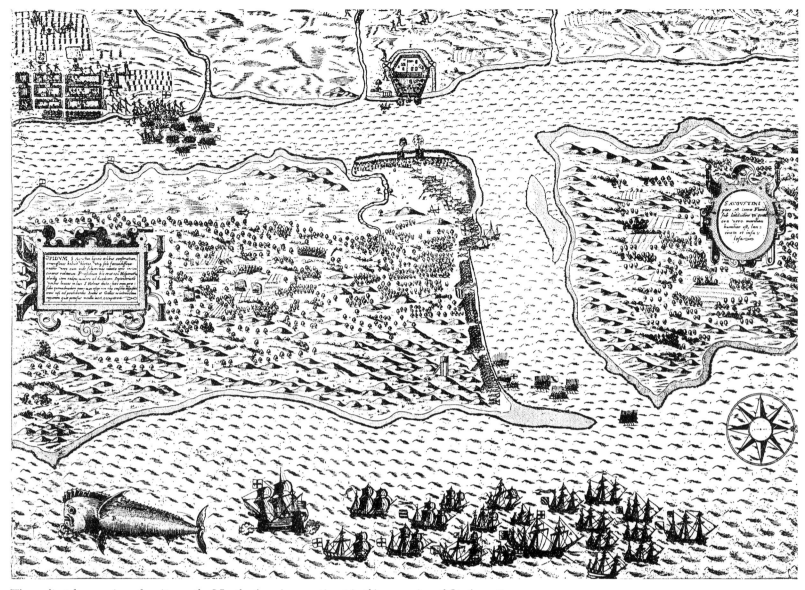

The earliest known view of a city on the North American continent is this engraving of St Augustine in Florida. It is from a book published in 1588 on the expedition of Sir Francis Drake. St Augustine was at that time in fact nothing more than a stockade (in the upper left-hand corner) inhabited by 150 Spanish soldiers. The illustration describes a successful British attack on the settlement, which was burnt down.

upon which the city after 1940 improved. L'Enfant, supported by Washington and Jefferson, had laid out a plan for Washington which from the early years of the city was an object lesson to the whole land. In due course later city-planners, encouraged by Andrew Mellon as Secretary of the Treasury, made the most of the possibilities of L'Enfant's plan, so that Washington became after 1925 one of the noblest capitals of the globe. Late in the nineteenth century city-planning began to come into its own in numerous areas. Special impetus was lent the movement by the Chicago architect Daniel Burnham and the New York landscape architect Frederick Law Olmsted who, with a group of distinguished collaborators, made the Chicago World's Fair of 1893 a transcendent expression of the nation's capacities in sculpture, painting, landscape, and architectural design, all harmoniously united. Burnham followed the Fair with his epochal Chicago Plan, which had its influence upon the 'Plan of New York and Its Environs' worked out (on paper) by C. D. Norton and Frederic A. Delano.

One great city after another has taken up planning in the last generation. A smokeless Pittsburgh, making the most of its Monongahela and Allegheny River fronts, has pivoted its streets upon a newly rebuilt Golden Triangle looking down the Ohio River. After decades of aimless growth, Detroit recalled that an early fire had given it an ill-realized scheme based on L'Enfant's design for Washington, and undertook a remarkable work of renovation. It has spent huge sums in beautifying its waterfront, and in erecting a civic centre which adjoins its art gallery, public library, and the principal buildings of Wayne University. St Louis, not to be behindhand, has undertaken to do nearly as much for its Mississippi river-front as

Chicago has done for its sparkling lake-front. Still other municipalities might be named. San Francisco is one. With its island-studded bay, its half-hundred parks, its Golden Gate opening on the Pacific, and its Coastal Range stretching north and south, it is one of the most attractive cities in the world; and it has added to its scenic charms by an imposing cluster of national, state, and municipal buildings, including its library, art gallery, and opera house. Even sprawling Los Angeles has lavished money and pains upon a civic centre. In 1930 more than three hundred cities reported that they had agencies at work on comprehensive plans, and the number must since have doubled.

The special glory of the American city lies in its cultural apparatus, and its contribution to the spiritual and intellectual advancement of the people; its greatest blemish is its inability to rid itself of the slum, and its continuous nurture of seedbeds of poverty and crime that are both hideous and dangerous.

Even in young and small cities the theatre, concert auditorium, art gallery, and organized sports gave minds and manners a polish they never derived from the rural pastimes of riding, shooting, skating, and picnicking. A few of the important universities of the country emerged in small places – the University of Virginia in Charlottesville, the University of Wisconsin in Madison, and Cornell University in Ithaca. These were the exceptions. Columbia University in New York, Johns Hopkins in Baltimore, and the University of Chicago in the city of its name owed much of their strength to their urban environment. It has been impossible to think of Harvard without Boston, or of the University of California in Berkeley without San Francisco. President Charles W. Eliot of

Harvard liked to recall that his father had been mayor of Boston. The first large libraries were college and university libraries, and not very large at that. It was when John Jacob Astor bequeathed his splendid collection of books to New York in 1848, when George Ticknor and Edward Everett took their first important steps in 1851 to found the Boston Public Library, and George Peabody about the same time established his free library in Baltimore, that the truly great libraries of America rose hand in hand with the great cities.

The reasons why the United States has never had a metropolis – a capital city that is the head and centre of its wealth, power, thought, scholarship, literature, and art – are evident to all. It is too huge and too variegated. It is a country of sections, which change constantly in population and from time to time in rank. Boston could be the hub of New England, but not of the areas over which New York, Cincinnati, and New Orleans held sway; and New England itself has descended in the scale. Bryce, arguing that New York could not claim any enduring pre-eminence, predicted that the centre of gravity might finally fix itself in the Mississippi Valley; he could not foresee that California would become the most populous state, and that its two great cities would yield no precedence to New York or Chicago. The country will doubtless always have a set of regional capitals, which will serve it better than any counterpart of London, Paris, or Rome could. These regional centres will be the stimulating leaders of cultural progress. Washington is planning a great home for the performing arts, and New York is enriching itself with the varied attractions of Lincoln Center. But in each region some would-be metropolis also takes challenging steps. The Los Angeles area, for example, with one of the nation's best universities and best technological schools, with many theatres and the centre of the cinema world, with the Huntington Library and fine museums, has just added a great orchestral hall to its unrivalled outdoor concert bowl.

We need not fear any lessening in the cultural energies of our fast-growing urban seats. But the ugliness of the other side of the shield shows no lessening either. As Presidents Kennedy and Johnson called for a war upon poverty, which according to sociologists was blighting nearly one-fifth of the population at the beginning of the 1960s, everyone thought in large part of the slums and other depressed areas of our crowded cities. They also thought of Appalachia, where Johnson began his celebrated 'war'.

We are tempted to say that large-scale poverty has always been visible in American cities, but this is not true. Poverty, the slum, and the attendant tragedies of criminality and vice, as glaring evils, owed their existence to three main elements: industrialism, immigration, and municipal corruption. The first great cities were not the offspring of manufacturing industry, but primarily the production of the farm, forest, and mine, and of commerce. Boston grew vigorous on the export of lumber, fish, furs and rum; New York on much the same articles, with its maritime trade. Chicago became great as a shipping centre for wheat, corn, cattle, pork, and the white pine timber of the north-west. Minneapolis became known as a flouring centre, while New Orleans was an entrepôt for cotton, sugar, molasses, and all the commodities grown or used by the Deep South. Both urban poverty and rural poverty were always visible, but down to the panic year 1837 the city slum troubled few observers. It was not until industrialism became prominent in New York, Philadelphia, and Pittsburgh, and a flood of immigrants poured into the Atlantic cities, that grimy wards filled up with seemingly hopeless people.

Hopeless? Never so hopeless in the United States as in the crowded Old World. American society was always fluid, and always open in many senses of the word – open in opportunity, open in freedom from class-divisions, open in the ease of movement from place to place, and from one employment to another. The restlessness of the people contributed a great deal to the growth of cities, and also to an air of impermanence in many of their parts. It found one remarkable expression in the rise of the hotel, which appeared in greater numbers and elegance in the United States than anywhere else in the world. 'The American hotel is to the English hotel what an elephant is to a periwinkle', wrote the British journalist George Augustus Sala. 'An American hotel is [in the chief cities] as roomy as Buckingham Palace, and is not much inferior to a palace in its interior fittings.' Dickens thought the St Nicholas in New York 'the lordliest caravanserai in the world', and the St Charles in New Orleans and the

This impression of Boston in 1768 was the work of Paul Revere, silversmith, engraver and revolutionary. Established in 1630, Boston proved to be an extremely successful settlement and for a long time one of the most important harbours on the American Atlantic coast.

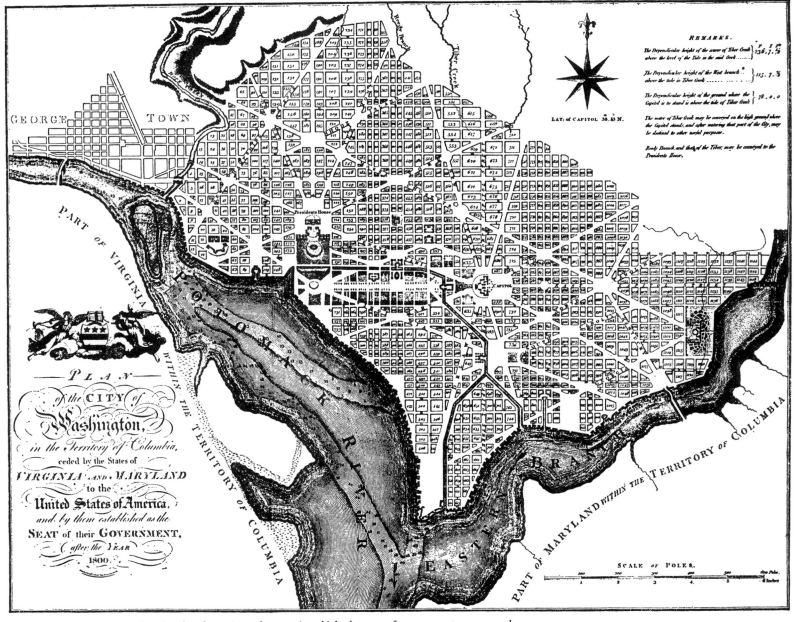

Plan of Washington, D.C., shortly after 1800, the year in which the seat of government was moved there. The designer of this capital, Major Pierre Charles L'Enfant, sought a grandiose effect: broad avenues for ceremonial occasions and many large circles and squares appropriate for monuments and statues.

Palmer House in Chicago rivalled it. On a lower level the multitudinous boarding-houses also catered for American mobility. Nothing was static in the cities; the indigent of today were the affluent of tomorrow; and this fact made people slow to feel anxiety about the slums.

Slum, semi-slum and super-slum

Yet even before the Civil War the slums of Boston, New York, Philadelphia, Baltimore, St Louis, and other cities were gangrenous sores, full of poverty, vice, crime and disease. They scattered the seeds of typhus, cholera, yellow fever and other maladies through the town. They were hiding places for criminals; they trained the waifs of the streets to be first juvenile delinquents, and then hoodlums. They absorbed the immigrants from Ireland, Germany, Italy, Poland and Greece, and held them in tight pockets, resistant to Americanization, giving industrial bosses and grafting politicians their opportunity. By 1890 the misery and general social deformity of the slums constituted a clear national problem. The vivid books of the Danish immigrant Jacob Riis, such as *How the Other Half Lives*, aroused a humanitarian fervour on behalf of the worst districts of New York. The writings of Jane Addams showed how terrible were the Chicago rookeries, and how much their denizens needed such helpful institutions as the Hull House which she founded and inspired.

The problem of the slum did not diminish, although philanthropic ventures in model housing and home nursing, labour union action

to destroy sweatshops, municipal ordinances on tenement house design and sanitation, and the creation of small parks and playgrounds were all helpful. The social settlements, the YMCA and YWCA, the Charity Organization Societies, and the Salvation Army – all imported from Britain, with its older slums – let a little sunshine into grubby areas. But as ever greater numbers of almost penniless immigrants poured through gates kept wide open until the First World War, congestion increased. When restrictive laws reduced overseas immigration to a trickle, a new influx of Puerto Ricans, Mexicans, and Negroes into the northern industrial centres perpetuated the old difficulties. In recent years prostitution has been driven off the streets of practically all American cities; the liquor traffic has been brought under firmer control; unceasing battle has been waged against drug addiction; and juvenile delinquency has been given the more civilized treatment that Judge Ben Lindsey made famous in Denver. But a spasmodic washing of the dirty face of a city too often accomplishes little permanent good.

Luther H. Gulick, the dean of American municipal administrators, declared in 1962 that as he explored the country he saw failure on all sides. 'In every big city the slums are spreading faster than they are being cleared up.' The slums of East Harlem in Manhattan vie in ugliness with those of Marseilles. A Swiss architect teaching in St Louis in 1950 said that he was familiar with the slums and war-damaged districts of Europe – 'But I've never seen anything like this.' Max Lerner told us in 1957 that the pattern of ethnic ghettoes is the same in all American cities. That is, the Negro slums of

Birmingham, Atlanta and Jacksonville are alike; the Mexican-American slums of San Antonio, Los Angeles and Denver are alike; the Puerto Rican slums of New York and Philadelphia, and the Polish slums of Buffalo and Chicago, are alike. William Bolitho called the slums of Glasgow 'the cancer of the Empire', their squalor contrasting with its wealth and pride; just so, the American slums contrast with the power and glitter of the affluent society about them. It is small comfort to reflect that all over the globe, from Naples to Moscow, from Istanbul to Buenos Aires, the scene is much the same. Patrick Geddes spoke for the whole world when he said: 'Slum, semi-slum, and super-slum – to this has come the evolution of our cities.'

In the growth of American cities the multiplicity of ever-new problems is always disconcerting, sometimes appalling. At the beginning of the twentieth century the character of cities seemed fairly well fixed. They were compact and crowded nuclei of humanity, solving the problem of housing by vertical expansion. The safety elevator that Elisha Otis introduced in the United States in 1854 and the wrought iron beams that the Cooper, Hewitt and other mills sold to builders in the 1850s and 1860s, revolutionized the urban outlook. Men could work in skyscraper office-buildings and dwell in high blocks of flats. Suburbs were still small, for down to 1900 they had to be built close to the railroad stations that gave commuters their only form of rapid transit.

The advent of the cheap mass-produced automobile and the hard road, however, altered the pattern. By 1930 it seemed plain that the great urban centre of the future would be a cluster-city. This would be a group of dormitory suburbs gathered in a fast-widening circle about a hard core containing the older city, with its factories, businesses, department stores, universities, theatres, museums and slums. A few neighbourhoods in the hard core would contain fine apartment houses; others would contain tenements of varying quality. But an increasing proportion of the affluent and cultured citizens would spend their nights and week-ends in the suburbs, enjoying the fresh air, quiet and greenery; getting into town by buses, automobiles and a shrinking service of railroad trains. The suburbs, writes Raymond Vernon, author of *Anatomy of a Metropolis*, would swell with the population explosion, 'spreading thinly over the landscape, and using up large quantities of land which not so long ago were cow-pastures and cornfields'. This development will increase as industries move out to the dormitory suburbs. Some of the newest cluster-cities, like Detroit, expanded over wide areas before the hard-core centre had time to reach maturity, and depended so overwhelmingly upon the automobile that they never developed a usable rapid-transit system for masses of passengers.

The new problems: towards Megalopolis

Among the host of difficulties engendered by this change, those of transportation easily stood first. They have not been happily solved. Hardly a single big city in America, by 1965, was not deformed by freeways, 'thruways', or (euphemistically) parkways, that cut great gashes through the town. All are tormented by traffic jams; in midtown New York the citizen riding in a powerful motor-car takes about three times as long to cover twenty blocks as his father took a half-century ago in a horse-drawn buggy. Traffic experts, invited to visit Los Angeles, turn in shuddering despair from that city without a centre, without a mile of mass rapid transit, and without any mode of travel that does not waste money, time and nervous energy on a frightening scale. An observer in Pasadena can stand any morning on an arterial street and watch many thousands of powerful automobiles pour past him into Los Angeles, each costly two-ton car, a marvellous combination of steel, chrome, electric wiring, glass, plastics, leather upholstery and rubber, carrying one man to business – if he can get there without a collision. In the evening the observer can watch these countless thousands of cars, bearing their load of one exhausted driver each, streaming out of the city again. Only the richest nation in the world could afford such a spectacle. Yet it is partly duplicated in Chicago, in Detroit, and in nearly all the cluster-cities of the day.

Problems of water supply, of decent cheap housing, of the reclamation of decaying business blocks and obsolete factory facilities, of modernized schools, of policing and courts, and of a hundred social services, have to be met in their new contexts. Meanwhile automation and other technological advances reduce the demand for manpower, and compel cities to provide for the advent of the four-day working week, and for more unemployment. Meanwhile, too, the atomic age complicates the task of planning, for vast concentrations of population may be viewed as prime targets for enemy weapons.

The development of suburbia – and of the belt beyond it called exurbia – has posed grim governmental problems; for many New Yorkers, Chicagoans and San Franciscans with the leisure and education for a steady display of civic consciousness have moved into the outer reaches, leaving the central core of the city to people less well equipped. And ahead lie still more daunting heights to scale. We are told by experts that within the lifetime of youths now in college – that is, within fifty years – the United States will have one city, or several, of 25 million people. We are told that in the same period the great reach from Boston through New Haven, New York, Philadelphia, and Baltimore to Washington will become solidly urban, a true Megalopolis.

The cities of the United States were swelled throughout the nineteenth century by a steady flow of immigrants from Europe. This scene of a group arriving in New York was an almost daily event.

MID-TWENTIETH-CENTURY NEW YORK

'The long shrill city'

was Henry James's epithet for New York in 1904–5. Since then the city has certainly grown shriller and, if not longer, higher. Little of what James saw and described some sixty years ago has survived into the mid-century, for New York is a city of continuous and intensive change. This is not a new phenomenon; even those two assiduous diarists of nineteenth-century New York, Philip Hone and George Templeton Strong, complained that their beloved city was like a snake that changed its skin every ten years. It has never been able to tolerate being called old-fashioned.

Like most visitors, James was equating New York with Manhattan – an inaccuracy ever since, in 1898, Manhattan joined with its four neighbouring boroughs, Brooklyn, the Bronx, Queens and Staten Island, to form the administrative unit called Greater New York, thus taking the first step towards Megalopolis. True enough, Manhattan has always remained the vital core and the quintessence of New York, but the peripheral areas furnish the essential manpower that keeps the city in perpetual motion.

The fantastic growth of New York was not foreseen by the Commissioners who, in 1811, prepared the grid plan of numbered streets and avenues, which has persisted, with surprisingly few alterations, up to the present. In their report they suggested that it might be 'a subject of merriment' that they had provided space for 'a greater population than is collected on any spot on this side of China'. The merriment stopped shortly after the turn of the century when it began to seem likely that New York, the gateway to the country, would one day – and soon – reach the point of saturation. Yet year after year New York seems to have more people, more cars, more office buildings, more and higher apartment houses – and consequently more problems. Nevertheless, the true New Yorker, who may have been born in Oregon, Iowa, Tennessee, New Hampshire or more remote places, would not exchange his city for all the peaceful backwaters of the world. The very hecticness of the city still draws great numbers to it and, because it is the financial, artistic and communications centre of the country, it remains a mecca for the young, optimistic and ambitious.

At all stages of its relatively short history, New York has been formed by foreigners. After the first Dutch and English settlers, there came the Germans, Irish, eastern European Jews and Italians; the latest arrivals have been the Puerto Ricans. During the greatest wave of European immigration – the thirty years before the First World War – the Statue of Liberty (opposite), which stands in the mouth of the harbour, became the symbol not only of New York, but of the whole land of hope and opportunity. Unveiled in 1886, the work of Frédéric-Auguste Bartholdi, it was a gift, more remarkable as an engineering feat than an aesthetic object, from the people of France to the people of the United States. (1)

Broadway,

the legendary avenue running the whole length of Manhattan, has always been its most important single artery. Beginning at the southern end, where the shipping offices are centred, it follows a somewhat jagged route northwards – cutting through the garment district, the theatre and entertainment section, the grey residential areas of upper Manhattan (relics of a turn-of-the-century speculators' boom), the halls and dormitories of Columbia University, Harlem and a complex of museums around 155th Street – until it reaches the northern end of the island. Although now clotted at most hours of day and night with heavy traffic, Broadway was once a wide and peaceful thoroughfare, as is evident from the early-nineteenth-century engraving (top left). St John's Chapel, whose spire used to dominate the area, is still standing today, but dwarfed by its towering neighbours. The second illustration, an 1855 lithograph, shows St Nicholas Hotel at Broadway and Spring Street, when that was considered an 'uptown' address. On a visit in 1842, Dickens described this hotel as 'the lordliest caravanserai in the world'. By 1859, however, the residential character of Broadway had given way almost entirely to trade (third photograph at left). The 1660 plan of New Amsterdam (bottom) shows Broadway's geographical and historical origins. The settlement's first road, and of course broader than the others, it led from the fort built by the Dutch towards the protective wall, which survives today in name only as Wall Street. (2–5)

Manhattan,

bounded on the west by the Hudson (or North) River and on the east by the East River, is only $12\frac{1}{2}$ miles long and $2\frac{1}{2}$ miles wide at its greatest width. The population density is over 75,000 per square mile, and had to be accommodated by vertical expansion when all other directions were exhausted. By far the greatest part of New York's business activity is concentrated within the constricted area between 59th Street and the lower end of the island. In the linked aerial views of midtown and downtown Manhattan at right, two clusters of skyscrapers are apparent: one south-east of Central Park and the other in the Wall Street area at the southern tip. At the bottom left of the photograph is a small portion of the New Jersey shore which, having been incorporated into the Port of New York Authority, supplements the vast wharfage of Manhattan and Brooklyn that makes New York one of the greatest and most convenient ports in the world. (6)

Three examples of Manhattan's diverse and changing architecture. Above, the twin Gothic spires of **St Patrick's Cathedral** on Fifth Avenue, seat of the Archbishop of New York. When designed by James Renwick, Jr., in the mid-nineteenth century, it stood well beyond the residential limits of the growing city. Now it is embedded in the most fashionable shopping district. Above right is the **Empire State Building,** the tallest skyscraper ever built. Completed in 1931 in the early days of the Depression, it supplanted the famous original Waldorf-Astoria Hotel, which about forty years earlier had itself replaced two Fifth Avenue mansions of the Astor family. Right: the **Solomon R. Guggenheim Museum,** designed by Frank Lloyd Wright, widely held to be America's most original architect. An example of Wright's functional aesthetic, this controversial building, which was opened in 1959, runs entirely counter to the large cubes of glass and steel which have been the mainstay of New York architecture since the Second World War. (7, 8, 9)

The varied face of the city. Central Park (the lake, below), acknowledged as one of the finest urban parks in existence, was designed by Frederick Law Olmsted and Calvert Vaux in 1857. Even so exacting a critic as Lewis Mumford has praised its conception: 'In its provisions for unhampered circulation and safe crossings, this scheme made a unique contribution to city planning.' Right top: national flags in front of the slab-like Secretariat Building of the United Nations. Right centre: one of the vanishing five-passenger 'yellow cabs' complements a temporary wall of colourful posters. Right bottom: Chinatown, most fascinating of the many ethnic cities within the city, each of which maintains, to a greater or lesser degree, its discrete cultural identity. (10–13)

The vertical horizon from above: this photograph, taken with a 'fish-eye' lens, shows still another dimension of Manhattan's concrete mountain range. Soaring upwards from the centre is the headquarters of the Chase Manhattan Bank, and around it loom the various other buildings of lower Manhattan's Wall Street area – world-wide symbol of high finance. (14)

Eight million New Yorkers: occasionally, on a summer afternoon, they all seem to be on the beach at Coney Island (right). They also swarm in the old Lower East Side, now the so-called East Village (below), for many years a deteriorated slum, which has recently been reviving into one of the most vital and colourful parts of the city. Here can be seen with-it boutiques and art galleries, racially mixed couples, poets, artists and hangers-on, among Jewish, Polish, Italian restaurants, delicatessens and push-carts. The revival has been caused in large part by the gradual desertion of Greenwich Village, the traditional artists' quarter between the two World Wars, which has become expensive, on the one hand, and Philistine, on the other. Drawn by its past reputation and its more recent honky-tonk night-clubs and coffee-bars, multitudes of tourists still come to Greenwich Village, and sidewalk-artists are there to serve them (bottom left). New Yorkers also sit on the steps of the New York Public Library (bottom centre) on Fifth Avenue, exclusive precinct of millionaires during the nineteenth century. In the depressed Puerto Rican sections, people with time on their hands spend it on sidewalks, and add Spanish to the polyglot city (bottom, third photograph). (15–19)

Whole streets change their identity within a matter of twenty years. Park Avenue, north of Grand Central (top right), was pre-eminently the street of expensive apartment houses between the two World Wars; now it has become increasingly the setting for prestige business buildings, such as Union Carbide, Seagram and Lever House. Resisting change for the moment are Shubert Alley (far right centre), in the heart of the Times Square theatre area; and Washington Mews, reconverted stables of the 1830 brick houses on Washington Square North, another aspect of Greenwich Village (far right bottom. (20, 21, 22)

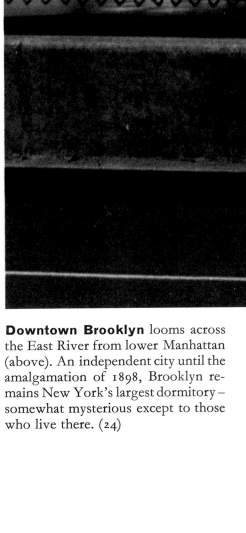

Brooklyn Bridge was the first traffic link with Manhattan, replacing a ferry service. When opened in 1883, after thirteen years of construction, the design of John A. Roebling was acclaimed as a wonder of engineering and beauty. (23)

Downtown Brooklyn looms across the East River from lower Manhattan (above). An independent city until the amalgamation of 1898, Brooklyn remains New York's largest dormitory – somewhat mysterious except to those who live there. (24)

New York roars all night long. This southwards view of Park Avenue (see Plate 20) shows the Grand Central Tower silhouetted against the Pan Am Building, New York's largest single office building, whose roof is a heliport. (25)

A hub of communications.

Every day, Manhattan sucks in a staggering number of workers, not only from the four neighbouring boroughs but also from Long Island, Connecticut, New Jersey and deep into Pennsylvania. These people pour in and out through tunnels, over bridges and water, by subway, bus, private car and ferry. Transportation is a vital and chronically insoluble problem which concerns commuters as well as those millions of less regular visitors who arrive and depart each year. Grand Central Terminal (right) serves commuters to the north of the city, but also those transcontinental travellers who still use trains. The Port Authority Bus Terminal (below) has the same dual function. Its roof provides extensive space for parking; the ramp connects with the Lincoln Tunnel under the Hudson River.

New York is also the focus of most transatlantic traffic. Opposite top: the *Queen Elizabeth* offers her passengers a view of Manhattan's incomparable skyline. Opposite centre: Saarinen's spectacular design for the TWA terminal at Kennedy International Airport, one of the most successful combinations of beauty and efficiency in modern architecture. (26–29)

The money and art markets.

The New York Stock Exchange (opposite, bottom left) is a primary centre of the financial world; activities on 'The Floor' affect most countries of the world as well as the American man in the street. More than half of the American population owns some form of securities. The Parke-Bernet Galleries (opposite, bottom right), now controlled by the London auction-house Sotheby's, has become one of the leading clearing houses for art, jewellery, furniture, etc., reflecting New York's current pre-eminence in the art world. (30, 31)

Cultural facilities for New Yorkers have traditionally been provided by the philanthropic gestures of rich benefactors. The Lincoln Center for the Performing Arts, an ambitious undertaking to create a co-ordinated city-complex devoted to music and theatre, comprises the new Metropolitan Opera House (right), Philharmonic Hall (the yellow reflection in the photograph), the New York State Theater, the Vivian Beaumont Theater – and there are other buildings yet to come.

Columbia University, founded as King's College in 1754, is now one of the oldest and most important universities in the country. The statue of Alma Mater (below), in front of Low Memorial Library, serves as a central meeting-point for Columbia students.

The marble building (below right), designed by Edward Durell Stone and standing on Columbus Circle, is the Gallery of Modern Art. (32, 33, 34)

ANDREW SINCLAIR

IN ITS GOLDEN AGE, New York City plays five roles. As the home of the United Nations and as the richest seaport in the world, it is the centre of the globe. As the hub of the great American Megalopolis of some 40 million people, that stretches from Boston to Washington and from the Atlantic to the Appalachian Mountains, it is the laboratory of the gigantic cities of tomorrow. With its heart in Manhattan Island, the city shows others how to create infinite riches in a little room. With its districts and its ghettoes, it explains how the immigrants of the world may live together in opportunity if not always in amity. And, within its varied streets, New York City produces the most complex and diverse culture that has been known to man.

Historically, New York differs from the past great cities of the world. In only three centuries it has grown up from a wilderness. It is not the capital of its country. Its local government is permanently a people's government, not that of aristocrats. Mobs or social revolution have never overthrown that government. The urban masses do not come from one culture, but from many. Race and religion matter to them more than class. Opportunity matters more than the fair division of riches. The future matters more than the past, rebuilding more than conservation. New York is the first great city with a stable government and unstable architecture and social life. It is the first to live, as William James lamented, in 'permanent earthquake conditions'. Its example girdles the globe and breeds imitations; but that example is itself in a continual flux.

The stream of immigrants

The condition for the rise of New York has been a constant stream of resourceful people immigrating to a deserted and rich continent. As the clearing-house between Europe and the wilderness, New York has called in the Old World to redress the emptiness of the New.

Two other cities could have dominated the eastern coast of America: Boston and Philadelphia. The Yankees of Boston were as shrewd merchants and more skilful sailors than those of New York; but Massachusetts lacked a good route through the mountains at its back towards the West. Philadelphia, too, was blessed by its good harbour and climate; but mountains also cut it off from the hinterlands.

New York, however, was destined to become the bridge between Europe and the American West. The Hudson Valley was a natural way into the continent; at its end, it branched down the Mohawk Valley into the Mid-West and along Lake Champlain into Canada. The enterprising New Yorkers were the first to build a canal to the Great Lakes, the Erie Canal, and the first to span the continent with railways. Thus they exploited their geographical advantages to become the bridge between the North American continent and Europe.

By doing this, New York attracted the best part of the huge immigrant mass that was to build up the United States on the backs of the refugees from Europe. In 1760, one American in three was foreign-born; by 1900, despite enormous native fertility, one American in six was still foreign-born. The dispossessed of the Old World became the cheap construction-labour and skilled industrial workers of the New. Curiously enough, many of the immigrants found a greater opportunity for making money in the familiar ghettoes of New York than in the virgin lands of the West. New York, with its early Irish, German, Jewish and Italian ghettoes, became a little urban Europe in the land of opportunity, despite the fact that the banks remained in the hands of the old-stock Americans.

Through immigration from Europe and from the American farm, the little city of New York grew from 25,000 inhabitants in 1775 to 3,437,000 in 1900 and to 7,782,000 in 1960. More than one New Yorker in three in 1900 was still born abroad; but in 1924 a quota was put on immigration, so that, by 1960, less than one in five New Yorkers was born overseas. Despite the quota, 2.5 million immigrants still entered the United States in the decade of the 1950s – and many of these settled in New York. The city has remained the special city of change and social mobility, of exiles and expatriates, of refugees from farm and slum, ready to throw their skills into the vast ferment of a metropolis made for metamorphosis.

New York's success has been based on its financial opportunities. It has attracted those who want to become rich. As the writer of the leading Victorian guide-book to the city declared, New York was founded merely in hope of commercial gain, in order to become the 'comprehensive emporium' of the world. Geography chose and man disposed. The trading spirit of the New Yorkers quickly made of the city 'a huge, continuous fifty-floored conspiracy against the very idea of the ancient graces'. There, Henry James continued, history had given up totally to commerce, and New York was 'indistinguishably sunk in the common fund of mere economic convenience'.

Yet this merchant city, which sacrificed all to trade and the making of money, attracted by its restless spirit. To those who felt cramped by the restrictions of hierarchy or town-life, New York was a free state of mind, where neither buildings nor social position remained constant with the years. A ferryboat captain, Cornelius Vanderbilt, could become the richest man in the city, and his children were its arbiters of fashion. The change from rags to riches could take place in one generation. As Melville's Pierre found, New York was a place where 'families rise and burst like bubbles in a vat'. Without the favour of the great, a poor man could become a robber baron on his own.

New York accelerated all the processes of growth and decay, and became a desperate free-for-all where the richest man won. Fortunes could not be kept without being increased; thus they had to be risked again. Banks rose and fell with families; there were fourteen severe slumps in the sixty-five years between the Civil War and the Great Depression, and banks failed in all of them. In the days of unrestrained capitalism, New York remained nervous with the expectation of imminent loss or gain.

Thus New York was in a position to exploit the revolution in communications of the twentieth century. As it had once seized the opportunity of canals and railways and book-publishing to peddle its influence over the continent, now it exploited radio and advertising and television. In the twentieth century it defeated expanding Chicago and became the centre of mass-communications in the United States. Its taste became broadcast across the continent and diffused round the world, and those who wished to influence public opinion had to congregate in Madison Avenue to influence the makers of that opinion.

Geography did not help the New Yorkers to capture the new world of communications, which favoured no particular location. It was their developed business acumen, trained by their early exploitation of natural advantages, which made them ready to incorporate and profit from the new frontiers of technology.

George Santayana found modern New York a place where 'everything is miscellaneous, urgent, and on an overwhelming scale, and where nothing counts but realization'. In the dedicated pursuit of that which is, New York has sucked in the seekers of Paradise on Earth. And if that paradise contains something of Sodom as well as something of Sybaris, it is still the most powerful and wealthy city in all history.

World capital

At the close of the Second World War, when the United Nations chose New York as its base, it recognized the reality of global power and communications. As Wendell Willkie had told his fellow Americans, all people now lived in One World.

Americans had not always thought so. In 1919, Geneva had been chosen as the home-city of the League of Nations, although New York was then already the banker of the world. The Senate, and later the American people – true to their traditional policy of keeping out of Europe's affairs – rejected America's entrance into the League, leaving the Geneva body a rump without a head. The United States, however, became more and more financially committed to Europe. By 1924, Europe owed American bankers and investors seven billion dollars, and these creditors were chiefly concentrated in New York.

Thus, when the New York Stock Exchange collapsed in 1929, it ruined Europe in its downfall. Despite its political rejection of the Old World, New York was entangled in a world-wide financial web. Economics and trade had made the world one, and the collapse of the American giant brought down the pigmies.

With the Great Depression and the New Deal, New York turned its attention to looking after its own millions of unemployed and starving people. World trade declined by two-thirds. The wharves of Manhattan were idle. Not until the Second World War brought a boom to all the seaports of the Atlantic did New York resume its position as the bridge between the riches of a continent and the demands of Europe.

The post-war leaders of America were determined not to repeat the mistake of 1919. The new United Nations was housed in New York. Symbolically as well as financially and politically, Manhattan Island became the centre of the world. The chiefs of all nations made their pilgrimages to this new Rome of international understanding. Money for intervention in the quarrels of Africa and Asia was immediately on hand. Moreover, the continuing presence of the United Nations in New York is a daily reminder that the United States is underwriting much of the stability and economy of the world. Since America is the leading nuclear power, the life of the human race has come to depend increasingly on the decision of the American President, while its feeding often depends on the surplus of American wealth and food.

The presence of the United Nations building in New York is also a daily reminder to the city of its own power and prestige. To be part of a great nation on a detached continent is to feel self-contained, and although New York has always been a city of immigrants, it is becoming more and more a suburb of Americans. It needs every stranger it can find to recollect its polyglot past and international future.

New York has always seemed to western Americans a city of aliens, where new immigrants arrived in their millions to dispute control of the United States with the old immigrants. But New York no longer stands alone. It is now joined with the old Yankee cities of Providence and Boston to the north and with Philadelphia and Baltimore and Washington to the south in a housing sprawl 400 miles long. At the time of writing the Governor of Massachusetts bears an Italian name, and Barry Goldwater has been quoted as wishing to saw off the whole of the Eastern Seaboard from the true America so that it can float out to sea.

This Megalopolis along the East Coast of some 40 million people has the highest density of population over a comparable area in the world, except for some areas of north-western Europe, northern Italy, the Nile Valley, and some parts of Japan, India and China. Usually the concentration of people in little spaces means mass-poverty; but in Megalopolis it means mass-wealth. Economic opportunity has become a permanent feature of the narrow strip between mountain and sea on the site of the old northern colonies of America. Megalopolis is bound together by surface and underground railways, by airlines and by roads. Its ports carry only freight and tourists. Without the commuting trains and cars, it could not function. Twice every weekday, Megalopolis acts as a pair of gigantic bellows, sucking in millions of morning commuters to work round its focal points of industry and management, and exhaling them in the evening.

The effect of improved communications has been to remove working people farther and farther from their place of work. More women now work in Megalopolis than ever before in any great city. For the modern city is particularly the frontier of opportunity for emancipated women, since fewer and fewer jobs there need manual strength. More than one in three of the labour-force is a woman. These women travel with the working men great distances to their jobs; four hours daily can be wasted in commuting alone. The very efficiency of communications has led to their over-use. Every improvement has encouraged its immediate congestion.

In fact, the effect of the revolution in communications has not been to decentralize industry, but to concentrate it. For, as industries become more automated and interdependent, their white-collar managers wish to gather more and more in the same places, to meet one another and make decisions affecting all. The answer of Megalopolis to the problems of work has been to pile office on office in what Lewis Mumford has called 'a sort of vertical human filing case, with uniform windows, a uniform façade, uniform accommodations, rising floor by floor in competition for light and air and, above all, financial prestige with other skyscrapers'.

Yet, while areas of white-collar operations concentrate, heavy industry has largely left Megalopolis for the shores of the Great Lakes and elsewhere. Megalopolis is interested in *control* rather than manufacture, in *services* rather than raw materials. And here it resembles many of the great cities of the past, where labour became specialized in the arts of government and luxury trades. Megalopolis contains one-fifth of the population of the United States, but two-fifths of the nation's bank deposits. Thus, through the control of capital, it organizes the work of others and reaps its profits.

City of perpetual motion

As Megalopolis increasingly becomes a vast reservoir of white-collar workers of both sexes – these already outnumber the blue-collar workers there – so its divisions of class and caste become more and more visible in the land of democracy. The white-collar workers no longer live in the cities, nor do the richer blue-collar workers. These dwell in the suburban sprawls which connect the old cities that were once distinct and now make up Megalopolis.

Meanwhile, the poorer blue-collar workers of Megalopolis, which even now has many hard and dirty jobs for manual labourers, still live near their work on the docks or in the streets. They have taken over the old middle-class areas round the skyscrapers of the financial districts. Thus the poor live the most rationally of all people in Megalopolis, except for the very rich, who can afford large apartments or town houses in segregated spaces near their work. And even the poor are sometimes forced to commute *out* to the fringes of Megalopolis, where the remaining heavy industries are. The inhabitants of Megalopolis, by divorcing their homes from their jobs, have made their city one of perpetual human motion.

This divorce has destroyed one of the chief reasons for urban life – its convenience. By making it both difficult and necessary to move about Megalopolis, the inhabitants of the place are forced, in Henry James's words, 'to move, move, move, as an end in itself, an appetite at any price'. The gift of great cities, the possibility of individual privacy and stability as well as a bustling public life, is rare and expensive in the hub of Megalopolis, the city of New York. Only in a few areas can a *vie de quartier* be found. And, even in these areas, the permanent speculative rebuilding of Megalopolis is a daily threat to the many people who seek there a precarious stability amidst the general hubbub of gain.

From the air, Manhattan Island looks like a liner, docked in between irregular piers of land. The wharves of Manhattan – its reason for existence as a city – project like davits into the rivers that flow on either side of the bow of the island, and its great bridges are steel hawsers anchoring it to the American continent. From the Hudson River, Henry James snorted, Manhattan is 'a pin-cushion in profile'. The skyscrapers bunch in the prow of the island round Wall Street, and on the bridge of the island in the mid-town section. From their eagles' nests, the captains of industry navigate towards El Dorado.

New York grew in layers from the tip of the island, where the Dutch first built a fort and named their town New Amsterdam. Like a stalagmite, with the years it added street after street in its expansion up the island. First, it swallowed up outlying Greenwich Village, and then plunged forwards in long tongues between straight avenues towards Harlem. Below Washington Square, New York shares the crazy-paving pattern of the haphazard streets of ancient European cities. Above it, the gridiron pattern makes long corridors of space between the buildings. The architecture of Manhattan makes visible the way in which the functional order of the New World leapt out of the disorder of the Old.

When Manhattan Island was swallowed up, New York City spilled over on to its surrounding islands and shores, on to Staten Island, the Bronx, Brooklyn, Queens and Long Island. Now Manhattan is surrounded by a ring of suburbs, from which the commuters ebb and flow more regularly than the tides.

Private speculation and building has kept Manhattan Island in a continual state of construction and 'permanent earthquake conditions'. Since an acre of ground can be worth a fortune in mid-town, the builders there have taken to constructing vertical streets, enclosed within skyscrapers. New York is the first city to *live* in three dimensions, and to house most of its working population in the air above its streets.

Added to the turmoil of private development, which often destroys a good building merely to replace it with an inferior but taller one, is the planned destruction of public housing. The incredible mobility of New Yorkers and the flight to the suburbs has led to the rapid slide of much of the middle-class housing in Manhattan down to slum conditions. These slums are equally rapidly torn down – usually to be replaced by taller slums, in which vertical streets of corridors and elevator shafts allow more unwatched crimes than the open streets of the old slums. Now a thousand families live in discomfort and some danger where a hundred once lived in the same condition. It is noticeable that, when a building is destroyed in New York, the rats and cockroaches in it merely emigrate to the new block next door; they are not exterminated. The evils of the old slum life are often transferred to the new and taller slum, and continue to plague the people there.

Decisions ruled by cost

The way to improve housing in New York is to preserve and modify the old and to integrate the new buildings into existing patterns of life. But cost governs decisions over public housing as it does over private. The City Council in New York is weak, and the real power over public finances lies in the hands of the Mayor and other elected or appointed officials on the Board of Estimate. This Board is made up of the Mayor, the five Borough Presidents, the Comptroller, and the President of the City Council. Once a fortnight, it holds a public hearing, where citizens can protest against proposed plans to demolish and to rebuild in this city of change. The protests are rarely effective, unless they can threaten the Mayor with the loss of a bloc of votes, which he may need to win the next election. The public hearings, like the Greek *agora*, perform a useful psychological function by allowing every citizen to feel that he can speak directly to his governors; but the decisions which affect him are rarely effected by him. In Megalopolis, the individual is too little.

Both private and public effort in New York is ruled by the same concept, that of cost. Skyscrapers and tall housing-blocks are built because they house the most people in new buildings for the least money. Considerations of aesthetics rarely apply. The very convenience of the people is hardly considered, nor is the fact that most of them prefer to live near the street – even in a so-called slum. Two of the curious features of American democracy have always been the urge to crowd together instead of filling the wilderness and the arrogance of city governments in these crowded spaces. 'There is no

Earliest known view of New York: Manhattan Island in 1626, the year it was bought from the Indians by the Dutch. The fort was the most important building, around which clustered some thirty dwellings and a windmill.

denying', Lord Bryce wrote in 1888, 'that the government of cities is the one conspicuous failure of the United States.' He would not change his opinion in Manhattan today.

The fault of inefficient city-government does not lie so much in its officials as in its structure. The organs of city government were set up for little cities; they do not suit great ones. The powers of officials have grown, until the users of that power no longer have any contact with the effects of that power in use. City government in New York is too far removed from district-control. It is a vast and segregated bureaucracy now, that tends to forget, until election time, that grass roots grow beneath the asphalt.

What Baron Haussmann was to Paris under Louis Napoleon, Robert Moses has been to New York in the last thirty years. He has destroyed and rebuilt great sections of the city in order to drive wide highways from the suburbs into the heart of Manhattan. He has also built vast buildings in order to accumulate people and prestige. The net result of all this planning has been to cause a permanent traffic-jam on the New York parkways, as at the Étoile. In his effort to make New York accessible to cars, Moses has transformed parts of the city into little more than a garage and an office. Large-scale planning can bring in the new, but only at the cost of destroying the urban values of the old.

New York is most successful, as a city, where the districts have kept a life and flavour of their own, which has endured through successive waves of immigration. Greenwich Village has housed the Irish and the Italians and the bohemians, although it is now giving way before the pressure of the immigrating executives – in search of the very people whom they are displacing. The Lower East Side has developed its Chinatown and its Little Italy, which still endure because they remain set in surrounding industrial areas or slums; it has also attracted the creative refugees from Greenwich Village, who find the low rents and decaying lofts and bubbling ghettoes there give them the space and stimulus to produce their experimental films and plays; for them, the further downtown means the further way-out. Spanish Harlem once provided a way of life for the Jews and the Italians, before the Puerto Ricans moved in; but the encroaching jungle of Negro Harlem has largely swallowed it up.

Harlem itself could provide an exciting and entertaining way of life with its old brownstone houses and its border on the far end of Central Park; but permanent poverty and high unemployment among the Negro men has kept large bodies of them on the streets, in continual revolt against white society and their own matriarchy, which has ruled Negro family-life since the days of slavery.

A city of ghettoes

New York has always been a city of ghettoes. In its early days, the conquering English were separated from the founding Dutch. When the Irish and the Germans began to immigrate in the 1840s, they settled in their own neighbourhoods in the city – largely because they were excluded from all except the worst housing. By 1855 the Irish-born numbered twenty-eight per cent of the population of New York, and the German-born sixteen per cent. By the end of the century the children of the Irish- and the German-Americans were in a majority in the city.

The immigrant waves, like the animals in Noah's Ark, seem always to have come in two by two. The next wave consisted of the Jews and the Italians, who poured out of the steerage-holds of the ships from the 1880s till the First World War. By 1920, the Italians made up fourteen per cent of the city's population, and the Jews perhaps one-quarter. The German-Americans began to lose their identity and be assimilated into the old-stock British-Americans of New York, while the Irish gradually began to lose their political power to the Italians and the Jews.

At this point the quota limit on immigration was imposed, and the new immigrants to New York came from *within* the North American continent. The Negro-Americans began their great trek north after the First World War, and the Puerto Ricans after the Second. By 1960 the Negroes made up fourteen per cent of the city's population, and the Puerto Ricans eight per cent. Of the older immigrant groups in 1960, perhaps a tenth of the population was of Irish stock and a tenth of German stock, a sixth of Italian origins and a quarter of Jewish origins. The remainder consisted of the old-stock Americans and a scattering of refugees from all over the globe.

New York City has kept its vitality because of its successive waves of immigration. The continual arrival of newer and poorer immigrants has urged the older immigrants to move ahead into the middle classes and make use of the inflow of cheap labour. Until the coming of automation, cheap labour always on tap was one of the conditions for the remarkable mushrooming of Manhattan. Now, unskilled labour is more of a problem than an advantage within a city. This fact helps to explain the failure of the Negroes to make any significant economic breakthrough in their forty years of life in Harlem.

The new immigrants, by organizing themselves into voting blocs and by exerting pressure on the elected officials of the urban (and even national) government, have always managed to extract many concessions from the dominant powers in New York. The Irish, who brought with them the art of ward-politics based on the village saloon of Ireland, dominated the city's politics through Tammany Hall from 1880 to 1932. They instituted the first permanent urban government by the people rather than by an aristocracy. It was not a good government; but, in the absence of any federal welfare-programme, it provided the only mechanism through which the poor could find occasional relief and jobs. In the time of naked capitalism, Tammany Hall was the necessary friend of the struggling family and the failures.

The strange thing about the Irish control of New York City has been that the Irish themselves have benefited so little from it. They neither grew particularly rich, nor did they produce a class of governing aristocrats. Although there was some corruption, they could stand amazed, like Clive in India, at their own moderation. Most of their profits went into the making of the Catholic Church, which became one of the most powerful national religious bodies in the world. The Irish bosses of New York used the riches of this world to pave their way to the next.

In 1932, with the Great Depression, the conservative Irish control of city politics was broken, and it passed over to the Italians, who produced one great leader, Fiorello La Guardia, and one efficient boss, Carmine de Sapio. Increasingly, however, Italian control over city politics was disputed by splintered reform groups, a combination of old-stock Americans and Jewish intellectuals – disenchanted with the failure of socialism in America. To this day, party affiliations mean less than ethnic background in this city of recent aliens. To be of an Italian or a Jewish family means more than to be of a Republican or a Democratic one.

In the heyday of Manhattan, nothing has seemed more chaotic – or more predictable – than its politics. Within the two-party system, the reform element, which usually has a slight majority within New York City itself, has struggled to elect its candidates against a combination of conservative votes in the city and in upstate New York. But the reformers are moderate. No man who questions the basic tenets of modified capitalism has any chance of support or election, although the Jewish community elected an occasional Socialist candidate in the early 1920s and 1930s. Each year the role of the 'independent' voter within the narrow choice of the conservative two-party system has decreased, until the chance of a great social change in the city through political means has become almost impossible. Most New Yorkers came to the city to make money and they do not wish to change the economic system which brought them there in the first place.

In fact, New York has demonstrated the failure of the idea that America would quickly become the melting-pot of all nations. Of the six great immigrant waves, only the Germans have been easily assimilated among the old-stock Americans; and even they, despite the wish to hide their origins because of America's intervention against Germany in two World Wars, have recently instituted Steuben's Day in New York in answer to St Patrick's Day, Columbus Day and Rosh Hashana. The Irish, the Italians, the Jews, the Negroes and the Puerto Ricans still live in distinct communities and keep their distinctive customs, although the families of some of them have been in New York for more than three generations.

Until recent years, there was practically no intermarriage between people of different religious and ethnic backgrounds. Most Italians still consider any education which is not professional or technical as a waste of time and money. There is still an expensive parochial school system for Roman Catholics. Many Jews still refuse to marry Gentiles.

The Negroes still have failed to develop a business class, even for the needs of Harlem and their other ghettoes in Queens, Brooklyn and the Bronx. And most Puerto Ricans still view their stay as temporary, a mere meal-ticket back to Puerto Rico.

A mecca for artists

The melting-pot, such as it is, only takes place in the segregated apartments of the very rich, where wealth is the chief criterion, and in the few bohemian areas, such as Greenwich Village, where a mixture of marriages and minds still develops the most creative and attractive group of people on the North American continent. Neither high rents nor police persecution can wholly drive out the artists and the writers from Manhattan Island or the Village. Indeed, the Village organized itself so effectively that it brought about the downfall of de Sapio, when he tried to push Fifth Avenue through the middle of Washington Square.

In fact, the flight of industry from Manhattan Island has turned over the deserted lofts on the Lower East Side to the artists, and has made New York the painting Mecca of the world. In these lofts, sculptors and painters have found the cheap urban space necessary for their vast creations, which more and more serve to decorate the vaster skyscrapers of the city.

The patronage of the numerous wealthy in their apartment-fortresses and the decaying lofts of industrial Manhattan have made New York into the art emporium of the world as well as 'the vast wilderness of the wholesale' which Henry James feared. The enlightened policy of the cultural foundations, set up by the conscience-stricken billionaires of the past, and of the Museum of Modern Art, has further encouraged creative work through grants and purchases. Meanwhile, New York's construction as a city of adjoining ghettoes has allowed the easy integration of the talents of any alien in a little Europe of a few slum streets. By always welcoming the stranger and allowing him a familiar urban village to live in, New York has kept many of the best of its immigrants. It is the *true* melting-pot of the undistinguished suburbs in parts of Brooklyn and the Bronx and Queens which loses its creative minds. From the mediocrity of uniformity, talented people flee towards the distinction and the particularity of the ghetto or the bohemia.

The streets – divisions and meeting-places

> From Eighth Street down, the men are earning it.
> From Eighth Street up, the women are spending it.
> That is the manner of this great town,
> From Eighth Street up and Eighth Street down.

So ran the jingle of the 1880s. For streets can be divisions as well as meeting-places. The streets of New York mark out the areas of work and consumption, the territory of gangs and the playgrounds of the rich. Only the location of these lines of division has changed as the city has grown.

Now the great areas of work are declining downtown and growing in mid-town. The luxurious consumer's street is still Fifth Avenue, now from Thirty-Fourth Street up to Central Park, and there the women are spending it still. Even in Dreiser's time, at the beginning of the century, Fifth Avenue was already 'all that it should be – the one really perfect show street of the world'.

The great division-street for living in New York is Forty-Second Street. Those who live uptown rarely manage to cross this busy ditch to reach downtown, and the subway system – the most inefficient and complicated in the world – can carry away visitors who would venture uptown through the bowels of earth in the wrong direction. Equally, Central Park divides the gang territories on the West Side from the preserves of the rich on the East Side, and the landscaped walks of the Park become a jungle of mayhem at night.

Yet the streets of New York can also lead on to some of the more charming meeting-places of the city. In the delicatessens, the coffee-houses, the bars and the laundromats, casual encounters develop the relationships that make a city-neighbourhood seem as safe – and ten times as interesting – as a small town. The atmosphere of New York round Washington Square is as casual and relaxed as any loafer could wish; and if, in the cinemas and bars round Times Square, an in-visible hostility from each passer-by seems to punch the stranger, yet he can find places of quietness and repose.

The street-life of New York in poor areas is dominated by teen-age gangs in a fashion unacceptable in other great cities since the cruel days of the Mohocks in London. Yet the fault lies in the very Constitution of the rebellious United States. The possession of fire-arms is guaranteed to every citizen as a protection against tyranny. Thus the threat of violence is almost hallowed. The police are armed and quick on the trigger, because the criminals are also armed. Mock-Gothic fortresses dot the city in strategic places, and will issue weapons to the numerous National Guardsmen in case of riot. Social revolution could never succeed in New York, because the forces of law and order are too well equipped and because the outbreak of a riot (as among the Irish in the nineteenth century or the Negroes in the twentieth) seems to make the population of all the other ghettoes in New York rally behind the city government. New York is armoured against its mobs as Paris has never been, because its poor find their separate backgrounds more important than their common poverty, and because most of its people are now moderately well-to-do or hope to become so.

Yet, while the streets of New York are safe from social revolution, they suffer more than European cities from individual crime. It has been the American tradition to work alone. New York has always been a city of suspicion and of aliens, where the new arrivals feel rejected by the old. In a way, crime has been one of the alien's ways to make good, as prize-fighting has been another. The criminals of the city have come from all races, not from the Mafia alone. If the Mafia or the Cosa Nostra are more successful than their competitors, it is, ironically, proof of the solidarity of Italian family-life.

Yet many millions frequent and enjoy the streets of New York. The rate of major crimes there is less than half that of the newer and more violent city of Los Angeles. Settled patterns of life in the older ghettoes and streets have preserved certain values of order and decency. The Greeks thought that men were city-loving animals, and even the Americans do not so much hate their cities as the failures of areas within those cities.

Decline or growth?

If New York imitates the great cities of the past, it must decline. Already California has overtaken New York State in population, and Los Angeles sprawls and sprawls and sprawls, growing on the riches of defence contracts.

Yet New York's supremacy should endure for many decades. Until the United States opens up its trade with the Far East and particularly with China, the docks of Los Angeles will not prosper. Meanwhile, the docks of Manhattan will remain the best port on the Atlantic seaboard, and New York will remain the main bridge between expanding Europe and the North American continent. Madison Avenue shows no sign of decline. It is Hollywood which shows signs of losing control over its dominant field in mass-communications – the film industry – to the managers of New York. If the decline of Manhattan comes about, it will be because no more aliens venture there to enrich the city, and because its people may lose the resource and sagacity which they have shown over three centuries of making money and piling up towers as high as their ambitions.

Until that time, short of a nuclear holocaust, New York will remain the economic and cultural capital of Megalopolis – which includes on its southern fringe the federal capital at Washington. Its efforts to solve its problems of living and transportation and mass-communications will be observed and copied by the emerging Megalopolises of the world.

By its very dedication to the pursuit of gain and its relative indifference to a pleasant way of life, New York's manner will continue to be what Dreiser found it, 'at once an invitation and a repulsion – the two carefully balanced so as to produce a static and yet an irritating state'. Now more than one man in five lives in a city; at the end of the century, at the present rate of urban growth, one man in two will do so. If the capital of the first Megalopolis fails, the future of urban mankind is dim.

THE COMING WORLD-CITY: ECUMENOPOLIS

The present and the past

IT IS DIFFICULT to foresee the future. I do not believe that we have developed this ability, nor do I believe that it will be easy to develop, for many subjects, even in the future. It is much safer to speak about the city of the past, or even the city of the present. It is therefore quite evident that the present chapter has a different character from those describing the cities of the past. Needless to say, we do not know everything about the cities of the past. However, enough of the shell has been left behind, and enough information about life in the past has been handed down, to allow us an attempt at description. But this is not so for the future.

Yet there is an imperative necessity to attempt to foresee the future. For, otherwise, many forces will develop in such a way as to lead to anarchy. We definitely need the freedom to develop ourselves in the future to the best of our ability on the basis of our desire and will; yet, if we speak of urban affairs, we must confess that we are gradually depriving ourselves of this freedom by committing our cities to many projects which will have a very important effect on the lives of our children and our grandchildren. Speaking of the city of the future, we recognize that our challenge is not whether we should commit ourselves to the future. Our real challenge is that, once we do commit ourselves to projects for the future, we have to try to do this in a way that will guarantee the best life possible, and the greatest degree of freedom, for those who succeed us.

Thinking in this way, we can recognize that it is easier for man to predict in urban affairs than in other fields. The reason is that in urban affairs we have forces of inertia as well as forces of investment which commit us for the future. For example, when we open a street and divide up land with specific ownership on both sides of it, then, even if we do not build on the street, we are committed, by the interests that have been created, to maintain this situation for as long as possible. The present owners will be succeeded by their descend-ants; all of them will want to maintain the *status quo*; and, even if they wanted to change the set-up, they would not all be wanting to change it at the same moment. Alternatively, we may build on the street, and then the buildings that we create will have a long period of amortization, much longer than we think. In urban affairs a much greater percentage of the present survives than in other fields of human creation. For example, twenty years from now, probably no car which is running at present is going to exist except as a museum or collection piece; yet more than 95 per cent of the present-day streets are still going to be in use, to judge by our present practice.

Even if we assume that we are going to have changes in the next twenty years, we cannot expect these to have an impact on our cities, as there is a great time-lag between a new discovery and its practical implementation, and between the practical implementation and the impact that this can have on the form of the city. Let us think of the automobile. It began its life in the city of man at the beginning of this century, but it is only now that its problems have accumulated to such a degree that man has begun to demand a change in the city in order to accommodate this new 'inhabitant' better. The conclusion, therefore, is that although it is difficult to predict the future, it is more necessary to try to do so in urban affairs than in other fields.

If we predict properly, we can recognize the problems that we are going to meet, and we can then invent new solutions which will relieve us from these problems and thus create the proper city for the future. It is possible to foresee, invent, and create the city of the future, and this is what I am going to attempt in this chapter.

In order to foresee the future properly, we have to study and understand the present. And, in order to do this, we must understand the past, as best we can. We shall thus have a safer launching ground from which to attempt our flight into the future.

CONSTANTINOS A. DOXIADIS

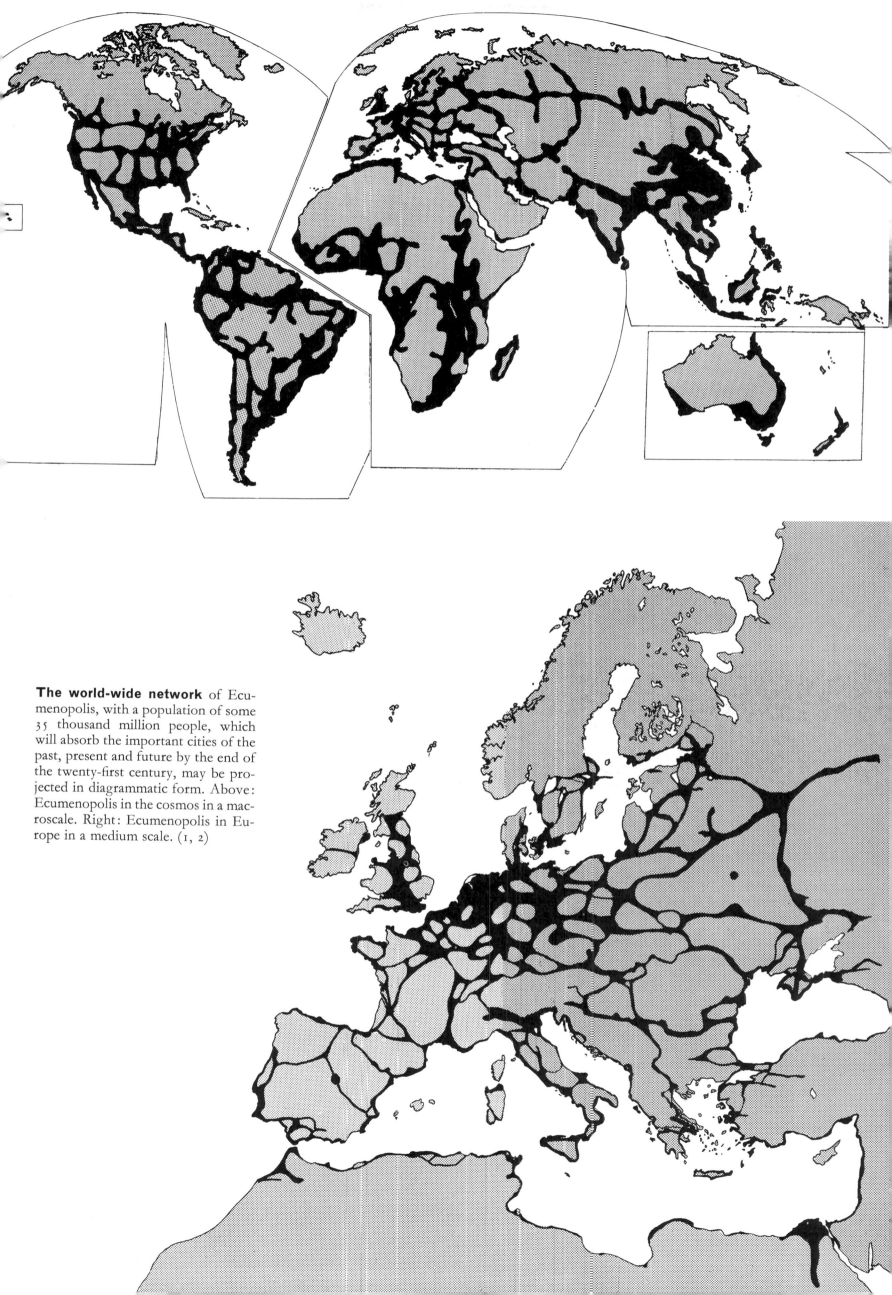

The world-wide network of Ecumenopolis, with a population of some 35 thousand million people, which will absorb the important cities of the past, present and future by the end of the twenty-first century, may be projected in diagrammatic form. Above: Ecumenopolis in the cosmos in a macroscale. Right: Ecumenopolis in Europe in a medium scale. (1, 2)

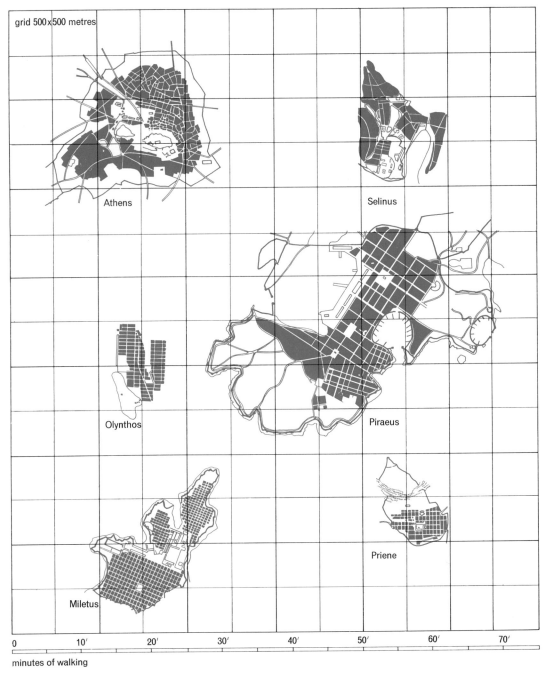

grid 500 x 500 metres

Athens

Selinus

Olynthos

Piraeus

Miletus

Priene

0   10'   20'   30'   40'   50'   60'   70'

minutes of walking

The physical dimensions of the city of the past were such that men could easily walk from one end to the centre in less than 15 minutes. Above: the ancient Greek cities, Athens, Selinus, Olynthos, Piraeus, Miletus and Priene, on a grid which indicates their size in relation to walking-time. (3)

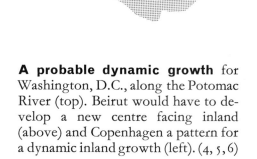

A probable dynamic growth for Washington, D.C., along the Potomac River (top). Beirut would have to develop a new centre facing inland (above) and Copenhagen a pattern for a dynamic inland growth (left). (4, 5, 6)

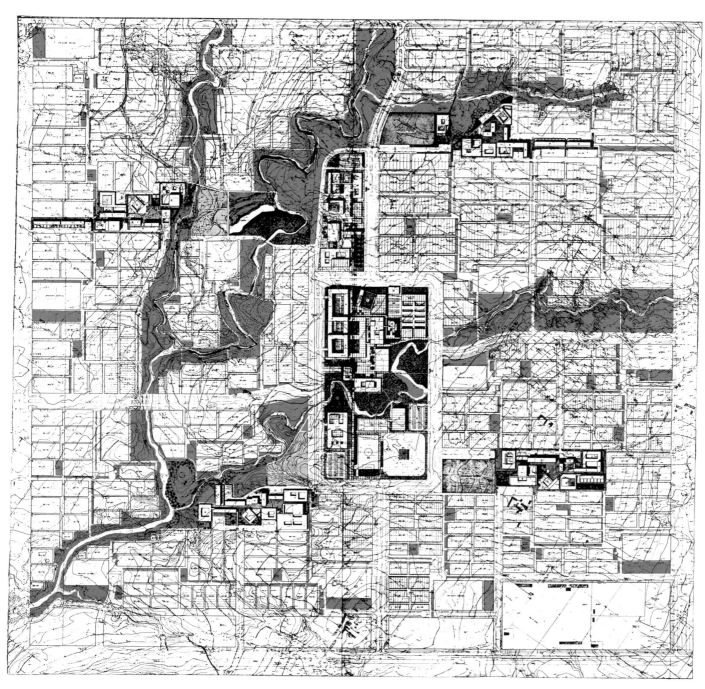

Islamabad, the new capital of Pakistan:
example of a system of major and minor
communities with a network of interconnected areas of natural landscape, providing an environment on a human scale
(see Plate 21). (7)

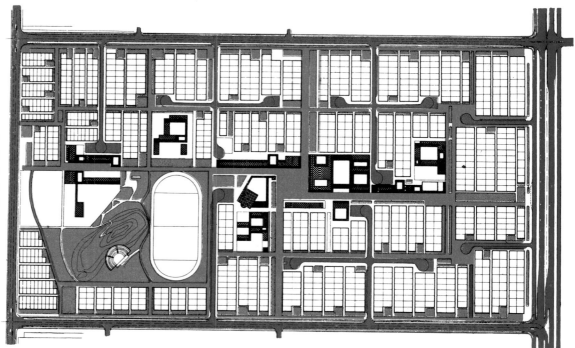

A representative human community
being built in Western Baghdad. The
blue areas are traffic arteries organized so
as to serve the practical needs of the
community but to leave large living areas
free of traffic. (8)

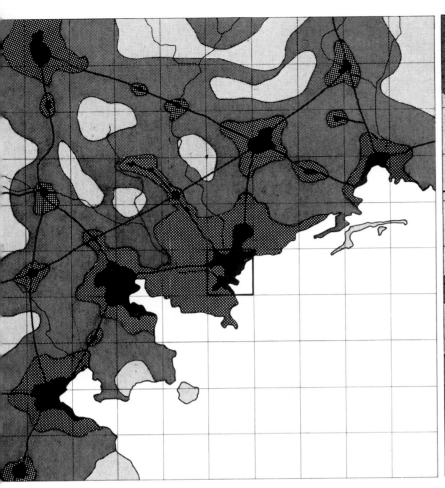

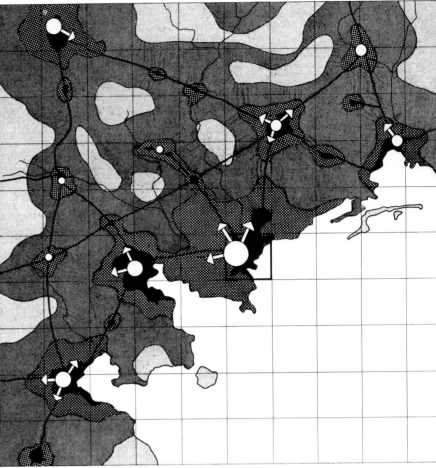

Ecumenopolis, the settlement of the future (above left). Huge pressures are exerted on the existing settlements: 33 times more people by the end of the twenty-first century in an area 60 to 100 times larger, with a much greater number of machines. The centres of existing cities are going to be choked to death, as indicated by the white circles and arrows (above right). Present urban areas should be turned into static ones and much larger centres should be established outside the built-up areas in order to relieve the pressure and serve both the existing cities and the new ones to be created in the surroundings (right). (9, 10, 11).

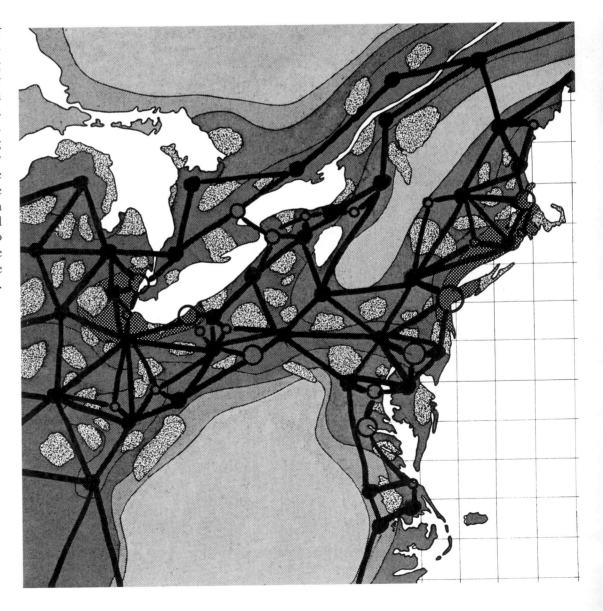

▨	13,000–52,000 inhabitants / sq. mile
▰	2,600–13,000 inhabitants / sq. mile
▰	520–2,600 inhabitants / sq. mile
▨	130–520 inhabitants / sq. mile
▨	0–130 inhabitants / sq. mile
▨	natural reserves

The Eastwick project of Philadelphia, Pennsylvania: one of the human communities that may form the cells of the city of the future. (12)

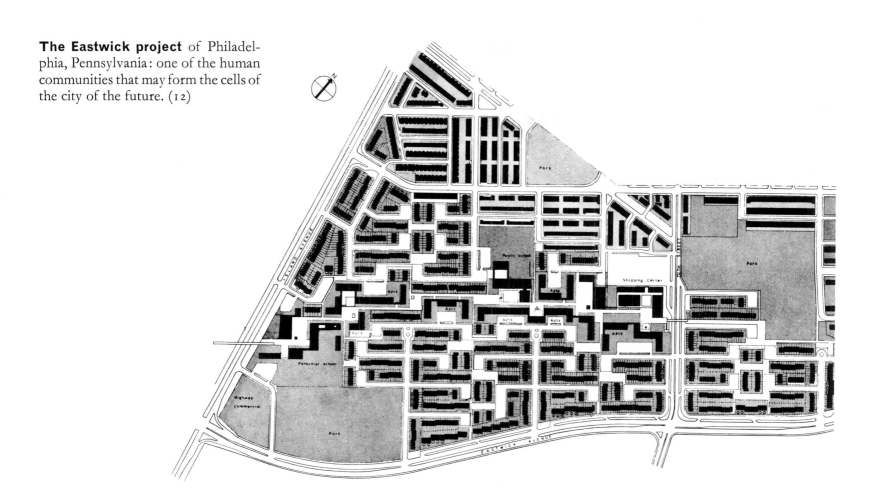

Louisville, Kentucky: model of the approved riverfront project to create human surroundings in an overcongested area. (13)

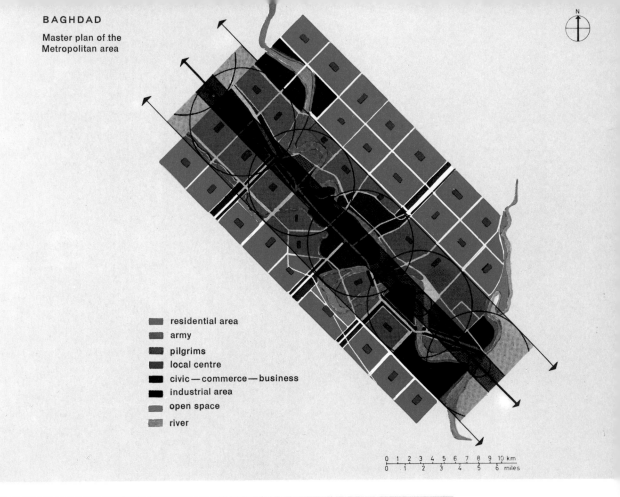

BAGHDAD

Master plan of the
Metropolitan area

residential area
army
pilgrims
local centre
civic—commerce—business
industrial area
open space
river

0 1 2 3 4 5 6 7 8 9 10 km
0 1 2 3 4 5 6 miles

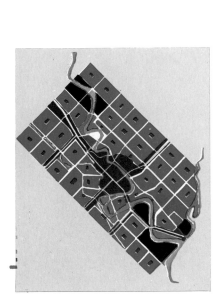

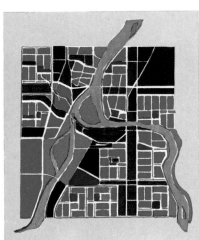

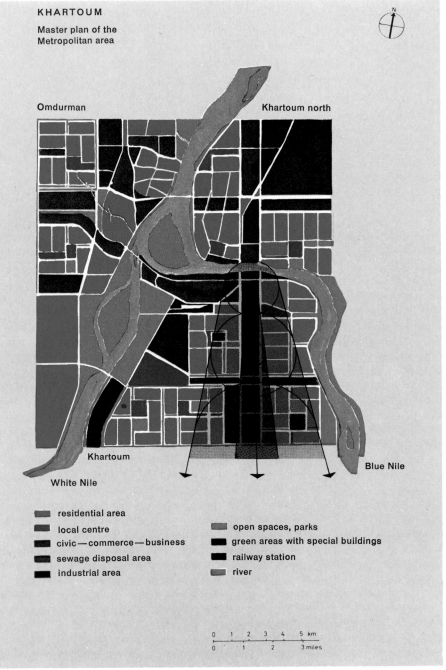

KHARTOUM

Master plan of the
Metropolitan area

Omdurman   Khartoum north

Khartoum   Blue Nile

White Nile

residential area   open spaces, parks
local centre   green areas with special buildings
civic—commerce—business   railway station
sewage disposal area   river
industrial area

0 1 2 3 4 5 km
0 1 2 3 miles

342

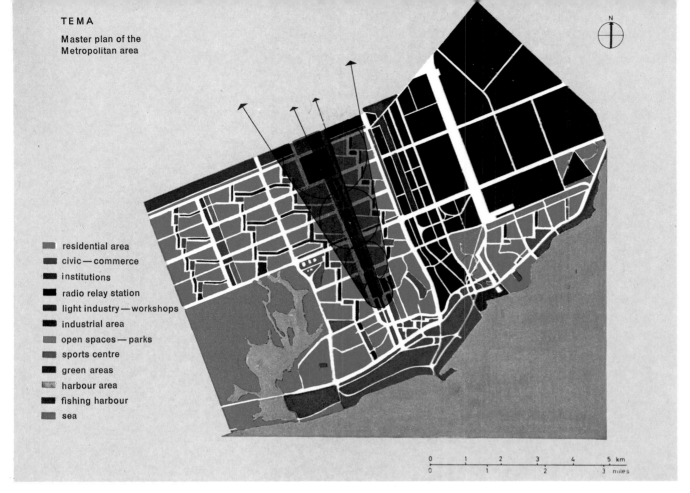

TEMA

Master plan of the
Metropolitan area

residential area
civic — commerce
institutions
radio relay station
light industry — workshops
industrial area
open spaces — parks
sports centre
green areas
harbour area
fishing harbour
sea

0   1   2   3   4   5 km
0   1   2   3 miles

New and old cities: the ideas behind
their construction, reshaping and extension into the future, as applied to the
plans at far left of Baghdad, Khartoum
and Tema. Above left: the overlay grid
with arrows shows that Baghdad will
have to grow at both ends of the existing
city in a vertical direction along parallel
lines in order to relieve pressures on the
centre. In the case of metropolitan Khartoum, which, at present, consists of three
components – Omduram, Khartoum
North and Khartoum – the overlay (left)
shows that expansion will be possible
only towards the south. The other two
components will remain static. Above:
the new port city of Ghana, Tema, has
been conceived as a Dynapolis and will
grow away from the sea, as indicated by
the arrows. (See p. 351)

The dark-blue ellipse in the plan at
right indicates the dimensions of ancient
Athens. Solutions for dynamic expansion, such as apply to Baghdad, Khartoum, Tema and other cities, are not
suitable for Athens, because of its topographical situation – surrounded by
mountains and confined to a valley. A
proposed solution is the creation of new
communities in areas not yet developed,
in order to reduce pressure on the centre
(14–20)

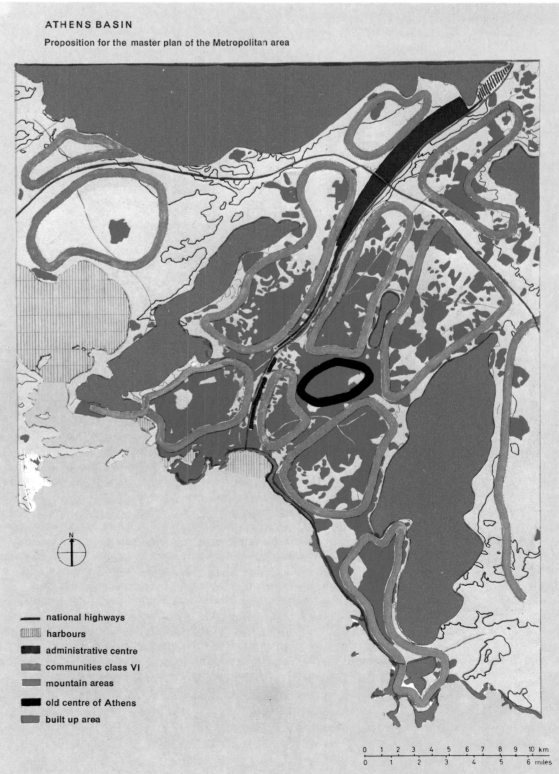

ATHENS BASIN

Proposition for the master plan of the Metropolitan area

national highways
harbours
administrative centre
communities class VI
mountain areas
old centre of Athens
built up area

0   1   2   3   4   5   6   7   8   9   10 km
0   1   2   3   4   5   6 miles

Bird's-eye view of Islamabad, showing the administrative centre which is planned to serve the whole country and two communities for about 40,000 people each. The city, which will grow continuously, is projected for an eventual population of 2,000,000 and will be able to grow even beyond that without changing its structure. (21)

344

CONSTANTINOS A. DOXIADIS

MAN HAS BEEN LIVING for thousands of years either in villages or in small static cities. Cities were always static; the symbol of their static nature was the wall. Walls did not exist merely in physical form; they were the most symbolic feature of the city for thousands of years. This can be understood by the fact that where there was no necessity for walls, for example, in the Spanish colonial cities which were created on the basis of well-conceived plans, the city walls which had so strongly influenced man were replaced by wide, well-planted avenues which did not present any hindrance to invaders, but none the less provided the inhabitants with those city limits which their predecessors had maintained for thousands of years.

It can be argued that several cities in the past were not static at all. Athens, for instance, underwent an important expansion under the Emperor Hadrian, and Constantinople moved its walls under the Emperor Justinian in order to cover a wider area. But these very examples confirm the theory of the existence of the static city. In both these cases, as in others, the city was not growing continuously in a dynamic way, but was simply revising the dimensions of its static nature at a particular critical historical moment, when its functions or its importance were changing.

The cities were also small. They ranged from a few thousand to scores of thousands of inhabitants. There were some larger cities like Alexandria and Rome, Constantinople and Peking, which contained hundreds of thousands of people, but these cities were quite exceptional and they did not maintain for very long such large populations. The overwhelming majority of the cities of the old civilizations, down to the seventeenth century, were small, with less than 100,000 inhabitants. It is quite characteristic that in the ancient Greek world, which created the famous city-states, the largest cities comprised only about 50,000 people; and such a famous cultural centre as Athens probably contained no more than 35–50,000 people. A comparative study of the populations of several Greek cities shows that their average population was below 28,000.

In these cities, the elements from which they were formed – the natural setting in which they were built, the man and society for whom they were built, their functions, and finally their physical

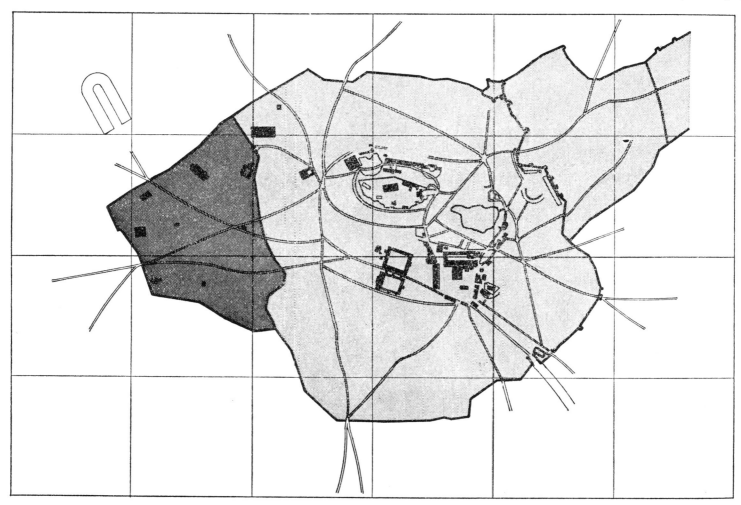

Athens, example of a revision of dimensions at a particular historical moment. The darker area shows the expansion under the Emperor Hadrian. (After the drawing by J. Travlos.)

345

structure, the shell – were all in balance. The inhabitants of these cities must have been happy in them, for they did not attempt to change their basic characteristics for thousands of years.

The physical dimensions of the city of the past, with few exceptions, were such that man could easily comprehend the whole, and could easily walk from one end to the centre in less than fifteen minutes. The structure of the city was simple: one main centre or, in the larger cities, one important centre and others of secondary importance. The central administration was responsible for all aspects of life. This administration was in most cases in charge of the whole area. In other cases there were also some small local administrative units, which were really only subordinate branches of the central city administration.

The city of the past, apart from being static and small, had a definite simple structure which allowed man, as an inhabitant, to comprehend it easily, to move without difficulty in a way that served all his needs, and to administer it properly.

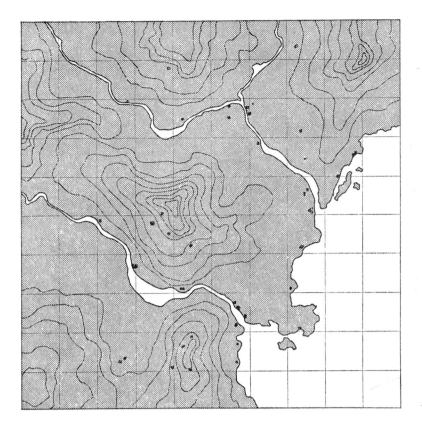

Constantinople in the fifth century, showing the double walls.

Dynamic evolution

On several occasions in this long history, several cities broke their walls and spread out into the countryside, but they have not survived. Those which survived were the typical static cities. It was only in the seventeenth century that cities began to break their way out and still to survive. This change, which coincides in date with the beginning of the scientific revolution, is related to the increase in population and to the new technology, both of peace and of war.

The construction of the first railway systems facilitated a much greater urban expansion. Several urban areas began, in the nineteenth century, to grow continuously at a rate which had no relation to the growth of the past. At the beginning of the twentieth century the introduction of the automobile produced a much wider spread of the urban tissue into the countryside.

The evolution of the several types of human settlements can be understood if we follow the patterns of the same area in different periods. First the villages, then the static city, then the dynamic city under the impact of the railway and car, and, finally, the present urban area. From the village through the city, we move to the Dynapolis, to the Metropolis, Dynametropolis, Megalopolis and, at present, the Dynamegalopolis.

The cause of this urban way of life was the great increase in population. We can easily understand this change if we follow the rate of growth of the population of the earth and of the urban population

of the earth. How this influences the city can be seen from the curve of the evolution of the population of the city of Athens, which for three thousand years had under 50,000 people, and then, within a single century, broke the barrier and has today reached the level of two million people.

The result of this population explosion was a great change in the physical dimensions of the city. The walls broke, and the city spread in all directions. The small cities of the past turned into the huge cities of the present.

In these cities, we completely lose the human scale. Man is unable to comprehend the whole. He cannot even see the city from end to end. He cannot understand how to move in it because, while the local areas have identical features, the totality makes no sense for him; he cannot find his way. More than anything, the dimensions have become non-human. Man can no longer walk from his home to the centre of the contemporary city. The example of Athens, where we can compare the dimensions of the city of the past with the city of the present (and Athens is not one of the largest cities in the present-day world), is characteristic of the change in the relationship between man and the city. Such a city has not just one centre, but many centres; not just one authority, but many authorities. It is no longer easy for man to comprehend, to live in, or to administer the contemporary city, because it has grown out of the human scale, grown out of control. What is more, it is continuously changing.

Actually, the contemporary city is no longer small, static, or comprehensible for the common man. It is a dynamic city. Athens, for example, is growing by 13.5 dwellings an hour. Contemporary cities are dynamic cities or Dynapolises, and very often they are systems of cities growing dynamically, Dynametropolises, and tending to be Dynamegalopolises. Thus, cities which remain small and static are no longer contemporary. This can be understood if we recollect that, although man has created and lived in cities for thousands of years, there are still villages which survive in the era of cities. In the same way, we can see several cities surviving in the era of Dynapolises. New types of human settlements do not eliminate the previous ones. They simply absorb the greatest part of the additional population.

The irrational city

The dynamic city which we have created today does not function properly. We only have to think of its five elements in order to see how irrational it is. Nature is spoiled with every passing day. Man finds himself in surroundings which are out of his direct control. Society is destroying the values that it has established in the past, without yet creating a system of values to replace the former ones and to give equivalent satisfaction to man. Functions are not operat-

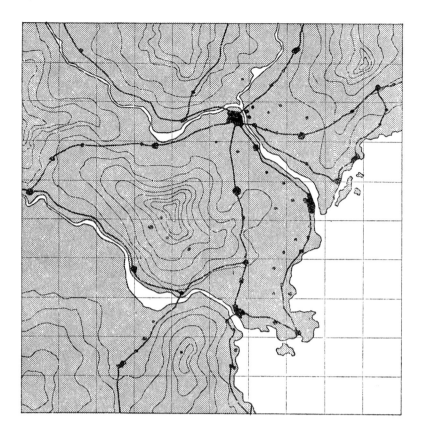
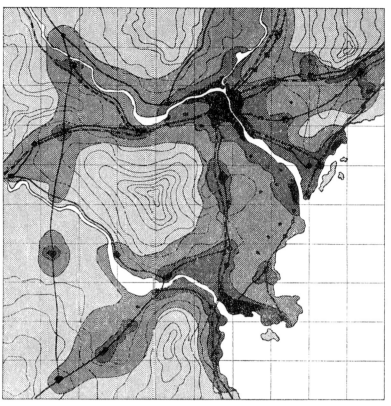
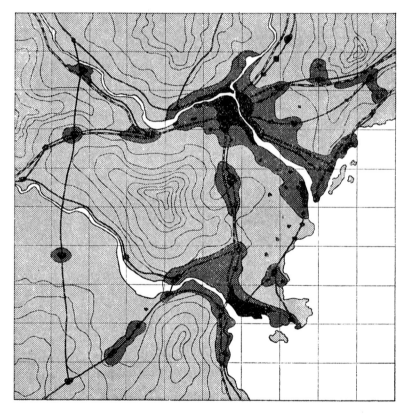
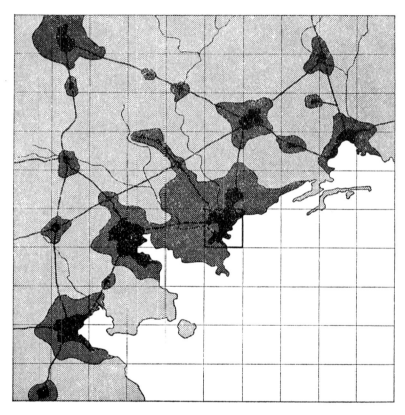

Stages in the development of the city. Villages in the pre-urban era (opposite top); city-states in the urban era (top left); cities as Dynapolis in the industrial and railroad era (top right); Metropolis in the motor-car era (above left); and Megalopolis, the beginning of a new era (above right).

ing properly; we need only realize that the greatest traffic volume is in the centre of the city, where we have the narrowest streets, in order to understand how irrationally we try to solve the problems of specific functions. Finally, the shell of the city is disintegrating; we do not have beautiful contemporary cities. When we talk about them it is only to veil the fact that we are changing them every day for the worse.

This irrational situation can be better understood if we think of the centres of our cities. We allow our cities to grow all round their centres, and they are being choked to death. Is it reasonable to expect

a small child to survive if we surround its heart with a steel frame? It will die. The same thing happens with our cities, the centres of which are surrounded by built-up areas, with the highest investment in the biggest buildings; and still we let our cities grow.

Distances are growing irrationally in the present-day city. We could even say that man has found himself in the following unreasonable situation; he is creating machines which can run at a higher speed, but he finds himself at longer distances from the centre of his cities. The speedier his machines, the longer it takes man to travel to the centre of his city. The very fact that today we cross the large

347

metropolitan areas at an average speed of 15 kilometres an hour by car, that is at the same speed at which we were crossing them at the beginning of the century, when we were using horses and carts, shows the irrationality of the systems that we are developing.

Our failure is due to the fact that everything is changing continuously; and, in spite of the cities being dynamic, we try to solve their problems as if they were static. As we cannot succeed in this, we continually revise our goals. We hear of cities with a maximum population of 2 million people which revise it to 3 million and 4 and 5, and so on, or we hear of cities which dream of surrounding themselves with a green coat, or green belt, in order not to grow, as if man could stop himself from putting on weight by wearing belts. Naturally they fail. The green belt of London is characteristic of these attempts.

In spite of these efforts and conceptions, we look upon the Dynapolis as a static city. But there is no city in the world which has managed to stop population growth. So it is not strange that all our plans have been failures. Because of such failures, we are trying to ameliorate the present cities with urban renewal plans, but we are not achieving anything, as the rate at which the problems are increasing is higher than the rate at which we can solve them so long as we view the city statically.

Thus, by the time when we may have solved problems of urban renewal at the centre of the city, we have a new ring of problems around the previous centre, and the problems have increased. It is a vicious circle.

If we follow this road, there is no way out. Our cities cannot survive in their present form, yet in spite of that we add population to them. The dynamic cities of the present are being led towards their destruction.

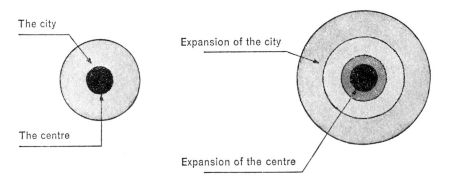

The city

The centre

Expansion of the city

Expansion of the centre

The concentric expansion strangles the centre which struggles with other functions

The static city. By the time problems of urban renewal have been solved at the centre, a new ring of problems around the previous one has been formed.

The future population increase

The most important characteristic of the city of the future is related to the increase in population. The present population of the earth exceeds 3 thousand million people. The rate of increase is growing. As things are at present, we should expect a continuing increase in the foreseeable future. There are, however, forces which are beginning to operate subconsciously (as we see in animal societies living in difficult situations) as well as consciously, such as the movements for birth-control.

What order of magnitude of population can we expect in the future? Because we are probably reaching a turning point, we cannot be certain at all. We must therefore satisfy ourselves by assuming a certain maximum and minimum. It is quite probable that the population of the earth is not going to be less than 12 thousand million people by the end of the twenty-first century. For, even if birth-control were to be imposed immediately on all nations, it would take a long period of time to implement such a policy, even if it was agreed upon at an international level. Thus, it has been estimated that we cannot expect a population of less than 12 thousand million people. However, it is much more probable that the minimum population will be of the order of 15 or 20 thousand million people.

Then what is the maximum? If we want to use the whole surface of the habitable earth, entirely for building a colossal world-city,

then we shall have a population of 500 thousand million people. This means that the food will have to be imported from other planets. As this may not be reasonable, it is estimated that not more than one-fifth of the total area can be taken over for these human settlements, which means that 100 thousand million people is the maximum reasonable population for the earth. But the earth cannot feed so many people, even at the present technological level. Assuming a normal development of technology, we can expect the population of the earth to reach the figure of 50 thousand million people. Some experts speak of 100 thousand million people; but, on the lines on which we have assumed a reasonable minimum of 20 thousand million, it is now reasonable to assume a probable maximum of 50 thousand million people.

Such considerations lead to the assumption of several curves of the evolution of population, ranging from a minimum of 20 thousand million to a maximum of 50, and pointing to an average of 35 thousand million people, to be reached towards the end of the twenty-first century. However, such a figure should not mislead us into assuming that the total population of the earth will be ten times larger and no more. First, we do not know whether it will break that barrier; second, and more important, the problem of our concern in urban affairs is not the problem of total population, but the problem of urban population. As we cannot expect an increase in the rural population beyond the present level of about 2 thousand million people (increase in productivity is going to allow them to produce enough food and raw materials for the whole population), a total population of 35 thousand million people means an urban population of 33 thousand million people.

As the present urban population of the earth is of the order of one thousand million people, we have to understand that, if the growth of the population is spread uniformly round the earth, the average city of the future is going, towards the end of the next century, to have 33 times more people than it has now. We have only to think of traffic in this city in order to understand how irrational such growth can be if we do not study the whole situation more carefully.

Dynamic change in the city

However, population growth is not the only dynamic change that we are going to witness in the city of the future. For, as a necessary condition for such growth in population, we shall witness a continuous increase of *per capita* income. Such an increase will proceed *pari passu* with the increase in the number of cars and other machines in use.

Thus, in order to understand the dynamic increase of the city of the future, we have to add all these forces together. When we have done that, we shall see that it is quite probable that the dynamic city is going to increase at a rate of more than 12 per cent per year. The population is increasing by 3 or 4 per cent per year, the *per capita* income is increasing by 4 to 5 per cent in the urban areas and, apart from that, there is a necessity for social programmes to catch up with the accumulated problems of the past; and we are going to have a greater increase of investment in the urban areas than in food production, for example, as gradually more and more people come to be adequately fed.

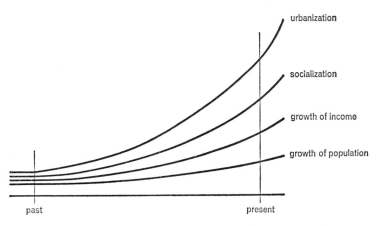

urbanization

socialization

growth of income

growth of population

past   present

It is probable that there will be a 12 per cent increase of the dynamic city, a population increase of 3–4 per cent yearly, a per capita *increase of income of 4–5 per cent.*

Apart from this higher rate of the dynamic change of the city, we also have to realize that, in consequence of the growth of cities, we shall have added functions because of the change of the order of magnitude in the city centre. In a small city with few functions in the centre, growth will demand that these functions shall be supplied to the whole population of the city, and therefore centres of this order will have to be multiplied. But in addition to this, we shall need new centres to offer services of a higher order, such as centres for administering the pre-existing centres of a lower order. In this way we not only have a dynamic increase of the city, but also have a change in its very structure as well, through the addition of functions of a higher order.

With all these additional functions that we have witnessed up to the present and shall witness even more in the future, there will be lower densities in relation to the area. This looks quite strange, because we normally think of London as the London confined within the city walls which are filled with multi-storey buildings, or of New York as the city of skyscrapers. But if we think of our metropolitan areas as the great urban agglomerations which they are, we shall find that their densities are continuously diminishing because a much larger space is required for the fringe: residential areas for systems of transportation of a higher order and modern industries, shopping-centres, etc., which are expanding in area more than in height. The result can be seen in the very fact that, whereas in the ancient walled cities we had densities from 150 to 200 persons per hectare in the ancient Greek cities and of several hundred per hectare in other over-congested cities – in ancient Rome or in the cities of medieval Europe and of the East – the densities of present metropolitan areas are below 100. Tokyo's density is 57, New York's is 42, and London's is 17 persons per hectare.

Towards a world-wide city

It is natural that, with a population of perhaps about 35 thousand million, and with diminishing densities in the urban areas, we may have a total city surface 33 times larger than the present one, and perhaps 60 or 100 times larger. When this happens – and we are heading in this direction – most of the cities of the world are going to be interconnected into a world-wide network, into a single world-wide city. This is not a new phenomenon. This evolution started in the seventeenth century when cities broke out of their walls and absorbed the villages next to them, and then absorbed other cities, till gradually the cities merged. The process is already in full swing. The Megalopolis of the East Coast of the United States – where we have practically one continuous urban area from Boston to Washington over a distance of hundreds of miles – shows what we have to expect.

This world-wide city or universal city is not going to be uniform. Unlike the city that we had in the era of static cities, when all cities were practically similar to each other in conception (small, static and simple in structure), the city of the future is going to have parts which will differ from each other, according to their main characteristics and the reason behind their creation. The city is going to have very large and wide areas expanding in all directions, and other areas which will be relatively thin and linear, connecting the massive expanding areas. This form is going to be imposed on the city of the future by three forces. Concentric force is going to bring people close to the existing urban centres, and this process of attraction is going to continue. If the expansion of some of them is checked by topographical and geographical features, as in Rio de Janeiro, then the city will flow into the nearest valleys or plains. Linear force is going to draw out branches of the city along the main lines of communication: roads, canals and railways. The third force will be aesthetic; big parts of the city of the future are going to be drawn towards the coastal regions: lakes, shores and other beautiful areas. What was impossible in the past can now become possible because of the automobile.

The approach of disaster

Let us now think of all these pressures which are going to be brought to bear on the existing urban settlements: 33 times more people in a century and a half, an area 60 to 100 times larger, and a much greater number of cars and machines. The centres of the existing cities are going to be choked to death. The world-wide city which is being born will be asphyxiated in its own cradle. Present-day city centres simply cannot withstand these pressures.

The city is going to destroy many parts of the natural landscape. At present it is spreading without any respect for natural contours or vegetation. The bulldozer technique shows on a small scale what we shall witness in the future on a much larger scale. The natural landscape is going to be lost. The natural skin of the earth is going to lose a large part of its vegetation as the city, in its spread, uses more and more chemicals and insecticides, and opens more and more stone-quarries in order to supply itself with additional materials for growth. All these forces will eliminate many of our areas of natural beauty. To this we must add the contamination of water and air, which is already dangerous and will grow worse at a much higher rate. Many natural values will be lost in the process of constructing the world-wide city.

In this city, man is going to find himself even more confused than at present. The scale of the city is going to be increased beyond his comprehension. He will have to rely almost completely on mechanical means for transportation and communication.

Society does not give any indication that it can be better organized in such a city. We simply do not see the trends yet. Man is already unable to impose metropolitan government in many of the cities of the world. The importance of the surviving local administration is over-emphasized in an organism which has nothing to do with the cities of the past. Many social phenomena, like the behaviour of youth, show that we have not been able to organize ourselves in the present city; and, if the present trends continue, these phenomena forbid us to hope for a better society in the city of the future.

Functions remain irrational. In the process of modernizing our cities we are eliminating the centres; two-thirds of the central four square miles of Los Angeles have been taken over by highways and parking. And we are losing many of the values created in the past; we can no longer see either the Piazza del Campidoglio or many other important squares of the past without being bothered by the omnibuses which stand between these monuments and us. There is no reason to expect that we shall behave better in the future.

Finally, there is the present ugliness of the shell of the city, where we have the contrast of the skyscraper with the slums which have survived from previous eras. Because of the irrational way in which the present city has grown, this ugliness is going to be accentuated still more acutely. Many of our streets are going to look much more like traffic-trains than streets for man. There will be nothing left of the public spaces which man has created for his service and pleasure for thousands of years.

In such a city, man is gradually going to escape more and more into buildings. He will gradually become a troglodyte. Buildings will be more effectively insulated from external noise, fumes and climate. And, finally, nobody will worry about what happens outside the big buildings when man, the displaced person of the city, is going to be in exile.

Such an evolution will lead the city and civilization towards disaster.

The march towards survival

There is a necessity for change. Present trends have to be studied, evaluated and, if necessary, reversed. It is quite clear that in many respects we have to change our road; we must set new goals. We cannot go on looking upon the city of the future as an extension of the city of the past. It is true that in some ways it is an extension of it. For example, the houses of the past and those of the present are not very different; they will probably not be very different in the future, as the dimensions of man have not changed, nor have his needs within a house. He always needs a bed of certain dimensions, a table of certain dimensions, a ceiling of a certain height. There is no necessity to think of a house in novel terms.

In the same way, however, we must think of minor units, the small public space, the neighbourhood, the small community – and these have at present been completely changed by the invasion of the automobile and machine, although this did not necessarily have to occur. We have to be careful to deal with these urban units with much greater respect than in the past. For thousands of years man created such units quite successfully. Why not learn from them and guarantee a historic continuity?

On the other hand, however, we are now dealing with cities which are changing. We are dealing with cities which in size, dimension and content, apart from man, have nothing to do with the cities of the past. It is quite clear that we have to change the course, especially in those units and elements which did not exist in the past. If we try to present the whole range of urban space in a logarithmic scale, we can see that a certain limit was inherent in the cities which man built in the past. This is the limit that is imposed by human scale. In dealing with cities, or with units within cities, that are comparable in their dimensions with cities of the past, we have to be very careful to preserve traditions as much as possible and to respect values which have been created. But, beyond it, we should think of the new solutions that are necessitated by new requirements.

With such a policy, we can save nature, create the proper habitat for man and society, organize the modern and future functions as they should be, and create a shell, a city which will correspond to the age-old as well as to the new requirements of man.

If we achieve this, we can guarantee the survival of the city and the survival of civilization. In order to achieve it, we have to coordinate action for the expansion and renewal of our cities.

Dynamic cities: towards proper solutions

We must march towards a world-city. How are we going to do this? We are certainly moving towards this city, but the way we are moving ensures disaster rather than survival and proper development. The question is not one of proceeding, but of how to proceed in the right manner.

To answer it, two goals must be defined. The first is to deflect the present line of march in order to save the existing human settlements which are being strangled. This operation, properly understood, will dictate our course in its first steps. Second, by properly picturing the world-city, we can gradually divert our efforts from the immediate solutions for survival towards long-term goals which will serve man positively. We cannot sacrifice the present in order to create the best solutions for the future. This is why we have to change our course immediately in order to meet the present situation. On the other hand, we cannot sacrifice the future in order to avoid inconveniencing our contemporaries. Thus we have to set long-term goals. It is the combination of short-term with long-term goals that will determine our line of march towards the future.

Our first goal is to achieve the best possible in the present. Our real problem today is that we are dealing with dynamically growing cities without really understanding that they are dynamic and no longer static. If we are to deal with such cities, we have to set the ideal goal for man. Up to now, man has conceived several types of ideals, but they have all been static. We now have to create the ideal dynamic city, or the ideal Dynapolis.

We have several cases to work with. The most typical is that of a round city which grows in concentric circles. This city has only a simple heart. If we let this city grow, as we are doing at present, it will finally strangle its centre. How can we avoid this? We are dealing with a city which is besieged by its own body. In seeking to escape from this besieged city, we cannot break out in all directions, as we are doing at present, for in every besieged city we have to break out in one direction only, the direction of least resistance. We have to

let the centre grow in this direction. It will grow into a larger area than the present one. This area is going to attract the new parts of the city all around it; but then we have to foresee the next stage, which is another expansion from the centre in the same direction, which again attracts the city all around it. By continuing this process we shall creat a dynamic city which is parabolic, with a parabolically expanding centre. If the city grows continuously, then it will continue as a parabola. This can be called the simplest form of the ideal Dynapolis. If this city later becomes static, then the parabola will close naturally at its end.

New Dynapolises – the axis of growth

We also have the opportunity for creating new cities. But this very seldom occurs. We have fewer opportunities for creating a dynamic city, because this kind of city has not been understood. Lately, though, we have had two cases of new cities that have been obeying the principles of dynamic growth. These are the cities of Islamabad, the new capital of Pakistan, and Tema, the new port town of Ghana, adjoining its capital. These are examples of ideal Dynapolises of the simplest form, implemented in cases in which there were no commitments at all (Islamabad), or in which there were few commitments, so that the areas took the proper shape right from the beginning.

Islamabad has been conceived as a dynamic city in a landscape at the foot of the Margalla hills. The heart of this new capital of Pakistan is now under construction. The city is going to be small at first. What else could it be? Any new organism has to start from a small nucleus. This nucleus is going to contain those functions that are indispensable for a new capital: an administrative centre for the whole country, a cultural centre, a bank, an institutional and business centre, with corresponding residential quarters and facilities. This city, which in its first phase will have 50,000 inhabitants, is going to grow continuously until it will contain 2 million people in the foreseeable future. It has been planned, therefore, for 2 million people. But it has been conceived as a city which can grow from 50,000 to 2 million people while remaining compact and self-sufficient in every phase, and it will also be able to grow from 2 million to 5 million and even more without changing its structure or sacrificing the first phases to the future phases or vice versa.

The city of Tema was conceived as a Dynapolis after the first communities were planned and built, though without any commitment towards its centre. Thus, it would be conceived as a city of 100,000 people in its first phase, and this initial figure would grow into hundreds of thousands. The fact that it is close to the sea and to the capital city of Accra, with which it will one day coalesce into a single urban area, has led to the decision to establish an axis of growth. With its back to the seafront, the city is going to grow inlandwards exactly as the capital city has already done, and this in a natural way, as many cities have grown under similar conditions, regardless of whether we have noticed that or not. A study of the whole area has proved that, between Accra and Tema, a third centre could and should exist, which, also having its back to the sea, would likewise grow inlandwards. Thus we should have three Dynapolises, all growing parallel to each other from the sea inlandwards, and this would allow the population of the metropolitan area to grow from some hundreds of thousands of people to millions.

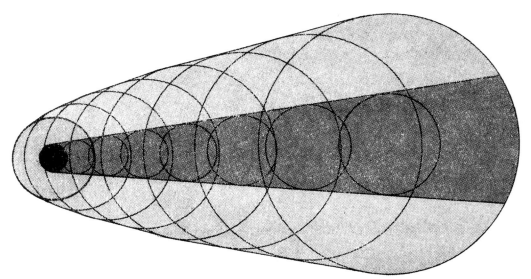

The simplest form of the ideal Dynapolis. The expansion in one direction allows the centre to expand without difficulty.

Re-shaping existing cities

There are cases in which the theory of the ideal Dynapolis can be implemented not only in new cities, but also in existing ones. Such proposals have been worked out for several major cities such as Washington, Copenhagen and Beirut, and they have been implemented in some – for instance, in Khartoum. In the metropolitan area of the new capital of the Sudan there are three cities, Khartoum, Khartoum North and Omdurman, on the three sides of the two Niles. The major problem of these cities lies in the fact that commuting from one to the other requires the construction of bridges or, perhaps in the future, tunnels which must be quite long and very expensive. The major problem, therefore, was how to create a city which would not be spending its budget on the crossing of rivers. An analysis has proved that the major part of the future expansion must be confined to one of the cities, with the others becoming static as soon as possible, in order to decrease the number of crossings over the river, which otherwise will increase enormously. Such an analysis has led to the formation of a plan for the metropolitan area of Khartoum which provides for the dynamic growth of the city of Khartoum and the gradual stabilization of conditions in Omdurman and Khartoum North.

Such a plan, which has been approved, is now being implemented. It allows for the growth of Khartoum in a dynamic way which will guarantee the proper functioning of the whole metropolitan area at a minimum cost for its inhabitants.

Similar solutions have been suggested for several types of cities such as Washington, which has to grow in one direction, probably along the Potomac River, in order to avoid the great pressures which are coming in from all directions; or Beirut, which has to develop a centre, far from the present one, with its back to the sea and facing inland; or Copenhagen, which, in order to save the cultural values invested in its centre, must develop a pattern of landward growth, for it has been estimated that the present population, which is about 1.5 million, is going to grow to 5–5.5 million a century from now.

There are cases, though, where it is impossible to impose a theoretically ideal Dynapolis on the existing city for a number of reasons. Such a case is the city of Baghdad, where the dominant feature is the river Tigris, along which Baghdad was developed in the past in a practically linear way, and along which it will have to be developed in the future for many topographical and climatic reasons. In this case the natural form of the city is dynamic along the river. Thus, Baghdad cannot turn into a uni-directional Dynapolis. Because of this, it will always be subject to pressure on its centre, which is preferably going to be in a central location receiving pressure from at least two directions. In order to avoid these pressures, the master-plan of Baghdad has been conceived with a view towards growth, not only along the Tigris, but also in a vertical direction, for otherwise the roads near the river would be choked to death. Such growth in a vertical direction is not going to succeed unless the new parts of the city have advantages over the parts near the river. This is why it has been suggested that the pattern of the river should be repeated by digging major canals parallel to it – a development which would draw the city out in parallel lines. Such a solution will not have the advantages of the ideal Dynapolis, but here the practical limitations set by the landscape show that we should not speak of theoretical solutions, but should try in every case to solve the problem in what is the best possible way in the local circumstances.

What is ideal for one city with one centre which is surrounded by a uniform plain, such as Tema, is not ideal for the city of Baghdad, where the dominant feature is a great river.

A different situation is represented by the city of Athens, which does not lend itself to the implementation of the ideal Dynapolis. Here the basic feature is the fact that the city is surrounded by four mountains and is confined to a valley which imposes its own rules. The major part of the valley has already been filled by densely built-up communities. Thus, there is only one direction for expansion, namely to the north-east of the city. This is the only natural direction for expansion, but it is no longer a practical direction because of the densely built-up central areas connecting the present centre with the new one that would have to be created to the north-east, at the cross-roads of the national highways. In such a case the dynamic solution for Athens turns out to be the creation of a new centre in the non-developed area. This will act to relieve the existing centre of

Athens from all the pressures on it, and will allow it to survive as a normal centre for a normal metropolitan area that now serves 2 million people. The additional millions that are to be expected by the end of this century, and the millions that are going to be added later, will need the new centre which has already been proposed and is now under discussion.

Network of cities

However, there are cases in which the situation is not so simple. These occur where we do not have one single city, or a metropolitan area with one definitely predominant centre, but rather networks or centres serving urban areas which have already coalesced with each other. In such cases the solution no longer consists in letting the present centres expand, for they are usually choked and cannot expand in any direction without affecting their own areas as well as the adjoining urban areas. In most of these cases the real solution lies in deciding that, as these areas have coalesced and have no more space in which to expand, they should be turned into static areas as soon as possible. The additional population which will be attracted by the major city will then have to be absorbed by new centres; and, as the whole area is going to grow into one of a higher order, a much greater centre has to be created outside the built-up areas in order to relieve pressure and to serve, not only the existing cities, but also the new cities that are going to be created in the surrounding areas.

It becomes quite clear that, in the near future, we shall have three phases in the development of dynamic cities: the new cities which, as Islamabad and Tema prove, can be a great success and which must be multiplied if we want to save our cities; dynamic cities following the principle of an ideal Dynapolis where this is possible (and here we shall have to conceive patterns allowing our present cities to expand dynamically); finally, as this is not going to be possible in all cases, we shall have to decide that several cities will have to stop at a certain stage, while other cities in their vicinity will have to cope with the new population, to become centres of a major order and to provide services for the widening urban areas.

We will certainly also have cities which will remain static because of their locality or their functions. These will be mostly small cities, in outlying areas which have been by-passed by present trends, or cities which are in such small areas or valleys that, for them, there is no possibility of major growth. Such cities are going to survive as remnants of the past; but, as the whole of the world's additional population is going to flow into major cities, the material importance of the old-fashioned cities will decrease, while their cultural importance will have great value for us, since these cities are going to be much better to live in than the cities that will be suffering from population pressure.

The survival of values

During this period of dynamic growth for so many cities, we shall have to consider very seriously the following facts. There are economic, historic, cultural and aesthetic values already invested in our present cities. These values are at present in danger of becoming completely lost under the pressures which are accumulating in the existing urban areas. In a few decades, man, by recognizing the necessity to act in a different way in shaping the surface of this earth, is going to change his policy. By then, though, there is a great danger that all values hitherto created by thousands of years of civilization in urban form are going to be lost. Man will have lost all the examples of the urban way of life which have been created after hard effort and by trial and error through hundreds of generations. And their loss will mean a great disaster, even if man averts the death of his civilization.

At this stage we have to draw one conclusion: there is an imperative necessity to save all existing cities which contain certain values for as long as possible, until the time for the proper formation of the new world-city comes, as these cities with values are going to be very important for historical continuity and for the survival of the values of the past in the city of the future.

These dynamically growing cities will have to take two factors into account:

1. How to save the values of the past.
2. How to create the best values for the future.

In pursuing this policy, we shall have to make sure that we have the best solution for all five elements that will enter into the formation of the city of the future. We have to protect the natural landscape. It is high time to decide in advance which parts of the natural landscape must be saved, and to keep them open and to protect them forever by acquiring the ownership of them for the community. Man and society have to be served in the best way. This can be achieved by respecting every form created by them in the past and by the development of the new city in such a way as to serve man and not the machine. City functions have to be served in the most reasonable way. If they are functions that are directly related to human dimensions, they should follow the experience of former generations. Man has not changed the dimensions of basic things. If, on the contrary, functions are the result of additional needs, such as commuting over distances unknown before in urban areas, then we should find the most rational solution corresponding to the new requirements and new possibilities.

Thus the form of the city to come is going to be the product of different forces: those derived from man and from human dimensions, as in the past, and those which correspond to the new dimensions imposed by the machine, which must be dynamic and be unrelated to the past, as there were no such problems and solutions in the past. This must be done with only one thing in mind: how to serve man best, and not how to expand and enlarge existing urban forms which are incommensurate in both scale and content with the forms that are now going to have to be created on a completely different scale. The coming dynamic city will be, of necessity, a combination of the city of the past and the city of the future. It will be traditional in its minor units and futuristic in its major units.

Ecumenopolis: a static world-wide city

The dimensions of the world-wide city are going to be, towards the end of the twenty-first century, the largest that will be compatible with man's survival. Certainly this is a flexible notion, based on modern technological progress. We assume that technology will continue to develop as at present; this is the only assumption on which we can imagine this earth being able to house some tens of thousands of millions of human beings. The moment will come, though, when even a technology that will allow of a much greater production of food than at present is not going to allow of any further expansion of population. There will be a limit to this because, even if we solve the problems of providing enough food, water and energy (we may take for granted a constant increase in food-production by an ever-developing technology, and also a full use of ocean water and energy sources), the population is going to reach a magnitude beyond which it should not expand. An increase beyond that magnitude would not leave enough space for the formation of a proper habitat for man, for the preservation of nature, and for the survival of open spaces in proper balance with the built-up areas of the world. At this point the population of the earth will reach its limit.

This limit, as I have already suggested, will probably be on the order of not less than 20 thousand million people and not more than 50; and for practical purposes, we can assume it to be something like 35 thousand million. As far as man can understand and imagine the future, this is the population of the world-wide city that we can expect by the end of the twenty-first century. As the city will then have attained its maximum population, and therefore its maximum physical dimensions, it will be static.

Humanity, after having lived for thousands of years in static settlements, villages and cities, and after having passed through a few centuries, four at the maximum, in dynamically growing settlements, will finally settle down in a world-wide, static, ecumenical city.

This city is already under construction. It will absorb almost all the important cities of the present, and will gradually grow out of them through their dynamic growth, as well as through the dynamic growth of the new settlements that are going to be created. It will be composed of almost all the major cities of the past and present. This city is going to expand widely over the plains and the great valleys, especially near the oceans, seas, great lakes and rivers, since the most restrictive factor in its formation will be the presence of water. Even when de-salinized water can be used economically for urban purposes, it will be available only near the level of the oceans

and lakes, so these will attract the city of the future, as the small rivers attracted primitive settlements.

The ecumenical city is going to pass through two phases. In the first phase, which has already started, it will gradually build up through the expansion of dynamically growing settlements. It will consist of dynamic parts and thus will change automatically from more primitive towards more developed forms. When it finally reaches the maximum calculable population and estimatable area, it will not expand any more, and in this phase it will undergo only those minor alterations that will be indispensable for the re-adjustment of the population, the economy, and the functions necessary for the world-wide city.

The shape of the Ecumenopolis

The city of the future is going to form a world-wide network. The centres of a higher order are going to be located mainly where the greatest concentrations of population are, i.e. in the greatest plains which have the best climate and the best water-resources. The connections between them will follow the natural lines of communication as well as some underground and submarine tunnels and the corresponding air-corridors.

In this network of major and minor centres, the Ecumenopolis will have a hierarchical structure of centres. The structure will range from the very small centre corresponding to present neighbourhoods, through centres of middle importance with a population corresponding to the large metropolitan areas of the present, i.e., from 5 to 10 million, to centres of the highest order with populations running to hundreds of millions. These centres are going to form networks of different orders within the major network.

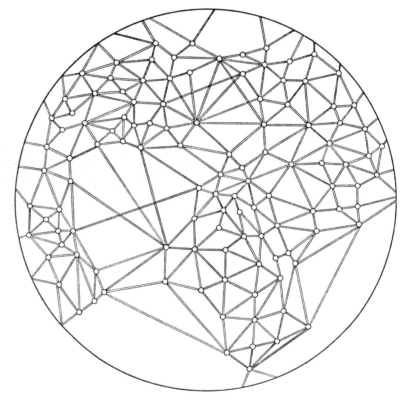

The city of the future will form a world-wide network consisting of centres of several orders interconnected by settled parts of various importance.

Several of these centres are going to comprise all types of functions, since they will provide administration, management, transportation, culture, production and pastime for a wide area. Several others, though, are going to be specialized centres catering for special local factors or traditions. Such cities – for example, Cambridge, Massachusetts – will attract all types of educational facilities and become important specialized centres of education of a very high order in the network of the world-wide city, while others will be important cultural, political or pleasure centres.

In this way the Ecumenopolis is going to be much more democratic in its nature than other cities of the past. The fact that it will be world-wide means that it will have no beginning and no end. It will, therefore, not have any central point that will be of much greater importance than the rest. By necessity it will lead to a much more democratic society, in which centres all round the world will be able to distinguish themselves by the type of services that they will provide, by the type of people that they will attract, and by their excellence in certain particular fields.

The notion of centrality is going to be different in the world-wide city. There will be no single central place, but a number distributed all round the world, which will be more important than the others of a lower order in their environs, but of equal importance with others not in their immediate vicinity. However, even centres in the immediate vicinity of the major centres will be able to distinguish themselves through achievements in specialized fields. There will no longer be any reason why a central area in the universal city of Africa should not be the seat of political power for at least a major African region, and why great centres of education and culture, deriving their forces from the roots of African traditions and civilizations, should not be developed near the lakes on the high plateau of eastern Africa.

Nature and the Ecumenopolis

The preservation of the natural landscape and natural elements like air and water is going to become increasingly important in the Ecumenopolis, since in many areas and in many respects we may be reaching the limits of the possible use of natural resources. What part of the natural landscape is to remain free and unencumbered with any type of construction will have to be determined by a calculation of the extent of the areas that must remain free of any man-made works in order to provide proper space for production, pre-

servation of wild life, leisure, and the proper balance of oxygen, hydrogen and nitrogen in the atmosphere. To infringe upon any part of the natural landscape or natural resources which have not been earmarked for development in advance is something that will not be allowed.

The areas to be preserved will fall into several different categories. Certainly the most beautiful areas will be preserved, so that we can expect the vicinity of minor lakes, hills, mountain-sides and waterfalls to be scheduled in this category. Areas which are potentially very productive will also have to be preserved, as well as those which cannot be built on in an economic way, either because they are at high altitudes to which water cannot be lifted at an economic cost, or because they cannot be built upon at a reasonable cost.

The total natural resources which are to be preserved will be broken up into areas of different orders of magnitude, varying from very big areas in deserts or in great forests to very small gardens or parks within the built-up areas.

These natural areas will either cover surfaces of different dimensions and shapes which will have a certain importance as natural areas, or they will form long strips connecting the areas of that kind, so as to allow man to move from a minor area towards a major one. As distinguished from the city of the past, which was a built-up area surrounded by natural landscapes, the natural landscapes of the future are going to be surrounded by built-up areas. But they will have to form a system of interconnected natural areas.

The natural landscapes that are to be left on the earth are not only going to be of different sizes; they are also going to be of different characters, ranging from those which will be left completely untouched by man, in order to preserve wild life to the greatest extent

Ecumenopolis in the North American continent in a medium scale. (See p. 336.)

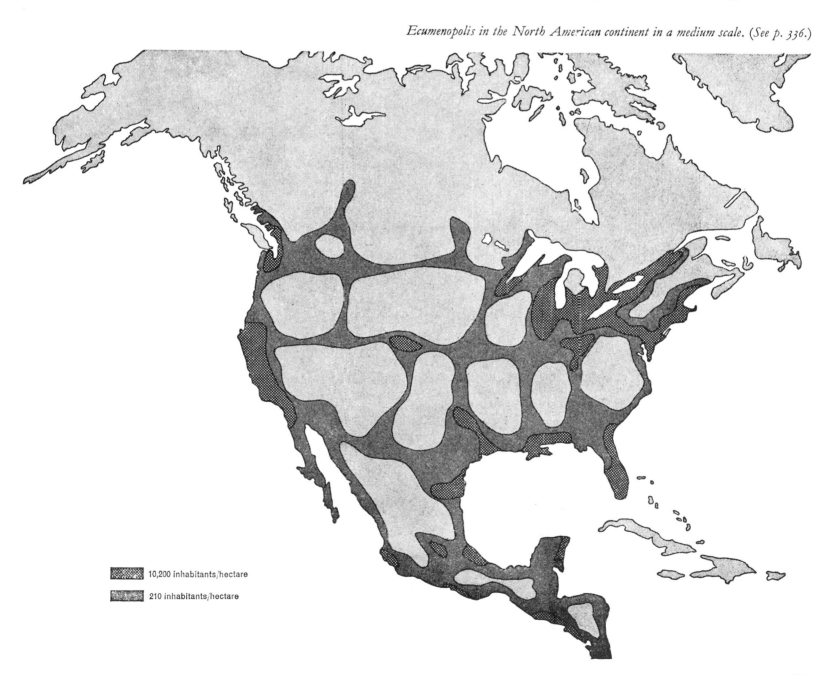

10,200 inhabitants/hectare

210 inhabitants/hectare

Ecumenopolis in Greece in a microscale. (See p. 336.)

possible, to those which will be gradually remodelled by man, down to the decorative gardens which will try to catch the meaning of the form of the whole earth and to present it on a very small scale in a symbolic way.

The small parks and gardens will, therefore, be of different kinds according to the area in which they are laid out. In India or Pakistan, for example, they should represent all the different landscapes from which the people come: the landscapes of the Indus Valley, Bengal and Sind. In these miniature natural landscapes man will find the reflection of the major landscapes from which he derives his ancestry.

These natural landscapes should offer man all the challenges which he will have lost through the construction of the world-wide city – the challenges of the open oceans and wild mountains which man should always try to conquer. As Bertrand Russell rightly tells us, 'Man should always be given the chance to cross the oceans on rafts like the Kon-Tiki.' These challenges will also exist on a very small scale in the gardens and nurseries where children will be given a replica of nature within the dimensions of childhood in order that they may start to conquer nature on this scale with their bodies and minds. Thus, every family garden and community garden will symbolize nature, its variety, its problems and its relation to man.

Man in the Ecumenopolis

This is the most difficult problem that will have to be faced by the people who will be responsible for the construction of the city of the future. It is much easier to speak of a system of transportation, of cars and machines, than of man, the great unknown. What kind of man will inhabit the city of the future? The kind that is closer to the classical ideal, or the kind equipped with all sorts of mechanical extensions that reduce man to a manipulator of machines? I myself hope that the kind of man that is going to inhabit the ecumenical city will be much closer to the Hellenic ideal. The reason is that this is an ideal which has appealed to the majority of people throughout the history of man. This is natural, if we remember that the Greeks idealized, not the Greek type of man, but a universal type derived from several parts of the world. They were able to understand this universal type better, because they were living at a cross-roads of civilization and in a type of landscape and area half-way between the cold and hot climates. It is natural for us to assume this kind of man to be the typical kind for the future, since this kind comes from an environment which was preferred by man in the past – the Mediterranean and Middle Eastern environment – and which is also going to be preferred in the future, as is indicated by the present trends towards the Mediterranean, Florida, and the West Coast of the United States.

However, we certainly cannot expect that there will be only one type of man in the Ecumenopolis. On the contrary, we should allow for all types of people. If I speak of one representative type, it is because I believe that we might be tending towards a single civilization which might have several of the characteristics of the ancient Greek culture. For similar reasons, the ancient Greek culture can be taken as being representative of several ancient civilizations.

The Ecumenopolis should, however, leave opportunities open for all types of people of the present and the future. We should not predetermine man's development, we should only set the frame for it. With this in mind, we should provide for the survival of all types of natural landscape and cultural values of the past, and we should create no more than a frame for the future life of man, leaving it to him in generation after generation to shape his proper habitat for himself.

If the Ecumenopolis ought not to predetermine the development of man, it also should not predetermine the development of society. The city should provide the physical shell for any type of society that may develop in the future.

As we do not know what political systems will finally survive or develop, any consideration of the city of the future should be based, not on political theories, but on dimensional considerations derived from such features and such forms as will probably remain unaltered in the city of the future. Among these then are the human dimensions, for example. As we do not expect man to double his physical size, we should always reckon with the existence of the human scale in the city. If we speak of the larger scale of the city – a scale that is no longer influenced by the physical dimensions of man and his human scale – we think of magnitudes derived from organizational considerations. Man is tending to form neighbourhoods and communities of certain dimensions which can be served best by one system of shopping-centres, irrespective of the political or social system.

In order to allow man and society to develop freely, the ecumenical city should respect the rules which are imposed by the structure of the landscape (plains and mountains, oceans and rivers), as well as those based upon the dimensions of man and the forms of organization in his social life.

Functions in the Ecumenopolis

Traffic is going to be the greatest problem of all in the Ecumenopolis. The number of the people and the amount of the goods that will have to circulate are virtually unimaginable in relation to present figures. Freedom of development will mean a much greater mobility of people; but, at the same time, these will need permanent settlements for their residence and for their places of culture and work. The city of the future will have new systems of transportation. The time that we spend in the most unreasonable way today is the time spent in moving about within our urban areas. We are going to need a completely different system of traffic for men and goods. This is going to be an underground system of very high-speed traffic for all types of vehicles both for mass transportation and for individual transportation.

In the city of the future both types will co-exist, and, as greater numbers of people will require individual means of transportation, the whole system is going to be based on tunnels connecting the main points of the ecumenical city. For the largest dimensions of all, transportation is going to be based on a system of rockets; for the very large dimensions short of that, a system of jets or their successors will be utilized. For distances of hundreds of miles, which will be of interest to the great bulk of people for their daily movement, man is going to rely on a system of radar-controlled cars in radar-controlled underground tubes, where millions of cars will move with the greatest safety at speeds of hundreds of miles an hour, allowing people, with a mere turn of the proper dial, to travel distances of miles in a few minutes and find themselves within a few hundred metres of their final destination, which they will then be able to reach by driving or walking.

If the traffic-problem is solved, then residence can be in the best locations of this world-city, as there will be no reason for people not to select the best beach or mountain or hillside for their residence,

many miles away from their employment and other functions, with no fear of losing an important part of their time in sitting idle and getting nervous in long queues on the highways and at the crossroads of the city.

Places of employment are going to be of two categories. The most important will be where the white-collar workers, working with computers and automatic machines, are going to be employed. These places could be everywhere, from the small communities to the major ones, as they will be clean and will not create any noise or obstruction for the neighbourhood. This is where the bulk of the people is likely to be employed. There will also be other places of employment which will be connected with the raw materials close to the bauxite mines, where we should expect the future aluminium plants to be. These will be so automated that they will employ only a few people who will be able to commute easily by airplane from their residences. Employment connected with natural resources will be much more scattered than it is now, and much more dense in the major concentrations of urban areas.

Opportunities for leisure will always exist near residences, but also in other appropriate locations (sports, for instance, near the oceans and lakes or mountains) since the transportation problem will be reduced in importance.

Many of the functions of the city are going to be underground, exactly as our body-functions are underneath the skin. Not only are the water-supply and sewage and power-distribution and communications systems going to be underground, but the whole system of transportation of man and goods is going to be buried deep in the earth as well, in order to leave the surface for man and his buildings.

Thus, buildings which are beginning to lose importance, architecture which is beginning to be forgotten, and art which is hidden between machines or inside buildings, are all going to come out into the open.

The natural landscape that is to be preserved and remodelled in the best possible way is going to provide the proper diagram for all types of buildings. As buildings are not only utilitarian but also create the cultural environment for man, and as man should be free to develop his culture, we have every reason to believe that buildings should not be as permanent as the underground networks of water and transportation will be. They should be lighter, so that they can be changed in accordance with changes in culture and in aesthetic habits in the city of the future, whereas the city's foundations should tend to become a permanent fixture, particularly the tunnels that will form networks for all types of movements. The superstructure of the city of the future should be light and interchangeable, in order that it may be developed gradually into the most ideal habitat for man

Is life to be tolerably human or even tolerable in this world-wide city? Is life even going to be possible in this monster city, controlled by machines which will encompass the earth? The answer is definitely 'No' if we allow this world-wide city to expand without any respect for man, as it has been expanding up to now. It should be 'Yes', though, if we recognize the fact that this city should be built for man, and if we take into consideration the necessity of creating the proper environment for him.

This new environment is going to expand over large distances, and it will have to be traversed by mechanical means. We shall have to hop in rockets or fly and drive at speeds of hundreds and thousands of miles an hour. This, of necessity, is going to have to be done in capsules. We are already being taught to live in capsules by travelling in modern jet-planes. Man will have to adjust himself to the notion of living in two types of space – in the static space on this earth which he controls, and in the fluid space which he will be able to control only within some kind of capsule.

The basic human community

Up to what size in the Ecumenopolis can the solid space under human control be carried? The answer can only be that it will have to correspond to human dimensions. We are used to the notion that our clothes must correspond to our body. We have to learn that our rooms do not appreciably change dimension when there are changes of culture, civilization and phase. This is also true of houses. On the other hand, we saw that this will not be possible for the ecumenical city, since this will expand beyond the human scale. Where should

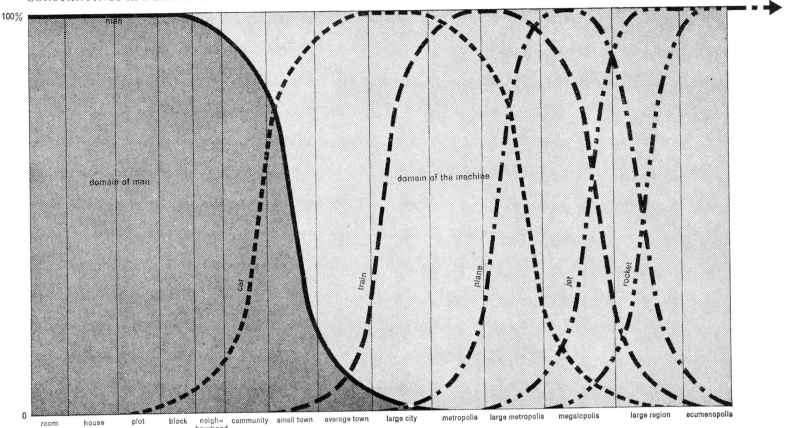

The efficiency and importance of different means of transportation in relation to the Ekistic logarithmic scale.

we stop, then, in expanding our static space for man, between the Ecumenopolis, which cannot have static space because man needs fluid space here, and the house, where space, we hope, will necessarily continue to be human?

If the present trends persist, man will continue to flee into the house and will become a troglodyte. This is not right; we should expand human space as much as possible. We have to find this human space and to form it into the basic cell of the ecumenical city. The dimensions of this basic cell will be those of the human community.

Is it right, however, to build the ecumenical city out of cells consisting of human communities? Yes, if we understand that we are only creating a shell, and that this shell is going to be re-built by every successive generation that uses it. What is necessary is to accept the principle that the ecumenical city will consist of cells of human communities, and that it will find their proper dimensions. Then every generation and every type of inhabitant will give the proper shape to the community in which he is going to live. As the construction, as we have already said, is going to be light and less permanent than it is now, this is a community that can be reshaped by succeeding generations.

This must be derived from human dimensions. We are now in a position to see where we stand. A study of the ancient city has shown the point at which man has set the limits of human dimensions in the past. Corresponding studies of present-day cities, in which people are still moving freely and forming natural communities, have confirmed these findings.

There are two types of communities which have been formed since ancient times. There are those which correspond to the minimum distances that man cares to walk, within which he can find the minimum of services, and there are those which correspond to the average maximum distances that man is willing to walk, within the radius of which he can find a large number of services.

The dimensions of the minor community are up to a length of 800 metres and a width of 400–500 metres. In such communities the people would never live at a distance of more than 400 metres from the centre. Such communities are represented by the minor cities of ancient times, like Priene, and by minor present-day communities, with facilities, shops, etc., that are to be found in many contemporary cities. The major group of the human community corresponds

to major cities of ancient times, like Athens, where the maximum distance in which people live from the centre is one kilometre. It also corresponds to the maximum distances covered by man in contemporary cities in search of almost all indispensable facilities.

In the light of these two considerations, we are now beginning to build communities which will form the cells of the city of the future. The basic principle in them is that man should be able to walk in order to satisfy all his needs in the community. The central part of them is the 'soft' part; there, man is in control and the space is formed with no influence of the machine. Outside, on the contrary, machines are free to run at very high speeds, using all their power, facilitating transportation and communication over longer distances.

Communities like those built in Baghdad in 1955, or like those now under construction in Eastwick, show how this principle can be implemented for lower or higher income areas, for a society with few or with many cars.

Communities like those of the University of the Punjab, which is now under construction, or like a major community corresponding to a small ancient city, show how the same ideas can be implemented in major institutions.

Communities like downtown Louisville, which has been approved and is going to be constructed, show how we can create human surroundings even in over-congested areas.

Finally, communities like those of Islamabad show how a whole system of major and minor communities can be created, and how, by expanding these, the system can cover wide urban areas while still allowing for the best type of metropolitan structure (proper systems of transportation, communications, facilities, etc.) with the best type of environment on a human scale.

A microcosm of the whole earth

The human community should be a replica of the whole surface of the earth on a human scale. It should consist of natural landscapes, either pre-existing or to be remodelled – an artificial landscape can be even more beautiful and more satisfactory than a natural one (consider the ability of the Japanese to create ideal gardens). In such a landscape, man is going to find all his opportunities for daily contact with nature. In a community of this kind, children will run free with no fear of the machine, and then will become used to growing up into being the normal citizens of the world-wide city which they will enter after the nursery age. Just as the house is still the breeding ground for babies, the human community should be the breeding ground for infants and young children.

Man will be in control of this community. His dimensions define the dimensions of the community, his walking-capacity defines the scale, his senses define the aesthetics of the community; architecture has a meaning, and landscape and works of art again have importance, because man is in rapport with them.

The future city's natural cells

Society will find its shell in this human community. Although we shall have all types of communities in the city of the future – communities based on common interests, on education, and on the professions – the human community will give man in the city of the future the opportunity to re-establish the community of the neighbourhood. There is no reason to think that this should be eliminated,

as it is being eliminated in the present-day city to the detriment of many social values.

Basic functions will be combined in the human community, as in the cities of the past. It will have its own system of transportation, based mainly on the concept of man circulating on the inner lines and machines only on the peripheral lines. It will be residential, and will have the corresponding services; it will have shopping, commercial, cultural, religious, administrative and recreational centres. It will have proper opportunities for employment (there is no reason why many places of employment, offices and small industries should not be incorporated into the human community, as they will not bother anyone) and leisure (parks, sports-grounds, etc.). Thus the major part of the needs of the inhabitants will be covered locally, so that they will have to go beyond their community only in order to find goods of a higher order. If these are available in the next community, they can walk to it by using a pedestrian bridge over the lines of transportation which, for a few more generations, are going

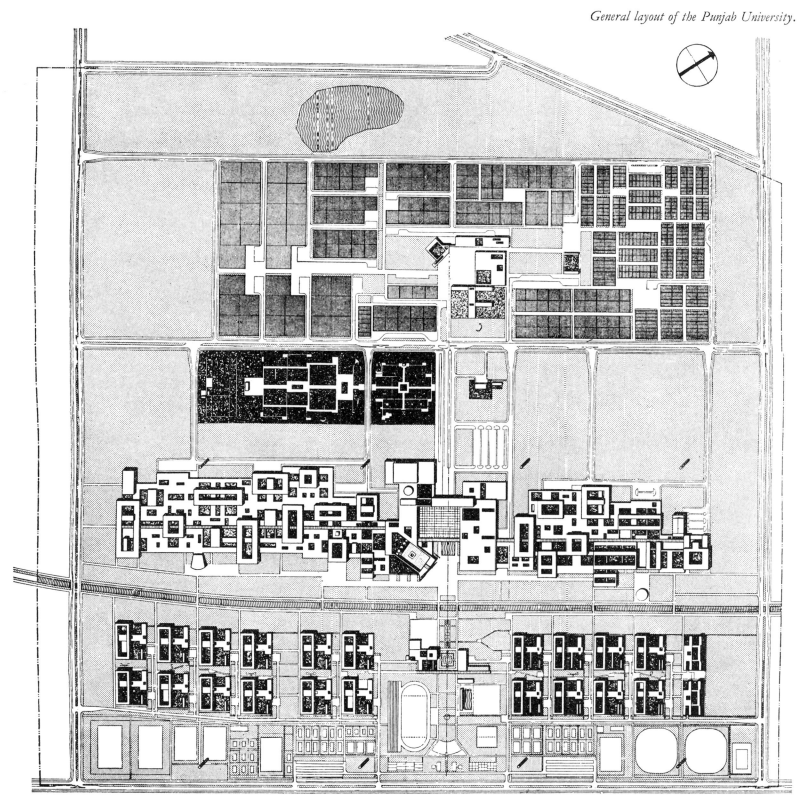

General layout of the Punjab University.

357

to be on the surface of the earth before they are finally buried deep underground. If these services of a higher order are at longer distances, then man will be able to use the system of transportation that is going to allow him to travel to the other communities at a very high speed.

The form of this community will correspond, to a large degree, to the city of the past. Man will again find himself in dimensions to which he is accustomed and in which he has expressed himself for thousands of years in a certain way. He will probably follow many of the rules of the city of the past. He will emphasize public space, the small street, the squares and the central functions which will be expressed in more monumental buildings. This is an emphasis that has been obliterated lately by the invasion of the automobile.

It is in these millions of communities which will be the cells of the Ecumenopolis that man is going to re-establish democratic institutions on a very low level, by expressing his own desires, his own heart, through trial and error. In these great numbers of communities, man is going to create again the best type of habitat on a human scale. It is this habitat of man, the human community, the natural cell of the city of the future, that, by being properly interconnected with the other representatives of its kind, is going to form the texture which will cover the whole city. It is in this basic element that the life of man can be preserved and can be properly developed. This is why it is important that this community should be shaped at every phase, in every locality, by the people who are going to live in it themselves. This is the community of democratic expression and democratic life.

The city as a whole will be the result of good programming and planning, based on very careful calculations of man's needs and of the possibilities of modern technology. The universal city of the future should be, as a whole and as a frame, the product of the creative work of every able mind which can comprehend, and give shape to, the total habitat of man on this earth. The human community is the one in which the ordinary human being will find the opportunity to express himself in the best possible way.

In the past, the city plan was defined by the city authority, by the ruler. Man had the opportunity of expressing himself personally in his own architecture, by building with his own hands or by choosing his master-builder. In the future, organized society is going to take care of the universal city as a whole, and man is going to express himself in his own architecture and in his own human community. This is the great challenge for the builders of the city of the future; how to build the frame without predetermining the life of the man who is going to inhabit it. The objective is to leave him free to express himself within the best possible frame.

We are moving into the unknown. We do not know how man is going to express himself, but this is no reason why we should not build the proper frame round him. Otherwise, we shall be heading towards anarchy. We must build the frame. We must re-create the earth's skin which, in our forests, has been burnt, and in our hills has been cut away, and in our cities has been covered by a cancer. We have to build the frame of the universal city. How is man going to express himself within it? We do not know. We do not know whether he will create larger buildings, or will try to cover neighbourhoods or whole communities with a single structure, as Buckminster Fuller suggests. We only know that something like this may be dangerous, as it may gradually isolate man from the elements of nature, and this isolation may turn him into an inhabitant of the earth who is not interested in what happens outside his shell. We may have several ideas on the formation of the city of the future, but we must allow man to express himself in the best possible way according to his desires and according to the current phase of his evolution. One thing that we must not and cannot do is to allow this city to grow and to develop haphazardly, for then it will asphyxiate man. We have to foresee, imagine and develop the proper evolution, invent the right solution, and then build our city on the basis of these.

NOTES TO THE TEXT

Quattrocento Venice

p. 62 *Canon Pietro Casola's Pilgrimage to Jerusalem in the Year 1494* (ed. and trans. by M. Margaret Newett), Manchester 1907, pp. 124–5.
The Memoirs of Philip de Commines (ed. A.R. Scoble), London 1856, II, pp. 169–70.
Casola, *op. cit.*, p. 338.
F.C. Lane, *Andrea Barbarigo, Merchant of Venice 1418–1449*, Baltimore 1944, p. 48.

p. 64 Casola, *op. cit.*, p. 141.
Quoted in F.C. Lane, *Venetian Ships and Shipbuilders*, Baltimore 1934, p. 172.

p. 67 Quoted in Horatio Brown, *Venice, an Historical Sketch*, London 1895, pp. 325–9.

Goethe's Weimar

p. 97 C.E. Dodd, *An Autumn near the Rhine*, London 1818, p. 15.

p. 97-8 S.T. Coleridge, *Constitution of Church and State*, quoted by R. Williams, *Culture and Society*, London 1958, p. 61.

p. 99 Siegmund von Seckendorff, letter quoted by W. Bode, *Karl August von Weimar, Jugendjahre*, Berlin 1913, p. 306.

p. 102 Friedrich von Schiller, letter to F.H. Jacobi, 25 January 1795.

Alexandria under the Ptolemies

p. 111 Homer, *Odyssey* (trans. by A.J. Murray), London 1946, Book IV, pp. 354–9.
Plutarch, *Life of Alexander*, v. VII, p. 26.

p. 112 *The Geography of Strabo* (trans. by H.L. Jones), London 1949, Book XVII, C 791.
Ibid., C 794.
Ibid., C 795.
Ibid., C 793.

p. 113 *Ibid.*, C 794.

p. 114 Philo, *Legatio ad Gaium* (trans. by E. Mary Smallwood), Leiden 1961, p. 151.
Aristotle, *Politique*, Book VII, 1326a.

p. 116 Caesar, *De Bello Civili*, Book III, 110.
Callixenus, *Athénée*, Book v, 203 C.
Strabo, *op. cit.*, C 793.

Changan

p. 145 Alexander C. Soper, translating from a T'ang stone inscription commemorating The Hall of the Pure Land Paradise erected at the end of the seventh century in the precincts of the Shih-chi Ssŭ in Changan. See his volume *The Evolution of Buddhist Architecture in Japan*, Princeton 1942, p. 124, n. 208.

p. 147 Adapted from the translation in William Hung, *Tu Fu, China's Greatest Poet*, Cambridge, Mass., 1952, pp. 125–6.

p. 148 Arthur Waley, *Translations from the Chinese*, New York 1941, p. 146.

p. 149 Edward H. Schafer, 'The Last Years of Changan' in *Oriens Extremus*, x (1963), p. 138. For full treatment of exotic products in T'ang life, see his excellent volume *The Golden Peaches of Samarkand*, Berkeley, Calif., 1963.
Lionel Giles, translating 'The Lament of the Lady of Ch'in' by Wei Chuang (d. 910) in *T'oung Pao*, XXIV (1926), pp. 305–80.
In 904 what was left of the city was ordered to be destroyed and the usable building materials to be rafted down to Kai-fêng. Two years later the T'ang line was extinguished.

Muslim Cordoba

All the Ibn Hazm passages are from *The Ring of the Dove*. The quotations from Ibn Sa'id are translated by A.J. Arberry.

p. 177 Amados de los Rios: quoted from A.F. Calvert and W.M. Gallichan, *Cordova*, London 1907, pp. 96–7.

Mexico-Tenochtitlan

p. 203 'La Historia de Tlatelolco desde los tiempos más remotos' (1528), in *Anales de Tlatelolco*, Mexico City 1948, p. 31.
Hernando Alvarado Tezozomoc, *Cronica Mexicayotl*, Mexico City 1949, p. 51.
Ibid., p. 65.

p. 204 *Ibid.*, p. 29.
Bernal Diaz del Castillo, *Historia Verdadera de la Conquista de la Nueva España*, Mexico City 1939, 3 vols, chapter 87.
Ibid., chapters 82, 88.

p. 205 *Ibid.*, chapter 88.

p. 206 Hernán Cortés, 'Cartas de Relación dirigidas al emperador Carlos v' (2nd *carta*), in *Biblioteca Histórica de la Iberia*, Mexico City 1870, I, p. 112.
Ibid., p. 156.

p. 209 Fernando de Alva Ixtlilxochitl, *Obras Históricas*, Mexico City 1891, I, p. 360.

Shah Abbas's Isfahan

p. 220 Sir Thomas Herbert, *Some Yeares Travels into Africa and Asia the Great ...*, London 1638, p. 160.
John Fryer, *A New Account of the East Indies and Persia ...*, London 1698, p. 260.

p. 222 Herbert, *loc. cit.*

p. 224 *Ibid.*, pp. 159–61.

Mid-twentieth-century New York

p. 331 See *The Letters of William James* (ed. Henry James), Boston 1920.
E. Porter Belden, *New York: Past, Present and Future*, New York 1849, p. 45.
Henry James, *The American Scene*, New York 1946, p. 92.
Herman Melville, 'Pierre, or, the Ambiguities,' in *The Works of Herman Melville*, London 1922, IX, p. 9.

p. 332 *The Philosophy of George Santayana* (ed. P.A. Schilpp), Evanston and Chicago 1940, p. 560.
Lewis Mumford, *The City in History: Its Origins, Its Transformations, and Its Prospects*, New York 1961, p. 535.

p. 333 Henry James, *op. cit.*, p. 84.
Ibid., p. 76.

p. 334 James Bryce, *The American Commonwealth* (2nd revised ed.). New York 1908, I, p. 681.

p. 335 See Spencer Brydon's vision of New York in Henry James's story, 'The Jolly Corner'.
Theodore Dreiser, *A Traveller at Forty*, New York 1913, p. 512.
Theodore Dreiser, *A Hoosier Holiday*, New York 1916, p. 365.

SELECT BIBLIOGRAPHY

Athens in the Age of Pericles

Beazley, J.D., and Ashmole, B. *Greek Sculpture and Painting* (Cambridge 1932)

Bowra, C. M. *The Greek Experience* (London 1957)

Ferguson, W. S. *Greek Imperialism* (London 1913)

Lesky, A. *Greek Tragedy,* trans. Frankfort, H.A. (London 1965)

Schede, M. *The Acropolis of Athens,* trans. Price, H.T. (London 1927)

Zielinski, T. *The Religion of Ancient Greece* (London 1926)

Zimmern, A. *The Greek Commonwealth* (London 1961)

Quattrocento Venice

Brown, H. 'Venice' in *The Cambridge Modern History,* v. 1 (Cambridge 1902)

La Civiltà Veneziana del Quattrocento (Florence 1957)

Molmenti, P. *Venice: the Middle Ages,* 2 vols (London 1906)

Venice: the Golden Age, 2 vols (London 1907)

Medicean Florence

Baron, H. *The Crisis of the Early Italian Renaissance,* 2 vols (Princeton 1955)

Bayley, C.C. *War and Society in Renaissance Florence* (Toronto 1961)

Berenson, B. *The Florentine Painters of the Renaissance* (New York/London 1909)

Brucker, G.A. *Florentine Politics and Society, 1343–1378* (Princeton 1962)

Burckhardt, J. *The Civilization of the Renaissance in Italy* (London 1951)

Davidsohn, R. *Geschichte von Florenz,* 4 vols (Berlin 1896–1927)

Hoover, R. de *The Medici Bank: Its Organisation, Management, Operations and Decline* (New York/London 1948)

Hyett, F.A. *Florence: Her History and Art to the Fall of the Republic* (London 1903)

Martines, L. *The Social World of the Florentine Humanists, 1390–1460* (Princeton 1963)

Pater, W. *The Renaissance: studies in Art and Poetry* (London 1877)

Perrens, F.T. *Histoire de Florence,* 6 vols (Paris 1877–83)

Ross, J. *Lives of the Early Medici* (London 1910)

Symonds, J.A. *Renaissance in Italy,* 7 vols (London 1875–86)

Goethe's Weimar

Bianquis, G. *La vie quotidienne en Allemagne à l'époque romantique* (Paris 1958)

Bruford, W. H. *Culture and Society in Classical Weimar* (Cambridge 1962)

Germany in the Eighteenth Century (Cambridge 1935)

Fairley, B. *A Study of Goethe* (Oxford 1947)

Kuhn, P. 'Weimar' in *Stätten der Kultur,* v. 13, 4th edition by Wahl, H. (Leipzig 1925)

Lewes, G. H. *The Life and Works of Goethe* (London 1855)

Alexandria under the Ptolemies

Adriani, A. *Annuaire du Musée gréco-romain d'Alexandrie* (1932)

Bell, H.I. 'Alexandria' in *Journal of Egyptian Archaeology,* 13 (1927)

Jews and Christians in Egypt (London 1924)

Breccia, E. *Alexandrea ad Aegyptum* (English edition, Bergamo 1922)

Brown, B.R. *Ptolemaic Paintings and Mosaics and the Alexandrian Style* (Cambridge, Mass., 1957)

Calderini, A. 'Alexandreia' in *Dizionario dei nomi geografici e topografici dell'Egitto greco-romano* (Cairo 1935)

Couat, A. *Alexandrian Poetry under the First Three Ptolemies* (London 1931)

Jones, A.H.M. 'Alexandria of Egypt' in *The Greek City from Alexander to Justinian* (Oxford 1940)

Jouguet, P. 'Les assemblées d'Alexandrie à l'époque ptolémaïque' in *Bulletin de la Société Royale d'Archéologie d'Alexandrie,* 37 (1948)

Lumbroso, G. 'Testi e commenti concernenti l'antica Alessandria' in *Glossario Lumbroso,* I, 1 (Milan 1934)

Musurillo, H. *Acts of the Pagan Martyrs. Acta Alexandrinorum* (Oxford 1954)

Parsons, E.A. *The Alexandrian Library, Glory of the Hellenic World* (London 1952)

Picard, C. 'Sur quelques représentations nouvelles du phare d'Alexandrie et sur l'origine alexandrine des paysages portuaires' in *Bulletin de Correspondance Hellénique,* 76 (1952)

Rostovtzeff, M. 'Alexandreia' in *Social and Economic History of the Hellenistic World,* v. III (Oxford 1941)

Rowe, A., and Brioton, E. *Discovery of the Famous Temple and Enclosure of Serapis at Alexandria* (Cairo 1946)

Tarn, W.W. *Hellenistic Civilisation,* 3rd edition with collaboration of Griffith, G.-T. (London 1952)

Thiersch, A. *Pharos, Antike Islam und Occident. Ein Beitrag zur Architekturgeschichte* (Leipzig 1909)

Rome of the Antonines

Carcopino, J. *Daily Life in Ancient Rome* (London 1941)

Dill, S. *Roman Society from Nero to Marcus Aurelius* (London 1904)

Henderson, B.W. *Principate of the Emperor Hadrian* (London 1923)

Paribeni, R. *Optimus Princips* (Messina 1926)

Rostovtzeff, M. *The Social and Economic History of the Roman Empire* (Oxford 1926)

Changan

Hung, W. *Tu Fu, China's Greatest Poet* (Cambridge, Mass., 1952)

Pulleyblank, E.G. *The Background of the Rebellion of An Lu-shan* (London 1955)

Schafer, E.H. *The Golden Peaches of Samarkand* (Berkeley and Los Angeles 1963)

Twitchett, D.C. *Financial Administration under the T'ang Dynasty* (Cambridge 1963)

Waley, A. *The Life and Times of Po Chü-i* (London 1949)

The Poetry and Career of Li Po (London 1950)

Christian Constantinople

Baynes, N.H. *The Byzantine Empire* (London 1925)

Beckwith, J. *The Art of Constantinople* (London 1961)

Cambridge Medieval History, v. IV, new edition, 2 vols

Hussey, J. M. *The Byzantine World* (London 1957)

Mathew, G. *Byzantine Aesthetics* (London 1963)

Ostrogorsky, G. *History of the Byzantine State,* trans. Hussey, J.M. (Cambridge 1955)

Runciman, S. *The Fall of Constantinople* (Cambridge 1965)

Sherrard, P. *Constantinople* (Oxford 1965)

Muslim Cordoba

Amador de los Rios y Villalta, R. *Inscripciones árabes de Córdoba,* 2nd edition (Madrid 1880)

Calvert, A.F., and Gallichan, W.M. *Cordova* (London 1907)
Hole, E. *Andalus* (London 1958)
Ibn Hazm *The Ring of the Dove,* trans. Arberry, A.J. (London 1953)
Lévi-Provençal, E. *Histoire de l'Espagne musulmane,* 2nd edition, 3 vols (Paris 1950–3)
Madrazo, P. de *Córdoba* (Barcelona 1884)
Sanchez-Albornoz C. *La España musulmana,* 2 vols (Buenos Aires 1960)

The Paris of Abelard and St Louis
Belloc, H. *Paris* (London 1907)
Evans, J. *Life in Medieval France* (London 1925)
Héron de Villefosse, R. *Histoire et géographie galantes de Paris* (Paris 1957)
Luchaire, A. *Social Life in France at the Time of Philip Augustus* (London 1912)
Rashdall, H. *The Universities of Europe of the Middle Ages* (Oxford 1942)
Tilley, A. *Medieval France* (Cambridge 1922)

Mexico-Tenochtitlan
Bernal, I. *Mexico Before Cortes* (New York 1964)
Caso, A. *People of the Sun* (University of Oklahoma 1962)
  'Los Barrios Antiguos de Tenochtitlan y Tlatelolco' in *Memorias de la Academia de Historia,* v. xv (Mexico City 1956)
Diaz del Castillo, B. *The True History of the Conquest of New Spain,* trans. Maudsley, A.P. (Mexico 1928)
Duran, D. de *The Aztecs,* trans. Heyden, D., and Horcasitas, F., intr. Bernal, I. (New York 1964)
Peterson, F.A. *Ancient Mexico* (London 1959)
Soustelle, J. *The Daily Life of the Aztecs* (London 1963)
Vaillant, G. *The Aztecs of Mexico* (Harmondsworth 1950)

Shah Abbas's Isfahan
Bruyn, C. de *Travels into Muscovy, Persia, and Part of the East-Indies* (London 1737), v. I, pp. 180–202, pl. 74–83
Chardin, J. *Voyages du Chevalier Chardin, en Perse et Autres Lieux de l'Orient,* ed. Langlès, L. (Paris 1811), vols VII–VIII
Costa, A., and Lockhart, L. *Persia* (London 1957)
Fryer, J. *A New Account of the East Indies and Persia in Eight Letters, being Nine Years Travels, begun 1672 and finished 1681* (London 1688)
Godard, A. 'Isfahan' in *Athar-e Iran* (Haarlem 1937), v. II, pp. 7–176
Herbert, T. *Some Yeares Travels into Africa and Asia the Great, Especially describing the Famous Empires of Persia and Industant. As also Divers other Kingdoms in the Orientall Indies, and Iles Adjacent* (London 1638), pp. 159–61
Lockhart, L. *Persian Cities* (London 1960)
Pope, A.U. (ed.) *A Survey of Persian Art from Prehistoric Times to the Present* (Oxford 1938), v. II, pp. 1179–1207, and v. v, pl. 283–300, 361–6, 396, 463–71, 473–86, 498, 501–7
Silva y Figueroa, G. de *L'Ambassade de D. Garcias de Silva Figueroa en Perse* (Paris 1667)

Mughal Delhi and Agra
Bernier, F. *Travels in the Mogul Empire,* edited by Constable, A., and Smith, V.A. (Oxford 1934)
Binyon, L. *Akbar* (London 1932)
Brown, P. *Indian Painting under the Mughals* (Oxford 1924)
Edwardes, S.M. *Babur, Diarist and Despot* (London 1926)
Fanshawe, H.C. *Delhi: Past and Present* (London 1902)
Havell, E.B. *Agra and The Taj* (London 1912)
Manucci, N. *Memoirs of the Mogul Court,* ed. Edwardes, M. (London 1957)
Sarkar, J. *History of Aurangzib,* 5 vols (Calcutta 1912–25)
  A Short History of Aurangzib, 1618–1707 (Calcutta 1930)
Smith, V.A. *Akbar, The Great Moghul* (Oxford 1927)
Spear, T.G.T. *Twilight of the Mughals* (Cambridge 1951)

Eighteenth-century St Petersburg
Bruce, H.J. *Silken Dalliance* (London 1946)
Byron, R. *First Russia Then Tibet* (London 1933)
Karsavina, T. *Theatre Street* (London 1930)
Marsden, C. *Palmyra of the North* (London 1942)
Sitwell, S. *Valse des Fleurs* (London 1941)

Vienna
Cecil, A. *Metternich, 1773–1859* (London 1933)
Gulick, C.A. *Austria from Habsburg to Hitler,* 2 vols (Berkeley and Los Angeles 1948)
Nicolson, H. *The Congress of Vienna* (London 1946)
Trollope, F. *Vienna and the Austrians,* 2 vols (London 1838)

Victorian and Edwardian London
Abercrombie, P. *County of London Plan* (London 1943)
Besant, W. *London* (London 1894)
Booth, C. *Life and Labour of the People in London,* 17 vols (London 1902)
Clunn, H. *London Rebuilt, 1897–1927* (London 1927)
Ensor, R.C. *England, 1870–1914* (Oxford 1936)
Hall, P. *London 2000* (London 1963)
Harling, R. *The London Miscellany – A Nineteenth-century Scrap-book* (Toronto 1937)
Jackson, W.E. *Achievement: a Short History of the L.C.C.* (London 1965)
Woodward, E.L. *The Age of Reform 1815–1870* (Oxford 1938)
Young, G.M. (ed.) *Early Victorian England 1830–65,* 2 vols (London 1934)

The American city in history
Gottman, J. *Megalopolis. The Urbanized Northeastern Seaboard of the United States* (New York 1961)
James, H. *The American Scene* (London 1907)
Lynd, R.S., and Lynd, H.M. *Middletown* (London 1929)
Mumford, L. *The Culture of Cities* (London 1938)
  City Development (New York 1945)
  The City in History (New York 1961)
Olmsted, D.L. (Jr), and Kimball, T. *Frederick Law Olmsted, Landscape Architect 1822–1903* (New York/London 1922)
Park, R. *Human Communities: The City and Human Ecology* (New York 1952)
Saarinen, E. *The City: Its Growth, Its Decay, and Its Future* (New York 1943)
Wright, F.L. *The Disappearing City* (New York 1938)

Mid-twentieth-century New York
Glazer, N., and Moynihan, D. *Beyond the Melting Pot* (Cambridge, Mass., 1963)
Gottman, J. *Megalopolis. The Urbanized Northeastern Seaboard of the United States* (New York 1961)
Jacobs, J. *The Death and Life of Great American Cities* (London 1962)
Mumford, L. *The City in History* (New York 1961)
Stein, M. *The Eclipse of Community* (Princeton 1960)
White, M., and White, L. *The Intellectual Versus the City* (Cambridge, Mass., 1962)

The coming world-city: Ecumenopolis
Doxiadis, C.A. *Architecture in Transition* (London 1963)
  Ecumenopolis: Towards the Universal City (Athens 1961)
  On the Measure of Man (Athens 1964)
  The New World of Urban Man (Athens 1965)
Geddes, P. *Cities in Evolution* (London 1949)
Giedion, S. *Space, Time and Architecture* (London 1956)
Gottman, J. *Megalopolis. The Urbanized Northeastern Seaboard of the United States* (New York 1961)
Mumford, L. *The City in History* (New York 1961)
Vernon, R. *Anatomy of a Metropolis* (Cambridge, Mass., 1959)

LIST OF ILLUSTRATIONS

In the following list the first numerals indicate the page numbers, and the second refer to plate numbers. Text illustrations are identified by page number only.

Nationale Forschungs- und Gedenkstätten, Weimar

Programme of the first performance of 'Wilhelm Tell', 17 March 1804. Nationale Forschungs- und Gedenkstätten, Weimar

Alexandria under the Ptolemies

107 1. Glass vase from Begram, Afghanistan, with representation of the Pharos of Alexandria; third–fourth century AD. Kabul Museum. Photo *Josephine Powell*

108–9 2. Silver coin of Lysimachus, King of Thrace, portrait of Alexander the Great deified; 306–281 BC. Courtesy *Museum of Fine Arts, Boston. Gift of Mrs George M. Brett*

3. Alexandria: bronze coin of Antoninus Pius, the Temple of Tyche; AD 138–61. British Museum. Photo *John Webb*

4. Roman clay lamp showing the port of Alexandria and the Royal Necropolis. Muzeum Narodowe, Poznan. Photo *L. Perz i F. Maćkowiak*

5. Alexandria: coin of Commodus, the Pharos and a ship; AD 187–8. British Museum. Photo *John Webb*

6. Alexandria: aerial view of the city. Photo *Radio Times Hulton Picture Library*

7. Alexandria: bronze coin of Antoninus Pius, the Temple of Serapis; AD 138–61. British Museum. Photo *John Webb*

8. Fragment of Greek Papyrus of the Book of Deuteronomy; second century AD. *John Rylands Library, Manchester*

110 9. Mosaic of a Nilotic scene from Praeneste, the Nile Delta in flood; Hellenistic. Museo Archeologico, Palestrina. Photo *Scala*

10. Mosaic from Thmuis, personification of Alexandria; Hellenistic copy of earlier original. Musée Gréco-Romain, Alexandria. (From Evaristo Breccia, *Le Musée Gréco-Romain 1925–1931*). Photo *John Webb*

113 Plan of Ptolemaic Alexandria. Drawn by Mrs Hanni Bailey

115 Portraits of Ptolemy II Philadelphus and Arsinoë on an engraved gem, from Georg Ebers, *Ägypten in Bild und Wort ...*, 1870

117 Reconstruction of bridges and palaces in Ptolemaic Alexandria. From Georg Ebers, *Ägypten in Bild und Wort ...*, 1870

The Rome of the Antonines

119 1. Rome: detail of Trajan's Column; AD 113. Photo *Josephine Powell*

120–1 2. Ostia: apartment house, the Cassegiato delle Trifore; second century AD. Photo *Fototeca Unione, Rome*

3. Ostia: public lavatory near the Forum; second century AD. Photo *Fototeca Unione, Rome*

4. Rome: relief from a sarcophagus, a money-changer; second century AD. Palazzo Salviati, Rome. Photo *Mansell-Alinari*

5. Ostia: mosaic floor of a shipping office in the Piazzale delle Corporazioni, ships in harbour; second century AD. Photo *Fototeca Unione, Rome*

6. Ostia: entrance of the Horrea Epagathiana; second century AD. Photo *Fototeca Unione, Rome*

122–3 7. Rome: the Colosseum seen from the Temple of Venus and Rome; late first century AD. Photo *Edwin Smith*

8. Mosaic of amphitheatre scene from Zliten, Tripolitania; late second century AD. Castello Museum, Tripoli. Photo *Roger Wood*

9. Rome: Trajan's Market; early second century AD. Photo *Josephine Powell*

124 10. Rome: relief showing Trajan and senators; early second century AD. Museo Profano Lateranense, Rome. Photo *Mansell-Alinari*

11. Rome: the library of Trajan's Baths; early second century AD. Photo *Fototeca Unione, Rome*

12. Ostia: floor-mosaic in the Piazzale delle Corporazioni, measuring corn; second century AD. Photo *Éditions Arthaud, Paris (Paul Ronald)*

13. Gallo-Roman relief from a sarcophagus found at Neumagen, payment of taxes; early third century AD. *Rheinisches Landesmuseum, Trier*

14. Rome: relief in the Forum Romanum showing the burning of tax records in AD 118; second century AD. Photo *Fototeca Unione, Rome*

15. Rome: coin-portrait of Hadrian; c. AD 132. *Trustees of the British Museum, London*

125 16. Rome: interior of the dome of the Pantheon; c. AD 126. Photo *Georgina Masson*

126–7 17. Rome: the Pons Aelius and mausoleum of Hadrian (Castel Sant'Angelo); second century AD. Photo *Josephine Powell*

18. Rome: detail of relief of the Apotheosis of Antoninus and Faustina; second century AD. *Musei e Gallerie Pontificie, Vatican City*

19. Rome: Temple of Antoninus and Faustina; dedicated AD 141. Photo *Georgina Masson*

20. Rome: bronze equestrian statue of Marcus Aurelius in the Campidoglio; second century AD. Photo *Josephine Powell*

21. Rome: detail of the Column of Marcus Aurelius; second century AD. Photo *Josephine Powell*

128 22. Rome: street of shops in Trajan's Market; early second century AD. Photo *Edwin Smith*

23. Gallo-Roman relief of a wine-shop; second century AD. Musée de Dijon. Photo *Mansell-Alinari*

24. Ostia: relief of a vegetable-stall; second–third century AD. Museo Ostiense, Ostia

25. Ostia: relief of shop selling poultry and vegetables; second century AD. Museo Ostiense, Ostia. Photo *Fototeca Unione, Rome*

26. Rome: left-bank ramp of the Pons Aelius as exposed in 1891; second century AD. Photo *Fototeca Unione, Rome*

129 27. Rome: relief of a cloth-merchant's shop; first century AD. Uffizi, Florence. Photo *Mansell-Alinari*

28. Ostia: relief of a butcher's shop; second century AD. Museo Ostiense, Ostia. Photo *Fototeca Unione, Rome*

29. Gallo-Roman relief found at Neumagen, weighing a bale of wool; second–third century AD. *Rheinisches Landesmuseum, Trier*

30. Rome: partial reconstruction (by A. Gismondi) of a five-storey *insula* at the foot of the Campidoglio; second century AD. Photo *Mansell-Alinari*

130 31. Relief from a marble sarcophagus found at Trier, scenes from the early life of a child; second–third century AD. Louvre, Paris. Photo *Giraudon*

32. Mosaic of a love-scene found at Centocelle, near Rome; first century AD. Kunsthistorisches Museum, Vienna. Photo *Erwin Meyer*, courtesy *Georg-Westermann-Verlag, Brunswick*

133 Plan of Antonine Rome. Drawn by Mrs Hanni Bailey

Changan

139 1. Wen-ti of Sui dynasty, detail from *Portraits of the Emperors* attributed to Yen Li-pen; early seventh century. Courtesy *Museum of Fine Arts, Boston*

140–1 2. Deep relief stone-panel from the tomb of the Emperor T'ai Tsung, showing a horse and groom; T'ang dynasty. *University Museum, Philadelphia*

3. Pottery figurines of camel and groom; T'ang dynasty. *Los Angeles County Museum of Art, Gift of the Hearst Foundation*

4. Group around bullock cart, pottery; T'ang dynasty. *Seattle Art Museum*

5. Pottery figure of merchant holding wine-skin vessel; T'ang dynasty. *Seattle Art Museum, Eugene Fuller Memorial Collection*

6. Pottery figure of a Persian; T'ang dynasty. *Royal Ontario Museum*

7. Pottery figure of a seated lady; T'ang dynasty. From Sian

8. Pottery figure of an official; T'ang dynasty. *Stanford University Art Gallery Collection*

9. Buddha Tejahprabha as the subduer of the Five Planets; painting on silk from Tun Huang, dated 897. British Museum. Photo *John Freeman*

10. Detail of *Manjuçrī visiting Vimalīkirti* showing Candracchatra, a legendary dignitary, with attendants; painting on paper from Tun Huang, tenth century. British Museum. Photo *John Freeman*

142 11. Stone image of the Taoist deity T'ien Tsun seated on a pedestal; from Sian, dated 709. *Chicago Natural History Museum*

12. Construction scene, from a copy of a wall-painting at Tun-huang (cave 445); T'ang period. From *Tun-huang pi-hua hsüan* (A Selection of Tun-huang wall-paintings), Peking, 1952

13. Ta-yen t'a, 'Great Wild Goose Pagoda'; T'ang period, later restored. From *Famous Historical Places and Cultural Relics of Sian*, Sian, 1959

14. The magic cosmic-quartered back of a bronze marriage mirror; T'ang dynasty. *Seattle Art Museum*

15. Detail of carved jade comb showing musician and dancers; T'ang dynasty. *Seattle Art Museum, Eugene Fuller Memorial Collection*

16. Engraved silver-gilt cup; T'ang dynasty. *Seattle Art Museum, Eugene Fuller Memorial Collection*

17. Pottery ewer; T'ang dynasty. *Ontario Museum, Toronto*

143 Changan: outline map of the city, based on historical research and recent excavations. Adapted from a map published in K'ao-ku ('Archaeology'), No. 11, 1963

145 Map of T'ang China. Drawn by Mrs Hanni Bailey after D. C. Twitchett, *Financial Administration under the T'ang Dynasty*, Cambridge University Press, 1963

Christian Constantinople

151 1. Constantine presenting the city of Constantinople to the Virgin, detail of mosaic in narthex of Hagia Sophia; tenth century. Photo *Byzantine Institute, Dumbarton Oaks*

152-3 2. Map of Constantinople by Buondelmonte; 1420. *Bibliothèque Nationale, Paris*

3. Istanbul: west side of the Obelisk of Theodosius I; 390. Photo *Martin Hürlimann*

4. Istanbul: exterior of St Irene; sixth century. Photo *Martin Hürlimann*

5. Istanbul: exterior of SS. Sergius and Bacchus; sixth century. Photo *YAN*

6. Istanbul: interior of St Irene; sixth century. Photo *Josephine Powell*

7. Istanbul: interior of SS. Sergius and Bacchus; sixth century. Photo *Hirmer Fotoarchiv, Munich*

8. Istanbul: city walls built by Theodosius II; 413. Photo *Martin Hürlimann*

9. Istanbul: the Golden Gate; *c.* 390. Photo *Hirmer Fotoarchiv, Munich*

10. Istanbul: ruins of Imperial Palace; early seventh century. Photo *Martin Hürlimann*

11-12. Details of ivory diptych of the Consul Flavius Anastasius; 517. Cabinet des Médailles, Paris. Photo *Hirmer Fotoarchiv, Munich*

13. Istanbul: interior of Cistern of Yerebatan Seray; sixth century. Photo *Hirmer Fotoarchiv, Munich*

154 14. Detail of mosaic in the Palace of the Byzantine emperors at Istanbul, girl carrying water; mid-sixth century. Photo *Josephine Powell*

15. Detail of mosaic in the Palace of the Byzantine emperors at Istanbul, water-mill; mid-fifth century. Photo *Josephine Powell*

16. Justinian presenting the church to the Virgin, detail of mosaic in narthex of Hagia Sophia; tenth century. Photo *Byzantine Institute, Dumbarton Oaks*

17. Istanbul: walls of Tekfur Saray, the Imperial Palace; twelfth century. Photo *Martin Hürlimann*

18. Istanbul: exterior of Hagia Sophia; 537. Photo *Hirmer Fotoarchiv, Munich*

155 19. Istanbul: interior of Hagia Sophia; 537. Photo *Othmar Pfserschy*

156-7 20-2. Details from the Sky-litzes MS showing the Byzantine emperor and empress receiving ambassadors; thirteenth century. *Biblioteca Nacional, Madrid*

23. Back panel of the Harbaville Triptych; tenth century. Photo *Hirmer Fotoarchiv, Munich*

24. Chalice bearing the name of the Emperor Romanos; *c.* 1070. Treasury of St Mark's, Venice. Photo *Osvaldo Böhm*

25. Ivory statuette of the Virgin and Child; tenth century. *Victoria and Albert Museum, London (Crown Copyright)*

26. Ivory relief showing Christ crowning Emperor Constantine VII Porphyrogenitus; *c.* 944. Museum of Fine Art, Moscow. Photo *Hirmer Fotoarchiv, Munich*

27. Crown of the Emperor Constantine Monomachus; mid-eleventh century. *Magyar Nemzeta Museum, Budapest*

28. Detail of Byzantine silk shroud of St Germain l'Auxerrois; late tenth century. Church of St Eusebius, Auxerre. Photo *Hirmer Fotoarchiv, Munich*

158 29. Detail of miniature showing a domed church, from the *Sermons of James of Kokkinobaphos*; twelfth century. *Bibliothèque Nationale, Paris*

30. Theodore Metochites, detail of mosaic tympanum of Kariye Cami, Constantinople; 1320-30. Photo *Byzantine Institute, Dumbarton Oaks*

160-1 Woodcut of Constantinople, from the *Liber Chronicarum* of Hartmann Schedel; Nuremberg, 1493

163 Plan of Constantinople

Muslim Cordoba

167 1. Cordoba: the Great Mosque (now the Cathedral), decorated archways near the Mihrab; mid-tenth century. Photo *YAN*

168-9 2. Cordoba: arched bays in the crypt of the Great Mosque (now the Cathedral); *c.* 848. Photo *J. E. Dayton*

3. Cordoba: interior of dome of the Great Mosque (now the Cathedral); mid-tenth century. Photo *J. E. Dayton*

4. Cordoba: detail of the east front of the Great Mosque (now the Cathedral); mid-tenth century. Photo *Diana Ashcroft*

5. Az-Zahra': arches from the excavated ruins; first half of tenth century. Photo *Diana Ashcroft*

6. Cordoba: water-wheel and Moorish bridge over the Guadalquivir; first half of tenth century. Photo *Diana Ashcroft*

170 7. Marble window grill from the Great Mosque at Cordoba; tenth century. Museo Arqueológico, Cordoba. Photo *Mas*

8. Ivory casket of Prince al-Mughira by Khalaf; from Cordoba, 968. Louvre, Paris. Photo *Giraudon*

9-10. Details of casket made for Ziyad ibn Aflah, showing a man on an elephant, and a man hawking; 969-70. *Victoria and Albert Museum, London (Crown Copyright)*

173 Map of Spain showing loss of Muslim territories, 756-1157. Drawn by John Woodcock

174-5 View of Cordoba from the *Civitates Orbis Terrarum* of Braun and Hogenberg; Cologne, 1573-1618

176 Cordoba: plan of Mosque (785-987). Adapted from G. Marçais, *L'Architecture Musulmane d'Occident*, 1954

The Paris of Abelard and St Louis

179 1. Detail of Notre-Dame from *The Descent of the Holy Spirit*, miniature by Jean Fouquet; mid-fifteenth century. *The Lehman Collection, New York*

180-1 2. St-Denis, near Paris: detail of stained-glass window in the abbey, showing Abbot Suger (prostrate at the feet of the Virgin); mid-twelfth century, reset in the fourteenth-century window of the Life of the Virgin. Photo *Jean Roubier*

3, 5, 6, 9. Paris: scenes of student life, reliefs on the south transept of Notre-Dame; *c.* 1260. Photo *Giraudon*

4. Paris: head of statue of Bishop Maurice de Sully, from the St Anne Portal of Notre-Dame; early thirteenth century. Photo *Martin Hürlimann*

7. Impression of the seal of the University of Paris; thirteenth century. Cabinet des Médailles, Bibliothèque Nationale, Paris. Photo *Archives Nationales*

8. Paris: head of Abelard, detail of capital in the Salle des Gardes of the Conciergerie; fourteenth century. Photo *Archives Photographiques*

10. Paris: relief from the tomb of Pierre Gougis, apology being made to the University of Paris; 1440. École des Beaux-Arts, Paris. Photo *Giraudon*

182-3 11. Paris: interior of upper church of the Sainte-Chapelle, looking east; *c.* 1239-58. Photo *A. F. Kersting*

12. Paris: detail of stained-glass window in the Sainte-Chapelle, St Louis carrying relics; mid-thirteenth century. Photo cour-

tesy *Éditions Robert Laffont, Paris*

184-5 13. Paris: section of wall constructed at the time of Philip Augustus, at the corner of Rue Cardinal-Lemoine and Rue Clovis; end twelfth-early thirteenth century. Photo *Eileen Tweedy*

14. Detail of miniature from the *Life of St Denis*, showing the bridges of Paris with a pilgrim and the transportation of wine and coal; French, 1317. *Bibliothèque Nationale, Paris*

15. Detail of miniature from the *Life of St Denis*, showing a flour-mill under the Grand-Pont; French, 1317. *Bibliothèque Nationale, Paris*

16. Detail of miniature from the *Life of St Denis* showing a covered wagon and barges containing barrels of wine; French, 1317. *Bibliothèque Nationale, Paris*

17. Detail of miniature from the *Life of St Denis*, showing a metal-working establishment; French, 1317. *Bibliothèque Nationale, Paris*

18. Reims: head of statue possibly representing Philip Augustus, on north transept façade of the cathedral; mid-thirteenth century. Photo *Archives Photographiques*

19. Miniature from the *Grandes Chroniques de France*, the Lendit Fair at St-Denis; French, fourteenth century. Musée Goya, Castres. Photo *Giraudon*

186 20. Detail of June miniature from the *Très Riches Heures du duc de Berry*, the Palace and Sainte-Chapelle; by the Limbourg brothers, 1413-16. Musée Condé, Chantilly. Photo *Giraudon*

21. Detail of October miniature from the *Très Riches Heures du duc de Berry*, the Louvre; by the Limbourg brothers, 1413-16. Musée Condé, Chantilly. Photo *Giraudon*

189 Obverse and reverse of the commemorative seal of the University of Paris; 1896. After an impression in the Archives Nationales, Paris

191 Plan of Paris, from Sebastian Münster's *Cosmographia Universalis*; Mainz, 1550. Courtesy Jean-Claude Peissel

Mexico-Tenochtitlan

195 1. Page of the *Codex Borbonicus* showing a pre-Conquest ritual calendar; Aztec. *Bibliothèque de l'Assemblée Nationale, Paris*

196-7 2. Painting from the *Codex Magliabecchi* (facsimile) showing a sacrifice. British Museum, London. Photo *John Freeman*

Rudolph. Photo *Robert Perron (Photo Researchers)*

28. Cambridge, Massachusetts: the Kresge Auditorium of the Massachusetts Institute of Technology; by Eero Saarinen, 1955. Photo *Mike Andrews, Copyright Bell Howarth Ltd*

308–9 29. *The Rocky Mountains* (detail), pioneers crossing the plains; Currier and Ives print, 1860–70. The American Museum in Britain, Claverton Manor, Bath. Photo *Desmond Tripp Ltd*

30. Studebaker in his wagon-shop at Hangtown, California, in 1850. *Private Collection, San Francisco*

31. New Orleans: hitching-post. Photo *Patrick O'Keeffe*

32. *Across the Continent;* Currier and Ives print, *c.* 1869. *Museum of the City of New York, Harry T. Peters Collection*

310–1 33. Chicago, Illinois: stockyards. Photo *Paul Popper Ltd*

34. Minneapolis, Minnesota: view of the city across the Mississippi. Photo *Paul Popper Ltd*

35. Houston, Texas: aerial view of the port and oil refineries. Photo *Houston Chamber of Commerce*

36. Toledo, Ohio: aerial view showing harbour on the Maumee River. Photo *Camera Press*

37. Pittsburgh, Pennsylvania: aerial view of the city showing the 'Golden Triangle'. Photo *Chamber of Commerce, Pittsburgh*

38. Mystic, Connecticut: the quayside. Photo *Mike Andrews, Bell Howarth Ltd*

39. Detroit, Michigan: exterior of General Motors building. Photo *Camera Press*

40. San Francisco, California: view towards the Bay. Photo *Arnold Gibbs*

41. Los Angeles, California: aerial view of the city. Photo *Camera Press*

314 Engraving of St Augustine, Florida, from *Expedito Francisci Draki equitis angli in Indias occidentilis;* 1588

315 Engraving of Boston harbour, Massachusetts; by Paul Revere, 1768

316 Plan for Washington, D.C., by Major Pierre Charles L'Enfant; *c.* 1800. The New-York Historical Society, New York City

317 Engraving showing emigrants landing in New York; late nineteenth century

Mid-twentieth-century New York

319 1. New York: the Statue of Liberty; by Frédéric-Auguste Bartholdi, 1884. Photo courtesy *Port of New York Authority*

320–1 2. Engraving of New York by S. Davenport; early nineteenth century. Photo *Radio Times Hulton Picture Library*

3. New York: St Nicholas Hotel at Broadway and Spring Street; lithograph, 1855. Photo courtesy *The New-York Historical Society, New York City*

4. New York: photograph of Broadway in 1859. Photo *Radio Times Hulton Picture Library*

5. The Castello Plan of New Amsterdam; 1660. *Museum of the City of New York*

6. New York: linked aerial views of midtown and downtown Manhattan. Photographs furnished courtesy *United States Department of Commerce, Coast and Geodetic Survey*

7. New York: detail of spires of St Patrick's Cathedral. Photo *Tom Blau (Camera Press)*

8. New York: Empire State Building; 1931. Photo *Infoplan*

9. New York: Solomon R. Guggenheim Museum; by Frank Lloyd Wright, 1959. Photo *Carl Frank (Photo Researchers)*

322–3 10. New York: view of Central Park. Photo *Martin Weaver*

11. New York: national flags in front of the Secretariat Building of the United Nations. Photo *Martin Weaver*

12. New York: taxi-cab in front of a hoarding. Photo *Martin Weaver*

13. New York: fire-escapes and signs on buildings in Chinatown. Photo *Martin Weaver*

14. New York: 'fish-eye' aerial view. Photo *Jay Maisel*

324–5 15. New York: scene in East Village. Photo *Ralph M. Toporoff*

16. New York: Coney Island Beach. Photo *Camera Press*

17. New York: sidewalk artists in Greenwich Village. Photo *D. Jordan Wilson (Camera Press)*

18. New York: steps of the New York Public Library. Photo *Infoplan*

19. New York: a Puerto Rican section of New York. Photo *Paul Popper Ltd*

20. New York: northwards view of Park Avenue from above. Photo *Arnold Gibbs*

21. New York: Shubert Alley in the Manhattan theatre district. Photo *United States Information Service*

22. New York: Washington Mews. Photo *John Minutoli (Department of Commerce and Public Events)*

326–7 23. New York: Brooklyn Bridge; by John A. Roebling, 1870–83. Photo *Martin Weaver*

24. New York: view of Brook-

lyn across the East River. Photo *Martin Weaver*

25. New York: night view of Park Avenue looking south to the Grand Central Tower. Photo *Martin Weaver*

328–9 26. New York: interior of Grand Central Station. Photo *Martin Weaver*

27. New York: aerial view showing the Port Authority Bus Terminal. Photo courtesy *Port of New York Authority*

28. The *Queen Elizabeth* arriving in New York. Photo courtesy *Port of New York Authority*

29. New York: exterior, TWA building at Kennedy International Airport; by Eero Saarinen, 1958. Photo *Ezra Stoller Associates*

30. New York: 'Floor' of the New York Stock Exchange. Photo *United States Information Service*

31. New York: auction at the Parke-Bernet Galleries. Photo *Camera Press*

330 32. New York: detail of the new Metropolitan Opera House, part of the Lincoln Center for the Performing Arts. Photo *Martin Weaver*

33. New York: part of the façade and steps of Low Memorial Library, Columbia University, with statue of Alma Mater. Photo *Martin Weaver*

34. New York: Huntington Hartford Gallery of Modern Art. Photo *Martin Weaver*

333 View of New Amsterdam, engraving by Hartger; 1626. Museum of the City of New York, J. Clarence Davies Collection

The coming world-city: Ecumenopolis

337 ff. All illustrations provided by Doxiadis Associates, Athens

INDEX

376